TELEPHONE AND FAX NUMBERS

HEADINGLEY CRICKET GROUND — **Tel: 0843 504 3099**
Fax: 0113 278 4099

NORTH MARINE ROAD, SCARBOROUGH — **Tel: 01723 365625**
Fax: 01723 364287

BURNLEY ROAD, TODMORDEN — **Tel: 01706 813140**

SHIPTON ROAD, YORK — **Tel: 01904 623602**

BRADFORD & BINGLEY — **Tel: 01274 775441**
Wagon Lane, Bingley

STAMFORD BRIDGE — **Tel: 01759 371545**
Low Catton Road

© The Yorkshire County Cricket Club Ltd 2017

Produced by:

Great Northern Books
PO Box 213, Ilkley LS29 9WS
www.greatnorthernbooks.co.uk

ISBN: 978-1-912101-71-9

CONTENTS

Colour Plates — Facing Pages 32 and 256

Officers for 2017

PATRONESS

THE DUCHESS OF KENT

PATRONS

PATRICIA,
COUNTESS OF HAREWOOD   The EARL OF MEXBOROUGH
DAVID LASCELLES, EARL OF HAREWOOD   LORD HAWKE

HONORARY LIFE MEMBERS

Mr J G BINKS
Mr H D BIRD, OBE
Mr G BOYCOTT, OBE
Mr D BYAS
Sir LAWRENCE BYFORD,
   QPM, LLD, DL
Mr D GOUGH
Mr J H HAMPSHIRE

Dr K HOWARD, OBE
Mr R ILLINGWORTH, CBE
Mr D S LEHMANN
Mr D E V PADGETT
Mr R K PLATT
Mr S R TENDULKAR
Mr M P VAUGHAN, OBE

PRESIDENT

Mr J H HAMPSHIRE

VICE-PRESIDENTS

Mr B BOUTTELL,
Mr I M CHAPPELL
Mr G A COPE
Mr G D DRABBLE
Mr S FIELDEN
Mr D S HALL, CBE, TD
Mr R A HILLIAM
Mr R A HUTTON
Sir DAVID JONES
Mr S J MANN

Mr K H MOSS MBE
Mr J W T MUSTOE
Mr R A SMITH, TD, DL
Mr W B STOTT
Mr K TAYLOR
Mr P W TOWNEND
Mr A L VANN
Mr D WARNER
Mr J D WELCH
Mr R D WILKINSON

THE BOARD

Mr S J DENISON (Chairman)
Mr R A SMITH TD, DL (Director)
Mr S WILLIS (Leeds Metropolitan University)
Mr M D MOXON
Mr M ARTHUR
SIR G K VERITY

MEMBERS' COMMITTEE

Chairman: Mr S J MANN

ELECTED MEMBERS

Ms C EVERS   Mr R LEVIN
Mr S J MANN

APPOINTED MEMBERS

Mr A KILBURN   Ms K MATHEW
Mr G GREENFIELD

ARCHIVES COMMITTEE

Chairman: Mr J C D ALLAN

Mr J C D ALLAN	Dr P E DUNN
Mr P E DYSON	Mr J M GREENFIELD
MR C HARDY	Mr B K SANDERSON
Mr D WARNER	Mr R D WILKINSON

**Changes announced after February 17 will be recorded in the
2018 edition of the Yorkshire County Cricket Club Yearbook**

Joe Root in the Top 10

The Club congratulates Joe Root on becoming the 10th Yorkshire
player to be invited to captain England in Tests. His predecessors
are Lord Hawke, Sir Stanley Jackson, Ronald Stanyforth,
Norman Yardley, Sir Leonard Hutton, Brian Close, Raymond
Illingworth, Geoffrey Boycott and Michael Vaughan.

A FANTASTIC SUMMER DESPITE JUST MISSING OUT ON TITLE

I can look back on my first year as Yorkshire President with immense pride. I have been well received and looked after at matches up and down the country, and I am extremely grateful for this.

To be elected Club President has meant a hell of a lot to me. It has been the icing on the cake and an amazing honour after well over half-a-century of active involvement in first-class cricket, starting out as a very young man dragging a big bag into Headingley hoping to get a second-team game.

By John Hampshire

It was a privilege to be there to watch Yorkshire's progress throughout 2016, and I have enjoyed every minute of it. It was a big disappointment to all concerned at the Club that we didn't quite manage to win the Specsavers County Championship title for a third consecutive year, the last time we did this being in 1966-68, when I played under Brian Close's captaincy.

But I do feel that this was mainly due to injuries to key players at various times, and also to Test calls. In the circumstances I think that Yorkshire have enjoyed a remarkably good season. Sometimes, by their own admission, they have perhaps not played quite as well as they could have done, but to finish where they did and to be in with a chance of the title right up to the end of the season was excellent.

Jason Gillespie did a great job as Yorkshire coach during his time with us, and we are indebted to him, as we are to Andrew Gale for his captaincy over the past five years.

Andrew has now taken over from Jason as Club Coach, and I am confident he will make a good job of it. I must admit that, like a lot of other people, I was taken aback a little when I heard of his appointment, and my immediate thought was: would he be too close to the dressing room?

I don't think this will be so, because Andrew has been a fine player, and he is a very good leader who has got the attention of the dressing room and has experienced success. If he carries on in the way that he has done so far I think we have a chance of winning the Championship again this year, particularly if we get one or two of our Test players back.

I have a nice feeling about Andrew coming in as coach, and I am looking forward to the team challenging strongly during my second year as President.

I hope that we can be just as successful in limited-overs cricket as we are in the Championship, because I think it is imperative in this day and age that we win a one-day trophy. It is very important that we do so.

One of us: President Hampshire caps the returning Azeem Rafiq

Although the so-called purists aren't bothered about one-day cricket I think that that is rubbish. One-day cricket is part and parcel of the game today. It brings in the crowds. Generally, the players enjoy it, and so do those who watch it. I think it is vital that we take both 50-over and Twenty20 cricket on board, and win some trophies in these competitions as well finishing top of the Championship table.

Looking beyond the team's own performances in 2016, it was a credit to the Yorkshire system to see so many of our players representing England at home and abroad in Test matches and one-day internationals.

I think it is something to be very proud of when any Yorkshire player makes it into the England team. It is terrific, not only for the Club and the Yorkshire side, but also for the whole of its membership as well.

Test calls can sometimes dilapidate the Yorkshire side. There is no doubt about that, but on the other hand they can give an opportunity to some of our younger players to get into the first team.

I congratulate all of our Test players, and wish them every success in the future, but I would particularly like to mention Jonny Bairstow, because I played alongside his dad, David, for so many years. Jonny is a top player now, and up there with some of the best in the world. Bluey would have been over the moon for him. He really would.

I must pay tribute to Headingley groundsman Andy Fogarty and his staff for preparing such excellent pitches throughout the season, and also congratulate Andy on retaining his title as Groundsman of the Year. The work of groundsmen often goes unnoticed by the watching public, and I also congratulate Scarborough groundsman John Dodds on his award for preparing the best outground pitches at North Marine Road.

Officials of the Yorkshire County Cricket Club

President	Treasurer	Captain	Captain (Contd)
T R Barker 1863	M J Ellison 1863-1893	R Iddison 1863-1872	P Carrick 1987-1989
M J Ellison 1864-97	M Ellison, jun 1894-1898	J Rowbotham 1873	M D Moxon 1990-1995
Lord Hawke 1898-1938	Chas Stokes 1899-1912	L Greenwood 1874	D Byas 1996-2001
Rt Hon Sir F S Jackson 1939-1947	R T Heselton 1913-1931	J Rowbotham 1875	D S Lehmann 2002
		E Lockwood 1876-1877	A McGrath 2003
T L Taylor 1948-1960	A Wyndham Heselton 1932-1962	T Emmett 1878-1882	C White 2004-6
Sir W A Worsley Bart 1961-1973	M G Crawford 1963-1979	Hon M B (Lord) Hawke 1883-1910	D Gough 2007-8
Sir K Parkinson 1974-1981	J D Welch 1980-1984	E J R H Radcliffe 1911	A McGrath 2009
		Sir A W White 1912-1918	A W Gale 2010-16
N W D Yardley 1981-1983	P W Townend 1984-2002	D C F Burton 1919-1921	G S Ballance 2017
The Viscount Mountgarret 1984-1989	*Chairman*	Geoff Wilson 1922-1924	*Secretary*
	A H Connell, DL 1971-1979	A W Lupton 1925-1927	Geo Padley 1863
Sir Leonard Hutton 1989-1990		W A Worsley 1928-1929	J B Wostinholm 1864-1902
Sir Lawrence Byford QPM, LLD, DL 1991-1999	M G Crawford 1980-1984	A T Barber 1930	F C (Sir Fredk.) Toone 1903-1930
	H R Kirk 1984-1985	F E Greenwood 1931-1932	J H Nash 1931-1971
R A Smith TD, LLB, DL 1999-2004	B Walsh, QC 1986-1991	A B Sellers 1933-1947	J Lister 1972-1991
David Jones CBE 2004-6	Sir Lawrence Byford CBE, QPM, LLD, DL 1991-1998	N W D Yardley 1948-1955	D M Ryder 1991-2002
Robert Appleyard 2006-8		W H H Sutcliffe 1956-1957	*Company Secretary*
	K H Moss MBE 1998-2002	J R Burnet 1958-1959	B Bouttell 2002-5
Brian Close CBE 2008-10		J V Wilson 1960-1962	C Hartwell 2011-14
	GA Cope 2002	D B Close 1963-1970	P Hudson 2014-
Raymond Illingworth CBE 2010-12	R A Smith TD, LLB, DL 2002-5	G Boycott 1971-1978	*Chief Executive*
			C D Hassell 1991-2002
Geoffrey Boycott OBE 2012-13		J H Hampshire 1979-1980	Colin J Graves 2002-5
	C J Graves 2005-15	C M Old 1981-1982	Stewart Regan 2006-10
Harold 'Dickie' Bird OBE 2014-15		R Illingworth 1982-1983	Colin J Graves 2012-13
John H Hampshire 2016-	S J Denison 2015-	D L Bairstow 1984-1986	Mark Arthur 2013-

8

IT'S NOT *JUST* CRICKET

IT'S AN INCREDIBLE DAY AT HEADINGLEY

1ST ROYAL LONDON ODI
ENGLAND v SOUTH AFRICA
24 MAY 2017, HEADINGLEY

2ND INVESTEC TEST
ENGLAND v WEST INDIES
25 - 29 AUGUST 2017, BANK HOLIDAY WEEKEND, HEADINGLEY

WE ARE
ENGLAND CRICKET

yorkshireccc.com
0843 504 3099

Calls are charged between 1p and 13p per minute for landline
customers. Calls from mobile phones may vary

COUNTY FIXTURES — 2017

LV COUNTY CHAMPIONSHIP — Division 1
(All four-day matches)

Date			Opponents	Venue
FRI	**7-10**	**APRIL**	**HAMPSHIRE**	**HEADINGLEY**
Fri	14-17	April	Warwickshire	Edgbaston
Fri	21-24	April	Hampshire	Southampton
Fri	19-22	MAY	Lancashire	Emirates Old Trafford
FRI	**2-5**	**JUNE**	**LANCASHIRE**	**HEADINGLEY**
Fri	9-12	June	Somerset	Taunton
Mon	19-22	June	Middlesex	Lord's
MON	**26-29**	**JUNE**	**SURREY**	**HEADINGLEY**
MON	**3-6**	**JULY**	**SOMERSET**	**SCARBOROUGH**
SUN	**6-9**	**AUGUST**	**ESSEX**	**SCARBOROUGH**
TUE	**5-8**	**SEPTEMBER**	**MIDDLESEX**	**HEADINGLEY**
Tue	12-15	September	Surrey	The Oval
TUE	**19-22**	**SEPTEMBER**	**WARWICKSHIRE**	**HEADINGLEY**
Mon	25-28	September	Essex	Chelmsford

ROYAL LONDON 50-OVER CUP

Sat	29	April	Nottinghamshire	Trent Bridge
MON	**1**	**MAY**	**LANCASHIRE**	**HEADINGLEY**
WED	**3**	**MAY**	**DURHAM**	**HEADINGLEY**
Fri	5	May	Worcestershire	Worcester
SUN	**7**	**MAY**	**DERBYSHIRE**	**HEADINGLEY**
Wed	10	May	Northamptonshire	Northampton
Sun	14	May	Warwickshire	Edgbaston
TUE	**16**	**MAY**	**LEICESTERSHIRE**	**HEADINGLEY**
Tue	13	June	Quarter-Finals	TBC
Fri	16-17	June	Semi-Finals	TBC
Sat	1	July	Final	Lord's
Sun	12	June	Derbyshire	Chesterfield

NATWEST T20 BLAST CUP

FRI	**7**	**JULY**	**NOTTINGHAMSHIRE**	**HEADINGLEY**
Sat	8	July	Derbyshire	Chesterfield
Tue	11	July	Northamptonshire	Northampton
Fri	14	July	Lancashire	Old Trafford
FRI	**21**	**JULY**	**BIRMINGHAM**	**HEADINGLEY**
SUN	**23**	**JULY**	**WORCESTERSHIRE**	**HEADINGLEY**
WED	**26**	**JULY**	**DURHAM**	**HEADINGLEY**
Fri	28	July	Birmingham	Edgbaston
Sun	30	July	Nottinghamshire	Trent Bridge
THU	**3**	**AUGUST**	**DERBYSHIRE**	**HEADINGLEY**
Fri	4	August	Durham	Chester-le-Street
FRI	**11**	**AUGUST**	**LANCASHIRE**	**HEADINGLEY**
Sat	12	August	Leicestershire	Leicester
THU	**17**	**AUGUST**	**NORTHAMPTONSHIRE**	**HEADINGLEY**
Tue	22-25	August	Quarter-Finals	TBC
Sat	2	September	Semi-Finals and Final	Edgbaston

OTHER MATCHES

SUN	**2-4**	**APRIL**	**LEEDS BRADFORD MCCU**	**HEADINGLEY**

TOUR MATCH

SAT	**27**	**MAY**	**SOUTH AFRICA A**	**HEADINGLEY**

INVESTEC TEST MATCHES

(All five-day matches)

ENGLAND v. SOUTH AFRICA

Thu	6-10	July	.......Lord's	Fri	14-18	July .... Trent Bridge
Thu	27-31	July	........The Oval	Fri	4-8	August ....Old Trafford

ENGLAND v. WEST INDIES

Thu	17-21	August	.....Edgbaston	**FRI**	**25-29**	**AUGUST ..HEADINGLEY**
Thu	7-11	September	...Lord's			

ROYAL LONDON ONE-DAY INTERNATIONALS

Fri	5	May	England v. Ireland ....Bristol
Sun	7	May	England v. Ireland ....Lord's
WED	**24**	**MAY**	**ENGLAND V. SOUTH AFRICA ....HEADINGLEY**
Sat	27	May	England v. South Africa ....Southampton
Mon	29	May	England v. South Africa.........................Lord's
Tue	19	September	England v. West Indies ....Old Trafford
Thu	21	September	England v. West Indies ....Trent Bridge
Sun	24	September	England v. West Indies ....Bristol
Wed	27	September	England v. West Indies ....The Oval
Fri	29	September	England v. West Indies ....Southampton

NATWEST INTERNATIONALS T20

Wed	21	June	England v. South Africa ....Southampton
Fri	23	June	England v. South Africa ....Taunton
Sun	25	June	England v. South Africa ....Cardiff
Sat	16	September	England v. West Indies ....Chester-le-Street

CHAMPIONS TROPHY ONE-DAY INTERNATIONAL TOURNAMENT

To be played from June 1 to 18 at Cardiff, Edgbaston and The Oval between the top eight teams in the ICC ODI Championship rankings as on September 30, 2015: England, Australia, Bangladesh, India, New Zealand, Pakistan, South Africa and Sri Lanka.

SECOND ELEVEN CHAMPIONSHIP

Wed	3-5	May	MCC Young Cricketers ....TBC
TUE	**9-11**	**MAY**	**WARWICKSHIRE ....HARROGATE**
Tue	30-1	May/June	Leicestershire ....TBC
TUE	**13-15**	**JUNE**	**LANCASHIRE ....SCARBOROUGH**
TUE	**20-22**	**JUNE**	**DERBYSHIRE ....YORK**
TUE	**27-29**	**JUNE**	**NOTTINGHAMSHIRE .....STAMFORD BRIDGE**
TUE	**11-13**	**JULY**	**NORTHAMPTONSHIRE ....YORK**
Tue	25-27	July	Worcestershire ....Upper Tything, Worcester
Tue	15-17	August	Durham ....Chester-le-Street
Tue	5-7	September	Final ....TBC

SECOND ELEVEN TROPHY

TUE	**25**	**APRIL**	**LANCASHIRE ....HEADINGLEY**
THU	**27**	**APRIL**	**DERBYSHIRE ....YORK**
Tue	2	May	MCC Young Cricketers ....TBC
MON	**8**	**MAY**	**WARWICKSHIRE ....YORK**
Mon	15	May	Leicestershire ....TBC
Fri	19	May	Durham ....Brandon CC
Fri	2	June	Semi-Finals ....TBC
Thu	8-9	June	Final ....TBC

SECOND ELEVEN TWENTY20 (TWO MATCHES IN THE SAME DAY)

MON	**26**	**JUNE**	**NOTTINGHAMSHIRE ....BARNSLEY**
Thu	6	July	Durham ....Marske-By-Sea CC
MON	**10**	**JULY**	**NORTHAMPTONSHIRE ....PUDSEY CONGS**
Mon	24	July	Worcestershire ....Upper Tything, Worcester
Mon	31	July	Derbyshire ....Alvaston and Boulton CC
Wed	2	August	Lancashire ....TBC
Thu	10	August	Semi-Finals and Final ....TBC

SECOND ELEVEN FRIENDLIES

Mon	3-4	April	Nottinghamshire	Lady Bay, West Bridgford
Mon	10-13	April	Lancashire	Old Trafford
WED	**19-21**	**APRIL**	**GLOUCESTERSHIRE**	**HEADINGLEY**
Mon	14	August	Durham	Chester-le-Street
Tue	29-31	August	Derbyshire	Harrogate
Wed	13-15	September	Surrey	TBC
TUE	**19-21**	**SEPTEMBER**	**DURHAM**	**SCARBOROUGH**

YORKSHIRE ACADEMY IN THE YORKSHIRE LEAGUE

Sat	22	April	Easingwold	Easingwold
Sat	29	April	Woodhouse Grange	Woodhouse Grange
Sat	6	May	Harrogate	Harrogate
SAT	**13**	**MAY**	**YORK**	**WEETWOOD**
Sat	20	May	Scarborough	Scarborough
SAT	**27**	**MAY**	**HULL**	**WEETWOOD**
Mon	29	May	Stamford Bridge	Stamford Bridge
Sat	3	June	Acomb	Acomb
SAT	**10**	**JUNE**	**CLIFTON ALLIANCE**	**WEETWOOD**
SAT	**17**	**JUNE**	**SHERIFF HUTTON BRIDGE**	**WEETWOOD**
Sat	24	June	Driffield Town	Driffield Town
SAT	**1**	**JULY**	**WOODHOUSE GRANGE**	**WEETWOOD**
Sat	8	July	York	York
Sat	15	July	Harrogate	Harrogate
SAT	**22**	**JULY**	**SCARBOROUGH**	**WEETWOOD**
Sat	29	July	Hull	Hull
SAT	**5**	**AUGUST**	**ACOMB**	**WEETWOOD**
Sat	12	August	Clifton Alliance	Clifton
Sat	19	August	Driffield Town	Weetwood
Sat	26	August	Sheriff Hutton Bridge	Sheriff Hutton Bridge
SAT	**2**	**SEPTEMBER**	**STAMFORD BRIDGE**	**WEETWOOD**
SAT	**9**	**SEPTEMBER**	**EASINGWOLD**	**WEETWOOD**

YORKSHIRE ACADEMY IN THE YORKSHIRE LEAGUE CUP

Sun	4	June	Wakefield Thornes	Wakefield Thornes

YORKSHIRE ACADEMY IN THE YORKSHIRE LEAGUE T20

Sun	11	June	Woodhouse Grange	Woodhouse Grange

YORKSHIRE ACADEMY FRIENDLIES

Wed	19	April	Durham Academy	Richmondshire CC
TBC		April	Durham Academy	Richmondshire CC
Wed	3	May	Sedburgh School	Sedburgh School
TUE	**4-5**	**JULY**	**SCOTLAND**	**WEETWOOD**
THU	**6**	**JULY**	**SCOTLAND**	**WEETWOOD**

YORKSHIRE UNDER-17s in THREE-DAY CHAMPIONSHIP

Tue	11-13	July	Lancashire	Away
TUE	**18-20**	**JULY**	**DURHAM**	**WEETWOOD**
TUE	1-3	August	Derbyshire	Away
TUE	**8-10**	**AUGUST**	**CHESHIRE**	**WEETWOOD**
Tue	15-17	August	Semi-Final	Home Tie
Tue	29-31	August	Final	TBC

YORKSHIRE UNDER-17s in ONE-DAY CHAMPIONSHIP

SUN	**14**	**MAY**	**PRACTICE MATCH**	**WEETWOOD**
Sun	28	May	Lancashire	Away
TUE	**30**	**MAY**	**DURHAM**	**WEETWOOD**
THU	**1**	**JUNE**	**CHESHIRE**	**WEETWOOD**
Sun	11	June	Derbyshire	Away
Sun	2	July	Semi-Final	Home Tie
Sun	9	July	Final	TBC

NEW REGIME ARE SEEKING EVEN GREATER SUCCESS

When the New Year was ushered in Yorkshire's new regime had all their plans in place for what they hope will be a period of success at least equal to that of the past five seasons under the guiding hand of Jason Gillespie.

The Australian's big shoes were filled in November by Andrew Gale, who did not apply for the job of coach but had it offered by Director of Cricket Martyn Moxon, who felt that Gale was better suited to the post than any who had put their names forward.

By David Warner

Gale understandably took a few days to mull things over, but then said, "Yes", admitting that it was an offer he simply could not refuse. Then he took his first important decision, and that was to announce the end of his playing career so that he could concentrate fully on his new and demanding role.

At only 32 it was a hard decision for the Club's first-class captain to take, because he potentially had several years still in front of him as an attractive and powerful batsman. But it was undoubtedly the right choice to make. Gale has always put team before self — as he once did when he dropped himself because he felt others were in better nick. Last summer he went through a similar loss of form, making only 525 Championship runs at an average of 21, and he was aware that an improvement would be needed quickly in 2017 to safeguard his place.

Had this season started badly for him the pressure would have increased as captain, player and coach, but now his only concern is to get the best out of the team that he possibly can without having to worry about himself.

He can go about his work with confidence, because he has already earned the complete respect of his teammates through his considerable achievements as captain during the past seven seasons when his side were county champions twice and strong contenders for the title on another couple of occasions. And although not one-day captain in 2016 he had already led Yorkshire to their first appearance in a T20 final in 2012.

Having terminated his own playing career, Gale's next big job was to decide who should succeed him as captain, and his choice of Gary Ballance in all formats ticked all the right boxes.

Before revealing that Ballance was his choice Gale had already admitted that he favoured one captain for all competitions, and this was understandable after he had learned at first hand how losing the one-day captaincy and his place led to weeks of being on the fringe with little real involvement.

It's different at England level. where the various squads are chosen separately and have their own structure, but at county level there are long stretches when 50-over and 20-over cricket take centre stage with Championship cricket virtually redundant.

As overall captain Ballance will not lose any of his authority, and he should benefit enormously from being in charge from the beginning of the season until the end.

The only loser to the Ballance appointment was Alex Lees, who led the one-day side capably last season and guided them through to the semi-finals of both the Royal London 50-overs Cup and the NatWest T20 Blast Cup. Lees, however, was fully understanding of the situation, and he could see that relinquishing the one-day captaincy would allow him to concentrate on continuing the improvement in his batting that was evident last season.

If Ballance should get the England call again this summer, then Gale, of course, will have other decisions to make, but with Tim Bresnan and Lees on hand, plus Ryan Sidebottom, he should not be short of options.

With the coach and captain sorted out, the only remaining big issue was who would be Yorkshire's overseas player. This was resolved shortly before Christmas, when it was announced that Australia's up-and-coming star batsman, Peter Handscomb, would be arriving at Headingley and playing in all formats.

It was hoped he would be available for most of the season — although Yorkshire know from their own experience that things do not always turn out that way with overseas signings.

No season ever pans out exactly as the pundits predict, but Gale, Moxon, Ballance and Co will be desperately keen that Yorkshire continue to be among the Championship's top-dogs while at the same time being able to take that one step forward that is still required in the one-day arena.

YORKSHIRE JUST FALL SHORT IN GILLESPIE'S FAREWELL SEASON

By Graham Hardcastle

The chase for a rare hat-trick of County Championship titles was on right down to the final session of the 2016 season against Middlesex at Lord's, but unfortunately it proved to be a step too far for Yorkshire's impressive group of cricketers.

Middlesex eventually took the crown away from Yorkshire and from under the noses of Somerset, the other of the three challengers, and nobody from Headingley had any complaints. Members of the playing and coaching staff readily admitted that the White Rose had not been at their best with the red ball throughout a summer which could have turned out so differently.

In mid-August they were on course to win all three trophies. They were firmly in the Championship race and also through to the semi-finals of the two limited-overs competitions — the NatWest T20 Blast and the Royal London one-day Cup. They were knocked out of the Blast by Durham in the second semi-final of Finals Day before losing a Headingley semi against Surrey the following weekend.

Ultimately, having played their part in a thrilling finale, Andrew Gale's men fell short in the Championship, too, as they could not quite match the achievements of Brian Close's great side of the 1960s, who won three titles in three years.

Yorkshire were set to make 240 in 40 overs as part of a contrived fourth day run chase at Lord's, with a Toby Roland-Jones hat-trick sealing success for the hosts. Middlesex went unbeaten throughout the campaign, and did the double over the defending champions, starting with a thrilling win at Scarborough's North Marine Road.

It was a particular disappointment that success could not be achieved in Jason Gillespie's final year as first-team coach. He had made the decision to return home to Adelaide for family reasons, and a third title would have provided the perfect send-off for the popular Aussie. Instead, he had to settle for two in five years, having taken over ahead of 2012 with the club languishing in Division Two of the Championship.

Yorkshire failed to find top gear for long enough last season as they won only five matches and lost three. There were glimpses of the dominance which was evident throughout the whole of 2015, hammering Surrey and Durham at Headingley at either end of the campaign.

Yorkshire's top-order batting, despite 1,000-run seasons for openers Alex Lees and Adam Lyth, is something the Club's new coach must try to address during 2017.

They often had to fight back from positions of weakness. The prime examples came against Nottinghamshire at Scarborough, when they were 51-6 in their first innings before winning by 305 runs, and against Middlesex at Lord's, when they were 53-4 needing 350 to pick up a fourth batting point to keep the title race alive.

Too often the middle and lower

Cast of 1,000s: Opening pair Adam Lyth and Alex Lees

order were forced into a patch-up job. Against Middlesex it was led by their resident rescue agent, Tim Bresnan, whose magnificent 145 not out was one of a series of crucial middle-order contributions on his way to being named as the Players' and Members' Player of the Year. It was probably Yorkshire's best innings of the season.

When Bresnan was handed his awards at the Club's Gala dinner in October, Ryan Sidebottom was also honoured for taking his 1,000th career wicket across all forms of senior cricket, domestic or international, during the early stages of the campaign.

Yorkshire's decision not to attempt a last-day run chase against Roses rivals Lancashire at Emirates Old Trafford was questioned at the time. Surely, had Gale and Gillespie et al been given the decision again it would have been a different one. Chasing 367, they were 148-0 at tea, needing 219 more runs from 30 overs. Albeit a task likely to be too tall, they should really have given it a crack, and not ended up shaking hands on a 10-point draw at 188-0.

Their limited-overs campaign proved a real rollercoaster, which started and ended badly, though ultimately showed signs of considerable promise under new full-time white-ball captain Lees. They won only one of their first seven Blast matches before surging through to the Club's second Finals Day appearance.

Disappointingly, they lost all three of their 50-over matches at

Headingley, including an opening-day hammering by Worcestershire when their batting was particularly limp on the way to 170 all out. It proved a watershed moment for their whole white-ball summer, with the White Rose determined to attack, attack, attack from then on.

Lyth led the way with scintillating 50-over centuries on successive days in mid-June against Northamptonshire and Lancashire. Yorkshire scored 200-plus in successive T20 home games against Durham and Northamptonshire in late July, and the 223-6 against Durham proved to be a Club record.

A number of Yorkshire players, including Azeem Rafiq, pointed to the calming influence of New Zealand captain Kane Williamson in the squad, but Rafiq should take a great deal of credit himself, because he ended up with 15 Blast wickets after nearly two years away from the professional game.

In truth, Yorkshire's overseas signings complicated things somewhat, although not through any fault of the players in question. Williamson needed to be rested during his short spell to avoid burnout, and Travis Head had to leave early to join Australia's squad just after a magnificent 175 in an RL50 win at Leicestershire, the Club's second highest personal score in List A cricket.

Head's replacement, a fellow South Australian in Jake Lehmann, impressed by averaging over 50 in five Championship matches with a century in the costly home defeat to Somerset during the last-but-one week — but he also was called away, this time by his state side before the Middlesex fixture.

Yorkshire continued to be hit by England unavailability, most notably during the last week of the campaign when Jonny Bairstow was ordered to rest and Adil Rashid asked to be rested.

Injuries gave Yorkshire a frustrating summer. Bresnan, Sidebottom and new signing David Willey all spent significant spells on the side-lines during the first half of the season. Teenage seamer Matthew Fisher, a sure-fire starter in limited-overs cricket and a valuable Championship squad member, did not play a single first-team match, having suffered three separate injuries to his left hamstring, starting on the Club's pre-season tour of the United Arab Emirates in mid-March.

A year of disappointment? Yes. But there were enough positive signs to indicate that the 2017 summer will be a fruitful one for Yorkshire County Cricket Club's first-team.

Graham Hardcastle writes on Yorkshire cricket for the Bradford Telegraph & Argus, The Press, York, and The Northern Echo

GALE CAN LOOK BACK WITH PRIDE ON PLAYING RECORD

By David Warner

Andrew Gale's sensible decision to end his playing career on accepting the position of Club Coach following the departure of Jason Gillespie robbed him of a few more years competing at first-class level.

At 32 years of age it could not have been an easy decision to make, but he can take immense satisfaction from knowing that he was one of the leading Yorkshire batsmen of his generation as well as the most successful captain in almost half a century.

It was a big challenge when Andrew agreed to take over the captaincy

ANDREW GALE: Most successful Yorkshire captain in half a century

from Anthony McGrath ahead of the 2010 season. Yorkshire had generally performed poorly. They had only just avoided relegation in the Championship, and were in some disarray.

He did not own up to it at the time, but there were some fleeting doubts in the back of his mind that he may not have been sufficiently experienced to take on such an exacting role.

Andrew need not have worried. In his first season in charge, Yorkshire lifted themselves to third place in the table — and could even have won the Championship but for a bizarre final day of the campaign. Behind the scenes, however, things were not running smoothly, and in 2011 immediate relegation resulted in big changes to the coaching structure and the appointment of Gillespie as first-team coach.

With strong backing, Andrew was able to bring Yorkshire on a regular basis the success they craved. They bounced straight out of the Second

19

Division in 2012, were runners-up to Durham the next season after a late falter, and clinched the title in 2014 before holding on to it.

Right up to the final day of last summer Andrew had the chance to become the first Yorkshire captain to lead his side to three consecutive titles since Brian Close in 1966-68.

The fact that they missed out was a disappointment, but Andrew had already done enough over seven seasons to earn the gratitude of both the Club and the fans.

Sad exit from Lord's...but Andrew Gale was the first to captain Yorkshire to back-to-back Championships since Brian Close

He was always very much the man-in-charge on the field, although keeping his finger on the pulse must have been even harder last season when Yorkshire replaced him as one-day captain with Alex Lees, while at the same time saying that they had no immediate plans to play him in limited-overs cricket which now takes up so much of the summer.

A fine and often powerful batsman, Andrew always found Scarborough a happy hunting ground, and it was fitting that he made his maiden century there, 149 against Warwickshire in 2006, although it did not bring him an instant regular place. Five of his 19 first-class centuries for Yorkshire came at North Marine Road, including a career-best 272 against Nottinghamshire in 2013, his most prolific season, when he hit 1,076 runs and also plundered consecutive centuries, the first against Middlesex at Lord's, 103, and then against Surrey, 148, at Headingley.

During his first-class career, which began against Somerset at Scarborough in July 2004, Andrew played in 149 matches for Yorkshire, scoring 7,726 runs at an average of 35.44.

Although eventually not called upon in white-ball cricket, it should not be forgotten than Andrew led Yorkshire to their only appearance so far in a Twenty20 Final — against Hampshire at the Swalec Stadium, Cardiff, in 2012, when his side went down by just 10 runs. Up to his retirement he was way ahead of any of his teammates in one-day runs — 3,256 at 31 with two centuries and 17 half-centuries in List A cricket and 2,260 at 25.39 with 16 half-centuries in Twenty20 contests.

If Andrew the young coach proves as successful in his new job as he was as captain and player, then Yorkshire should have little to fear over the next few years.

MANY HAPPY RETURNS — BUT NOT MUCH TO CELEBRATE

By Howard Clayton

Back in 2015 a film called *The Revenant* — he who returns — grossed 640 million dollars at the box office world-wide, and won four Oscars, having been nominated in 11 categories. To a certain extent season 2016 was a tale of those who returned for Yorkshire Second Eleven.

Firstly, Callum Geldart, released in 2011, was reinvited to open the innings after scoring a bucketful of runs in the Bradford League. He began well with an unbeaten 75 as Northamptonshire were beaten twice in the opening T20 encounters in the delightful setting of Stowe School in Buckinghamshire...but he failed to pass 50 again in any format, and had drifted out of contention by the end of the season.

Secondly came Azeem Rafiq, released in 2014 but attracting attention with Sheffield and Phoenix United. His return was almost immediately successful, bringing glowing praise for his refound enthusiasm from Director of Professional Cricket Martyn Moxon. A contract to the end of the season and his First Eleven cap were splendid returns for his rebirth.

Finally, the last game of the season was against Nottinghamshire at Scarborough, and down the pavilion steps came one Jonathan Tattersall, released 12 months earlier. In many ways his return was the most striking, as he made 101 out of a total of 232, or 43.53 per cent.

In the Championship two games were won against Leicestershire and Northamptonshire. Yorkshire were set to make 300 against Leicestershire at York, and at 129-4 it was anybody's game. At least it was until Ryan Gibson came in to destroy the bowling with an unbeaten 162. Azeem Rafiq, 72 not out, gave him solid support, and victory was achieved by six wickets. In all games Gibson scored just over 2,000 runs, gaining his Second Eleven cap in the course of the season.

The Northamptonshire game lost the first day to weather, and early declarations set Yorkshire a target of 220. Again, wickets fell, but this time Matthew Waite stood firm, and his unbeaten 103 saw them home by three wickets. Waite also gained his Second Eleven cap in 2016.

James Wainman with 24 wickets and Ben Coad, 20, led the way with the ball. Karl Carver, 11 wickets, was the leading spinner. Wainman received his Second Eleven cap as well. Three games were lost and four drawn to round off a moderate season. There was one notable black spot, and that was the team's dismissal for 66 against Nottinghamshire at Trent College in the second innings. This is the lowest total for which the Second Eleven have ever been dismissed against any opponent in the Championship. On the other side of the coin, after conceding 502-4 declared to Warwickshire, Yorkshire reduced them to 43-7 in their second innings — chasing 56 in seven overs — to almost pull off the most astounding victory.

There was no more success in white-ball cricket either. The Trophy saw three of the first four games lost, with the Leicestershire fixture at Pudsey Congs abandoned without a ball bowled. The last two games, against Durham and Derbyshire, were both won to illustrate perfectly the statement that too little is too late.

The game against Durham at York saw Alex Lees lead the way with 119 not out, but Gibson, 87, and Will Rhodes, 56 not out, stayed with him to see it through. Gibson, 70, and Harry Brook, 69, gave promise of a massive total against Derbyshire at Alvaston and Boulton, but the innings fell away to 270 with five of the 50 overs disappointingly unused. It was enough, however, as the home side succumbed almost 50 runs short.

Finally to T20: the first two games were won against Northamptonshire and the last two against Worcestershire, the second of these by one run as Jordan Thompson bowled a superb over to tie the batsmen down. Six other games were lost with the two against Lancashire at York severely curtailed by the weather.

Jordan also showed what he can do with the bat, as his unbeaten 146 at Scarborough, also against Worcestershire, almost pulled off a remarkable victory. This innings was in the running for the Second Eleven Performance of the Year, but the award finally went to Will Rhodes, who against Lancashire at Liverpool scored 137 and 114 not out opening the innings. Will also had an unbelievable spell of bowling against the Scotland Development Eleven at Harrogate in September. He returned 5-43, but those wickets came in nine deliveries for four runs and included a quadruple wicket maiden with scalps on the first, second, fourth and final deliveries of the over.

The Club's congratulations go to two young and talented players. Ed Barnes represented his country at Under-19 level against Sri Lanka, and Harry Brook was included in a National Training Camp at the National Centre for Performance in Cricket at Loughborough University with a three-week camp in Dubai following in December.

Howard Clayton is the Yorkshire CCC Second Eleven Scorer

LEAGUE CUP HAT-TRICK IN A RESPECTABLE SEASON

On the back of a successful 2015 season in which the Academy won the Black Sheep Champions' Trophy at the first time of trying, and retained the Yorkshire League Cup for the second year running, the lads were hoping for more success last summer.

The annual Sheriff Hutton Bridge v. Yorkshire Academy pre-season friendly had to be cancelled due to SHB gaining promotion to the Premier League, but it was not long before we were due to face them on the opening week of the season. This was not to be either, as typical English weather had its say on the first day.

The following week brought us our first game against Driffield, resulting in a 117-run win and 10 points. James Logan took his first wickets of the season with 7-16 from nine overs. Next came another rain-affected game at Dunnington, who were newly promoted to the Premier League, and a late start turned it into a T20-type contest. On a tricky, wet pitch, the Academy reached 137-7 and managed to contain Dunnington to 51-8 as a result of some very tight bowling from all five who were used. Eight points were taken from a winning draw.

The first loss of the season was at the hands of another newly promoted team, Stamford Bridge. A strong outfit saw the return of Will Rhodes for the home side. Stamford Bridge reached 231-8, with the Academy bowlers not quite up to their usual standards. Early wickets made it tough for the Academy to form any sort of partnership. Mosun Hussain and Jordan Thompson managed a stand of 50, but it did not go any further. The Academy ended on 191 all out, 40 short of Stamford's target, Thompson unbeaten on 71.

After this disappointing defeat normal service was resumed the following week in a comfortable 10-point victory over Acomb, Logan again among the wickets with six dismissals. Yet another reduced game followed, this time against Woodhouse Grange, which went to the wire. Woodhouse reached 97 from 23 overs, and again the Academy batters struggled to form any partnerships. It went all the way to the final over: a clever paddle sweep from wicket-keeper Jonny Read went all the way to the boundary, leaving one to win from the last ball. We managed to scrape over the line and pick up eight points.

A trip to the seaside was in order on May 28 to play Scarborough on a very hard pitch, It favoured the batsmen, as the result showed, only 11 wickets falling in the day. The Academy reached 272-5 from their 50 overs, Matthew Waite making 74 and Hussain 61, but a hard battle was on with the ball as Scarborough closed on 175-6, leaving us with a winning draw. A frustrating day to not come away with 10 points.

Two of the top performances of the season followed. Home to Castleford, Harry Brook hit his maiden ton for the Academy, helping us to reach 233-5. The second half brought something incredible: Castleford were reduced to 15-6, Jared Warner taking all six in a very sharp spell, but Castleford fought hard to make it to 107-9 in the 48th over. From being a couple of wickets away from victory in no more than 15 overs we were still in the field 30 overs later needing one more wicket. It eventually came, Warner picking up his ninth of the match to finish with the incredible figures of 9-19 from 10.2 overs.

A few weeks later took us to eventual champions Harrogate in what proved to be the first of two nail-biters against them. The Academy struggled to 185-9 in 50 overs, and Harrogate looked as if they were going to cruise to their target. Another five-wicket haul from Logan restricted them to nine down and needing five from the last over. Unfortunately, they made it over the line with four balls to spare.

It proved to be a shaky few weeks for the Academy, as we were to lose the following week to a good York side. We managed to get back to winning ways the next week at Driffield by knocking off 197, Thompson hitting 80 and Barnes striking a six to clinch it and reach his 50. The rain again beat us when up against Sheriff Hutton Bridge, three quarters of the game being completed before heavy showers took over. A comprehensive win over Dunnington came a week later with contributions from most of the order and another seven-wicket haul for Logan.

A winning draw against Stamford Bridge brought us eight points, but we could not get the extra two to enable us to creep up the table. Fine performances from Brook, 84, and Ainsley, 92, got us to 253, but we were unable to bowl Stamford out, their West Indian overseas hitting a brilliant 107. Three comfortable wins in consecutive weeks followed against Acomb, Woodhouse Grange and Scarborough, but wins around other grounds were still restricting us to third position in the league.

Our second game against Harrogate was a case of bad batting from both sides. The Academy fell to 85 all out, a very poor performance. Strong words at the break spurred us on to go out and make a game of it, which is exactly what we did. The return of Matthew Fisher was a great help as he managed to remove Harrogate's top two early. He was supported by the rest of the attack, and came back to pick up the last wicket to give the Academy a fantastic win by 12 runs.

The last three games were all rain-affected. Castleford had us 54-4 chasing 90 before rain intervened, and the matches against York and

Hull saw no play at all. This left us sitting in third place at the end of the season, a respectable position taking into account some of the injuries we had and calls to the first team.

In the Black Sheep Trophy we were drawn away to Scholes. It was a tough batting pitch, but we managed to scrape to 220. Our bowling proved too strong for the Huddersfield team as we shot them out for just above 100. The clash with York proved a step too far as we were comfortably beaten, and failed to retain the Trophy.

On the other hand we continued our great form in the Yorkshire League Cup as three comfortable wins against Castleford, Cleethorpes and Woodhouse Grange saw us reach the final for the third year running.

We faced Sheriff Hutton Bridge in a full game for the first time this season in the final at Stamford Bridge. Another century from Brook and contributions from the other batsmen saw us to 282 from our 50 overs, and Sheriff Hutton Bridge fell well short, with Fisher picking up five wickets against his home club and his two brothers.

The Academy came out of a respectable season with another Cup triumph. A few of the older end have moved on, but the young ones look promising. Hopefully, they can bring more success in 2017, winning the League Cup for the fourth year in a row, along with more trophies!

(Photo by Coach Richard Damms appears in our colour pages.)

YORKSHIRE ACADEMY BATTING IN LEAGUE AND CUP MATCHES

Player	M.	I.	N.O.	Runs	H.S.	Avge	100s	50s	Strike Rate	ct/st
H Brook	17	16	1	721	119	48.07	2	3	85.43	5
M Hussain	24	22	4	724	77	40.22	6	0	63.12	12
B Ainsley	23	22	4	700	103*	38.89	6	1	63.69	4
M Waite	19	19	2	588	74	34.59	4	0	87.50	2
J Thompson	24	20	4	473	80	29.56	3	0	79.63	15
J Warner	14	9	3	137	39	22.83	0	0	74.46	5
J Read	18	8	5	67	17	22.33	0	0	48.55	15/6
M Fisher	6	4	1	58	28	19.33	0	0	70.73	0
J Brown	19	17	5	191	44	15.92	0	0	61.41	9
E Barnes	18	17	4	199	50*	15.31	1	0	93.43	3
Y Imtiaz	19	14	5	129	37*	14.33	0	0	53.53	1
J Shutt	25	7	4	42	18*	14.00	0	0	46.15	6
R Brown	4	3	0	33	30	11.00	0	0	62.26	1
B Birkhead	8	4	1	30	13*	10.00	0	0	46.88	3
J Logan	26	7	3	38	15	9.50	0	0	50.67	5

YORKSHIRE ACADEMY BOWLING IN LEAGUE AND CUP MATCHES

Player	Overs	Mdns	Runs	Wkts	Avge	Best	5wI	Econ.	Strike Rate
M Fisher	43.4	9	91	13	7.00	5-20	1	2.08	20.15
J Logan	261.2	69	805	76	10.59	7-16	6	3.08	20.63
J Warner	69.4	9	229	20	11.45	9-19	1	3.29	20.90
M Waite	83	9	298	19	15.68	4-9	0	3.59	26.21
M Taylor	46	6	156	9	17.33	2-20	0	3.39	30.67
J Shutt	197.1	37	676	36	18.78	5-20	2	3.43	32.86
J Brown	21	5	66	3	22.00	1-5	0	3.14	42.00
J Thompson	108	12	397	18	22.06	3-12	0	3.68	36.00
H Brook	26	6	81	3	27.00	2-14	0	3.12	52.00
E Barnes	78.3	7	320	9	35.56	2-27	0	4.08	52.33

CHANGES AHEAD BUT YSCA WILL CONTINUE TO THRIVE

By David Warner

There was sadness in the air, but also a sense of great achievement when the Yorkshire Schools' Cricket Association, founded in 1930, held their final presentation dinner in the Headingley Long Room last November in front of a packed house.

In a YSCA report president Chris Hassell and chairman Dr Bernard Knowles MBE wrote that the Association heard in late 2015 that it was planned that county and recreational cricket would all come under the banner of "Yorkshire Cricket" and within that organisation an "Elite Junior Management Group" would be established to run county age group cricket. YSCA was allocated two places on the group of about 10, which would operate on majority decisions and be responsible for the appointment of team managers, coaches and officials to oversee fixtures and all matters relating to CAGC.

Last July it was confirmed that the YSCA would no longer be responsible for county age-group cricket as in the past.

"So, what of the future?" they asked. "The YSCA is an independent body, and will continue to run the six inter-school competitions which attract more entries than at any other county as well as the long-standing Under 19s Festival at St Peter's School, York, now in its 48th year.

"In addition, we will be introducing an Under 16/17 squad to take part in a five-day festival at Ampleforth College in order to cater for those boys who miss out on selection for the Yorkshire Academy and YCB Under 17s squads. This initiative will provide further opportunities for boys over 15. We now look forward with interest to see how the new arrangements work out, and hope that the standards we have carefully established are maintained.

"We are immensely proud of what YSCA has achieved since 1923, and would like to acknowledge the wonderful service our managers, coaches and officials have rendered by asking them to accept a special YSCA crystal memento to remind them of their valued contribution to the development of not only so many county and international cricketers but also very many other players who will have benefited from their time when playing for Yorkshire Schools." The YSCA annual report, entitled *The End of an Era*, said they could celebrate another excellent season in 2016 with some resounding successes.

The Under-14s were unbeaten, and won the ECB Royal London County Cup North Division and the 13s won the Taunton Festival for the fourth year as well the ESCA Northern Counties Cup for the third year.

The 12s were unbeaten, and won their Festival at Taunton, and the 11s were also unbeaten, completing their fifth consecutive win at the Taunton Festival. The 10s enjoyed a good season during their introduction to county fixtures.

The 15s were somewhat disappointing, and failed to make the national finals, a stage they had previously reached on many occasions. The B teams recorded some very good results and provided opportunities for a number of players to show their potential in moving to the A squads. A total of 198 scheduled fixtures were arranged.

All team captains and managers came forward to give their reports at the presentation dinner, when the guest speaker was John Abrahams, the former Lancashire captain and ECB England Development Programme Under 19s manager.

There was also an attendance of over 320 in the Long Room the previous week at the final Junior presentation evening when the awards were presented by Yorkshire and England's Tim Bresnan.

£4,500 raised at bookstall

The second-hand book stall at Headingley Cricket Ground, run on match days by Vivien Stone, Geoff Holmes, Jeremy Wimbush and new helper Trevor Horner, brought in £4,500 last season, taking the total amount raised since it started 18 years ago to £111,175. Proceeds are for the John Featherstone Foundation and go to the Yorkshire Schools' Cricket Association.

On the move

Two young players no longer with Yorkshire at the end of the 2016 season are Danish Hussain, Bradford-born opening batsman who played for the Academy, and James William Peter Brown, Sheffield-born left-arm all-rounder who played in three Second Eleven *T20* matches.

DIAMONDS FIND SPARKLE AHEAD OF ROSES CLASH

Yorkshire County Cricket Club were awarded hosting rights for a team in the KIA Super League by the England and Wales Cricket Board in January 2016, and Yorkshire Diamonds were formed with Richard Pyrah appointed as Head Coach.

On the day of the announcement Yorkshire's Chief Executive, Mark Arthur, said: "This is a momentous day for Yorkshire Cricket. We are delighted to welcome Yorkshire Diamonds to the family. Cricket is one of the fastest-growing female sports in

By Jane Hildreth

the country, and to be part of the inaugural Women's Cricket Super League is very special for the Club and the local region.

"We aim to make the Yorkshire Diamonds, through our partnership with Leeds Beckett University, an integral part of the Yorkshire sporting landscape, and ultimately see the Diamonds become the most prosperous professional female team in the region through success on the field and a vibrant supporter base off it."

The KIA Super League is designed to attract the best players in the women's game and bridge the gap between county and international cricket. The new competition would also attract new fans and players.

Through the support of the Yorkshire Cricket Board and the Yorkshire Cricket Foundation events were run around the county to engage children and their families in the KIA Super League. Yorkshire Diamonds players in their Chance to Shine Ambassador roles took part in the activities, signed autographs and "selfies".

A wide range of events were organised, including taking cricket road shows to clubs, school competitions, beach cricket, Junior Diamonds pre-match coaching, matchday mascots and guard of honour. As well as attracting a new audience to matches the events were aimed at encouraging girls and women to play cricket.

Working with the ECB all teams were allocated a squad of 15 players to include those from overseas, England players and county players.

Yorkshire were very excited to announce their team, which had a strong balance of strength and experience. A fantastic opportunity was given to younger county players to experience a high-performance environment and to train with international cricketers.

The Yorkshire Diamonds squad was:

Lauren Winfield (captain), Katherine Brunt, Danielle Hazell, Jenny Gunn, Alex Blackwell (Australia), Beth Mooney (Australia), Shabnim Ismail (South Africa), Hollie Armitage, Steph Butler, Alice Davison Richards, Katie Levick, Katie Thompson, Laura Spragg, Anna Nicholls, Teresa Graves.

Headingley hosted the inaugural match on Saturday, July 30, when the team played Loughborough Lightning. Despite the disappointing result it was fantastic to have almost 1,000 people watching the game.

With away matches against Surrey Stars at the KIA Oval under floodlights and Southern Vipers at the Ageas Bowl, the team had the opportunity to play at first-class grounds. They were unable to win either game despite some fine individual performance with bat and ball.

The Diamonds recorded their first victory at Emirates Old Trafford against Lancashire Thunder. The anticipation of a *Roses* game gave the Diamonds a boost, and they did not disappoint.

The final match of the competition on Sunday, August 14, at Headingley, versus Western Storm, gave the Diamonds a very slim chance of gaining a place at Finals Day. Only a win and a superior run rate would have been sufficient. This was not to be, and the Diamonds lost their final fixture of the competition to finish in fifth place.

A comprehensive review of the KIA Super League involving the ECB and all hosts was undertaken at the end of the playing season. A review document has been published including actions for 2017, when the KIA Super League will take place after the Women's World Cup. The timing allows for the continuation of support and engagement of new fans and players. Yorkshire Diamonds will again play in five T20 league games, and will be pushing for a place at Finals Day in early September.

The competition is expanding in 2018, which will give Yorkshire County Cricket Club the opportunity to host five games.

Jane Hildreth is General Manager
of Yorkshire Diamonds

FLOODS TASKFORCE STOPS CLUBS FROM GOING UNDER

By John Fuller

Nothing is more likely to chill the blood of those involved at cricket clubs than the imminent threat of flooding.

Twenty clubs contacted Yorkshire Cricket Board after the Boxing Day deluge of 2015 to seek urgent assistance, and in the aftermath of the unprecedented rainfall the Yorkshire Cricket Floods Taskforce was set up. It included representatives from the England and Wales Cricket Board, the then Yorkshire captain, Andrew Gale, Chief Executive Mark Arthur and ex-Yorkshire cricketer Neil Hartley, chairman of the Yorkshire CCC Players' Association.

Each club was visited and assessed, with rapid funding made available from the board's Emergency Fund and further monetary aid through Sport England and the Yorkshire Cricket Floods Appeal, all adding to expertise offered to begin the onerous task of repairing and rebuilding.

Time tends to blur our memories which is where the unbelievable photos and video taken across the county in December 2015 and into the New Year jolt us into a double-take. We live in an age of hyperbole. The longest, fastest, oldest, heaviest comparisons are trotted out with such frequency that it is hard not to be cynical, but that winter was worse than any Hollywood disaster blockbuster. No exaggeration required.

On Boxing Day my wife and I began a walk along the River Aire, a route we had taken many times, but we were pulled up open-mouthed at the way the river had burst its banks and swallowed huge swathes of land. Walkers milled about, shocked at scenes some had never witnessed in their lifetime. We are not complete novices to freak weather in this country, but Storms Desmond and Eva flooded 16,000 homes in December alone.

Last season I visited Bradford and Bingley Cricket Club on a scorching summer's day where the firsts were at home to Cleckheaton in the Bradford Premier League. The Wagon Lane deck still had some life in it, a miracle considering that the whole complex had been submerged with extensive damage to the grounds, equipment and machinery.

Bolton Percy is a tiny North Yorkshire village a few miles east of

DOWN BUT NOT OUT: Bradford and Bingley CC rose from the floods to produce a strip which still had some life in it

Tadcaster, and their cricket club play in the York and District Senior League. The area caught the national headlines when Tadcaster Bridge collapsed on December 30, 2015, under pressure from the swollen waters of the River Wharfe, and residents were evacuated.

Bolton Percy CC are familiar with water on their pitch. It had crept up to the doorsteps the winter before, but the decision to close a sluice gate to protect the village meant that metres of floodwater turned their pavilion into an isolated island surrounded on all sides.

Club secretary Bill Preacher shuddered at what the floods ruined several years after their HQ had been expanded and completely redecorated: "Everything was knackered. Like all old buildings, it's not exactly level, so it was up to 15 inches in places. The fridges had been swimming in water."

Nonetheless, among the now-useless machinery, a few trusty faithfuls refused to give up. Once the waters had receded things considered ancient like the roller "which dates back to Noah's Ark" miraculously started first time. At times like these clubs needs their volunteers to step up and, literally, wade in. Repairs take many months, and there is the headache of insurance – what is covered and what not in the fine print, and how to make up any shortfall.

There were no sudden, rampant torrents at Bolton Percy. The water eerily rose...and then gradually sank back down, but damage from standing water was plentiful, with the outdoor nets one of the casualties. As the water disappeared trees that had been ripped up were revealed on the cricket square and outfield. Little bits of bark were still being plucked out of the ground the following September.

In Bolton Percy's case the insurance payout was appreciatively speedy, but as a rural club they had not managed to afford cover for the outdoor nets, so the Yorkshire Cricket Floods Appeal stumped up a sizeable grant to replace them.

Are they better prepared for another flood? Lessons have been learned about storing machinery out of the clutches of nature, but there are no cast-iron fail-safes, as with Bill's verdict: "Unless we knock down the pavilion and start again the water will get in."

If that prognosis sounds too gloomy, the club has bounced back from adversity, and out in the middle their first team avoided relegation from Division 1 of the York Senior League with the last game of 2016. Fundraising was appreciatively up as the community rallied, and if there is anything positive to be gleaned from something like this then, thanks to the generosity of many, Bolton Percy Cricket Club's facilities are now better than ever before.

The list of Yorkshire clubs struck by the 2015 floods was indicative of the might of the county's river system fuelled by unprecedented rainfall. The Calder, Aire, Wharfe and Ure all rose up in unison.

A year on the incredulity in treasurer David Young's voice at Tong Park Esholt Cricket Club was palpable: "We had debris all over the field. It took six weeks for the water to recede. It was horrendous...like nothing we'd ever seen."

The Aire swallowed up the cricket and football fields as well as the caravan and camping park. Eight residents needed picking up by West Yorkshire Fire and Rescue in a boat, though cricket-club president Bob Wilkinson chose to stay in the clubhouse, where he lives in a connecting flat. By the second week of January three caravans that had been picked up by the currents like rubber ducks were still on the Tong Park outfield.

David was keen to highlight the help of the England and Wales Cricket Board, particularly Dan Musson in their Facilities Team, without whose support he believes Tong Park Esholt CC would no longer exist. David stressed how the club pulled together to get things back on track, though even now their ground is not ready for play, with June or July 2017 – some 18 months after the event – the goal for cricket's return.

The square and outfield needed relaying, while five feet of standing water in the changing rooms necessitated a refit. the total bill estimated at £150,000. Our interview coincided with the first storm of the season, Angus, which had David anxiously rooted to his hourly flood alerts and painting a stark picture post-2015: "We're under no illusion. If we have it that bad again I don't think we'll be able to continue, as we'll no longer get insurance. It's always there hanging over you."

They could at least count their blessings by virtue of having two

BALLANCE OF POWER: Gary Ballance takes on added responsibilities this year with his appointment as Yorkshire captain in all forms of cricket. He takes over as first-class captain from new coach Andrew Gale and as one-day captain from Alex Lees, who will now concentrate solely on his batting.

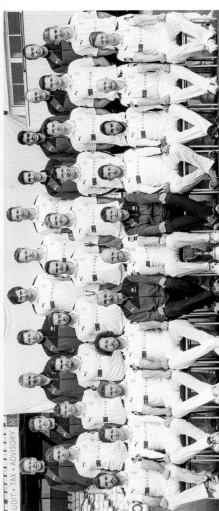

YORKSHIRE 2016: Back Row, left to right: Ian Fisher, Lead Strength and Conditioning Coach; Blaine Clancy, Academy Strength and Conditioning Coach; Richard Pyrah, Club Coach; Ian Dews, Second Eleven Coach and Academy Director; Richard Damms, Academy Head Coach. Middle row: Ben Coad, Karl Carver, Will Rhodes, Jack Leaning, Jack Brooks, David Willey, Andy Hodd, Matthew Fisher, Alex Lees and Jared Warner. Front row: Liam Plunkett, Gary Ballance, Jonathan Bairstow, Ryan Sidebottom, Jason Gillespie, First Eleven Coach; Andrew Gale, Captain; Martyn Moxon, Director of Cricket; Tim Bresnan, Adil Rashid, Adam Lyth and Steven Patterson.

THE FAMILY WAY: Four generations of Roots line up on the sofa with Joe's mother, Helen, behind the camera. Grandfather Don, extreme left, played for Rotherham Town, as did a long line of cricketing Roots — they formed a Sunday team called *The Rooters* — and Don was chief sport chauffeur throughout the childhood of Joe and his brother, Billy. Father Matt, centre, a former Nottinghamshire Second Eleven player, started Joe and Billy off at his Yorkshire League club, Sheffield Collegiate...and how long will it be before Alfred William, born to Joe and Carrie at New Year, gets off his father's knee to pick up a bat? Joe was able to play in only two Championship matches in 2016 because of England commitments, but ¬ Yorkshire's innings victory against rrey, right, he piled up 213 and ijoyed a stand of 372 for the fourth wicket with Jonny Bairstow (198).

BRESNAN THE BRAVE: Tim Bresnan during his epic 142 not out against Middlesex at Lord's in the final game of the season. His fighting spirit gave Yorkshire a chance of retaining their Specsavers County Championship title until the last few overs, when Middlesex gained the upper hand to take their crown. Tim, who scooped both the Players' Player of the Year and the Supporters' Player of the Year awards, was appointed Yorkshire vice-captain in January.

TRIUMPH FROM TRAGEDY: Floods cover the pitch at Riddlesden to a depth of several feet. The garage was five feet deep in water and the clubhouse two feet deep, and everything had to be stripped out – including internal walls. Yet such was the devotion of members that the pitch was cleared of debris and walls and club rose from the abyss.

grounds – Esholt was put out of action, but Tong Park thankfully escaped attention: that was where the firsts and seconds played, while the thirds hired Shipley Providence's Salts ground.

Emergency funding was sought from Yorkshire Cricket Board and Sport England, the latter awarding a £25,000 grant that at the time of writing was dependant on Bradford Council renewing the ground's lease. In a striking act of generosity the members of Tong Park Esholt CC have put their hands in their pockets to loan the thousands of pounds for repairs to speed up the recovery process.

Once finished, Tong Park Esholt will have an all singing all dancing drainage system, a relaid cricket square and brand-new practice facilities. They wish the horror of the floods had never happened, but the money has been found and something good will come out of all of this destruction.

Collective, dogged endeavour got countless clubs through a grim time, and while the weather is unlikely to be becalmed anytime soon, communities across Yorkshire rallied when they were really needed.

John Fuller is a cricket journalist who runs the website *cricketyorkshire.com*

MAJOR BOOTH MEMORABILIA IS BROUGHT TO HEADINGLEY

By J C David Allan

Those members of Yorkshire CCC who are readers of *The Times* will undoubtedly look forward to each Thursday when Michael Atherton, the paper's Chief Cricket Correspondent, writes his weekly column on a current topic of interest. One certain member of the Archives Committee was absolutely fascinated by Atherton's chosen subject in mid-July; the first day of that month had seen the 100th anniversary of the Battle of the Somme, and the writer's piece featured a review of a play which had been presented by schoolchildren at Lord's.

The venue for this performance was chosen because the storyline related the experience of Major William Booth, who tragically had lost his life in that fateful conflict. Booth, Pudsey-born, was a young Yorkshire all-rounder who had made his Test debut prior to the outbreak of war. However, the section of the article which caught our reader's eye more than any other related how Atherton had met Booth's great-nephew, and had been able to peruse a considerable amount of his memorabilia which had been passed down through the family.

Our committee member, Paul Dyson, who had himself written an article on Booth which was published in *The Cricketer* in 1987 to coincide with the 100th anniversary of his birth, thought this too good an opportunity to miss, and immediately wrote to Atherton stating that the Archives Committee would be most interested in the items mentioned in the piece. Nothing happened for a few weeks until a phone call was received from a Martin Bradford, who was a resident in London. Mr Bradford stated that he would be spending a week in Yorkshire in October. He would gladly meet some members of the committee and show them what he had.

Naturally enough, this offer was seized upon with great enthusiasm by the committee and the date of October 17 was fixed. Mick Pope, who had also written about Booth in his *Tragic White Roses*, was invited to the meeting, and it turned out that Mr Bradford was a keen cricket enthusiast, being a member of MCC, and had read Mick's book. The amount of memorabilia, as well as its quality, was most impressive.

The year as a whole must rank as one of the most productive ever in the amount of cricket memorabilia to be logged by the Archives

Committee, and much of this came from the families of two of Yorkshire CCC's greatest cricketers, Bob Appleyard and Brian Close.

Most of Bob's large collection was handed over by his family for scheduling following his death in March 2015, and when Brian died later that year his devoted wife, Vivien, generously passed on the vast majority of his memorabilia for the committee to assess.

Several visits were made to the Close household in Baildon to collect an amazing array of items, including scores of letters and postcards which Brian had written during his younger days as an England and Yorkshire cricketer — and also a top soccer player — and they give an unprecedented insight into one of the most versatile sportsmen this country has ever produced.

The work of putting all of this together and making out an inventory is still very much ongoing, and in the case of the collections of both Bob and Brian I would like to pay special mention to Ron Deaton, who has spent countless hours neatly cataloguing everything that has found its way into our hands. Although Ron no longer has a seat on the Archives Committee he is as committed and as meticulous as ever in his archivist's role, and we are extremely grateful to him.

We hope that in the fullness of time it will be possible to acquire some or all of the Appleyard/Close collections either by way of gift, loan or outright purchase.

Each and every member of my committee has played an important role in making sure that as much general Yorkshire cricket memorabilia as possible either remains in the collection or is added to it, and numerous interesting items have come into our possession over the past year.

At various times in 2016 the committee made enquiries about the feasibility of blue plaques being issued for three great Yorkshire players in Bob Appleyard, Maurice Leyland and Willie Watson, but late in the year it was decided not to proceed for the time being because of a reluctance by other bodies to assist with the funding.

In February 2016 David Gent, then chairman of Yorkshire Cricket Foundation, was invited to an Archives meeting to give an update on the Foundation's activities, and he briefed us on the Foundation's intention to apply for Heritage Lottery Funding. He was able to report that Brian Heywood had been appointed a Foundation consultant.

Since then Brian has regularly sat in at Archives meetings, and we have been very impressed with his hard work and expertise. He has kept us up to date with various aspects of the Foundation's work, and we have continued to ensure that the Archive and the Museum are made accessible to benefit the wider community within and beyond cricket. At the YCF's request the committee prepared their own job description for the post of Heritage Officer and, in the end, this varied, from the one used.

The lost legend: What heights Yorkshire and England all-rounder Major Booth might have reached between the two world wars of the 20th Century can never be known. Second Lieutenant Booth was one of 20,000 British soldiers killed on the first day of the Battle of the Somme on July 1, 1916. To mark the centenary of Booth's death his great nephew, Martin Bradford, unveils the family's priceless collection of memorabilia in the Long Room at Headingley.

The cabinets in the Long Room at Headingley are viewed with great interest by Yorkshire members and many others with access to the room.

Showing at various times in 2016 were items associated with the Maurice Dover collection, Philip Sharpe, Brian Close, Bob Appleyard, Ted Lester, Sir Leonard Hutton, Gerald Smithson, Darren Lehmann and other overseas players. Also displayed were items relating to the Great War and the Leeds Pals.

As well as memorabilia on display in the Museum and Long Room cabinets, items have been selected for the mobile museum, which travels to various venues around the county and was frequently visited during the Scarborough Cricket Festival.

36

The Archives Committee held several Open Days at Headingley in 2016 during County Championship matches with Brian Sanderson and Chris Hardy regularly on hand to answer queries and inspect memorabilia brought in by supporters.

The Yorkshire and Lancashire Cup (formerly the Duke of Leeds Cup) has recently been engraved with updates, and following Yorkshire's *Roses* victory in the Championship match at Headingley it was handed to first-team captain Andrew Gale by Lieutenant Colonel David O'Kelly, the Regimental Secretary of the Yorkshire Regiment.

The committee also managed to acquire the 2014 and 2015 County Championship pennants. which had proudly flown at Headingley, and these are now on display in the Museum. A professional valuation of all items in the archives possession that belong to YCCC was carried out in 2016, and Brian Sanderson and Chris Hardy spent countless hours at Morley sifting through the many items stored there.

The archives collection was added to through the year as a result of outstanding pieces being obtained either at sales or on E-bay, and one particularly noteworthy item secured was the gold cigarette case of a former Yorkshire captain, Frank Greenwood. Some items not directly connected with Yorkshire cricket were also sold.

A total of 54 pieces of correspondence have been dealt with by the committee, mainly by Paul Dyson, during the course of the year. These relate to almost the whole range of cricket memorabilia, including bats, balls, ties, photographs, fixture cards, books, dinner menus, autographs as well as specially presented items such as glasses and silver salvers.

Many of the inquiries concern valuation and advice on disposal, but particular pleasure has been derived from there being an increasing number of letters of thanks which have been sent to people who, completely out of the blue, have donated items to our collection. Pride of place among these must be a rare photograph of the 1874 Yorkshire side, and the committee was particularly grateful to receive this. Another feature of the year has been the connections with two of the county's cricket societies, who have loaned items.

The committee is always looking to increase its stock of memorabilia. Suitable items which come its way, whether they be bought, borrowed or given, are always most gratefully received.

This annual report would be incomplete if I did not place on public record our thanks to members of this committee who give most generously, in varying degrees, of their time and wide experience for our mutual benefit.

David Allan is Chairman of the Yorkshire Cricket Foundation Archives Committee

YORKSHIRE AT THE DOUBLE — DESPITE CLOSE CENSURE

By Anthony Bradbury

Yorkshire had won the County Championship in 1966. So the aim for 1967 was to achieve a "double". Thoughts of a hat-trick could wait until the end of the season. At the start of the 1967 summer Yorkshire had a strong side, and were clear favourites to win the title again.

They had a considerable coterie of established players, led by England captain Brian Close, with Freddie Trueman as his deputy, and with such well established players as Raymond Illingworth, Philip Sharpe, Geoffrey Boycott, John Hampshire, Jimmy Binks, Ken Taylor, Don Wilson and Tony Nicholson available to play in many of the matches. Others seeking to secure a regular place included Geoff Cope, Chris Old and Richard Hutton.

At the season's end the top 13 in the Yorkshire batting averages had all played or would play for England — a startling indication of Yorkshire talent, and all, of course, born in Yorkshire. But in late 1967 a regulation was introduced for 1968 and later years, namely that one overseas-born player could immediately play for their chosen county without further qualification. No one had too many qualms about that in 1967, but the introduction of that regulation was to have profound implications for the success of Yorkshire cricket in the years ahead.

The season started in a tumult of rain and generally bad weather. The 17 counties were each due to play 26 matches, so the concept of every team playing its opposition home and away was never a consideration. Of Yorkshire's first six Championship games two were abandoned without a ball, including the May Bank Holiday clash with Lancashire.

One other early fixture – that against Nottinghamshire – only achieved a result with three declarations: Nottinghamshire 159-5, Yorkshire 62-3 and Nottinghamshire 52-0 before Yorkshire scored 150 to win in two hours, the last 50 coming in 20 minutes. Yorkshire historian Tony Woodhouse was later to write: "There were some who were incensed at the methods used to reach that situation." Was this a forerunner of the tossed-up bowling seen at Lord's in the decider of 2016?

Geoffrey Boycott, now well installed as an England opener, had a curate's egg of a season. Early on he scored 10 runs in five successive Championship innings, including a pair of 0s against Kent at Bradford, each time falling to that industrious bowler Norman Graham. Shortly afterwards he had two consecutive innings of 98 not out and 220 not out.

He had just been dropped by England for slow scoring in his 246 not out against India – so he had a point to prove – but curiously in his undefeated 98 against Gloucestershire he had not been given, or taken, the opportunity to make a century to win the match with minutes and wickets in hand.

Even more curiously, Fred Trueman was on the field at the time as a runner for Boycott's partner, Sharpe (71 not out). In a generally low-scoring summer Boycott still scored 1,260 Championship runs at an average of 48.46. Padgett and Sharpe also

Daily Express 1967: Grim classic from the Mick Pope Archive

scored over 1,000 runs, Sharpe without completing a century, the other centuries being Taylor and Hampshire.

Five bowlers finished the season with an average of under 20 per wicket, and top of the pile was Cope who, despite the wet conditions, took 32 Championship wickets at 12.78. The ever consistent Tony Nicholson claimed 90 wickets in the Championship and 101 wickets in all Yorkshire matches at an average of 17.07. Illingworth, Wilson and Trueman each took more than 50 Championship wickets, and Illingworth joined Close and Boycott in the Test side.

Matches are often only noticed in retrospect, but by early August it was becoming clear that either Kent or Yorkshire could well become Champions. The two sides then met at Canterbury – both having lost players to England, Cowdrey and Boycott opening together for England, and Close and Knott. In that Canterbury week of two consecutive first-class games 40,000 people attended. Compare that with the Championship decider of Middlesex v. Yorkshire at Lord's in 2016.

With Knott unavailable for Kent, Godfrey Evans was recalled for his first Championship match in eight years. The battle for first innings was tenacious, Kent scrambling to 223. Yorkshire were eight down for 157 when captain Fred Trueman, coming in at No. 10, struck a lively 33 before being caught by Alan Ealham with an outstanding boundary catch. Yorkshire 217-9, but Don Wilson, after a simple dropped catch, steered the visitors to 225 and four precious first-innings points. Kent then lost all momentum: they were three wickets down for five runs in their second innings, 100 all out, and Yorkshire cantered to victory.

A drawn rain-ruined match with Derbyshire was followed by the tragedy of Brian Close at Edgbaston in mid-August. After another fierce battle for first-innings points — Yorkshire 238, Warwickshire 242 — Yorkshire had a poor second innings and were all out for 145. That left Warwickshire one hour and 40 minutes to score 142. They were 133-5 when stumps were drawn. Yorkshire in that time had bowled 24 overs — maybe a reasonable rate in 2016, but not so in 1967. In the last 15 minutes Yorkshire bowled two overs and once left the field briefly during drizzle and without the consent of the umpires. There were no stipulations then about the number of overs to be bowled in the final hour.

By obtaining the draw Yorkshire saved for themselves two points. Close as captain was censured for time-wasting, a censure he never accepted as being just, and a greater penalty came when he was removed from the England captaincy before that winter's tour of the West Indies. The captaincy instead went to Kent's Colin Cowdrey, a decision that added salt to the wounds. Perhaps there is significance in trying to see where the reality of the situation lay in reading the words of a great Yorkshire cricket writer, Jim Kilburn, in *Wisden* 1967: "Yorkshire indulged in blatant time-wasting tactics which brought down the wrath of spectators and disapproval of the critics. Report of this conduct raised an enquiry by the County Advisory Executive Committee, which resulted in a public censure for the team with full responsibility laid on the Yorkshire captain."

Eight months later, in March 1968, the counties collectively decided that from the start of the last hour of a match at least 20 overs would be bowled whatever the official closing time might be. That new rule stood the test of time. The Edgbaston saga received not a single mention in Yorkshire CCC's Annual Report for 1967, where the opening sentence (before any mention of the Championship) read: "Your Committee regrets to report a loss on the year of £5,260."

This controversy did damage and sully Yorkshire's march over the last games of the season to the Championship. After the Edgbaston match they stuttered briefly by losing to Essex by nine runs at Scarborough, where they were bowled out for 109 in the fourth innings. They recovered to beat Sussex at Eastbourne, drew with Nottinghamshire at Trent Bridge, and then had to play Warwickshire

YORKSHIRE 1967. Back row, left to right: Geoffrey Cope, Philip Sharpe, Tony Nicholson, Peter Stringer, John Waring, John Hampshire and Geoffrey Boycott. Front row: Doug Padgett, Jimmy Binks, Freddie Trueman, Brian Close (captain) Raymond Illingworth, Ken Taylor and Don Wilson.
(Photo: Ron Deaton Archive)

again at Middlesbrough. Kent at that stage were just ahead, but had played a game more than Yorkshire. The atmosphere must have been tense at Middlesbrough, not least when Boycott was almost immediately out for one run. Then Yorkshire recovered to reach a respectable 250, and Warwickshire collapsed twice to the spin of Don Wilson, 6-31 and 7-21. Yorkshire had a few days off before their last game at Harrogate.

Meantime, Kent had played and won their last two matches, both at Dover, and were top of the table, albeit by only two points. To win the title Yorkshire could take first-innings points against Gloucestershire in their final game, or, of course, win. They did both, though being sent in on a damp wicket. Boycott and Sharpe eased nerves with a fine opening partnership of 127; Yorkshire reached 307, and on the second day they bowled out Gloucestershire for 134 and 99. Illingworth was master of the day, taking 7-58 and then an amazing 7-6: that final analysis was 13 overs, nine maidens, six runs, seven wickets. The Yorkshire crowd revelled in Yorkshire's 28th Championship success since 1893. Yorkshire's 12 wins were the lowest number by a Champion county since 1895.

The Gillette Cup competition scarcely troubled Yorkshire supporters. It was a straight 60-overs-per-side knockout tournament with no preliminary league rounds. Minor Counties had a few places in the draw, and not all first-class sides played in the first round. Yorkshire were given a bye in that round, and in the second they were drawn at home to

Scars of victory: Skipper Brian Close was suffering from more than physical wounds at the champagne celebration of Yorkshire's 1967 triumph. *(Photo: Mick Pope Archive)*

Cambridgeshire with three days allocated. No play was possible on any day. Twelve days later, on the rearranged date, Headingley was under water, so the teams moved to Castleford 12 miles away. There, despite more rain, a 10-over thrash was arranged. Cambridgeshire managed 43-8 and Yorkshire, batting in a torrent, won with 46-4 in 6.5 overs. Johnny Wardle, playing for Cambridgeshire nine years after his last match for Yorkshire, bagged in vain the scalps of Taylor and Hampshire.

The next round was at Old Trafford. There were 12,000 spectators, and in a thrilling match both sides at times had the edge. Lancashire prevailed by four runs with an lbw decision in the last permitted over. So, Yorkshire's interest in one-day cricket in 1967 was over by mid-June.

One of Yorkshire's finest batsmen, Maurice Leyland, died on January 1, 1967. In memory he has been overshadowed by the overlapping careers of Herbert Sutcliffe and Len Hutton, but for Yorkshire from 1920 to 1946 he scored over 26,000 runs with 62 centuries. Only Sutcliffe, Hutton and Boycott have made more centuries. He played in 41 Tests scoring nine centuries, seven of them against Australia. His highest Test score was 187 against Australia at The Oval in 1938, and his second-wicket partnership of 382 with Hutton remains an England record.

Could Yorkshire achieve a hat-trick of Championships in 1968? That had last been obtained in 1937, 1938, and 1939 — and actually added to in 1946. Could it be done once more?

YORKSHIRE'S FIRST CLASS HIGHLIGHTS OF 1967

Win by an innings (7)

Leicestershire (161 and 96) lost to Yorkshire (380) by an innings and 123 runs at Leicester

Northamptonshire (173 and 99) lost to Yorkshire (388-5 dec) by an innings and 116 runs at Sheffield

Yorkshire (300) defeated Surrey (118 and 90) by an innings and 92 runs at Leeds

Yorkshire (309) defeated Gloucestershire (134 and 99) by an innings and 76 runs at Harrogate

Cambridge University (174 and 142) lost to Yorkshire (359) by an innings and 43 runs at Scarborough

Yorkshire (380) defeated India (188 and 186) by an innings and 6 runs at Sheffield

Worcestershire (119 and 197) lost to Yorkshire (318-4 dec) by an innings and 2 runs at Kidderminster

Win by 10 wickets (1)

Glamorgan (141 and 273) lost to Yorkshire (389 and 27-0) at Swansea

Win by over 200 runs (1)

Yorkshire (250 and 197-5 dec) defeated Warwickshire (148 and 70) by 229 runs at Middlesbrough

Totals of 400 and over (1)

414-3 dec v. Pakistan at Leeds

Opponents dismissed for under 100 (7)

70	v. Warwickshire at Middlesbrough	96	v. Leicestershire at Leicester
74	v. Worcestershire at Hull	99	v. Northamptonshire at Sheffield
87	v. Essex at Scarborough	99	v. Gloucestershire at Harrogate
90	v. Surrey at Leeds		

Century Partnerships (13)

For the 1st wicket (4)

210	G Boycott and P J Sharpe	v. Pakistan at Leeds
128	G Boycott and K Taylor	v. Worcestershire at Kidderminster
127	G Boycott and P J Sharpe	v. Gloucestershire at Harrogate
100	G Boycott and P J Sharpe	v. Hampshire at Bournemouth

For the 2nd wicket (2)

192	P J Sharpe and D E V Padgett	v. Pakistan at Leeds
103	G Boycott and D E V Padgett	v. Derbyshire at Chesterfield

For the 3rd wicket (2)

158	G Boycott and J H Hampshire	v. Glamorgan at Harrogate
148	P J Sharpe and J H Hampshire	v. Glamorgan at Swansea

Century Partnerships *(Continued)*

For the 4th wicket (3)

126	J H Hampshire and D B Close	v. MCC at Lord's
109	J H Hampshire and J C Balderstone	v. India at Sheffield
100	D E V Padgett and D B Close	v. Worcestershire at Hull

For the 5th wicket (2)

162*	G Boycott and J G Binks	v. Northamptonshire at Sheffield
114	D B Close and R Illingworth	v. Gloucestershire at Bristol

Centuries (9)

G Boycott (3)

220*	v. Northamptonshire at Sheffield
128	v. Pakistan at Leeds
102	v. Glamorgan at Harrogate

J H Hampshire (2)

107	v. MCC at Lord's
102	v. Warwickshire at Birmingham

D E V Padgett (2)

139	v. Nottinghamshire at Nottingham
111	v. Middlesex at Sheffield

P J Sharpe (1)

197	v. Pakistan at Leeds

K Taylor (1)

162	v. Worcestershire at Kidderminster

5 wickets in an innings (18)

A G Nicholson (6)

9-62	v. Sussex at Eastbourne
6-34	v. Somerset at Bradford
6-50	v. Warwickshire at Birmingham
5-24	v. Derbyshire at Bradford
5-30	v. Essex at Scarborough
5-37	v. Kent at Canterbury

R Illingworth (5)

7- 6	v. Gloucestershire at Harrogate 2nd innings
7-58	v. Gloucestershire at Harrogate 1st innings
6-34	v. Worcestershire at Hull
6-52	v. Leicestershire at Leicester 1st innings
5-27	v. Leicestershire at Leicester 2nd innings

D Wilson (3)

7-21	v. Warwickshire at Middlesbrough 2nd innings
7-50	v. Somerset at Bath
6-31	v. Warwickshire at Middlesbrough 1st innings

G A Cope (2)

5-23	v. Surrey at Leeds
5-95	v. MCC at Scarborough

F S Trueman (2)

5-39	v. Glamorgan at Harrogate
5-59	v. Cambridge University at Scarborough

10 wickets in a match (5)

R Illingworth (2)

| 14-64 | (7-58 and 7- 6) | v. Gloucestershire at Harrogate |
| 11-79 | (6-52 and 5-27) | v. Leicestershire at Leicester |

D Wilson (2)

| 13-52 | (6-31 and 7-21) | v. Warwickshire at Middlesbrough |
| 11-123 | (4-73 and 7-50) | v. Somerset at Bath |

A G Nicholson (1)

| 12-102 | (9-62 and 3-40) | v. Sussex at Eastbourne |

3 catches in an innings (11)

P J Sharpe (4)

3	v. Cambridge University at Scarborough
3	v. Middlesex at Sheffield
3	v. Lancashire at Sheffield 1st innings
3	v. Lancashire at Sheffield 2nd innings

F S Trueman (3)

4	v. Northamptonshire at Sheffield
3	v. Nottinghamshire at Nottingham
3	v. Gloucestershire at Harrogate

J H Hampshire (2)

| 3 | v. Cambridge University at Scarborough |
| 3 | v. MCC at Scarborough |

J G Binks (1)

| 3 | v. Worcestershire at Kidderminster |

D B Close (1)

| 3 | v. Warwickshire at Middlesbrough |

3 dismissals in an innings (1)

J G Binks (1)

3 (2ct, 1st) v. Gloucestershire at Bristol

5 catches in a match (4)

J H Hampshire (2)

| 5 (2 + 3) | v. Cambridge University at Scarborough |
| 5 (3 + 2) | v. MCC at Scarborough |

P J Sharpe (1)

6 (3 + 3)   v. Lancashire at Sheffield

F S Trueman (1)

5 (4 + 1)   v. Northamptonshire at Sheffield

Debut (1)

In First Class cricket: P M Stringer

50 YEARS AGO

YORKSHIRE AVERAGES 1967

ALL FIRST-CLASS MATCHES

Played 31   Won 16   Lost 5   Drawn 10   Abandoned 2

County Championship: Played 26   Won 12   Lost 5   Drawn 9   Abandoned 2

BATTING AND FIELDING *(Qualification 10 completed innings)*

Player	M.	I.	N.O.	Runs	H.S.	Avge	100s	50s	ct/st
G Boycott	20	33	2	1530	220*	49.35	3	12	6
D B Close	15	20	2	643	98	35.72	0	7	21
P J Sharpe	29	46	5	1352	197	32.97	1	10	39
R Illingworth	23	30	8	718	65*	32.63	0	4	6
J H Hampshire	30	46	7	1244	107	31.89	2	7	29
D E V Padgett	30	47	5	1284	139	30.57	2	5	17
J C Balderstone	10	13	1	334	82	27.83	0	3	5
J G Binks	31	33	3	650	70*	21.66	0	3	37/10
K Taylor	23	39	2	771	162	20.83	1	2	4
D Wilson	29	35	6	523	52	18.03	0	3	14
R A Hutton	10	13	2	164	57	14.90	0	1	9
F S Trueman	30	33	5	342	34	12.21	0	0	31
A G Nicholson	25	23	6	105	33	6.17	0	0	11

Also batted

C M Old	10	10	1	183	57	20.33	0	1	7
P M Stringer	7	7	5	24	10	12.00	0	0	4
B Leadbeater	8	9	1	59	19	7.37	0	0	1
G A Cope	11	13	6	38	15*	5.42	0	0	5

BOWLING *(Qualification 10 wickets)*

Player	Overs	Mdns	Runs	Wkts	Avge	Best	5wI	10wM
G A Cope	277.4	129	553	40	13.82	5-23	2	0
R Illingworth	681	272	1289	78	16.52	7-6	5	2
A G Nicholson	740.3	202	1725	101	17.07	9-62	6	1
D Wilson	708.1	293	1368	76	18.00	7-21	3	2
C M Old	154.3	34	456	24	19.00	3-34	0	0
P M Stringer	131	45	305	15	20.33	4-33	0	0
F S Trueman	578	130	1571	71	22.12	5-39	2	0
R A Hutton	190.2	49	543	21	25.85	4-43	0	0
D B Close	250.1	96	565	18	31.38	3-34	0	0

Also bowled

D E V Padgett	8	6	6	1	6.00	1-6	0	0
J C Balderstone	34	13	71	6	11.83	3-22	0	0
P J Sharpe	6	2	14	1	14.00	1-14	0	0
G Boycott	14	1	50	1	50.00	1-10	0	0
K Taylor	64	18	158	3	52.66	1-12	0	0
J H Hampshire	51	11	165	0	—	—	0	0
J G Binks	2	0	8	0	—	—	0	0

50 YEARS AGO

YORKSHIRE AVERAGES 1967

LIST A KNOCKOUT COMPETITION — GILLETTE CUP

Played 2   Won 1   Lost 1

BATTING AND FIELDING

Player	M.	I.	N.O.	Runs	H.S.	Avge	100s	50s	ct/st
P J Sharpe	2	1	0	33	33	33.00	0	0	3
K Taylor	2	2	0	51	30	25.50	0	0	1
F S Trueman	2	2	1	25	14	25.00	0	0	3
D E V Padgett	2	1	0	22	22	22.00	0	0	0
G Boycott	2	1	0	19	19	19.00	0	0	0
J H Hampshire	2	2	0	33	32	16.50	0	0	1
D Wilson	2	2	0	23	12	11.50	0	0	1
J G Binks	2	1	0	9	9	9.00	0	0	3
R Illingworth	2	2	1	2	1*	2.00	0	0	1
D B Close	1	1	0	1	1	1.00	0	0	1
C M Old	1	1	0	0	0	0.00	0	0	1
A G Nicholson	2	1	1	0	0*	—	0	0	1

BOWLING

Player	Overs	Mdns	Runs	Wkts	Avge	Best	4wI	RPO
D B Close	2	0	8	2	4.00	2-8	0	4.00
C M Old	12	2	32	4	8.00	4-32	1	2.66
K Taylor	12	1	29	3	9.66	3-29	0	2.41
A G Nicholson	13.5	2	46	4	11.50	3-11	0	3.32
F S Trueman	14	3	49	3	16.33	2-34	0	3.50
D Wilson	10	2	49	2	24.50	2-8	0	4.90
R Illingworth	4	0	16	0	—	—	0	4.00

THE TRIP OF A LIFETIME FOR PREMIER LEAGUE FINALISTS

By Alan Birkinshaw

The first season of Yorkshire Premier League cricket could not have had a better climax than the play-offs provided.

The tone was set in the two nail-biting semi-finals, which saw the Yorkshire League South champions, Wakefield Thornes, defeat the Yorkshire League North title-winners, Harrogate, by three wickets at Scarborough, and Bradford Premier League champions Pudsey St Lawrence beat the North Yorkshire South Durham League's top Yorkshire side, Great Ayton, by seven runs at Headingley.

The final in Abu Dhabi exceeded the most optimistic expectations, and it was fitting that it was between two clubs who reflect the template for a Premier League club. Both invest in their facilities consistently and have outstanding junior set-ups. It was described by both clubs as a trip of a lifetime, and everything they did during their stay in Abu Dhabi was a great advertisement for Yorkshire Premier League cricket.

Whether it be on the plane, in and around the hotel or on the training ground, the two teams conducted themselves in an exemplary manner. Much of the credit for this had to go to the two captains, Tom Froggett. Wakefield Thornes, and James Smith, Pudsey St Lawrence, who set the tone by the way they handled their media duties prior to the trip at Yorkshire TV with Andrew Watson and at BBC Radio Leeds with Mark Arthur. In Abu Dhabi they set the example for their teams, and ensured that everything was done in a professional manner.

It was clear before the final that there was a strong bond between the two teams, and that came through on the day. The following little touches made the final at the magnificent Sheik Zayeed Stadium extra special:

* A match programme was produced as a souvenir for the players.
* Each club had their own coach to the ground with the name on the windscreen
* A poster with each team's name was produced with pictures of all the players
* The match was played with the Test quality pink Dukes ball.
* The match was live-streamed, thanks to a donation from Keith Moss and the 364 Club.
* Special commemorative medals were purchased for all the players.

48

It was great for the players that in addition to the 34 supporters on the official trip others flew in from the UK in the 24 hours before the game, and more travelled up from Dubai. Their efforts were rewarded as they witnessed a superb match, which was viewed by more than 12,000 people worldwide thanks to the video stream.

Establishing the video link was fraught with teething problems, but thanks to the persistence of Bradford Premier League chairman David Young and officials of the Abu Dhabi Cricket Club it went ahead with Pudsey St Lawrence secretary Richard Brown acting as cameraman.

The temperature at the start of the match was 36C, and it said much for the players that they produced a compelling contest.

Centuries in finals are a rare commodity, but to get two in conditions which were more extreme than the players were used to was exceptional. David Toft's 137 was a high-quality innings for Wakefield Thornes and helped them to post a total of 296-6, while Mark Robertshaw's 112 for St Lawrence was great effort of endurance as he had fielded for 50 overs in the heat of the day before batting under floodlights for the first time.

St Lawrence were dismissed eventually for 257 to lose by 39 runs, so Thornes were crowned as the first Yorkshire Premier League champions. For a club that had finished fourth in the Central Yorkshire League in 2015 to take the title was incredible, and it showed that aspirational clubs can rise to the top.

To crown a wonderful match the two teams insisted on having a special picture taken together. There was to be no regimented line-up as the two teams wanted to be mixed up together to reflect the respect they had for each other. This picture is reproduced in the *Yorkshire Yearbook's* colour-page section.

The teams had also agreed that whoever won would invite their opponents into their dressing room for a beer afterwards, and it was uplifting to see the players sitting and talking to each other. The Spirit of Cricket is alive and kicking. The two sides demonstrated that you can play hard, have respect for each other and be friends off the field too.

The two clubs plan to build on the bond between them with a pre-season match. They have set the template for future finals, and they will be a hard act to follow.

Alan Birkinshaw is Chairman of the Yorkshire Cricket Premier League

Yorkshire Premier League Play-Offs
Pudsey St Lawrence v. Wakefield Thornes

Played at Zayed Cricket Stadium on Thursday, October 27, 2016

Wakefield Thornes 1st XI won By 39 runs

Toss won by Wakefield Thornes 1st XI

WAKEFIELD THORNES

J Wolfenden, c Duce b Lamb	14
T Marsden, c Duce b Hudson	22
D Toft, lbw b Parker	137
M Jordan, run out (Goldthorp)	48
F Irfin, b Watts	22
A Isanka, c Duce b Lamb	18
G Wadsworth, not out	6
M Varley, not out	5
* § T Froggett	
S Morgan	Did not bat
M Rasool	
Extras lb 5, nb 3, w 16	24
Total (6 wkts, 50 overs)	296

FoW: 1-23 (Wolfenden), 2-67 (Marsden), 3-171 (Jordan), 4-245 (Irfin), 5-282 (Toft), 6-290 (Isanka)

	O	M	R	W
Parker	10	0	69	1
Lamb	9	0	56	2
Marsden	9	2	43	0
Hudson	10	0	49	1
Watts	7	0	44	1
Smith	2	0	16	0
Robertshaw	3	0	14	0

PUDSEY ST LAWRENCE

M Robertshaw, c Toft b Morgan	112
A Waite, lbw b Rasool	0
C Goldthorp, c Froggett b Irfin	0
Frankland, b Varley	15
* J Smith, c Marsden b Toft	65
C Marsden, b Morgan	46
§ M Duce, c Froggett b Toft	1
R Lamb, b Toft	7
S Watts, st Froggett b Morgan	1
T Hudson, b Isanka	1
C Parker, not out	1
Extras lb 2, w 6	8
Total	257

FoW: 1-5 (Waite), 2-6 (Goldthorp), 3-28 (Frankland), 4-150 (Smith), 5-234 (Marsden), 6-239 (Duce), 7-251 (Lamb), 8-255 (Robertshaw), 9-255 (Watts), 10-257 (Hudson)

	O	M	R	W
Irfin	4	1	10	1
Rasool	7	4	17	1
Varley	10	0	50	1
Morgan	10	0	53	3
Isanka	7.3	0	53	1
Toft	10	0	63	3
Wadsworth	1	0	9	0

THE CAP, THE BENEFIT...
AND THE TESTIMONIAL

By Andrew Bosi

The award of a county cap has for many years marked a major milestone in a player's career. Unlike international caps, which are awarded for being selected, and in other sports even to substitutes, the county cap signifies a degree of seniority. At the peak of its importance (sorry for the pun), a capped player would expect to be selected every match if fit.

Yet the award was for many years given little prominence. Cricket annuals might record the caps awarded in a year, but not list or identify the capped players in a side. Cricket histories — the *Wisden Book of County Cricket* or various publications devoted to single counties — give the dates of the first and last seasons in which players appeared.

The list of players in our *Yearbook* maintains that tradition. Anthony Woodhouse in *The History of Yorkshire CCC* reflects the prevailing mood when he writes of Maurice Leyland "gaining a regular place in the side" in 1923. He is photographed proudly wearing a Yorkshire cap. In later years Ashley Metcalfe is recorded as "celebrating the award of his Yorkshire cap" with a century, and the photograph of Paul Jarvis is of him receiving his county cap from the skipper.

Early editions of the *Playfair Cricket Annual* record caps only in the potted biography of players. In the mid-50s the date capped was added to the county averages, a practice copied by *Wisden* almost half a century later. By that time the status of the cap was on the wane in many counties. Worcestershire abandoned the traditional system in 2002, and awarded caps on the same basis as England.

Our two most recent capped players to become President — Geoffrey Boycott and John Hampshire — both received their awards one October evening at a Committee meeting, and even as recently as 1976 this was commonplace. In the 1980s the award of caps became a feature of visits to Scarborough, with speculation as to likely recipients in the weeks before. The award might be made before the start of play, but even that was insufficient for the popular appetite.

So David Byas went one step further, going on to the field with an extra sweater and presenting it to the player in question at some suitable break in play. This had to be done at Scarborough: nowhere else could you guarantee a stiff breeze from the North Sea.

Last year Yorkshire marked a further departure from tradition with the award of three caps during an away match with little ceremony. None of the recipients would have qualified under the old definition.

The fact that first-class cricket is interrupted for long periods by one-day cricket, together with the ever-increasing demands of the ECB, requires us to maintain a squad of players far beyond the 11 and two reserves who brought success in the 1960s.

One-day cricket may come to be recognised as a separate sport, and there is a need for a career path for those who are mainstays of the shorter form.

The date of award of a cap has traditionally been linked to the date of a benefit. At one time 10

Beneficiary 2017: Steven Patterson was awarded his cap in 2012...but that May at Scarborough he was happier with something warmer after taking eight wickets in the match against Leicestershire.

years was seen as the norm. In the beginning the benefit comprised gate receipts from a match chosen by the beneficiary. The last time more people watched a Championship match at Lord's prior to our game in September was J T Murray's benefit in 1966. The most famous benefit game is that chosen by Bertie Buse of Somerset. It was over in a day. Buse took a hatful of wickets to ensure that there was no second pay day.

The distinction between a benefit and a testimonial was clear cut when the former was defined by a designated match. As the scope of benefits expanded to a year the term *testimonial* was used for a second benefit to mark the long careers of the likes of Brian Close, Boycott and Doug Padgett, this last extended by captaincy of the Second Eleven.

Now the concept of a testimonial is being further refined. Both Ryan Sidebottom, who has been awarded a testimonial, and Steve Patterson, this year's beneficiary, have given sterling service to Yorkshire and will prove popular beneficiaries. There is no appropriate word that can be derived from testimonial.

BEVIN BOY WHO ALSO
PLAYED FOR ENGLAND

By Michael Pulford

Gerald Smithson, the post-war Yorkshire, Leicestershire and England batsman, rose suddenly and dramatically to national cricket and political prominence 70 years ago, in 1947, when after a highly promising start to his county career, including a memorable innings against Lancashire, he was unexpectedly selected for the MCC tour of the West Indies, following which his employment as a "Bevin Boy" in the coalmines caused his availability to be discussed in the House of Commons.

Gerald was born in 1926 at Spofforth, near Harrogate, hailing from a family imbued with cricket. His grandfather, George, played for 50 years with Spofforth CC until 1937, while his father, Harold, was a professional cricketer and groundsman who took up engagements in many parts of the country, being good enough to make appearances for Berkshire in 1938.

As a boy Gerald lived very near Maurice Leyland. He told a story of waiting with friends for the great man to return home and garage his car, hoping that he would bowl a few balls to them. The ever generous Maurice obliged. Later Gerald was to be coached by the Yorkshire and England batsman, and regarded him as a big influence in his career.

The young Gerald was doubtless taken down to Spofforth CC to see his father and grandfather play, but his first known club cricket was as a 13- year-old with Sidmouth, Devon, in 1940 during his father's second year there. Harold took Gerald to Lord's during the war years, perhaps with a mind to him being taken on the MCC ground staff, but despite reported interest Gerald and his father seem to have preferred that he try and make his way in the Yorkshire system. In 1944, when only 17, he became a player and groundsman at Queensbury CC near Bradford. Gerald did indeed make an impression, for he was selected for a Colts match at Headingley that summer and also for a Bradford League XI which included Len Hutton.

Gerald was awaiting conscription, but when his call-up came it was to work underground in a coal mine as a Bevin Boy. Gerald was allotted to Askern Main Colliery between Doncaster and Pontefract, where Norman Horner, one of his teammates at Queensbury and a future county cricketer, was already working. Gerald and Norman's cricket ability was quickly utilised by Askern CC, and both were monitored by Yorkshire. In 1946, when peacetime cricket returned, Gerald was selected to play for Yorkshire Seconds, and also made two appearances for the first team.

The following year was Gerald's third and last underground, but he was nevertheless able to make many more appearances in the Yorkshire team, with notable success and quite remarkable consequences.

A half-century against Nottinghamshire and a century against a Surrey attack which included both Bedsers and Jim Laker brought him to the notice of Yorkshire supporters,

He followed up with a truly memorable 98 against Lancashire at Bramall Lane. Remarkably, his 50 came up in the hour, with Jim Kilburn writing in *Yorkshire Post* that the 60 minutes — most of which was in partnership with Len Hutton — was "as happy an exhibition of left-handed batting as any young cricketer could dream",

GERALD SMITHSON: Fluent left-handed batsman who rose to the heights, only to leave promise unfulfilled
(Photo: Ron Deaton Archive)

adding that it was "an occasion when everything goes well". This innings was recalled by Michael Parkinson over 20 years later in his book, *Cricket Mad*.

Gerald was in full flow, and in the next match against Leicestershire he made169. Kilburn wrote glowingly that "the excellence of the timing and the power of the strokes made his batsmanship a thing of great joy and beauty. He is a cricketer of the proper temper for distinction". Memorable praise indeed. At the next game, against Gloucestershire at Park Avenue, Yorkshire gave caps to three players — Johnny Wardle, Don Brennan and Gerald. It was rapid elevation, but more was to come.

Gerald also made a number of low scores, but his best innings had clearly impressed important people, for when the MCC selectors met to choose the party for the forthcoming tour of the West Indies — and had to replace a number of established players who were resting for the 1948 home series against the Australians – they selected some younger men including Gerald, along with Jim Laker, who became a good friend, and Johnny Wardle, who was to be a regular roommate.

Much had happened in a short time, but much more was to come before Gerald was able to tour. This was because of his special work circumstances. Yorkshire had to seek Gerald's release from his employment in the mine, but in mid-October the Ministry of Labour wrote to the Secretary, Mr. John Nash, telling him that Gerald had to fulfil his duties and continue in employment until at least December and possibly January, the date of his release not being precise.

The touring party were due to leave just before Christmas, so it was not clear whether Gerald would be able to travel with rest of the players, an unsatisfactory situation which obviously jeopardised his place. This decision was widely criticised and led to the question being raised in the House of Commons. Gerald, who was soon to turn 21, must have felt an air of unreality. A few days later he learned that the decision had been reversed, though he would be required to complete his time as a coalminer after his return from the tour.

The under-strength MCC struggled against a West Indian team which was about to become a rising force in international cricket with the three Ws — Worrell, Walcott and Weekes — playing together for the first time. Gerald was selected for the First Test in Barbados, which England managed to draw, but he failed to score in his only innings.

Gerald was selected for the Second Test in Trinidad, due in part to injuries to others, when England packed their batting. He batted down the order, and though he made only 35 in each innings the runs and the partnerships they contributed to were very valuable. Gerald's first knock lasted nearly two hours, and with Sussex's Billy Griffith put on 87 for the seventh wicket, while the second on the last afternoon helped to add 74 for the eighth wicket with Middlesex's Jack Robertson and effectively saved the game.

Len Hutton was flown out to strengthen the side, and Gerald did not play in any of the three remaining Tests. He also suffered an elbow injury. He returned home with the problem, which eventually required an operation, and he missed much of the county season, managing only three Second Eleven matches. He was unable to return to the pit and complete his three years as a Bevin Boy.

This lengthy absence undoubtedly set Gerald's Yorkshire career back. Not only was he unable to build on his previous season's success, but he had to look on while Willie Watson, Ted Lester, Harry Halliday and Vic Wilson established themselves and received caps. Other young cricketers made their debuts in the Second Eleven, including Brian Close and Frank Lowson. Competition for batting places was intense.

In 1949 Gerald was fit, but he managed only half a dozen Championship appearances. He appeared to lose confidence, while his technique was questioned, though another report said his method was still sound. Gerald's Championship season in 1950 mirrored 1949, and in mid-season Yorkshire informed him that he was not being kept on. It was a real disappointment to the Club as well as to the individual.

What had gone wrong? Had he become too attack-minded? Did his early success against Lancashire based on shot-making undermine his strategy? Not judging by his dogged innings at Port of Spain. Had those early successes and appearances for England made him a target for opposing bowlers, or had the associated high expectations become too great a burden? Did he not quite have the required technique to be a consistent run maker? Or was it a matter of confidence?

It is unclear, though I have an inclination that the last point was especially important to Gerald. When he was batting at his fluent best he was clearly an impressive sight, but those times had become too few. Gerald had lost confidence, and his career had lost momentum.

Gerald left a number of friends behind in the Yorkshire camp, and two players, fast bowler Bill Foord and batsman Ted Lester, were kind enough to recall Gerald for me in 2013. Bill remembered Gerald as "a very, very nice lad...a good fellow, a team man". He remembered Gerry with his "sleek back hair....an attractive left-hand bat...a great fielder in the outfield...very fast across the ground". Ted told me that he and Gerald had got on very well together: "A great pity he left Yorkshire..."a very athletic outfielder, a good striker of the ball".

Gerald's first-class career was far from over. He was only 23, and at his best had impressed many opponents. Like countless Yorkshiremen before and since he signed for another county, Leicestershire, against whom he had made his highest score in that glorious spell during 1947.

He gave six years good service to Leicestershire, scoring over 5,000 runs for them and taking over 100 catches, while his calm and kind influence was much appreciated in the dressing room. His last season for them was 1956. He started the summer marvellously well, highlighted by an impressive 60 against the touring Australians in front of a large crowd. but the runs then stopped coming. Unfortunately, he was not offered another contract.

Gerald had experienced truly the precarious existence of a county cricketer and, moreover, had been released without receiving a benefit, though he had played for Yorkshire and Leicestershire for a total of 11 seasons. He had married Anne in her native Berkshire in 1954, and in 1956 became a father to the first of four daughters. Gerald was 29 and sought financial stability. He found it as coach and groundsman at Abingdon School in north-western Berkshire. By happy coincidence this was two miles from Radley School, where his father and brother Malcolm were working.

Abingdon was where Gerald and his growing family settled, and where he was recognised and respected as an excellent coach and an integral part of the school community. He continued to play cricket when time allowed, appearing for Abingdon CC, where his father was also groundsman, while from 1957 to 1962 he represented Hertfordshire when the school term was over.

Two Abingdon old boys, John Bunce and Julian Shellard, have excellent memories of Gerald as a coach and a man. John described him as a "consummate professional" who transformed Abingdon's cricketers and teams from wayward and often ordinary to very good and competitive. He taught technique, and demanded high standards of behaviour. John said Gerald liked people "in his gruff Yorkshire way" and the boys responded enthusiastically and positively to his influence. Julian remembers Gerald as a "fantastic coach", who was highly demanding in his pursuit of excellence, noting: "He could see talent at a very young age and nurture it."

Gerald established himself firmly in his role at Abingdon, developing the game there until his untimely death in 1970 in his early 40s. The following summer a benefit match was played for the family at the Abingdon CC ground on the Abbey Meadow, now the home of Abingdon Vale CC. One of the sides was a Sir Leonard Hutton XI and featured the great cricketer himself, Julian Shellard recalling that Hutton spoke fondly of Gerald at the proceedings.

Gerald's work and personality were so well respected and fondly remembered by the former pupils who were coached by him that when a *T20* cricket competition was started in 2009 by the Abingdon Old Boys' Association it was named in his memory. Some 40 years after his sudden death there could have been no finer tribute to this impressive batsman and outstanding coach.

HODGSON AND SLINN — THE COUNTY'S FIRST GREAT PAIR

By Jeremy Lonsdale

In his great history of Yorkshire County Cricket Club the Rev. R S Holmes commented that the names of William Slinn and Isaac Hodgson were "as inseparably connected as were those of Freeman and Emmett, Peate and Bates, Hirst and Rhodes of later date". Many years later Anthony Woodhouse called them "Yorkshire's first notable bowling partnership". Despite this praise the two played together for Yorkshire on only 15 occasions in a short period from 1861 to 1864. Three years later Slinn's county career was long over, and tragically — 150 years ago this year — Hodgson was dead.

Both missed out on the expansion of county cricket that took place shortly afterwards, yet they played a crucial part in laying the ground for the game's transformation, and they hold a particularly significant place in Yorkshire cricket history. Slinn bowled during the first-ever innings at Bramall Lane on its opening in 1855, while the two opened the bowling for the newly formed Yorkshire County Cricket Club in its first match – against Surrey at The Oval in June 1863. The first wicket that fell was recorded as "caught Slinn bowled Hodgson"

Both contributed significant performances when Yorkshire were finding their feet, at a time when inter-town differences and player disputes threatened to derail the new club. In the 15 games in which they bowled together for Yorkshire they took more than 12 of the 20 wickets on 10 occasions — including 17 out of 20 against Surrey in 1862. George Parr, considered the best batsman in the world at the time, particularly feared Hodgson, while Slinn was considered "one of the most effective bowlers of the day". In 1862 *Sporting Life* described the two as "peerless".

Yet it was not only for Yorkshire that Slinn and Hodgson played a pioneering role. It was as the "given men" for numerous local sides opposing the All England Eleven and United England Eleven during the late 1850s and 1860s that they arguably made their greatest contributions to the development of English cricket. Selected to augment often weak sides of local players, both frequently bowled throughout the two innings of professional touring sides, trying to contain some of the best players of the day. Without their skill and endurance many fixtures would have been even less competitive than they often were but, more importantly, they would have been over well within the allotted three days, making them a commercial disaster. This would have jeopardised the ability of the touring sides to take their message around the country.

It is therefore little exaggeration to say that Hodgson and Slinn helped to provide credibility for a form of cricket which transformed the game from a folk pastime to a nationwide, commercial sport. Individually and together, they played a hugely important – and much neglected – role in sustaining cricket at a crucial stage of its development.

Slinn and Hodgson epitomise the northern professionals of the period. Both were from poor backgrounds with little schooling, whose ability at a sport that was capturing the public's imagination gave them an escape route – at least for some of the year – from their existing employment. In Slinn's case this was as a scissor smith and in Hodgson's a factory overseer. Both were brought up in the hard, competitive cricket environments of their native towns – Bradford for Hodgson, Sheffield for Slinn. They were sometime adversaries in the games played between these towns in the 1850s, but more often they teamed up to wreak havoc.

In exchanging a routine existence for professional sport both Hodgson and Slinn found their lives shaped by two significant pressures – the constant travel and the relentless exertion on the field. Both had to travel considerable distances to piece together a living and, in the case of Isaac Hodgson – a weak man who suffered ill health throughout his career – this travelling almost certainly contributed to his premature death. During the 1860s Hodgson covered more than 2,500 miles each summer, including over 4,000 in 1863, when he made five trips to London and back. From the start of May to the end of September every week involved several journeys to play in different parts of the country.

Such exhausting travel regularly came at the end of a long day of bowling and a six o'clock finish, the players often travelling overnight to begin next day many miles away, or on a Sunday to start a fresh game on the Monday. They frequently had little time for rest, even before or after appearing in county games. In June 1863 after Yorkshire's much celebrated victory over Nottinghamshire at Bradford, Hodgson – who had bowled 95 four-ball overs – appeared next day at Redditch 140 miles away against the All England Eleven. In 1866 in one week he played the Monday, Tuesday and Wednesday in Bradford for Yorkshire and the Thursday, Friday and Saturday against the United South of England in Glasgow 200 miles away before returning to Bradford for a another three-day match starting on the Monday.

Once at a match, Slinn and Hodgson made long, physically demanding contributions to almost all games, and reporters frequently marvelled at their stamina. They might bowl unchanged throughout both innings of the touring sides over three days, often clocking up more than 50 to 70 four-ball overs an innings. In July 1860 Slinn bowled more than 80 overs in an innings twice in a week.

Two years later he played five three-day games between September 11 and October 1, bowling over 320 overs, and in the course of the season delivered 5,500 balls in 40 innings, being so accurate that he conceded only three wides. In 1863 Hodgson appeared in six three-day matches in the first 23 days of September. In the two matches for Yorkshire against Nottinghamshire the same year he sent down 95 and 96 overs, and in the one-sided Yorkshire v. All England game in 1865 he returned innings figures of 98-44-127-5.

A third factor which shaped their lives was their ambiguous social status. In Bradford Hodgson was "our townsman" or "Ike" as the local paper referred to him, a man whose successes were praised and celebrated. In Sheffield in the early 1860s Slinn's name featured regularly in the regional papers, his contributions to the town's reputation as a cricket centre justly highlighted. Yet neither was anything like as well known or valued in the South, and whatever their fame they were treated as servants of the clubs who engaged them, performing alongside far less skilled local players. No doubt they were feted on many grounds, and might leave with the results of a collection, but it was a wearing existence, affected by the uncertainties of the weather and personal form.

If there were similarities in the lives of the two bowlers it is also important to recognise the differences. Slinn was a fast right-handed bowler, Hodgson a slow left-hander. Although the younger of the two, Hodgson's career got going more quickly – three appearances for Yorkshire sides in 1847, 1852 and 1855, a position in the Bradford side early on, and games against the All England XI in the mid-1850s. He sustained his standing through the 1860s until his career came to an abrupt end. A year later – 1867 – he was dead, a victim of consumption.

In contrast Slinn's was both a more gradual development and decline, as well as a shorter period at the top. He contributed modestly to local Sheffield cricket for much of the 1850s, played against Bradford for the first time in 1855, and made appearances in All England games from 1859. Thereafter a change in his approach to bowling seemed to have helped him to make big strides very quickly, but his county career was compressed into the period from 1861 to 1864.

The manner of their deaths were also quite different. Hodgson's health was a cause for concern in the 1850s, but in 1866 he overworked himself so much that he abandoned his final engagements of the season in order to rest. The following summer, benefit matches were organised when it became clear that he could no longer play cricket. A sum of over £300 was raised for his widow before – in November 1867 – he died aged 39. The same week his fellow Yorkshire bowling hero, William Slinn – described as a tobacconist as well as a professional cricketer – was declared bankrupt. He continued as a respected coach – including at Oxford and Cambridge universities 100– and appeared in Lancashire club cricket until in 1888 the second member of Yorkshire's first great bowling partnership died.

Ike Hodgson	**Born 1828, Died 1867**
21 first-class matches for Yorkshire	**88 wickets at 17.46**
William Slinn	**Born 1826, Died 1888**
Nine first-class matches for Yorkshire	**48 wickets at 15.45**

Park Avenue progress

The redevelopment of Bradford Park Avenue cricket ground by the England and Wales Cricket Board is moving along nicely, and the plan is to have it up to first class standard again by 2019. The restructuring of the famous ground is being done in five stages, and the first two have been completed with the laying of eight artificial pitches and the building of a community pavilion (Phase 1) and the upgrading of current pitches (Phase 2). Although Park Avenue is an ECB community project Yorkshire may use the ground in 2019 when Headingley will be staging an *Ashes* Test and also some World Cup fixtures.

Moxon gives it a Bash

Martyn Moxon, Yorkshire's Director of Cricket, did not take long in teaming up again with former *White Rose* coach Jason Gillespie. Martyn flew out to Australia for a fortnight in the winter to get a taste of Big Bash cricket, working alongside Jason, who is Adelaide Strikers' coach. Other players involved in the competition with Yorkshire connections were Tim Bresnan, Peter Willey, Travis Head, Jake Lehmann, Peter Handscomb, and Glenn Maxwell.

DETAILS ON YORKSHIRE PLAYERS UNEARTHED

By Mick Pope

A few additional birth-and-death details of Yorkshire cricketers were included in the 2011 *Yearbook*. Here are a few more, uncovered since that last collection, with notes and more details of sources, where relevant. For further reading on these players, with the exceptions of Albert Champion, Fred Blake and George Pollitt, members are directed to *Headingley Ghosts* (Scratching Shed Publishing) published in 2013. All new details, apart from Blake's, were correctly updated in the 2016 *Yorkshire Yearbook*.

Walter Aspinall (discovery of circa date of death)

Elland-born Aspinall played two first-class matches for Yorkshire, both in August 1880: v. Surrey at Kennington Oval and v. Middlesex at Bramall Lane, Sheffield. He replaced veteran wicket-keeper George Pinder behind the stumps, but his brief "trial" as Pinder's successor did not work out — 16 runs, highest score 14 and one catch.

Pinder made specific reference to Aspinall's poor match at Sheffield in his discussion with sports journalist A W Pullin (*Old Ebor*) in the book *Talks with Old Yorkshire Cricketers* (pg.82): "At Bramall Lane he was not successful, and on the Tuesday the county officials sent for me, and said they wanted me to finish the season out." Aspinall played one other first-class fixture, Over 30 v. Under 30 at Lord's in May 1882. Joe Hunter became Pinder's long-term replacement, but what happened to Aspinall? His place and date of death went unrecorded by the Club.

Some time after 1882 Aspinall emigrated to Australia. He settled at Townsville in Queensland, and there continued to work at his trade as a plumber and tinsmith in partnership with a well-known Townsville local, Mr Luby. He married Jane Sarah Hannant, originally of Norfolk, in January 1888. They had at least three children — Albert, Elsie and Dolly. Between 1904 and March 1906 the Aspinalls returned to England, but late in 1906 they moved to South Brisbane, and in 1907 Walter bought the licence of the Boundary Hotel and the lease for £2,500.

At about 1.30pm on Thursday, January 27, 1910, a full suit of male attire was found on the riverbank in the West End Cricket Reserve. Police established that the clothes belonged to Aspinall. Reports stated that he had left home at about 10.30 that morning. The *Brisbane Courier* reported that soon afterwards Aspinall "...was seen in the reserve by a man named Matthew Pitt (employed cutting back the weeds there).

About midday Pitt noticed him sitting close to the water's edge, smoking, and on visiting the spot later found the clothes lying on the bank. It is supposed that the missing man, who is said to have been unable to swim, entered the water and was carried downstream by the ebb tide."

Aspinall's wife and two daughters were on a holiday visit to the Blue Mountains in New South Wales at the time. It seems reasonable to assume that

FRED BLAKE
Sketch dated 1900

Aspinall's intentions, for reasons unknown, were planned and deliberate. The body was discovered floating near North Quay, and a post mortem examination established that Aspinall had died of asphyxia caused by drowning. On June 15, 1910, the *Courier* carried details under the heading of Probates and Administrations confirming that Aspinall, 51, formerly of Charters Towers, licensed victualler, had died on or about January 27, 1910, leaving his entire estate to his wife.

Wilfred Blake (date and place of death)

Wilfred or Fred Blake, as he was commonly known, made only three first-class appearances. In July 1877 he was chosen by Lancashire for the *Roses* match at Huddersfield. Three years later he made two appearances for Yorkshire in August 1880, against Derbyshire and Gloucestershire. He did nothing remarkable in any of those fixtures, although he did take the wicket of W G Grace in his third and final first-class game at the Clifton College Close ground.

Born at Embsay, near Skipton, he moved with his family to Burnley when he was still very young, and became a cotton weaver. A prolific club cricketer, Blake's first professional engagement was with Keighley in 1877. He also had seasons with Bacup, Lockwood and a spell with Settle. A large part of his playing career was spent with his adopted Burnley CC. A date and place of death had eluded cricket historians until very recently, but an obituary in the *Burnley Express* of December 2, 1931, solved the mystery. Wilfred Blake Uttley (the ancient family name and that recorded on his death certificate) died on November 28, 1931. The incorrect date of death recorded in the 2016 *Yearbook* was of the

63

newspaper report, but not the actual date of death.

Albert Champion (correction to date of death)

Champion represented Yorkshire in 14 first-class matches between 1876 and 1879. He was born near Handsworth, Sheffield, in December 1851, and *Scores & Biographies* (Vol XIII, pg.905) described him as "a good batsman, left-handed, but a right middle-paced round-armed bowler, while in the field he generally takes long-leg or cover-point."

His date of death in various records and sources is recorded as June 30, 1909, but a report in the *Sheffield Independent* of Friday, July 2, 1909, states: "The death took place on Saturday last (June 26) at the Wadsley Asylum of Albert Champion, the once well-known Sheffield cricketer." The obituary notice goes on to record that he had been an inmate at the asylum "for the past four months" and had been interred at Handsworth on Wednesday, June 30. The Civil Register for the South Yorkshire Asylum confirms that Champion, a widower, was admitted on March 13, 1909. His certificate confirms a date of death as June 26, and notes his occupation as "Cricket Groundsman of 4 Richmond Park Cottages, Handsworth". Cause of death is recorded as "General Paralysis".

Thomas Darnton (correction to date of death)

Born at Stockton-on-Tees, Darnton played a lot of his cricket in the North East during the 1850s and 1860s with the Stockton and Middlesbrough clubs. He played for Yorkshire in the pre-1863 Club era, and then 13 first-class matches for the newly formed County Club between 1863 and 1868. His playing days ended around 1872, and his health soon gave way. A fortnight before his death Darnton was "compelled to his room."

His date of death is generally recorded as October 25, 1874, but he actually died at about 2am on the morning of Sunday, October 18, at the home of his cousin, Mr W Salmon, chemist, of High Street, Stockton. The *Northern Echo* of October 20 carried the notice of Darnton's demise, recording that he was a victim of consumption in his 39th year. The certificate confirms the date of death as the 18th, registered on the 20th, and details Darnton as a "retired butcher".

James Dearman (confirmation of date of birth)

"Little Jimmy" Dearman was one of the best-known players in Sheffield district and in the North during the late 1820s and the 1830s. An all-round player, a fast round-arm bowler who generally fielded at middle-wicket and occasionally kept wicket, he played alongside W H Woolhouse and Tom Marsden in Sheffield's regular encounters with Nottingham from 1827 as well as other fixtures, and he was a member of the "Yorkshire" side who beat Norfolk in 1833.

He was still playing when William Clarke took his All England Eleven to Hyde Park, Sheffield, for their inaugural match in 1846. After going fishing in early September 1854 he contracted the symptoms of cholera, and died of "Asiatic cholera in its most malignant form" on Sunday, September 3. He was interred speedily in the burial ground of Hill Top Chapel, Attercliffe, the following day. He left a widow and 11 children in "rather straightened circumstances", according to the *Sheffield Times*.

Cricket records show Dearman as having been Christened on January 31, 1808. The Sheffield Parish registers confirm, supported by records on the *familysearch.org* website, that Dearman was born on December 7. 1807, the son of James and Elizabeth Dearman.

George Pollitt (date and place of death)

Born at Chickenley, near Dewsbury, on June 3,1874, Pollitt owed his one and only first-class appearance to injury and Test commitments. In August 1899 Stanley Jackson, David Denton and Wilfred Rhodes were chosen to represent England in the Fifth Test at The Oval (although Denton did not make the final 11) against Australia. The opening batsman, J T Brown, had suffered a hand injury in July, and was not fit for the Championship match at Bradford against Hampshire. Lord Hawke was also unavailable for the fixture.

Pollitt was to be 12th man, but then J T Brown, the fast bowler from Darfield, Barnsley, was ruled out due to a knee injury, and thus the 25-year-old batsman from Chickenley was handed his debut. He made a chanceless 51 in Yorkshire's first innings of 456. Hampshire salvaged a draw, having followed-on early on the final day. Pollitt, despite a debut half-century, never played again for Yorkshire at first-class level. What became of him thereafter?

With Yorkshire's batting resources rich and deep, Pollitt chose to take up a professional engagement at the recently formed Bedfordshire club in 1900, and his association with the Minor County lasted until 1907. In 75 matches there he scored 2,630 runs, with three hundreds. Around 1905 his occupation is stated as "Engineer Clerk". In 1908 he married Annie Waterhouse, and on March 9, 1909, a son, Ernest Barrington, was born. By the 1911 census Pollitt and his family had moved to Blackpool, and were living at 56 Egerton Road. His occupation is given as "professional cricketer", but where he was playing at the time remains unknown. Thirty-one years later the *Blackpool Evening Gazette* recorded his death on May 19, 1942. There was no mention of his cricketing deeds or that distant innings of 51 made for Yorkshire at Bradford.

George Steer, Darnall cricket ground proprietor (date and circumstances of death previously unrecorded)

A significant but largely forgotten character in the early development and advancement of cricket in Sheffield and Yorkshire in the 1820s, George Steer was responsible for preparing and establishing the Darnall cricket grounds. The son of John Steer, George was born at Attercliffe on April 29, 1764. He was a partner in a firm of scissor manufacturers called Steers and Wilkinson, and later invested in the construction of an enclosed arena for the game in Sheffield. The rise and fall of the two Darnall grounds, Old and New, from 1822 to 1830 is well chronicled, but what became of Steer has previously gone unrecorded.

In April 1826 he formally handed over the proprietorship and management of the new Darnall venue to his son-in-law. Only 18 months later the *Sheffield Independent* and *Sheffield Mercury* carried detailed reports of the inquest on George Steer, whose body had been recovered from the Sheffield canal between 7 and 8pm on the evening of November 16, 1827. Steer's hat and stick were found carefully laid on the bank. The pockets of his breeches were turned inside out: in one of his waistcoat pockets was 3½d and a spring knife, and in the other pocket a pair of spectacles.

A medical examination indicated no signs of violence, although conflicting witness statements suggested that others might have been present when Steer entered the icy waters. A verdict of "found drowned in the Sheffield Canal" was returned, but whether Steer met his death by accident, self-destruction or by a more sinister method it was a sad end for the entrepreneur who did so much to foster the development of cricket in Sheffield in the first half of the 1820s.

John Thewlis (amendment to date of birth)

Thewlis, a handloom weaver from Lascelles Hall, Huddersfield, played 44 first-class matches for Yorkshire between 1861 and 1875. Scorer of Yorkshire's first-ever "official" century — 108 v. Surrey at The Oval in 1868 — Thewlis was tragically immortalised by A W Pullin, *Talks with Old Yorkshire Cricketers 1898*, who discovered him eking out a meagre existence in very poor circumstances at Failsworth, Manchester, and long since forgotten by the Club.

The YCCC *Yearbook* and several other major sources of players' birth-and-death records have given June 30, 1828, as the date when Thewlis was born. *Scores and Biographies* (Vol.VII, p.273) gave it as January 30, 1828, and added "...other dates of his birth as given in various cricket publications are erroneous, the above (i.e. January 30, 1828) being corrected by Thewlis himself." J R Ellam in his excellent but not well-known small book, *Huddersfield's Nineteenth-Century Yorkshire XI*, gives the date as March 11,1828. The Kirkheaton St John The Baptist Parish records show that he was baptised at Kirkheaton Parish Church on April 16, the 12th child of John and Francis Thewlis, and notes "Bn 11 March, 1828", although the figure eight has been overwritten with a seven, and is given on the *Ancestry.com* transcription of his birth date thus as 1827. From the available evidence, and after examining the parish document, it can be stated that the correct date of birth for John Thewlis should be recorded as March 11, 1828.

John Usher (date of death amendment)

A slow left-arm bowler of "deadly cunning", safe left-handed batsman and useful fielder, Usher was a prolific league player. It was thought until recently that he had been born in Staincliffe, near Batley, but some newspapers of the time say he was a native of

JOHN USHER
Drowned himself

Liversedge, near Bradford. In fact he was born on February 26, 1859, in Templemore in the north of County Tipperary, Ireland. Among the Yorkshire clubs he served in his early career were Heckmondwike, Holbeck, Holmfirth and Wortley. Usher played only one first-class match for Yorkshire, v. MCC at Lord's in 1888.

Jack Usher drowned himself in the mill reservoir at Haslingden, Lancashire, in the wake of his financial ruin. (See David Frith's *Silence of the Heart*, pgs.152-153). His date of death has been variously recorded as August 10, 1905 (YCCC *Yearbook*) or August 8 (*Who's Who of Cricketers* and *CricketArchive*). Usher's death certificate records the date as August 9, confirming the cause of death thus: "Drowned himself whilst not of sound mind by reason of his adverse circumstances."

Brian Wilkes Waud (correction to date of death)

Known as "The Major", Waud was a stylish amateur batsman and wicket-keeper who represented Yorkshire in their pre-and-post County Club formation years, 1862 to 1864, including the inaugural 1863 fixture at The Oval against Surrey.

When the Yorkshire Gentlemen's Cricket Club was formed in 1864 Waud was a founding member, but his work and business commitments gradually curtailed his playing days. He was called to the bar of the Inner Temple in 1862, and pursued a career as a barrister. Around 1871 the Waud family left Yorkshire for a new life in Canada. The cricket historian Arthur Haygarth noted (*Scores & Biographies, Vol.V*, pg.89) that by 1874 Waud was a journalist in Toronto. In 1879 and until at least 1881 the former Yorkshire player returned to cricket, batting and keeping wicket for Hamilton, whose ground was chosen in late August 1881 to host the oldest of all international fixtures — Canada v. USA. Waud at 44 not only played and kept wicket, but captained the Canadian team.

Waud's date of death is widely recorded as May 30, 1889, but several original documents provide evidence that the correct date is May 31, 1889. On February 1, 1889, Waud was admitted to the Toronto asylum for the insane. The medical records for the asylum have survived, and they show that he had been ill for at least a year. Waud's occupation was recorded as "agent", his status "single", and the apparent cause of his disorder was "financial difficulties". His actual symptoms included "loss of memory, change of habit from clean to the reverse, morose and suspicious". Waud's diagnosis was that he was suffering from "GP" or general paralysis of the insane.

The condition, also known as paralytic dementia, affected the brain and central nervous system, and was generally caused by syphilis. Waud was in the Queen West Asylum for just over three months, and died from his affliction a few days short of his 52nd birthday on May 31, 1889, not May 30, as most cricket sources detail. The date is consistent with the death records for the County of York, Toronto — although they incorrectly listed him as Brian Wilkes WAND, aged 52 — and the National probate records for 1906. His death was registered on June 1, 1889, but it took until September 1906 for his financial affairs to be resolved, when probate (effects £1,713 5s 3d — did he really have financial difficulties?) was granted to Katharine Burgoyne.

Deaths of Committee men

The following are former Yorkshire County Criket Club General Committee members whose deaths have not previously been recorded in the Yearbook:

GEOFF DENTON, a Hull District representative, died on December 16, 2015, aged 84. Geoff took up his seat in 1986 following the resignation of Reg Kirk, and he served until the Committee was reduced from 23 elected members to 12 in 1993. For many years he attended Scarborough Cricket Festival.

TONY BOOT, a Sheffield district representative, died on September 11, 2013, aged 71. He won a place on the Committee in March 1984, and served until he lost his seat to David Tunbridge in 1991. Tony played an important role in the Sheffield Cricket League, where he umpired for several years.

TERRY JARVIS, another Sheffield district representative to gain a seat in 1984, has also died.

The *Yearbook's* annual Obituary section follows.

BILL HOLDSWORTH

By David Warner

BILL HOLDSWORTH
(Ron Deaton Archive.)

Bill Holdsworth, one of several bowlers to play alongside Fred Trueman in the early 1950s, died on July 31 last year at the age of 87.

Born in Armley, Bill lived in Tockwith, North Yorkshire, with his wife, Janet, and was a staunch member of the Yorkshire CCC Players' Association, regularly attending the annual meeting as well as a variety of other functions.

Following the retirement of Alex Coxon, Bill was one of several fast bowlers Yorkshire called upon at a time when a young and fiery Trueman was also making his mark. He played in 27 first-class matches for his native county in the 1952 and 1953 seasons, and he began the 1953 campaign by capturing 5-21 in the Essex second innings in the opening fixture at Hull, the visitors' last pair holding out to save the game.

Later that season he enjoyed his career-best figures of 6-58 against Derbyshire at Scarborough to bring Yorkshire victory by 109 runs.

Although he claimed 35 of his total of 53 wickets in 1953 he was not called upon again. He remained a very keen and effective league cricketer. A baker by trade, he was with Lidget Green in 1950, and went as professional to Stalybridge the following year. In 1953 he played for Chester-le-Street, and moved to Farsley in 1954.

Bill switched to Bradford for the 1959 and 1960 seasons, when they won the Priestley Cup. He was president of Otley Golf Club in 1990.

William Edgar Newman Holdsworth **Born: September 17, 1928**
Died: July 31, 2016

PETER KIPPAX

By David Warner

PETER KIPPAX
(Ron Deaton Archive.)

Peter Kippax, a talented leg-spin bowler and right-hand batsman, who played in four first-class matches for Yorkshire, died in Berwick Grange care home in Harrogate on January 17 this year. He was 76.

His first-class career spanned 27 seasons, for as well as his four matches for Yorkshire in 1961-62 he turned out once for MCC against Yorkshire at Scarborough in 1987.

Peter was a regular member of the Yorkshire Second Eleven from 1957 to 1963, and he enjoyed spells with Northumberland and Durham as well as giving splendid service to league clubs, including Harrogate and Idle.

His father, Horace, also played for Yorkshire Colts.

Peter founded the Kippax bat manufacturing firm in 1976, which was then known as Peter Kippax Sports Ltd. He wanted to follow the vision of Gray Nicolls to make bats from their own trees. After Peter was diagnosed with Alzheimer's in 2001 his son Chris left his career with Total Oil, and took over the business which is now known as Kippax Willow Limited. The business has over 4,000 trees in its portfolio, and ships willow clefts and bats all over the world.

Born in Huddersfield, Peter claimed eight first-class wickets for Yorkshire with a career-best 5-74 against Leicestershire at Grace Road in 1962, a game which Yorkshire surprisingly lost by 149 runs.

One of Peter's closest friends was his county teammate, Peter Chadwick, who was his captain when Kippax joined Harrogate in 1980. Peter Chadwick said: "We had known each other for over 50 years, and we used to go together to the Johnny Lawrence Indoor School at Tadcaster on Sunday mornings. I got a lot of experience there from Johnny about batting against leg-spinners, but he would not bowl to Peter or show him any of his tricks because he was a fellow leg-spinner.

"In my opinion Peter was one of the finest leg-spinners in the country, because he rarely bowled a bad ball. In my experience leg-spinners usually bowled a long hop or full toss now and again, but Peter rarely did, and he turned his googly more than any other googly bowler I have played against. He was immensely proud of the fact that he bowled Viv Richards with a googly while playing for Durham in a Gillette Cup match against Somerset, and Richards said 'Well bowled' to him as he headed for the pavilion.

"Peter could be a bit temperamental on the field, but I had no problems with him at Harrogate. He did not like to be taken off, but when I brought him back on he often broke a partnership by taking a wicket."

Former Yorkshire and England off-spinner and Yorkshire CCC Vice-President Geoff Cope also had happy memories of playing alongside Peter when they were in the same Leeds side. "He was a very accurate leg-spinner, who thoroughly enjoyed his cricket, and will be much missed," Geoff said.

Peter leaves a widow, Anne, two sons, a daughter and six grandchildren.

Peter John Kippax   **Born: October 15,1940**
                                       Died: January 17, 2017

BOB STOTT

Bob Stott, right, who was awarded the Yorkshire CCC President's Medal in 2014 for outstanding services to the Club, died on September 15, 2016, aged 73.

Bob, a former chief executive of the Bradford-based supermarket chain Morrisons, had a life-long interest in cricket, but it was not until after his retirement in 2006 that he became actively involved with Yorkshire CCC. He wrote to Yorkshire Board chairman Robin Smith to ask if he could be of service in any way, and his offer was readily accepted.

Bob became involved with the Yorkshire Pride Appeal, and he was later invited to join the Members' Committee as a Board nominee.

He was then asked by the Board to chair a committee to organise the 2013 celebrations to mark the Club's 150th anniversary, and the work of that committee which he led was a resounding success.

Born in Huddersfield and educated at Huddersfield College Grammar School, Bob at the age of 12 joined Paddock Cricket and Bowling Club, where their star man was Chris Balderstone, the Yorkshire, Leicestershire and England cricketer who also played football for Huddersfield Town and Carlisle United.

He moved to Bradford in 1959, and became a stalwart of Thornbury Cricket Club, where he opened the bowling for the first team for the best part of 20 years and for a while shared a place in the side with his son, Andrew. He was made a life member of the club, and when he moved to Lincolnshire he was able to take with him the mounted ball he had been given to mark his hat-trick for Thornbury against Pudsey St Lawrence in the Pudsey Jubilee Cup.

As well as cricket and soccer, Bob had a passion for Rugby League, and at one stage he took on a non-executive role at the Rugby Football League.

DESMOND BAILEY

Captain Desmond Bailey, who gave continuous service on Yorkshire County Cricket Club's General Committee from 1969 to 1984, died in hospital in Estepona, Southern Spain, on June 27, 2016, aged 89.

He was the North Riding district representative on the committee and he served on several of the sub-committees, including finance, grounds and public relations. Captain Bailey was an outspoken critic of Geoffrey Boycott during the controversies surrounding the former captain in the early 1980s, but he lost his North Riding seat to the pro-Boycott Peter Quinn in elections after the General Committee had been brought down at a special general meeting.

He was particularly well known throughout Yorkshire for being actively involved in forming The Saints nomadic cricket team in 1959, captaining the side for a while and later becoming the club's chairman and then president. It was one of the strongest amateur sides around, and those who turned out for it included Fred Trueman, John Hampshire, Philip Sharpe, A C Smith, Brian Bolus, Geoff Cope and Bob Platt. Those well acquainted with Captain Bailey will know that the cricket and the socialising were on a grand scale.

He bought a villa in Southern Spain many years ago, and went to live there permanently about three years ago. He still kept his home at Aldbrough Hall, Aldbrough St John, North Yorkshire.

PETER BRIGGS

Peter Briggs, one of the key figures in the successful bid to have Geoffrey Boycott reinstated as a Yorkshire player after his sacking at the end of the 1983 season, died on October 11, 2016, aged 80.

Mr Briggs, from Davyhulme, Manchester, was chairman of the Yorkshire Reform Group which opposed Geoffrey losing the captaincy following the 1977 season, and he later became chairman of Yorkshire

Members 1984, which forced the special general meeting that overturned the decision not to renew Geoffrey's contract. The Yorkshire Committee were forced to resign, and fresh elections brought in a committee comprised mainly of Boycott sympathisers, including the Club's new chairman, Reg Kirk, from Hull.

Mr Briggs, right, who had been diagnosed with cancer a year before his death, was born in Sowerby Bridge, but the family moved to Brighouse when he was two upon the birth of

his sister, Dorothy. Following National Service he moved to Manchester, where he worked for GEC as an accountant upon qualifying. His love of cricket took him to Australia for three months each winter for the last 13 years of his life. He was a regular at the MCG for the Boxing Day Test, and then at the SCG for the New Year Test.

Yorkshire Vice-President Tony Vann said: "While Peter was part of the Reform Group who tried unsuccessfully to keep the captaincy in the hands of Geoffrey Boycott, I did not meet him until the Yorkshire Members' meeting in September 1983. Over 500 people turned up after the Committee had sacked GB, and at a second meeting two weeks later Peter was appointed chairman of the 1984 Group. Bob Slicer became treasurer. Following a request for a secretary, I put my hand up, and the rest is history.

"From that moment Peter would ring me three or four times a day with information to give to the Press to keep our story in the news. I hate to think how much we spent on telephone calls, but we achieved our objective in Harrogate on January 22, 1984, by winning all three resolutions."

The funeral of Mr Briggs was held at St Mary The Virgin Church, Davyhulme Road, Davyhulme, followed by cremation at Dunham Crematorium, Dunham Massey, Altrincham.

CHRISTINE KILBURN

Christine Kilburn, a long-serving and popular member of Yorkshire County Cricket Club, died suddenly on June 21, 2016.

Christine, and her husband, Sam, lived in Halifax, and were Yorkshire CCC debenture-holders. They first met on Yorkshire's pre-season tour of South Africa in 1998 and were immediately attracted to each other.

Sam lived in Brighton at the time but returned to Yorkshire to marry Christine. They particularly enjoyed following Yorkshire on their pre-season tours, and for several years they regularly attended Yorkshire CC Supporters' Association events.

IN SEARCH OF CRICKET —
AND A BREAK FOR TEA!

By David Warner

ALL WICKETS GREAT AND SMALL: In search of Yorkshire's Grassroots Cricket John Fuller
(Pitch Publishing £9.99)

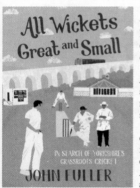

All cricket is important in Yorkshire, whether it be an international match at Headingley or a second-team game on a cow-pat field in some far-flung corner of the county.

Nobody appreciates this more than John Fuller, and it is the lesser games and the rituals which surround them that mostly capture his imagination in this splendid book.

John runs the website www.cricketyorkshire.com, and one of the reasons for its success is that it features articles and comment on cricket around the Broad Acres. Enjoy the website, and you are almost certain to enjoy the book.

Results matter far less to the author than the grounds he visits and the personalities of the players who make up the teams. Often, he has left a venue before the game has actually finished because, a non-driver himself, he has to rely upon trains, buses or a lift in someone else's car.

His journey is never in vain, because once there he soaks up the history of the place, and he will leave content, particularly if he has sampled a good tea in the clubhouse — which he invariably does!

Before starting this book John took himself off to Headingley to seek out the Yorkshire Cricket Board office for information that would help him to decide which clubs and grounds to visit.

He starts off at Bradford Park Avenue, a ground with a famous past which is having life breathed into it again through being extensively redeveloped by the England and Wales Cricket Board. It is a community project, and the aim is to have it up and running before 2019, when Yorkshire could well make use of it again while their headquarters are being used for an *Ashes* Test and some World Cup matches. His main purpose for this visit was to watch a pre-2015 season friendly between Omar and Interlink, two local league sides, and although the redevelopment work had not then started the pitch was a good one — they always were at Park Avenue — the teams were hospitable, and John was left hoping that there would still be room for Omar once the ground transformation has taken place.

Visits are made to St George's Road, Harrogate, where Yorkshire also used to play, and North Marine Road, Scarborough, where they still do, but most of his excursions are to grounds and clubs that will be new to many readers of his book — and they will find them fascinating.

Copies can be obtained by contacting the author at john@cricketyorkshire.com

REBEL WITH A CAUSE: The Life and Times of Jack Crawford Keith and Jennifer Booth (Chequered Flag Publishing, £11.99)

When Yorkshire met Surrey at The Oval towards the end of the 2013 season they were flogged for 242 by Dominic Sibley who, at 18 years and 21 days, became the youngest Surrey batsman to hit a double first-class century.

He was over three years younger than the previous holder of that record, Jack Crawford, who, in 1905 struck 232 against Somerset, also at The Oval, at the age of 21 years and 186 days. Sibley and Crawford are also the youngest players to hit centuries for the county.

Crawford was a young man from a family steeped in cricket, and the early signs were that here was an England captain in the making with an impeccable pedigree: captain of Repton School, Surrey Cap in 1906, *Wisden* Cricketer of the Year in 1907 and playing Test cricket for England before he was 21.

A fallout with Surrey over their team selection against the Australian tourists when he was acting captain escalated into his sacking when he refused to apologise for standing down from the match on a matter of principle and, unlike Geoffrey Boycott in his wrangle with Yorkshire, there was no people power on hand to overturn the decision.

Crawford's career was not over, however, and there were remarkable twists and turns, including spells with South Australia and Otago which also ended in controversy.

Surrey first-team scorer Keith Booth and his wife, Jennifer, the county's second-team scorer, have written this fascinating and thoroughly researched book on Crawford, which contains several references to Yorkshire CCC that will be of particular interest to readers from these parts. Keith has already written several biographies on great Surrey players, and this is a worthy addition to the list.

The Players

Gary Simon BALLANCE

Left-hand batsman, leg-break bowler
Born: Harare, Zimbabwe, November 22, 1989

First-Class Cricket:
Debut: v Kent at Canterbury, 2008
Highest score: 210 for Mid-West Rhinos v.
Southern Rocks at Masvingo, Zimbabwe, 2011-12
For Yorkshire: 174 v. Northamptonshire
at Leeds, 2014

One-Day:
Highest score: 139 v. Unicorns at Leeds, 2013

t20:
Highest score: 68 v Durham
at Chester-le-Street, 2013

Joe Edward ROOT
Right-hand batsman, right-arm off-spin bowler
Born: Sheffield, December 30, 1990
First-Class cricket:
Debut: v. Loughborough MCCU at Leeds, 2010
Highest score: 254 for England v. Pakistan
at Manchester, 2016
Highest for Yorkshire: 236 v. Derbyshire at Leeds, 2013
Best bowling: 3-33 v. Warwickshire
at Birmingham, 2011
One-Day:
Highest score: 121 for England v. Sri Lanka
at Wellington, 2015
Hiighest for Yorkshire: 63 v. Essex at Leeds, 2009
Best bowling: 2-10 for England Lions v. Bangladesh A
at Sylhet, 2011/12
For Yorkshire: 2-14 v. Kent at Leeds, 2012
t20:
Highest score: 92* v. Lancashire at Manchester, 2016
Best bowling: 1-12 v. Warwickshire at Leeds, 2011

Jonathan Marc BAIRSTOW

Right-hand batsman, wicket-keeper
Born: Bradford, September 26, 1989

First-Class Cricket:
Debut: v Somerset at Leeds, 2009
Highest score: 246 v. Hampshire at Leeds, 2016

One-Day:
Highest score: 123 for England Lions
v. New Zealand A at Bristol, 2014
Highest score: 114 v. Middlesex at Lord's, 2011

t20:
Highest score: 102* v. Durham
at Chester-le-Street, 2014

Timothy Thomas BRESNAN
Right-hand batsman, right-arm medium-fast bowler
Born: Pontefract, February 28, 1985
First-Class cricket:
Debut: v. Northamptonshire at Northampton, 2003
Highest score: 169* v. Durham
at Chester-le-Street, 2015
Best bowling: 5-36 v. Nottinghamshire
at Scarborough, 2016
One-Day:
Highest score: 95* v. Nottinghamshire
at Scarborough, 2016
Best bowling: 4-25 v. Somerset at Leeds, 2005
t20:
Highest score: 51 v. Lancashire at Manchester, 2015
Best bowling: 3-10 England v. Pakistan
at Cardiff, 2010
Best bowling for Yorkshire: 3-15 v. Northamptonshire
at Northampton, 2016

Adam LYTH
Left-hand batsman, right-arm medium bowler
Born: Whitby, September 25, 1987
First-Class cricket:
Debut: v. Loughborough UCCE at Leeds, 2007
Highest score: 251 v. Lancashire
at Manchester, 2014
Best bowling: 2-9 v. Middlesex at Scarborough, 2016
One-Day:
Highest score: 136 v. Lancashire at Manchester, 2016
Best bowling: 1-6 v Middlesex at Leeds, 2013
t20:
Highest score: 87 v. Durham at Leeds, 2016
Best bowling: 2-5 v. Derbyshire
at Chesterfield, 2014

Ryan Jay SIDEBOTTOM
Left-hand bat, left-arm fast-medium bowler
Born: Huddersfield, January 15, 1978
First-Class cricket:
Debut: v. Leicestershire at Leicester, 1997
Highest score: 61 v. Worcestershire
at Worcester, 2011
Best bowling: 7-37 v. Somerset at Leeds 2011
One-Day:
Highest score: 32 for Nottinghamshire v. Middlesex
at Nottingham, 2005
Highest score for Yorkshire: 30* v. Glamorgan
at Leeds, 2002
Best bowling: 6-40 v. Glamorgan at Cardiff, 1998
t20:
Highest score for Yorkshire: 16* v. Worcestershire
at Worcester, 2011
Best bowling: 4-25 v. Durham
at Chester-le-Street, 2012

Adil Usman RASHID

Right-hand batsman, leg-break bowler
Born: Bradford, February 17, 1988
First-Class cricket:
Debut: v. Warwickshire at Scarborough, 2006
Highest score: 180 v Somerset at Leeds, 2013
Best bowling: 7-107 v. Hampshire
at Southampton, 2008

One-Day:
Highest score: 71 v. Gloucestershire at Leeds, 2014
Best bowling: 5-33 v. Hampshire
at Southampton, 2014

t20:
Highest score: 36* v Uva Next
at Johannesburg, 2012/3
Best bowling: 4-20 v. Leicestershire at Leeds, 2010

Steven Andrew PATTERSON

Right-hand batsman, right-arm medium-fast bowler
Born: Beverley, October 3, 1983
First-Class cricket:
Debut: v. Bangladesh 'A' at Leeds, 2005
Highest score: 63* v. Warwickshire at Leeds, 2016
Best bowling: 6-56 v. Durham
at Chester-le-Street, 2016

One-Day:
Highest score: 25* v. Worcestershire at Leeds, 2006
Best bowling: 6-32 v. Derbyshire at Leeds, 2010

t20:
Highest score: 3* v. Derbyshire at Leeds, 2010
Best bowling: 4-30 v. Lancashire at Leeds, 2010

Alexander Zak LEES

Left-hand batsman
Born: Halifax, April 14, 1993
First-Class Cricket:
Debut: India A at Leeds, 2010
Highest score: 275* v Derbyshire
at Chesterfield, 2013
Best bowling: 2-51 v. Middlesex at Lord's, 2016

One-Day:
Highest score: 102 v. Northamptonshire
at Northampton, 2014

t20:
Highest score: 67* v. Derbyshire
at Chesterfield, 2014

Liam Edward PLUNKETT

Right-hand batsman, right-arm fast-medium bowler
Born: Middlesbrough, April 6, 1985
First-Class cricket:
Debut: For Durham v. Durham UCCE
at Durham, 2003
Yorkshire Debut: v. Leeds/Bradford MCCU
at Leeds, 2013
Highest score: 126 v. Hampshire at Leeds, 2016
Best bowling: 6-33 v. Leeds/Bradford MCCU
at Leeds 2013
One-Day:
Highest score: 72 for Durham v. Somerset
at Chester-le-Street, 2008
Highest for Yorkshire: 53 v. Leicestershire
at Scarborough, 2013
Best bowling: 4-15 for Durham v. Essex
at Chester-le-Street, 2007
For Yorkshire: 4-52 v. Kent at Canterbury, 2016
t20:
Highest score: 41 for Durham v. Lancashire at Manchester, 2011
For Yorkshire: 36 v. Northamptonshire at Leeds, 2014
Best bowling: 5-31 for Durham v. Lancashire at Chester-le-Street, 2011
For Yorkshire: 3-49 v. Worcestershire at Leeds, 2015

Jack Alexander BROOKS

Right-hand batsman, right-arm medium-fast bowler
Born: Oxford, June 4, 1984
First-Class Cricket:
Debut: For Northamptonshire v. Australia
at Northampton, 2009
Debut for Yorkshire: v. Leeds/Bradford MCCU
at Leeds, 2013
Highest score: 53 for Northamptonshire
v. Gloucestershire at Bristol, 2010
For Yorkshire: 50* v. Middlesex at Lord's 2015
Best bowling: 6-65 v. Middlesex at Lord's, 2016
One-Day:
Highest Score: 10 for Northamptonshire
v. Middlesex at Uxbridge, 2009
For Yorkshire: 6 v. Somerset at Scarborough, 2015
Best bowling: 3-30 v. Hampshire
at Southampton, 2014
t20:
Highest score: 33* for Northamptonshire v. Warwickshire at Birmingham, 2011
Highest for Yorkshire: Has not batted
Best bowling: 5-21 v Leicestershire at Leeds, 2013

David Jonathan WILLEY

Left-hand batsman, left-arm fast-medium
Born: Northampton, February 28, 1990

First-Class cricket:
Debut: for Northamptonshire v. Leicestershire
at Leicester, 2009
Highest score: 104* for Northamptonshire
v. Gloucestershire at Northampton, 2015
Highest for Yorkshire: 22 v Middlesex
at Lord's, 2016
Best bowling: 5-29 for Northamptonshire
v. Gloucestershire at Northampton, 2011
For Yorkshire: 3-55 v. Surrey at Leeds, 2016

One-Day:
Highest score: 167 for Northamptonshire
v. Warwickshire at Birmingham, 2013
Highest for Yorkshire: 27 v. Warwickshire at Leeds, 2016
Best bowling: 5-62 for England Lions v. New Zealand A at Bristol, 2014
For Yorkshire: 3-34 v. Kent at Canterbury, 2016

t20:
Highest score: 100 for Northamptonshire v. Sussex at Hove, 2015
Highest for Yorkshire: 79 v. Glamorgan at Cardiff, 2016
Best bowling: 4-9 for Northamptonshire v. Surrey at Cardiff, 2013
For Yorkshire: 2-28 v. Warwickshire at Leeds, 2016

Andrew John HODD

Right-hand batsman, wicket keeper
Born: Chichester, January 12, 1984
First-Class cricket:
Debut: Sussex v. Zimbabwe at Hove, 2003
Debut for Yorkshire: v. Derbyshire at Leeds, 2012
Highest score: 123 for Sussex v. Yorkshire
at Hove, 2007
Highest score for Yorkshire: 96* v. Nottinghamshire
at Scarborough, 2016
One-Day:
Highest score: 91 for Sussex v. Lancashire
at Hove, 2010
For Yorkshire: 69* v. Leicestershire
at Leicester, 2014
t20:
Highest score: 70 v. Nottinghamshire
at Leeds, 2015

Jack Andrew LEANING

Right-hand batsman, right-arm medium
and off-break bowler
Born: Bristol, October 18, 1993
First-Class cricket:
Debut: v. Surrey at Leeds, 2013
Highest score: 123 v. Somerset at Taunton, 2015
Best bowling: 2-30 v. MCC at Abu Dhabi, 2016

One-Day:
Highest score: 131* v. Leicestershire
at Leicester, 2016
Best bowling: 5-22 v Unicorns at Leeds, 2013

t20:
Highest score: 60* v. Worcestershire at Leeds, 2015
Best bowling: 0-12 v. Derbyshire at Leeds, 2014

Azeem RAFIQ

Right-hand batsman, off-break bowler
Born: Karachi, Pakistan, February 27, 1991
First-Class cricket:
Debut: v. Sussex at Leeds, 2009
Highest score: 100 v. Worcestershire
at Worcester, 2009
Best bowling: 5-50 v. Essex at Chelmsford, 2012
One-Day:
Highest score: 34* v. Unicorns at Leeds, 2012
Best bowling: 5-30 v. Bangladesh A at Leeds, 2013
t20:
Highest score: 21* v. Durham at Leeds 2012
Best bowling: 3-15 v. Lancashire
at Manchester, 2011

William Michael Harry RHODES

Left-hand batsman, right-arm medium fast
Born: Nottingham, March 2, 1995
First-Class Cricket:
Debut: v. MCC at Abu Dhabi, 2015
Highest score: 95 v. MCC at Abu Dhabi, 2016
Best bowling: 3-42 v. Middlesex at Leeds, 2015

One-Day:
Highest score: 46 v. Leicestershire at Leeds, 2015
Best bowling: 2-22 v. Essex at Chelmsford, 2015

t20:
Highest score: 45 v. Leicestershire at Leeds, 2016
Best bowling: 3-27 v. Warwickshire at Leeds, 2015

Karl CARVER

Left-hand batsman, slow left-arm orthodox bowler
Born: Northallerton, March 26, 1996
First-Class Cricket:
Debut for Yorkshire: v. Warwickshire
at Birmingham, 2014
Highest score: 16 v. Leeds/Bradford MCCU
at Leeds, 2015
Best bowling: 4-106 v. MCC at Abu Dhabi, 2016

One-Day:
Highest score: 35* v. Somerset
at Scarborough, 2015
Best bowling: 3-5 v. Lancashire
at Manchester, 2016

t20:
Highest score: 2 v. Worcestershire at Leeds, 2015
Best bowling: 3-40 v. Durham at Leeds, 2016

Benjamin Oliver COAD

Right-hand batsman, right-arm fast-medium bowler
Born: Harrogate, January 10, 1994
First-Class Cricket:
Debut: v. Durham at Chester-le-Street, 2016
Highest score: 17* v. Durham
at Chester-le-Street, 2016
Best bowling: 1-57 v. Pakistan A at Leeds, 2016

One-Day:
Highest score: 2* v. Sri Lanka A at Leeds, 2014
Best bowling: 1-34 v. Gloucestershire
at Bristol, 2013

t20:
Highest score: 2* v. Northamptonshire
at Northampton, 2015
Best bowling: 2-24 v. Northamptonshire
at Northampton, 2015

Matthew David FISHER

Right-hand batsman, right-arm fast-medium bowler
Born: York, November 9, 1997
First-Class Cricket:
Debut: v. Nottinghamshire at Nottingham, 2015
Highest score: 0* v. Warwickshire at Leeds, 2015
Best bowling: 2-61 v. Hampshire
at West End, Southampton, 2015

One-Day:
Highest score: 34 v. Somerset at Scarborough, 2015
Best bowling: 3-32 v. Leicestershire at Leeds, 2015

t20:
Highest score: 0* v. Worcestershire at Leeds, 2015
Best bowling: 5-21 v. Derbyshire at Leeds, 2015

Peter Stephen Patrick HANDSCOMB
Right-hand batsman
Born: Melbourne, April 26, 1991
Awaiting Yorkshire debut
First-Class Cricket:
Debut: For Victoria v. Queensland
at Brisbane, 2011
Highest score: 215 for Victoria v New South Wales
at Sydney, 2016
One-Day:
Highest score: 72 for Victoria v Queensland
at Sydney, 2014
t20:
Highest score: 103* for Melbourne Stars
v. Perth Scorchers at Melbourne 2015

Handscomb celebrates in style

Only days after signing as Yorkshire's overseas player for 2017 Peter Handscomb celebrated by hitting 110 for Australia against Pakistan at the SCG in January. This was his second century in his first four Tests, taking his tally to 359 from six innings at an average of 89.95, the highest by any Aussie in his first four Tests and overtaking the 89.75 set by Michael Hussey in 2005.

Andy is pitch perfect again

Headingley groundsman Andy Fogarty retained his title of Groundsman of the Year in 2016 for producing the best four-day pitches in the country. It was the third time in six years that Andy has scooped the prize at the annual awards night for first-class groundsmen, while Scarborough groundsman John Dodds won the award for preparing the best outground pitches at North Marine Road.

YORKSHIRE'S FIRST-CLASS HIGHLIGHTS OF 2016

Win by an innings (1)

    Surrey (330 and 207) lost to Yorkshire (557-6 dec) by an innings and 20 runs at Leeds

Wins by over 200 runs (2)

    Yorkshire (282 and 263-4 dec) defeated Nottinghamshire (94 and 146) by 305 runs
       at Scarborough
    Yorkshire (460 and 225-2 dec) defeated Durham (265 and 192) by 228 runs at Leeds

Totals of 400 and over (5)

593-9 dec	v. Hampshire at Leeds
557-6 dec	v. Surrey at Leeds
460	v. Durham at Leeds
407	v. Surrey at The Oval
406	v. Middlesex at Scarborough

Opponents dismissed for under 100 (1)

    94   v. Nottinghamshire at Scarborough

Century Partnerships (19)

For the 1st wicket (4)

188*	A Lyth and A Z Lees	v. Lancashire at Manchester
185	A Lyth and A Z Lees	v. Durham at Leeds
112	A Lyth and A Z Lees	v. Durham at Chester-le-Street
103	A Lyth and A Z Lees	v. Somerset at Taunton

For the 2nd wicket (2)

163	A Z Lees and G S Ballance	v. Durham at Leeds
116	A Z Lees and G S Ballance	v. Nottinghamshire at Nottingham

For the 3rd wicket (2)

150	A Lyth and A W Gale	v. Surrey at The Oval
130	A Z Lees and A W Gale	v. Lancashire at Manchester

For the 4th wicket (2)

372	J E Root and J M Bairstow	v. Surrey at Leeds
205	A Lyth and J M Bairstow	v. Hampshire at Leeds

For the 5th wicket (3)

126	G S Ballance and T T Bresnan	v. Middlesex at Scarborough
116	T T Bresnan and A J Hodd	v. Middlesex at Lord's
102	G S Ballance and J A Leaning	v. Warwickshire at Birmingham

For the 6th wicket (2)

136	A U Rashid and T T Bresnan	v. Lancashire at Leeds
125	G S Ballance and w M H Rhodes	v. MCC at Abu Dhabi

For the 7th wicket (3)

227	J M Bairstow and L E Plunkett	v. Hampshire at Leeds
132	A J Hodd and Azeem Rafiq	v. Nottinghamshire at Scarborough
114	T T Bresnan and Azeem Rafiq	v. Middlesex at Lord's

For the 8th wicket (1)

101	J S Lehmann and L E Plunkett	v. Somerset at Leeds

Centuries (16)

A Lyth (4)

202	v. Surrey at The Oval
114*	v. Durham at Leeds
111	v. Hampshire at Leeds
106	v. Somerset at Taunton

G S Ballance (3)

132	v. Middlesex at Scarborough
105	v. MCC at Abu Dhabi
101*	v. Nottinghamshire at Scarborough

A Z Lees (3)

132	v. Durham at Leeds
114*	v. Lancashire at Manchester
107	v. Nottinghamshire at Nottingham

J M Bairstow (2)

246	v. Hampshire at Leeds
198	v. Surrey at Leeds

T T Bresnan (1)

142*	v. Middlesex at Lord's

J S Lehmann (1)

116	v. Somerset at Leeds

L E Plunkett (1)

126	v, Hampshire at Leeds

J E Root (1)

213	v. Surrey at Leeds

5 wickets in an innings (6)

J A Brooks (3)

6-65	v. Middlesex at Lord's
5-53	v. Hampshire at West End, Southampton
5-137	v. Middlesex at Scarborough

T T Bresnan (1)

5-36	v. Nottinghamshire at Scarborough

S A Patterson (1)

6-56	v. Durham at Chester-le-Street

R J Sidebottom (1)

5-51	v. Somerset at Leeds

3 catches in an innings (8)

A J Hodd (4)

4	v. Lancashire at Manchester
3	v. Lancashire at Leeds
3	v. Nottinghamshire at Scarborough
3	v. Hampshire at West End, Southampton

A Lyth (3)

3	v. Warwickshire at Birmingham
3	v. Durham at Leeds
3	v. Middlesex at Lord's

T T Bresnan (1)

4	v. Middlesex at Scarborough

J Read (1)

4	v. Pakistan A at Leeds

5 catches in a match (3)

A J Hodd (3)

    6 (4+2)   v. Lancashire at Manchester

    5 (2+3)   v. Lancashire at Leeds

    5 (2+3)   v. Nottinghamshire at Scarborough

5 dismissals in a match (2)

A J Hodd (2)

    6 (5ct+1st)   v. Lancashire at Leeds

    5 (2ct+3st)   v. MCC at Abu Dhabi

Debuts (9)

In first-class cricket: H C Brook, E Callis, B O Coad, R Gibson and J Read

In first-class cricket for Yorkshire: T M Head, J S Lehmann, J Shaw and D J Willey

Caps (3)

A J Hodd on May 29, 2016

Azeem Rafiq, J A Leaning and D J Willey, all on August 13, 2016

SPECSAVERS COUNTY CHAMPIONSHIP FACTFILE

Compiled by John T Potter

Versus HAMPSHIRE at Leeds

1. Yorkshire's 593-9 dec was their highest total against Hampshire
2. It was their fifth highest total at Headingley, all of the top five scored in the present century
3. J M Bairstow's 246 was a First Class career-best
4. L E Plunkett's 126 was his First Class career-best and his maiden First Class century for Yorkshire
5. J M Bairstow added 102 runs to his score during the morning session on the second day. His father, D L Bairstow, also scored a century before lunch (100*) v. Leicestershire at Bradford in 1985
6. Yorkshire had three centurions in their innings — Lyth, Bairstow and Plunkett. This was last achieved in a Championship match in 2007 v. Surrey at The Oval — J A Rudolph, T T Bresnan and J N Gillespie. This was last achieved in a Championship match at Headingley by M J Lumb, D S Lehmann and M J Wood v. Leicestershire in 2001
7. S M Ervine was R J Sidebottom's 1,000th career wicket in all three forms of cricket
8. Hampshire's seventh-wicket partnership of 143 between S M Ervine and A J Wheater was a club record against Yorkshire
9. The result of this match, a draw, brought an end to Yorkshire's run of seven consecutive Championship home wins

Versus WARWICKSHIRE at Birmingham

1. G S Ballance played his 100th First Class match
2. S A Patterson's 63* was a First Class career-best
3. Yorkshire failed to make it four wins in a row at Edgbaston, but did make it eight without losing, four wins and four draws in a row

Versus NOTTINGHAMSHIRE at Nottingham

1. D J Willey made First Class debut for Yorkshire
2. A Z Lees passed 3,000 First Class career runs
3. L E Plunkett passed 4,000 First Class career runs

SPECSAVERS CHAMPIONSHIP FACTFILE *(Continued)*

Versus SURREY at Leeds

1. Yorkshire's 557-6 dec was their highest total v. Surrey at Leeds
2. J E Root's century was Yorkshire's 50th Championship century v. Surrey in Yorkshire
3. J E Root and J M Bairstow's fourth-wicket partnership of 372 was a record for Yorkshire against any county, the 358 by D S Lehmann and M J Lumb against Durham at Leeds being the previous highest
4. This was Yorkshire's highest partnership v. Surrey for any wicket
5. It was the fifth highest partnership in Yorkshire's history, the four higher all being for the first wicket
6. An innings victory against Surrey was last achieved in 1977 at Abbeydale Park, Sheffield. The last one at Leeds was in 1967

Versus SOMERSET at Taunton

1. Somerset's 562-7 dec was their third-highest total v. Yorkshire at Taunton. behind 592 in 1892 and 581 in 2005
2. A Lyth passed 7,500 First Class career runs

Versus LANCASHIRE at Leeds

1. A U Rashid passed 6,000 First Class career runs
2. S A Patterson passed 1,500 First Class runs for Yorkshire
3. K R Brown became S A Patterson's 300th First Class wicket for Yorkshire

Versus DURHAM at Chester-le-Street

1. B O Coad made his First Class debut
2. J Shaw, son of C Shaw, made his First Class debut for Yorkshire
3. S A Patterson's 6-56 was a First Class career-best
4. K K Jennings's 221* was his maiden First Class double-century
5. It was the fourth-highest individual score at Riverside, and the highest by a Durham player against Yorkshire

Versus PAKISTAN A at Headingley

1. This was the second match between the two sides. The first was also at Leeds in 1997, when M D Moxon hit 155 and P M Hutchison took 7-38, his first five-wicket haul in an innings
2. First Class debuts for H C Brook, E Callis, R Gibson and J Read
3. The match was ruined by the weather. The second day saw a full day's play, the fourth none at all and a total of 825 minutes were lost

Versus MIDDLESEX at Scarborough

1. Middlesex'ss 577 was their highest total against Yorkshire
2. Middlesex's last two First Class innings against Yorkshire produced 1,150 runs
3. T S Roland-Jones's contribution to this total was 103* plus 79*
4. Middlesex last defeated Yorkshire by an innings in 1995 at Leeds. This was their ninth win by an innings against Yorkshire
5. This was Yorkshire's first loss by an innings in a Championship match at Scarborough, and was only their second innings defeat at the ground. The first was against MCC in 1881

Versus SURREY at The Oval

1. This match was ruined by rain, 247 minutes lost on the first day and 311 on the second
2. A Lyth, who was eighth out at 400, had contributed 202 of those runs (50.50 per cent)

Versus WARWICKSHIRE at Leeds

1. T M Head made his First Class debut for Yorkshire
2. A W Gale passed 8,000 First Class career runs
3. J A Brooks took his 300th Championship wicket when he dismissed I R Bell

Versus LANCASHIRE at Manchester

1. J S Lehmann, son of D S Lehmann, made his First Class debut for Yorkshire
2. A Z Lees passed 3,000 First Class career runs
3. J A Brooks passed 1,000 First Class career runs
4. Lancashire's 10th-wicket partnership of 107 between J Clark and K M Jarvis was their highest against Yorkshire
5. H Hameed passed 1,000 Championship runs for the season
6. Hameed also became the first Lancashire player to score a century in each innings — 114 and 100* — in a Roses match, and only the third player to do this. The other two were Yorkshire's P Holmes — 126 and 111* — in 1920 and E I Lester — 125* and 138— in 1948, both at Manchester

SPECSAVERS CHAMPIONSHIP FACTFILE *(Continued)*

Versus NOTTINGHAMSHIRE at Scarborough

1. A J Hodd passed 3,000 First Class career runs
2. A Lyth passed 7,000 Championship runs
3. S J Mullaney passed 1,000 First Class runs for the season
4. Mullaney was dismissed by R J Sidebottom to give the bowler his 600th Championship wicket
5. T T Bresnan's 5-36 was his First Class career best
6. Bresnan's dismissal of L Wood gave him his 350th Championship wicket
7. Yorkshire's victory margin of 305 runs was their best by runs against Nottinghamshire
8. This was also Yorkshire's best victory by runs at Scarborough

Versus HAMPSHIRE at West End, Southampton

1. G S Ballance passed 8,000 First Class career runs

Versus DURHAM at Headingley

1. A Z Lees and A Lyth both passed 1,000 Championship runs for the season
2. M D Stoneman passed 1,000 First Class runs for the season
3. J A Brooks's dismissal of M D Stoneman in the second innings was his 50th Championship wicket of the season and 350th of his career

Versus SOMERSET at Headingley

1. P D Trego passed 1,000 First Class runs for the season for the first time
2. A U Rashid passed 450 First Class career wickets and 400 Championship wickets
3. J S Lehmann scored his maiden First Class century for Yorkshire

Versus MIDDLESEX at Lord's

1. N R T Gubbins's 125 was the 600th Championship century against Yorkshire in away matches
2. J A Brooks's 6-56 was his First Class career-best
3. T S Roland-Jones finished the match with a hat-trick — Azeem Rafiq, A J Hodd and R J Sidebottom. This was the second of his career: his first was against Derbyshire in 2013 at Lord's
4. This was the first hat-trick by a Middlesex player against Yorkshire
5. Middlesex last did the double over Yorkshire in 1961
6. The last team to do the double over Yorkshire was Lancashire in 2011. They also won the Championship that year
7. Yorkshire last lost two matches in a row in 2011. They were against Lancashire at Liverpool, from May 18 to 21, and Somerset at Taunton, from May 24 to 27

Specsavers Championship Division 1, 2016

Captain: A W Gale

*Captain

§ Wicket-Keeper

Figures in brackets ( ) indicate position in 2nd Innings batting order,
where different from 1st Innings.

DETAILS OF PLAYERS WHO APPEARED FOR YORKSHIRE IN 2015
(ALL FIRST-CLASS MATCHES)

Player	Date of Birth	Birthplace	First-Class debut for Yorkshire	Date Capped
A W Gale	November 28, 1983	Dewsbury	July 21, 2004	Sept. 18, 2008
R J Sidebottom	January 15, 1978	Huddersfield	July 2, 1997	July 23, 2000
T T Bresnan	February 28, 1985	Pontefract	May 14, 2003	July 19, 2006
A U Rashid	February 17, 1988	Bradford	July 19, 2006	Sept. 18, 2008
A Lyth	September 25, 1987	Whitby	May 16, 2007	Aug. 22, 2010
R M Pyrah	November 1, 1982	Dewsbury	August 24, 2004	Aug. 22 ,2010
J M Bairstow	September 26, 1989	Bradford	June 11, 2009	Aug. 17, 2011
S A Patterson	October 3, 1983	Beverley	August 3, 2005	May 16, 2012
G S Ballance	November 22, 1989	Harare, Zim	July 11, 2008	Sept 4, 2012
J A Brooks	June 4, 1984	Oxford	April 5, 2013	Aug. 2, 2013
L E Plunkett	April 6, 1985	Middlesbrough	April 5, 2013	Aug. 2, 2013
J A Finch	November 17, 1986	Colac, Australia	May 31, 2014	May 31, 2014
A Z Lees	April 14, 1993	Halifax	June 5, 2010	Sept 23, 2014
C A Pujara	January 25, 1988	Rajkot, India	April 12, 2015	Apr. 12, 2015
G J Maxwell	October 14, 1988	Kew, Melbourne	May 24, 2015	May 24, 2015
J D Middlebrook	May 13, 1977	Leeds	June 27, 1998	—
A J Hodd	January 12, 1984	Chichester	August 15, 2012	—
J A Leaning	October 18, 1993	Bristol	June 21, 2013	—
D M Hodgson	February 26, 1990	Northallerton	April 1, 2014	—
K Carver	March 26, 1996	Northallerton	June 22, 2014	—
W M H Rhodes	March 2, 1995	Nottingham	March 22, 2015	—
M D Fisher	November 9, 1997	York	April 19, 2015	—

Match-By-Match Reports   NIGEL PULLAN

Specsavers County Championship Division 1
Yorkshire v. Hampshire

Played at Headingley, Leeds, on April 17, 18, 19 and 20, 2016
Match drawn at 4.50pm on the Fourth Day

Hampshire opted to field — Yorkshire 12 points, Hampshire 10 points

Close of play: First Day, Yorkshire 270-5 (Bairstow 107*, Rashid 7*); Second Day, Hampshire 141-5 (Vince 76*, Ervine 7*); Third Day, Hampshire 450-8 (McLaren 55*, Wood 28*)

YORKSHIRE

	First Innings		Second Innings	
A Lyth, lbw b Ervine	111		c Wheater b McLaren	15
A Z Lees, c Vince b Tomlinson	7		lbw b Tomlinson	1
G S Ballance, c Wheater b Wood	12		c Alsop b Tomlinson	4
* A W Gale, c Wheater b McLaren	0		c Wheater b Wood	46
§ J M Bairstow, c Tomlinson b Alsop	246		c Wheater b McLaren	5
J A Leaning, c Wheater b Wood	1		b Smith	18
A U Rashid, c Wheater b Tomlinson	34		c Smith b Tomlinson	22
L E Plunkett, b Smith	126		not out	27
S A Patterson, lbw b Alsop	5		c Tomlinson b Vince	1
J A Brooks, not out	13		not out	15
R J Sidebottom	Did not bat			
Extras b 5, lb 12, w 3, nb 18	38		Extras b 1, lb 20, nb 8	29
Total (9 wkts dec)	593		Total (8 wkts dec)	183

Bonus points — Yorkshire 5, Hampshire 2 — Score at 110 overs: 526-6

FoW: 1-16 (Lees), 2-36 (Ballance), 3-41 (Gale), 4-246 (Lyth), 5-249 (Leaning), 1st 6-348 (Rashid), 7-575 (Bairstow), 8-575 (Plunkett), 9-593 (Patterson)

FoW: 1-3 (Lees), 2-13 (Ballance), 3-35 (Lyth), 4-43 (Bairstow), 5-116 (Gale), 2nd 6-120 (Leaning), 7-148 (Rashid), 8-156 (Patterson)

	O	M	R	W		O	M	R	W
Edwards	23	2	145	0	Tomlinson	16	7	31	3
Tomlinson	21	4	74	2	Wood	16	8	21	1
$ Wood	18.4	6	79	2	Vince	10	1	43	1
McLaren	19	4	85	1	McLaren	10	2	26	2
Dawson	3	0	7	0	Smith	16.3	5	41	1
Ervine	12	4	32	1					
$ Vince	1.2	0	15	0					
Smith	12	0	80	1					
Alsop	8	0	59	2					

$ Wood was unable to complete his 19th over, which was finished by Vince

HAMPSHIRE

M A Carberry, c Lees b Plunkett	19	
T P Alsop, lbw b Sidebottom	1	
* J M Vince, lbw b Patterson	119	
W R Smith, lbw b Brooks	11	
L A Dawson, c Bairstow b Sidebottom	16	
J A Tomlinson, c Leaning b Plunkett	2	
S M Ervine, c Bairstow b Sidebottom	123	
§ A J A Wheater, c Ballance b Patterson	62	
R McLaren, not out	55	
C P Wood, c Lyth b Sidebottom	31	
F H Edwards	Did not bat	
Extras lb 9, w 1, nb 4	14	
Total (9 wkts dec)	453	

Bonus points — Hampshire 3, Yorkshire 2 — Score at 110 overs: 306-6

FoW: 1-9 (Alsop), 2-34 (Carberry), 3-66 (Smith), 4-125 (Dawson), 5-128 (Tomlinson), 1st 6-203 (Vince), 7-346 (Wheater), 8-391 (Ervine), 9-453 (Wood)

	O	M	R	W
Sidebottom	27.4	10	80	4
Brooks	32	11	103	1
Plunkett	25	6	75	2
Patterson	31	8	75	2
Rashid	32	4	85	0
Lyth	4	2	15	0
Ballance	1	0	11	0

Umpires: S C Gale and N J Llong — Scorers: J T Potter and K R Baker

Bairstow starts with double ton

This was a remarkable match to begin the season. On two days of biting winds with reports of ice under the covers Yorkshire gained an ascendancy that should have been decisive.

They made a massive first-innings score with a double-century from Bairstow and hundreds from Lyth and Plunkett.

Hampshire had lost Topley and Berg preseason, Dawson and Wood were restricted

JONATHAN BAIRSTOW: Outstanding innings of uninhibited strokeplay

by injury and poor Edwards suffered a broken ankle before the final day.

Bairstow's was an outstanding innings of uninhibited strokeplay, and he was especially severe on Edwards. His 246 was a career-best, with 29 fours and three sixes. Lyth made a responsible 111, starting the season with a first-ball cover-drive for four and batting with concentration and skill, assisted by Rashid. Plunkett struck the ball with immense power to make his first Championship hundred and he reached 94 by lunch, having come in at 11.52 on the second morning. When Plunkett joined Bairstow both were scoring at a great rate, and then Bairstow allowed Plunkett plenty of strike. Yorkshire made 236 in two hours up to lunch.

On two early-summer sunny days Hampshire showed great character in fighting back, refusing to concede a defeat that had seemed inevitable. Vince, their captain, led the way with a classical defensive innings as wickets fell around him, but most credit should go to Ervine, apparently suffering a broken index finger, whose stubborn determination and solid defence moved the score gradually towards the 444 required to save the follow-on. This would not have been achieved without Wheater's 62 and McLaren and Wood, who came together for the ninth wicket with 53 still needed. Yorkshire's bowlers persisted, but lacked inspiration on a wicket that gave them little assistance.

There was more disappointment when Yorkshire batted again. Batsmen who had the opportunity to spend time in the middle failed again. Hampshire produced the best bowling performance of the match, but no result was possible, Yorkshire having a lead of 323.

Specsavers County Championship Division 1
Warwickshire v. Yorkshire

Played at Edgbaston, Birmingham, on April 24, 25, 26 and 27, 2016
Match drawn at 4.51pm on the Fourth Day

Toss won by Yorkshire   Warwickshire 13 points, Yorkshire 11 points
Close of play, First Day, Yorkshire 177-4 (Balance 50*, Leaning 50*); Second Day, Yorkshire 368-9 (Patterson 62*, Sidebottom 6*); Third Day, Warwickshire 205-2 (Chopra 101*, Trott 38*)

	First Innings	YORKSHIRE			Second Innings	
A Lyth, c Bell b Rankin			19	lbw b Patel		8
A Z Lees, b Clarke			19	c Woakes b Rankin		20
G S Ballance, c Ambrose b Barker			68	not out		21
* A W Gale, b Barker			5	not out		13
§ J M Bairstow, b Woakes			20			
J A Leaning, c Ambrose b Woakes			51			
A U Rashid, b Woakes			63			
L E Plunkett, c Ambrose b Clarke			26			
S A Patterson, not out			63			
J A Brooks, c Ambrose b Barker			2			
R J Sidebottom, c Clarke b Woakes			15			
Extras b 19, lb 7, w 2			28	Extras b 5, lb 4, nb 2		11
Total			379	Total (2 wkts dec)		73

Bonus points — Yorkshire 4, Warwickshire 3

FoW: 1-46 (Lees), 2-50 (Lyth), 3-56 (Balance), 4-85 (Bairstow), 5-187 (Leaning),
1st   6-209 (Ballance), 7-252 (Plunkett), 8-343 (Rashid), 9-352 (Brooks), 10-379 (Sidebottom)
2nd   1-19 (Lyth), 2-37 (Lees)

	O	M	R	W		O	M	R	W
Barker	28	6	101	3	Rankin	6	1	18	1
Woakes	28	6	87	4	Patel	9	1	24	1
Clarke	20	7	46	2	Barker	3	0	12	0
Rankin	24	2	93	1	Hain	2	0	8	0
Patel	8	2	26	0	Bell	1	0	2	0
					Ambrose	1	1	0	0

WARWICKSHIRE

V Chopra, c Lyth b Patterson		107
I J Westwood, b Brooks		4
* I R Bell, c Lyth b Rashid		59
I J L Trott, c Lees b Lyth		74
S R Hain, st Bairstow b Lyth		15
§ T R Ambrose, not out		61
C R Woakes, c Lyth b Rashid		15
R Clarke, c and b Rashid		51
K H D Barker, b Rashid		18
J S Patel, b Patterson		9
W B Rankin, not out		16
Extras b 6, lb 8		14
Total (9 wkts dec)		443

Bonus points — Warwickshire 5, Yorkshire 2   Score at 110 overs: 410-7
FoW: 1-18 (Westwood), 2-150 (Bell), 3-220 (Chopra), 4-253 (Hain), 5-270 (Trott),
6-305 (Woakes), 7-387 (Clarke), 8-410 (Barker), 9-423 (Patel)

	O	M	R	W
$ Sidebottom	5.3	1	19	0
Brooks	24	3	105	1
$ Patterson	25.3	4	80	2
Plunkett	24	1	79	0
Rashid	31	4	127	4
Lyth	7	1	19	2

$ Sidebottom was unable to complete his sixth over, which was finished by Patterson

Umpires: N G C Cowley and J W Lloyds   Scorers: J T Potter and M D Smith

Top knock warms Patterson

STEVEN PATTERSON
Determined and aggressive

There was insufficient time because of poor weather for a positive result, and both sides batted with the object of gaining the bonus points available.

Warwickshire were perhaps the better side, but Yorkshire's middle and lower order, led by Ballance, compensated for early failures.

From a spectator's point of view it was cold and wet stadium cricket in April, with even some sleet and snow flurries, and no encouragement to first-class cricket followers.

Yorkshire lost four early wickets before Ballance and Leaning put on 102. Warwickshire relied on four good seam bowlers: Barker, Woakes, Clarke and Rankin. Woakes bowled Bairstow with an in-swinging yorker. On the second day Yorkshire fought back after the early loss of Ballance and Leaning, and a stand between Rashid, in good form with the bat, and a determined and aggressive Patterson restored Yorkshire's fortunes. Patterson's 63 not out was a career-best and only his second 50 in 122 first-class matches.

Woakes, on the fringes of the England side, took 4-87.

Warwickshire's batting had been reinforced by the return of Bell and Trott from Test duties, and both batted very well, although it was Chopra who dominated the third day and reached 107. Yorkshire were handicapped by an injury to Sidebottom's left ankle, and so were a bowler short. Bell and Chopra put on 132 for the second wicket, Bell showing that he remains a classical batsman with a fine technique, but it was Bell who was dismissed first by Rashid and an agile Lyth at slip.

A draw was the only outcome on the last day. Warwickshire also batted deep to gain full batting points as Clarke and Ambrose took them towards 400 after Chopra and Trott had both fallen to catches by Lyth. Rashid persisted in cold, windy conditions inimical to spin bowling, and ended with four wickets. In the limited time left both Lyth and Lees lost their wickets. Lees in particular will have to make some runs after too long in the doldrums for a quality player.

Specsavers County Championship Division 1
Nottinghamshire v. Yorkshire

Played at Trent Bridge, Nottingham, on May 1, 2, 3 and 4, 2016
Match drawn at 6.37pm on the Fourth Day

Yorkshire opted to field   Nottinghamshire 10 points, Yorkshire 10 points
Close of play: First Day, Nottinghamshire 261 all out; Second Day, Yorkshire 170-4 (Lees 91*, Gale 21*); Third Day, Nottinghamshire 151-5 (Patel 51*, Read 13*)

First Innings	NOTTINGHAMSHIRE	Second innings	
S J Mullaney, c Lees b Patterson	78	lbw b Willey	2
A D Hales, c Root b Brooks	36	b Brooks	34
G P Smith, b Brooks	0	b Patterson	17
M J Lumb, lbw b Brooks	49	c Lyth b Patterson	9
M H Wessels, c Root b Plunkett	12	b Plunkett	15
S R Patel, lbw b Rashid	16	c Root b Brooks	51
* § C M W Read, c Bairstow b Brooks	5	c Rashid b Patterson	101
S C J Broad, run out (Brooks/Bairstow)	36	c Lyth b Brooks	55
J T Ball, c Brooks b Rashid	7	b Willey	22
J M Bird, lbw b Rashid	4	lbw b Patterson	23
H F Gurney, not out	8	not out	3
Extras lb 9, w 1	10	Extras b 8, lb 6, w 2	16
Total	261	Total	348

Bonus points — Nottinghamshire 2, Yorkshire 3

FoW: 1-77 (Hales), 2-89 (Smith), 3-132 (Mullaney), 4-163 (Wessels), 5-195 (Patel),
1st   6-201 (Lumb), 7-214 (Read), 8-225 (Ball), 9-238 (Bird), 10-261 (Broad)
FoW: 1-0 (Mullaney), 2-28 (Smith), 3-47 (Lumb), 4-75 (Hales), 5-98 (Wessels),
2nd   6-151 (Patel), 7-255 (Broad), 8-289 (Ball), 9-341 (Bird), 10-348 (Read)

	O	M	R	W		O	M	R	W
Willey	14	3	54	0	Willey	21	5	68	2
Brooks	16	4	74	4	Brooks	23	6	69	3
Patterson	17.2	4	48	1	Plunkett	13	1	52	1
Plunkett	10	1	38	1	Patterson	23.3	8	57	4
Rashid	11	3	29	3	Rashid	17	1	79	0
Lyth	1	0	9	0	Root	3	0	9	0

First Innings	YORKSHIRE	Second innings	
A Lyth, lbw b Ball	0	c Read b Ball	4
A Z Lees, c Read b Gurney	92	c Bird b Gurney	107
G S Ballance, c Read b Ball	7	c Mullaney b Patel	43
J E Root, c Wessels b Ball	0	c Smith b Ball	27
§ J M Bairstow, lbw b Gurney	29	c Broad b Ball	35
* A W Gale, c Mullaney b Ball	44	(8) lbw b Gurney	2
A U Rashid, c Ball b Patel	1	(9) not out	1
LE Plunkett, c Smith b Bird	51	(6) c Lumb b Gurney	11
D J Willey, c Read b Bird	18	(7) lbw b Gurney	5
S A Patterson, c Ball b Patel	1	lbw b Broad	1
J A Brooks, not out	0	not out	4
Extras lb 25, nb 4	29	Extras b 1, lb 11, w 3, nb 2	17
Total	290	Total (9 wkts)	257

Bonus points — Yorkshire 2, Nottinghamshire 3

FoW: 1-0 (Lyth), 2-24 (Ballance), 3-24 (Root), 4-107 (Bairstow), 5-173 (Lees),
1st   6-216 (Gale), 7-250 (Rashid), 8-279 (Willey), 9-284 (Patterson), 10-290 (Plunkett)
FoW: 1-4 (Lyth), 2-120 (Ballance), 3-173 (Root), 4-227 (Bairstow), 5-234 (Lees),
2nd   6-247 (Plunkett), 7-252 (Gale), 8-252 (Willey), 9-253 (Patterson)

	O	M	R	W		O	M	R	W
Ball	18	4	57	4	Ball	15	1	68	3
Broad	14	3	48	0	Broad	11	2	60	1
Bird	17.2	1	76	2	Gurney	16	3	53	4
Gurney	16	0	60	2	Bird	6	0	34	0
Patel	11	2	24	2	Patel	5	0	30	1

TV Man of the match: A Z Lees

Umpires: M A Gough and R A Kettleborough   Scorers: J T Potter and R Marshall
Third Umpire: R K Illingworth

Plucky Yorkshire cling on

It was a close match which Yorkshire, but for Read, might have won and, but for Rashid and Brooks, they might have lost.

On a bleak first morning Yorkshire bowled badly as runs flowed from an array of half volleys. Mullaney played well, but before lunch Brooks redeemed himself by removing Hales and Smith, while Patterson had Mullaney caught by Lees as Nottinghamshire reached 132-3.

Yorkshire regained some composure as Brooks and Rashid bowled Nottinghamshire out just before bad light ended play.

On a shortened second day Ball was impressive as he bowled Lyth and Root for golden ducks and had Ballance caught by Read. Subsequent evidence suggested that both Lyth and Root might

ALEX LEES: Recovered form with 199 in the two innings

have been unlucky, but Ball has a good action, commendable accuracy and moves the ball off the seam. It was good to see Lees unbeaten on 92 recovering form to show his quality as an opener. Lees soon left next morning, but Yorkshire built a lead of 29 and took five wickets before the close. Willey claimed his first for his new county, and Brooks bowled Hales, who showed uncharacteristic restraint under selectorial gaze. Nottinghamshire led by only 122.

No one should underestimate Read, who made his 25th first-class century in defiance of a disappointing Yorkshire attack. He had support, especially from Broad, to set Yorkshire 320 in a minimum of 53 overs. To their credit Yorkshire took up the challenge. Ball dismissed Lyth, but Lees and Ballance put on 116, although they took over half of the allocated overs. Root was caught on the boundary by Wessels. Bairstow swept Broad for six from outside off-stump, but was also caught on the boundary. Gurney dismissed Lees and Plunkett, so Yorkshire put up the shutters. Gurney had Gale and Willey lbw, leaving Yorkshire on 252-8 with two overs to go. The first was survived, so Patterson had to face the final over from Broad: he fell to the fourth, and Broad had two balls in which to dismiss Brooks — who hit a four and survived the last one.

Specsavers County Championship Division 1
Yorkshire v. Surrey

Played at Headingley, Leeds, on May, 8, 9, 10 and 11, 2016
Yorkshire won by an innings and 20 runs at 5.42pm on the Fourth Day

Toss won by Surrey   Yorkshire 24 points, Surrey 5 points

Close of play: First Day, Yorkshire 15-0 (Lyth 6*, Lees 5*), Second Day, Yorkshire 486-5 (Root 190*, Rashid 21*); Third Day, Yorkshire 557-6 (Rashid 60*, Plunkett 4*)

SURREY	First Innings		Second innings	
R J Burns, c Bairstow b Willey	12	lbw b Brooks	8
A Harinath, c Ballance b Plunkett	12	c Root b Plunkett	21
K C Sangakkara, c Lees b Plunkett	73	c Ballance b Root	61
S M Davies, c Plunkett b Patterson	117	lbw b Root	52
J J Roy, c Root b Brooks	1	c Rashid b Brooks	4
§ B T Foakes, c Lees b Patterson	45	b Patterson	21
J E Burke, lbw b Willey	6	lbw b Brooks	0
T K Curran, b Brooks	32	b Patterson	22
* G J Batty, lbw b Willey	0	c Bairstow b Patterson	0
R Rampaul, c Bairstow b Brooks	12	not out	4
M P Dunn, not out	5	lbw b Plunkett	2
Extras lb 13, nb 2	15	Extras b 7, lb 5	12
Total	330	Total	207

Bonus points — Surrey 3, Yorkshire 3

FoW: 1-14 (Burns), 2-38 (Harinath), 3-160 (Sangakkara), 4-161 (Roy), 5-264 (Davies),
1st   6-273 (Foakes), 7-309 (Burke), 8-309 (Batty), 9-321 (Curran), 10-330 (Rampaul)
FoW: 1-14 (Burns), 2-34 (Harinath), 3-138 (Sangakkara), 4-143 (Roy), 5-151 (Davies),
2nd   6-152 (Burke), 7-194 (Curran), 8-194 (Batty), 9-205 (Foakes), 10-207 (Dunn)

	O	M	R	W		O	M	R	W
Willey	20	7	55	3	Brooks	20	6	65	3
Brooks	18.4	3	73	3	Plunkett	14.1	4	46	2
Plunkett	18	2	77	2	Patterson	9	5	15	3
Patterson	21	6	53	2	Rashid	18	5	46	0
Rashid	10	1	42	0	Root	12	3	23	2
Root	3	0	17	0					
Lyth	1	1	0	0					

YORKSHIRE

A Lyth, lbw b Rampaul		13
A Z Lees, c Foakes b Curran		16
G S Ballance, b Rampaul		8
J E Root, c Batty b Rampaul		213
§ J M Bairstow, c Sangakkara b Burke		198
* A W Gale, c Foakes b Rampaul		18
A U Rashid, not out		60
L E Plunkett, not out		4
D J Willey		
S A Patterson	Did not bat	
J A Brooks		
Extras b 7, lb 10, w 4, nb 6		27
Total (6 wkts dec)		557

Bonus points — Yorkshire 5, Surrey 2   Score at 110 overs: 551-6

FoW: 1-27 (Lyth), 2-41 (Ballance), 3-45 (Lees), 4-417 (Bairstow), 5-452 (Gale),
6-547 (Root)

	O	M	R	W
Curran	31	0	139	1
Rampaul	32.2	0	153	4
Burke	12	0	74	1
Dunn	17	2	79	0
Batty	9	1	58	0
Harinath	10	1	37	0

Umpires: S A Garratt and A G Wharf   Scorers: J T Potter and K R Booth

Root and Bairstow set record

RUNNING INTO HISTORY: Jonny Bairstow, left; and Joe Root during their 372 stand

Yorkshire won in a tense final session on a cloudy afternoon by bowling Surrey out with 4.5 overs to spare.

Fine knocks from Davies and Sri Lankan Test player Sangakkara, with support from Foakes, were the main features of Surrey's first innings. Davies made a century and Sangakkara played some beautifully timed shots. Brookes and Willey, who later retired with an abdominal strain, took three wickets apiece.

The second day was distinguished by wonderful batting from Root and Bairstow. They put on a record 372 for the fourth wicket, surpassing Lehmann and Lumb's marathon against Durham, and taking only 67 overs. It was high quality batting, off-side and straight-driving off front and back foot, and they ran between wickets like greyhounds. Root (213) began with his characteristic drive behind square in a masterly innings. Bairstow (198) was even more adventurous, at one point doubling Root's score. A day of sunshine saw 471 runs scored.

It was another matter for Surrey. They had an inexperienced attack, the benign wicket was ideal for batting and the batsmen were two of the three best in England. Tom Curran, with 76 wickets in his first season, should benefit from the experience and Rampaul, a West Indian Test cricketer, more runs than Curran.

Surrey will be more disappointed not to have saved the game on an interrupted final day that started at 11.45. They appeared safe as Sangakkara and Davies renewed their partnership; then Sangakkara hit Root — leading the side after Gale had hobbled off with a knee injury — to Ballance in the covers. Roy fell to Brooks, and Root had Davies lbw. Root bowled well, getting turn with fielders around the bat. Foakes and Curran suggested stability until Patterson was recalled and bowled Curran with his first ball. Both Foakes, who batted well, and Batty played casual shots. Dunn and Rampaul, two insecure left-handers, were reluctant to depart until Plunkett administered the coup de grace.

Specsavers County Championship Division 1
Somerset v. Yorkshire

Played at The County Ground, Taunton, on May, 15, 16, 17 and 18, 2016
Match drawn at 5.57pm on the Fourth Day

Yorkshire opted to field   Somerset 12 points, Yorkshire 9 points

Close of play: First Day, Somerset 342-4 (Hildreth 68*, Trego 7*); Second Day, Yorkshire 127-1 (Lyth 80*, Rhodes 6*); Third Day, Yorkshire 306-9 (Patterson 32*, Brooks 34*)

SOMERSET

M E Trescothick, c and b Rashid		97
T B Abell, b Patterson		8
* C J L Rogers, c Hodd b Rashid		91
J C Hildreth, c and b Rashid		166
J Allenby, c Ballance b Rhodes		51
P D Trego, c Hodd b Rashid		94
J Overton, c Lees b Patterson		23
L Gregory, not out		7
T D Groenewald		
§ R C Davies	Did not bat	
M J Leach		
Extras b 11, lb 7, w 5, nb 2		25
Total (7 wkts dec)		562

Bonus points — Somerset 5, Yorkshire 1   Score at 110 overs: 387-4

FoW: 1-30 (Abell), 2-178 (Trescothick), 3-247 (Rogers), 4-332 (Allenby), 5-531 (Trego), 6-544 (Hildreth), 7-562 (Overton).

	O	M	R	W
Brooks	25	2	106	0
Plunkett	19	1	87	0
Patterson	27.2	8	80	2
Rhodes	21	2	70	1
Lyth	12	1	41	0
Rashid	34	2	160	4

YORKSHIRE

First Innings		Second innings	
A Lyth, c Allenby b Gregory	106	b Overton	18
A Z Lees, c Trego b Overton	33	b Overton	11
W M H Rhodes, c Overton b Trego	15	c Abell b Leach	18
G S Ballance, c Davies b Groenewald	37	c Leach b Overton	18
* A W Gale, c Allenby b Leach	8	c Leach b Groenewald	13
J A Leaning, c Davies b Gregory	17	not out	29
A U Rashid, run out(Abell/Groenewald)	0	c Allenby b Groenewald	0
L E Plunkett, c Davies b Groenewald	4	not out	20
§ A J Hodd, b Groenewald	0		
S A Patterson, b Overton	32		
J A Brooks, not out	38		
Extras b 6, lb 5, nb 10	21	Extras lb 9, w 5	14
Total	311	Total (6 wkts)	141

Bonus points — Yorkshire 3, Somerset 3   Score at 110 overs: 306-9

FoW: 1-103 (Lees), 2-145 (Rhodes), 3-172 (Lyth), 4-189 (Gale), 5-226 (Leaning), 1st 6-232 (Rashid), 7-232 (Ballance), 8-232 (Hodd), 9-237 (Plunkett), 10-311 (Patterson)
FoW: 1-19 (Lyth), 2-45 (Rhodes), 3-49 (Lees), 4-69 (Gale), 5-88 (Ballance), 2nd 6-99 (Rashid)

	O	M	R	W		O	M	R	W
Gregory	21	9	55	2	Groenewald	15	5	32	2
Groenewald	20	4	54	3	Gregory	14	4	32	0
Overton	27.1	7	87	2	Leach	21	8	33	1
Leach	27	10	64	1	Overton	17	7	26	3
Allenby	6	0	15	0	Trego	4	1	3	0
Trego	12	3	25	1	Allenby	0.4	0	6	0

Umpires: S J O'Shaughnessy and B V Taylor   Scorers: J T Potter and L M Rhodes

Somerset v. Yorkshire

Lyth ton can't save follow-on

Somerset dominated this game, but were unable to gain the success they deserved. Having been asked to bat first, they compiled an impregnable total.

All four high-scoring batsmen had previous achievements at Yorkshire's expense — Trescothick, who was 40 last Christmas Day, almost reached his sixth century against the White Rose.

We have encountered Rogers at Lord's, and now the new Somerset captain added 148 with Trescothick.

ADAM LYTH: Three sixes in 106

The enterprising Trego was the third batsman in the 90s, but it was Hildreth, surely as accomplished a batsman as many who have played for England, who made the big century with 166. Neither Brooks nor Plunkett took a wicket and conceded almost 200 runs, while Rashid did take four at high cost. With injury problems among the bowlers and displays like this Yorkshire must be concerned about the prospects of retaining the Championship.

Lyth and Lees began well, although both were missed early on. At the close Yorkshire were 127-1, and seemed secure. On a cloudy third day a batting collapse made the follow-on inevitable, but Lyth hit a good 106 with three sixes before being smartly caught at slip by Allenby. Ballance and Leaning were still there, but after a delay play resumed under heavy cloud and Yorkshire lost five wickets for 11 runs, subsiding to 237-9. A last-wicket stand of 74 by Patterson and Brooks, ending early on Wednesday, left Yorkshire 74 overs to survive.

No one epitomised dour resolution better than Lees, whose 11 runs occupied two hours and nine minutes. Yorkshire made their runs at two an over, but each batsman stuck to his task, and Leaning and Plunkett together averted defeat which had been a real prospect. Somerset bowled well with a mainly home-produced attack of Gregory, Jamie Overton and Leach, supplemented by the experience of Groenewald. Jamie Overton bowled Lyth and Lees, and also dismissed Ballance. Last year at Headingley his identical twin Craig bowled well, and at Taunton they added 76 together for the last wicket.

Specsavers County Championship Division 1
Yorkshire v. Lancashire

Played at Headingley, Leeds, on May 29, 30 and 31 and June 1, 2016
Yorkshire won by 175 runs at 3.35pm on the Fourth Day

Lancashire opted to field   Yorkshire 22 points, Lancashire 3 points

Close of play: First Day, Yorkshire 301-9 (Patterson 41*); Second Day, Yorkshire 77-3 (Lyth 44*, Patterson 0*); Third Day, Lancashire 41-1 (Hameed 16*, Procter 6*)

First Innings	YORKSHIRE	Second innings	
A Lyth, c Croft b Bailey	4	b Wagner	48
A Z Lees, c Brown b Jarvis	0	c Croft b Smith	17J
A Leaning, c Smith b Jarvis	10	c Smith b Wagner	4
G S Ballance, c Smith b Jarvis	0	c Croft b Wagner	8
* A W Gale, lbw b Wagner	36	(6) c Hameed b Wagner	7
A U Rashid, c Procter b Kerrigan	88	(7) c Croft b Kerrigan	34
T T Bresnan, c Croft b Wagner	69	(8) c Livingstone b Procter	29
L E Plunkett, c Procter b Jarvis	3	(9) c Petersen b Kerrigan	57
§ A J Hodd, c Livingstone b Wagner	40	(10) not out	15
S A Patterson, c Smith b Wagner	45	(5) c Croft b Smith	1
J A Brooks, not out	3	b Procter	5
Extras b 1, lb 7, nb 2	10	Extras b 1, lb 6, nb 4	11
Total	308	Total	236

Bonus points — Yorkshire 3, Lancashire 3

FoW: 1-4 (Lyth), 2-6 (Lees), 3-14 (Ballance), 4-29 (Leaning), 5-74 (Gale),
1st   6-210 (Rashid), 7-215 (Plunkett), 8-226 (Bresnan), 9-301 (Hodd), 10-308 (Patterson)
FoW: 1-41 (Lees), 2-54 (Leaning), 3-70 (Ballance), 4-81 (Lyth), 5-89 (Patterson),
2nd   6-89 (Gale), 7-130 (Bresnan), 8-204 (Rashid), 9-221 (Plunkett), 10-236 (Brooks)

	O	M	R	W		O	M	R	W
Bailey	17	2	48	1	Wagner	24	3	71	4
Jarvis	20	5	74	4	Jarvis	23	5	72	0
Smith	16	2	54	0	Smith	14	8	20	2
Wagner	24.1	5	75	4	Kerrigan	11	1	36	2
Kerrigan	20	3	49	1	Procter	12.2	1	30	2

First Innings	LANCASHIRE	Second innings	
T C Smith, c Ballance b Patterson	26	c Plunkett b Patterson	15
H Hameed, c Lyth b Bresnan	17	c Hodd b Rashid	20
L A Procter, lbw b Brooks	6	c Bresnan b Lyth	16
A N Petersen, lbw b Brooks	8	lbw b Bresnan	24
* § S J Croft, c Leaning b Bresnan	14	b Hameed	5
K R Brown, c Hodd b Patterson	0	c Ballance b Bresnan	51
L S Livingstone, not out	60	c Plunkett b Rashid	24
T E Bailey, c Hodd b Plunkett	0	c Hodd b Rashid	2
N Wagner, lbw b Rashid	12	c Hodd b Bresnan	2
K M Jarvis, st Hodd b Rashid	33	lbw b Rashid	0
S C Kerrigan, lbw b Rashid	6	not out	0
Extras b 5, lb 5, nb 4	14	Extras b 4, lb 10	14
Total	196	Total	173

Bonus points — Yorkshire 3

FoW: 1-46 (Smith), 2-56 (Hameed), 3-59 (Procter), 4-68 (Petersen), 5-69 (Brown),
1st   6-91 (Croft), 7-92 (Bailey), 8-126 (Wagner), 9-174 (Jarvis), 10-196 (Kerrigan)
FoW: 1-28 (Smith), 2-55 (Hameed), 3-55 (Procter), 4-71 (Croft), 5-98 (Petersen),
2nd   6-161 (Livingstone), 7-169 (Bailey), 8-172 (Wagner), 9-173 (Brown), 10-173 (Jarvis)

	O	M	R	W		O	M	R	W
Bresnan	14	2	50	2	Bresnan	22	9	36	4
Brooks	17	7	39	2	Brooks	17	8	43	0
Patterson	14	6	22	2	Patterson	15	5	26	1
Plunkett	10	1	38	1	Plunkett	14	4	29	0
Rashid	5.4	0	37	3	Rashid	14.4	7	17	4
					Lyth	4	0	8	1

Umpires: M Burns and P J Hartley   Scorers: J T Potter and C Rimmer

Yorkshire v. Lancashire
Joint top after Roses win

ADIL RASHID: Two vital innings and the wickets that brought victory

On a competitive first day fortunes swung between red and white rose. and play ended with Yorkshire having a slight advantage.

After Croft chose to bowl Lancashire reduced Yorkshire to 29-4. Lyth went to his fourth ball from Bailey, who was impressive until suffering an injury, and Jarvis accounted for Lees, Ballance and Leaning.

Gale showed aggressive intent, but Bresnan and Rashid led Yorkshire's recovery with a sixth-wicket stand of 136. Rashid batted very well for 88, while Bresnan, back after injury in Dubai, demonstrated his value in the middle-order. Then Jarvis and Wagner broke through, leaving Yorkshire on a precarious 226-8. Patterson and Hodd, who had received his county cap before play, added 75, and the adhesive Patterson was out next morning for 45.

Lancashire started confidently, but after Hameed and Smith fell no other batsman could play the major innings that the situation required. It was left to Jarvis and Livingstone to avert the follow-on, which Livingstone achieved with a six off Rashid. Yorkshire bowled well as a unit, but Brooks's dismissal of Petersen was the significant break-through. Patterson's removal of Brown was his 300th first-class wicket.

Yorkshire were 77-3 overnight on Monday, and on a bleak third day they gradually batted Lancashire out of contention. Wagner made early inroads until again Rashid and Bresnan began the recovery. Rashid's innings was most significant in that it enabled Yorkshire to bat longer and Plunkett to hit an attacking fifty. Wagner took 8-146 in the match with his left-arm seamers.

Lancashire may have been optimistic starting on Wednesday at 41-1, but in reality it was a question of survival. Yorkshire did bowl well again, Bresnan dismissing the middle-order and Rashid with 4-17 ensuring that the visitors' resistance was ended before bad light could bring about an early closure. Victory for the champions moved them level on points at the top of the table with their opponents.

Specsavers County Championship Division 1
Durham v. Yorkshire

Played at Riverside, Chester-le-Street, on June 20, 21, 22 and 23, 2016

Match drawn at 6.05pm on the Fourth Day

Yorkshire opted to field

Yorkshire 11 points, Durham 8 points

Close of play: First Day, Yorkshire 129-4 (Balance 35*, Gale 1*); Second Day, Durham 98-3 (Jennings 46*, Richardson 3*); Third Day, Durham 452-8 (Jennings 185*, Rushworth 16*)

First Innings	DURHAM		Second Innings	
M D Stoneman, lbw b Patterson	45		c and b Bresnan	28
K K Jennings, b Shaw	20		not out	221
S G Borthwick, run out (Gale)	2		b Lyth	4
J T A Burnham, c Williamson b Patterson	49		lbw b Patterson	8
§ M J Richardson, c Hodd b Patterson	18		run out (Coad)	13
* P D Collingwood, c Ballance b Patterson	4		lbw b Williamson	61
R D Pringle, b Patterson	3		b Bresnan	20
U Arshad, c Hodd b Bresnan	3		c Hodd b Coad	84
B J McCarthy, c and b Shaw	9		c Hodd b Patterson	11
C Rushworth, c Leaning b Patterson	13		not out	31
G Onions, not out	0			
Extras b 1, lb 5	6		Extras b 11, lb 9, w 2, nb 4	26
Total	172		Total (8 wkts dec)	507

Bonus points — Yorkshire 3

FoW: 1-49 (Jennings), 2-56 (Borthwick), 3-74 (Stoneman), 4-98 (Richardson), 5-106 (Collingwood),
1st 6-110 (Pringle), 7-122 (Arshad), 8-148 (McCarthy), 9-172 (Rushworth), 10-172 (Burnham)
FoW: 1-46 (Stoneman), 2-65 (Borthwick), 3-83 (Burnham), 4-105 (Richardson), 5-222
2nd (Collingwood), 6-252 (Pringle), 7-408 (Arshad), 8-425 (McCarthy)

	O	M	R	W		O	M	R	W
Bresnan	14	3	34	1	Bresnan	35	5	145	2
Coad	17	5	38	0	Coad	18	5	70	1
Patterson	20.1	4	56	6	Patterson	38	17	77	1
Shaw	10	1	38	2	Shaw	19	2	81	0
					Lyth	15	3	54	1
					Williamson	14	2	40	1
					Leaning	6	1	20	0

First Innings	YORKSHIRE		Second innings	
A Lyth, c Borthwick b Rushworth	12		c sub (B A Stokes) b McCarthy	50
A Z Lees, b Rushworth	71		b Pringle	74
K S Williamson, c Jennings b Rushworth	10		lbw b McCarthy	0
G S Ballance, c Borthwick b Onions	78		c Richardson b Onions	32
S A Patterson, b Rushworth	0			
* A W Gale, c Stoneman b Pringle	28		(5) c Richardson b Pringle	17
J A Leaning, b Onions	9		(6) not out	22
T T Bresnan, c Burnham b McCarthy	63		(7) not out	27
§ A J Hodd, lbw b Rushworth	3			
J Shaw, b Borthwick	24			
B O Coad, not out	17			
Extras lb 8	8		Extras b 12, lb 4	16
Total	323		Total (5 wkts)	238

Bonus points — Yorkshire 3, Durham 3

FoW: 1-30 (Lyth), 2-54 (Williamson), 3-125 (Lees), 4-125 (Patterson), 5-193 (Gale),
1st 6-210 (Leaning), 7-229 (Ballance), 8-236 (Hodd), 9-279 (Shaw), 10-323 (Bresnan)
2nd 1-112 (Lyth), 2-112 (Williamson), 3-149 (Ballance), 4-176 (Gale), 5-179 (Lees)

	O	M	R	W		O	M	R	W
Rushworth	25	3	95	5	Rushworth	10	1	25	0
Onions	24	3	90	2	Onions	15	5	29	1
McCarthy	17.1	0	67	1	Borthwick	20	7	70	0
Arshad	16	3	46	0	Pringle	16	3	35	2
Borthwick	6	2	9	1	Arshad	9	1	31	0
Pringle	2	0	10	1	McCarthy	11	2	27	1
					Stoneman	1	0	5	0

Umpires: S A Garratt and J W Lloyds

Scorers: J T Potter and B Hunt

Durham v. Yorkshire
Patterson's best in vain

Yorkshire were without six bowlers. Sidebottom, Brooks and Fisher were injured, and Plunkett, Rashid and Willey with the England team.

Coad and Shaw, recalled from his loan to Gloucestershire, made their Yorkshire Championship debuts. Durham had two England bowlers, Stokes and Wood, also absent through injury.

At the close on the second day Yorkshire had the advantage, but that was lost as Jennings made a dominant double-century with good support from Collingwood and Arshad. Requiring 357 to win, Yorkshire began with a challenging opening stand of 112, but once wickets fell they had to defend for a draw.

STEVEN PATTERSON: Man for a crisis with career-best 6-56

Durham batted first after an uncontested toss, and began well until Jennings was bowled by Shaw with his seventh ball and Borthwick run out as Gale hit the stumps. Patterson, responding to the bowling crisis, was as accurate as usual but also took six wickets, four between lunch and tea, as Durham slumped from 72-2 to 155-8. His 6-56 was a career-best. Durham's 172 was disappointing, but the day ended on parity as Rushworth took four wickets. He had New Zealander Williamson brilliantly caught in the gully by Jennings.

Next day Yorkshire's recovery centred around Ballance and Bresnan, who put on 87 with debutants Shaw and Coad for the last two wickets. Shaw batted sensibly until tempted by Borthwick's leg-spin, and Coad helped to add 44 for the 10th wicket. Rushworth took 5-95, and his admirers must wonder why he apparently is not considered by England.

The third day belonged to Jennings, who batted all day for his fourth century of the summer, so Durham had a lead of 301 by the close. Coad took his first wicket when Hodd caught Arshad who had been dropped off him earlier. On Wednesday Durham batted on for an hour, and Jennings finished undefeated on 221. They set Yorkshire a virtually impossible 357 to win, and after the openers' early aggression it was a matter of survival to save a game that neither side deserved to lose.

Specsavers County Championship Division 1
Yorkshire v. Middlesex

Played at North Marine Road, Scarborough, on July, 3, 4, 5 and 6, 2016
Middlesex won by an innings and 4 runs at 5.24pm on the Fourth Day

Toss won by Yorkshire   Middlesex 21 points, Yorkshire 4 points

Close of play: First Day, Yorkshire 291-5 (Ballance 106*, Rhodes 12*); Second Day, Middlesex 130-2 (Eskinazi 19*, Bailey 19*); Third Day, Middlesex 470-8 (Roland-Jones 14*, Murtagh 7*)

First Innings	YORKSHIRE		Second innings	
A Lyth, c Simpson b Murtagh	0		c Franklin b Roland-Jones	23
A Z Lees, c Rayner b Murtagh	63		c Simpson b Rayner	26
K S Williamson, c Simpson b Franklin	28		c Simpson b Roland-Jones	4
G S Ballance, c and b Franklin	132		c Simpson b Finn	3
* A W Gale, lbw b Roland-Jones	7		c Simpson b Rayner	7
T T Bresnan, b Murtagh	63		b Murtagh	39
W M H Rhodes, c Robson b Roland-Jones	20		c Simpson b Finn	20
§ A J Hodd, c Robson b Roland-Jones	37		c Rayner b Murtagh	6
Azeem Rafiq, c Simpson b Franklin	0		not out	8
S A Patterson, b Finn	13		c Rayner b Roland-Jones	3
J A Brooks, not out	19		c Robson b Murtagh	6
Extras b 4, lb 14, nb 6	24		Extras b 5, lb 7, nb 10	22
Total	406		Total	167

Bonus points — Yorkshire 3, Middlesex 2   Score at 110 overs: 332-6

FoW: 1-0 (Lyth), 2-85 (Williamson), 3-111 (Lees), 4-131 (Gale), 5-257 (Bresnan), 1st 6-300 (Rhodes), 7-334 (Ballance), 8-334 (Rafiq), 9-371 (Patterson), 10-406 (Hodd)
FoW: 1-41 (Lyth), 2-47 (Williamson), 3-63 (Lees), 4-63 (Bresnan), 5-89 (Gale), 2nd 6-136 (Rhodes), 7-144 (Bresnan), 8-147 (Hodd), 9-156 (Patterson), 10-167 (Brooks)

	O	M	R	W		O	M	R	W
Murtagh	31	4	100	3	Murtagh	18	4	44	3
Roland-Jones	29.5	7	88	3	Finn	15	2	54	2
Finn	30	8	90	1	Roland-Jones	17	5	34	3
Franklin	21	6	62	3	Rayner	19	9	23	2
Rayner	15	6	44	0					
Stirling	1	0	4	0					

MIDDLESEX

S D Robson, c Rhodes b Brooks	40
N R T Gubbins, lbw b Rhodes	43
S S Eskinazi, c Williamson b Brooks	157
G J Bailey, c Bresnan b Rhodes	62
§ J A Simpson, c Bresnan b Brooks	15
* J E C Franklin, c Williamson b Brooks	99
P R Stirling, c Bresnan b Brooks	5
O P Rayner, c Lees b Williamson	0
T S Roland-Jones, not out	79
T J Murtagh, c and b Lyth	47
S T Finn, c Azeem Rafiq b Lyth	0
Extras b 10, lb 5, w 1, nb 14	30
Total	577

Bonus points — Middlesex 3, Yorkshire 2   Score at 110 overs: 338-4
FoW: 1-87 (Robson), 2-94 (Gubbins), 3-215 (Bailey), 4-256 (Simpson), 5-428 (Eskinazi), 6-436 (Stirling), 7-439 (Rayner), 8-454 (Murtagh), 9-577 (Murtagh), 10-577 (Finn)

	O	M	R	W
Bresnan	35	11	112	0
Brooks	37	12	137	5
Patterson	29	3	119	0
Azeem Rafiq	21	5	99	0
Rhodes	20	3	67	2
Lyth	2.4	0	9	2
Williamson	4	0	19	1

Umpires: J H Evans and P J Hartley   Scorers: J T Potter and D K Shelley

Yorkshire v. Middlesex

Last-day slip, first defeat

Yorkshire lost their first Championship match of the season to a good Middlesex side.

It had looked destined to be a draw after some loss to rain until the last day, when Middlesex gained a lead of 171 and Yorkshire did not bat well enough to save the game.

Middlesex have good pace bowlers: Murtagh, accurate and skilful, swung the ball around, and Finn from the Trafalgar

TAKE THAT: Gary Ballance leaves wicket-keeper Simpson on the hop

Square End looked to have regained rhythm and pace despite some inaccuracy. Roland-Jones, a genuine quick bowler of potential Test standard, took his wickets next day, but Yorkshire finished on Sunday at 291-5. Ballance reached a determined unbeaten century, helped by good innings from Lees and Bresnan. Lees was caught once — but it was by a spectator at the back of the stand.

Eventually Yorkshire reached 406, but they found Middlesex's batsmen equally resolute as Robson and Gubbins, who had played for Leeds/Bradford MCCU, put on 87. On Tuesday Eskinazi, South African-born, educated in Western Australia and a British passport holder who had made his debut against Yorkshire at Lord's the previous September, made an excellent century, his second of the summer. This saw Middlesex to a substantial lead. Eskinazi received good support from Bailey and Franklin, who was unlucky to be caught for 99.

Middlesex seized the initiative on the last day. First, they made 107 runs off 9.4 overs with devastating hitting from Roland-Jones and Murtagh. At one stage they hit six sixes off seven balls, and Roland-Jones hit three in succession off Brooks. Brooks did finish with five wickets, but Patterson, Bresnan and Rafique conceded 315 runs between them without taking a wicket.

Then no Yorkshire batsman played a major innings on a pitch which had seen 983 first-innings runs. The three visiting seam bowlers, assisted by off-spinner Rayner, sustained the pressure and catches were taken, including five by wicketkeeper Simpson. Middlesex are a good side who went to the top of the table, but Yorkshire should have saved the game.

Specsavers County Championship Division 1
Surrey v. Yorkshire

Played at The Oval on July 11, 12, 13 and 14, 2016
Match drawn at 5pm on the Fourth Day

Toss won by Surrey   Yorkshire 13 points, Surrey 10 points

Close of play: First Day, Surrey 95-2 (Ansari 35*, Finch 34*); Second Day, Surrey 164-5 (Davies 29*, Foakes 14*); Third Fay, Yorkshire 207-3 (Lyth 116*, Patterson 5*)

First Innings	SURREY	Second Innings	
R J Burns, lbw b Willey	8	c and b Azeem Rafiq	14
D P Sibley, c Hodd b Patterson	17	not out	54
Z S Ansari, b Willey	40	not out	24
A J Finch, c Leaning b Patterson	52		
J J Roy, c Hodd b Willey	0		
§ S M Davies, lbw b Bresnan	56		
B T Foakes, c Lyth b Patterson	14		
S M Curran, not out	59		
T K Curran, lbw b Rashid	6		
* G J Batty, lbw b Rashid	0		
S C Meaker, c Lyth b Azeem Rafiq	4		
Extras b 2, lb 7, nb 2	11	Extras b 8, nb 6	14
Total	267	Total (1 wkt)	106

Bonus points — Surrey 2, Yorkshire 3

FoW: 1-13 (Burns), 2-36 (Sibley), 3-121 (Ansari), 4-121 (Finch), 5-121 (Roy),
1st   6-164 (Foakes), 7-239 (Davies), 8-254 (T K Curran), 9-254 (Batty), 10-267 (Meaker)
2nd   1-20 (Burns)

	O	M	R	W		O	M	R	W
Bresnan	10	4	22	1	Bresnan	2	0	10	0
Willey	18	3	59	3	Willey	3	1	6	0
Plunkett	9	2	26	0	Rashid	13	1	37	0
Patterson	18	5	58	3	Lyth	3	1	11	0
Rashid	14	2	47	2	Azeem Rafiq	11	5	12	1
Azeem Rafiq	13.3	2	46	1	Plunkett	1	0	1	0
					Leaning	4	1	7	0
					Hodd	1	0	14	0

YORKSHIRE

A Lyth, c Davies b Meaker	202
A Z Lees, b S M Curran	15
J A Leaning, b Meaker	0
* A W Gale, c Davies b T K Curran	61
S A Patterson, b Ansari	51
A U Rashid, c Finch b Ansari	16
T T Bresnan, lbw b Batty	3
L E Plunkett, run out (sub M W Pillans/Davies)	37
D J Willey, c S M Curran b Meaker	2
§ A J Hodd, c Burns b T K Curran)	5
Azeem Rafiq, not out	0
Extras b 6, lb 3, w 6	15
Total	407

Bonus points — Yorkshire 5, Surrey 3

FoW: 1-28 (Lees), 2-47 (Leaning), 3-197 (Gale), 4-288 (Patterson), 5-324 (Rashid),
       6-330 (Bresnan), 7-388 (Plunkett), 8-400 (Lyth), 9-406 (Hodd), 10-407 (Willey)

	O	M	R	W
T K Curran	19	2	73	2
S M Curran	11	2	58	1
Meaker	11.2	1	66	3
Ansari	34	8	98	2
Batty	31	4	103	1

Umpires: N L Bainton and M J Saggers   Scorers: J T Potter and K R Booth

Outstanding Lyth leathers 202

Too much play was lost on the first two days for any positive result to be achieved, but Yorkshire did gain maximum bonus points from the drawn match.

Both sides hoped to bat first, but Surrey won the toss and went in on a dismal morning, losing two wickets, one to a brilliant catch by wicket-keeper Hodd.

By the end of the second day Surrey had reached 164-5, only 16.4 overs being possible. The former Yorkshire player, Finch, made 52 and the promising Ansari 40.

Willey took three wickets, and his yorker to Ansari removed two stumps. Davies and Sam Curran enabled Surrey to reach 267 by lunch on the third morning, and

ADAM LYTH: Battered 17 fours and five sixes in graceful innings

Yorkshire took full bowling points, thanks to Patterson, as ever, and Willey, who was keen to establish himself in the Championship side.

Lyth now played one of his outstanding innings, going on to a double-century. He did receive support, especially from Gale and Patterson, but it was Lyth's innings which took Yorkshire past the 400 mark. Once he is established and in good form there is no one more graceful and accomplished than this son of Whitby, who hit 17 fours and five sixes. His off-side shots are a hallmark of his quality, but he can hit a ball hard as his sixes on this large ground demonstrated.

Gale would be pleased with his valuable 61, and nightwatchman Patterson enjoyed himself next morning, when watchmen should be asleep, with some selective hitting and his third 50 for Yorkshire.

Curran brothers Tom and Sam, sons of Kevin who took part in Zimbabwe's victory over Australia in the 1983 World Cup, bowled well, and Sam at 18 is a fine prospect. Meaker took three wickets and Ansari, a left-handed all-rounder who had to withdraw from England's winter tour of the United Arab Emirates, had a long bowl. So did Yorkshireman Gareth Batty, captain of Surrey, whose side lost one wicket in 38 overs.

Specsavers County Championship Division 1
Yorkshire v. Warwickshire

Played at Headingley, Leeds, on August 4, 5 and 6, 2016
Yorkshire won by 48 runs at 6.30pm on the Third Day

Toss won by Yorkshire

Yorkshire 21 points, Warwickshire 3 points

Close of play: First Day, Yorkshire 252-9 (Patterson 35*, Sidebottom 11*); Second Day, Yorkshire 78-5 (Lees 39*, Rashid 3*)

First Innings	YORKSHIRE		Second innings	
A Lyth, c Ambrose b Hannon-Dalby	24		c Chopra b Clarke	20
A Z Lees, lbw b Clarke	10		c Ambrose b Wright	70
T M Head, c Umeed b Barker	54		c Chopra b Clarke	2
* A W Gale, c Ambrose b Barker	14		c Clarke b Patel	1
J A Leaning, c Clarke b Barker	42		b Clarke	3
A U Rashid, c Clarke b Patel	6		(7) c Hain b Patel	17
T T Bresnan, c Patel b Hannon-Dalby	28		(8) c Barker b Patel	5
§ A J Hodd, lbw b Patel	7		(9) c Ambrose b Wright	8
S A Patterson, c Trott b Wright	38		(6) lbw b Clarke	0
J A Brooks, b Barker	5		not out	0
R J Sidebottom, not out	13		c Clarke b Patel	9
Extras b 6, lb 8, nb 2	16		Extras b 5, lb 8, nb 2	15
Total	257		Total	150

Bonus points — Yorkshire 2, Warwickshire 3

FoW: 1-18 (Lees), 2-57 (Lyth), 3-90 (Gale), 4-109 (Head), 5-130 (Rashid),
1st 6-190 (Leaning), 7-199 (Bresnan), 8-199 (Hodd), 9-204 (Brooks), 10-257 (Patterson)
FoW: 1-43 (Lyth), 2-50 (Head), 3-53 (Gale), 4-68 (Leaning), 5-68 (Patterson),
2nd 6-99 (Rashid), 7-115 (Bresnan), 8-134 (Hodd), 9-141 (Lees), 10-150 (Sidebottom)

	O	M	R	W		O	M	R	W
Barker	22	8	55	4	Barker	9	2	23	0
Wright	20.3	5	53	1	Wright	6	1	18	2
Clarke	11	2	41	1	Patel	29.3	11	49	4
Patel	32	8	55	2	Clarke	20	5	45	4
Hannon-Dalby	13	2	39	2	Hannon-Dalby	1	0	2	0

First Innings	WARWICKSHIRE		Second Innings	
V Chopra, lbw b Sidebottom	23		(2) lbw b Brooks	4
A R I Umeed, c Leaning b Brooks	0		(1) lbw b Sidebottom	4
I J L Trott, c and b Brooks	3		c and b Brooks	59
* I R Bell, c Rashid b Patterson	0		lbw b Brooks	0
S R Hain, c Bresnan b Sidebottom	48		(7) c Lyth b Rashid	34
§ T R Ambrose, c Hodd b Patterson	11		(5) c Leaning b Sidebottom	36
R Clarke, not out	50		(6) lbw b Patterson	21
K H D Barker, lbw b Rashid	20		lbw b Rashid	2
J S Patel, c Sidebottom b Rashid	7		st Hodd b Rashid	4
C J C Wright, b Rashid	0		lbw b Rashid	8
O J Hannon-Dalby, c Hodd b Sidebottom	0		not out	0
Extras b 10, lb 5	15		Extras b 4, lb 7	11
Total	179		Total	180

Bonus points — Yorkshire 3

FoW: 1-4 (Umeed), 2-26 (Chopra), 3-26 (Trott), 4-40 (Bell), 5-80 (Ambrose),
1st 6-112 (Hain), 7-163 (Barker), 8-175 (Patel), 9-178 (Wright), 10-179 (Hannon-Dalby)
FoW: 1-0 (Umeed), 2-14 (Chopra), 3-14 (Bell), 4-105 (Ambrose), 5-109 (Trott),
2nd 6-141 (Clarke), 7-145 (Barker), 8-157 (Patel), 9-167 (Wright), 10-180 (Hain)

	O	M	R	W		O	M	R	W
Sidebottom	15	1	41	3	Sidebottom	11	2	30	2
Brooks	11	5	28	2	Brooks	17	3	48	3
Bresnan	3	0	14	0	Bresnan	7	2	14	0
Patterson	10	3	30	2	Patterson	12	4	21	1
Lyth	4	0	19	0	Rashid	13.3	1	29	4
Rashid	9	0	32	3	Head	4	1	16	0
					Lyth	4	0	11	0

Umpires: J H Evans and S J O'Shaughnessy

Scorers: J T Potter and R J Dickinson

Lees vigilance pays off

ALEX LEES: All might have been lost

This was an interesting, competitive game in which the batsmen had to work hard for their runs.

Yorkshire won by only 48 runs, and it was their first-innings superiority and an excellent defensive second knock of 70 from Lees that enabled them to prevail against a good Warwickshire team.

Barker, a tall, strong left-arm bowler who took four wickets, was the best of a skilful visiting attack. Travis Head, an Australian on debut for Yorkshire, made 54, and Leaning batted well for 42, but Yorkshire had lost nine wickets for 204 before a last-wicket stand of 53 by Patterson and Sidebottom which was higher than the winning margin.

The Yorkshire bowling was at full strength with Brooks and Sidebottom recovered from injury and Rashid returning from the England squad. Brooks demonstrated his ability to take early wickets as Umeed and Trott succumbed, while Patterson claimed the important wicket of Bell, who had a disappointing match.

It was always a struggle for the visitors, although Hain made a dogged 48 and Clarke was unbeaten on 50 as Rashid took three wickets and Sidebottom came back to dismiss Hannon-Dalby.

Yorkshire did not bat well in their second innings, and all would have been lost but for an outstanding 70 out of 150 by Lees. Patel is arguably the best off-spinner in county cricket, and Clarke always does well against Yorkshire, but Lees remained vigilant, played straight, showed sound judgment to score when he could, but maintained his concentration. His runs were critical in a closely contested match.

Then Brooks and Sidebottom took three wickets, including Bell without scoring, and as a stand was developing Leaning launched himself to his right to catch Ambrose one-handed at third slip. Trott was twice caught and bowled by Brooks. Rashid took four wickets, including Hain, who batted courageously after injuring his shoulder in the field. It was an important win against close Championship rivals.

Specsavers County Championship Division 1
Lancashire v. Yorkshire

Played at Old Trafford, Manchester, on August 13, 14, 15 and 16, 2016
Match drawn at 5.pm on the Fourth Day

Toss won by Lancashire   Lancashire 11 points, Yorkshire 10 points

Close of play: First Day, Lancashire 299-7 (Clark 4*); Second Day, Yorkshire 136-2 (Lees 62*, Gale 36*); Third Day, Lancashire 70-0 (Smith 35*, Hameed 30*)

First Innings	LANCASHIRE	Second Innings	
T C Smith, lbw b Sidebottom	46	c Hodd b Bresnan	87
H Hameed, c and b Bresnan	114	not out	100
L A Procter, c Hodd b Bresnan	79		
A N Petersen, b Brooks	32	(3) c and b Rashid	2
* § S J Croft, c Bresnan b Brooks	13	(4) c Hodd b Bresnan	3
L S Livingstone, c Hodd b Sidebottom	0	(5) not out	31
S C Kerrigan, c Hodd b Brooks	2		
J Clark, not out	84		
A M Lilley, c Hodd b Patterson	45		
N L Buck, lbw b Bresnan	1		
K M Jarvis, lbw b Rashid	57		
Extras b 4, lb 11, nb 6	21	Extras b 4, lb 1, nb 4	9
Total	494	Total (3 wkts dec)	232

Bonus points — Lancashire 4, Yorkshire 3   Score at 110 overs: 387-9

FoW: 1-86 (Smith), 2-238 (Procter), 3-247 (Hameed), 4-268 (Croft), 5-279 (Livingstone),
1st   6-286 (Kerrigan), 7-299 (Petersen), 8-386 (Lilley), 9-387 (Buck), 10-494 (Jarvis)
2nd   1-168 (Smith), 2-172 (Petersen), 3-177 (Croft)

	O	M	R	W		O	M	R	W
Sidebottom	24	6	81	2	Sidebottom	9	0	52	0
Brooks	23	3	81	3	Brooks	4	0	25	0
Bresnan	24	4	80	3	Bresnan	11	1	60	2
Patterson	26	8	69	1	Rashid	16	1	68	1
Rashid	32	2	149	1	Patterson	4	1	22	0
Lyth	4	1	19	0					

First Innings	YORKSHIRE	Second Innings	
A Lyth, lbw b Jarvis	25	not out	63
A Z Lees, lbw b Jarvis	85	not out	114
J A Leaning, c Livingstone b Smith	7		
* A W Gale, c Kerrigan b Smith	83		
J S Lehmann, b Jarvis	46		
A U Rashid, c Hameed b Kerrigan	16		
T T Bresnan, lbw b Jarvis	7		
§ A J Hodd, c Livingstone b Kerrigan	43		
S A Patterson, b Buck	20		
J A Brooks, not out	6		
R J Sidebottom, c Croft b Kerrigan	3		
Extras b 9, lb 4, nb 6	19	Extras b 10, lb 1	11
Total	360	Total (0 wkts)	188

Bonus points — Yorkshire 2, Lancashire 2   Score at 110 overs: 290-7

FoW: 1-38 (Lyth), 2-55 (Leaning), 3-185 (Lees), 4-237 (Gale), 5-272 (Rashid), 6-272
1st   (Lehmann), 7-283 (Bresnan), 8-341 (Hodd), 9-357 (Patterson), 10-360 (Sidebottom)

	O	M	R	W		O	M	R	W
Jarvis	25	5	70	4	Jarvis	13	2	39	0
Buck	25	5	65	1	Kerrigan	11	3	33	0
Smith	14	3	38	2	Buck	10	2	43	0
Clark	15	2	46	0	Clark	5	0	28	0
Lilley	15	5	31	0	Lilley	8	1	20	0
Kerrigan	38.5	7	91	3	Livingstone	5	0	14	0
Livingstone	2	1	6	0					

Umpires: P K Baldwin and D J Millns   Scorers: J T Potter and C Rimmer

Lancashire v. Yorkshire

Red Rose record for Hameed

ANDREW GALE: Century beckoned

Hameed had an outstanding match, in which he made 114 in the first innings and 100 not out in the second.

He will not be 20 years of age until January 2017. He has been a correct and patient batsman with a sound defence since his days at Bolton School, and is now playing more shots, especially through the off side.

Hameed's accomplished Roses century in partnership with Smith and then with Procter gave Lancashire an impressive start at 238-1, but by the close Yorkshire had reduced them to 299-7 as Brooks and Bresnan each took two wickets. On Sunday morning Yorkshire's attack was devastated by Lancashire's tail as Clark, Lilley and Jarvis put on 195 in 37.2 overs before a delayed lunch. Clark and Jarvis added 107 for the last wicket, and Jarvis reached his first 50 with a straight six.

Yorkshire had to face the possibility of a follow-on, which at 283-7 seemed a distinct possibility. Gale played well, but was caught in the gully when a century beckoned, and Jake Lehmann, son of Darren, made 46. Jarvis and Smith took wickets, and at one stage three fell for 11 runs. It was left to Hodd and Patterson to see Yorkshire to safety, although Livingstone showed Olympic standard sprinting and diving to catch Hodd just before the 345 was achieved.

Lancashire added 70 before the close of the third day, and on the final morning Hameed made his second century of the match. It was the first time a Lancashire batsman had done this in a Roses match. They declared to set Yorkshire 367 in a minimum of 71 overs. Lyth and Lees batted very well, and were undefeated. Lees outpaced Lyth to make 114 not out, and showed his potential as an international opening batsman. Some thought Yorkshire might have gone for a win, but it was the fourth innings on a wicket with some uneven bounce, so they were content to draw a game they might well have lost.

Specsavers County Championship Division 1
Yorkshire v. Nottinghamshire

Played at North Marine Road, Scarborough, on August 23, 24, 25 and 26, 2016
Yorkshire won by 305 runs at 1.58pm on the Fourth Day

Nottinghamshire opted to field Yorkshire 21 points, Nottinghamshire 3 points
Close of play: First Day, Nottinghamshire 38-2 (Mullaney 15*); Second Day, Yorkshire 200-4 (Balance 75*, Bresnan 0*); Third Day, Nottinghamshire 61-3 (Moores 41*, Taylor 3*)

	First Innings		YORKSHIRE	Second Innings	
A Lyth, run out (Mullaney)		12	c and b Wood		41
A Z Lees, c Taylor b Mullaney		13	lbw b Hutton		30
* G S Ballance, lbw b Fletcher		1	not out		101
J S Lehmann, c Patel b Mullaney		5	c Wood b Patel		35
J A Leaning, c Patel b Hutton		5	st Read b Patel		15
T T Bresnan, lbw b Mullaney		10	not out		35
§ A J Hodd, not out		96			
Azeem Rafiq, lbw b Patel		74			
S A Patterson, lbw b Imran Tahir		2			
J A Brooks, b Hutton		48			
R J Sidebottom, lbw b Hutton		0			
Extras lb 12, w 2, nb 2		16	Extras lb 3, w 1, nb 2		6
Total		282	Total (4 wkts dec)		263

Bonus points — Yorkshire 2, Nottinghamshire 3

FoW: 1st 1-21 (Lyth), 2-26 (Lees), 3-36 (Lehmann), 4-36 (Ballance), 5-51 (Bresnan), 6-51 (Leaning), 7-183 (Rafiq), 8-192 (Patterson), 9-280 (Brooks), 10-281 (Sidebottom)
2nd 1-72 (Lees), 2-76 (Lyth), 3-137 (Lehmann), 4-194 (Leaning)

	O	M	R	W		O	M	R	W
Wood	9	0	35	0	Mullaney	8	0	40	0
Fletcher	18	5	43	1	Fletcher	16	1	57	0
Mullaney	16	6	54	3	Wood	18	4	67	1
Hutton	14.3	2	67	3	Hutton	16.2	6	53	1
Imran Tahir	13	1	48	1	Imran Tahir	4	1	10	0
Patel	11	1	23	1	Patel	11	0	33	2

	First Innings		NOTTINGHAMSHIRE	Second Innings	
S J Mullaney, lbw b Sidebottom		25	c Leaning b Brooks		2
J D Libby, lbw b Brooks		0	c Lehmann b Bresnan		9
T J Moores, c Lyth b Bresnan		23	c Lyth b Bresnan		41
M J Lumb, c Hodd b Sidebottom		0	c Hodd b Bresnan		0
B R M Taylor, b Patterson		14	c Lees b Brooks		38
S R Patel, c Bresnan b Sidebottom		4	c Hodd b Bresnan		5
* § C M W Read, c Lees b Brooks		7	c Lehmann b Bresnan		0
B A Hutton, c Lyth b Brooks		5	c Hodd b Sidebottom		20
L Wood, c Hodd b Bresnan		7	not out		16
L J Fletcher, c Leaning b Bresnan		6	b Brooks		0
Imran Tahir, not out		2	c Lees b Brooks		0
Extras lb 1		1	Extras b 8, lb 4, nb 2		14
Total		94	Total		146

Bonus points — Yorkshire 3

FoW: 1st 1-0 (Libby), 2-38 (Moores), 3-41 (Lumb), 4-48 (Mullaney), 5-52 (Patel), 6-61 (Read), 7-79 (Hutton), 8-79 (Taylor), 9-87 (Wood), 10-94 (Fletcher)
FoW: 2nd 1-3 (Mullaney), 2-34 (Libby), 3-34 (Lumb), 4-61 (Moores), 5-77 (Patel), 6-83 (Read), 7-130 (Hutton), 8-130 (Taylor), 9-130 (Read), 10-146 (Tahir)

	O	M	R	W		O	M	R	W
Sidebottom	12	3	21	3	Sidebottom	16	5	37	1
Brooks	11	1	41	3	Brooks	13.3	4	35	4
Patterson	7	3	16	1	Patterson	15	8	26	0
Bresnan	7.1	1	15	3	Bresnan	12	2	36	5
					Azeem Rafiq	1	1	0	0

Umpires: M Burns and N A Mallender Scorers: J T Potter and R Marshall

Yorkshire v. Nottinghamshire

Hodd stranded on 96

SEASIDE RECOVERY: Andy Hodd hits back as wicket-keeper Read looks on

Yorkshire struggled on the first morning on a lively pitch after being invited to bat first.

Lyth was unlucky to be run out when the bowler diverted the ball on to the stumps, but more wickets fell, three to Mullaney, leaving Yorkshire on a precarious 51-6 at lunch.

There followed a fine partnership from Rafiq, recently restored to the side and capped, and Hodd, who has been out of form with the bat. The more assertive Rafiq took command at first, but after his dismissal for 73 Hodd batted with growing assurance. He was assisted by some aggressive hitting from Brooks, but was stranded on 96 when the last wicket fell, Mullaney and Hutton each claiming three victims.

Nottinghamshire lost Libby first ball and Moores overnight, and showed little resolution next morning against Yorkshire's four quick bowlers, who shared the wickets. Their experienced middle-order did not show the anticipated resistance, and they were all out for 94. Yorkshire bowled a disciplined line and length, and had enough assistance to be always likely to take wickets. Around the ground there was talk of enforcing the follow-on, but it had been decided to bat again.

On a gloomy, damp third day Ballance, captain for this match, reached his century just before the declaration. Nottinghamshire again underperformed, but the quality of Yorkshire's bowling was the main factor in the visitors' defeat. Bresnan took important early wickets with movement off the seam; Brooks dismissed Mullaney, the obdurate Taylor and the last two batsmen, and Patterson and Sidebottom gave nothing away with their relentless accuracy.

On the last morning, with the sun out again, Nottinghamshire lost three more wickets, but then Hutton joined Taylor to bat until lunch. Any distant prospect of survival disappeared when the last four wickets toppled in 20 minutes, and Taylor, who had been so responsible and restrained, gave an easy catch to short cover. Yorkshire had won an important victory in their game in hand on Middlesex.

Specsavers County Championship Division 1
Hampshire v. Yorkshire

Played at The Rose Bowl, West End, Southampton, on August 31, September 1, 2, and 3, 2016
Match drawn at 4.40pm on the Fourth Day

Toss won by Yorkshire   Yorkshire 10 points, Hampshire 9 points

Close of play: First Day, Yorkshire 275-9 (Brooks 29*, Sidebottom 8*); Second Day, Yorkshire 69-1 (Lyth 37*, Ballance 17*); Third Day, Yorkshire 143-2 (Balance 46*, Gale 19*)

First Innings	YORKSHIRE		Second Innings	
A Lyth, c Smith b McLaren	24		c Ervine b Wheal	56
A Z Lees, c Smith b Wheal	10		b Wheal	12
G S Ballance, c McManus b Berg	10		b Berg	72
* A W Gale, c McManus b McLaren	26		c McManus b Wheal	19
J S Lehmann, c Adams b Berg	58		not out	35
T T Bresnan, b Berg	56		c Berg b Carter	27
§ A J Hodd, b Berg	17		not out	1
Azeem Rafiq, c McManus b Berg	5			
S A Patterson, c Alsop b Crane	7			
J A Brooks, not out	34			
R J Sidebottom, b Berg	9			
Extras b 5, lb 10, nb 10	25		Extras b 2, lb 6, nb 8	16
Total	281		Total (5 wkts dec)	238

Bonus points — Yorkshire 2, Hampshire 3

FoW: 1-22 (Lees), 2-39 (Lyth), 3-57 (Ballance), 4-119 (Gale), 5-143 (Lehmann), 1st 6-216 (Bresnan), 7-221 (Hodd), 8-224 (Rafiq), 9-234 (Patterson), 10-281 (Sidebottom)
2nd: 1-39 (Lees), 2-101 (Lyth), 3-143 (Gale), 4-189 (Ballance), 5-235 (Bresnan)

	O	M	R	W		O	M	R	W
McLaren	20	3	76	2	McLaren	17	1	60	0
Wheal	19	4	64	1	Berg	22	8	60	1
Berg	24.2	5	56	6	Wheal	19	5	79	3
Carter	9	1	27	0	Carter	4	0	23	1
Ervine	5	0	13	0	Ervine	2	0	8	0
Crane	11	3	30	1					

First Innings	HAMPSHIRE		Second Innings	
J H K Adams, c Lees b Patterson	23		(2) c Lyth b Brooks	30
W R Smith, lbw b Brooks	1		(1) lbw b Sidebottom	4
T P Alsop, lbw b Sidebottom	4		c Azeem Rafiq b Brooks	18
* J M Vince, c Lyth b Bresnan	60		c Bresnan b Brooks	16
S M Ervine, c Hodd b Sidebottom	80		not out	10
R McLaren, c Hodd b Sidebottom	26		not out	4
§ L D McManus, c Azeem Rafiq b Brooks	6			
G K Berg, c Hodd b Brooks	0			
M S Crane, not out	8			
B T J Wheal, b Brooks	0			
A Carter, b Brooks	4			
Extras lb 9, nb 2	11		Extras lb 2	2
Total	222		Total (4 wkts)	84

Bonus points — Hampshire 1, Yorkshire 3

FoW: 1-14 (Smith), 2-17 (Alsop), 3-38 (Adams), 4-145 (Vince), 5-199 (Ervine), 1st 6-208 (McManus), 7-210 (McLaren), 8-212 (Berg), 9-214 (Wheal), 10-222 (Carter)
2nd 1-8 (Smith), 2-50 (Alsop), 3-59 (Adams), 4-74 (Vince)

	O	M	R	W		O	M	R	W
Sidebottom	19	6	45	3	Sidebottom	8.4	1	36	1
Brooks	17.2	7	53	5	Brooks	9	3	24	3
Bresnan	10	1	49	1	Bresnan	6	3	9	0
Patterson	10	2	39	1	Patterson	6	3	9	0
Azeem Rafiq	8	0	27	0	Azeem Rafiq	2	1	4	0

Umpires: N G B Cook and N G C Cowley   Scorers: J T Potter and K R Baker

Hampshire v. Yorkshire

Brooks's best, but rain wins

JACK BROOKS: Inspired spells

The weather on the last two days prevented any positive result in a match Yorkshire would probably have won.

Gale chose to bat, but it soon became overcast, and Berg obtained significant movement so that batting was never straightforward.

Hampshire fielders Smith and Adams took excellent diving catches, so that despite some batting errors 275-9 was a good score at the close.

Smith caught both Lees and Lyth at backward point, but Lehmann hit his first Championship 50 while Bresnan and Hodd made valuable contributions.

It was the last-wicket stand between Brooks and Sidebottom that gained a second batting point. Berg took a career-best 6-56.

Vince, who has batted well against Yorkshire in an otherwise disappointing season, and Ervine, who had just made two hundreds in a match, took Hampshire to 199-4 after they had lost three wickets for 38. Around tea time Hampshire lost six wickets for 23 as one of Brooks's inspired spells brought him four wickets and a season's best of 5-53. Sidebottom took the important wicket of Ervine, and Yorkshire added 69 for the loss of Lees.

Now came two days of frustration as rain interruptions made a draw inevitable. Yorkshire batted well in the circumstances to reach 235-5. Ballance, not always at his best this year, made a good 72 and Lyth 56. Only 19 overs were possible on the third day as the South Coast suffered more than other venues. Brooks took three wickets in 12 balls after Yorkshire declared, but bad light and then rain brought an early conclusion. Hampshire were concerned about possible relegation, and would regard a draw as an achievement, but Yorkshire had played well enough to win. They have two games at Headingley and then a possible Championship decider against their main rivals, Middlesex, at Lord's.

Specsavers County Championship Division 1
Yorkshire v. Durham

Played at Headingley, Leeds, on September 6, 7, 8 and 9, 2016
Yorkshire won by 228 runs at 2.16pm on the Fourth Day

Durham opted to field

Yorkshire 23 points, Durham 4 points

Close of play: First Day, Yorkshire 341-5 (Bresnan 11*, Hodd 22*); Second Day, Durham 205-4 (Burnham 34*, Clark 17*); Third Day, Durham 39-3 (Borthwick 7*, Onions 2*)

First Innings	YORKSHIRE		Second innings	
A Lyth, c Jennings b Onions	2		not out	114
A Z Lees, c and b Pringle	132		c Richardson b Pringle	88
G S Ballance, Collingwood b McCarthy	71		b Pringle	20
* A W Gale, b Onions	17			
J S Lehmann, c Pringle b Rushworth	58			
T T Bresnan, b Rushworth	22			
§ A J Hodd, c Collingwood b McCarthy	31			
Azeem Rafiq, st Richardson b Borthwick	45			
S A Patterson, b McCarthy	4			
J A Brooks, b Collingwood	36			
R J Sidebottom, not out	7			
Extras b 21, lb 12, nb 2	35		Extras lb 3	3
Total	460		Total (2 wkts dec)	225

Bonus points — Yorkshire 4, Durham 2

Score at 110 overs: 392-6

FoW: 1-5 (Lyth), 2-168 (Ballance), 3-190 (Gale), 4-277 (Lees), 5-308 (Lehmann),
1st 6-355 (Bresnan), 7-392 (Hodd), 8-397 (Patterson), 9-444 (Rafiq), 10-460 (Brooks)
2nd 1-185 (Lees), 2-225 (Ballance)

	O	M	R	W		O	M	R	W
Rushworth	27	5	101	2	Rushworth	6	0	27	0
Onions	34	8	101	2	Onions	11	0	37	0
Collingwood	12.1	0	39	1	Pringle	13.4	0	69	2
McCarthy	20	1	103	3	Borthwick	14	0	74	0
Pringle	7	4	14	1	McCarthy	6	0	15	0
Jennings	13	6	30	0					
Borthwick	8	0	39	1					

First Innings	DURHAM		Second Innings	
M D Stoneman, c Lyth b Brooks	38		c Gale b Brooks	10
K K Jennings, c Hodd b Patterson	40		c Hodd b Brooks	8
S G Borthwick, c Lyth b Patterson	53		lbw b Sidebottom	9
J T A Burnham, b Sidebottom	49		lbw b Patterson	9
* P D Collingwood, b Bresnan	6		(6) lbw b Sidebottom	9
G Clark, lbw b Brooks	25		(7) c Hodd b Bresnan	25
§ M J Richardson, c Lyth b Brooks	4		(8) c Bresnan b Sidebottom	33
R D Pringle, lbw b Brooks	9		(9) not out	57
B J McCarthy, c Hodd b Bresnan	10		(10) c Lyth b Bresnan	3
G Onions, b Sidebottom	19		(5) c Ballance b Sidebottom	6
C Rushworth, not out	0		b Brooks	6
Extras b 10, lb 8, nb 2	20		Extras b 5, lb 6, nb 6	17
Total	265		Total	192

Bonus points — "Durham 2, Yorkshire 3

FoW: 1-56 (Stoneman), 2-113 (Jennings), 3-154 (Borthwick), 4-165 (Collingwood), 5-227 (Clark),
1st 6-235 (Burnham), 7-235 (Richardson), 8-236 (Pringle), 9-265 (McCarthy), 10-265 (Onions)
FoW: 1-17 (Stoneman), 2-18 (Jennings), 3-31 (Burnham), 4-49 (Onions), 5-56 (Borthwick), 6-63
2nd (Collingwood), 7-112 (Clark), 8-149 (Richardson), 9-171 (McCarthy), 10-192 (Rushworth)

	O	M	R	W		O	M	R	W
Sidebottom	22.1	6	55	2	Sidebottom	15	3	34	4
Brooks	19	2	76	4	Brooks	15.2	4	55	3
Bresnan	21	9	44	2	Patterson	16	5	41	1
Patterson	15	4	35	2	Bresnan	12	3	44	2
Azeem Rafiq	13	4	19	0	Azeem Rafiq	5	2	7	0
Lyth	4	0	13	0					

Umpires: R J Evans and G D Lloyd

Scorers: J T Potter and W Dobson

EVEREST UNCONQUERED: Alex Lees just fails to become the first to score two centuries in a match at Headingley

Lees so close to record

Yorkshire made a good start against an experienced attack of Onions and Rushworth in mostly overcast conditions in which Durham had chosen to bowl first. Lyth went early, but Lees and Ballance added 163 for the second wicket. Lees was to have a very good match, and he was at his best in this innings, where his shot selection and especially his off-driving were impressive. He reached 1,000 runs for the first time, and made his third first-class century of the summer.

Lees was well supported by Ballance, and Lehmann, playing his initial first class innings at Headingley, made 58 after a shaky start. Rafiq's enterprise made a fifth batting point possible, but the opportunity was missed. Hodd failed to score off the first five balls of the last-but-one over, gave a catch off the sixth when Rafiq crossed, and Patterson could not make the eight needed off the 110th over.

By the end of the second day Durham were 205-4 and the match well balanced. Stoneman played with uninhibited aggression but gave his wicket away, and Yorkshire took the key wickets of Collingwood and Borthwick at the end of the day. Next morning they took six wickets for 38 with the second new ball. Clark did well, as had Burnham, a promising locally born player, but Richardson was restricted by a hand injury.

Yorkshire did not enforce the follow-on, and Lyth made a good century. Attention turned to Lees as he sought to become the first batsman to make two centuries in a match on this historic ground, but he was caught at the wicket for 88. Last year Westwood made 196 and 84 for Warwickshire. Yorkshire concluded a day of domination by taking three Durham wickets. Sidebottom has bowled excellently in his shortened season after injury, and on the final morning took three quick wickets to ensure Durham's inevitable demise.

The match ended with two of Rushworth's stumps flat on the ground and Yorkshire in optimistic mood.

Specsavers County Championship Division 1
Yorkshire v. Somerset

Played at Headingley, Leeds, on September 12, 13, and 14, 2016
Somerset won by 10 wickets at 5.04pm on the Third Day

Toss won by Yorkshire

Somerset 23 points, Yorkshire 3 points

Close of play: First Day, Somerset 107-1 (Trescothick 45*, Rogers 58*); Second Day, Somerset 107-1 (Trescothick 45*, Rogers 58*)

First Innings	YORKSHIRE		Second innings	
A Lyth, c Davies b Allenby	14		c Davies b Overton	49
A Z Lees, c Allenby b Overton	0		c Allenby b Gregory	9
G S Ballance, c Gregory b Overton	3		b Groenewald	1
* A W Gale, c Davies b Overton	29		b Groenewald	2
J S Lehmann, c Hildreth b Trego	31		lbw b Leach	116
A U Rashid, c Overton b Allenby	1		st Davies b Leach	16
T T Bresnan, not out	38		b Leach	4
§ A J Hodd, b Allenby	0		st Davies b Leach	73
L E Plunkett, c Allenby b Groenewald	10		c Trescothick b Leach	73
J A Brooks, b Groenewald	7		c and b Leach	0
R J Sidebottom, c Davies b Gregory	3		not out	2
Extras b 5, lb 2, nb 2	9		Extras b 7, lb 4, nb 2	13
Total	145		Total	286

Bonus points — Somerset 3

FoW: 1-1 (Lees), 2-19 (Ballance), 3-39 (Lyth), 4-86 (Lehmann), 5-87 (Gale),
1st 6-95 (Rashid), 7-97 (Hodd), 8-112 (Plunkett),9-122 (Brooks), 10-145 (Sidebottom)
FoW: 1-22 (Lees), 2-23 (Ballance), 3-37 (Gale), 4-99 (Lyth), 5-126 (Rashid),
2nd 6-156 (Bresnan), 7-162 (Hodd), 8-263 (Lehmann), 9-265 (Brooks), 10-286 (Plunkett)

	O	M	R	W		O	M	R	W
Overton	15	3	32	3	Overton	16	1	57	1
Gregory	7.2	0	32	1	Gregory	18	5	41	1
Allenby	15	8	16	3	Groenewald	18	6	55	2
Groenewald	12	1	43	2	Allenby	7	0	27	0
Leach	2	1	1	0	Leach	24.3	4	64	6
Trego	10	5	14	1	Trego	13	4	31	0

First Innings	SOMERSET		Second Innings	
M E Trescothick, b Plunkett	73		not out	37
T B Abell, lbw b Brooks	0		not out	7
* C J L Rogers, c Lyth b Sidebottom	63			
J C Hildreth, b Sidebottom	2			
J Allenby, lbw b Rashid	50			
P D Trego, c Hodd b Sidebottom	46			
L Gregory, not out	73			
C Overton, lbw b Rashid	38			
§ R C Davies, c Bresnan b Sidebottom	9			
M J Leach, b Sidebottom	1			
T D Groenewald, st Hodd b Rashid	13			
Extras lb 21, w 1	22		Extras	0
Total	390		Total (0 wkts)	44

Bonus points — Somerset 4, Yorkshire 3

FoW: 1-0 (Abell), 2-123 (Rogers), 3-125 (Hildreth), 4-164 (Trescothick), 5-228 (Trego), 6-257
1st (Allenby), 7-358 (Overton), 8-369 (Davies), 9-375 (Leach), 10-390 (Groenewald)

	O	M	R	W		O	M	R	W
Sidebottom	22	7	51	5	Sidebottom	3	0	10	0
Brooks	19	1	84	1	Brooks	5	3	24	0
Bresnan	17	1	74	0	Lyth	2.3	0	10	0
Plunkett	15	0	54	1					
Rashid	22.3	2	99	3					
Lyth	3	0	7	0					

Umpires: R A Kettleborough and J W Lloyds

Scorers: J T Potter and G A Stickley

Lehmann's farewell century

JAKE LEHMANN: Like father...

Somerset outplayed Yorkshire to win this important fixture.

Crucially, they bowled Yorkshire out for only 145, and a second-wicket stand of 123 between Trescothick and Rogers, experienced first-class batsmen, enabled their middle order to score freely.

Yorkshire's batsmen could not save the game in their second innings against some good spin bowling.

A depleted Yorkshire elected to bat first, as Somerset would have done, but Craig Overton removed Lees, Ballance and Gale, and Allenby bowled a fine spell at medium pace.

Lehmann, dropped at slip before he had scored, batted almost to lunch, when he misdirected a pull shot, and only Bresnan offered serious resistance.

Trescothick and Rogers had the patience and technical application that Yorkshire had lacked. Any prospect of recovery by the hosts disappeared next day as Gregory, Allenby, Trego and Overton all made runs. Sidebottom showed good control of line and length on a very warm day to dismiss Rogers and Hildreth, and Plunkett bowled Trescothick. Somerset's fortunes were then enhanced by two Devonian all-rounders when Gregory and Overton put on 101 for the seventh wicket and Gregory made his career-best score at Headingley for the second time.

On the third day Somerset gained their well merited victory, and there were two good individual performances. Leach bowled his left-arm spin from the Rugby Ground End, showing good control, flight and some spin. It is rare these days for a left-arm spinner to win a match as he undoubtedly did. He had to contend with Lehmann, recalled to Adelaide, who said farewell with a maiden century for Yorkshire. He has the same propensity as his father to tempt the slip fielders, but also has his cover -drives and adventurous approach to batting.

Plunkett ensured that Somerset had to bat again, but an elated Trescothick, Keynsham-born and 23 years a Somerset player, soon celebrated a win to keep their Championship hopes alive at Taunton.

Specsavers County Championship Division 1
Middlesex v. Yorkshire

Played at Lord's on September 20. 21, 22 and 23, 2016
Middlesex won by 61 runs at 5.30pm on the Fourth Day

Yorkshire opted to field   Middlesex 17 points, Yorkshire 7 points
Close of play: First Day, Middlesex 208-5 (Gubbins 120*, Franklin 21*); Second Day, Yorkshire 235-6 (Bresnan 72*, Rafiq 20*); Third Day, Middlesex 81-2 (Gubbins 39*, Malan 37*)

	First Innings	MIDDLESEX		Second Innings	
S D Robson, lbw b Brooks		0	(2) c Lees b Sidebottom		0
N R T Gubbins, c Lyth b Bresnan		125	(1) c and b Azeem Rafiq		93
N R D Compton, lbw b Brooks		8	b Brooks		1
D J Malan, b Willey		22	c Brooks b Lees		116
S S Eskinazi, b Brooks		12	not out		78
§ J A Simpson, lbw b Bresnan		15	b Lees		31
* J E C Franklin, c Hodd b Bresnan		48	c and b Lyth		30
O P Rayner, not out		15			
T S Roland-Jones, c Lyth b Brooks		7			
T J Murtagh, c Gale b Brooks		0			
S T Finn, c Lyth b Brooks		6			
Extras b 4, lb 6, nb 2		12	Extras b 1, lb 6, w 1, nb 2		10
Total		270	Total (6 wkts dec)		359

Bonus points — Middlesex 2, Yorkshire 3

FoW: 1-11 (Robson), 2-33 (Compton), 3-57 (Malan), 4-97 (Eskinazi), 5-154 (Simpson), 6-229
1st (Gubbins), 7-244 (Franklin), 8-254 (Roland-Jones), 9-258 (Murtagh), 10-270 (Finn)
FoW: 1-1 (Robson), 2-2 (Compton), 3-200 (Gubbins), 4-265 (Malan), 5-303 (Simpson),
2nd 6-359(Franklin)

	O	M	R	W		O	M	R	W
Sidebottom	22	12	29	0	Sidebottom	13	0	36	1
Brooks	23.3	2	65	6	Brooks	15	5	48	1
Willey	16	1	71	1	Bresnan	12	3	33	0
Patterson	17	9	32	0	Patterson	14	5	40	0
Bresnan	23	7	48	3	Willey	10	3	21	0
Azeem Rafiq	7	1	15	0	Azeem Rafiq	18	3	46	1
					Lyth	7.5	0	77	1
					Lees	4	0	51	2

	First Innings	YORKSHIRE		Second innings	
A Lyth, b Finn		43	c Robson b Roland-Jones		13
A Z Lees, b Roland-Jones		0	c Gubbins b Murtagh		20
G S Ballance, c Rayner b Roland-Jones		0	(4) c Robson b Finn		30
* A W Gale, c Rayner b Roland-Jones		0	(6) b Roland-Jones		22
T T Bresnan, not out		142	lbw b Roland-Jones		55
§ A J Hodd, lbw b Roland-Jones		64	(7) b Roland-Jones		17
D J Willey, lbw b Murtagh		22	(3) c Eskinazi b Murtagh		11
Azeem Rafiq, b Murtagh		65	c Simpson b Roland-Jones		4
S A Patterson, c Rayner b Finn		11	b Finn		2
J A Brooks, c Gubbins b Murtagh		0	not out		0
R J Sidebottom, b Rayner		23	b Roland-Jones		0
Extras lb 14, nb 6		20	Extras lb 4		4
Total		390	Total		178

Bonus points — Yorkshire 4, Middlesex 3   Over-rate deduction 4 points
Score at 110 overs: 363-9

FoW: 1-14 (Lees), 2-32 (Ballance), 3-32 (Gale), 4-53 (Lyth), 5-169 (Hodd),
1st 6-204 (Willey), 7-318 (Rafiq), 8-333 (Patterson), 9-334 (Brooks), 10-390 (Sidebottom)
FoW: 1-27 (Lyth), 2-39 (Lees), 3-48 (Willey), 4-98 (Ballance), 5-153 (Bresnan),
2nd 6-160 (Gale), 7-174 (Rafiq), 8-178 (Patterson), 9-178 (Hodd), 10-178 (Sidebottom)

	O	M	R	W		O	M	R	W
Murtagh	32	4	96	3	Murtagh	8	1	28	2
Roland-Jones	29	5	73	4	Roland-Jones	12.2	0	54	6
Franklin	9	1	32	0	Rayner	5	0	32	0
Finn	30	4	105	2	Finn	10	0	60	2
Rayner	16.3	1	70	1					

Umpires: R J Bailey and R T Robinson   Scorers: J T Potter and D K Shelley
Third Umpire: N L Bainton

Middlesex v. Yorkshire
Bresnan brilliant in decider

This excellent match was the decider, and Middlesex won by 61 runs to take their first Championship title since 1993.

Somerset had won at Taunton in three days, so whoever won this game would win the title if they had the necessary bonus points, but if it was a draw Somerset

TIM BRESNAN: Outstanding century, then gave Yorkshire glimpse of glory

would be champions. As the match developed on Friday it was clear that there would have to be some contrivance to obtain a result, so Yorkshire bowled eight overs giving Middlesex a hundred runs to enable them to set a target of 240 off 40 overs. This was controversial.

In my opinion you cannot expect two sides that can each win the Championship to settle for a draw in which case neither would win it. Yorkshire had failed to take enough Middlesex wickets on the fourth morning, and the declaration gave them at least an even chance of winning. Middlesex succeeded because all three seamers bowled well, the pitch had slowed down so that Yorkshire found boundaries harder to score, and they did not make enough runs by other means. Bresnan's 55 gave a glimpse of glory, but when Roland-Jones had him lbw defeat looked inevitable. It came when Roland-Jones took the hat-trick that won the Championship as he flattened Sidebottom's leg stump.

There were three outstanding performances in this match at Lord's. Gubbins made a determined 125 out of 270, and was unlucky to be out for 93 second time round. Roland-Jones dismissed Lees, Ballance and Gale for ducks and took 6-54 in the second innings. Both Gubbins and Roland-Jones had been at Leeds/Bradford MCCU.

For Yorkshire Bresnan played the best innings of his career. Coming in at 32-3 he was undefeated when the innings closed on 390, a lead of 120 that had seemed unattainable. Hodd and Rafiq gave valuable support, but Bresnan's 142 not out was outstanding. Yorkshire's fourth batting point was gained after a tense hour's rain interruption at 349-9, so Yorkshire could still win the Championship — at least for a further day.

123

LV COUNTY CHAMPIONSHIP 2016

DIVISION 1

	P	W	L	D	BAT	BOWL	Pen.	Points
					Bonus Points			
1 Middlesex (Div 1, 2)	16	6	0	10	48	40	4	230
2 Somerset (Div 1, 6)	16	6	1	9	44	41	0	226
3 Yorkshire (Div 1, 1)	**16**	**5**	**3**	**8**	**49**	**42**	**0**	**211**
4 Durham (Div 1, 4)	16	5	3	8	39	41	0	200
5 Surrey (Div 2, 1)	16	4	6	6	46	42	0	182
6 Warwickshire (Div 1, 5)	16	3	4	9	39	44	0	176
7 Lancashire (Div 2, 2)	16	3	5	8	39	38	0	165
8 Hampshire (Div 1, 7) *	16	2	4	10	41	35	3	155
9 Nottinghamshire (Div 1, 3) *	16	1	9	6	34	44	0	124

Pen. 1 point deducted for each over short in a match based on a rate of 16 overs per hour

* Hampshire and Nottinghamshire were expected to be relegated to Division 2 for 2017, but sactions imposed by the ECB consequent upon a financial bailout meant that Durham were relegated to Division 2 with a 48-point penalty for 2017.
Hampshire were reinstated to Division 1 for 2017.

DIVISION 2

	P	W	L	D	BAT	BOWL	Pen.	Points
					Bonus Points			
1 Essex (Div 2, 3) *	16	6	3	7	58	46	0	235
2 Kent (Div 2, 7)	16	5	2	9	49	38	0	212
3 Worcestershire (Div 1, 9)	16	6	4	6	42	35	0	203
4 Sussex (Div 1, 8)	16	4	2	10	40	38	0	192
5 Northamptonshire (Div 2, 5)	16	4	3	9	42	33	0	184
6 Gloucestershire (Div 2, 6)	16	4	5	7	44	40	0	183
7 Leicestershire (Div 2, 9)	16	4	4	8	39	40	1	182
8 Glamorgan (Div 2, 4)	16	3	8	5	34	42	1	148
9 Derbyshire (Div 2, 8)	16	0	5	11	32	32	0	119

Pen. 1 point deducted for each over short in a match based on a rate of 16 overs per hour

* Promoted to Division 1 for 2017.

(2015 positions in brackets)

YORKSHIRE AVERAGES 2016

SPECSAVERS COUNTY CHAMPIONSHIP

Played 16   Won 5   Lost 3   Drawn 8

BATTING AND FIELDING

(Qualification 10 completed innings)

Player	M.	I.	N.O.	Runs	H.S.	100s	50s	Avge	ct/st
T T Bresnan	11	19	4	722	142*	1	5	48.13	12
L E Plunkett	8	13	3	449	126	1	3	44.90	3
A Lyth	16	30	2	1133	202	4	3	40.46	25
A Z Lees	16	30	1	1165	132	3	7	40.17	12
G S Ballance	13	25	2	780	132	2	4	33.91	8
A U Rashid	10	16	2	393	88	0	3	28.07	7
A J Hodd	12	18	3	391	96*	0	2	26.06	35/3
A W Gale	15	26	1	525	83	0	2	21.00	2
J A Leaning	9	15	2	233	51	0	1	17.92	8
S A Patterson	15	20	1	300	63*	0	2	15.78	0

Also played

Player	M.	I.	N.O.	Runs	H.S.	100s	50s	Avge	ct/st
J M Bairstow	4	6	0	533	246	2	0	88.83	5/1
J E Root	2	3	0	240	213	1	0	80.00	5
J S Lehmann	5	8	1	384	116	1	2	54.85	2
Azeem Rafiq	6	8	2	201	74	0	1	33.50	5
T M Head	1	2	0	56	54	0	1	28.00	0
J A Brooks	14	20	11	250	48	0	0	27.77	4
J Shaw	1	1	0	24	24	0	0	24.00	1
W M H Rhodes	2	4	0	73	20	0	0	18.25	1
D J Willey	4	5	0	58	22	0	0	11.60	0
K S Williamson	2	4	0	42	28	0	0	10.50	3
R J Sidebottom	9	11	3	75	23	0	0	9.37	1
B O Coad	1	1	1	17	17*	0	0	—	0

BOWLING

(Qualification 10 wickets)

Player	Overs	Mdns	Runs	Wkts	Avge	Best	5wI	10wM
R J Sidebottom	245	63	657	31	21.19	5-51	1	0
J A Brooks	432.2	105	1501	60	25.01	6-65	3	0
S A Patterson	440.5	138	1146	39	29.38	6-56	1	0
T T Bresnan	297.1	71	934	31	30.12	5-36	1	0
A U Rashid	293.2	36	1083	32	33.84	4-17	0	0
L E Plunkett	172.1	23	602	10	60.20	2-46	0	0

Also bowled

Player	Overs	Mdns	Runs	Wkts	Avge	Best	5wI	10wM
J E Root	18	3	49	2	24.50	2-23	0	0
A Z Lees	4	0	51	2	25.50	2-51	0	0
K S Williamson	18	2	59	2	29.50	1-19	0	0
D J Willey	102	23	334	9	37.11	3-55	0	0
W M H Rhodes	41	5	137	3	45.66	2-67	0	0
A Lyth	79	10	322	7	46.00	2-9	0	0
J Shaw	29	3	119	2	59.50	2-38	0	0
Azeem Rafiq	99.3	24	275	3	91.66	1-12	0	0
B O Coad	35	10	108	1	108.00	1-70	0	0
J A Leaning	10	2	27	0	—	0-7	0	0
T M Head	4	1	16	0	—	0-16	0	0
G S Ballance	1	0	11	0	—	0-11	0	0
A J Hodd	1	0	14	0	—	0-14	0	0

University Match (Non First Class)
Yorkshire v. Leeds/Bradford MCCU

Played at Headingley, Leeds, on April 11, 12 and 13, 2016
Match drawn at 10.30am on the Third Day
Toss won by Leeds/Bradford MCCU

Close of play: First Day, Leeds/Bradford MCCU 225-8 (Weston 68*, Ogden 0*); Second and Third Day, no play

LEEDS/BRADFORD MCCU

S F G Bullen, b Brooks		9
H L Thompson, c Lees b Sidebottom		64
W T Root, c and b Brooks		0
C A L Davis, lbw b Carver		19
G F B Scott, lbw b Lyth		12
L P Weston, not out		68
L Watkinson, lbw b Brooks		17
§ A M Gowers, b Carver		8
* A E Lilley, c Rhodes b Carver		19
A Ogden, not out		0
M A Ashraf	Did not bat	
Extras lb 9		9
Total (8 wkts)		225

FoW: 1-11 (Bullen), 2-11 (Root), 3-59 (Davis), 4-92 (Scott), 5-109 (Thompson), 6-162 (Watkinson), 7-177 (Gowers), 8-225 (Lilley)

	O	M	R	W
Sidebottom	11	3	24	1
Brooks	13	3	36	3
Rhodes	12	3	49	0
Patterson	16	3	33	0
Carver	17.4	1	58	3
Lyth	5	2	16	1

YORKSHIRE

A Z Lees
A Lyth
G S Ballance
* A W Gale
J A Leaning
W M H Rhodes
§ J M Bairstow
S A Patterson
K Carver
J A Brooks
R J Sidebottom

Umpires: P K Baldwin and P J Hartley   Scorers: J T Potter and C N Rawson

Top class but not First Class!

JACK BROOKS
Troubled all batsmen

This game was ruined by the weather, play being possible for only 74.4 overs on the first day, but it still provided useful practice for both sides with the Universities' Henry Thompson and Logan Weston performing creditably with the bat, and Yorkshire's Jack Brooks and Karl Carver with the ball.

The students were miffed that the game was not deemed first class because they had already played two under that status —against Warwickshire and Sussex — and were not allowed a third.

For Lancashire-born Thompson and Bradford-born Weston to register half-centuries against the County Champions at a Test match venue was understandably frustrating for them.

It was a frustrating day, also, for Billy Root, brother of Joe, who was unable to enjoy his own moment of Headingley glory. Coming in after the early dismissal of Steve Bullen, Root lasted only five deliveries before giving a return catch to Brooks without having registered a run.

Opener Thompson remained firm, however, and completed a solid half-century before he was caught by Alex Lees off Ryan Sidebottom for 64 off 122 balls with nine fours. Leeds/Bradford were then 109-5, but the challenge was taken up by Weston, who had made a spirited 68 not out with four fours and a six when play came to a premature close.

All of the visiting batsmen found Brooks difficult to deal with, the paceman finishing with 3-36 off his 13 overs, while Carver's left-arm spin deservedly brought him 3-58 from 17.4 overs. His nerve held after soaking up some punishment in his first over, and he was quickly rewarded.

YORKSHIRE AVERAGES 2016
ALL FIRST-CLASS MATCHES

Played 18   Won 5   Lost 4   Drawn 9

BATTING AND FIELDING
(Qualification 10 completed innings)

Player	M.	I.	N.O.	Runs	H.S.	100s	50s	Avge	ct/st
L E Plunkett	8	13	3	449	126	1	3	44.90	3
T T Bresnan	12	21	4	731	142*	1	5	43.00	12
A Z Lees	18	34	2	1285	132	3	8	40.15	15
A Lyth	17	32	2	1153	202	4	3	38.43	25
G S Ballance	14	27	2	894	132	3	4	35.76	9
A U Rashid	10	16	2	393	88	0	3	28.07	7
A J Hodd	13	20	3	444	96*	0	2	26.11	37/6
J A Brooks	15	22	11	275	48	0	0	25.00	4
A W Gale	16	28	1	571	83	0	2	21.14	2
J S Leaning	11	18	2	285	51	0	1	17.81	9
S A Patterson	16	22	1	305	63*	0	2	14.52	1

Also played

E Callis	1	2	1	114	84	0	1	114.00	1
J M Bairstow	4	6	0	533	246	2	0	88.83	5/1
J E Root	2	3	0	240	213	1	0	80.00	5
J S Lehmann	5	8	1	384	116	1	2	54.85	2
Azeem Rafiq	7	9	2	249	74	0	2	35.57	5
W M H Rhodes	4	7	0	220	95	0	1	31.42	3
J Shaw	2	2	1	31	24	0	0	31.00	1
K Carver	2	3	2	29	13	0	0	29.00	1
T M Head	1	2	0	56	54	0	1	28.00	0
B O Coad	2	2	1	18	17*	0	0	18.00	0
J Read	1	1	0	14	14	0	0	14.00	4
S J Willey	4	5	0	58	22	0	0	11.60	0
K S Williamson	2	4	0	42	28	0	0	10.50	3
R J Sidebottom	9	11	3	75	23	0	0	9.37	1
H C Brook	1	1	0	0	0	0	0	0.00	0
R Gibson	1	1	0	0	0	0	0	0.00	0

BOWLING
(Qualification 10 wickets)

Player	Overs	Mdns	Runs	Wkts	Avge	Best	5wI	10wM
R J Sidebottom	245	63	657	31	21.19	5-51	1	0
J A Brooks	459.2	112	1583	60	26.38	5-53	3	0
T T Bresnan	318.1	76	997	35	28.48	5-36	1	0
S A Patterson	465.5	145	1205	41	29.39	6-56	1	0
A U Rashid	293.2	36	1083	32	33.84	4-17	0	0
L E Plunkett	172.1	23	602	10	60.20	2-75	0	0

Also bowled

J E Root	18	3	49	2	24.50	2-23	0	0
A Z Lees	4	0	51	2	25.50	2-51	0	0
J A Leaning	14.4	3	57	2	28.50	2-30	0	0
K S Williamson	18	2	59	2	29.50	1-40	0	0
J Shaw	45.4	8	177	5	35.40	3-58	0	0
D J Willey	102	23	334	9	37.11	3-55	0	0
K Carver	71.2	20	285	7	40.71	4-106	0	0
R Gibson	12	1	42	1	42.00	1-42	0	0
A Lyth	94	13	365	8	45.62	2-19	0	0
Azeem Rafiq	119.3	31	335	6	55.83	3-60	0	0
W M H Rhodes	74	11	240	4	60.00	2-67	0	0
B O Coad	53	16	165	2	82.50	1-57	0	0
T M Head	4	1	16	0	—	0-16	0	0
G S Ballance	1	0	11	0	—	0-11	0	0
A J Hodd	1	0	14	0	—	0-14	0	0

Champion County Match — First Class
MCC v. Yorkshire

Played at Sheikh Zayed Cricket Stadium, Abu Dhabi, on March 20, 21, 22 and 23, 2016

MCC won by 4 wickets

Toss won by Yorkshire

Close of play: First Day, MCC 0-0 (Harris 0*, Browne 0*); Second Day, MCC 282-6 (Foakes 83*, Clarke 56*); Third Day, Yorkshire 239-7 (Rhodes 41*, Patterson 5*)

YORKSHIRE

	First Innings			Second Innings	
A Lyth, c Patel b Clarke		13	lbw b Treadwell		7
A Z Lees, lbw b Ball		0	b Patel		86
G S Ballance, lbw b Patel		105	b Harris		9
* A W Gale, c Foakes b Tredwell		23	lbw b Patel		23
J A Leaning, b Tredwell		6	c Clarke b Tredwell		13
T T Bresnan, c Foakes b Tredwell		3	c Harris b Tredwell		6
W M H Rhodes, c Foakes b Clarke		95	c Foakes b Onions		43
§ A J Hodd, b Ball		9	lbw b Ball		44
S A Patterson, b Onions		0	b Onions		5
J A Brooks, lbw b Onions		0	st Foakes b Patel		25
K Carver, not out		0	not out		12
Extras b 3, lb 7, w 5, nb 2		17	Extras b 1, lb 5		6
Total		275	Total		279

FoW: 1-0 (Lees), 2-21 (Lyth), 3-64 (Gale), 4-82 (Leaning), 5-88 (Bresnan),
1st 6-213 (Ballance), 7-233 (Hodd), 8-234 (Patterson), 9-234 (Brooks), 10-275 (Rhodes)

FoW: 1-21 (Lyth), 2-60 (Ballance), 3-108 (Gale), 4-137 (Leaning), 5-147 (Lees),
2nd 6-147 (Bresnan), 7-227 (Hodd), 8-241 (Rhodes), 9-242 (Patterson), 10-279 (Brooks)

	O	M	R	W		O	M	R	W
Onions	14	4	39	2	Onions	12	2	32	2
Ball	14	3	41	2	Ball	11	1	44	1
Clarke	14.2	3	39	2	Tredwell	40	13	79	3
Harris	13	2	48	0	Clarke	8	1	23	0
Tredwell	25	8	53	3	Harris	13	0	43	1
Patel	8	2	28	1	Patel	23	4	52	3
Westley	4	0	17	0					

MCC

	First Innings			Second innings	
J A R Harris, c Leaning b Patterson		4	(8) not out		0
N L J Browne, c Rhodes b Bresnan		2	c Lees b Lyth		13
R J Burns, c Hodd b Bresnan		51	(1) run out (Ballance)		27
* I R Bell, c Patterson b Carver		44	(3) c Lees b Carver		66
S R Patel, lbw b Bresnan		5	c Ballance b Leaning		22
T Westley, c Hodd b Patterson		22	(4) st Hodd b Carver		58
§ B T Foakes, b Carver		94	(6) not out		32
R Clarke, lbw b Bresnan		58	(7) st Hodd b Leaning		33
J T Ball, st Hodd b Carver		1			
J C Tredwell, not out		2			
G Onions, b Carver		3			
Extras b 5, lb 8, w 1, nb 2		16	Extras b 4, lb 2		6
Total		299	Total (6 wkts)		257

FoW: 1-2 (Browne), 2-14 (Harris), 3-103 (Burns), 4-109 (Bell), 5-114 (Patel),
1st 6-151 (Westley), 7-290 (Foakes), 8-292 (Ball), 9-296 (Clarke), 10-299 (Onions)

FoW: 1-29 (Browne), 2-54 (Burns), 3-138 (Westley), 4-173 (Patel), 5-199 (Bell),
2nd 6-246 (Clarke),

	O	M	R	W		O	M	R	W
Brooks	14	6	37	0	Bresnan	2	0	5	0
Bresnan	19	5	58	4	Brooks	13	1	45	0
Patterson	16	6	32	2	Patterson	9	1	27	0
Carver	30.2	10	106	4	Rhodes	6	1	25	0
Rhodes	11	2	41	0	Lyth	8	1	31	1
Lyth	7	2	12	0	Carver	25	7	88	2
					Leaning	4.4	1	30	2

Umpires: N A Mallender and D J Millns

First Investec Test Match
England v. Sri Lanka

Played at "Headingley, Leeds, on May 19, 20 and 21, 2016
England won by an innings and 88 runs at 5.09pm on the Third Day
Toss won by Sri Lanka

Close of play: First Day, England 171-5 (Hales 71*, Bairstow 54*); Second Day, Sri Lanka Second Innings 1-0 (Karunaratne 0*, Silva 0*)

ENGLAND

* A N Cook, c Chandimal b Shanaka		16
A D Hales, c Chameera b Herath		86
N R D Compton, c Thirimanne b Shanaka		0
J E Root, c Mendis b Shanaka		0
J M Vince, c Mendis b Eranga		9
B A Stokes, c Mathews b Pradeep		12
§ J M Bairstow, c Pradeep b Chameera		140
M M Ali, c Mendis b Chameera		0
S C J Broad, b Chameera		2
S T Finn, st Chandimal b Herath		17
J M Anderson, not out		1
Extras lb 8, w 4, nb 3		15
Total		298

FoW: 1-49 (Cook), 2-49 (Compton), 3-51 (Root), 4-70 (Vince), 5-83 (Stokes), 6-224 (Hales), 7-231 (Ali), 8-233 (Broad), 9-289 (Bairstow), 10-298 (Finn)

	O	M	R	W
Eranga	19	4	68	1
Pradeep	19	7	56	1
Mathews	11	2	31	0
Chameera	17	0	64	3
Shanaka	13	3	46	3
Herath	11.3	1	25	2

First Innings			Second innings	
F D M Karunaratne, c Bairstow b Broad	0		c Bairstow b Anderson	7
J K Silva, c Bairstow b Anderson	11		c Bairstow b Anderson	14
B K G Mendis, c Bairstow b Broad	0		b Anderson	53
§ L D Chandimal, c Vince b Stokes	15		b Ali	8
* A D Mathews, lbw b Anderson	34		c Bairstow b Broad	5
H D R L Thirimanne, c Finn b Broad	22		c Root b Finn	16
M D Shanaka, c Bairstow b Anderson	0		c Bairstow b Anderson	4
H M R K B Herath, c Stokes b Anderson	1		c Broad b Finn	4
P V D Chameera, c Finn b Broad	2		c Compton b Finn	0
R M S Eranga, c Bairstow b Anderson	1		not out	2
A N P R Pradeep, not out	0		b Anderson	0
Extras nb 5	5		Extras lb 5, nb 1	6
Total	91		Total	119

FoW: 1-10 (Karunaratne), 2-12 (Silva), 3-12 (Mendis), 4-43 (Chandimal), 5-77 (Mathews),
1st   6-81 (Shanaka), 7-83 (Herath), 8-90 (Chameera), 9-91 (Thirimanne), 10-91 (Eranga)
FoW: 1-10 (Karunaratne), 2-35 (Silva), 3-79 (Chandimal), 4-93 (Mathews), 5-93 (Mendis),
2nd   6-101 (Shanaka), 7-111 (Herath), 8-117 (Chameera), 9-118 (Thirimanne), 10-119 (Pradeep)

	O	M	R	W		O	M	R	W
Anderson	11.4	6	16	5	Anderson	13.3	5	29	5
Broad	10	1	21	4	Broad	13	0	57	1
Stokes	7	2	25	1	Finn	8	0	26	3
Vince	1	0	10	0	Ali	1	0	2	1
Finn	7	0	19	0					

Man of the Match: J M Bairstow

Umpires: Aleem Dar and R J Tucker   Scorers: J T Potter and H Clayton
Third Umpire: S Ravi   Fourth Umpire: P J Hartley   Match Referee: A J Pycroft

Tourist Match — First Class
Yorkshire v. Pakistan A

Played at Headingley, Leeds, on June 26, 27, 28 and 29, 2016
Match drawn at 12.55pm on the Fourth Day
Toss won by Pakistan A

Close of play: First Day, Yorkshire 243-8 (Shaw 7*, Carver 12*); Second Day, Pakistan A 341-8 (M Hasan 88*, Asghar 11*); Third Day, Yorkshire 57-0 (Callis 30*, Lees 17*)

First Innings	YORKSHIRE	Second innings
E Callis, b Bilawal Bhatti	84	not out ... 30
* A Z Lees, b Mir Hamza	17	not out ... 17
H C Brook, b Mir Hamza	0	
J A Leaning, lbw b Hasan Ali	33	
W M H Rhodes, c Mohammad Asghar b Mir Hamza	9	
R Gibson, lbw b Mohammad Asghar	0	
Azeem Rafiq, lbw b Mohammad Asghar	48	
§ J Read, b Hasan Ali	14	
J Shaw, not out	7	
K Carver, c Sharjeel Khan b Hasan Ali	13	
B O Coad, c Mohammad Hasan b Mir Hamza	1	
Extras b 7, lb 5, w 1, nb 7	20	Extras b 5, lb 2, nb 3 ... 10
Total	246	Total (0 wkts) ... 57

FoW: 1-19 (Lees), 2-19 (Brook), 3-91 (Leaning), 4-123 (Rhodes), 5-124 (Gibson), 1st 6-189 (Callis), 7-222 (Read), 8-222 (Rafiq), 9-245 (Carver), 10-246 (Coad)

	O	M	R	W		O	M	R	W
Mir Hamza	19.4	5	53	4	Mir Hamza	9	2	31	0
Hasan Ali	18	4	69	3	Hasan Ali	4.2	1	8	0
Bilawal Bhatti	15	2	46	1	Bilawal Bhatti	5	2	11	0
Mohammad Asghar	16	3	50	1					
Sharjeel Khan	1	1	0	0					
Mohammad Nawaz	6	1	16	1					

PAKISTAN A

Sharjeel Khan, c Carver b Coad	25
Jaahid Ali, c Read b Azeem Rafiq	64
Fakhar Zaman, c Read b Carver	49
* Babar Azam, c Read b Rhodes	45
Umar Siddiq, lbw b Azeem Rafiq	0
Mohammad Nawaz, c sub (J C Wainman) b Azeem Rafiq	0
§ Mohammad Hasan, c Lees b Shaw	98
Bilawal Bhatti, c Read b Gibson	0
Hasan Ali, c Rhodes b Shaw	41
Mohammad Asghar, c Callis b Shaw	15
Mir Hamza, not out	1
Extras b 8, lb 4, nb 7	19
Total	357

FoW: 1-29 (Sharjeel), 2-142 (Zaman), 3-160 (Jaahid), 4-170 (Siddiq), 5-174 (Nawaz), 1st 6-214 (Azam), 7-215 (Bhatti), 8-305 (Hasan Ali), 9-356 (Asghar), 10-357 (M Hasan)

	O	M	R	W
Shaw	16.4	5	58	3
Coad	18	6	57	1
Rhodes	16	3	37	1
Gibson	12	1	42	1
Azeem Rafiq	20	7	60	3
Carver	16	3	91	1

Umpires: G D Lloyd and T Lungley   Scorers: J T Potter and H Clayton

PAUL GRAYSON APPOINTED DIAMONDS' HEAD COACH

Yorkshire Diamonds in February provided proof of their determination to succeed by appointing Bedale-born former Yorkshire all-rounder Paul Grayson as head coach.

Paul, who went on to become a leading player with Essex before a successful spell as their head coach, signed a contract with the KIA Super League team until 2019, and will continue to coach Durham University MCCU alongside his new role.

Paul, who played for Yorkshire between 1990 and 1995, scoring 1,958 first-class runs and taking 13 wickets, succeeded Richard Pyrah, who is placing emphasis on assisting Yorkshire's

PAUL GRAYSON
Ex-Yorkshire all-rounder

First Eleven coach Andrew Gale. Paul said: "I am delighted to be joining as head coach for the Yorkshire Diamonds. The opportunity to work with an elite female team is really exciting for me and a role which gives me a fantastic opportunity to use my first-class coaching experience.

"I am looking forward to meeting up with players and the Diamonds support staff, and preparing for Super League competition."

Yorkshire Diamonds General Manager Jane Hildreth said: "I am thrilled that we have been able to recruit Paul as head coach. He has a wealth of experience in the game, having had a successful coaching career with Essex County Cricket Club and Durham University MCCU.

"Paul will take the Yorkshire Diamonds forward and build a team who will be challenging for the title in 2017."

ROYAL LONDON ONE-DAY CUP
HIGHLIGHTS OF 2016

WINNERS
Warwickshire, who defeated Surrey by 8 wickets

Wins by 100 or more runs (2)
Yorkshire (325-7) defeated Lancashire (84) by 242 runs (*DLS*) at Manchester
Yorkshire (376-3) defeated Leicestershire (185) by 191 runs at Leicester

Totals of 250 and over (6)
376-3	v. Leicestershire at Leicester (won)
325-7	v. Lancashire at Manchester (won)
314-8	v. Northamptonshire at Scarborough (won)
266-8	v. Durham at Chester-le-Street (lost)
256-9	v. Kent at Canterbury (won)
254-8	v. Nottinghamshire at Scarborough (won)

Opponents dismissed for under 100 (1)
84   v. Lancashire at Manchester

Match aggregates of 450 and over (7)
624   Northamptonshire (310-7) lost to Yorkshire (314-8) by 2 wickets
           at Scarborough
561   Yorkshire (376-3) defeated Leicestershire (185) by 191 runs at Leicester
547   Durham (281-7) defeated Yorkshire (266-8) by 15 runs at Chester-le-Street
505   Nottinghamshire (251-9) lost to Yorkshire (254-8) by 2 wickets
           at Scarborough
501   Yorkshire (256-9) defeated Kent (245) by 11 runs at Canterbury
491   Surrey (255-7) defeated Yorkshire (236) by 19 runs at Headingley
450   Warwickshire (283-6) defeated Yorkshire (167) by 114 runs (*DLS*) at Leeds

Century Partnerships (3)
For the 1st wicket (1)
106   A Lyth and A Z Lees v. Northamptonshire at Scarborough

For the 2nd wicket (1)
111   A Lyth and K S Williamson v. Lancashire at Manchester

For the 3rd wicket (1)
274   T M Head and J A Leaning v. Leicestershire at Leicester
(Yorkshire's highest List A partnership)

Centuries (4)
A Lyth (2)
   136   v. Lancashire at Manchester
   125   v. Northamptonshire at Scarborough
(Consecutive days)

T M Head (1)
   175   v. Leicestershire at Leicester

J A Leaning (1)
   131*   v. Leicestershire at Leicester

4 wickets in an innings (1)
L E Plunkett (1)
   4-52   v. Kent at Canterbury

3 catches in an innings (1)
A Z Lees(1)
    3   v. Nottinghamshire at Scarborough

List A Debuts for Yorkshire (2): T M Head and D J Willey

Match-By-Match Reports	**DAVE CALDWELL**

Royal London One-Day Cup — North Group
Yorkshire v. Worcestershire

Played at Headingley, Leeds, on June 7, 2016
Worcestershire won by 7 wickets

Toss won by Yorkshire　　　　　　　　　　　Worcestershire 2 points, Yorkshire 0 points

YORKSHIRE

A Lyth, c Cox b Shantry		9
* A Z Lees, lbw b Rhodes		19
J A Leaning, c Cox b Barnard		23
G S Ballance, lbw b D'Oliveira		30
W M H Rhodes, c Mitchell b Rhodes		17
A U Rashid, c Barnard b D'Oliveira		9
T T Bresnan, c Clarke b Shantry		24
D J Willey, c and b Mitchell		15
L E Plunkett, b Leach		19
§ A J Hodd, lbw b Leach		2
S A Patterson, not out		0
Extras lb 1, w 2		3
Total (45.2 overs)		170

FoW: 1-13 (Lyth), 2-50 (Leaning), 3-54 (Lees), 4-94 (Ballance), 5-108 (Rashid), 6-109 (Rhodes), 7-136 (Willey), 8-166 (Plunkett), 9-170 (Hodd), 10-170 (Bresnan)

	O	M	R	W
Leach	9	2	30	2
Shantry	7.2	1	10	2
Barnard	6	0	31	1
Rhodes	10	1	34	2
D'Oliveira	10	1	49	2
Mitchell	3	0	15	1

WORCESTERSHIRE

J Leach, c Ballance b Rashid		63
T Kohler-Cadmore, lbw b Plunkett		42
* D K H Mitchell, not out		23
J M Clarke, c and b Rashid		26
A N Kervezee, not out		13
B L D'Oliveira		
R A Whiteley		
§ O B Cox	Did not bat	
G H Rhodest		
E G Barnard		
J D Shantry		
Extras lb 4		4
Total (3 wkts, 25.3 overs)		171

FoW: 1-107 (Kohler-Cadmore), 2-111 (Leach), 3-148 (Clarke)

	O	M	R	W
Bresnan	2	0	25	0
Willey	5	0	36	0
Patterson	5	0	29	0
Plunkett	6	0	38	1
Rashid	7.3	1	39	2

Man of the Match: J Leach

Umpires: R T Robinson and M J Saggers　　　　Scorers: J T Potter and S M Drinkwater
Third Umpire: M A Gough

The scoresheet for Yorkshire's match against Derbyshire at Chesterfield on June 12, which was abandoned after one over, appears at the end of this section

Yorkshire v. Worcestershire

Another TV horror show

GARY BALLANCE: More like his old self

Yorkshire crashed to their fourth consecutive limited-overs defeat and third in front of the TV cameras.

The Royals' impressive young side dominated their more illustrious counterparts.

From the onset Worcestershire's bowlers held the upper hand as Lyth and Lees both struggled on a sluggish pitch against an accurate seam attack. Lyth edged in indeterminate fashion to Cox before Leaning and Lees provided a patient stand of 37, Leaning then edging a beauty from Barnard into Cox's safe hands. Yorkshire were 50-2 after 17 overs, and from this point two young spinners took centre stage: Rhodes and D'Oliveira gave their side control and guile as the Vikings again struggled with tempo and shot selection.

Lees played across the line for 19, but Ballance began to look like his old self until he fell for 30 to an attempted swipe at D'Oliveira. From 94-4 it was a steady procession of wickets. Rashid got out to an ungainly slog, while Rhodes was caught at short mid-off from a leading edge. Willey, curiously coming in at No. 8, played a cameo before an excellent return catch by Mitchell accounted for him. Bresnan and Plunkett briefly looked to have the appetite to post a competitive score, but the seamers finished the job with over four overs still be bowled.

Worcestershire's approach to the 171 run chase was apparent with the promotion of pinch-hitter Leach to open with Kohler-Cadmore, and 16-0 after two overs became 38-0 after three as Bresnan was shown no respect, Leach carving him to all parts. The Worcestershire pair ran amok, Leach passing his 50 off 25 deliveries to give him a career best. The 100 partnership followed in the 12th over before Plunkett finally made the breakthrough by trapping Kohler-Cadmore lbw for 42. Leach holed out for 63, caught at long-off, his innings spanning only 35 balls. Rashid grabbed a late return catch to capture Clarke for 26, but Mitchell and Kervezee saw their side home inside 26 overs.

Royal London One-Day Cup — North Group
Yorkshire v. Northamptonshire

Played at North Marine Road, Scarborough, on June 14, 2016
Yorkshire won by 2 wickets

Toss won by Yorkshire   Yorkshire 2 points, Northamptonshire 0 points

NORTHAMPTONSHIRE

J J Cobb, c Williamson b Plunkett		23
A M Rossington, lbw b Willey		8
§ B M Duckett, c Leaning b Rashid		121
* A G Wakely, c and b Lyth		71
R I Keogh, c Bresnan b Plunkett		0
S P Crook, not out		46
R I Newton, c and b Patterson		26
G G White, c Plunkett b Willey		6
R J Gleeson, not out		1
M Bahaullah		
B W Sanderson	Did not bat	
Extras lb 1, w 7		8
Total (7 wkts, 50 overs)		310

FoW: 1-20 (Rossington), 2-35 (Cobb), 3-201 (Wakely), 4-206 (Keogh), 5-246 (Duckett),
6-296 (Newton), 7-304 (White).

	O	M	R	W
Bresnan	10	0	76	0
Willey	10	2	55	2
Plunkett	10	1	33	2
Patterson	8	0	49	1
Rashid	8	0	67	1
Lyth	4	0	29	1

YORKSHIRE

A Lyth, c Gleeson b White		125
* A Z Lees, c Sanderson b Crook		20
K S Williamson, b Gleeson		10
G S Ballance, b Azharullah		80
J A Leaning, c and b Cobb		0
A U Rashid, c Rossington b White		1
T T Bresnan, c Cobb b White		38
D J Willey, not out		26
L E Plunkett, b Azharullah		0
§ A J Hodd, not out		4
S A Patterson	Did not bat	
Extras lb 2, w 4, nb 4		10
Total (8 wkts, 47.3 overs)		314

FoW: 1-106 (Lees), 2-132 (Williamson), 3-189 (Lyth), 4-189 (Leaning), 5-192 (Rashid),
6-250 (Bresnan), 7-303 (Ballance), 8-303 (Plunkett).

	O	M	R	W
Gleeson	10	0	56	1
Azharullah	9	0	62	2
Sanderson	4	0	38	0
Cobb	9	0	43	1
Crook	7.3	0	68	1
White	8	1	45	3

Umpires: P R Pollard and M J Saggers   Scorers: J T Potter and A C Kingston

Brutal Lyth's timely century

ADAM LYTH: Masterful display of clean hitting

A brutal 60-ball century from Adam Lyth, his second List A hundred, gave Yorkshire a timely limited-overs boost as the *White Rose* chased an imposing 310.

Lyth's innings spanned a mere 78 deliveries for his 125, which contained 10 fours and eight sixes in a masterful display of clean hitting.

An opening stand of 106 in under 12 overs had been dominated by Lyth when Lees fell for 20, taken on the leg side off Crook. The returning Kane Williamson made 10 before chopping into his stumps, but Ballance gave Lyth a solid anchor as the pair added 57. Lyth then finally fell, caught at mid-on.

Leaning offered a return catch to Cobb off his second ball, closely followed by Rashid to make it 192-5...but Lyth's explosive innings had gone at such a pace that the run rate was unlikely to be an issue. Ballance passed his half-century, and found a reliable partner in Bresnan, the pair adding 58 before Bresnan went for a 45-ball 38.

A late wobble led to two wickets falling on 303, Ballance bowled by Azharullah for 80 and Plunkett going the same way two balls later. Willey held his nerve with 26, and won the game in fine fashion with a six off Crook with 15 balls remaining.

Yorkshire had won the toss and begun well on a greener than normal Scarborough pitch. Northamptonshire's openers were dismissed inside nine overs with only 35 runs scored, Willey and Plunkett, Yorkshire's best bowlers on the day, taking the wickets. The visitors then seized control, Duckett and Wakeley adding 166 for the third wicket, helped by some lacklustre fielding, which gave Wakeley, 71, two lives. Duckett went to his maiden hundred, and when he was taken on the leg-side boundary off Rashid for 121 off 113 balls with 15 fours and two sixes his side were well placed at 246-5 in the 43rd over. Crook and Newton continued to blaze away, ensuring Yorkshire's chase would be sizeable.

Royal London One-Day Cup — North Group
Lancashire v. Yorkshire

Played at Old Trafford, Manchester, on June 15, 2016
Yorkshire won by 242 runs(D/L method)

Toss won by Yorkshire   Yorkshire 2 points, Lancashire 0 points

YORKSHIRE

A Lyth, c Brown b Livingstone	136
* A Z Lees, c and b Clark	20
K S Williamson, run out (Procter)	40
G S Ballance, c Mahmood b Livingstone	34
A U Rashid, c Buck b Livingstone	13
T T Bresnan, c Buttler b Buck	10
D J Willey, b Parry	21
L E Plunkett, not out	25
§ A J Hodd, not out	13
K Carver	
S A Patterson Did not bat	
Extras b 1, lb 3, w 5, nb 4	13
Total (7 wkts, 47 overs)	325

FoW: 1-65 (Lees), 2-176 (Williamson), 3-218 (Lyth), 4-250 (Ballance), 5-252 (Rashid), 6-283 (Willey), 7-285 (Bresnan)

	O	M	R	W
Mahmood	7	0	57	0
Buck	6	0	61	1
Croft	10	0	51	0
Clark	5	0	37	1
Livingstone	8	0	51	3
Parry	10	0	50	1
Procter	1	0	14	0

LANCASHIRE

Target to win: 327 runs off 47 overs

M J Guptill, b Willey	45
A N Petersen, c Hodd b Bresnan	6
K R Brown, c Lees b Bresnan	7
L S Livingstone, b Rashid	6
§ J C Buttler, c Hodd b Willey	0
* S J Croft, c Williamson b Willey	0
L A Procter, c Lees b Carver	1
J Clark, b Carver	4
S D Parry, st Hodd b Carver	9
N L Buck, b Rashid	0
S Mahmood, not out	0
Extras b 1, lb 2, w 3	6
Total (17.3 overs)	84

FoW: 1-39 (Petersen), 2-53 (Guptill), 3-64 (Brown), 4-65 (Buttler), 5-65 (Croft), 6-68 (Livingstone), 7-68 (Procter), 8-75 (Clark), 9-84 (Parry), 10-84 (Buck)

	O	M	R	W
Willey	6	0	44	3
Bresnan	5	0	22	2
Rashid	3.3	0	10	2
Carver	3	0	5	3

Umpires: N G C Cowley and M A Gough   Scorers: J T Potter and C Rimmer

Lyth lathers record 136

A second List A hundred in less than 24 hours from Adam Lyth propelled Yorkshire to their biggest margin of victory in List A cricket as Lancashire were swept aside at Old Trafford.

Lyth continued from where he had left off in Scarborough the previous day, instantly on the attack with consecutive sixes as early as the second over.

Vikings were 60-0 in six overs before a 30-minute break for light rain curtailed the carnage. Three overs were lost, but Lyth soon settled back into his stride, despite losing opening partner Lees for 20 when he gifted Clark a return catch.

Lyth brought up his half century in 28 deliveries and found the patient Williamson to be the perfect foil as the two combined effortlessly in a century partnership off 86 balls.

The left-hander was dropped on 83, a sharp diving chance spilled by Guptill, before com-

ADAM LYTH: 12 fours, seven sixes in 136-run carnage

pleting his century in 64 balls. Williamson was run out after fine work from Procter for 40, and Lyth was caught at long-off for the highest one-day Roses score for Yorkshire, 136 from 92 balls with 12 fours and seven sixes. Ballance provided a typically industrious 34, and Willey threatened to catch fire before he was bowled for 21. An eighth-wicket stand of 42 between Plunkett and Hodd ensured a stiff target.

Duckworth-Lewis recalculations added one run to Yorkshire's total, but this proved immaterial despite a rapid-fire opening by Guptill: the big-hitting Kiwi, dropped by Carver on the mid-wicket fence, raced to 45 before Willey bowled him. Lancashire were 53-2, and at 64 they lost the first of five wickets for four runs in a spectacular 16-ball spell. Willey had Buttler caught at the wicket, and Croft first ball, slicing to Williamson at point. Rashid and Carver combined beautifully to complete the rout, both spinners appearing unplayable as Lightning meekly surrendered inside 18 overs to their heaviest List A defeat.

Royal London One-Day Cup — North Group
Leicestershire v. Yorkshire

Played at Grace Road, Leicester, on July 24, 2016
Yorkshire won by 191 runs

Toss won by Yorkshire   Yorkshire 2 points, Leicestershire 0 points

YORKSHIRE

A Lyth, run out (N J O'Brien)		2
* A Z Lees, st N J O'Brien b Sayer		32
T M Head, c N J "Brien b K J O'Brien		175
J A Leaning, not out		131
T T Bresnan, not out		24
D J Willey		
A U Rashid		
L E Plunkett	Did not bat	
§ A J Hodd		
Azeem Rafiq		
S A Patterson		
Extras b 4, lb 6, w 2		12
Total (3 wkts, 50 overs)		376

FoW: 1-13 (Lyth), 2-51 (Lees), 3-325 (Head)

	O	M	R	W
McKay	10	1	57	0
Raine	9	0	88	0
Sayer	10	1	52	1
Dexter	8	0	65	0
K J O'Brien	6	0	48	1
Cosgrove	7	0	56	0

LEICESTERSHIRE

A J Robson, c Hodd b Bresnan		16
* M L Pettini, b Willey		1
K J O'Brien, c Plunkett b Bresnan		34
M J Cosgrove, c Lyth b Patterson		6
L J Hill, st Hodd b Azeem Rafiq		55
P J Horton, lbw b Patterson		8
§ N J O'Brien, lbw b Rashid		17
N J Dexter, c Plunkett b Rashid		11
R J Sayer, not out		12
C J McKay, c Lees b Azeem Rafiq		12
B A Raine, lbw b Rashid		4
Extras lb 5, w 4		9
Total (33.3 overs)		185

FoW: 1-6 (Pettini), 2-46 (Robson), 3-55 (K J O'Brien), 4-69 (Cosgrove), 5-88 (Horton), 6-135 (N J O'Brien), 7-154 (Hill), 8-156 (Dexter), 9-180 (McKay), 10-185 (Raine)

	O	M	R	W
Willey	5	0	35	1
Bresnan	7	1	26	2
Patterson	5	0	30	2
Plunkett	5	0	20	0
Azeem Rafiq	7	0	46	2
Rashid	4.3	0	23	3

Umpires: S A Garratt and P J Hartley   Scorers: J T Potter and P J Rogers

Head, Leaning 275 best yet

TRAVIS HEAD: 18 fours and four sixes in his brutal 175

Hundreds from Travis Head and Jack Leaning, who set Yorkshire's List A partnership record of 275, kept them in pole position for a quarter-final slot.

Head struck a sublime 175 from only 139 deliveries, and Leaning thrashed his second one-day century in contributing an unbeaten 131 from 110 balls.

Yorkshire amassed 376-3, their highest total against first-class opposition, but this looked some way off when Lyth was run out for two in a mix-up with opening partner Lees, who advanced to 32 before he was stumped, aiming wildly at Sayer.

Head had settled into his stride, and Leaning greeted his third delivery by hitting it straight back over the bowler's head for six. Head reached 50 in 60 balls and his second half-century 39 deliveries later. Both batsmen had one blot on their copybooks: Head was dropped by Sayer on the long-off fence on 116, and Leaning was inexplicably put down at deep mid-wicket on 83. The pair continued striking the ball cleanly and decisively, overtaking the previous best partnership for any wicket of 242 in 1990 by Moxon and Metcalfe. Head finally fell for a brutal 175, containing 18 fours and four sixes. Bresnan joined in the carnage at the end of the innings to finish on 24 from 13 balls as the Foxes' bowlers sought refuge.

What Leicester did not need was an early wicket, but Pettini went for a solitary run as Willey castled the former Essex man with a vicious in-swinger. What Yorkshire did not need was some spirited hitting from Kevin O'Brien, 34, and top-scorer Hill, 55. Robson was caught down the leg side for 16, and O'Brien holed out at mid-wicket, both falling to Bresnan. Rashid and Rafiq took the Vikings to what was already a foregone conclusion, the Foxes subsiding to 185 all out in the 34th over. Rafiq took 2-46 and Rashid 3-23 to complete the rout as Yorkshire prevailing by a mammoth 191 runs.

Royal London One-Day Cup — North Group
Yorkshire v. Nottinghamshire

Played at North Marine Road, Scarborough, on July 27, 2016
Yorkshire won by 2 wickets

Toss won by Yorkshire   Yorkshire 2 points, Nottinghamshire 0 points

NOTTINGHAMSHIRE

M J Lumb, c Lees b Bresnan		9
M H Wessels, c Lees b Plunkett		36
G P Smith, c Head b Willey		0
B R M Taylor, c Hodd b Bresnan		0
S R Patel, lbw b Plunkett		0
D T Christian, c Lees b Patterson		52
S J Mullaney, not out		89
* § C M W Read, c Hodd b Willey		15
L J Fletcher, st Hodd b Azeem Rafiq		13
J T Ball, b Patterson		27
H F Gurney, not out		1
Extras b 4, w 3, nb 2		9
Total (9 wkts, 50 overs)		251

FoW: 1-24 (Lumb), 2-30 (Smith), 3-38 (Taylor), 4-39 (Patel), 5-46 (Wessels), 6-131 (Christian), 7-162 (Read), 8-183 (Fletcher), 9-225 (Ball)

	O	M	R	W
Bresnan	8	2	24	2
Willey	10	1	55	2
Plunkett	10	0	35	2
Patterson	7	0	36	2
Rashid	10	0	48	0
Azeem Rafiq	5	0	49	1

YORKSHIRE

A Lyth, c Fletcher b Gurney		39
* A Z Lees, c Read b Ball		7
T M Head, c Fletcher b Gurney		0
J A Leaning, c Read b Ball		0
A U Rashid, c Fletcher b Christian		41
T T Bresnan, not out		95
D J Willey, c Ball b Fletcher		15
L E Plunkett, c Fletcher b Christian		10
§ A J Hodd, lbw b Christian		12
Azeem Rafiq, not out		17
S A Patterson	Did not bat	
Extras lb 12, w 4, nb 2		18
Total (8 wkts, 49.4 overs)		254

FoW: 1-45 (Lyth), 2-45 (Head), 3-46 (Leaning), 4-50 (Lees), 5-147 (Rashid), 6-191 (Willey), 7-205 (Plunkett), 8-224 (Hodd)

	O	M	R	W
Ball	8	0	47	2
Gurney	10	0	53	2
Fletcher	9.4	0	41	1
Patel	8	1	37	0
Mullaney	4	0	20	0
Christian	10	0	44	3

Umpires: P K Baldwin and G D Lloyd   Scorers: J T Potter and R Marshall

Yorkshire v. Nottinghamshire

Bresnan's best does it

A scintillating clash saw the points go the way of the White Rose after a fine all-round display from Tim Bresnan proved the difference between two evenly matched sides.

Bresnan saw his team home with a List A best unbeaten 95.

Chasing 252, Yorkshire got off to a flier with Lyth striking the ball serenely and racing to 39 from 26 balls before mistiming a drive to mid-on off Gurney.

This signalled a dramatic collapse as two wickets fell in no time. Head miscued a pull, and Leaning was caught at the wicket, neither troubling the scorers.

Lees fell soon afterwards, taken at second slip, and Vikings were staring down the barrel at 50-4 inside 10 overs. Rashid was spilled at second slip on nought, and this let-off allowed him to add 97 for the fifth wicket with Bresnan before departing for a

TIM BRESNAN: Key wickets and an undefeated 95

typically busy 41 from 65 balls, and caught in the deep off Christian.

Partners for Bresnan came and went after making minor contributions. Willey struck two boundaries before falling to Fletcher for 15, and it was only the arrival of Rafiq that brought calmness to the chase. Needing 15 from two overs with two wickets in hand, Rafiq took control, and the winning boundary was struck with two balls remaining.

Earlier, the Outlaws had recovered from a dire situation after being inserted by Lees and slumping to 46-5. Bresnan took the two key wickets of Lumb, caught at mid-on, and Taylor, caught at the wicket. Plunkett impressed early on in a fearsome spell, finishing with 2-35 from his 10 overs. Christian and Mullaney repaired the damage with a fine stand of 85, but the Vikings kept the run rate to manageable proportions with only the spinners coming in for any fierce treatment.

Mullaney finished unbeaten on 89 from 94 balls, and with Ball helped to build a ninth-wicket stand of 42 in nigh on five overs to ensure the visitors a score worthy of defence.

Royal London One-Day Cup — North Group
Durham v. Yorkshire

Played at Riverside, Chester-le-Street, on July 31, 2016
Durham won by 15 runs

Toss won by Durham   Durham 2 points, Yorkshire 0 points

DURHAM

M D Stoneman, c Hodd b Bresnan	14
K K Jennings, st Hodd b Azeem Rafiq	24
S G Borthwick, c Patterson b Plunkett	84
J T A Burnham, c Lees b Carver	21
* P D Collingwood, c Azeem Rafiq b Carver	16
M J Richardson, c Bresnan b Patterson	53
R D Pringle, c Azeem Rafiq b Bresnan	27
§ S W Poynter, not out	27
U Arshad, not out	2
M A Wood	
C Rushworth	Did not bat
Extras b 2, lb 6, w 3, nb 2	13
Total (7 wkts, 50 overs)	281

FoW: 1-31 (Stoneman), 2-58 (Jennings), 3-103 (Burnham), 4-129 (Collingwood), 5-185 (Borthwick), 6-229 (Pringle), 7-262 (Richardson).

	O	M	R	W
Bresnan	9	1	65	2
Willey	8	0	49	0
Azeem Rafiq	7	0	43	1
Patterson	10	1	43	1
Plunkett	10	0	43	1
Carver	6	0	30	2

YORKSHIRE

A Lyth, c Richardson b Jennings	24
D J Willey, c Poynter b Rushworth	19
* A Z Lees, b Wood	1
T M Head, c and b Borthwick	49
J A Leaning, c Pringle b Wood	35
T T Bresnan, c sub b Rushworth	92
§ A J Hodd, run out (sub P Coughlin/Poynter)	13
L E Plunkett, c Wood b Rushworth	8
Azeem Rafiq, not out	4
S A Patterson, not out	8
K Carver	Did not bat
Extras lb 5, w 2, n b6	13
Total (8 wkts, 50 overs)	266

FoW: 1-30 (Willey), 2-31 (Lees), 3-75 (Lyth), 4-111 (Head), 5-187 (Leaning), 6-218 (Hodd), 7-238 (Plunkett), 8-254 (Bresnan).

	O	M	R	W
Rushworth	10	0	67	3
Wood	10	0	43	2
Arshad	7	0	34	0
Jennings	6	0	34	1
Borthwick	10	0	48	1
Pringle	7	0	35	0

Man of the Match: S G Borthwick

Umpires: J W Lloyds and D J Millns   Scorers: J T Potter and B Hunt
Third Umpire: R T Robinson

Bresnan's 92 in vain

TIM BRESNAN: Strong all-round performance

Yorkshire slipped to their second defeat in the competition, despite a fine 92 from Bresnan, falling 15 short of a challenging 282. They will look at Durham's last 10 overs, where the hosts stacked up 97 runs after the Vikings had seemed to have the contest under control.

Early exchanges were dominated by the visitors. Tight opening bursts from Bresnan and Willey restricted Durham as Stoneman fell after seven overs, taken at the wicket off Bresnan, and Jennings departed for 24 from 29 balls, smartly stumped by Hodd off Rafiq.

Borthwick and Burnham recovered to enjoy a partnership of 45 for the fourth wicket before Carver snared Burnham. Borthwick moved through the gears to ease past his half-century, and despite losing Collingwood he went on to a 102-ball 84-run stay before a miscued stroke off Plunkett foound Patterson at long-leg.

Richardson struck a half-century as Yorkshire's out-cricket became more desperate, Bresnan's final two overs costing 31 runs as Durham surged to 281-7 from their 50 overs.

Lyth and Willey made a solid start to the run chase, reaching 30 in the seventh over before Rushworth found the edge of Willey's bat for 19. The impressive Wood, bowling at venomous pace, caused Lees to play on for one, and the winning line looked a long way away for the Vikings.

Lyth advanced to 24 in 37 balls, but tried to strike down the ground, only to be taken at mid-on with the total on 75. Head and Leaning both played compact, low-risk cricket, but the asking rate was starting to rise, and the scoreboard pressure brought wickets. Head offered a return catch to Borthwick for 49, while the in-form Leaning was pouched at backward-point for 35. Bresnan reached his half-century from 58 balls as Yorkshire needed 82 from the last 10 overs, but the game slipped away, Bresnan's dismissal leaving Yorkshire to get 28 from 12 balls. Wood conceded only one from the last-but-one over to put paid to that.

Royal London One-Day Cup — North Group
Yorkshire v. Warwickshire

Played at Headingley, Leeds, on August 1, 2016
Warwickshire won by 114 runs (D/L method)

Toss won by Warwickshire   Warwickshire 2 points, Yorkshire 0 points

WARWICKSHIRE

W T S Porterfield, c Plunkett b Patterson		7
S R Hain, c Hodd b Plunkett		10
I J L Trott, c Leaning b Patterson		118
* I R Bell, c Willey b Plunkett		21
§ T R Ambrose, c Rhodes b Azeem Rafiq		34
L J Evans, not out		48
R Clarke, c Lyth b Azeem Rafiq		18
A Javid, not out		2
J S Patel		
R O Gordon	Did not bat	
C J C Wright		
Extras b 4, lb 5, w 5, nb 6, p 5		25
Total (6 wkts, 50 overs)		283

FoW: 1-16 (Porterfield), 2-40 (Hain), 3-92 (Bell), 4-185 (Ambrose), 5-214 (Trott), 6-250 (Clarke)

	O	M	R	W
Willey	10	1	53	0
Patterson	10	0	50	2
Plunkett	10	0	58	2
Rhodes	6	0	32	0
Azeem Rafiq	10	0	56	2
Carver	4	0	20	0

YORKSHIRE
(Target to win: 282 runs off 49 overs)

A Lyth, c Evans b Wright		12
D J Willey, lbw b Javid		27
* A Z Lees, run out (Bell/Ambrose)		2
T M Head, b Javid		53
J A Leaning, c Hain b Javid		3
W M H Rhodes, c Bell b Javid		17
§ A J Hodd, lbw b Patel		14
L E Plunkett, st Ambrose b Patel		13
Azeem Rafiq, lbw b Gordon		0
S A Patterson, b Patel		7
K Carver, not out		12
Extras lb 1, w 6		7
Total (37.4 overs)		167

FoW: 1-22 (Lyth), 2-26 (Lees), 3-71 (Willey), 4-79 (Leaning), 5-120 (Rhodes), 6-125 (Head), 7-143 (Hodd), 8-144 (Rafiq), 9-148 (Plunkett), 10-167 (Patterson)

	O	M	R	W
Clarke	6	0	41	0
Wright	5	1	12	1
Gordon	8	0	37	1
Patel	8.4	0	34	3
Javid	10	0	42	4

Man of the Match: I J L Trott

Umpires: N L Bainton and P J Hartley   Scorers: J T Potter and M D Smith
Third Umpire: N G C Cowley

Defeat ends home tie hope

Yorkshire began by bowling tight lines and keeping Warwickshire's openers at arm's length, Willey and Patterson combining well as the Bears limped along at barely two runs an over.

First blood was drawn by Patterson as Porterfield drove on the up to cover for seven. The score had advanced in unspectacular fashion to 40 in the 12th over when Plunkett found the edge of Hain's bat and he was superbly taken by the diving Hodd.

Bell and Trott moved the total on to 92 before Bell drove Plunkett into the waiting hands of Willey in the covers. Trott, playing in typically unflappable fashion, reached his half-century from 62 balls, and in tandem with Ambrose provided the meat for the Bears.

TRAVIS HEAD: Style and power in his half-century

While never accelerating to unmanageable levels the experienced pair added 93 for the fourth wicket before Ambrose picked out Rhodes off Rafiq for 34. The Bears did accelerate arrive after Trott had reached his century in 122 balls, his dismissal bringing Clarke to join Evans, who helped himself to an unbeaten 48 from 30 balls as the visitors piled on 104 runs from the final 10 overs.

Yorkshire found themselves on 26-2 with both Lyth and Lees gone, Lees run out attempting a second that was simply never on. Willey and Head enjoyed a spirited stand of 45 before Willey was trapped in front to give Javed the first of four wickets in a career-best performance.

The Vikings' run chase was littered with false starts, and in truth never looked like challenging the stiff target. Lyth on 12 fell to a fine diving catch at second slip, and Lees followed almost immediately. Head batted with style and power for his 53, which came from 63 balls and contained five boundaries. Once the young Australian had been bowled by a beauty from Javid the wickets fell with alarming regularity

As results started to filter in from round the country it was seen that the score Yorkshire needed to guarantee a quarter-final home tie was 189. Despite a valiant last-wicket stand of 19 they fell 114 runs short of victory and 22 runs shy of that elusive home tie.

Royal London One-Day Cup — Quarter-Final
Kent v. Yorkshire

Played at St Lawrence Ground, Canterbury, on August 18, 2016
Yorkshire won by 11 runs
Toss won by Kent

YORKSHIRE

A Lyth, c Billings b Coles	88
* A Z Lees, c Blake b Claydon	7
J E Root, c Blake b Hartley	45
§ J M Bairstow, c Bell-Drummond b Hartley	9
G S Ballance, run out (Bell-Drummond/Billings/Claydon)	37
T T Bresnan, c Northeast b Gilman	10
D J Willey, c Billings b Gidman	0
L E Plunkett, c Northeast b Coles	16
A U Rashid, not out	24
Azeem Rafiq, b Coles	1
S A Patterson, not out	3
Extras b 2, lb 4, w 8, nb 2	16
Total (9 wkts, 50 overs)	256

FoW: 1-27 (Lees), 2-117 (Root), 3-140 (Bairstow), 4-167 (Lyth), 5-191 (Bresnan), 6-192 (Willey), 7-219 (Plunkett), 8-237 (Ballance), 9-241 (Rafiq)

	O	M	R	W
Claydon	10	0	65	1
Coles	10	1	39	3
Stevens	3	0	16	0
Gidman	7	0	36	2
Tredwell	10	0	52	0
Hartley	10	0	42	2

KENT

D J Bell-Drummond, lbw b Willey	2
J L Denly, c Willey b Plunkett	31
* S A Northeast, c Ballance b Plunkett	23
§ S W Billings, lbw b Patterson	1
D I Stevens, c and b Plunkett	54
A J Blake, c Bairstow b Willey	50
W R S Gidman, c and b Plunkett	19
M T Coles, st Bairstow b Rashid	22
J C Tredwell, lbw b Willey	17
C F Hartley, lbw b Rashid	15
M E Claydon, not out	2
Extras b 2, lb 3, w 2, nb 2	9
Total (47.5 overs)	245

FoW: 1-3 (Bell-Drummond), 2-53 (Northeast), 3-54 (Billings), 4-66 (Denly), 5-152 (Blake), 6-180 (Stevens), 7-191 (Gidman), 8-212 (Coles), 9-241 (Hartley), 10-245 (Tredwell)

	O	M	R	W
Bresnan	10	1	45	0
Willey	8.5	1	34	3
Plunkett	10	0	52	4
Patterson	6	0	25	1
Rashid	8	0	43	2
Azeem Rafiq	5	0	41	0

Man of the Match: L E Plunkett

Umpires: N A Mallender and A G Wharf   Scorers: J T Potter and L A R Hart
Third Umpire: P K Baldwin

Kent v. Yorkshire

Lyth, Plunkett excel

LIAM PLUNKETT
Awesome catch

Yorkshire marched into the semi-finals for the second consecutive season after a tense tussle in front a capacity crowd.

Lyth, 88, and Plunkett, 4-52, were the outstanding performers as Yorkshire admirably defended a total of 256 to prevail by 11 runs. Put in to bat, Yorkshire were soon without skipper Lees, who miscued a drive at Claydon.

An innings-defining partnership between Lyth and Root then added 90 for the second wicket, Lyth's innings from 95 deliveries proving to be a vital contribution. The pitch was slow, offering a modicum of assistance and making free scoring a challenge. Root consolidated rather than dominated before he was caught in the deep on the leg side for 45 to make it 117-2, ending a stand of 18 overs.

Yorkshire, brimming with internationals, struggled to achieve their intended 280-plus, Bairstow, Bresnan and Willey all failing to contribute significantly — Willey because of a contentious leg-side catch at the wicket. Only a late flurry from Rashid boosted the total.

Coles was the outstanding bowler with 3-39, ably supported by Gidman and Hartley.

Not one to stay out of the limelight for long, Willey trapped Bell-Drummond lbw with a beautiful in-swinger in the second over. Denly and Northeast repaired the damage with a 50 partnership, but neither ever looked settled. Plunkett removed Northeast, clipping to Ballance at mid-wicket for 23, before Patterson had the dangerous Billings lbw with the total on 54. Plunkett grabbed his second scalp, Denly, for a 45-ball 31, but Stevens, so often a thorn in Yorkshire's flesh, combined superbly with Blake as the pair took a particular liking to the spin of Rashid and Rafiq. They added 86 in 13 overs before Blake edged behind off Willey.

Kent were in the ascendancy, needing 109 from 20 overs, but the key wicket of Stevens by Plunkett for 54 turned the game Yorkshire's way as a leading edge was taken one-handed at full stretch by the bowler in a superb show of athleticism. Plunkett added a further wicket before Rashid was reintroduced: he pinned Hartley lbw to make it 241-9, and the win was secured when Willey similarly dismissed Tredwell for 17 with 13 balls remaining, Willey closing with 3-34.

Royal London One-Day Cup Semi-Final
Yorkshire v. Surrey

Played at Headingley, Leeds, on August 28, 2016
Surrey won by 19 runs
Toss won by Yorkshire

SURREY

S M Davies, c Rhodes b Waite		104
D P Sibley, lbw b Brooks		0
K C Sangakkara, c Azeem Rafiq b Bresnan		4
R J Burns, c Patterson b Waite		12
§ B T Foakes, c Brooks b Bresnan		90
S M Curran, b Waite		18
O J Pope, run out (Bairstow/Patterson)		20
T K Curran, not out		2
* G J Batty		
S C Meaker	Did not bat	
J W Dernbach		
Extras lb 2, w 3		5
Total (7 wkts, 50 overs)		255

FoW: 1-3 (Sibley), 2-8 (Sangakkara), 3-61 (Burns), 4-191 (Davies), 5-214 (S M Curran), 6-249 (Foakes), 7-255 (Pope)

	O	M	R	W
Bresnan	10	0	52	2
Brooks	10	1	42	1
Patterson	10	0	53	0
Waite	10	1	48	3
Rhodes	4	0	24	0
Azeem Rafiq	6	0	34	0

YORKSHIRE

A Lyth, c Sibley b Dernbach	4
* A Z Lees, b Batty	26
G S Ballance, c Foakes b Meaker	32
§ J M Bairstow, c Sibley b Meaker	13
J A Leaning, b Meaker	3
T T Bresnan, c Sibley b Dernbach	68
M J Waite, c Batty b S M Curran	38
W M H Rhodes, run out (T K Curran)	23
Azeem Rafiq, c Burns b T K Curran	6
S A Patterson, c Sangakkara b T K Curran	0
J A Brooks, not out	1
Extras lb 11, w 9, nb 2	22
Total (48.5 overs)	236

FoW: 1-10 (Lyth), 2-54 (Lees), 3-75 (Bairstow), 4-80 (Ballance), 5-81 (Leaning), 6-161 (Waite), 7-207 (Rhodes), 8-231 (Rafiq), 9-234 (Patterson), 10-236 (Bresnan)

	O	M	R	W
Dernbach	9.5	0	45	2
S M Curran	10	0	47	1
Batty	10	0	37	1
T K Curran	9	0	35	2
Meaker	10	0	61	3

Man of the Match: S M Davies

Umpires: P J Hartley and J W Lloyds   Scorers: J T Potter and K R Booth
Third Umpire: N G B Cook

Yorkshire v. Surrey

Bresnan's fling in vain

Vikings fell short for the second consecutive season in the semi-finals, Stuart Meaker's pace proving the difference on a sluggish pitch.

A target of 256 was made all the more difficult by a mid-innings collapse before a valiant 68 from Bresnan proved to be in vain.

With a depleted attack, Yorkshire skipper Lees opted to bowl first under leaden skies with moisture in the air.

The pacemen did not quite get their lines right in the opening exchanges

UP AND OVER: Bresnan heaves Meaker for the maximum as Foakes looks on

despite Brooks trapping Sibley lbw without scoring and two balls later Sangakkara mistiming an attempted drive off Bresnan to Rafiq, who held a sharp catch at cover. With Surrey 8-2 Yorkshire were cock-a-hoop, but the elegant poise of Davies became the feature of the opening 20 overs. The same could not be said for Burns, who struggled manfully to break the shackles of an accurate but circumspect attack. He had made 12 from 31 balls when he helped Waite's first delivery straight to long-leg and the hands of Patterson, Surrey 61-3 in the 15th.

The game began to be taken away from Yorkshire by Davies and Foakes. Davies passed his half-century, but Foakes was the main aggressor, the promising wicket-keeper/batsmen reaching his 50 in 61 balls as the pair added a hundred in 120 balls. Davies effortlessly strode to his own landmark, a century off 112 balls, but clubbed a full toss from Waite straight to Rhodes patrolling the leg-side boundary.

The departure of Davies seemed to galvanise the Vikings. Waite added a third wicket after being scooped twice in succession by Sam Curran — a quicker, fuller delivery then disturbing the timbers to give

151

him career-best figures of 3-48. Having eclipsed his highest List A score, Foakes lobbed a simple catch off Bresnan to Brooks at short-fine-leg to depart for 90 from 100 balls.

Patterson and Bresnan closed out the final overs expertly with Surrey struggling to find the boundaries, only 31 coming in the last five overs.

UP AND IN: Patterson catches Burns

Yorkshire ran into early difficulties as Dernbach celebrated the wicket of Lyth. The ball seemed to stop on the batsmen, who sent an attempted drive to cover. Lees and Ballance added 44 with minimal fuss, but the introduction of Batty and Meaker turned the game on its head. Lees made a fluent 26 before he played down the wrong line of a straight one from Batty, and Bairstow hit a curious shot off Meaker to mid-wicket for 13. Ballance looked comfortable, but edged an upper-cut for 32, and Leaning played on to give Meaker a trio of wickets in nine balls for two runs.

A spirited partnership of 80 between Bresnan and Waite brought Yorkshire back into the contest, Bresnan taking stock while allowing his young charger the freedom to play as expansively as he saw fit. The asking rate crept over seven as the final 15 overs arrived, Waite falling on his sword for 38 when he was caught at mid off. The colt left the arena to a standing ovation. Rhodes rode his luck, but began to fashion a worthy partnership with his more experienced partner. They pushed the ball into the gaps, but did not have the wickets in hand to take huge risks.

The final six overs left Yorkshire needing 54 before Rhodes was superbly run out by Tom Curran's direct hit. Meaker's last over went for 13 as Bresnan, having passed his half-century from 70 balls, heaved him for a maximum over long-on. Dernbach came back with a fine over. and Yorkshire needed 27 from three overs. Rafiq could only help a full toss from Tom Curran to Burns on the long-on fence, and it was all on Bresnan to take his side home. Patterson lobbed his first delivery, a slower-ball long-hop, straight to mid-wicket, leaving 21 to get from the last two overs. The end came with the last-but-one ball of the 49th over, with Bresnan caught on the long-off fence for 68. Dernbach was the jubilant bowler as Surrey celebrated a quick return to Lord's.

Royal London One-Day Cup — Group A
Derbyshire v. Yorkshire

Played at Queen's Park, Chesterfield, on June 12, 2016
No result

Toss won by Yorkshire   Yorkshire 1 point, Derbyshire 1 point

DERBYSHIRE

B T Slater, not out		0
B A Godleman, not out		0
H D Rutherford		
W L Madsen		
N T Broom		
S J Thakor		
* A L Hughes	Did not bat	
§ T Poynton		
B D Cotton		
W S Davis		
A Carter		
Extras		0
Total (0 wkts, 1 over)		0

	O	M	R	W
Bresnan	1	1	0	0

YORKSHIRE

A Lyth
* A Z Lees
K S Williamson
G S Ballance
J A Leaning
T T Bresnan
D J Willey
L E Plunkett
§ A J Hodd
S A Patterson
K Carver

Umpires: I D Blackwell and N A Mallender   Scorers: J T Potter and J M Brown

Royal London One-Day Cup

FINAL TABLES 2016

NORTH GROUP

		P	W	L	T	NR/A	PTS	NRR
1	Northamptonshire Steelbacks (A 5) * ...	8	4	3	0	1	9	0.784
2	Warwickshire Bears (B 6) *	8	4	3	0	1	9	0.740
3	**Yorkshire Vikings (A 3) * ....**	**8**	**4**	**3**	**0**	**1**	**9**	**0.596**
4	Worcestershire (A 8) *	8	4	3	0	1	9	0.040
5	Durham (A 4)	8	4	3	0	1	9	-0.634
6	Nottinghamshire Outlaws (B 1)	8	3	4	0	1	7	0.228
7	Derbyshire Falcons (A 7)	8	2	3	0	3	7	-0.335
8	Leicestershire Foxes (A 9)	8	2	3	0	3	7	-0.486
9	Lancashire Lightning (B 5)	8	2	4	0	2	6	-1.328

SOUTH GROUP

		P	W	L	T	NR/A	PTS	NRR
1	Somerset (A 6) *	8	6	1	1	0	13	-0.087
2	Kent Spitfires (B 4) *	8	5	3	0	0	10	0.587
3	Essex Eagles (B 2) *	8	4	2	1	1	10	-0.119
4	Surrey (A 1) *	8	4	3	0	1	9	0.992
5	Hampshire Royals (B 3)	8	4	4	0	0	8	0.393
6	Middlesex Panthers (B 7)	8	4	4	0	0	8	0.117
7	Glamorgan (B 8)	8	3	4	0	1	7	-0.320
8	Gloucestershire (A 2)	8	2	5	0	1	5	-0.709
9	Sussex Sharks (B 9)	8	1	7	0	0	2	-0.679

* Qualified for Quarter-Finals

(2015 group positions in brackets)

YORKSHIRE AVERAGES 2016
ROYAL LONDON ONE-DAY CUP

Played 10　　Won 5　　Lost 4　　No Result 1

BATTING AND FIELDING

(Qualification 4 completed innings)

Player	M.	I.	N.O.	Runs	H.S.	100s	50s	Avge	ct/st
T M Head	4	4	0	277	175	1	1	69.25	1
T T Bresnan	9	8	2	361	95*	0	3	60.16	2
A Lyth	10	9	0	439	136	2	1	48.77	3
G S Ballance	6	5	0	213	80	0	1	42.60	2
J A Leaning	8	7	1	195	131*	1	0	32.50	2
A U Rashid	6	5	1	88	41	0	0	22.00	1
D J Willey	9	7	1	123	27	0	0	20.50	2
L E Plunkett	9	7	1	91	25	0	0	15.16	6
A Z Lees	10	9	0	134	32	0	0	14.88	7
A J Hodd	8	6	2	58	13*	0	0	14.50	7
Also played									
J E Root	1	1	0	45	45	0	0	45.00	0
M J Waite	1	1	0	38	38	0	0	38.00	0
K S Williamson	3	2	0	50	40	0	0	25.00	2
W M H Rhodes	3	3	0	57	23	0	0	19.00	2
J M Bairstow	2	2	0	22	13	0	0	11.00	1/1
Azeem Rafiq	6	5	2	28	17*	0	0	9.33	3
S A Patterson	10	5	3	18	8*	0	0	9.00	3
K Carver	4	1	1	12	12*	0	0	—	0
J A Brooks	1	1	1	1	1*	0	0	—	1

BOWLING

(Qualification 4 wickets)

Player	Overs	Mdns	Runs	Wkts	Avge	Best	4wI	RPO
K Carver	13	0	55	5	11.00	3-5	0	4.23
A U Rashid	41.3	1	230	10	23.00	3-23	0	5.54
L E Plunkett	61	1	279	12	23.25	4-52	1	4.57
D J Willey	62.5	5	361	11	32.81	3-34	0	5.74
T T Bresnan	62	6	335	10	33.50	2-22	0	5.40
S A Patterson	61	1	315	9	35.00	2-30	0	5.16
Azeem Rafiq	40	0	269	6	44.83	2-46	0	6.72
Also bowled								
M J Waite	10	1	48	3	16.00	3-48	0	4.80
A Lyth	4	0	29	1	29.00	1-29	0	7.25
J E Brooks	10	1	42	1	42.00	1-42	0	4.20
W M H Rhodes	10	0	56	0	—	0-24	0	5.60

Fourth Royal London One-Day International
England v. Pakistan

Played at Headingley, Leeds, on September 1, 2016

England won by 4 wickets

Toss won by Pakistan

PAKISTAN

Sami Asiam, c Stokes b Plunkett		24
Sharjeel Khan, c Stokes b Jordan		16
* Azhar Ali, c Willey b Rashid		80
Babar Azam, c Plunkett b Ali		12
§ Sarfraz Ahmed, c Plunkett b Rashid		12
Mohammad Rizwan, lbw b Rashid		6
Mohammad Nawaz, st Bairstow b Ali		13
Imad Wasim, not out		57
Hasan Ali, c Root b Jordan		9
Umar Gul, not out		6
Mohammad Irfan Did not bat		
Extras lb 3, w 6, nb 3		12
Total (8 wkts, 50 overs)		247

FoW: 1-24 (Sharjeel), 2-61 (Sami), 3-110 (Babar), 4-136 (Sarfraz), 5-152 (Rizwan), 6-169 (Azhar Ali), 7-180 (Nawaz), 8-236 (Hasan Ali)

	O	M	R	W
Willey	8	2	40	0
Jordan	9	1	42	2
Stokes	4	0	15	0
Plunkett	9	0	61	1
Rashid	10	0	47	3
Ali	10	0	39	2

ENGLAND

J J Roy, c M Rizwan b M Irfan		14
A D Hales, c Sarfraz Ahmed b M Irfan		8
J E Root, c M Irfan b Hasan Ali		30
* E J G Morgan, c Sharjeel Khan b Umar Gul		11
B A Stokes, c Babar Azam b Imad Wasim		69
§ J M Bairstow, run out (Azhar Ali)		61
M M Ali, not out		45
D J Willey, not out		4
LE Plunkett		
A U Rashid Did not bat		
C J Jordan		
Extras lb 3, w 7		10
Total (6 wkts, 48 overs)		252

FoW: 1-15 (Roy), 2-36 (Hales), 3-59 (Root), 4-72 (Morgan0, 5-175 (Stokes), 6-225 (Bairstow)

	O	M	R	W
Mohammad Irfan	5	1	26	2
Umar Gul	10	1	39	1
Hasan Ali	10	0	53	1
Imad Wasim	10	0	50	1
Mohammad Nawaz	10	0	54	0
Azhar Ali	3	0	27	0

Man of the Match: J M Bairstow

Umpires: M Erasmus and R T Robinson   Scorers: J Virr and H Clayton
Third Umpire: S D Fry   Fourth: R J Bailey   Match Referee: J J Crowe

NATWEST T20 BLAST HIGHLIGHTS OF 2016

WINNERS

Northamptonshire, who defeated Durham by 4 wickets

Totals of 150 and over (9)

223-6	v, Durham at Leeds (won)
215-6	v. Northamptonshire at Leeds (won)
180-8	v. Glamorgan at Cardiff (won)
178-7	v. Lancashire at Manchester (lost)
177-5	v. Northamptonshire at Northampton (won)
173-5	v. Worcestershire at Worcester (lost)
166-6	v. Derbyshire at Derby (won)
160-7	v. Nottinghamshire at Nottingham (lost)
156-6	v. Warwickshire at Leeds (won)

Match aggregates of 350 and over (3)

397	Yorkshire (223-6) defeated Durham (174-8) by 49 runs at Leeds
382	Lancashire (204-7) defeated Yorkshire (178-7) by 26 runs at Manchester
355	Yorkshire (215-6) defeated Northamptonshire (140) by 75 runs at Leeds

Century Partnerships (2)

For the 2nd wicket (1)

106	D J Willey and A Z Lees	v. Northamptonshire at Leeds

For the 4th wicket (1)

100	A Z Lees and J A Leaning	v. Northamptonshire at Leeds

4 wickets in an innings (1)

A U Rashid (1)

4-26	v. Glamorgan at Cardiff

3 catches in an innings (1)

A Lyth (1)

3	v. Lancashire at Leeds

Debuts (3)

t 20 cricket: J C Wainman
For Yorkshire: T M Head and D J Willey

Match-By-Match Reports   DAVE CALDWELL

NatWest T20 BLAST — North Group
Yorkshire v. Leicestershire

Played at Headingley, Leeds, on May 27, 2016
Leicestershire won by 54 runs

Toss won by Yorkshire

Leicestershire 2 points, Yorkshire 0 points

LEICESTERSHIRE

* M L Pettini, c Rhodes b Bresnan	0
M J Cosgrove, c Coad b Wainman	20
K J O'Brien, c Rashid b Plunkett	21
B A Raine, c Lyth b Rhodes	48
U Akmal, c Ballance b Plunkett	8
§ N J O'Brien, c Bresnan b Coad	39
T J Wells, c Coad b Bresnan	3
L J Hill, not out	24
N Dexter, not out	5
C J McKay	
J K H Naik	Did not bat
Extras lb 1, w 1, nb 4	6
Total (7 wkts, 20 overs)	174

FoW: 1-0 (Pettini), 2-25 (Cosgrove), 3-51 (K J O'Brien), 4-72 (Akmal), 5-121 (Raine), 6-145 (N J O'Brien), 7-145 (Wells)

	O	M	R	W
Bresnan	4	1	28	2
Wainman	3	0	27	1
Plunkett	4	0	23	2
Rashid	4	0	33	0
Lyth	2	0	17	0
Rhodes	1	0	11	1
Coad	2	0	34	1

YORKSHIRE

A Lyth, c Pettini b Raine	11
* A Z Lees, c McKay b K J O'Brien	3
A U Rashid, c N J O'Brien b Raine	2
J A Leaning, c Raine b Wells	9
G S Ballance, c Naik b K J O'Brien	17
W M H Rhodes, c Wells b Dexter	45
TT Bresnan, c Dexter b Naik	10
L E Plunkett, c K J O'Brien b Dexter	0
§ A J Hodd, b K J O'Brien	1
J C Wainman, not out	12
B O Coad, b Raine	1
Extras lb 2, w 7	9
Total (18.4 overs)	120

FoW: 1-13 (Lyth), 2-16 (Lees), 3-20 (Rashid), 4-32 (Leaning), 5-62 (Ballance), 6-89 (Bresnan), 7-89 (Plunkett), 8-98 (Hodd), 9-109 (Rhodes), 10-120 (Coad)

	O	M	R	W
McKay	3	0	20	0
Raine	3.4	1	7	3
K J O'Brien	4	0	27	3
Dexter	4	0	26	2
Wells	2	0	19	1
Naik	2	0	19	1

Man of the Match: B A Raine

Umpires: R J Evans and M A Gough

Scorers: J T Potter and P J Rogers

Runs leaked, catches dropped

WILL RHODES
Fight in his classy 45

Yorkshire's *T20* woes of earlier years manifested themselves at the first hurdle. They seemed to have a lid on the Foxes as their fifth wicket fell at 121 in the 16th over, but they haemorrhaged runs, Niall O'Brien and Hill making them pay for sloppy out cricket and ill-disciplined bowling.

Bresnan announced his return from injury with a wicket maiden, Pettini finding the waiting hands of Rhodes at point. Wainman, marking his *T20* debut for Yorkshire, bagged the wicket of Cosgrove for 20, Coad holding the catch on the square-leg fence.

Three catches were spilled. Plunkett's dropped chance off Rashid as Raine was starting to cut loose was certainly the most charitable of the let-offs. Raine top-scored with 48 from 43 balls, but it was the final 10 overs that effectively cost Yorkshire the game as 104 runs were amassed.

The last four overs bled 51 runs, 22 coming in the final over as Hill laid siege on the beleaguered Coad.

Vikings were never in the hunt. Lyth was caught driving at mid-off after a promising start, while Lees, who had struggled with his timing, was taken round the leg-side corner off Kevin O'Brien.

Rashid and Leaning fell in rapid succession, reducing Vikings to 32-4 and leaving them with a mountain to climb. Rhodes showed some fight in a classy innings of 45 from 26 deliveries, but he could not find a partner to mount a challenge with him.

Ballance and Bresnan both showed some appetite for the job, but any faint hopes were extinguished as Ballance fell to Kevin O'Brien for his second of three wickets for 17. Rhodes's best efforts were in vain. He was ninth out in the 17th over, by which point the game had long been decided. Coad was last out, bowled by Raine, as the Vikings were routed by 54 runs.

NatWest T20 BLAST — North Group
Worcestershire v. Yorkshire

Played at New Road, Worcester, on June 2, 2016
Worcestershire won by 7 wickets

Toss won by Yorkshire — Worcestershire 2 points, Yorkshire 0 points

YORKSHIRE

* A Z Lees, b Mitchell		46
D J Willey, b Barnard		6
A U Rashid, run out (Kervezee/Cox)		1
J A Leaning, c Cox b Leach		24
G S Ballance, b Leach		24
W M H Rhodes, b Leach		3
T T Bresnan, not out		29
L E Plunkett, not out		34
§ A J Hodd		
J C Wainman	Did not bat	
B O Coad		
Extras lb 2, w 2, nb 2		6
Total (6 wkts, 20 overs)		173

FoW: 1-34 (Willey), 2-36 (Rashid), 3-74 (Lees), 4-92 (Leaning), 5-99 (Rhodes), 6-112 (Ballance).

	O	M	R	W
Leach	4	0	33	3
Henry	4	0	32	0
Barnard	4	0	45	1
D'Oliveira	3	0	25	0
Russell	2	0	21	0
Mitchell	3	0	15	1

WORCESTERSHIRE

T Kohler-Cadmore, b Plunkett		19
* D K H Mitchell, c Ballance b Plunkett		29
J M Clarke, c Ballance b Rashid		34
A N Kervezee, not out		52
B L D'Oliveira, not out		34
R A Whiteley		
§ O B Cox		
J Leach	Did not bat	
M J Henry		
E G Barnard		
C J Russell		
Extras lb 1, w 5		6
Total (3 wkts, 19.1 overs)		174

FoW: 1-44 (Mitchell), 2-57 (Kohler-Cadmore), 3-108 (Clarke).

	O	M	R	W
Wainman	2	0	22	0
Bresnan	4	0	29	0
Plunkett	4	0	29	2
Rhodes	2	0	24	0
Rashid	4	0	39	1
Coad	3.1	0	30	0

Man of the Match: J Leach

Umpires: N L Bainton and A G Wharf — Scorers: J T Potter and S M Drinkwater
Third Umpire: S C Gale

Plunkett's efforts in vain

The Vikings' unconvincing form continued as the Royals gave their 4,000-strong support a convincing victory.

Despite an excellent all-round performance from Plunkett, his efforts were to be in vain, his side losing by seven wickets.

Yorkshire's batsmen were peering straight down the barrel at one stage before a stunning late rally from Bresnan and Plunkett produced 61 from the final 17 balls.

Plunkett hammered an unbeaten 34 from a mere 10 deliveries, while Bresnan struck 29 from 13 balls.

Batsmen had found the sluggish pitch hard to get to

LIAM PLUNKETT: Hammered 34 in 10 balls, and took two wickets

grips with as they came and went in relatively meek fashion. Willey, appearing only as batsmen, played on for six, and Rashid, promoted to No. 3, fell short of his ground attempting an ill-advised second run. Lees looked in good touch before he was castled by Mitchell for a 36-ball 46, the score having advanced to 74 in the 11th over.

The middle overs proved a struggle as boundaries dried up and wickets fell, but the late onslaught brought a seventh-wicket undefeated stand of 61 and a total that few in the ground had thought achievable. Thirty runs were plundered from the last-but-one over as Barnard's bowling fell to pieces.

Wainman and Bresnan both struggled to pin down the Royals' opening pair of Mitchell and Kohler-Cadmore, but Plunkett made a much needed breakthrough, Mitchell driving straight to mid-on and the hands of Ballance with the total on 44. Plunkett gathered his second victim as Kohler-Cadmore was deceived by a slower one and bowled for 19.

Worcestershire never looked likely to stutter in pursuit of the target, runs coming at a steady eight an over as the game drifted to its conclusion without a hint of trepidation. Kervezee and D'Oliveira completed the task with an unbeaten stand of 66 with five balls remaining, but in truth the Royals' triumph was far more emphatic.

Played at Old Trafford, Manchester, on June 3, 2016
Lancashire won by 26 runs

Toss won by Yorkshire   Lancashire 2 points, Yorkshire 0 points

LANCASHIRE

M J Guptill, c Lees b Bresnan		13
A N Petersen, c Bairstow b Patterson		16
K R Brown, c Ballance b Patterson		54
L S Livingstone, c Coad b Plunkett		55
§ J C Buttler, c Bresnan b Coad		23
* S J Croft, not out		9
J Clark, c Bairstow b Bresnan		28
N Wagner, c Root b Bresnan		2
A M Lilley		
S D Parry		
G A Edwards		
Extras lb 1, w 3		4
Total (7 wkts, 20 overs)		204

FoW: 1-24 (Guptill), 2-31 (Petersen), 3-129 (Livingstone), 4-160 (Buttler), 5-167 (Brown), 6-202 (Clark), 7-204 (Wagner)

	O	M	R	W
Root	2	0	25	0
Bresnan	4	0	24	3
Patterson	4	0	35	2
Rhodes	1	0	15	0
Plunkett	4	0	39	1
Coad	3	0	36	1
Rashid	2	0	29	0

YORKSHIRE

* A Z Lees, c Lilley b Edwards		16
D J Willey, c Croft b Wagner		10
J E Root, not out		92
§ J M Bairstow, c Buttler b Lilley		18
G S Ballance, c Petersen b Parry		8
T T Bresnan, c Brown b Lilley		3
L E Plunkett, c Clark b Edwards		22
W M H Rhodes, c Parry b Edwards		0
A U Rashid, not out		1
S A Patterson		
B O Coad		
Extras lb 5, w 1, nb 2		8
Total (7 wkts, 20 overs)		178

FoW: 1-29 (Lees), 2-29 (Willey), 3-69 (Bairstow), 4-86 (Ballance), 5-98 (Bresnan), 6-174 (Plunkett), 7-175 (Rhodes)

	O	M	R	W
Wagner	4	0	39	1
Clark	3	0	30	0
Edwards	4	0	33	3
Parry	4	0	32	1
Lilley	3	0	23	2
Croft	2	0	16	0

Man of the Match: L S Livingstone

Umpires: R T Robinson and A G Wharf   Scorers: J T Potter and and C Rimmer
Third Umpire: G D Lloyd

The scoresheet for Yorkshire's match against Warwickshire at Edgbaston on June 10, which was abandoned without a ball bowled, appears at the end of this section.

Lancashire v. Yorkshire

Root 92, but Red Rose win

Yorkshire fell to a third consecutive defeat when a 205-run target proved far too much as their hosts out-spun, out-hit and out-fielded them in front of the now obligatory capacity crowd.

With both sides containing big international names, Yorkshire got on top first: Guptill aimed to the long-off boundary, miscued and fell to a sprawling catch over his shoulder by Lees. Petersen soon followed, skying a good-length Patterson delivery for Bairstow to take a steepler.

The complexion of the innings changed swiftly as Livingstone and Brown set about the beleaguered attack with a savage display of clean and powerful hitting. The pair had added 98 in just over eight overs when Livingstone, having completed the fastest *T20* half century for the hosts from only 21 balls, was caught by Coad at extra-cover off Plunkett.

Rashid, Rhodes and Root all struggled to contain their *Red Rose* adversaries as Buttler joined Brown to

JOE ROOT: Stranded on 92 as target got away

show his international credentials with a wonderful ramp for six off Plunkett in his cameo 23 from 11 balls. The Vikings stuck gamely to their plans, and were rewarded with wickets in the final five overs. They were thankful to the miserly Bresnan, whose 3-24 kept the total down.

Vikings began brightly, Lees striking the ball nicely through the covers before he picked out the lone fielder on the leg-side boundary. Willey fell next ball, caught at mid-off, and the score had slipped to 29-2. The partnership between Bairstow and Root escalated until Bairstow was harshly adjudged caught at the wicket off Lilley. Ballance and Bresnan came and went, while Root went through his repertoire, but the asking rate became unmanageable. Plunkett and Root put on 76 in seven overs, but a target of 31 in the last over was far too much. Plunkett fell for 22, and Rhodes went first ball, leaving the shell-shocked Root unbeaten on 92 from 53 balls with eight fours and three sixes.

NatWest T20 BLAST — North Group
Yorkshire v. Nottinghamshire

At Headingly, Leeds, on June 17, 2016
Match abandoned without a ball bowled
Yorkshire 1 point, Nottinghamshire 1 point

Umpires: N G C Cowley and G D Lloyd   Scorers: J T Potter and R Marshall

Yorkshire v. Derbyshire

Played at Headingley, Leeds, on June 19, 2016
Yorkshire won by 1 run (D/L method)

Toss won by Yorkshire   Yorkshire 2 points, Derbyshire 0 points

DERBYSHIRE

N T Broom, c Bairstow b Willey	5
H D Rutherford, c Lyth b Azeem Rafiq	15
C F Hughes, c Plunkett b Azeem Rafiq	4
S J Thakor, b Bresnan	30
W L Madsen, c Azeem Rafiq b Carver	10
J D S Neesham, c Ballance b Plunkett	29
* A L Hughes, c Azeem Rafiq b Bresnan	23
§ T Poynton, run out (Williamson/Bairstow)	13
M J J Critchley, b Bresnan	10
B D Cotton, not out	0
A Carter	Did not bat
Extras b 4, lb 6, w 4	14
Total (9 wkts, 20 overs)	153

FoW: 1-18 (Broom), 2-23 (C F Hughes), 3-35 (Rutherford), 4-49 (Madsen), 5-93 (Thakor), 6-113 (Neesham), 7-142 (Poynton), 8-144 (A L Hughes), 9-153 (Critchley)

	O	M	R	W
Willey	4	0	29	1
Bresnan	3	0	22	3
Azeem Rafiq	4	0	33	2
Carver	3	0	17	1
Patterson	4	0	29	0
Plunkett	2	0	13	1

YORKSHIRE
(D/L par score at stoppage: 66-3)

A Lyth, lbw b Critchley	30
D J Willey, lbw b Madsen	8
* K S Williamson, run out (A L Hughes)	21
J E Root, not out	5
§ J M Bairstow, not out	3
G S Ballance	
T T Bresnan	
L E Plunkett	Did not bat
S A Patterson	
K Carver	
Azeem Rafiq	
Extras	0
Total (3 wkts, 9 overs)	67

FoW: 1-26 (Willey), 2-52 (Lyth), 3-61 (Williamson)

	O	M	R	W
Madsen	3	0	17	1
Cotton	1	0	13	0
Neesham	2	0	21	0
Critchley	2	0	13	1
A L Hughes	1	0	3	0

Man of the match: Azeem Rafiq

Umpires: R J Bailey and D J Millns   Scorers: J T Potter and J M Brown

Yorkshire v. Derbyshire

Rafiq helps break duck

ADAM LYTH: Beating the rain

At last Yorkshire's *T20* campaign found the winning formula, albeit in fortunate circumstances as the Duckworth-Lewis method yielded a one-run victory after persistent rain finally broke from the clouds.

A 7,000-strong crowd, buoyed by the news that their England stars would be available, were greeted with the reintroduction of Azeem Rafiq after a two-year absence.

Electing to field, Yorkshire always held the upper hand, regularly taking wickets to keep Falcons' progress in check. Willey claimed the first wicket, strangling Broom down the leg side at 18, before Rafiq was introduced by stand-in skipper Williamson during the power play.

Rafiq was soon rewarded as Plunkett held on to a miscue from Chesney Hughes, and then Rutherford was caught in the deep. The first six overs had brought 40 runs when the fourth wicket fell in the ninth over, Madsen finding the waiting hands of Rafiq, Carver the gleeful bowler.

The most productive partnership came from Neesham and Thakor, ensuring that the visitors would have some platform for a late assault. Neesham was beaten for pace by Plunkett, Ballance taking the catch, and a disciplined 30 from Thakor was ended by a Bresnan yorker. Yorkshire conceded only 25 runs from the last four overs.

The Vikings' reply was swift with the clouds ominous. They had eclipsed 50 at the end of the powerplay for the loss of Willey, lbw playing across the line. Williamson lofted a straight six into the stands, but was caught short of his ground at the non-striker's end when Lyth drove hard down the pitch. 52-2. Lyth was trapped in front for 30 before Root and Bairstow negotiated the ninth over with no further alarms and, more crucially, one run ahead of the required rate as the heavens opened.

NatWest T20 BLAST — North Group
Durham v. Yorkshire

Played at Riverside, Chester-le-Street, on June 24, 2016
Durham won by 6 runs (D/L method)

Toss won by Durham   Durham 2 points, Yorkshire 0 points

YORKSHIRE

A Lyth, b Rushworth		4
* A Z Lees, c Richardson b Borthwick		43
K S Williamson, b Rushworth		8
J A Leaning, c Rushworth b Arshad		48
G S Ballance, c Mustard b Borthwick		2
T T Bresnan, c Mustard b Coughlin		19
§ A J Hodd, c Muchall b Arshad		1
Azeem Rafiq, c and b Rushworth		1
J Shaw, run out (Stoneman)		1
S A Patterson, c Mustard b Coughlin		3
K Carver, not out		0
Extras lb 2, w 2		4
Total (19.3 overs)		134

FoW: 1-4 (Lyth), 2-34 (Williamson), 3-60 (Lees), 4-69 (Ballance), 5-102 (Bresnan), 6-111 (Hodd), 7-114 (Rafiq), 8-118 (Shaw), 9-134 (Leaning), 10-34 (Patterson)

	O	M	R	W
Rushworth	4	1	14	3
Arshad	4	0	41	2
Coughlin	3.3	0	27	2
Borthwick	3	0	24	2
Pringle	3	0	20	0
Jennings	2	0	6	0

DURHAM
(D/L par score at stoppage: 62-3)

* M D Stoneman, c Ballance b Azeem Rafiq		25
§ P Mustard, c Shaw b Bresnan		8
B A Stokes, c Williamson b Lyth		5
G J Muchall, not out		9
R D Pringle, not out		20
S G Borthwick		
K K Jennings		
P Coughlin	Did not bat	
U Arshad		
C Rushworth		
M J Richardson		
Extras w 1		1
Total (3 wkts, 9.5 overs)		68

FoW: 1-26 (Mustard), 2-37 (Stoneman), 3-38 (Stokes)

	O	M	R	W
Bresnan	2	0	23	1
Shaw	1	0	10	0
Azeem Rafiq	3.5	0	22	1
Lyth	1	0	2	1
Carver	2	0	11	0

Man of the Match: C Rushworth

Umpires: S A Garratt and J W Lloyds   Scorers: J T Potter and B Hunt

Durham v. Yorkshire

Ballance drop proves costly

JACK LEANING: Workmanlike 48

Lightning did not strike twice for the Vikings as Duckworth-Lewis this time conspired against them. Lightning lit up the sky, and play was ended by a deluge.

Durham, 68-3 in the 10th over, were six runs to the good. That would not have been the case four balls earlier had Ballance held on to a relatively straight forward chance at long-off.

Instead, Pringle got away with two runs and the Vikings were left bottom of the group.

Yorkshire's batting had again been inauspicious as they mustered a meagre 134 all out. Lees provided the meat of the entertainment as he struck a 24-ball 43 before he was third out, caught superbly at long-on by Richardson off the leg-spin of Borthwick. His innings took some time to catch fire with only three scored from his first 11 deliveries, in stark contrast to 34 from his next nine.

Lyth and Williamson both fell early, but Leaning fought his way through a recent poor spell with a workmanlike 48 from 36 balls. Wickets fell at increasingly regular intervals at the other end, and no batsman other than the reliable Bresnan, 19, could give Leaning the support he needed. Leaning was ninth out in the 19th over, Arshad recovering from an earlier buffeting from Lees to have him caught. Rushworth was the pick of the attack with sterling figures of 3-14.

Durham lost Mustard in the fourth over off Bresnan as Josh Shaw, recalled from Gloucestershire, took the catch. Stoneman clearly had one eye on the gathering clouds as he quickly got into his stride before Rafiq ended his offensive on 25. Stokes, playing only as batsmen in this game, fell to a superb catch at short extra-cover by Williamson, who parried a fierce drive before diving full length to complete the catch off Lyth. The contest was concluded as the storm broke, Muchall hitting what was to be the final delivery for four to ensure a home victory.

NatWest T20 BLAST — North Group
Yorkshire v. Lancashire

Played at Headingley, Leeds, on July 1, 2016
Yorkshire won by 5 runs

Toss won by Lancashire   Yorkshire 2 points, Lancashire 0 points

YORKSHIRE

A Lyth, c Procter b Buck		23
* A Z Lees, c Livingstone b Buck		5
K S Williamson, b Parry		28
JA Leaning, b Clark		29
G S Ballance, c Petersen b Buck		12
T T Bresnan, c Clark b Edwards		5
W M H Rhodes, not out		24
§ A J Hodd, c Clark b Edwards		2
Azeem Rafiq, not out		6
S A Patterson		
K Carver	Did not bat	
Extras lb 1, w 6		7
Total (7 wkts, 18 overs)		141

FoW: 1-32 (Lyth), 2-32 (Lees), 3-76 (Leaning), 4-97 (Williamson), 5-107 (Bresnan), 6-116 (Ballance), 7-130 (Hodd)

	O	M	R	W
Buck	4	0	25	3
Clark	3	0	37	1
Edwards	4	0	24	2
Lilley	2	0	14	0
Parry	3	0	21	1
Croft	2	0	19	0

LANCASHIRE

J Clark, c Lyth b Patterson		9
A N Petersen, c Leaning b Rhodes		15
K R Brown, c Azeem Rafiq		19
L S Livingstone, c Ballance b Carver		36
* S J Croft, c Leaning b Carver		5
L A Procter, c Carver b Bresnan		16
A M Lilley, c Carver b Rhodes		2
§ T M Moores, c Lyth b Patterson		9
S D Parry, c Hodd b Patterson		15
N L Buck, c Lyth b Bresnan		0
G A Edwards, not out		2
Extras b 3, lb 4, w 1		8
Total (17.4 overs)		136

FoW: 1-23 (Clark), 2-26 (Petersen), 3-49 (Brown), 4-87 (Croft), 5-87 (Livingstone), 6-92 (Lilley), 7-112 (Procter), 8-117 (Moores), 9-123 (Buck), 10-136 (Parry)

	O	M	R	W
Bresnan	4	0	30	2
Patterson	3.4	0	23	3
Rhodes	2	0	18	2
Azeem Rafiq	4	0	20	1
Carver	3	0	34	2
Lyth	1	0	4	0

Man of the Match: Azeem Rafiq

Umpires: N G B Cook and J H Evans   Scorers: J T Potter and C Rimmer
Third Umpire: S A Garratt

Yorkshire v. Lancashire

Carver carves Roses win

Yorkshire won this vital clash in front of a packed house and under devilish grey skies.

Lancashire needed 74 from eight overs with seven wickets in hand after Yorkshire had scrambled to 141-7 from their rain-reduced allocation of 18.

Carver then found himself despatched for three successive sixes by Livingstone before clawing the game back with two quick wickets, Livingstone for an 18-ball 36 and Croft per-ishing in the deep.

Safe hands: Carver pouches Lilley

With rain starting to fall, Lancashire had one eye on the Duckworth-Lewis requirement, but they were pegged back by Carver again, this time as catcher. Procter offered a simple catch to mid-wicket off Bresnan, making Lightning 112-7 with 19 balls remaining. It was one of two catches for Carver in addition to his brace of wickets.

Bresnan and Patterson showed steely determination and no little guile in the closing four overs. Lancashire were left needing 12 from the last over and a solitary wicket remaining. Six runs came from the first three deliveries before Patterson found the edge of Parry's bat to end the contest. Notably, Yorkshire's fielding in the closing stages was of the highest calibre, with some exemplary out-cricket.

Earlier, Yorkshire had got off to a flier in the first three overs. Lyth continued his purple patch with aggressive strokes aplenty, but his cameo of 23 runs from 14 balls was ended by the impressive Buck, one of three victims for the medium-pacer. Lees departed with the score still on 32, but Yorkshire ended the power play positively enough on 40-2.

Mini partnerships followed, Ballance and Williamson both making reasonable contributions, but Lancashire's bowlers were responsive as a unit and never let Vikings break the shackles. A late cameo of 24 in 14 balls by Rhodes helped Yorkshire to make 25 from the final three overs, giving them a total worthy of defending on a sluggish pitch.

169

NatWest T20 BLAST — North Group
Yorkshire v. Warwickshire

Played at Headingley, Leeds, on July 8, 2016
Yorkshire won by 2 runs

Toss won by Yorkshire   Yorkshire 2 points, Warwickshire 0 points

YORKSHIRE

A Lyth, c Javid b Hannon-Dalby		12
D J Willey, c Porterfield b Hannon-Dalby		10
* A Z Lees, b Poysden		23
K S Williamson, run out (Wade)		48
G S Ballance, b Clarke		33
T T Bresnan, c Porterfield b Gordon		10
L E Plunkett, not out		2
J A Leaning, not out		6
A U Rashid		
§ A J Hodd	Did not bat	
Azeem Rafiq		
Extras b 1, lb 6, w 3, nb 2		12
Total (6 wkts, 20 overs)		156

FoW: 1-13 (Lyth), 2-34 (Willey), 3-53 (Lees), 4-131 (Ballance), 5-147 (Bresnan), 6-147 (Williamson)

	O	M	R	W
Clarke	4	0	30	1
Hannon-Dalby	4	0	33	2
Gordon	4	0	27	1
Patel	4	0	22	0
Poysden	3	0	26	1
Javid	1	0	11	0

WARWICKSHIRE

S R Hain, lbw b Willey		0
* I R Bell, st Hodd b Rashid		30
W T S Porterfield, c Hodd b Bresnan		48
§ M S Wade, c Lees b Rashid		6
L J Evans, c Williamson b Azeem Rafiq		37
R Clark, run out (Willey)		9
A Javid, run out (Lyth/Bresnan)		8
J S Patel, c Leaning b Willey		0
R O Gordon, c and b Bresnan		0
J E Poysden, run out (Hodd)		0
O J Hannon-Dalby, not out		2
Extras b 1, lb 2, w 11		14
Total (20 overs)		154

FoW: 1-1 (Hain), 2-52 (Bell), 3-60 (Wade), 4-120 (Evans), 5-141 (Porterfield), 6-145 (Clarke), 7-146 (Patel), 8-146 (Gordon), 9-147 (Poysden), 10-154 (Javid)

	O	M	R	W
Willey	4	0	28	2
Bresnan	4	0	31	2
Plunkett	3	0	37	0
Azeem Rafiq	4	0	21	1
Rashid	4	0	30	2
Lyth	1	0	4	0

Man of the Match : K S Williamson

Umpires: R J Evans and S J O'Shaughnessy   Scorers: J T Potter and M D Smith

Williamson stars in nail-biter

KANE WILLIAMSON: Winning 48

Yorkshire claimed a second nail-biting victory in a week after a dramatic comeback against a Birmingham side cruising to victory in pursuit of a below-par 156.

With six wickets in hand and 16 needed from 13 balls, the visitors imploded as tight bowling and livewire fielding brought another tense finale.

Hain fell without scoring to the first ball of the innings before Bell and Porterfield added a half-century partnership for the second wicket.

A fourth-wicket stand of 60 appeared to have the match won for Bears but Bresnan and Willey bowled with economy and skill as Porterfield edged behind to Hodd off Bresnan for a well-constructed 48, and Clarke was needlessly run out by Lyth for nine. The 19th over was closed by Willey removing Patel for a duck, thus crucially exposing the tail. Gordon offered a return catch to Bresnan with the first ball of the last over and the score on 146. A further run was added before Hodd ran out Poysden.

It all came down to the final ball with a boundary to tie the game. Javid hit hard towards the long-on fence, only for a supremely athletic effort from Lyth to thwart the ball on its intended destination. The fielder then fired in an arrow-like return to find Javid short of his ground, and the Vikings had secured the points by the narrowest of margins.

Yorkshire had struggled with the bat, again finding the initial power-play overs hard to negotiate. Indeterminate stroke-play again proved to be the downfall for openers Lyth and Willey as former Yorkshire seamer Hannon-Dalby bagged both scalps, caught in the circle.

Lees made some inroads with a breezy 23, but at 53 in the eighth over a significant contribution was needed. Williamson and Ballance provided a welcome partnership of 78 from 59 deliveries before Ballance was bowled by Clarke for 33. Williamson was run out in the final over for a 42-ball 48, but he had been pivotal in Yorkshire breaching 150 and, as it transpired, his innings was a match-winning one.

NatWest T20 BLAST — North Group
Derbyshire v. Yorkshire

Played at The County Ground, Derby, on July 10, 2016
Yorkshire won by 1 run

Toss won by Derbyshire

Yorkshire 2 points, Derbyshire 0 points

YORKSHIRE

A Lyth, c Critchley b Carter		19
D J Willey, c Madsen b Durston		33
* A Z Lees, c Hosein b Thakor		0
K S Williamson, b Neesham		65
J A Leaning, lbw b Critchley		1
W M H Rhodes, c Madsen b Durston		8
T T Bresnan, not out		24
L E Plunkett, not out		9
A U Rashid		
§ A J Hodd	Did not bat	
Azeem Rafiq		
Extras lb 6, w 1		7
Total (6 wkts, 20 overs)		166

FoW: 1-46 (Lyth), 2-48 (Lees), 3-80 (Willey), 4-91 (Leaning), 5-101 (Rhodes), 6-149 (Williamson)

	O	M	R	W
Durston	4	0	17	2
Thakor	4	0	34	1
Carter	4	0	40	1
Neesham	4	0	41	1
A L Hughes	1	0	11	0
Critchley	3	0	17	1

DERBYSHIRE

H D Rutherford, st Hodd b Rashid		44
* W J Durston, lbw b Bresnan		5
N T Broom, lbw b Rashid		37
C F Hughes, c Bresnan b Willey		35
W L Madsen, st Hodd b Rashid		13
J D S Neesham, c Plunkett b Willey		9
S J Thakor, run out (Azeem Rafiq)		3
A L Hughes, c Willey b Azeem Rafiq		3
M J J Critchley, not out		6
§ H R Hosein, not out		0
A Carter	Did not bat	
Extras b 2, lb 3, w 5		10
Total (8 wkts, 20 overs)		165

FoW: 1-7 (Durston), 2-80 (Rutherford), 3-102 (Broom), 4-124 (Madsen), 5-151 (C F Hughes), 6-153 (Neesham), 7-156 (A L Hughes), 8-159 (Thakor)

	O	M	R	W
Willey	4	0	33	2
Bresnan	3	0	28	1
Plunkett	3	0	35	0
Azeem Rafiq	4	0	28	1
Rashid	4	0	20	3
Rhodes	2	0	16	0

Man of the Match: A U Rashid

Umpires: P J Hartley and N J Llong

Scorers: J T Potter and J M Brown

Derbyshire v. Yorkshire

The 'Rash and Raf' show

ADIL RASHID: Craft and skill

Another tense affair brought Yorkshire a one-run victory as the spin duo of Rashid and Rafiq bowled beautifully to leave Derbyshire short at the death.

The hosts seemed to have the game wrapped up needing 25 with six wickets in hand and three overs remaining.

Rafiq went for eight in the 18th over before Willey turned the game on its head: Chesney Hughes, 35, was caught at extra-cover and Plunkett's fine catch on the leg boundary accounted for Neesham. More importantly, only four had been conceded.

The last over was entrusted to Rafiq. Alex Hughes fell to the second ball, and the last-but-one delivery was driven straight back to the bowler, who ran out Thakor backing up.

This left Derbyshire wanting eight off the last ball: it sailed over long-on for six. Rashid had bowled with craft and skill to earn outstanding figures of 3-20, including the big wicket of Rutherford, who looked well set on 44 before he was drawn down the track, Hodd gleefully whipping off the bails.

Yorkshire's innings was given early impetus as Lyth and Willey looked in ominously good form. They raced to 43 from four overs, 21 coming from the last of them as Willey unleashed his trademark pickup shot to good effect. The middle overs became a struggle on a slow pitch against a disciplined attack. Lyth went for 19, upper-cutting to deep third-man, and Lees fell without scoring, caught behind on the drive.

Williamson and Willey mounted a recovery of sorts, but both found boundaries hard to come by. Willey drove to Madsen at long-off for 33 from 28 deliveries. Williamson passed his half century after two more cheap dismissals, and with Bresnan plundered 48 in just over four overs before he was bowled by Neesham for 65 from 45 balls with six fours and two sixes. A flurry from Plunkett and Bresnan brought 16 in the last over, Bresnan striking the final ball into the marquee.

NatWest T20 BLAST — North Group
Nottinghamshire v. Yorkshire

Played at Trent Bridge, Nottingham, on July 15, 2016
Nottinghamshire won by 3 wickets

Toss won by Yorkshire   Nottinghamshire 2 points, Yorkshire 0 points

YORKSHIRE

A Lyth, c Imran Tahir b Patel		39
* A Z Lees, b Gurney		1
K S Williamson, c Imran Tahir b Mullaney		39
T M Head, c Wessels b Gurney		40
T T Bresnan, b Gurney		17
L E Plunkett, st Read b Imran Tahir		6
W M H Rhodes, run out (Smith/Read)		8
A U Rashid, not out		2
§ A J Hodd		
Azeem Rafiq	Did not bat	
S A Patterson		
Extras lb 1, w 5, nb 2		8
Total (7 wkts, 20 overs)		160

FoW: 1-12 (Lees), 2-55 (Lyth), 3-122 (Head), 4-138 (Williamson), 5-146 (Plunkett), 6-155 (Bresnan), 7-160 (Rhodes)

	O	M	R	W
Patel	4	0	35	1
Gurney	4	0	16	3
Fletcher	4	0	20	0
Christian	1	0	23	0
Mullaney	3	0	30	1
Imran Tahir	4	0	35	1

NOTTINGHAMSHIRE

M J Lumb, b Azeem Rafiq		8
M H Wessels, c Bresnan b Patterson		2
G P Smith, c Rashid b Rhodes		32
* D T Christian, c Lyth b Patterson		12
S R Patel, c Lees b Plunkett		58
B R M Taylor, lbw b Rashid		1
S J Mullaney, run out (Patterson)		1
§ C M W Read, not out		35
L J Fletcher, not out		0
Imran Tahir		
H F Gurney	Did not bat	
Extras b 6, lb 1, w 4, nb 2		13
Total (7 wkts, 19.4 overs)		162

FoW: 1-10 (Lumb), 2-25 (Wessels), 3-47 (Christian), 4-98 (Smith), 5-100 (Taylor), 6-102 (Mullaney), 7-158 (Patel)

	O	M	R	W
Bresnan	3	0	34	0
Azeem Rafiq	4	0	21	1
Patterson	4	0	30	2
Plunkett	2.4	0	31	1
Rashid	4	0	23	1
Rhodes	1	0	11	1
Lyth	1	0	5	0

Man of the Match: C M W Read

Umpires: J H Evans and M J Saggers   Scorers: J T Potter and R Marshall

Nottinghamshire v. Yorkshire

Rule break proves costly

The Vikings' qualification hopes were hanging by a thread after this controversial defeat. The talking point was a no-ball called because Yorkshire had too many fielders inside the circle.

Lees was the man in question, and as captain he was censured later by his club for criticising the umpires' decision. He went on to give a full apology.

The free hit awarded went for a boundary, while the extra ball sailed over the ropes for six, a huge penalty for the White Rose in a game of small margins.

Yorkshire batted first and

TRAVIS HEAD: Tucking in for 40

recovered well after the early dismissal of Lees, bowled by Gurney for one. Lyth and Williamson had reached 55 early in the seventh over when Lyth, having struck 18 in one Dan Christian over, found Tahir on the cover fence and left for 39 in 21 balls.

Debutant Australian Travis Head, while enjoying some luck, tucked into Mullaney and Tahir before he fell for a 25-ball 40. With the score advanced to 138 in the 16th over, Williamson, who had played second fiddle to his partners, went for 39. This signalled a halt to Yorkshire's chance of a big score as the Outlaws turned the screw, taking three further wickets and conceding only 16 runs from the last three overs.

A score of 160 seemed 20 light. Early wickets were needed, and they duly arrived as Lumb was bowled by Rafiq, who shared the new ball with Bresnan. Wessels fell at 25, and Vikings were in the ascendancy. Their vice-like grip brought a third wicket, Christian becoming Patterson's second scalp, and Rafiq and Rashid then bowled beautifully in tandem, each conceding less than six an over.

The Outlaws slipped to 100-5 in the 13th over before a match-winning half-century from Patel turned the game in their favour. He kept one end ticking over as the evergreen Read joined him, striking 35 from 17 balls. Despite losing Patel in the last over for 58, Read struck the winning boundary with two balls remaining.

175

NatWest T20 BLAST — North Group
Yorkshire v. Durham

Played at Headingley, Leeds, on July 20, 2016
Yorkshire won by 49 runs

Toss won by Yorkshire   Yorkshire 2 points, Durham 0 points

YORKSHIRE

A Lyth, c Richardson b Rushworth	....	87
D J Willey, c Richardson b Pringle	....	32
* A Z Lees, b Jennings	....	5
T M Head, c Muchall b Harrison	....	34
J A Leaning, c Pringle b Harrison	....	32
T T Bresnan, c Richardson b Rushworth	....	12
L E Plunkett, not out	....	8
W M H Rhodes, not out	....	0
§ A J Hodd		
K Carver	Did not bat	
Azeem Rafiq		
Extras lb 4, w 9	....	13
Total (6 wkts, 20 overs)		223

FoW: 1-64 (Willey), 2-82 (Lees), 3-165 (Head), 4-174 (Lyth), 5-210 (Bresnan), 6-217 (Leaning)

	O	M	R	W
Rushworth	4	0	41	2
Harrison	4	0	47	2
Arshad	4	0	63	0
Pringle	2	0	21	1
Jennings	4	0	32	1
Borthwick	2	0	15	0

DURHAM

* M D Stoneman, c Azeem Rafiq b Willey	....	15
§ P Mustard, c Willey b Carver	....	15
C S MacLeod, c Lees b Plunkett	....	12
G J Muchall, c Bresnan b Carver	....	25
K K Jennings, c Plunkett b Azeem Rafiq	....	21
M J Richardson, c Leaning b Carver	....	11
R D Pringle, st Hodd b Azeem Rafiq	....	10
U Arshad, c Lyth b Rhodes	....	43
S G Borthwick, not out	....	13
C Rushworth, not out	....	0
J Harrison	Did not bat	
Extras lb 2, w 2, nb 5	....	9
Total (8 wkts, 20 overs)		174

FoW: 1-23 (Stoneman), 2-40 (MacLeod), 3-56 (Mustard), 4-68 (Muchall), 5-95 (Richardson), 6-104 (Jennings), 7-114 (Pringle), 8-173 (Arshad)

	O	M	R	W
Bresnan	1	0	17	0
Willey $	3.5	0	39	1
Plunkett	4	0	13	1
Azeem Rafiq	4	0	27	2
Carver	4	0	40	3
Rhodes	3	0	32	1
Head $	0.1	0	4	0

$ Willey was not allowed to complete his fourth over. Head bowled the final ball.

Man of the Match: A Lyth

Umpires: R J Bailey and R A Kettleborough   Scorers: J T Potter and W Dobson
Third Umpire: B V Taylor

Yorkshire v. Durham

Career-best from Lyth

Over the top: Adam lyth shows Phil Mustard how it is done

Adam Lyth's career-best 87 thrilled the 8,000-strong Yorkshire crowd, but most of his partners were in no mood to stand on ceremony.

Openers Willey and Lyth had surged to 64 in the fifth over when Willey, dropped on 21, lofted to Richardson for a lusty 32 from 14 balls.

Lees dragged on trying a sweep, but this brought Head to the crease. In tandem with Lyth the Aussie blasted away merrily, reminiscent of David Miller in 2012. Lyth's half-century arrived in 34 balls as Yorkshire romped past 100 in the ninth over, and the pace never relented.

Head, having been given a life on five, played with serious power and precision for his 32 until he holed out to long-on at 165 in the 16th.

Lyth eclipsed his previous highest score, and looked well set for a century when he unselfishly went searching for his fourth six, only to be caught on the long-off fence to end an innings that also contained 11 fours, and spanned 54 balls. Leaning found welcome form in the closing stages, striking 32 from 11 balls, including some lusty blows into the West Stand, aided by a couple of dropped chances in the deep. Yorkshire's record innings contained 20 fours and 11 maximums.

Durham's reply, though spirited, never looked like ensuring a close finish. Willey provided Yorkshire's first success, Stoneman caught by Rafiq at mid-off with the score on 26. Plunkett bowled beautifully in his spell, 1-13 in four overs. Carver gained a wicket with his first delivery, disappeared for sixes off the next two, and netted his second wicket with his fourth ball. Carver went on to his best *T20* analysis when a fine Leaning catch on the mid-wicket fence brought him his third victim.

Rafiq contributed a lovely spell in the middle overs, conceding only 27 and claiming two key wickets as Durham fell away, despite a jaunty 43 from Arshad. The Vikings' momentum continued to grow.

NatWest T20 BLAST — North Group
Yorkshire v. Northamptonshire

Played at Headingley, Leeds, on July 22, 2016
Yorkshire won by 75 runs

Toss won by Yorkshire

Yorkshire 2 points, Northamptonshire 0 points

YORKSHIRE

A Lyth, c Prasanna b Gleeson		10
D J Willey, c Prasanna b Ashraf		74
* A Z Lees, c Levi b Crook		35
T M Head, b Ashraf		22
J A Leaning, c Wakely b Crook		30
T T Bresnan, not out		26
L E Plunkett, run out (Wakely)		1
W M H Rhodes, not out		0
§ A J Hodd		
A U Rashid	Did not bat	
Azeem Rafiq		
Extras lb 7, w 10		17
Total (6 wkts, 20 overs)		215

FoW: 1-11 (Lyth), 2-117 (Lees), 3-137 (Willey), 4-184 (Leaning), 5-207 (Head), 6-209 (Plunkett)

	O	M	R	W
Ashraf	4	0	42	2
Gleeson	4	0	31	1
Kleinveldt	4	0	33	0
Prasanna	2	0	35	0
Crook	3	0	26	2
Cobb	2	0	33	0
White	1	0	8	0

NORTHAMPTONSHIRE

J J Cobb, c and b Bresnan		7
§ A M Rossington, c Willey b Plunkett		12
B M Duckett, st Hodd b Rashid		51
* A G Wakely, c Lyth b Plunkett		0
S P Crook, lbw b Azeem Rafiq		43
S Prasanna, run out (Rashid/Hodd)		1
R K Kleinveldt, c Willey b Rashid		1
G G White, b Azeem Rafiq		17
R J Gleeson, c Hodd b Rhodes		3
M A Ashraf, not out		0
R E Levi	absent hurt	0
Extras lb 1, w 2, nb 2		5
Total (15.2 overs)		140

FoW: 1-10 (Cobb), 2-47 (Rossington), 3-47 (Wakely), 4-89 (Duckett), 5-103 (Prasanna), 6-105 (Kleinveldt), 7-133 (Crook), 8-140 (Gleeson), 9-140 (White)

	O	M	R	W
Willey	2	0	17	0
Bresnan	2	0	30	1
Plunkett	4	0	32	2
Azeem Rafiq	2.2	0	21	2
Rashid	4	0	36	2
Rhodes	1	0	3	1

Man of the Match: D J Willey

Umpires: N G B Cook and S C Gale

Scorers: J T Potter and A C Kingston

Yorkshire v. Northamptonshire

Willey leads the charge

An explosive first half-century in Yorkshire colours by David Willey provided the meat of a savage batting display which proved too much for *T20* North leaders Northamptonshire.

For the second time in three days the Vikings' new found energy and intent produced an unassailable total with almost all of the top order contributing to a wonderful exhibition of aggressive batting.

The only man to miss out was Lyth, who made 10 from six balls before the pace of Gleeson forced a false stroke, Prasanna taking the catch.

Willey and Lees proceeded to go through their repertoire, adding 106 in 10 overs. Willey passed his 50 in 31 balls before the stand ended with a stunning

DAVID WILLEY: Savage display with five fours and six sixes

one-handed take by Levi at point to send back Lees for 35. Willey accelerated through the gears until he was caught in the deep by former Yorkshire paceman Ashraf for 74 from 46 balls with five fours and six sixes. Head and Leaning combined effectively in a brisk stand of 47 before Leaning was caught by Wakely, having surged to 30 in 14 balls. Vikings passed 200 before losing Head in the last over for 22, Bresnan completing the carnage with three sixes in his nine-ball onslaught of 26.

Steelbacks soon lost Cobb, caught and bowled by Bresnan, but the much talked about left-hander Duckett proved himself up to the task, striking Bresnan for five boundaries in an over. Two wickets in consecutive balls from Plunkett ended Rossington and Wakely's involvement in the fifth over with the score on 47. Duckett passed his half-century before Rashid tempted him down the track, allowing Hodd to finish the job. Duckett had made 51 from 23 balls.

A steady stream of wickets followed as the target receded into the distance. The spin twins of Rashid and Rafiq gave Yorkshire control and cutting edge. A spirited knock from Crook aside, Northamptonshire meekly surrendered, nine down in the 16th over with Levi unable to bat and Rashid, Rafiq and Plunkett claiming two scalps apiece.

NatWest T20 BLAST — North Group
Northamptonshire v. Yorkshire

Played at Wantage Road, Northampton, on July 29, 2016
Yorkshire won by 14 runs

Toss won by Yorkshire

Yorkshire 2 points, Northamptonshire 0 points

YORKSHIRE

A Lyth, c White b Gleeson		5
D J Willey, c White b Crook		17
* A Z Lees, b Gleeson		59
T M Head, b White		17
J A Leaning, c Keogh b Azharullah		64
T T Bresnan, not out		7
L E Plunkett, not out		0
W M H Rhodes		
A U Rashid	Did not bat	
§ A J Hodd		
Azeem Rafiq		
Extras lb 3, w 3, nb 2		8
Total (5 wkts, 20 overs)		177

FoW: 1-9 (Lyth), 2-29 (Willey), 3-63 (Head), 4-163 (Lees), 5-173 (Leaning)

	O	M	R	W
Kleinveldt	4	0	38	0
Gleeson	3	0	15	2
Crook	2	0	17	1
Azharullah	4	0	39	1
White	3	0	27	1
Cobb	1	0	11	0
Prasanna	3	0	27	0

NORTHAMPTONSHIRE

J J Cobb, lbw b Willey		0
§ A M Rossington, c Rashid b Bresnan		1
B M Duckett, c Willey b Azeem Rafiq		41
* A G Wakely, c Lyth b Bresnan		64
S P Crook, b Rashid		10
R I Keogh, b Willey		28
R K Kleinveldt, c Azeem Rafiq b Bresnan		13
S Prasanna, not out		1
G G White, not out		1
R J Gleeson		
M Azharullah	Did not bat	
Extras lb 1, w 3		4
Total (7 wkts, 20 overs)		163

FoW: 1-0 (Cobb), 2-20 (Rossington), 3-46 (Duckett), 4-71 (Crook), 5-137 (Keogh), 6-161 (Wakely), 7-161 (Kleinveldt)

	O	M	R	W
Willey	4	0	32	2
Bresnan	4	1	15	3
Plunkett	3	0	37	0
Azeem Rafiq	4	0	37	1
Rashid	4	0	28	1
Rhodes	1	0	13	0

Man of the Match: J A Leaning

Umpires: M Burns and A G Wharf   Scorers: J T Potter and A C Kingston
Third Umpire: R J Bailey

Northamptonshire v. Yorkshire

Leaning's six-hit mayhem

JACK LEANING: Scant regard for public safety

Yorkshire completed a remarkable turn-around in their *T20* campaign to secure a quarter-final place with an excellent 14-run victory to give them their seventh win in nine matches.

The welcome return to form of Leaning and Lees provided the bulk of the runs after the Vikings had slipped to 63-3 in a shade over 10 overs.

Lyth and Willey were both taken at point by the effervescent White before the fielder bowled Head, who was aiming at something substantial towards the leg side. Lees took anchor, allowing his partner to blaze away with little regard for public safety, "cow corner" being cleared five times as Leaning raced to his half-century in 22 balls.

The catalyst appeared to be the 13th over, bowled by Kleinveldt, which disappeared for 20 runs and gave Vikings the impetus required. Lees completed his first 50 of the tournament in a less brutal 45 deliveries, but his contribution was not to be under-estimated.

The skipper's innings was given some discomfort when Azharullah struck him on the arm with a beamer. He fell just after the pair had brought up their century partnership in a little over eight overs, the impressive Gleeson bowling him. Leaning was caught in the deep for 64 from 29 balls as Yorkshire completed their innings with an above par 177.

Willey struck with the first ball of the Steelbacks innings, a perfect in-swinger trapping Cobb lbw. Duckett was clearly in no mood to stand on ceremony as he raced to 41 from 26 balls, despite losing Rossington to Bresnan for one. The key wicket of Duckett fell as Rafiq induced a false stroke and the dangerous left-hander was caught at short fine-leg. 46-3 after six overs. Rashid bowled beautifully mid-innings to stem the tide, including a perfect leg-break to account for Crook. As the asking rate began to climb Wakely produced a fine innings of 64 from 42 balls, but the reintroduction of Bresnan at the death ensured that there would be no tight finish, and he ended with 3-15, the best analysis of the day.

181

NatWest T20 BLAST — Quarter-Final
Glamorgan v. Yorkshire

Played at Sophia Gardens, Cardiff, on August 11, 2016
Yorkshire won by 90 runs
Toss won by Yorkshire

YORKSHIRE

A Lyth, c Rudolph b Tait		8
D J Willey, b Ingram		79
* A Z Lees, c Hogan b Wagg		36
J A Leaning, b Ingram		10
W M H Rhodes, lbw b Ingram		1
T T Bresnan, c Ingram b van der Gugten		9
L E Plunkett, c Wagg b Ingram		3
M J Wait, not out		19
A U Rashid, c Hogan b van der Gugten		5
§ A J Hodd, not out		1
Azeem Rafiq	Did not bat	
Extras b 1, lb 2, w 2, nb 4		9
Total (8 wkts, 20 overs)		180

FoW: 1-36 (Lyth), 2-110 (Lees), 3-134 (Willey), 4-141 (Leaning), 5-146 (Rhodes), 6-154 (Plunkett), 7-156 (Bresnan), 8-169 (Rashid)

	O	M	R	W
van der Gugten	4	0	22	2
Wagg	2	0	25	1
Hogan	4	0	39	0
Tait	4	0	34	1
Meschede	1	0	10	0
Salter	1	0	15	0
Ingram	4	0	32	4

GLAMORGAN

D L Lloyd, b Bresnan		0
§ M A Wallace, c Plunkett b Bresnan		6
C A Ingram, c Rhodes b Waite		16
A H T Donald, b Willey		1
* J A Rudolph, c Lyth b Azeem Rafiq		26
G G Wagg, b Plunkett		2
C A J Meschede, c Plunkett b Rashid		1
A G Salter, b Rashid		9
T van der Gugten, c Waite b Rashid		13
M G Hogan, b Rashid		12
S W Tait, not out		0
Extras lb 2, nb 2		4
Total (13 overs)		90

FoW: 1-0 (Lloyd), 2-21 (Wallace), 3-24 (Donald), 4-28 (Ingram), 5-34 (Wagg), 6-37 (Meschede), 7-65 (Salter), 8-71 (Rudolph), 9-86 (van der Gugten), 10-90 (Hogan)

	O	M	R	W
Bresnan	2	0	13	2
Willey	2	0	11	1
Waite	2	0	6	1
Plunkett	3	0	19	1
Rashid	3	0	26	4
Azeem Rafiq	1	0	13	1

Man of the Match: D J Willey

Umpires: N G B Cook and D J Millns   Scorers: J T Potter and A K Hignell
Third Umpire: S J O'Shaughnessy

Glamorgan v. Yorkshire

Willey's blast paves way

Yorkshire strode confidently into Finals Day, overcoming their Welsh counterparts through a swashbuckling 38-ball 79 by David Willey which paved the way for a huge 90-run victory.

It could have been a far closer contest when Glamorgan wrestled their way back after the Vikings had mustered only 46 from the last eight overs, losing six wickets in the process.

This was after Willey and Lees had propelled the total past the century in the first 10 overs. Willey was nigh on impossible to bowl to. Yorkshire raced to 61-1 during the power play overs, Lyth the wicket to fall when he mistimed a Tait slower ball to mid-off.

DAVID WILLEY: Impossible to bowl to with swashbuckling 79

Willey tucked in to all and sundry, Wagg's first over going for a couple of boundaries, while Hogan was given short shrift, three strikes bringing 14 runs. Willey brought up his half-century from 28 balls with a huge maximum blow off a visibly disbelieving Hogan. Lees perished for a more circumspect 36 from 24 balls, offering a simple chance to Hogan in the deep off Wagg. Willey was bowled having an agricultural heave at Ingram.

Vikings then came unstuck, Ingram's leg-spin causing all sorts of problems as he collected career-best figures of 4-32. Despite a jaunty 19 from Waite, 180 seemed a good 30 short of what had looked likely.

Glamorgan's riposte hit the buffers immediately as Bresnan found the bottom edge of Lloyd's bat, the ball clipping the base of the stumps. Ingram went on the attack. only to see his opening partner, Wallace, drive straight to cover, Bresnan again the bowler. Donald came and went, Willey producing a lovely ball to disturb his stumps, while young Waite removed the dangerous Ingram for 16, taken at fine-leg by Rhodes. The score became 34-5 as Plunkett beat Wagg with a snorter.

The disparity between the sides was all too evident. Rudolph, 26, manfully kept the board ticking over, but the result was never in doubt as Rashid, released by England earlier, cleaned up the tail with four wickets in his three overs, the hosts subsiding to 90 all out in 13 overs.

Durham v. Yorkshire

Played at Edgbaston, Birmingham, on August 20, 2016
Durham won by 7 runs
Toss won by Durham

DURHAM

M D Stoneman, b Plunkett		25
K K Jennings, st Bairstow b Azeem Rafiq		11
B A Stokes, c Bresnan b Azeem Rafiq		56
§ M J Richardson, lbw b Rashid		29
J T A Burnham, c Bairstow b Bresnan		17
R D Pringle, b Plunkett		10
* P D Collingwood, not out		2
U Arshad, not out		1
S G Borthwick		
M A Wood	Did not bat	
C Rushworth		
Extras lb 4, w 1		5
Total (6 wkts, 20 overs)		156

FoW: 1-31 (Jennings), 2-47 (Stoneman), 3-119 (Richardson), 4-128 (Stokes), 5-144 (Pringle), 6-154 (Burnham)

	O	M	R	W
Willey	4	0	25	0
Bresnan	4	0	29	1
Azeem Rafiq	4	0	34	2
Plunkett	4	0	22	2
Rashid	2	0	22	1
Root	2	0	20	0

YORKSHIRE

A Lyth, c Stoneman b Rushworth		64
D J Willey, c Collingwood b Rushworth		3
J E Root, c Burnham b Rushworth		7
* A Z Lees, c Stokes b Borthwick		22
§ J M Bairstow, b Wood		3
G S Ballance, c Collingwood b Wood		0
J A Leaning, c Pringle b Arshad		19
T T Bresnan, b Wood		9
L E Plunkett, b Wood		9
A U Rashid, not out		5
Azeem Rafiq, not out		6
Extras lb 1, w 1		2
Total (9 wkts, 20 overs)		149

FoW: 1-21 (Willey), 2-30 (Root), 3-75 (Lees), 4-86 (Bairstow), 5-86 (Ballance), 6-120 (Lyth), 7-122 (Leaning), 8-138 (Plunkett), 9-139 (Bresnan)

	O	M	R	W
Rushworth	4	0	19	3
Wood	4	0	25	4
Arshad	4	0	42	1
Pringle	2	0	17	0
Borthwick	4	0	31	1
Jennings	2	0	14	0

Man of the Match: M A Wood

Umpires: N A Mallender and A G Wharf   Scorers: J T Potter and W Dobson
Third Umpire: R T Robinson   Fourth Umpire: D J Millns

Reverse-sweep: Adam Lyth hits a boundary on the way to his top-score 64 as wicket-keeper Richardson looks on

Wood wrecks the Vikings

Durham's England stars proved too much for the Vikings as Stokes with the bat and Wood with the ball made the difference in this tense encounter which Yorkshire lost by seven runs. Yorkshire were able to name a full strength side, welcoming back Bairstow, Ballance and Root, with Leaning deservedly keeping his place.

Durham elected to bat, and Willey and Bresnan showed supreme control in the opening two overs. Willey then dropped a devilishly hard return catch off Stoneman, injuring his wrist. Stoneman got into his stride with three boundaries in four balls as Durham advanced to 29 in four overs. Rafiq came to the fore almost instantly, turning a ball sharply round the legs of the advancing Jennings for Bairstow to complete a smart stumping.

The powerplay overs left Durham on 39-1, and with Willey still in significant discomfort Lees decided to bowl him for one more over before he left the field for treatment. Plunkett's pace found a way through Stoneman's indecisive shot, the opener making 25 from 20 balls. Durham's first maximum arrived in the ninth over as Stokes lofted the returning Willey over deep square-leg.

A heavy shower stopped play with Jets 60-2 and needing to accelerate. Rashid was straight into the attack on the resumption as light rain returned, and Stokes immediately launched an assault on him. Root nearly had a wicket with his second ball, Bairstow missing a regulation stumping to reprieve Richardson. Durham crept through the gears. Their century arrived in the 13th over, signalling the 50 partnership between

Stokes and Richardson. The stand was worth 72 when it was broken, Rashid's quicker ball trapping Richardson in front for 29. Stokes reached his half-century off 32 balls, but there was another short rain delay before the key wicket of Stokes for 56 provided Vikings with the perfect fillip as he drove Rafiq straight to short extra-cover, where Bresnan took a tumbling catch.

Root dropped Burnham off Bresnan at short fine-leg in the 18th over before Plunkett returned to york Pringle and end with the outstanding figures of 2-21. Bresnan provided a master class in death bowling as the final over yielded only two runs and the wicket of Burnham, Durham finishing on a seemingly below par 156-6.

Lyth and Willey began well enough. Lyth's pull shot for six off Wood was an early highlight, but Willey could not capitalise, splicing a ball from Rushworth to Collingwood at cover for three. Root, having been discomforted by some searing Wood deliveries, fell after an unconvincing knock, scooping an attempted pull straight into the air to be caught at square-leg for seven. Yorkshire reached the powerplay at 43-2 after Arshad conceded three boundaries in the fifth over to boost the total.

A reverse-sweep from Lyth brought up the 50 in 43 balls as Borthwick's introduction was met with 15 runs. The score had reached 75 when Lees mis-pulled and was taken at mid-wicket by Stokes for 22. The key wicket of Bairstow followed, Wood's recall in the 12th over paying instant dividends with a rapid full ball breaching his defences. Ballance fell two balls later when he was unsettled by Wood, and could only nudge to leg gully where Collingwood produced a catch of some distinction. Lyth brought up his half-century in 31 balls as Yorkshire needed consolidation before the final onslaught with rain again in the air.

Lyth and Leaning enjoyed a partnership of 34, but when Lyth found Stoneman at gully off Rushworth to end his top-score innings of 64 the Vikings still needed 37 from 21 balls. Bresnan was dropped first ball at the wicket, and it was now or never for the victory charge.

Leaning's inauspicious innings ended in the hands of Pringle at long-on, leaving it to Bresnan and Plunkett to take up the mantle. The 18th over yielded 13 runs, with Plunkett striking the final ball for six over cow corner. Plunkett's edge off Wood raced for four, leaving Yorkshire requiring 19 off 11 balls before Wood bowled Plunkett.

The key wicket of Bresnan came two balls later, thanks to the whirlwind fast bowling from Wood once again as he finished with a career-best 4-25. Yorkshire were left needing 15 runs from the last over, but Rafiq and Rashid could not muster a boundary between them as the White Rose left the competition eight runs short.

NatWest T20 BLAST — North Group
Warwickshire v. Yorkshire

At Edgbaston. Birmingham, on June 10, 2016
No result

Toss won by Yorkshire   Yorkshire 1 point, Warwickshire 1 point

Rain fell after the toss, and the match was abandoned without a ball bowled

WARWICKSHIRE

S R Hain
* I R Bell
W T S Porterfield
L J Evans
§ L Ronchi
R Clarke
A Javid
J S Patel
M R Adair
O J Hannon-Dalby
J E Poysden

YORKSHIRE

* A Z Lees
D J Willey
K S Williamson
G S Ballance
J A Leaning
T T Bresnan
L E Plunkett
S A Patterson
A U Rashid
§ A J Hodd
K Carver

Umpires: R J Bailey and I D Blackwell   Scorers: J T Potter and M D Smith

NatWest T20 BLAST in 2016

NORTH GROUP

		P	W	L	T	NR/A	PTS	NRR
1	Nottinghamshire Outlaws (N 5) *	14	8	2	0	4	20	0.741
2	Northamptonshire Steelbacks (N 3) *	14	7	5	0	2	16	0.265
3	**Yorkshire Vikings (N 8) ***	**14**	**7**	**5**	**0**	**2**	**16**	**0.223**
4	Durham Jets (N 6) *	14	6	6	0	2	14	-0.050
5	Lancashire Lightning (N 4)	14	6	7	0	1	13	0.200
6	Birmingham Bears (N 1)	14	6	7	0	1	13	-0.215
7	Derbyshire Falcons (N 9)	14	5	7	0	2	12	0.021
8	Worcestershire Rapids (N 2)	14	5	7	0	2	12	-0.862
9	Leicestershire Foxes (N 7)	14	4	8	0	2	10	-0.180

SOUTH GROUP

		P	W	L	T	NR/A	PTS	NRR
1	Gloucestershire (S 5) *	14	10	3	0	1	21	0.518
2	Glamorgan (S 6) *	14	8	3	0	3	19	1.005
3	Middlesex Panthers (S 9) *	14	7	6	0	1	15	0.395
4	Essex Eagles (S 4) *	14	7	6	0	1	15	0.174
5	Surrey (S 7)	14	7	7	0	0	14	0.153
6	Sussex Sharks (S 2)	14	5	6	0	3	13	-0.053
7	Kent Spitfires (S 1)	14	6	8	0	0	12	-0.643
8	Hampshire Royals (S 3)	14	4	8	0	2	10	-0.691
9	Somerset (S 7)	14	3	10	0	1	7	-0.660

* Qualified for the Quarter-Finals

(2015 group positions in brackets)

YORKSHIRE AVERAGES 2016

NATWEST T20 BLAST

Played 15   Won 8   Lost 6   No Result 1   Abandoned 1

BATTING AND FIELDING

(Qualification 4 completed innings)

Player	M.	I.	N.O.	Runs	H.S.	100s	50s	Avge	ct/st
K S Williamson	7	6	0	209	65	0	1	34.83	2
T M Head	4	4	0	113	40	0	0	28.25	0
J A Leaning	12	11	1	272	64	0	1	27.20	4
D J Willey	11	10	0	272	79	0	2	27.20	5
A Lyth	12	12	0	312	87	0	2	26.00	10
A Z Lees	14	13	0	294	59	0	1	22.61	4
T T Bresnan	15	13	4	180	29*	0	0	20.00	8
L E Plunkett	13	11	5	94	34*	0	0	15.66	5
W M H Rhodes	10	9	3	89	45	0	0	14.83	2
G S Ballance	9	7	0	96	33	0	0	13.71	7
Also played									
J E Root	3	3	2	104	92*	0	1	104.00	1
Azeem Rafiq	11	3	2	13	6*	0	0	13.00	4
J M Bairstow	3	3	1	24	18	0	0	12.00	4/1
A U Rashid	11	6	3	16	5*	0	0	5.33	3
S A Patterson	6	1	0	3	3	0	0	3.00	0
A J Hodd	12	4	1	5	2	0	0	1.66	3/5
B O Coad	3	1	0	1	1	0	0	1.00	3
J Shaw	1	1	0	1	1	0	0	1.00	1
—J C Wainman	2	1	1	12	12*	0	0	—	0
K Carver	5	1	1	0	0*	0	0	—	2

BOWLING

(Qualification 4 wickets)

Player	Overs	Mdns	Runs	Wkts	Avge	Best	4wI	RPO
S A Patterson	15.4	0	117	7	16.71	3-23	0	7.46
T T Bresnan	44	2	353	21	16.80	3-15	0	8.02
K Carver	12	0	102	6	17.00	3-40	0	8.50
Azeem Rafiq	39.1	0	277	15	18.46	2-21	0	7.07
A U Rashid	35	0	286	15	19.06	4-26	1	8.17
D J Willey	27.5	0	214	9	23.77	2-28	0	7.68
W M H Rhodes	14	0	143	6	23.83	2-18	0	10.21
L E Plunkett	40.4	0	330	13	25.38	2-22	0	8.11
Also bowled								
M J Waite	2	0	6	1	6.00	1- 6	0	3.00
A Lyth	6	0	32	1	32.00	1-2	0	5.33
J C Wainman	5	0	49	1	49.00	1-27	0	9.80
B O Coad	8.1	0	100	2	50.00	1-34	0	12.24
J E Root	4	0	45	0	—	0-20	0	11.25
J Shaw	1	0	10	0	—	0-10	0	10.00
T M Head	0.1	0	4	0	—	0-4	0	24.00

Second Eleven 2016

PLAYERS WHO APPEARED FOR YORKSHIRE SECOND ELEVEN IN 2016
(excluding First Eleven capped players)

Player	Date of Birth	Birthplace	Type
K Carver *	March 26, 1996	Northallerton	LHB/SLA
B O Coad *	January 10, 1994	Harrogate	RHB/RMF
M D Fisher *	November 9, 1997	York	RHB/RMF
R Gibson *	January 22, 1996	Middlesbrough	RHB/RM
W M H Rhodes *	March 2, 1995	Nottingham	LHB/RM
J Shaw *	January 3, 1996	Wakefield	RHB/RMF
J A Tattersall *	December 15, 1994	Knaresborough	RHB/LB
J C Wainman *	January 25, 1993	Harrogate	RHB/LMF
M J Waite *	December 24, 1995	Leeds	RHB/RMF
B L Ainsley	November 19, 1997	Middlesbrough	RHB/OB
E Barnes	November 26, 1997	York	RHB/RFM
B D Birkhead	October 28, 1998	Halifax	RHB/WK
H C Brook	February 22, 1999	Keighley	RHB/RM
J W P Brown	March 27, 1998	Sheffield	LHB/LM
E Callis	November 8, 1994	Doncaster	RHB
G J Finn $	March 16, 1988	Halifax	RHB/WK
C J Geldart	December 17, 1991	Huddersfield	LHB
M Hussain	March 27, 1997	Leeds	RHB/LM
Y Imtiaz	March 9, 1998	Huddersfield	RHB/OB
J E G Logan	October 12, 1997	Wakefield	LHB/SLA
A MacQueen	January 12, 1993	Chertsey, Surrey	RHB/OB
L J McKendry	April 25, 1991	Northallerton	RHB/OB
J Read	February 2, 1998	Scarborough	RHB/WK
J W Shutt	June 24, 1997	Barnsley	RHB/OB
J A Thompson	October 9, 1996	Leeds	LHB/RMF
J D Warner	November 14, 1996	Wakefield	RHB/RFM

* Second Eleven cap

$ *G J Finn was due to make his Second Eleven debut v. Leicestershire at Pudsey Congs in the Second Eleven Trophy, but the game was abandoned without a ball bowled.*

SECOND ELEVEN HIGHLIGHTS OF 2016

CHAMPIONSHIP

Century partnerships (5)

For the 1st wicket (1)

   100   B L Ainsley and M Hussain   v. Durham at York

For the 3rd wicket (1)

   160   L J McKendry and A W Gale   v. Durham at York

For the 5th wicket (1)

   172 *   R Gibson and Azeem Rafiq   v. Leicestershire at York

For the 7th wicket (1)

   101   Azeem Rafiq and E Barnes   v. Warwickshire at Edgbaston Foundation
                                                                    Sports Ground

For the 8th wicket (1)

   131   J A Thompson and J C Wainman v. Worcestershire at Scarborough
This was the highest 8th-wicket stand nationally in the 2016 Championship

Centuries (5)

  R Gibson (1)

    162* v. Leicestershire at York

  J A Thompson

    146* v. Worcestershire at Scarborough

  E Callis

    125 v. Warwickshire at Edgbaston Foundation Sports Ground

  L J McKendry

    121 v. Durham at York

  M J Waite

    103* v. Northamptonshire at Market Harborough

Five wickets in an innings (7)

  B O Coad (2)

    6-57 v. Northamptonshire at Market Harborough
    6-58 v. Leicestershire at York

  J C Wainman (2)

    5-24 v. Warwickshire at Edgbaston Foundation Sports Ground
    5-49 v. Worcestershire at Scarborough

  R J Sidebottom (1)

    5-19 v. Nottinghamshire at Trent College

  J A Thompson (1)

    5-60 v. Derbyshire at Belper Meadows

  M D Fisher (1)

    5-70 v. MCC Universities at Stamford Bridge

CHAMPIONSHIP MILESTONES IN 2016

Ryan Gibson completed his 1,000 runs in Second Eleven Championship cricket.

Jordan Thompson hit his maiden Championship century, 146* v. Worcestershire at Scarborough, and took his maiden five-wicket haul, 5-60 v. Derbyshire at Belper Meadows

Karl Carver, with 4-47 v. Northamptonshire at Market Harborough, recorded his best figures in Second Eleven Championship cricket.

TROPHY

Century Partnerships (3)

For the 2nd wicket (2)

143	A Z Lees and R Gibson	v. Durham at York
104	H C Brook and R Gibson	v. Derbyshire at Alvaston and Boulton

For the 3rd wicket (1)

127*	A Z Lees and W M H Rhodes	v. Durham at York

Centuries (1)

A Z Lees (1)

119* v. Durham at York

5 wickets in an innings: None

The best figures were 4-27 by B O Coad v. Derbyshire at Alvaston and Boulton

Five victims in an innings: None

TROPHY MILESTONE FOR 2016

Will Rhodes has 531 runs, and is the leading scorer in the Trophy competition, regularly playing Second Eleven cricket. Azeem Rafiq has 35 wickets, and is the leading bowler among present participants in the competition.

T20 COMPETITION

Century Partnerships: None

The highest stand was 85 for the second wicket between D J Willey and R Gibson v. Durham at Brandon CC (second game)

Centuries (1)

D J Willey (1)

108 v. Durham at Brandon CC (second game)

5 wickets in an innings: None

The best return was 3-16 by M J Waite v. Northamptonshire at Stowe School (first game)

Four victims in an innings: None

The best performance was three by B D Birkhead v. Durham at Brandon CC (first game)

Debuts (5)

E Barnes, B D Birkhead, A MacQueen, L J McKendry and J W Shutt

T20 MILESTONE FOR 2016

Ryan Gibson has 447 runs, 45 behind Jack Leaning. Gibson also has 20 outfield catches, 10 more than Alex Lees. Karl Carver, with 22 wickets, leads the bowlers.

Second Eleven Championship
Warwickshire v. Yorkshire

Played at Edgbaston Foundation Community Sports Ground on June 7, 8 and 9, 2016
Match drawn at 7.34pm on the Third Day

Toss won by Warwickshire   Warwickshire 13 points, Yorkshire 9 points
Close of play: First Day, Warwickshire (1) 136-3 (Westwood 64, Thomason 3, 39 overs), Second
Day, Warwickshire (1) 502-4 (Westwood 230, Mellor 51, 103 overs)

YORKSHIRE

First Innings		Second Innings	
E Callis, b H Brookes	27	run out (Thomason)	125
C J Geldart, c Mellor b Parker	45	c Parker b B L Brookes	7
R Gibson, c Mellor b Parker	42	lbw b Parker	21
* M J Waite, c Mellor b B L Brookes	15	b Jones	33
M Hussain, lbw b Parker	16	c Westwood b Thornton	4
Y Imtiaz, lbw b Parker	0	c Mellor b Thornton	12
Azeem Rafiq, b Sukhjit Singh	40	b Thornton	0
E Barnes, not out	44	b Sukhjit Singh	49
§ B D Birkhead, c Umeed b Sukhjit Singh	0	c Mellor b B L Brookes	0
J C Wainman, c and b Sukhjit Singh	6	not out	6
K Carver, c H Brookes b Sukhjit Singh	10	c Westwood b Thornton	1
J D Warner	Did not bat		
Extras b 8, lb 5, nb 2, w 1	16	Extras b 20, lb 7, nb 10, w 1	38
Total (64.1 overs)	261	Total (91.1 overs)	296

FoW: 1-67 (Geldart), 2-81 (Callis), 3-126 (Waite), 4-150 (Hussain), 5-150 (Imtiaz),
1st 6-151 (Gibson), 7-225 (Rafiq), 8-229 (Birkhead), 9-251 (Wainman), 10-261 (Carver)
FoW: 1-14 (Geldart), 2-79 (Gibson), 3-129 (Waite), 4-138 (Hussain), 5-160 (Imtiaz),
2nd 6-172 (Azeem Rafiq), 7-273 (Barnes), 8-274 (Birkhead), 9-294 (Callis), 10-296 (Carver)

	O	M	R	W		O	M	R	W
Thornton	14	3	47	0	B L Brookes	13	4	47	2
B L Brookes	17	3	75	1	Thornton	18	4	37	3
H Brookes	11	2	50	1	Parker	12.1	1	41	2
Parker	15	5	45	4	H Brookes	11	1	52	0
Sukhjit Singh	7.1	2	31	4	Sukhjit Singh	19	4	31	1
					Jones	18	3	61	1

WARWICKSHIRE

First innings		Second innings	
I J Westwood, not out	230	(5) c Carver b Barnes	4
* A R I Umeed, b Waite	4	(1) c Carver b Wainman	1
L Banks, c Imtiaz b Barnes	26		
M Lamb, b Wainman	136	(3) c Gibson b Barnes	6
A D Thomason, b Carver	136	(2) b Wainman	11
§ A J Mellor, not out	51	(4) c Carver b Wainman	11
G T Thornton		(6) c Carver b Wainman	8
L Jones		(8) not out	0
C R M Parker	Did not bat		
B L Brookes		(7) c Waite b Wainman	0
Sukhjit Singh		(9) not out	0
H Brookes			
Extras b 5, lb 2, nb 12, w 7	26	Extras lb 1, w 1	2
Total (4 wkts dec, 103 overs)	502	Total (7 wkts, 7 overs)	43

FoW 1st   1-12 (Umeed), 2-54 (Banks), 3-132 (Lamb), 4-376 (Thomason)
       2nd   1-2 (Umeed), 2-15 (Thomason), 3-25 (Lamb), 4-33 (Mellor), 5-40 (Westwood),
             6-43 (Thornton), 7-43 (B L Brookes)

	O	M	R	W		O	M	R	W
Wainman	22	1	80	1	Wainman	4	0	24	5
Warner	10	0	78	1	Barnes	3	0	18	2
Barnes	12	0	65	1					
Azeem Rafiq	23	2	95	0					
Carver	19	2	65	1					
Gibson	11	0	68	0					
Imtiaz	6	0	44	0					

Umpires: N L Bainton and S Redfearn   Scorers: S Smith and H Clayton

Second Eleven Championship
Yorkshire v. Leicestershire

Played at York CC on June 13, 14 and 15, 2016
Yorkshire won by 6 wickets at 5.55pm on the Third Day

Toss won by Leicestershire

Yorkshire 22 points, Leicestershire 6 points

Close of play: First Day, Leicestershire 267-6 (Dearden 114, Sayer 58, 75 overs); Second Day, Leicestershire (2) 39-1 (Dearden 26, Lambert 6, 16 overs)

LEICESTERSHIRE

	First Innings		Second Innings	
H E Dearden, c Birkhead b Coad	132	c Gale b Rafiq	30
O M D Kolk, c Birkhead b Coad	0	b Warner	6
S J W Lambert, c Warner b Coad	2	st Birkhead b Rafiq	97
I A Karim, lbw b Rafiq	52	c Callis b Wainman	34
M W R Stokes, c Coad b Barnes	6	lbw b Shutt	6
O H Freckingham, c Rhodes b Coad	9	c Gibson b Barnes	9
§ L G Cammish, b Warner	3	c Gale b Warner	19
R J Sayer, not out	94	not out	1
* J S Sykes, c Rhodes b Coad	4		
C A Barrett, c Gibson b Coad	1		
M B Wareing, c Rhodes b Wainman	2		
C E Shreck	Did not bat		
Extras b 6, lb 12, nb 8	26	Extras lb 4, nb 2	6
Total (89.1 overs)	331	Total (7 wkts dec, 52.5 overs)	208

FoW: 1-1 (Kolk), 2-9 (Lambert), 3-94 (Karim), 4-105 (Stokes), 5-122 (Freckingham), 1st 6-135 (Cammish), 7-302 (Dearden), 8-306 (Sykes), 9-312 (Barrett), 10-331(Wareing).
FoW: 1-20 (Kolk), 2-44 (Dearden), 3-103 (Karim), 4-113 (Stokes), 5-132 (Freckingham), 6-192 (Cammish), 7-208 (Lambert)

	O	M	R	W		O	M	R	W
Coad	23	6	58	6	Coad	5	0	17	0
Wainman	13.1	3	67	1	Warner	9	2	26	2
Warner	12	0	45	1	Rafiq	14.5	3	66	2
Rhodes	10	1	32	0	Wainman	8	1	22	1
Azeem Rafiq	15	3	38	1	Rhodes	4	1	26	0
Barnes	10	2	33	1	Shutt	7	1	28	1
Shutt	6	0	40	0	Barnes	5	0	19	1

YORKSHIRE

	First Innings		Second Innings	
E Callis, c Karim b Sykes	78	(2) lbw b Wareing	3
W M H Rhodes, b Barrett	2	(1) b Barrett	15
* A W Gale, lbw b Wareing	1	c and b Barrett	31
R Gibson, c Dearden b Shreck	36	not out	162
M J Waite, c Wareing b Sykes	69	b Sykes	11
Azeem Rafiq, not out	26	not out	72
E Barnes, not out	14		
§ B D Birkhead			
B O Coad			
J W Shutt	Did not bat		
J C Wainman			
J D Warner			
Extras b 4, lb 9, w 1	14	Extras b 4, lb 2, w 1	7
Total (5 wkts dec, 69 overs)	240	Total (4 wkts, 53.2 overs)	301

FoW: 1st 1-4 (Rhodes), 2-7 (Gale), 3-86 (Gibson), 4-176 (Callis), 5-211 (Waite)
2nd 1-17 (Callis), 2-21 (Rhodes), 3-110 (Gale), 4-129 (Waite)

	O	M	R	W		O	M	R	W
Barrett	15	4	44	1	Barrett	12	0	56	2
Wareing	13	1	27	1	Wareing	12	2	57	1
Stokes	9	3	21	0	Shreck	6	2	28	0
Sykes	16	3	71	2	Sayer	9	0	54	0
Shreck	7	2	18	1	Sykes	11.2	0	82	1
Sayer	7	1	40	1	Stokes	3	0	18	0
Kolk	2	0	6	0					

Umpires: I D Blackwell and J D Middlebrook

Scorers: H Clayton and P N Johnson

Second Eleven Championship
Yorkshire v. Worcestershire

Played at North Marine Road, Scarborough, on June 21, 22 and 23, 2016
Match drawn at 6.12pm on the Third Day

Toss won by Worcestershire   Yorkshire 9 points, Worcestershire 9 points
Close of play: First Day, no play; Second Day, Yorkshire (1) 20-1 (Gildart 0, Gibson 20, 2 overs)

WORCESTERSHIRE
(Second innings forfeited)

* G H Rhodes, c Callis b Wainman		50
O E Westbury, c Read b Wainman		8
T C Fell, c Rhodes b Wainman		1
A Hepburn, b Rafiq		121
Z Ul-Abideen Malik, c Rhodes b Thompson		41
W A R Fraine, not out		87
B J Twohig, lbw b Wainman		21
J C Tongue, c Hussain b Wainman		2
§ J M H Dodd, c Gibson b Thompson		27
C A J Morris, b Gibson		0
G L S Scrimshaw, b Thompson		2
A J Willerton	Did not bat	
Extras b 8, lb 1, b 4		13
Total (99.2 overs)		373

FoW: 1-13 (Westbury), 2-17 (Fell), 3-86 (G H Rhodes), 4-169 (Ul-Abideen Malik), 5-244 (Hepburn), 6-279 (Twohig), 7-299 (Tongue), 8-364 (Dodd), 9-370 (Morris), 10-373 (Scrimshaw)

	O	M	R	W
Wainman	20	6	49	5
W M H Rhodes	16	4	34	0
Azeem Rafiq	24	7	95	1
Warner	5.2	1	30	0
Carver	20.4	1	71	0
Thompson	9.2	0	52	3
Gibson	4	0	33	1

YORKSHIRE

First Innings		Second Innings	
E Callis, lbw b Tongue	0	c Twohig b Morris	5
C J Geldart, not out	0	c Dodd b Tongue	4
R Gibson, not out	20	c Dodd b Morris	1
* W M H Rhodes		b G H Rhodes	21
M J Waite		b Tongue	1
M Hussain,		c Dodd b Willerton	46
Azeem Rafiq		c G H Rhodes b Hepburn	37
J A Thompson Did not bat		not out	146
K Carver		c Twohig b Rhodes	47
§ J Read		not out	3
J D Warner			
Extras	0	Extras b 5, lb 8, nb 2, w 2	17
Total (1 wkt dec, 2 overs)	20	Total (8 wkts, 97 overs)	328

FoW: 1st   1-0 (Callis)
     2nd   1-7 (Geldart), 2-10 (Gibson), 3-13 (Callis), 4-16 (Waite), 5-61 (W M H Rhodes), 6-99 (Hussain), 7-183 (Rafiq), 8-314 (Wainman)

	O	M	R	W		O	M	R	W
Tongue	1	0	5	1	Tongue	9	3	18	2
Morris	1	0	15	0	Morris	18	2	64	2
					Scrimshaw	10	0	61	0
					Rhodes	23	5	57	2
					Willerton	11	3	43	1
					Twohig	13	4	43	0
					Ul-Abideen Malik	2	0	4	0
					Hepburn	11	3	25	1

Umpires: P R Pollard and I J Dixon   Scorers: J R Virr and P M Mellish

Second Eleven Championship
Lancashire v. Yorkshire

Played at Todmorden CC on July 4, 5 and 6, 2016
Lancashire won by 176 runs at 6.01pm on the Third Day

Toss won by Lancashire

Lancashire 24 points, Yorkshire 3 points

Close of play: First Day, Lancashire (1) 239-3 (Jones 50, Bohannon 27, 76 overs), Second Day, Yorkshire (2) 0-0 (Callis 0, Geldart 0, 2 overs)

LANCASHIRE	First Innings		Second Innings	
L M Reece, c Carver b Waite		17	c Gibson b Wainman	26
C K Turner, c Geldart b Barnes		103	lbw b Wainman	24
§ B D Guest, c Read b Shaw		27	c Hussain b Carver	48
R P Jones, b Wainman		81	not out	45
J J Bohannon, c Thompson b Carver		28		
D J Lamb, lbw b Shaw		8		
* S D Parry, not out		43		
A M Lilley, c Thompson b Wainman		27		
N L Buck				
T J Lester	Did not bat			
S Mahmood				
Extras b 4, lb 12, w 5		21	Extras lb 4, w 1	5
Total (7 wkts dec, 96.4 overs)		355	Total (3 wkts dec, 28.5 overs)	148

FoW: 1-47 (Reece), 2-124 (Guest), 3-185 (Turner), 4-240 (Bohannon), 5-262 (Lamb),
1st 6-327 (Jones), 7-355 (Lilley).
2nd 1-53 (Turner); 2-56 (Reece); 3-148 (Guest).

	O	M	R	W		O	M	R	W
Shaw	16	7	50	2	Shaw	4	1	22	0
Coad	20	9	48	0	Coad	4	1	15	0
Wainman	13.4	3	44	2	Carver	10.5	1	62	1
Waite	12	2	75	1	Wainman	7	1	24	2
Carver	13	3	52	1	Waite	3	0	21	0
Barnes	11	2	34	1					
Thompson	4	0	19	0					
Gibson	7	1	17	0					

YORKSHIRE	First Innings		Second Innings	
E Callis, lbw b Lester		1	lbw b Parry	45
C J Geldart, lbw b Buck		0	b Lester	8
R Gibson, b Buck		8	lbw b Lester	6
M J Waite, lbw b Mahmood		35	lbw b Parry	67
M Hussain, b Lester		0	lbw b Parry	11
J A Thompson, b Parry		31	lbw b Lilley	10
E Barnes, c Lester b Mahmood		23	b Parry	4
J C Wainman, lbw b Parry		1	b Parry	0
J Shaw, lbw b Parry		2	lbw b Lilley	13
§ J Read, c Lilley b Mahmood		0	not out	13
K Carver, not out		6	c Guest b Lilley	0
* B O Coad	Did not Bat			
Extras b 7, lb 5, nb 4, w 1		17	Extras b 23, lb 3	26
Total (46 overs)		124	Total (97.2 overs)	203

FoW: 1-1 (Geldart), 2-1 (Callis), 3-13 (Gibson), 4-18 (Hussain), 5-77 (Thompson),
2nd 6-95 (Waite), 7-110 (Wainman), 8-110 (Barnes), 9-114 (Read), 10-124 (Shaw)
FoW: 1-10 (Geldart), 2-16 (Gibson), 3-105 (Callis), 4-123 (Hussain), 5-146 (Thompson),
2nd 6-154 (Barnes), 7-156 (Wainman), 8-163 (Waite), 9-203 (Shaw), 1-203 (Carver)

	O	M	R	W		O	M	R	W
Buck	7	1	31	2	Lester	12	7	23	2
Lester	8	2	17	2	Parry	31	17	33	5
Lamb	6	2	11	0	Buck	15	4	37	0
Lilley	7	1	14	0	Lamb	7	2	34	0
Parry	11	5	14	3	Mahmood	9	6	10	0
Mahmood	7	2	25	3	Lilley	23.2	8	40	3

Umpires: I L Herbert and M D Watton

Scorers: M Dixon and J R Virr

Second Eleven Championship
Nottinghamshire v. Yorkshire

Played at Trent College on July 19 and 20, 2016

Nottinghamshire won by 7 wickets at 5.17pm on the Second Day

Toss won by Yorkshire   Nottinghamshire 21 points, Yorkshire 5 points

Close of play: First Day, Nottinghamshire (1) 109-3 (Gidman 59, Brown 25, 45 overs)

First Innings	YORKSHIRE		Second Innings	
E Callis, c Carter b Gidman	2		lbw b L Wood	1
B L Ainsley, b L Wood	2		c Carter b Kitt	4
C J Geldart, lbw b Brown	9		c Gidman b L Wood	0
R Gibson, c Gidman b Kitt	19		c Shafique b Kitt	0
M J Waite, lbw b L Wood	2		lbw b L Wood	3
J A Thompson, c Shafique b Brown	31		lbw b Brown	16
§ J Read, c Gidman b Kitt	21		b Brown	10
J C Wainman, run out (Dal)	18		lbw b Brown	1
R J Sidebottom, not out	5		(10) c and b Gidman	4
* B O Coad, lbw b L Wood	5		(9) c Shafique b Gidman	12
J E G Logan, b L Wood	0		not out	0
J W Shutt	Did not bat			
Extras b 9, lb 10, nb 20	39		Extras b 1, lb 10, nb 4	15
Total (56.1 overs)	157		Total (28.1 overs)	66

FoW: 1-3 (Callis), 2-16 (Geldart), 3-23 (Ainsley), 4-33 (Waite), 5-39 (Gibson),
1st 6-84 (Thompson), 7-128 (Wainman), 8-138 (Read), 9-151 (Coad), 10-157 (Logan)
FoW: 1-6 (Callis), 2-6 (Ainsley), 3-6 (Gibson), 4-6 (Geldart), 5-11 (Waite),
2nd 6-44 (Read), 7-49 (Thompson), 8-50 (Wainman), 9-55 (Sidebottom), 10-66 (Coad)

	O	M	R	W			O	M	R	W
Brown	10	4	19	2	L Wood		9	4	13	3
Gidman	10	3	25	1	Kitt		8	3	19	2
L Wood	13.1	2	42	4	Brown		6	3	17	3
Kitt	12	2	38	2	Gidman		5.1	3	6	2
Carter	11	5	14	0						

First Innings	NOTTINGHAMSHIRE		Second Innings	
J H Barrett, lbw b Sidebottom	6		c Thompson b Logan	27
W T Root, lbw b Sidebottom	3		lbw b Sidebottom	9
* W R S Gidman, lbw b Sidebottom	66		b Shutt	8
A K Dal, lbw b Wainman	5		not out	10
D D A Brown, c Geldart b Sidebottom	33		not out	19
S K W Wood, b Sidebottom	0			
§ A A Shafique, c Waite b Logan	21			
L Wood, c Callis b Logan	6			
C R Marshall, c and b Wainman	1			
M Carter, lbw b Logan	0			
B M Kitt, not out	0			
Extras lb 3, nb 8	11		Extras nb 2	2
Total (46 overs)	152		Total (3 wkts, 23.4 overs)	75

FoW: 1-10 (Barrett), 2-19 (Root), 3-33 (Dal), 4-123 (Brown), 5-123 (S K W Wood),
1st 6-126 (Gidman), 7-145 (L Wood), 8-152 (Shafique), 9-152 (Marshall), 10-152 (Carter)
2nd 1-17 (Root), 2-32 (Gidman), 3-52 (Barrett)

	O	M	R	W			O	M	R	W
Sidebottom	12	5	19	5	Sidebottom		3	1	10	1
Coad	12	6	19	0	Coad		3	0	14	0
Shutt	18	5	51	0	Wainman		4	1	18	0
Waite	5	1	15	0	Shutt		8.4	3	19	1
Wainman	7	3	18	2	Logan		5	1	14	1
Logan	13.1	7	27	3						

Umpires: R J Evans and B Jones   Scorers: Mrs A Cusworth and J R Virr

Second Eleven Championship
Derbyshire v. Yorkshire

Played at Christchurch Meadows, Belper, on July 26, 27 and 28, 2016
Match drawn at 12.19pm on the Third Day

Toss won by Yorkshire

Derbyshire 12 points, Yorkshire 11 points

Close of play: First Day, Yorkshire 27-1 (Brook 17, Gibson 2, 13 overs); Second Day, Derbyshire 37-5 (Cork 1, Milnes 5, 24 overs)

DERBYSHIRE

	First Innings			Second Innings	
G H Sellars, c Read b Brooks		2	lbw b Brooks		3
T A Wood, c Callis b Thompson		39	c Thompson b Brooks		3
J Clarke, c Callis b Thompson		43	c Brook b Brooks		0
C M Macdonnell, c Thompson b Shutt		6	lbw b Thompson		17
C A Brodrick, c Read b Thompson		16	lbw b Carver		8
G T G Cork, c Read b Thompson		16	c Read b Sidebottom		1
* T P Milnes, c Carver b Brooks		89	c Thompson b Wainman		24
R P Hemmings, lbw b Sidebottom		23	(11) not out		26
C F Parkinson, c Thompson b Sidebottom		0	(8) c Read b Thompson		1
§ J H Sookias, not out		15	(9) c Brook b Waite		4
S Conners, b Thompson		20	(10) b Waite		6
D J Gibbs	Did not bat				
Extras b 1, lb 5, nb 4		10	Extras lb 6, nb 4		10
Total (92.1 overs)		279	Total (41.2 overs)		103

FoW: 1-5 (Sellers), 2-85 (Clarke), 3-86 (Wood), 4-113 (Macdonnell), 5-113 (Brodrick),
1st 6-148 (Cork), 7-244 (Milnes), 8-244 (Hemmings), 9-251 (Parkinson), 10-279 (Conners)
FoW: 1-3 (Sellars), 2-3 (Clarke), 3-8 (Wood), 4-31 (Macdonnell), 5-31 (Brodrick),
2nd 6-38 (Cork), 7-70 (Milnes), 8-77 (Sookias), 9-95 (Conners), 10-103 (Parkinson)

	O	M	R	W		O	M	R	W
Sidebottom	15	4	27	2	Sidebottom	10	1	20	1
Brooks	16	1	52	2	Brooks	7	4	7	3
Wainman	8	1	30	0	Thompson	7.2	1	17	2
Waite	9	1	34	0	Wainman	8	0	38	1
Carver	13	4	34	0	Carver	4	3	1	1
Thompson	16.1	2	60	5	Waite	5	1	14	2
Shutt	13	2	32	1					
Gibson	2	0	4	0					

YORKSHIRE

E Callis, c Hemmings b Cork		6
H C Brook, lbw b Gibbs		39
R Gibson, c Clarke b Parkinson		76
* A W Gale, c sub (S Gadsby) b Gibbs		33
M J Waite, c Brodrick b Parkinson		11
J A Thompson, b Milnes		17
§ J Read, c Sookias b Cork		15
J C Wainman, c Sookias b Milnes		0
J A Brooks, c Sookias b Conners		0
K Carver, not out		19
R J Sidebottom, b Milnes		0
J W Shutt	Did not bat	
Extras b 1, nb 20, w 11		32
Total (90.1 overs)		248

FoW: 1-19 (Callis), 2-70 (Brook), 3-148 (Gale), 4-188 (Gibson), 5-191 (Waite),
6-217 (Thompson), 7-217 (Wainman), 8-217 (Brooks), 9-243 (Read), 10-248 (Sidebottom)

	O	M	R	W
Milnes	15.1	9	21	3
Hemmings	6	2	14	0
Cork	18	7	25	2
Parkinson	18	8	54	2
Conners	16	3	68	1
Gibbs	15	3	49	2
Macdonnell	2	0	16	0

Umpires: B V Taylor and I N Ramage

Scorers: Mrs J E M Hough and J R Virr

Second Eleven Championship
Northamptonshire v. Yorkshire

Played at Market Harborough CC on August 2, 3 and 4, 2016
Yorkshire won by 3 wickets at 6.32pm on the Third Day

Toss won by Yorkshire   Northamptonshire 1 point, Yorkshire 20 points

Close of play: First Day, no play; Second Day, Northamptonshire (2) 33-2 (Thomas 21, Bell 1, 11 overs)

First Innings	NORTHAMPTONSHIRE	Second Innings	
* C O Thurston, lbw b Thompson	19	b Coad	6
H R Adair, c Read b Thompson	15	b Coad	3
R Henry, c Thompson b Carver	24	(5) c Gibson b Coad	9
W D Thomas, b Shutt	8	(3) b Carver	26
M Bell, lbw b Shutt	0	(4) lbw b Coad	6
§ A E King, lbw b Wainman	38	lbw b Carver	31
C A Barrett, c Thompson b Shutt	4	b Coad	9
M A Richardson, c Read b Rhodes	20	lbw b Coad	0
L J Hurt, c Gibson b Waite	15	c Coad b Carver	22
M J G Taylor, not out	4	not out	23
M A Ashraf, st Read b Carver	16	c Ainsley b Carver	4
T W Holmes	Did not bat		
Extras b 4, lb 2, nb 2, w 1	13	Extras b 1, lb 3	4
Total (66 overs)	176	Total (38 overs)	143

FoW: 1st 1-27 (Thurston), 2-42 (Adair), 3-73 (Thomas), 4-73 (Bell), 5-73 (Henry), 6-82 (Barrett), 7-133 (King), 8-145 (Richardson), 9-159 (Hurt), 10-176 (Ashraf)

FoW: 2nd 1-7 (Adair), 2-30 (Thurston), 3-38 (Bell), 4-44 (Thomas), 5-58 (Henry), 6-78 (Barrett), 7-78 (Richardson), 8-109 (Hurt), 9-127 (King), 10-143 (Ashraf)

	O	M	R	W		O	M	R	W
Coad	12	2	34	0	Coad	14	2	57	6
Wainman	9	1	28	1	Wainman	4	1	10	0
Thompson	9	1	19	2	Rhodes	2	1	4	0
Rhodes	9	1	27	1	Carver	14	5	47	4
Carver	13	4	32	2	Shutt	4	0	21	0
Shutt	10	4	19	3					
Waite	4	0	7	1					

First Innings	YORKSHIRE	Second Innings	
H C Brook, b Hurt	25	b Hurt	1
B L Ainsley, not out	24	b Taylor	8
R Gibson, c Hurt b Taylor	21	lbw b Taylor	22
* W H M Rhodes, not out	13	c King b Richardson	35
M J Waite		not out	103
J A Thompson		b Holmes	9
§ J Read		lbw b Ashraf	17
J C Wainman	Did not bat	lbw b Ashraf	1
K Carver		not out	13
E Callis			
B O Coad			
J W Shutt			
Extras lb 7, nb 10	17	Extras b 1, lb 6, nb 4	11
Total (2 wkts dec, 24.4 overs)	100	Total (7 wkts, 53.4 overs)	220

FoW: 1st 1-36 (Brook), 2-84 (Gibson)

FoW: 2nd 1-2 (Brook), 2-29 (Ainsley), 3-48 (Gibson), 4-90 (Rhodes), 5-109 (Thompson), 6-184 (Read), 7-196 (Wainman)

	O	M	R	W		O	M	R	W
Barrett	3	0	18	0	Hurt	11	1	33	1
Ashraf	8	0	25	0	Ashraf	10.4	2	38	2
Hurt	7	0	23	1	Taylor	10	0	38	2
Richardson	4	0	10	0	Barrett	6	0	21	0
Taylor	2.4	0	17	1	Richardson	8	2	33	1
					Taylor	8	1	50	1

Umpires: P R Pollard and R P Medland   Scorers: M E Woolley and J R Virr

Second Eleven Championship
Yorkshire v. Durham

Played at York CC on August 9, 10 and 11, 2016
Match drawn at 5.19pm on the Third Day

Toss won by Yorkshire   Yorkshire 13 points, Durham 9 points

Close of play: First Day, Yorkshire 310-3 (Gale 54, Y Imtiaz 2, 91 overs); Second Day, Durham (2) 47-2 (Hickey 16, S M Imtiaz 0, 14 overs)

YORKSHIRE

B L Ainsley, lbw b McCarthy	57
M Hussain, c S M Imtiaz b Harrison	47
L J McKendry, c S M Imtiaz b Chase	121
* A W Gale, c Hobson b Harrison	74
Y Imtiaz, c Weighell b Chase	2
J A Thompson, lbw b Harrison	4
§ J Read, not out	36
M D Fisher, lbw b Harding	32
J C Wainman, not out	10
B O Coad	
J W Shutt Did not bat	
J E G Logan	
Extras b 5, lb 27	32
Total (7 wkts dec, 115 overs)	415

FoW: 1-100 (Ainsley), 2-148 (Hussain), 3-308 (McKendry), 4-330 (Y Imtiaz), 5-335 (Thompson), 6-338 (Gale), 7-396 (Fisher)

	O	M	R	W
Chase	18	4	52	2
Harrison	25	11	41	3
Main	15	2	81	0
Hart	9	2	30	0
Harding	24	2	97	1
McCarthy	9	2	31	1
Hickey	15	1	51	0

DURHAM

First Innings		Second Innings (following on)	
G Clark, lbw b Coad	10	c Read b Coad	4
N R Hobson, c McKendry b Wainman	16	c McKendry b Logan	19
A J Hickey, c Read b Coad	0	c Fisher b Wainman	29
§ S M Imtiaz, c Y Imtiaz b Wainman	1	lbw b Fisher	8
* W J Weighell, c and b Thompson	54	not out	61
B A Carse, c Fisher b Shutt	39	not out	56
A J H A Hart, c Coad b Shutt	4		
B J McCarthy, not out	41		
G H I Harding, c Read b Fisher	0		
G T Main, lbw b Shutt	17		
P K D Chase, b Thompson	1		
J Harrison Did not bat			
Extras b 6, lb 11	17	Extras b 8, lb 1, nb 12	21
Total (62 overs)	200	Total (4 wkts, 56 overs)	198

FoW: 1-25 (Clark), 2-31 (Hickey), 3-32 (S M Imtiaz), 4-41 (Hobson), 5-105 (Weighell),
1st   6-138 (Hart), 7-147 (Carse), 8-160 (Harding), 9-189 (Main), 10-200 (Chase)
2nd   1-4 (Clark), 2-43 (Hobson), 3-56 (S M imtiaz), 4-82 (Hickey)

	O	M	R	W		O	M	R	W
Fisher	10	2	34	1	Coad	11	1	39	1
Coad	12	4	36	2	Wainman	13	3	56	1
Wainman	10	1	38	2	Shutt	12	1	35	0
Thompson	13	4	49	2	Logan	7	0	26	1
Shutt	14	8	17	3	Fisher	7	2	14	1
Logan	3	1	9	0	Thompson	4	1	16	0
					Ainsley	2	0	3	0

Umpires: S C Gale and G M Roberts   Scorers: H Clayton and G Maddison

Second Eleven Championship
Yorkshire v. MCC Universities

Played at Stamford Bridge CC on August 15, 16 and 17, 2016
MCC Universities won by 6 wickets at 5.37pm on the Third Day

Toss won by Yorkshire   Yorkshire 5 points, MCC Universities 23 points

Close of play: First Day, MCC Universities 88-1 (Azad 38, Kumar 44, 34 overs); Second Day, Yorkshire 84-3 (Gibson 48, Hussain 3, 45 overs)

YORKSHIRE

Batsman	First Innings		Second Innings	
H C Brook	lbw b Owen	13	c Azad b Lilley	2
B L Ainsley	lbw b Grundy	46	c Lowen b Grundy	18
L J McKendry	c Azad b Grundy	17	b Owen	3
R Gibson	lbw b Lilley	0	run out (Kumar)	52
M Hussain	c Norris b Lilley	0	not out	48
J A Thompson	c Azad b Owen	12	lbw b Lilley	0
M D Fisher	c Sehmi b Lilley	8	b Kumar	26
§ J Read	lbw b McIver	42	c Lowen b Grundy	30
J C Wainman	c Lilley b McIver	11	lbw b Grundy	4
K Carver	not out	29	b Lilley	4
* B O Coad	b McIver	0	lbw b Lilley	2
J W Shutt	Did not bat			
Extras	lb 7, nb 8, w 1	16	b 4, lb 2, nb 8	14
Total	(70 overs)	194	Total (101 overs)	203

FoW: 1-21 (Brook), 2-48 (McKendry), 3-51 (Gibson), 4-55 (Hussain), 5-87 (Thompson),
1st 6-101 (Fisher), 7-109 (Ainsley), 8-139 (Wainman), 9-194 (Read), 10-194 (Coad)

FoW: 1-2 (Brook), 2-9 (McKendry), 3-58 (Ainsley), 4-91 (Gibson), 5-95 (Thompson),
2nd 6-140 (Fisher), 7-191 (Read), 8-196 (Wainman), 9-201 (Carver), 10-203 (Coad)

Bowler	O	M	R	W		O	M	R	W
Lilley	23	6	51	3		29	10	51	4
Owen	16	5	55	2		23	11	30	1
Grundy	18	3	45	2		17	5	43	3
McIver	11	1	30	3		10	6	14	0
Thomson	2	0	6	0		10	3	29	0
Akram						7	1	21	0
Kumar						5	2	9	1

MCC UNIVERSITIES

Batsman	First Innings		Second Innings	
M H Azad	c Thompson b Fisher	45	lbw b Coad	2
M J Norris	c Thompson b Fisher	4	lbw b Fisher	9
N R Kumar	lbw b Thompson	79	lbw b Coad	0
§ C T Lowen	b Fisher	14	c Thompson b Coad	2
S F G Bullen	c Hussain b Carver	19	not out	43
B M R Akram	lbw b Shutt	51	not out	37
R T Sehmi	lbw b Fisher	1		
A T Thomson	b Coad	54		
J N McIver	c Gibson b Fisher	4		
* A E Lilley	c Read b Coad	8		
J O Grundy	not out	6		
X G Owen	Did not bat			
Extras	b 2, lb 7, nb 4	13	b 6, lb 1, nb 2	9
Total	(90.1 overs)	298	Total (4 wkts, 27.5 overs)	102

FoW: 1-11 (Norris), 2-102 (Azad), 3-147 (Kumar), 4-156 (Lowen), 5-180 (Bullen),
1st 6-181 (Sehmi), 7-252 (Akram), 8-272 (McIver), 9-291 (Thomson), 10-298 (Lilley)
2nd: 1-3 (Azad), 2-3 (Kumar), 3-7 (Lowen), 4-23 (Norris)

Bowler	O	M	R	W		O	M	R	W
Fisher	22	4	70	5		8	3	11	1
Coad	20.1	5	58	2		11	4	23	3
Wainman	14	2	52	0		2	0	17	0
Thompson	7	1	28	1		3	0	23	0
Carver	15	3	42	1		2.5	0	9	0
Shutt	11	2	36	1		1	0	12	0
Brook	1	0	3	0					

Umpires: C M Watts and G M Roberts   Scorers: H Clayton and C N Rawson

SECOND ELEVEN CHAMPIONSHIP 2016

FINAL

Durham (504) beat Middlesex (202 and 185) by an innings and 117 runs

NORTHERN GROUP FINAL TABLE

	P	W	L	D	Tied	Aban.	Bat	Bowl	Ded	Points
1 Durham (2)	9	5	1	3	0	0	23	30	0	148
2 Lancashire (3)	9	4	0	3	0	2	17	25	0	131
3 MCC Universities (9) ...	9	2	1	6	0	0	26	31	0	119
4 Worcestershire (8)	9	3	3	3	0	0	25	28	0	116
5 Yorkshire (7)	9	2	3	4	0	0	13	32	0	97
6 Warwickshire (5)	9	0	0	8	0	1	27	23	0	95
7 Nottinghamshire (1)	9	2	4	2	0	1	17	29	0	93
8 Derbyshire (6)	9	1	2	5	0	1	8	25	0	89
9 Leicestershire (4)	9	1	3	4	0	1	21	24	0	86
10 Northamptonshire (10) ..	9	0	3	4	0	2	14	20	0	64

SOUTHERN GROUP FINAL TABLE

	P	W	L	D	Tied	Aban.	Bat	Bowl	Ded	Points
1 Middlesex (1)	9	5	1	3	0	0	22	26	0	143
2 Sussex (7)	9	4	2	3	0	0	24	25	1	127
3 MCC Young Cricketers (10)	9	2	1	6	0	0	21	26	0	109
4 Glamorgan (9)	9	2	2	5	0	0	22	27	0	106
5 Kent (3)	9	3	3	3	0	0	18	26	2	105
6 Essex (8)	9	2	2	5	0	0	21	29	2.5	104.5
7 Surrey (4)	9	2	3	4	0	0	23	30	2	103
8 Hampshire (6)	9	1	2	6	0	0	29	21	0	96
9 Somerset (2)	9	1	3	5	0	0	29	25	0	95
10 Gloucestershire (5)	9	1	4	4	0	0	11	21	0	68

Ded. Points deducted for slow over-rates

(2015 group positions in brackets)

SECOND ELEVEN CHAMPIONS

In the seasons in which Yorkshire have competed. The Championship has been split into two groups since 2009, the group winners playing off for the Championship. These groups were deemed North and South from the 2012 season.

Season	Champions	Yorkshire's Position	Season	Champions	Yorkshire's Position
1959	Gloucestershire	7th	1995	Hampshire	5th
1960	Northamptonshire	14th	1996	Warwickshire	4th
1961	Kent	11th	1997	Lancashire	2nd
1975	Surrey	4th	1998	Northamptonshire	9th
1976	Kent	5th	1999	Middlesex	14th
1977	**Yorkshire**	**1st**	2000	Middlesex	5th
1978	Sussex	5th	2001	Hampshire	2nd
1979	Warwickshire	3rd	2002	Kent	3rd
1980	Glamorgan	5th	**2003**	**Yorkshire**	**1st**
1981	Hampshire	11th	2004	Somerset	8th
1982	Worcestershire	14th	2005	Kent	10th
1983	Leicestershire	2nd	2006	Kent	3rd
1984	**Yorkshire**	**1st**	2007	Sussex	10th
1985	Nottinghamshire	12th	2008	Durham	5th
1986	Lancashire	5th	2009	Surrey	A 2nd
1987	**Yorkshire and Kent**	**1st**	2010	Surrey	A 8th
1988	Surrey	9th	2011	Warwickshire	A 10th
1989	Middlesex	9th	2012	Kent	North 9th
1990	Sussex	17th	2013	Lancashire & Middlesex	
1991	**Yorkshire**	**1st**			(North) 4th
1992	Surrey	5th	2014	Leicestershire	(North) 4th
1993	Middlesex	3rd	2015	Nottinghamshire	(North) 7th
1994	Somerset	2nd	2016	Durham	(North) 5th

SECOND ELEVEN CHAMPIONSHIP
AVERAGES 2016

Played 9   Won 2   Lost 3   Drawn 4

BATTING AND FIELDING
(Qualification 5 innings)

Player	M.	I.	N.O.	Runs	H.S.	Avge	100s	50s	ct/st
Azeem Rafiq	3	5	2	175	72*	58.33	0	1	0
E Barnes	3	5	2	134	49	44.66	0	0	0
R Gibson	8	15	2	486	162*	37.38	1	2	8
M J Waite	7	11	1	350	103*	35.00	1	2	2
J A Thompson	7	10	1	276	146*	30.66	1	0	13
B L Ainsley	4	7	1	163	57	27.16	0	1	1
E Callis	7	11	0	293	125	26.63	1	1	5
J Read	7	9	2	184	42	26.28	0	0	13/1
M Hussain	5	8	1	172	48*	24.57	0	0	3
W M H Rhodes	3	5	1	86	35	21.50	0	0	5
K Carver	6	9	5	85	29*	21.25	0	0	6
H C Brook	3	5	0	80	39	16.00	0	0	2
J C Wainman	9	12	2	105	47	10.50	0	0	1
C J Geldart	4	8	1	73	45	10.42	0	0	2

Also played

L J McKendry	2	3	0	141	121	47.00	1	0	2
A W Gale	3	4	0	139	74	34.75	0	1	2
M D Fisher	2	3	0	66	32	22.00	0	0	2
J Shaw	1	2	0	15	13	7.50	0	0	-
B O Coad	6	4	0	19	12	4.75	0	0	3
Y Imtiaz	2	3	0	14	12	4.66	0	0	2
R J Sidebottom	2	3	1	9	5*	4.50	0	0	0
B D Birkhead	2	2	0	0	0	—	0	0	2/1
J A Brooks	1	1	0	0	0	—	0	0	0
J E G Logan	2	2	1	0	0*	—	0	0	0
J W Shutt	6	0	0	0	—	—	0	0	0
J D Warner	3	0	0	0	—	—	0	0	0

BOWLING
(Qualification 10 wickets)

Player	Overs	Mdns	Runs	Wkts	Avge	Best	5wI	10wM
J A Thompson	72.5	10	283	15	18.86	5-60	1	0
B O Coad	147.1	40	418	20	20.90	6-57	2	0
J C Wainman	166.5	28	615	24	25.62	5-24	2	0
J W Shutt	104.4	26	310	10	31.00	3-17	0	0
K Carver	125.2	26	415	11	37.72	4-47	0	0

Also bowled

R J Sidebottom	40	11	76	9	8.44	5-19	1	0
J A Brooks	23	5	59	5	11.80	3-7	0	0
J E G Logan	28.1	9	76	5	15.20	3-27	0	0
M D Fisher	47	11	129	8	16.12	5-70	1	0
E Barnes	41	4	169	6	28.16	2-18	0	0
J Shaw	20	0	72	2	36.00	2-50	0	0
M J Waite	38	5	166	4	41.50	2-14	0	0
J D Warner	36.2	3	179	4	44.75	2-26	0	0
Azeem Rafiq	76.5	15	294	4	73.50	2-66	0	0
R Gibson	24	1	122	1	122.00	1-33	0	0
W M H Rhodes	41	8	123	1	123.00	1-27	0	0
B L Ainsley	2	0	3	0	—	—	0	0
H C Brook	1	0	3	0	—	—	0	0
Y Imtiaz	6	0	44	0	—	—	0	0

Second Eleven Trophy
Yorkshire v. Unicorns

Played at Barnsley CC on May 3, 2016
Unicorns won by 33 runs at 5.50pm

Toss won by Unicorns

Yorkshire 0 points, Unicorns 2 points

UNICORNS

S Kelsall, c Wainman b Rhodes		15
T A Wood, c Thompson b Wainman		0
* C J Whittock, c and b Carver		55
M A Gouldstone, run out (Rhodes)		46
§ L J Thomason, c Rhodes b Coad		40
H C Stephens, c Leaning b Wainman		4
B S Phagura, c Gibson b Rhodes		5
M G Coxon, c Carver b Rhodes		10
M H McKiernan, not out		1
T Bulcock		
A J Syddall	Did not bat	
Extras b 5, nb 2, nb 2, w 5		14
Total (8 wkts, 50 overs)		190

FoW: 1-0 (Wood), 2-32 (Kelsall), 3-109 (Whittock), 4-143 (Gouldstone), 5-153 (Stephens), 6-172 (Phagura), 7-179 (Thomason), 8-190 (Coxon)

	O	M	R	W
Waite	7	3	15	0
Wainman	7	1	18	2
Coad	8	0	38	1
Rhodes	7	0	34	3
Warner	7	0	30	0
Carver	7	0	31	1
MacQueen	7	0	17	0

YORKSHIRE

R Gibson, c Whittock b Coxon		11
§ A J Hodd, lbw b Stephens		28
J A Leaning, st Thomason b McKiernan		45
* W M H Rhodes, c Thomason b Stephens		0
M J Waite, b Bulcock		8
J A Thompson, st Thomason b Stephens		15
J C Wainman, c Stephens b Bulcock		4
A MacQueen, lbw b McKiernan		0
K Carver, lbw b McKiernan		13
B O Coad, not out		11
J D Warner, run out (Kelsall)		2
Extras b 4, nb 2, w 14		20
Total (45 overs)		157

FoW: 1-15 (Gibson), 2-55 (Hodd), 3-62 (Rhodes), 4-79 (Waite), 5-108 (Thompson), 6-118 (Leaning), 7-121 (MacQueen), 8-126 (Wainman), 9-149 (Carver), 10-157 (Warner)

	O	M	R	W
Syddall	8	1	23	0
Coxon	5	0	19	1
Stephens	10	1	38	3
Phagura	3	0	18	0
Bulcock	9	1	33	2
McKiernan	10	3	22	3

Umpires: G D Lloyd and I J Dixon

Scorers: H Clayton and K B O'Connell

Second Eleven Trophy
Warwickshire v. Yorkshire

Played at Knowle and Dorridge CC, Solihull, on June 6, 2016
Warwickshire won by 5 runs at 6.34pm

Toss won by Warwickshire — Warwickshire 2 points, Yorkshire 0 points

WARWICKSHIRE

* A R I Umeed, c Birkhead b Warner	98
§ A J Mellor, c Birkhead b Warner	10
L Banks, c Birkhead b Wainman	0
M Lamb, c Carver b Gibson	63
A D Thomason, c and b Azeem Rafiq	12
R A Jones, c Gibson b Azeem Rafiq	8
M R Adair, b Gibson	16
G D Panayi, not out	22
R O Gordon, run out (Gibson)	1
B L Brookes, b Barnes	25
Sukhjit Singh, not out	1
Extras b 5, lb 13, nb 4, w 6	28
Total (9 wkts, 50 overs)	284

FoW: 1-15 (Mellor), 2-16 (Banks), 3-181 (Lamb), 4-195 (Umeed), 5-217 (Jones), 6-226 (Thomason), 7-237 (Adair), 8-241 (Gordon), 9-283 (Brookes)

	O	M	R	W
Warner	10	2	53	2
Waite	1	0	1	0
Wainman	10	0	50	1
Barnes	6	0	42	1
Azeem Rafiq	10	0	37	2
Carver	8	0	54	0
Gibson	5	0	29	2

YORKSHIRE

M Hussain, c Jones b Adair	48
C J Geldart, b Jones	4
R Gibson, b Sukhjit Singh	46
* M J Waite, c sub b Jones	6
E Callis, c sub b Jones	1
Azeem Rafiq, lbw b Panayi	1
E Barnes, run out (Sukhjit Singh)	58
§ B D Birkhead, c Mellor b Brookes	5
J C Wainman, lbw b Sukhjit Singh	5
K Carver, not out	66
J D Warner, b Panayi	19
Extras nb 14, w 6	20
Total (49.4 overs)	279

FoW: 1-7 (Geldart), 2-76 (Gibson), 3-100 (Waite), 4-106 (Callis), 5-107 (Azeem Rafiq), 6-120 (Hussain), 7-153 (Birkhead), 8-164 (Wainman), 9-230 (Barnes), 10-279 (Warner)

	O	M	R	W
Jones	10	0	59	3
Adair	10	0	48	1
Brooks	10	1	54	1
Sukhjit Singh	10	0	81	2
Panayi	9.4	1	37	2

Umpires: I D Blackwell and M Qureshi — Scorers: S Smith and H Clayton

Second Eleven Trophy
Yorkshire v. Leicestershire

At Pudsey Congs CC on June 16, 2016
Match abandoned without a ball bowled

No toss made   Yorkshire 1 point, Leicestershire 1 point

Lancashire v. Yorkshire

Played at the Tyldesleys, Westhoughton, on July 7, 2016
(Reduced before the start to 33 overs per side)
Lancashire won by 7 wickets at 6.09pm

Toss won by Lancashire   Lancashire 2 points, Yorkshire 0 points

YORKSHIRE

R Gibson, c Bohannon b Edwards		31
E Callis, lbw b Lilley		34
E Barnes, c Turner b Edwards		2
* J A Leaning, st Guest b Lilley		18
M J Waite, b Lilley		6
J A Thompson, b Reece		8
§ B D Birkhead, st Guest b Lilley		14
J C Wainman, c Turner b Edwards		8
J Shaw, c Lilley b Mahmood		18
K Carver, run out (Lamb)		1
B O Coad, not out		5
Extras b 2, lb 9, w 3		14
Total (30.4 overs)		159

FoW: 1-54 (Gibson), 2-59 (Barnes), 3-83 (Leaning), 4-100 (Callis), 5-105 (Waite), 6-126 (Birkhead), 7-130 (Thompson), 8-143 (Wainman), 9-149 (Carver), 10-159 (Shaw)

	O	M	R	W
Mahmood	5.4	0	27	1
Lester	2	0	17	0
Edwards	6	0	34	3
Lamb	3	0	16	0
Reece	7	0	30	1
Lilley	7	1	24	4

LANCASHIRE

L M Reece, lbw b Wainman		15
C K Turner, c Leaning b Carver		44
§ B D Guest, not out		65
R P Jones, c Birkhead b Gibson		26
J J Bohannon, not out		3
D J Lamb		
T J Lester		
S Mahmood	Did not bat	
* A M Lilley		
G A Edwards		
C Laker		
Extras lb 1, nb 4, w 5		10
Total (3 wkts, 24.1 overs)		163

FoW: 1-40 (Reece), 2-86 (Turner), 3-146 (Jones)

	O	M	R	W
Shaw	3	0	20	0
Coad	3	0	20	0
Wainman	3	1	14	1
Waite	2	0	21	0
Leaning	3	0	28	0
Carver	6.1	0	37	1
Gibson	4	0	22	1

Umpires: M A Gough and A Davies   Scorers: M Dixon and J R Virr

Second Eleven Trophy
Derbyshire v. Yorkshire

Played at Raynesway, Alvaston, on July 25, 2016
Yorkshire won by 66 runs at 5.28pm

Toss won by Yorkshire   Derbyshire 0 points, Yorkshire 2 points

YORKSHIRE

H C Brook, st Sookias b Gibbs	....	69
B L Ainsley, c Clarke b Milnes	....	26
R Gibson, c Wood b Cork	....	70
* W M H Rhodes, lbw b Cork	....	4
M J Waite, c and b Clarke	....	41
J A Thompson, lbw b Clarke	....	22
§ J Read, c Milnes b Parkinson	....	0
J C Wainman, c and b Parkinson	....	13
K Carver, run out (Cork)	....	9
J A Brooks, b Milnes	....	2
B O Coad, not out	....	0
Extras lb 2, nb 4, w 8	....	14
Total (47 overs)	....	270

FoW: 1-46 (Ainsley), 2-150 (Brook), 3-161 (Rhodes), 4-194 (Gibson), 5-222 (Waite) 6-223 (Read), 7-243 (Wainman), 8-266 (Thompson), 9-270 (Carver), 10-270 (Brooks)

	O	M	R	W
Milnes	8	1	42	2
Hemmings	6	0	29	0
Conners	4	0	24	0
Cork	6	1	36	2
Parkinson	10	0	48	2
Gibbs	4	0	28	1
Clarke	9	0	61	2

DERBYSHIRE

G H Sellars, c Read b Brooks	....	4
T A Wood, c Brook b Wainman	....	0
J Clarke, c Thompson b Coad	....	14
C M Macdonnell, run out (Thompson)	....	34
G T G Cork, b Rhodes	....	38
* T P Milnes, b Coad	....	6
R P Hemmings, c Carver b Brooks	....	36
C F Parkinson, c Thompson b Coad	....	26
§ J H Sookias, c Coad b Waite	....	21
S Conners, c Read b Coad	....	2
D J Gibbs, not out	....	7
Extras lb 6, nb 8, w 2	....	16
Total (47 overs)	....	204

FoW: 1-4 (Sellars), 2-4 (Wood), 3-51 (Clarke), 4-75 (Macdonnell), 5-84 (Milnes), 6-144 (Hemmings), 7-147 (Cork), 8-192 (Sookias), 9-194 (Parkinson), 10-204 (Conners)

	O	M	R	W
Brooks	9	1	41	2
Wainman	6	0	39	1
Rhodes	10	0	36	1
Coad	9	1	27	4
Carver	10	1	39	0
Waite	3	0	16	1

Umpires: S J O'Shaughnessy and H Adnan   Scorers: Mrs J E M Hough and H Clayton

Second Eleven Trophy
Yorkshire v. Durham

Played at York CC on August 8, 2016
Yorkshire won by 8 wickets at 5.47pm

Toss won by Durham   Yorkshire 2 points, Durham 0 points

DURHAM

G Clark, b Carver	....	43
N R Hobson, c Thompson b Rhodes	....	43
J T A Burnham, c Thompson b Carver	....	42
R D Pringle, not out	....	70
* A J Hickey, lbw b Shutt	....	1
§ S M Imtiaz, c Gibson b Carver	....	9
U Arshad, c Thompson b Shutt	....	16
B A Carse, run out (Read)	....	43
B J McCarthy, b Thompson	....	5
P K D Chase		
J Harrison	Did not bat	
Extras b 1, lb 4, w 16	....	21
Total (8 wkts, 50 overs)	....	293

FoW: 1-81 (Hobson), 2-138 (Clark), 3-144 (Burnham), 4-147 (Hickey), 5-158 (Imtiaz), 6-196 (Arshad), 7-288 (Carse), 8-293 (McCarthy)

	O	M	R	W
Wainman	7	0	49	0
Waite	6	0	28	0
Coad	9	0	45	0
Rhodes	8	0	47	1
Carver	8	0	52	3
Shutt	8	0	46	2
Thompson	4	0	21	1

YORKSHIRE

A Z Lees, not out	....	119
B L Ainsley, b Harrison	....	11
R Gibson, c Hobson b Hickey	....	87
* W M H Rhodes, not out	....	56
M J Waite		
J A Thompson		
J C Wainman		
K Carver	Did not bat	
B O Coad		
§ J Read		
J W Shutt		
Extras lb 9, w 12	....	21
Total (2 wkts, 47.3 overs)	....	294

FoW: 1-24 (Ainsley), 2-167 (Gibson)

	O	M	R	W
Arshad	9	0	52	0
Harrison	7.3	0	46	1
Chase	10	1	43	0
Pringle	6	0	54	0
Hickey	10	0	61	1
McCarthy	5	0	29	0

Umpires: S C Gale and G M Roberts   Scorers: H Clayton and G Maddison

SECOND ELEVEN TROPHY 2016

SEMI-FINALS

Lancashire (156-5) beat Kent (164-7) by 11 runs *(DLS)*

The match was reduced to 33 overs per side before play began, and then further reduced to 22 overs per side. At this point Kent's target was 176 in 22 overs

Leicestershire (186-9) lost to Somerset (190-3) by seven wickets

FINAL

Somerset (209-9) lost to Lancashire (77-0) by 10 wickets *(DLS)*

Somerset's innings was reduced to 44 overs before play began, and then Lancashire's innings was further reduced

NORTHERN GROUP – FINAL TABLE *(2015 in brackets)*

		P	W	L	Aban/NR	Points	Net Run Rate
1	Lancashire (6)	6	4	1	1	9	0.772
2	Leicestershire (5)	6	3	0	3	9	1.018
3	Nottinghamshire (8)	6	4	2	0	8	0.750
4	Derbyshire (1)	6	3	2	1	7	0.169
5	Warwickshire (9)	6	3	3	0	6	-0.018
6	Durham (2)	6	2	3	1	5	0.385
7	**Yorkshire (10)**	**6**	**2**	**3**	**1**	**5**	**-0.031**
8	Unicorns (4)	6	2	3	1	5	-0.125
9	Northamptonshire (7)	6	2	3	1	5	-1.293
10	Worcestershire (3)	6	0	5	1	1	-1.540

SOUTHERN GROUP – FINAL TABLE *(2015 in brackets)*

		P	W	L	Aban/NR	Points	Net Run Rate
1	Somerset (1)	6	5	0	1	11	1.226
2	Kent (4)	6	4	1	1	9	0.385
3	Hampshire (6)	6	4	2	0	8	0.711
4	Sussex (7)	6	4	2	0	8	0.625
5	Surrey (2)	6	3	3	0	6	0.154
6	Essex (3)	6	3	3	0	6	-0.163
7	Middlesex (5)	6	2	4	0	4	-0.226
8	Gloucestershire (8)	6	2	4	0	4	-0.547
9	MCC Young Cricketers (10)	6	1	4	1	3	-1.574
10	Glamorgan (9)	6	0	5	1	1	-0.708

SECOND ELEVEN TROPHY

PREVIOUS WINNERS

1986	**Northamptonshire**, who beat Essex by 14 runs
1987	**Derbyshire**, who beat Hampshire by 7 wickets
1988	**Yorkshire**, who beat Kent by 7 wickets
1989	**Middlesex**, who beat Kent by 6 wickets
1990	**Lancashire**, who beat Somerset by 8 wickets
1991	**Nottinghamshire**, who beat Surrey by 8 wickets
1992	**Surrey**, who beat Northamptonshire by 8 wickets
1993	**Leicestershire**, who beat Sussex by 142 runs
1994	**Yorkshire**, who beat Leicestershire by 6 wickets
1995	**Leicestershire**, who beat Gloucestershire by 3 runs
1996	**Leicestershire**, who beat Durham by 46 runs
1997	**Surrey**, who beat Gloucestershire by 3 wickets
1998	**Northamptonshire**, who beat Derbyshire by 5 wickets
1999	**Kent**, who beat Hampshire by 106 runs.
2000	**Leicestershire,** who beat Hampshire by 25 runs.
2001	**Surrey**, who beat Somerset by 6 wickets
2002	**Kent**, who beat Hampshire by 5 wickets
2003	**Hampshire**, who beat Warwickshire by 8 wickets
2004	**Worcestershire**, who beat Essex by 8 wickets
2005	**Sussex**, who beat Nottinghamshire by 6 wickets
2006	**Warwickshire**, who beat Yorkshire by 93 runs
2007	**Middlesex**, who beat Somerset by 1 run
2008	**Hampshire**, who beat Essex by 7 runs
2009	**Yorkshire**, who beat Lancashire by 2 wickets
2010	**Essex**, who beat Lancashire by 14 runs
2011	**Nottinghamshire**, who beat Lancashire by 4 wickets
2012	**Lancashire**, who beat Durham by 76 runs
2013	**Lancashire**, who beat Nottinghamshire by 76 runs
2014	**Leicestershire**, who beat Lancashire by 168 runs
2015	**Derbyshire**, who beat Durham by 10 runs

SECOND ELEVEN TROPHY
AVERAGES 2016

Played 6   Won 2   Lost 3   Abandoned 1

BATTING AND FIELDING

(Qualification 3 innings)

Player	M.	I.	N.O.	Runs	H.S.	Avge	Strike Rate	100s	50s	ct/st
R Gibson	5	5	0	245	87	49.00	103.37	0	2	3
W M H Rhodes	3	3	1	60	56*	30.00	85.71	0	1	1
K Carver	5	4	1	89	66*	29.66	90.81	0	1	4
M J Waite	5	4	0	61	41	15.25	79.22	0	0	0
J A Thompson	4	3	0	45	22	15.00	51.13	0	0	6
J C Wainman	5	4	0	30	13	7.50	69.76	0	0	1
B O Coad	4	3	3	16	11*	—	48.48	0	0	1

Also played

H C Brook	1	1	0	69	69	69.00	102.98	0	1	1
M Hussain	1	1	0	48	48	48.00	65.75	0	0	0
J A Leaning	2	2	0	63	45	31.50	67.02	0	0	2
E Barnes	2	2	0	60	58	30.00	100.00	0	1	0
A J Hodd	1	1	0	28	28	28.00	70.00	0	0	0
B L Ainsley	2	2	0	37	26	18.50	61.66	0	0	0
J Shaw	1	1	0	18	18	18.00	100.00	0	0	0
E Callis	2	2	0	35	34	17.50	58.33	0	0	0
J D Warner	2	2	0	21	19	10.50	53.84	0	0	0
B D Birkhead	2	2	0	19	14	9.50	70.37	0	0	4
C J Geldart	1	1	0	4	4	4.00	80.00	0	0	0
J A Brooks	1	1	0	2	2	2.00	40.00	0	0	0
Azeem Rafiq	1	1	0	1	1	1.00	50.00	0	0	0/1
A Z Lees	1	1	1	119	119*	—	93.70	1	0	0
A MacQueen	1	1	0	0	0	—	—	0	0	0
J Read	2	1	0	0	0	—	—	0	0	2
J W Shutt	1	0	0	0	0	—	—	0	0	1

BOWLING

(Qualification 5 wickets)

Player	Overs	Mdns	Runs	Wkts	Avge	Best	4wI	Strike Rate	Econ.
W M H Rhodes............	25	0	117	5	23.40	3-34	0	30.00	4.68
B O Coad	29	1	130	5	26.00	4-27	1	34.80	4.48
J C Wainman	33	2	170	5	34.00	2-18	0	39.60	5.15
K Carver....................	39.1	1	213	5	42.60	3-52	0	47.00	5.43

Also bowled

R Gibson...................	9	0	51	3	17.00	2-29	0	18.00	5.66
Azeem Rafiq...............	10	0	37	2	18.50	2-37	0	30.00	3.70
J A Brooks	9	1	41	2	20.50	2-41	0	27.00	4.55
J A Thompson	4	0	21	1	21.00	1-21	0	24.00	5.25
J W Shutt	8	0	46	2	23.00	2-46	0	24.00	5.75
J D Warner.................	17	2	83	2	41.50	2-53	0	51.00	4.88
E Barnes...................	6	0	42	1	42.00	1-42	0	36.00	7.00
M J Waite..................	19	3	81	1	81.00	1-16	0	114.00	4.26
J A Leaning................	3	0	28	0	—	—	0	—	9.33
A MacQueen...............	7	0	17	0	—	—	0	—	2.42
J Shaw......................	3	0	20	0	—	—	0	—	6.66

Second Eleven Twenty20
Northamptonshire v. Yorkshire

Played at Stowe School, Buckinghamshire, on May 16, 2016
Yorkshire won by 33 runs at 2.09pm

Toss won by Yorkshire

Northamptonshire 0 points, Yorkshire 2 points

YORKSHIRE

M Hussain, run out (sub T B Sole)		28
C J Geldart, c Crook b White		19
R Gibson, c Crook b White		7
M J Waite, b Jakeman		18
Y Imtiaz, run out (White)		21
J A Thompson, c Kendall b Jakeman		12
§ B D Birkhead, c Kendall b Sanderson		5
A MacQueen, not out		12
K Carver		
* B O Coad	Did not bat	
J D Warner		
Extras b 1, nb 2, w 9		12
Total (7 wkts, 20 overs)		134

FoW: 1-50 (Geldart), 2-56 (Hussain), 3-67 (Gibson), 4-90 (Waite), 5-106 (Thompson), 6-115 (Birkhead), 7-134 (Imtiaz)

	O	M	R	W
Branston	3	0	29	0
Sanderson	4	0	27	1
Griggs	1	0	7	0
Crook	4	0	27	0
White	4	0	20	2
Jakeman	4	0	23	2

NORTHAMPTONSHIRE

S A Zaib, c Thompson b Waite		10
* R A Newton, b Warner		2
S P Crook, c Birkhead b Waite		1
L C Paternott, c Coad b Carver		18
W D Thomas, c Warner b Waite		0
G G White, c Geldart b Coad		3
§ J S Kendall, c Coad b Gibson		23
S R Branston, b MacQueen		23
B W Sanderson, b Coad		10
J Jakeman, b Coad		2
C R Griggs, not out		1
Extras b 1, nb 4, w 3		8
Total (18 overs)		101

FoW: 1-11 (Zaib), 2-16 (Newton), 3-16 (Crook), 4-16 (Thomas), 5-19 (White), 6-57 (Paternott), 7-84 (Branston), 8-90 (Kendall), 9-96 (Jakeman), 10-101 (Sanderson)

	O	M	R	W
Waite	4	0	16	3
Warner	2	0	8	1
Coad	3	1	17	3
Carver	4	0	25	1
MacQueen	4	0	29	1
Gibson	1	0	5	1

Umpires: J R Cousins and T Lungley

Scorers: M E Woolley and H Clayton

Second Eleven Twenty20
Northamptonshire v. Yorkshire

Played at Stowe School, Buckinghamshire, on May 16, 2016
Yorkshire won by 8 wickets at 5.12pm

Toss won by Northamptonshire   Northamptonshire 0 points, Yorkshire 2 points

NORTHAMPTONSHIRE

S A Zaib, c Waite b Gibson		15
* R A Newton, b Coad		22
S P Crook, b MacQueen		15
L C Paternott, c Callis b Carver		14
W D Thomas, not out		37
§ J S Kendall, not out		14
T B Sole		
S R Branston		
B W Sanderson	Did not bat	
J Jakeman		
C R Griggs		
Extras b 4, w 1		5
Total (4 wkts, 20 overs)		122

FoW:1-24 (Zaib), 2-49 (Newton), 3-60 (Crook), 4-71 (Paternott)

	O	M	R	W
Waite	2	0	12	0
Warner	2	0	10	0
Gibson	4	0	34	1
Coad	4	0	19	1
Carver	4	0	26	1
MacQueen	4	0	17	1

YORKSHIRE

E Callis, run out (Paternott)		5
C J Geldart, not out		75
R Gibson, c Kendall b Sanderson		13
M J Waite, not out		19
M Hussain		
J A Thompson		
A MacQueen		
§ B D Birkhead	Did not bat	
K Carver		
* B O Coad		
J D Warner		
Extras lb 2, nb 2, w 8		12
Total (2 wkts, 16.1 overs)		124

FoW: 1-37 (Callis), 2-76 (Gibson)

	O	M	R	W
Crook	4	0	29	0
Griggs	2	0	27	0
Branston	2	0	11	0
Sanderson	3	0	22	1
Jakeman	4	0	27	0
Zaib	1	0	2	0
Paternott	0.1	0	4	0

Umpires: J R Cousins and T Lungley   Scorers: M E Woolley and H Clayton

Second Eleven Twenty20
Yorkshire v. Lancashire

Played at York CC on May 25, 2016
Match abandoned at 3.15pm. No Result

Toss won by Yorkshire   Yorkshire 1 point, Lancashire 1 point

YORKSHIRE

A W Gale, b Mahmood		3
* A Z Lees, not out		36
R Gibson, c Yates b Mahmood		0
J A Leaning, not out		18
M J Waite		
W M H Rhodes		
J A Thompson		
C J Geldart	Did not bat	
§ B D Birkhead		
K Carver		
J D Warner		
Extras lb 1, w 2		3
Total (2 wkts, 9 overs)		60

FoW: 1-15 (Gale), 2-15 (Gibson)

	O	M	R	W
Clark	2	0	14	0
Buck	2	0	15	0
Edwards	1	0	6	0
Mahmood	2	0	9	2
Parry	1	0	6	0
Lilley	1	0	9	0

LANCASHIRE

* K R Brown	
L M Reece	
J Clark	
R P Jones	
D J Lamb	
S D Parry	Did not bat
A M Lilley	
§ B J Yates	
G A Edwards	
N L Buck	
S Mahmood	
T J Lester	

Umpires: I J Dixon and P R Pollard   Scorers: H Clayton and M Dixon

Second Eleven Twenty20
Yorkshire v. Lancashire

(Second game)

At York CC on May 25, 2016
Match abandoned without a ball bowled

No toss made   Yorkshire 1 point, Lancashire 1 point

Second Eleven Twenty20
Nottinghamshire v. Yorkshire

Played at Trent College, Long Eaton, on May 27, 2016
Nottinghamshire won by 2 wickets at 2.11pm

Toss won by Nottinghamshire   Nottinghamshire 2 points, Yorkshire 0 points

YORKSHIRE

H C Brook, c Marshall b D D A Brown	12
C J Geldart, c Carter b D D A Brown	35
R Gibson, c Wyatt b Kitt	40
* M J Waite, c Kitt b Root	30
E Callis, b D D A Brown	16
J A Thompson, b Kitt	5
J W P Brown, not out	1
§ B D Birkhead, not out	4
J D Warner	
J E G Logan Did not bat	
J W Shutt	
Extras w 2	2
Total (6 wkts, 20 overs)	145

FoW: 1-34 (Brook), 2-72 (Geldart), 3-116 (Gibson), 4-127 (Waite), 5-139 (Callis), 6-141 (Thompson)

	O	M	R	W
Carter	4	0	32	0
Kitt	4	0	31	2
Root	3	0	18	1
D D A Brown	4	0	12	3
Marshall	3	0	32	0
Wood	2	0	20	0

NOTTINGHAMSHIRE

S K W Wood, b Warner	13
§ T J Moores, c Birkhead b Waite	0
A K Dal, b Warner	10
W T Root, c Callis b Logan	16
D D A Brown, c and b Shutt	28
S T Ashraf, c Gibson b Thompson	22
T R Wyatt, run out (Warner)	7
M Carter, b Thompson	8
* P J Franks. not out	13
B M Kitt, not out	17
C R Marshall Did not bat	
Extras b 3, nb 6, w 3	12
Total (8 wkts, 19 overs)	146

FoW: 1-1 (Moores), 2-26 (Wood), 3-27 (Dal), 4-42 (Root), 5-92 (Brown), 6-92 (Ashraf), 7-106 (Wyatt), 8-124 (Carter)

	O	M	R	W
Waite	4	0	23	1
Warner	4	0	14	2
Gibson	3	0	28	0
Shutt	3	0	34	1
Logan	2	0	15	1
Thompson	2.4	0	24	2
J W P Brown	0.2	0	5	0

Umpires: S A Garratt and B Jones   Scorers: Mrs A Cusworth and H Clayton

Second Eleven Twenty20
Nottinghamshire v. Yorkshire

Played at Trent College, Long Eaton, on May 27, 2016
Nottinghamshire won by 2 wickets at 5.49pm

Toss won by Yorkshire   Nottinghamshire 2 points, Yorkshire 0 points

YORKSHIRE

H C Brook, b D D A Brown	....	29
C J Geldart, c Moores b S K W Wood	....	0
R Gibson, c Moores b Kitt	....	4
* M J Waite, run out (Marshall)	....	10
E Callis, not out	....	66
J A Thompson, lbw b S K W Wood	....	3
J W P Brown, lbw b Marshall	....	4
§ B D Birkhead, lbw b D D A Brown	....	0
J D Warner, run out (Ashraf)	....	4
J E G Logan, not out	....	0
J W Shutt	Did not bat	
Extras b 5, lb 6, w 7	....	18
Total (8 wkts, 20 overs)	....	138

*FoW:*1-1 (Geldart), 2-15 (Gibson), 3-36 (Waite), 4-62 (Brook), 5-81 (Thompson), 6-104 (J W P Brown), 7-105 (Birkhead), 8-136 (Warner)

	O	M	R	W
S K W Wood	4	0	20	2
L Wood	4	0	34	0
Kitt	4	0	25	1
D D A Brown	4	0	23	2
Carter	2	0	15	0
Marshall	2	0	10	1

NOTTINGHAMSHIRE

* S K W Wood, c Gibson b Logan	....	28
§ T J Moores, st Birkhead b Logan	....	13
W T Root, b Shutt	....	5
D T Christian, lbw b Warner	....	31
D D A Brown, not out	....	45
S T Ashraf, b Warner	....	0
A Aldred, run out (Waite)	....	0
L Wood, b Gibson	....	2
M Carter, c Gibson b Thompson	....	8
B M Kitt, not out	....	3
C R Marshall	Did not bat	
Extras b 2, w 2	....	4
Total (8 wkts, 20 overs)	....	139

*FoW:*1-44 (S K W Wood), 2-45 (Moores), 3-57 (Root), 4-105 (Christian), 5-105 (Ashraf), 6-109 (Aldred), 7-113 (L Wood), 8-126 (Carter)

	O	M	R	W
Waite	4	0	24	0
Warner	4	0	18	2
Gibson	3	0	27	1
Shutt	4	0	37	1
Logan	4	0	20	2
Thompson	1	0	11	1

Umpires: S A Garratt and B Jones   Scorers: Mrs A Cusworth and H Clayton

Second Eleven Twenty20
Durham v. Yorkshire

Played at Brandon CC on May 31, 2016
Durham won by 23 runs at 2.19pm

Toss won by Yorkshire

Durham 2 points, Yorkshire 0 points

DURHAM

A J Hickey, c Gibson b Willey	6
P Mustard, c Birkhead b Rhodes	29
C S MacLeod, c Gibson b Wainman	9
§ S W Poynter, c Birkhead b Waite	29
G J Muchall, c Callis b Wainman	18
* P Coughlin, c Brook b Waite	3
U Arshad, run out (Rhodes)	1
G S Randhawa, c Birkhead b Willey	0
J Coughlin, not out	13
G H I Harding, run out (Coad)	3
J Harrison, not out	6
Extras nb 2, w 2	4
Total (9 wkts, 20 overs)	121

FoW: 1-26 (Hickey), 2-43 (MacLeod), 3-49 (Mustard), 4-86 (Muchall), 5-95 (P Coughlin), 6-95 (Poynter), 7-96 (Arshad), 8-101 (Randhawa), 9-110 (Harding)

	O	M	R	W
Willey	4	0	31	2
Wainman	4	0	32	2
Rhodes	3	0	20	1
Carver	4	0	19	0
Coad	3	0	14	0
Waite	2	0	5	2

YORKSHIRE

H C Brook, c Poynter b Arshad	2
D J Willey, c Poynter b Arshad	2
R Gibson, c Harrison b J Coughlin	14
* W M H Rhodes, c Mustard b J Coughlin	10
M J Waite, st Poynter b Randhawa	17
E Callis, b Randhawa	20
§ B D Birkhead, run out (Poynter)	5
J C Wainman, run out (Hickey)	1
K Carver, c Harding b Harrison	6
B O Coad, not out	5
J W Shutt, c P Coughlin b Arshad	7
Extras lb 1, nb 6, w 2	9
Total (19.5 overs)	98

FoW: 1-6 (Willey), 2-8 (Brook), 3-27 (Rhodes), 4-41 (Gibson), 5-59 (Waite), 6-75 (Birkhead), 7-78 (Wainman), 8-83 (Callis), 9-87 (Carver), 10-98 (Shutt)

	O	M	R	W
Harrison	4	0	16	1
Arshad	3.5	0	17	3
P Coughlin	4	0	17	0
J Coughlin	4	0	28	2
Randhawa	4	0	19	2

Umpires: M A Gough and N Pratt

Scorers: K Telford and H Clayton

Second Eleven Twenty20
Durham v. Yorkshire

Played at Brandon CC on May 31, 2016
Durham won by 14 runs at 5.47pm

Toss won by Yorkshire   Durham 2 points, Yorkshire 0 points

DURHAM

A J Hickey, c Callis b Coad		36
§ P Mustard, c Willey b Rhodes		104
C S MacLeod, c Callis b Rhodes		40
S W Poynter, not out		12
G J Muchall, not out		0
U Arshad		
J Harrison		
* P Coughlin	Did not bat	
G S Randhawa		
J Coughlin		
G H I Harding		
Extras lb 8, nb 2, w 3		13
Total (3 wkts, 20 overs)		205

FoW: 1-98 (Hickey), 2-171 (Mustard), 3-201 (MacLeod)

	O	M	R	W
Wainman	3	0	28	0
Warner	4	0	37	0
Waite	1	0	7	0
Rhodes	4	0	50	2
Coad	4	0	40	1
Carver	4	0	35	0

YORKSHIRE

H C Brook, run out (MacLeod)		16
D J Willey, c Mustard b Harrison		108
R Gibson, c Poynter b J Coughlin		23
* W M H Rhodes, c MacLeod b Randhawa		20
M J Waite, c MacLeod b Randhawa		1
E Callis, not out		11
§ B D Birkhead, not out		4
J C Wainman		
K Carver	Did not bat	
B O Coad		
J D Warner		
Extras lb 6, w 2		8
Total (5 wkts, 20 overs)		191

FoW: 1-62 (Brook), 2-147 (Willey), 3-153 (Gibson), 4-156 (Waite), 5-178 (Rhodes)

	O	M	R	W
Harrison	4	0	26	1
Arshad	4	0	44	0
P Coughlin	4	0	24	0
Harding	1	0	21	0
J Coughlin	4	0	33	1
Hickey	1	0	21	0
Randhawa	2	0	16	2

Umpires: M A Gough and N Pratt   Scorers: K Telford and H Clayton

Second Eleven Twenty20
Yorkshire v. Derbyshire

Played at Harrogate CC on June 1, 2016
Derbyshire won by 5 wickets at 2.14pm

Toss won by Derbyshire
Yorkshire 0 points, Derbyshire 2 points

YORKSHIRE

H C Brook, b Neesham		16
* C J Geldart, c Tattersall b Carter		8
R Gibson, c Hemmings b Neesham		7
M J Waite, c Knight b Elstone		23
E Callis, c Davis b Elstone		26
Azeem Rafiq, c White b Elstone		11
J A Thompson, c Hemmings b Neesham		13
E Barnes, lbw b Carter		3
§ J Read, not out		5
J D Warner, b Neesham		0
J E G Logan, not out		1
Extras lb 2, nb 2, w 9		13
Total (9 wkts, 20 overs)		126

FoW: 1-19 (Geldart), 2-30 (Gibson), 3-41 (Brook), 4-84 (Waite), 5-96 (Callis), 6-115 (Azeem Rafiq), 7-120 (Barnes), 8-124 (Thompson), 9-125 (Warner).

	O	M	R	W
Davis	3	0	22	0
Carter	3	0	13	2
Neesham	4	0	21	4
White	2	0	17	0
Hughes	2	0	14	0
Hemmings	3	0	16	0
Elstone	3	0	21	3

DERBYSHIRE

S L Elstone, c Read b Waite		4
J A Tattersall, c Thompson b Warner		19
J P Webb, c Brook b Barnes		9
J D S Neesham, c Thompson b Gibson		22
* A L Hughes, not out		56
T C Knight, lbw b Logan		9
§ H R Hosein, not out		5
R P Hemmings		
W S Davis	Did not bat	
H J White		
A Carter		
Extras lb 1, nb 2, w 4w		7
Total (5 wkts, 18.3 overs)		131

FoW: 1-4 (Elstone), 2-21 (Webb), 3-35 (Tattersall), 4-68 (Neesham), 5-105 (Knight).

	O	M	R	W
Waite	1	0	4	1
Warner	4	1	29	1
Barnes	3	0	25	1
Azeem Rafiq	4	0	28	0
Thompson	1	0	6	0
Gibson	3	0	23	1
Logan	2.3	0	15	1

Umpires: R J Warren and G M Roberts   Scorers: H Clayton and J A Wallis

Second Eleven Twenty20
Yorkshire v. Derbyshire

Played at Harrogate CC on June 1, 2016
Derbyshire won by 43 runs at 5.45pm

Toss won by Derbyshire   Yorkshire 0 points, Derbyshire 2 points

DERBYSHIRE

§ H R Hosein, b Logan		10
J P Webb, c Warner b Thompson		5
J A Tattersall, not out		40
* A L Hughes, b Warner		20
J D S Neesham, lbw b Gibson		2
S L Esltone, c Hussain b Gibson		12
T C Knight, lbw b Thompson		61
R P Hemmings, not out		17
A Carter		
W S Davis	Did not bat	
C F Parkinson		
Extras lb 1, nb 5, w 8		14
Total (6 wkts, 20 overs)		181

FoW: 1-11 (Hosein), 2-18 (Webb), 3-46 (Hughes), 4-54 (Neesham), 5-76 (Elstone), 6-151 (Knight)

	O	M	R	W
Warner	4	0	46	1
Logan	4	0	39	1
Thompson	4	0	29	2
Gibson	4	0	37	2
Azeem Rafiq	4	0	29	0

YORKSHIRE

H C Brook, b Parkinson		1
C J Geldart, c Parkinson b Carter		1
R Gibson, c Hosein b Parkinson		0
* M J Waite, c Parkinson b Carter		49
E Callis, c Hemmings b Neesham		13
M Hussain, c and b Hemmings		36
J A Thompson, c Hughes b Davis		17
Azeem Rafiq, c Knight b Hemmings		5
§ J Read, not out		5
J D Warner, not out		5
J E G Logan	Did not bat	
Extras lb 3, w 3		6
Total (8 wkts, 20 overs)		138

FoW: 1-2 (Brook), 2-2 (Geldart), 3-5 (Gibson), 4-47 (Callis), 5-101 (Waite), 6-107 (Hussain), 7-128 (Thompson), 8-132 (Azeem Rafiq)

	O	M	R	W
Parkinson	4	0	17	2
Carter	4	0	15	2
Neesham	3	0	12	1
Hughes	2	0	20	0
Davis	3	0	41	1
Hemmings	4	0	30	2

Umpires: R J Warren and G M Roberts   Scorers: H Clayton and J A Wallis

Second Eleven Twenty20
Yorkshire v. Worcesterhire

Played at Marske CC on June 20, 2016
Yorkshire won by 5 runs at 2.20pm

Toss won by Worcestershire   Yorkshire 2 points, Worcestershire 0 points

YORKSHIRE

R Gibson, c Twohig b Scrimshaw		38
C J Geldart, c Ul-Abideen Malik b Rhodes		18
M J Waite, st Dodd b Twohig		11
M Hussain, c Russell b Rhodes		2
E Callis, c Westbury b Rhodes		3
* Azeem Rafiq, c Fraine b Rhodes		7
J A Thompson, c Twohig b Russell		26
§ B D Birkhead, lbw b Russell		16
J C Wainman, b Morris		4
J D Warner, c Rhodes b Russell		1
J W Shutt, not out		0
Extras lb 2, nb 2, w 6		10
Total (19.2 overs)		136

FoW: 1-57 (Gibson), 2-69 (Geldart), 3-75 (Hussain), 4-79 (Callis), 5-79 (Waite), 6-100 (Rafiq), 7-125 (Thompson). 8-131 (Wainman), 9-136 (Warner), 10-136 (Birkhead)

	O	M	R	W
Morris	3	0	25	1
Tongue	2	0	19	0
Scrimshaw	2	0	9	1
Hepburn	1	0	17	0
Russell	3.2	0	22	3
Rhodes	4	0	19	4
Twohig	4	0	23	1

WORCESTERSHIRE

* G H Rhodes, c Gibson b Shutt		33
Z Ul-Abideen Malik, c Thompson b Warner		5
W A R Fraine, b Azeem Rafiq		18
A Hepburn, b Azeem Rafiq		26
O E Westbury, c Gibson b Shutt		6
B J Twohig, c Azeem Rafiq b Wainman		16
J C Tongue, not out		10
§ J M H Dodd, run out (Waite)		3
C J Russell, not out		0
C A J Morris		
G L S Scrimshaw Did not bat		
Extras lb 10, nb 2, w 2		14
Total (7 wkts, 20 overs)		131

FoW: 1-24 (Ul-Abideen Malik), 2-59 (Rhodes), 3-63 (Fraine), 4-76 (Westbury), 5-106 (Hepburn), 6-123 (Twohig), 7-130 (Dodd)

	O	M	R	W
Wainman	4	0	29	1
Warner	4	0	21	1
Gibson	3	0	29	0
Shutt	4	0	18	2
Azeem Rafiq	4	0	20	2
Thompson	1	0	4	0

Umpires: P R Pollard and J D Middlebrook   Scorers: H Clayton and P M Mellish

Second Eleven Twenty20
Yorkshire v. Worcesterhire

Played at Marske CC on June 20, 2016
Yorkshire won by 1 run at 5.48pm

Toss won by Yorkshire　　　　　　　　　　Yorkshire 2 points, Worcestershire 0 points

YORKSHIRE

R Gibson, c Dodd b Morris		11
C J Geldart, b Russell		7
M J Waite, c Fraine b Scrimshaw		35
M Hussain, c Rhodes b Scrimshaw		41
E Callis, lbw b Scrimshaw		0
* Azeem Rafiq, c Hepburn b Scrimshaw		1
J A Thompson, st Dodd b Twohig		16
§ B D Birkhead, c Morris b Hepburn		4
J C Wainman, not out		1
J D Warner, b Twohig		1
J W Shutt, c Ul-Abideen Malik b Twohig		0
Extras lb 1, lb 4, nb 2, w 7		14
Total (20 overs)		131

FoW: 1-8 (Gledart), 2-20 (Gibson), 3-86 (Waite), 4-86 (Callis), 5-96 (Azeem Rafiq), 6-111 (Hussain), 7-128 (Birkhead), 8-129 (Thompson), 9-131 (Warner), 10-131 (Shutt)

	O	M	R	W
Morris	3	0	16	1
Russell	3	0	33	1
Rhodes	3	0	23	0
Hepburn	3	0	22	1
Twohig	4	0	12	3
Scrimshaw	4	0	20	4

WORCESTERSHIRE

A Hepburn, c Birkhead b Azeem Rafiq		34
Z Ul-Abideen Malik, run out (Waite)		0
W A R Fraine, c Callis b Shutt		26
* G H Rhodes, not out		28
O E Westbury, c Thompson b Shutt		7
B J Twohig, b Thompson		17
§ J M H Dodd, run out (Thompson)		5
S Harvey		
C A J Morris	Did not bat	
C J Russell		
G L S Scrimshaw		
Extras lb 2, w 11		13
Total (6 wkts, 20 overs)		130

FoW: 1-0 (Ul-Abideen Malik), 2-63 (Fraine), 3-81 (Hepburn), 4-98 (Westbury), 5-124 (Twohig), 6-130 (Dodd)

	O	M	R	W
Wainman	4	0	35	0
Warner	3	0	26	0
Thompson	4	0	20	1
Gibson	1	0	6	0
Azeem Rafiq	4	0	19	1
Shutt	4	0	22	2

Umpires: P R Pollard and J D Middlebrook　　　　Scorers: H Clayton and P M Mellish

SECOND ELEVEN TWENTY20 2016

Two matches played against the same opponents at the same venue on the same day.

SEMI-FINALS

Middlesex (199-5)	beat Durham (191-6)	by eight runs
Somerset (151-7)	beat Warwickshire (94)	by 57 runs

FINAL

Somerset (161-7)	lost to Middlesex (162-8) by two wickets

NORTHERN GROUP – FINAL TABLE *(2015 in brackets)*

		P	W	L	T	Aban/NR	Points	Net Run Rate
1	Durham (2)	12	7	1	0	4	18	1.595
2	Warwickshire (7)	12	7	1	0	4	18	0.866
3	Lancashire (1)	12	6	1	0	5	17	1.251
4	Derbyshire (5)	12	7	3	0	2	16	0.727
5	Leicestershire (10)	12	4	3	0	5	13	0.168
6	Nottinghamshire (4)	12	4	5	0	3	11	-0.558
7	**Yorkshire (8)**	**12**	**4**	**6**	**0**	**2**	**10**	**-0.186**
8	Northamptonshire (6)	12	3	6	0	3	9	-0.824
9	Unicorns (9)	12	2	8	0	2	6	-1.049
10	Worcestershire (3)	12	0	10	0	2	2	-1.155

SOUTHERN GROUP – FINAL TABLE *(2015 in brackets)*

		P	W	L	T	Aban/NR	Points	Net Run Rate
1	Somerset (6)	12	8	4	0	0	16	1.146
2	Middlesex (2)	12	6	3	0	3	15	0.536
3	Kent (1)	12	6	4	0	2	14	0.300
4	Glamorgan (8)	12	6	4	0	2	14	-0.066
5	Hampshire (4)	12	4	3	0	5	13	0.078
6	Surrey (10)	12	5	4	1	2	13	-0.052
7	Gloucestershire (7)	12	3	3	0	6	12	-0.371
8	MCC Young Cricketers (9)	12	2	5	0	5	9	-0.473
9	Sussex (3)	12	1	5	1	5	8	-0.847
10	Essex (5)	12	1	7	0	4	6	-1.175

PREVIOUS WINNERS

2011	**Sussex**, who beat Durham by 24 runs
2012	**England Under-19s**, who beat Sussex by eight wickets
2013	**Surrey**, who beat Middlesex by six runs
2014	**Leicesterhire**, who beat Somerset by 11 runs
2015	**Middlesex**, who beat Kent by four wickets

SECOND ELEVEN TWENTY20
AVERAGES 2016

Played 12   Won 4   Lost 6   No Result 1   Abandoned 1

BATTING AND FIELDING
(Qualification 3 innings)

Player	M.	I.	N.O.	Runs	H.S.	Avge	50s	Strike Rate	Ct/St
M Hussain	5	4	0	107	41	26.75	0	108.08	1
M J Waite	11	10	1	213	49	23.66	0	105.97	1
C J Geldart	9	8	1	163	75*	23.28	1	117.26	1
E Callis	9	9	2	160	66*	22.85	1	94.67	6
R Gibson	11	11	0	157	40	14.27	0	106.08	7
J A Thompson	9	7	0	92	26	13.14	0	105.74	5
H C Brook	6	6	0	76	29	12.66	0	84.44	2
B D Birkhead	9	7	2	38	16	7.60	0	95.00	6/1
A Rafiq	4	4	0	24	11	6.00	0	88.88	1
J W Shutt	5	3	1	7	7	3.50	0	87.50	1
J C Wainman	4	3	1	6	4	3.00	0	100.00	0
J D Warner	10	5	1	11	5*	2.75	0	64.70	2

Also batted

Player	M.	I.	N.O.	Runs	H.S.	Avge	100s	Strike Rate	Ct/St
D J Willey	2	2	0	110	108	55.00	1	215.68	1
Y Imtiaz	1	1	0	21	21	21.00	0	95.45	0
W M H Rhodes	3	2	0	30	20	15.00	0	120.00	0
K Carver	5	1	0	6	6	6.00	0	75.00	0
J W P Brown	2	2	1	5	4	5.00	0	83.33	0
E Barnes	1	1	0	3	3	3.00	0	60.00	0
A W Gale	1	1	0	3	3	3.00	0	25.00	0
B O Coad	4	1	1	5	5*	—	0	41.66	2
J A Leaning	1	1	1	18	18*	—	0	100.00	0
A Z Lees	1	1	1	36	36*	—	0	156.52	0
J E G Logan	4	2	2	1	1*	—	0	100.00	0
A MacQueen	2	1	1	12	12*	—	0	100.00	0
J Read	2	2	2	10	5*	—	0	125.00	1

BOWLING
(Qualification 5 wickets)

Player	Overs	Mdns	Runs	Wkts	Avge	Best	Strike Rate	Econ.	4wI
M J Waite	18	0	91	7	13.00	3-16	15.42	5.05	0
J A Thompson	13.4	0	94	6	15.66	2-24	13.66	6.87	0
J E G Logan	12.3	0	89	5	17.80	2-20	15.00	7.12	0
B O Coad	14	1	90	5	18.00	3-17	16.80	6.42	0
J W Shutt	15	0	111	6	18.50	2-18	15.00	7.40	0
J D Warner	31	1	209	8	26.12	2-14	23.25	6.74	0
R Gibson	22	0	189	6	31.50	2-37	22.00	8.59	0

Also bowled

Player	Overs	Mdns	Runs	Wkts	Avge	Best	Strike Rate	Econ.	4wI
D J Willey	4	0	31	2	15.50	2-31	12.00	7.75	0
A MacQueen	8	0	46	2	23.00	1-17	24.00	5.75	0
W M H Rhodes	7	0	70	3	23.33	2-50	14.00	10.00	0
E Barnes	3	0	25	1	25.00	1-25	18.00	8.33	0
Azeem Rafiq	16	0	96	3	32.00	2-20	32.00	6.00	0
J C Wainman	15	0	124	3	41.33	2-32	30.00	8.26	0
K Carver	16	0	105	2	52.50	1-25	48.00	6.56	0
J W P Brown	2	0	5	0	—	—	—	15.00	0

Other Second Eleven Matches
Gloucestershire v. Yorkshire

Played at Bristol on April 11, 12 and 13, 2016

Gloucestershire 220 (G T Hankins 110, J R Bracey 43) and 166-2 dec (G T Hankins 78*, M A H Hammond 75*). **Yorkshire** 67-1 dec (A J Hodd 40*) and 320-9 (R Gibson 97, B L Ainsley 61, M D Fisher 40, T M J Smith 3-84).

Yorkshire won by 1 wicket   Toss: Gloucestershire

Lancashire v. Yorkshire

Played at Aigburth, Liverpool, on April 19, 20 and 21, 2016

Yorkshire 361 (W M H Rhodes 137, R Gibson 53, A J Hodd 51, H C Brook 36) and 193-1 dec (W M H Rhodes 114*, R Gibson 51). **Lancashire** 250-7 dec (L M Reece 134, T C Smith 32) and 273-9 (R P Jones 81, T E Bailey 69, D J Lamb 41, B O Coad 3-34).

Match drawn   Toss: Yorkshire

Glamorgan v. Yorkshire

Played at the SSE SWALEC Stadium, Cardiff, on April 26, 27 and 28, 2016

Glamorgan 201 (A O Morgan 46, M A Wallace 41, N J Selman 31, J R Murphy 30, K Carver 4-58) and 200-0 dec (M A Wallace 128*, N J Selman 68*). **Yorkshire** 81-4 dec (R Gibson 30) and 273 (Y Imtiaz 63*, R Gibson 50, W M H Rhodes 49, A O Morgan 4-72, D A Cosker 4-77).

Glamorgan won by 47 runs   Toss: Glamorgan

Kent v. Yorkshire

Played at Beckenham on May 9, 10, 11 and 12, 2016

Yorkshire 268-8 dec (T T Bresnan 66, A J Hodd 53, J A Leaning 35, J C Wainman 35, D A Griffiths 3-30) and 29-1 dec. **Kent** innings forfeited and 140-5 (F K Cowdrey 65, J A Lewis 46).

Match drawn   Toss: Yorkshire

Yorkshire v. Somerset

Played at Headingley on July 11, 12 and 13, 2016

Somerset 359-6 dec (R E van der Merwe 111, G A Bartlett 106, J H Davey 59*) and 216-7 dec (A J Hose 68, G A Bartlett 59, M A Leask 31, K Carver 4-39). **Yorkshire** 151 (R Gibson 55, R E van der Merwe 3-4, O R T Sale 3-33) and 233 (M J Waite 83, R Gibson 50, P A van Meekeren 4-38, O R T Sale 3-38).

Somerset won by 191 runs   Toss: Yorkshire

Yorkshire v. Scotland Development XI

Played at Harrogate on September 6 and 7, 2016

Scotland Development XI 120 (F R J Coleman 59*, W M H Rhodes 5-43) and 184 (M Jones 46, R Henry 39. K Carver 4-29, J W Shutt 3-17). **Yorkshire** 346 (M D Fisher 96*, E Barnes 68, W M H Rhodes 38, A Neill 4-81).

W M H Rhodes ended the Scotland first innings with a spell of five wickets for four runs in nine balls. Four of those wickets came in a quadruple wicket maiden, with wickets on the first, second, fourth and final deliveries.

Yorkshire won by an innings and 42 runs   Toss: Yorkshire

Yorkshire v. Nottinghamshire

Played at Scarborough on September 12, 13 and 14, 2016

Yorkshire 232 (J A Tattersall 101, K Carver 31, M J Waite 30, M E Milnes 4-54) and 107 (B L Ainsley 32, B M Kitt 6-43). **Nottinghamshire** 243 (L Patterson-White 58, A K Dal 55, J H Barrett 37, K Carver 4-75, E Barnes 3-23) and 97-5 (M D Fisher 3-41).

Nottinghamshire won by 5 wickets   Toss: Nottinghamshire

YORKSHIRE DIAMONDS

Inaugural Season

Captain: Lauren Winfield

General Manger Jane Hildreth   Head Coach Richard Pyrah

KIA SUPER LEAGUE 2016 (T20)

2016 WINNERS: Southern Vipers, who beat Western Storm by 7 wickets

LEAGUE TABLE

2 points awarded for a win, plus 1 bonus point for any team that
achieves victory with a run rate 1.25 times that of the opposition.

		P	W	L	T	NR/A	PTS	NRR
1	Southern Vipers	5	4	1	0	0	11	1.437
2	Western Storm	5	4	1	0	0	9	0.838
3	Loughborough Lightning	5	3	2	0	0	8	0.170
4	Surrey Stars	5	2	3	0	0	5	-0.274
5	**Yorkshire Diamonds ....**	**5**	**1**	**4**	**0**	**0**	**3**	**-0.362**
6	Lancashire Thunder	5	1	4	0	0	2	-1.724

YORKSHIRE DIAMONDS 2016 KIA SUPER LEAGUE SQUAD5

Player	Date of Birth	Birthplace	Type
L Winfield (captain)	August 16 1990	York	RHB
H J Armitage	June 14 1997	Huddersfield	RHB, LB
A J Blackwell	August 31 1983	Wagga Wagga, New South Wales	RHB, RAM
K H Brunt	July 2 1985	Barnsley	RHB, RAMF
S Butler	April 23 1994	Stoke on Trent	LHB, RAOS
A N Davidson-Richards	May 29 1994	Tunbridge Wells	RHB, RAFM
T Graves	October 10 1998	Halifax	RHB
J L Gunn MBE	May 9 1986	Nottingham	RHB, RAMF
D Hazell	May 13 1988	Durham	RHB, OS
S Ismail	October 5 1988	Cape Town, Cape Province	LHB, RAFM
K A Levick	July 17 1991	Sheffield	RHB, LB
B L Mooney	January 14 1994	Shepperton, Victoria, Australia	LHB, WK
A L Nicholls	October 30 1997	Barnet	RHB, RAM
L Spragg	June 16 1982	Keighley	LHB, LAM
K C Thompson	September 28 1996	Harrogate	RHB, LAS

Kia Super League
Yorkshire Diamonds v. Loughborough Lightning

Played at Headingley, Leeds, on Saturday, July 30, 2016
Loughborough Lightning won by 43 runs

Toss won by Loughborough   Yorkshire 0 points, Loughborough 3 points

LOUGHBOROUGH

* G A Elwiss, st Mooney b Hazell	....	10
D van Nierkerk, c Armitage b Brunt	....	1
S F M Devine, c Gunn b Levick	....	52
E A Perry, run out (Mooney)	....	17
§ A E Jones, lbw b Hazell	....	0
S B Odedra, c and b Gunn	....	9
E Jonesc, c Gunn b Ismail	....	12
T F Brookes, run out (Ismail)	....	0
P J Scholfield, not out	....	13
B A Langstonc, c Levick b Gunn	....	1
R L Grundy, not out	....	3
Extras lb 5, w 5	....	10
Total (9 wkts, 20 overs)	....	128

FoW: 1-6, 2-30, 3-85, 4-85, 5-96, 6-96, 7-97, 8-118, 9-119

	O	M	R	W
Ismail	4	0	27	1
Brunt	4	1	15	1
Hazell	4	0	22	2
Thompson	1	0	7	0
Levick	3	0	32	1
Gunn	4	1	20	2

YORKSHIRE

* L Winfield, run out (Langstone)	....	23
H J Armitage, lbw b Perry	....	9
A N Davidson, c Perry b Grundy	....	3
§ B L Mooney, lbw b Grundy	....	0
A J Blackwell, lbw b Grundy	....	3
K H Brunt, b Elwiss	....	16
J L Gunn, lbw b van Nierkerk	....	6
D Hazellc, c Elwiss b Devine	....	15
S Ismail, st Jones b Elwiss	....	0
K A Levick, st Jones b Devine	....	1
K C Thompson, not out	....	2
Extras lb 1, w 6	....	7
Total (17.1 overs)	....	85

FoW: 1-11, 2-37, 3-37, 4-37, 5-47, 6-64, 7-70, 8-71, 9-75. 10-85

	O	M	R	W
Devine	3.1	0	27	2
Perry	3	0	17	1
Grundy	4	0	21	3
van Nierkerk	4	0	13	1
Elwiss	3	0	6	2

Umpires: B J Debenham and T Lungley   Scorers: K Motley and K Oliver

Kia Super League
Surrey Stars v. Yorkshire Diamonds

Played at The Oval on Thursday, August 4, 2016 *(Day/Night)*
Surrey Stars won by 6 wickets

Toss won by Yorkshire   Surrey 2 points, Yorkshire 0 points

YORKSHIRE

* L Winfield, c and b Hartley		29
H J Armitage, b A Hartley		43
§ B L Mooney, run out (Sciver)		9
A J Blackwell, b Farrell		23
A N Davidson-Richards, run out (Smith)		10
K H Brunt, not out		15
D Hazell, not out		1
J L Gunn		
S Ismail	Did not bat	
S Butler		
L Spragg		
Extras lb 2 w 2		4
Total (5 wkts, 20 overs)		134

FoW: 1-74, 2-75, 3-92, 4-113, 5-125

	O	M	R	W
Knapp	2	0	15	0
Marsh	3	0	19	0
Sciver	4	0	28	0
Tahuhu	3	0	24	0
Hartley	4	0	18	2
Farrell	4	0	28	1

SURREY

§ T T Beaumont, c Spragg b Butler		47
B F Smith, c Blackwell b Gunn		31
C L Griffith, st Mooney b Gunn		7
* N R Sciver, not out		29
M Knapp, b Butler		0
B L Morgan, not out		0
N D Dettani		
R M Farrell		
L A Marsh	Did not bat	
L M M Tahuhu		
A Hartley		
Extras b 2, lb 8, w 11		21
Total (4 wkts, 18.1 overs)		135

FoW: 1-65, 2-73, 3-130, 4-131

	O	M	R	W
Brunt	4	0	34	0
Spragg	1	0	16	0
Ismail	2	0	14	0
Hazell	3.1	0	18	0
Gunn	4	0	19	2
Butler	4	0	24	2

Umpires: I D Blackwell and R J Warren

Kia Super League
Southern Vipers v. Yorkshire Diamonds

Played at Ageas Bowl, Southampton, on Monday, August 8, 2016
Southern Vipers won by 54 runs

Toss won by Southern Vipers   Southern Vipers 3 points, Yorkshire 0 points

SOUTHERN VIPERS

S W Bates, not out	....	45
* C M Edwards, c Mooney b Brunt	....	0
I V Collis, lbw b Ismail	....	1
S J McGlashan, c Armitage b Brunt	....	6
L S Greenway, c Ismail b Levick	....	5
A Brindle, not out	....	45
§ C E Rudd		
N E Farrant		
M J G Nielsen	Did not bat	
F M K Morris		
L C N Smith		
Extras b 6, lb 7, w 3	....	16
Total (4 wkts, 20 overs)	....	118

FoW: 1-1, 2-2, 3-9, 4-19

	O	M	R	W
Brunt	4	0	26	2
Ismail	4	0	9	1
Levick	4	0	10	1
Gunn	4	0	32	0
Hazell	4	0	28	0

YORKSHIRE

* L Winfield, c Brindle b Bates	....	8
H J Armitage, run out (Edwards)	....	7
A N Davidson-Richards, st Rudd b Smith	....	7
§ B L Mooney, b Nielsen	....	17
A J Blackwell, c and b Smith	....	6
K H Brunt, c Farrant b Smith	....	4
J L Gunn, b Smith	....	1
D Hazell, b Morris	....	5
S Butler, st Rudd b Nielsen	....	0
S Ismail, not out	....	1
K A Levick, c Brindle b Bates	....	1
Extras lb 1, w 4, nb 2	....	7
Total ((16.3 overs)	....	64

FoW: 1-10, 2-19, 3-32, 4-44, 5-48, 6-49, 7-52, 8-56, 9-61, 10-64

	O	M	R	W
Nielsen	4	0	18	2
Farrant	3	0	11	0
Bates	2.3	0	8	2
Morris	3	0	16	1
Smith	4	1	10	4

Umpires: B J Debenham and C M Watts   Scorer: Cecilia Allen

Kia Super League
Lancashire Thunder v. Yorkshire Diamonds

Played at Old Trafford, Manchester, on Friday, August 12, 2016 *(Day/Night)*
Yorkshire Diamonds won by 95 runs

Toss won by Yorkshire   Lancashire 0 points, Yorkshire 3 points

YORKSHIRE

* L Winfield, st Threlkeld b Ecclestone	....	14
H J Armitage, c Ecclestone b Satterthwaite	....	1
§ B L Mooney, b Dottin	....	18
A J Blackwell, c Ecclestone b Cross	....	59
K H Brunt, run out (Brown)	....	36
A N Davidson-Richards, not out	....	7
D Hazell, c Wyatt b Matthews	....	3
J L Gunn, not out	....	8
S Ismail		
K A Levick	Did not bat	
S Butler		
Extras b 4, lb 3, w 7, pen 6	....	20
Total (6 wkts, 20 overs)	....	166

FoW: 1-11, 2-16, 3-63, 4-132, 5-135, 6-147

	O	M	R	W
Satterthwaite	3	0	28	1
Ecclestone	4	0	25	1
Matthews	4	1	21	1
Cross	4	0	34	1
Dottin	4	0	33	1
Brown	1	0	12	0

LANCASHIRE

H K Matthews, c Armitage b Ismail	....	3
E L Lamb, b Hazell	....	10
* A E Satterthwaite, b Ismail	....	16
D N Wyatt, st Mooney b Levick	....	1
D J S Dottin, lbw b Hazell	....	25
§ E Threlkeld, c Davidson-Richards b Hazell	....	7
N Brown, b Hazell	....	0
L K Macleod, c Gunn b Brunt	....	1
K L Cross, not out	....	2
S Ecclestone, lbw b Brunt	....	0
N K A Patel, lbw b Brunt	....	0
Extras w 2, nb 4	....	6
Total (15 overs)	....	71

FoW: 1-4, 2-33, 3-34, 4-40, 5-60, 6-68, 7-69, 8-71, 9-71, 10-71

K H Brunt took a hat-trick with the wickets of L K Newton, K L Cross and N K A Patel

	O	M	R	W
Brunt	3	0	6	3
Ismail	4	0	23	2
Hazell	4	0	10	4
Levick	3	0	24	1
Gunn	1	0	8	0

Umpires: B J Debenham and C M Watts   Scorers: M Cregan and K Motley

Kia Super League
Yorkshire Diamonds v. Western Storm

Played at Headingley, Leeds, on Sunday, August 14, 2016
Western Storm won by 6 wickets

Toss won by Yorkshire   Yorkshire 0 points, Western Storm 2 points

YORKSHIRE

* L Winfield, c Priest b Davies	....	32
H J Armitage, b Shrubsole	....	0
§ B L Mooney, b Taylor	....	56
A J Blackwell, run out (Lee)	....	20
K H Brunt, c Wilson b Taylor	....	0
A Nicholls, lbw b Hennessy	....	2
D Hazell, c Davies b Shrubsole	....	4
J L Gunn, b Shrubsole	....	1
S Butler, not out	....	0
S Ismail, st Priest b Shrubsole	....	0
K A Levick, b Shrubsole	....	0
Extras lb 1, w 2	....	3
Total (20 overs)	....	118

FoW: 1-14, 2-54, 3-83, 4-84, 5-89, 6-116, 7-118, 8-118, 9-118, 10-118

	O	M	R	W
Knight	4	0	20	0
Davies	3	0	21	1
Shrubsole	4	2	23	5
Hennessy	3	0	16	1
Dibble	2	0	17	0
Taylor	4	0	20	2

WESTERN STORM

S R Taylor, c Blackwell b Ismail	....	45
§ R H Priest, c and b Ismail	....	50
L Lee, c Winfield b Levick	....	8
* H C Knight, c Brunt b Hazell	....	7
F C Wilson, not out	....	2
S N Luff, not out	....	1
G M Hennessy		
A Shrubsole		
J M Dibble	Did not bat	
C O'Keefe		
F R Davies		
Extras lb 1, w 3, nb 2	....	6
Total (4 wkts, 16.3 overs)	....	119

FoW: 1-101, 2-101, 3-111, 4-117

	O	M	R	W
Brunt	2	1	10	0
Hazell	3.3	0	22	1
Ismail	2	0	16	2
Levick	4	0	25	1
Butler	2	0	20	0
Gunn	1	0	12	0
Armitage	2	0	13	0

Umpires: P R Pollard and C M Watts   Scorers: K Motley and H Barr

KIA SUPER LEAGUE 2016

YORKSHIRE DIAMONDS AVERAGES

Played 5   Won 1   Lost 4

BATTING AND FIELDING

Player	M.	I.	N.O.	Runs	H.S.	100s	50s	Avge	ct/st
A J Blackwell	5	5	0	111	59	0	1	22.20	2
L Winfield	5	5	0	106	32	0	0	21.20	1
B L Mooney	5	5	0	100	56	0	1	20.00	0/3
K H Brunt	5	5	1	71	36	0	0	17.75	1
H J Armitage	5	5	0	60	43	0	0	12.00	3
AN Davidson-Richards	4	4	1	27	10	0	0	9.00	1
D Hazell	5	5	1	28	15	0	0	7.00	0
J L Gunn	5	4	1	16	8*	0	0	5.33	4
A Nicholls	1	1	0	2	2	0	0	2.00	0
K A Levick	4	3	0	2	1	0	0	0.67	1
S Ismail	5	3	1	1	1*	0	0	0.50	2
S Butler	4	2	1	0	0*	0	0	0.00	0
K C Thompson	1	1	1	2	2*	0	0	—	0
L Spragg	1	0	0	0	—	0	0	—	1

BOWLING

Player	Overs	Mdns	Runs	Wkts	Avge	Best	4wI	Econ
D Hazell	18.4	0	100	7	14.29	4-10	1	5.36
S Ismail	16	0	89	6	14.83	2-16	0	5.56
K H Brunt	17	2	91	6	15.17	3-6	0	5.35
S Butler	6	0	44	2	22.00	2-24	0	7.33
K A Levick	14	0	91	4	22.75	1-10	0	6.50
J L Gunn	14	1	91	4	22.75	2-19	0	6.50
H J Armitage	2	0	13	0	—	—	0	6.50
K C Thompson	1	0	7	0	—	—	0	7.00
L Spragg	1	0	16	0	—	—	0	16.00

RECORDS SECTION

All records in this section relate to First-Class Yorkshire matches except where stated

HONOURS

County Champions (34)
1867, 1870, 1893, 1896, 1898, 1900, 1901, 1902, 1905, 1908, 1912, 1919,
1922, 1923, 1924, 1925, 1931, 1932, 1933, 1935, 1937, 1938, 1939,
1946, 1959, 1960, 1962, 1963, 1966, 1967, 1968, 2001, 2014, 2015

Joint Champions (2)
1869, 1949

Promoted to Division 1
2005, 2012

Gillette Cup Winners (2)
1965, 1969

Cheltenham & Gloucester Trophy (1)
2002

Benson & Hedges Cup Winners (1)
1987

John Player Special League Winners (1)
1983

Fenner Trophy Winners (3)
1972, 1974, 1981

Asda Challenge Winners (1)
1987

Ward Knockout Cup (1)
1989

Joshua Tetley Festival Trophy (7)
1991, 1992 (Joint), 1993, 1994, 1996, 1997 and 1998

Tilcon Trophy Winners (2)
1978 and 1988

Pro-Arch Trophy (1)
2007-08

Emirates Airlines T20 (2)
2015 and 2016

Second Eleven Champions (4)
1977, 1984, 1991, 2003

Joint Champions (1)
1987

Minor Counties Champions (5)
1947, 1957, 1958, 1968, 1971

Under-25 Competition Winners (3)
1976, 1978, 1987

Bain Clarkson Trophy Winners (2)
1988 and 1994

Second Eleven Trophy (1)
2009

YORKSHIRE'S CHAMPIONSHIP CAPTAINS

1867 to 2016

* R Iddison (2)	1867, 1870
Lord Hawke (8)	1893, 1896, 1898, 1900, 1901, 1902, 1905, 1908
Sir Archibald White (1)	1912
D C F Burton (1)	1919
G Wilson (3)	1922, 1923, 1924
A W Lupton (1)	1925
F E Greenwood (2)	1931, 1932
A B Sellers (6)	1933, 1935, 1937, 1938, 1939, 1946
J R Burnet (1)	1959
J V Wilson (2)	1960, 1962
D B Close (4)	1963, 1966, 1967, 1968
D Byas (1)	2001
A W Gale (2)	2014, 2015

Joint Champions

* R Iddison (1)	1869
N W D Yardley (1)	1949

* R Iddison was captain when Yorkshire were Champion county, the County Championship starting in 1890.

RECORDS SECTION INDEX

CHAMPION COUNTIES SINCE 1873

The County Championship

The County Championship was officially constituted in 1890, and before that Yorkshire were generally considered Champions by the Press in 1867 and 1870, and equal top in 1869. From 1873 the list was generally accepted in the form as it is today.

		Yorkshire's Position
1873	Gloucestershire / Nottinghamshire	7th
1874	Gloucestershire	4th
1875	Nottinghamshire	4th
1876	Gloucestershire	3rd
1877	Gloucestershire	7th
1878	Middlesex	6th
1879	Nottinghamshire/Lancashire	6th
1880	Nottinghamshire	5th
1881	Lancashire	3rd
1882	Nottinghamshire/Lancashire	3rd
1883	Nottinghamshire	2nd
1884	Nottinghamshire	3rd
1885	Nottinghamshire	2nd
1886	Nottinghamshire	4th
1887	Surrey	3rd
1888	Surrey	2nd
1889	Surrey/Lancashire / Nottinghamshire	7th
1890	Surrey	3rd
1891	Surrey	8th
1892	Surrey	6th
1893	**Yorkshire**	**1st**
1894	Surrey	2nd
1895	Surrey	3rd
1896	**Yorkshire**	**1st**
1897	Lancashire	4th
1898	**Yorkshire**	**1st**
1899	Surrey	3rd
1900	**Yorkshire**	**1st**
1901	**Yorkshire**	**1st**
1902	**Yorkshire**	**1st**
1903	Middlesex	3rd
1904	Lancashire	2nd
1905	**Yorkshire**	**1st**
1906	Kent	2nd
1907	Nottinghamshire	2nd
1908	**Yorkshire**	**1st**
1909	Kent	3rd
1910	Kent	8th
1911	Warwickshire	7th
1912	**Yorkshire**	**1st**
1913	Kent	2nd
1914	Surrey	4th
1919	**Yorkshire**	**1st**
1920	Middlesex	4th
1921	Middlesex	3rd
1922	**Yorkshire**	**1st**
1923	**Yorkshire**	**1st**
1924	**Yorkshire**	**1st**
1925	**Yorkshire**	**1st**
1926	Lancashire	2nd
1927	Lancashire	3rd
1928	Lancashire	4th
1929	Nottinghamshire	2nd
1930	Lancashire	3rd
1931	**Yorkshire**	**1st**
1932	**Yorkshire**	**1st**
1933	**Yorkshire**	**1st**
1934	Lancashire	5th
1935	**Yorkshire**	**1st**
1936	Derbyshire	3rd
1937	**Yorkshire**	**1st**
1938	**Yorkshire**	**1st**
1939	**Yorkshire**	**1st**
1946	**Yorkshire**	**1st**
1947	Middlesex	7th
1948	Glamorgan	4th
1949	**Yorkshire**/Middlesex	**1st**
1950	Lancashire/Surrey	3rd
1951	Warwickshire	2nd
1952	Surrey	2nd
1953	Surrey	12th
1954	Surrey	2nd
1955	Surrey	2nd
1956	Surrey	7th
1957	Surrey	3rd

CHAMPION COUNTIES SINCE 1873 *(Continued)*

	Yorkshire's Position			*Yorkshire's Position*
1958	Surrey 11th		1988	Worcestershire 13th
1959	**Yorkshire 1st**		1989	Worcestershire 16th
1960	**Yorkshire 1st**		1990	Middlesex 10th
1961	Hampshire 2nd		1991	Essex 14th
1962	**Yorkshire 1st**		1992	Essex 16th
1963	**Yorkshire 1st**		1993	Middlesex 12th
1964	Worcestershire 5th		1994	Warwickshire 13th
1965	Worcestershire 4th		1995	Warwickshire 8th
1966	**Yorkshire 1st**		1996	Leicestershire 6th
1967	**Yorkshire 1st**		1997	Glamorgan 6th
1968	**Yorkshire 1st**		1998	Leicestershire 3rd
1969	Glamorgan 13th		1999	Surrey 6th
1970	Kent 4th		2000	Surrey 3rd
1971	Surrey 13th		**2001**	**Yorkshire 1st**
1972	Warwickshire 10th		2002	Surrey 9th
1973	Hampshire 14th		2003	Sussex ....Div 2, 4th
1974	Worcestershire 11th		2004	Warwickshire ....Div 2, 7th
1975	Leicestershire 2nd		2005	Nottinghamshire .....Div 2, 3rd
1976	Middlesex 8th		2006	Sussex ....Div 1, 6th
1977	Kent/Middlesex 12th		2007	Sussex ....Div 1, 6th
1978	Kent 4th		2008	Durham ....Div 1, 7th
1979	Essex 7th		2009	Durham ....Div 1, 7th
1980	Middlesex 6th		2010	Nottinghamshire .....Div 1, 3rd
1981	Nottinghamshire 10th		2011	Lancashire ....Div 1, 8th
1982	Middlesex 10th		2012	Warwickshire ......Div 2, 2nd
1983	Essex 17th		2013	Durham ....Div 1, 2nd
1984	Essex 14th		**2014**	**Yorkshire ....Div 1, 1st**
1985	Middlesex 11th		**2015**	**Yorkshire ....Div 1, 1st**
1986	Essex 10th		2016	Middlesex ....Div 1, 3rd
1987	Nottinghamshire 8th			

SEASON-BY-SEASON RECORD OF ALL FIRST-CLASS MATCHES PLAYED BY YORKSHIRE 1863-2016

Season	Played	Won	Lost	Drawn	Abd§	Season	Played	Won	Lost	Drawn	Abd§
1863	4	2	1	1	0	1921	30	17	5	8	0
1864	7	2	4	1	0	1922	33	20	2	11	0
1865	9	0	7	2	0	1923	35	26	1	8	0
1866	3	0	2	1	0	1924	35	18	4	13	0
1867	7	7	0	0	0	1925	36	22	0	14	0
1868	7	4	3	0	0	1926	35	14	0	21	1
1869	5	4	1	0	0	1927	34	11	3	20	1
1870	7	6	0	1	0	1928	32	9	0	23	0
1871	7	3	3	1	0	1929	35	11	2	22	0
1872	10	2	7	1	0	1930	34	13	3	18	2
1873	13	7	5	1	0	1931	33	17	1	15	1
1874	14	10	3	1	0	1932	32	21	2	9	2
1875	12	6	4	2	0	1933	36	21	5	10	0
1876	12	5	3	4	0	1934	35	14	7	14	0
1877	14	2	7	5	0	1935	36	24	2	10	0
1878	20	10	7	3	0	1935-6	3	1	0	2	0
1879	17	7	5	5	0	1936	35	14	2	19	0
1880	20	6	8	6	0	1937	34	22	3	9	1
1881	20	11	6	3	0	1938	36	22	2	12	0
1882	24	11	9	4	0	1939	34	23	4	7	1
1883	19	10	2	7	0	1945	2	0	0	2	0
1884	20	10	6	4	0	1946	31	20	1	10	0
1885	21	8	3	10	0	1947	32	10	9	13	0
1886	21	5	8	8	0	1948	31	11	6	14	0
1887	20	6	5	9	0	1949	33	16	3	14	0
1888	20	7	7	6	0	1950	34	16	6	12	1
1889	16	3	11	2	1	1951	35	14	3	18	0
1890	20	10	4	6	0	1952	34	17	3	14	0
1891	17	5	11	1	2	1953	35	7	7	21	0
1892	19	6	6	7	0	1954	35	16	3	16*	0
1893	23	15	5	3	0	1955	33	23	6	4	0
1894	28	18	6	4	1	1956	35	11	7	17	0
1895	31	15	10	6	0	1957	34	16	5	13	1
1896	32	17	6	9	0	1958	33	10	8	15	2
1897	30	14	7	9	0	1959	35	18	8	9	0
1898	30	18	3	9	0	1960	38	19	7	12	0
1899	34	17	4	13	0	1961	39	19	5	15	0
1900	32	19	1	12	0	1962	37	16	5	16	0
1901	35	23	2	10	1	1963	33	14	4	15	0
1902	31	15	3	13	1	1964	33	12	4	17	0
1903	31	16	5	10	0	1965	33	12	4	17	0
1904	32	10	2	20	1	1966	32	16	6	10	1
1905	33	21	4	8	0	1967	31	16	5	10	2
1906	33	19	6	8	0	1968	32	13	4	15	0
1907	31	14	5	12	2	1969	29	4	7	18	0
1908	33	19	0	14	0	1970	26	10	5	11	0
1909	30	12	5	13	0	1971	27	5	8	14	0
1910	31	11	8	12	0	1972	21	4	5	12	1
1911	32	16	9	7	0	1973	22	3	5	14*	0
1912	35	14	3	18	1	1974	22	6	7	9	1
1913	32	16	5	11	0	1975	21	11	1	9	0
1914	31	16	4	11	2	1976	22	7	7	8	0
1919	31	12	5	14	0	1977	23	7	5	11	1
1920	30	17	6	7	0	1978	24	10	3	11	1

SEASON-BY-SEASON RECORD OF ALL FIRST-CLASS
MATCHES PLAYED BY YORKSHIRE 1863-2016 *(Contd.)*

Season	Played	Won	Lost	Drawn	Abd§	Season	Played	Won	Lost	Drawn	Abd§
1979	22	6	3	13	1	1998	19	9	3	7	0
1980	24	5	4	15	0	1999	17	8	6	3	0
1981	24	5	9	10	0	2000	18	7	4	7	0
1982	22	5	1	16	1	2001	16	9	3	4	0
1983	23	1	5	17	1	2002	16	2	8	6	0
1984	24	5	4	15	0	2003	17	4	5	8	0
1985	25	3	4	18	1	2004	16	3	4	9	0
1986	25	4	6	15	0	2005	17	6	1	10	0
1986-7	1	0	0	1	0	2006	16	3	6	7	0
1987	24	7	4	13	1	2007	17	5	4	8	0
1988	24	5	6	13	0	2008	16	2	5	9	0
1989	22	3	9	10	0	2009	17	2	2	13	0
1990	24	5	9	10	0	2010	18	6	2	10	0
1991	24	4	6	14	0	2011	17	4	6	7	0
1991-2	1	0	1	0	0	2012	17	5	0	12	0
1992	22	4	6	12	1	2013	17	8	2	7	0
1992-3	1	0	0	1	0	2014	17	8	1	8	0
1993	19	6	4	9	0	2015	18	12	1	5	0
1994	20	7	6	7	0	2016	18	5	4	9	0
1995	20	8	8	4	0						
1995-6	2	2	0	0	0		3602	1516	653	1433	38
1996	19	8	5	6	0						
1997	20	7	4	9	0	*Includes one tie in each season.					

§ All these matches were abandoned without a ball being bowled, except Yorkshire v Kent at Harrogate, 1904, which was abandoned under Law 9. The two in 1914 and the one in 1939 were abandoned because of war. All these matches are excluded from the total played.

Of the 1,516 matches won 519 have been by an innings margin, 88 by 200 runs or more, and 133 by 10 wickets. Of the 653 lost 110 have been by an innings margin, 13 by 200 runs or more and 35 by 10 wickets.

ANALYSIS OF RESULTS VERSUS ALL FIRST-CLASS
TEAMS 1863-2016

COUNTY CHAMPIONSHIP

Opponents	Played	Won	Lost	Drawn	Tied
Derbyshire	205	103	19	83	0
Durham	36	16	8	12	0
Essex	160	84	25	51	0
Glamorgan	111	53	13	45	0
Gloucestershire	200	102	43	55	0
Hampshire	169	74	19	76	0
Kent	200	84	39	77	0
Lancashire	257	76	52	129	0
Leicestershire	166	84	15	66	1
Middlesex	233	82	58	92	1
Northamptonshire	142	67	26	49	0
Nottinghamshire	254	91	47	116	0
Somerset	173	90	23	60	0
Surrey	242	86	67	89	0
Sussex	199	85	33	81	0
Warwickshire	190	85	31	74	0
Worcestershire	140	70	21	49	0
Cambridgeshire	8	3	4	1	0
Total	3085	1335	543	1205	2Total

OTHER FIRST-CLASS MATCHES

Opponents	Played	Won	Lost	Drawn	Tied
Derbyshire	2	1	1	0	0
Essex	2	2	0	0	0
Hampshire	1	0	0	1	0
Lancashire	12	5	3	4	0
Leicestershire	2	1	1	0	0
Middlesex	1	1	0	0	0
Nottinghamshire	2	1	1	0	0
Surrey	1	0	0	1	0
Sussex	2	0	0	2	0
Warwickshire	2	0	0	2	0
Totals	**27**	**11**	**6**	**10**	**0**
Australians	55	6	19	30	0
Indians	14	5	1	8	0
New Zealanders	10	2	0	8	0
Pakistanis	4	1	0	3	0
South Africans	17	1	3	13	0
Sri Lankans	3	0	0	3	0
West Indians	17	3	7	7	0
Zimbabweans	2	0	1	1	0
Bangladesh A	1	1	0	0	0
India A	2	0	0	2	0
Pakistan A	2	1	0	1	0
South Africa A	1	0	0	1	0
Totals	**128**	**20**	**31**	**77**	**0**
Cambridge University/U C C E	88	42	17	29	0
Canadians	1	1	0	0	0
Combined Services	1	0	0	1	0
Durham MCCU	1	1	0	0	0
England XI's	6	1	2	3	0
Hon. M.B. Hawke's XI	1	0	1	0	0
International XI	1	1	0	0	0
Ireland	3	3	0	0	0
Jamaica	3	1	0	2	0
Leeds/Bradford MCCU	4	1	0	3	0
Liverpool and District*	3	2	1	0	0
Loughborough UCCE	2	1	0	1	0
MCC	155	55	40	60	0
Mashonaland	1	1	0	0	0
Matebeleland	1	1	0	0	0
Minor Counties	1	1	0	0	0
Oxford University	44	21	3	20	0
Philadelphians	1	0	0	1	0
Rest of England	16	4	5	7	0
Royal Air Force	1	0	0	1	0
Scotland**	11	7	0	4	0
South of England	2	1	0	1	0
C. I. Thornton's XI	5	2	0	3	0
United South of England	1	1	0	0	0
Western Province	2	0	1	1	0
Windward Islands	1	0	0	1	0
I Zingari	6	2	3	1	0
Totals	**362**	**150**	**73**	**139**	**0**
Grand Totals	**3602**	**1516**	**653**	**1431**	**2**

*Matches played in 1889, 1891, 1892 and 1893 are excluded. **Match played in 1878 is included

ABANDONED MATCHES (38)

1889	v. MCC at Lord's	1939	v. MCC at Scarborough (due to war)
1891 (2)	v. MCC at Lord's	1950	v. Cambridge University
	v. MCC at Scarborough		at Cambridge
1894	v. Kent at Bradford	1957	v. West Indians at Bradford
1901	v. Surrey at The Oval	1958 (2)	v. Nottinghamshire at Hull
1902	v. Leicestershire at Leicester (AR)		v. Worcestershire at Bradford
1904	v. Kent at Harrogate (Law 9	1966	v. Oxford University at Oxford
	— now Law 10)	1967 (2)	v. Leicestershire at Leeds
1907 (2)	v. Derbyshire at Sheffield		v. Lancashire at Manchester
	v. Nottinghamshire at Huddersfield	1972	v. Australians at Bradford
1912	v. Surrey at Sheffield	1974	v. Hampshire at Bournemouth
1914 (2)	v. England at Harrogate (due to war)	1977	v. Gloucestershire at Bristol
	v. MCC at Scarborough (due to war)	1978	v. Pakistan at Bradford
1926	v. Nottinghamshire at Leeds	1979	v. Nottinghamshire at Sheffield (AP)
1927	v. Kent at Bradford	1982	v. Nottinghamshire at Harrogate
1930 (2)	v. Derbyshire at Chesterfield*	1983	v. Middlesex at Lord's
	v. Northamptonshire at Harrogate*	1985	v. Essex at Sheffield (AP)
1931	v. Sussex at Hull	1987	v. Sussex at Hastings
1932 (2)	v. Derbyshire at Chesterfield	1992	v. Oxford University at Oxford
	v. Kent at Sheffield		
1937	v. Cambridge University at Bradford		

*Consecutive matches

ANALYSIS OF RESULTS ON GROUNDS IN YORKSHIRE USED IN 2016

FIRST-CLASS MATCHES

Ground	Played	Won	Lost	Drawn	Tied
Leeds Headingley 1891-2016	452	171 (37.83%)	79 (17.47%)	202 (44.69%)	0 (0.00%)
Scarborough North Marine Road 1874-2016	253	103 (40.71%)	36 (14.23%)	114 (45.06%)	0 (0.00%)

HIGHEST MATCH AGGREGATES – OVER 1350 RUNS

Runs	Wkts	
1665	33	Yorkshire (351 and 481) lost to Warwickshire (601:9 dec and 232:4) by 6 wkts at Birmingham, 2002
1606	31	Yorkshire (438 and 363:5 dec) lost to Somerset (326 and 479:6) by 4 wkts at Taunton, 2009
1479	28	Yorkshire (405 and 333:4 dec) lost to Somerset (377 and 364:4) by 6 wkts at Taunton , 2010
1473	17	Yorkshire (600:4 dec. and 231:3 dec.) drew with Worcestershire (453:5 dec. and 189:5) at Scarborough, 1995.
1442	29	Yorkshire (501:6 dec. and 244:6 dec.) beat Lancashire (403:7 dec. and 294) by 48 runs at Scarborough, 1991.
1439	32	Yorkshire (536:8 dec. and 205:7 dec.) beat Glamorgan (482: 7 dec. and 216) by 43 runs at Cardiff, 1996.
1431	32	Yorkshire (388 and 312:6) drew with Sussex (398 and 333:6 dec) at Scarborough, 2011
1417	33	Yorkshire (422 and 193:7) drew with Glamorgan (466 and 336:6 dec) at Colwyn Bay, 2003
1406	37	Yorkshire (354 and 341:8) drew with Derbyshire (406 and 305:9 dec) at Derby, 2004
1400	32	Yorkshire (299 and 439: 4 dec.) drew with Hampshire (296 and 366:8) at Southampton, 2007
1393	35	Yorkshire (331 and 278) lost to Kent (377 and 407:5 dec) by 175 runs at Maidstone, 1994.
1390	34	Yorkshire (431:8 dec and 265:7) beat Hampshire (429 and 265) by 3 wkts at Southampton, 1995.
1390	33	Durham (573 and 124:3) beat Yorkahire (274 and 419) by 7 wkts at Scarborough, 2013.
1376	33	Yorkshire (531 and 158:3) beat Lancashire (373 and 314) by 7 wkts at Leeds, 2001
1376	20	Yorkshire (677: 7 dec.) drew with Durham (518 and 181:3 dec.) at Leeds, 2006
1374	36	Yorkshire (594: 9 dec. and 266:7 dec.) beat Surrey (344 and 170) by 346 runs at The Oval, 2007
1373	36	Yorkshire (520 and 114:6) drew with Derbyshire (216 and 523) at Derby, 2005
1364	35	Yorkshire (216 and 433) lost to Warwickshire (316 and 399:5 dec.) by 66 runs at Birmingham, 2006
1359	25	Yorkshire (561 and 138:3 dec.) drew with Derbyshire (412:4 dec. and 248:8) at Sheffield, 1996.
1359	30	Yorkshire (358 and 321) lost to Somerset (452 and 228:0) by 10 wkts at Taunton, 2011
1353	18	Yorkshire (377:2 dec. and 300:6) beat Derbyshire (475:7 dec. and 201:3 dec.) by 4 wkts at Scarborough, 1990.

LOWEST MATCH AGGREGATES – UNDER 225 RUNS
IN A COMPLETED MATCH

Runs	Wkts	
165	30	Yorkshire (46 and 37:0) beat Nottinghamshire (24 and 58 by 10 wkts at Sheffield, 1888.
175	29	Yorkshire (104) beat Essex (30 and 41) by an innings and 33 runs at Leyton, 1901.
182	15	Yorkshire (4:0 dec. and 88.5) beat Northamptonshire (4:0 dec. and 86) by 5 wkts at Bradford, 1931.
193	29	Yorkshire (99) beat Worcestershire (43 and 51) by an innings and 5 runs at Bradford, 1900.
219	30	Yorkshire (113) beat Nottinghamshire (71 and 35) by an innings and 7 runs at Nottingham, 1881.
222	32	Yorkshire (98 and 14:2) beat Gloucestershire (68 and 42) by 8 wkts at Gloucester, 1924.
223	40	Yorkshire (58 and 51) lost to Lancashire (64 and 50)

LOWEST MATCH AGGREGATES – UNDER 325 RUNS
IN A MATCH IN WHICH ALL 40 WICKETS FELL

Runs	*Wkts*	
223	40	Yorkshire (58 and 51) lost to Lancashire (64 and 50) by 5 runs at Manchester, 1893.
288	40	Yorkshire (55 and 68) lost to Lancashire (89 and 76) by 42 runs at Sheffield, 1872.
295	40	Yorkshire (71 and 63) lost to Surrey (56 and 105) by 27 runs at The Oval, 1886.
303	40	Yorkshire (109 and 77) beat Middlesex (63 and 54) by 69 runs at Lord's, 1891.
318	40	Yorkshire (96 and 96) beat Lancashire (39 and 87) by 66 runs at Manchester, 1874.
318	40	Yorkshire (94 and 104) beat Northamptonshire (61 and 59) by 78 runs at Bradford, 1955.
319	40	Yorkshire (84 and 72) lost to Derbyshire (106 and 57) by 7 runs at Derby, 1878.
320	40	Yorkshire (98 and 91) beat Surrey (72 and 59) by 58 runs at Sheffield, 1893.
321	40	Yorkshire (88 and 37) lost to I Zingari (103 and 93) by 71 runs at Scarborough, 1877.
321	40	Yorkshire (80 and 67) lost to Derbyshire (129 and 45) by 27 runs at Sheffield, 1879.

LARGE MARGINS OF VICTORY – BY AN INNINGS
AND OVER 250 RUNS

Inns and 397 runs	Yorkshire (548:4 dec.) beat Northamptonshire (58 and 93) at Harrogate, 1921
Inns and 387 runs	Yorkshire (662) beat Derbyshire (118 and 157) at Chesterfield, 1898.
Inns and 343 runs	Yorkshire (673:8 dec) beat Northamptonshire (184 and 146) at Leeds, 2003.
Inns and 321 runs	Yorkshire (437) beat Leicestershire (58 and 58) at Leicester, 1908.
Inns and 314 runs	Yorkshire (356:8 dec) beat Northamptonshire (27 and 15) at Northampton, 1908. (Yorkshire's first match v. Northamptonshire).
Inns and 313 runs	Yorkshire (555:1 dec) beat Essex (78 and 164) at Leyton, 1932.
Inns and 307 runs	Yorkshire (681:5 dec.) beat Sussex (164 and 210) at Sheffield, 1897.
Inns and 302 runs	Yorkshire (660) beat Leicestershire (165 and 193) at Leicester, 1896.
Inns and 301 runs	Yorkshire (499) beat Somerset (125 and 73) at Bath, 1899.
Inns and 294 runs	Yorkshire (425:7 dec.) beat Gloucestershire (47 and 84) at Bristol, 1964.

LARGE MARGINS OF VICTORY – BY AN INNINGS
AND OVER 250 RUNS *(Continued)*

Inns and 284 runs	Yorkshire (467:7 dec) beat Leicestershire (111 and 72) at Bradford, 1932.
Inns and 282 runs	Yorkshire (481:8 dec) beat Derbyshire (106 and 93) at Huddersfield, 1901.
Inns and 280 runs	Yorkshire (562) beat Leicestershire (164 and 118) at Dewsbury, 1903.
Inns and 271 runs	Yorkshire (460) beat Hampshire (128 and 61) at Hull, 1900.
Inns and 271 runs	Yorkshire (495:5 dec) beat Warwickshire (99 and 125) at Huddersfield, 1922.
Inns and 266 runs	Yorkshire (352) beat Cambridgeshire (40 and 46) at Hunslet, 1869.
Inns and 260 runs	Yorkshire (521: 7dec.) beat Worcestershire (129 and 132) at Leeds, 2007.
Inns and 258 runs	Yorkshire (404:2 dec) beat Glamorgan (78 and 68) at Cardiff, 1922. (Yorkshire's first match v. Glamorgan).
Inns and 256 runs	Yorkshire (486) beat Leicestershire (137 and 93) at Sheffield, 1895.
Inns and 251 runs	Yorkshire (550) beat Leicestershire (154 and 145) at Leicester, 1933.

LARGE MARGINS OF VICTORY – BY OVER 300 RUNS

389 runs	Yorkshire (368 and 280:1 dec) beat Somerset (125 and 134) at Bath, 1906.
370 runs	Yorkshire (194 and 274) beat Hampshire (62 and 36) at Leeds, 1904.
351 runs	Yorkshire (280 and 331) beat Northamptonshire (146 and 114) at Northampton, 1947.
346 runs	Yorkshire (594: 9 dec. and 266: 7 dec.) beat Surrey (344 and 179) at The Oval, 2007.
328 runs	Yorkshire (186 and 318:1 dec) beat Somerset (43 and 133) at Bradford, 1930.
328 runs	Yorkshire (280 and 277:7 dec) beat Glamorgan (104 and 105) at Swansea, 2001.
320 runs	Yorkshire (331 and 353:9 dec) beat Durham (150 and 214) at Chester-le-Street, 2004
308 runs	Yorkshire (89 and 420) beat Warwickshire (72 and 129) at Birmingham, 1921.
308 runs	Yorkshire (89 and 420) beat Warwickshire (72 and 129)
305 runs	Yorkshire (370 and 305:4 dec) beat Hampshire (227 and 143) at Leeds, 2015
305 runs	Yorkshire (282 and 263:4 dec) beat Nottinghamshire (94 and 146) at Scarborough 2016

LARGE MARGINS OF VICTORY – BY 10 WICKETS (WITH OVER 100 RUNS SCORED IN THE 4th INNINGS)

4th Innings

167:0 wkt	Yorkshire (247 and 167:0) beat Northamptonshire 233 and 180) at Huddersfield, 1948.
147:0 wkt	Yorkshire (381 and 147:0) beat Middlesex (384 and 142) at Lord's, 1896.
142:0 wkt	Yorkshire (304 and 142:0) beat Sussex (254 and 188) at Bradford, 1887.
139:0 wkt	Yorkshire (163:9 dec and 139:0) beat Nottinghamshire (234 and 67) at Leeds, 1932.
138:0 wkt	Yorkshire (293 and 138:0) beat Hampshire (251 and 179) at Southampton, 1897.
132:0 wkt	Yorkshire (328 and 132:0) beat Northamptonshire (281 and 175) at Leeds, 2005.
129:0 wkt	Yorkshire (355 and 129:0) beat Durham MCCU (196 and 287) at Durham, 2011.
127:0 wkt	Yorkshire (258 and 127:0) beat Cambridge University (127 and 257) at Cambridge, 1930.
119:0 wkt	Yorkshire (109 and 119:0) beat Essex (108 and 119) at Leeds, 1931.
118:0 wkt	Yorkshire (121 and 118:0) beat MCC (125 and 113) at Lord's, 1883.
116:0 wkt	Yorkshire (147 and 116:0) beat Hampshire (141 and 120) at Bournemouth, 1930.
114:0 wkt	Yorkshire (135 and 114:0) beat Hampshire (71 and 176) at Bournemouth, 1948.
114:0 wkt	Yorkshire (135 and 114:0) beat Hampshire (71 and 176)
105:0 wkt	Yorkshire (307 and 105:0) beat Worcestershire (311 and 100) at Worcester, 2015

HEAVY DEFEATS – BY AN INNINGS AND OVER 250 RUNS

Inns and 272 runs	Yorkshire (78 and 186) lost to Surrey (536) at The Oval, 1898.
Inns and 261 runs	Yorkshire (247 and 89) lost to Sussex (597: 8 dec.) at Hove, 2007.
Inns and 255 runs	Yorkshire (125 and 144) lost to All England XI (524) at Sheffield, 1865.

HEAVY DEFEATS – BY OVER 300 RUNS

324 runs	Yorkshire (247 and 204) lost to Gloucestershire (291 and 484) at Cheltenham, 1994.
305 runs	Yorkshire (119 and 51) lost to Cambridge University (312 and 163) at Cambridge, 1906.

HEAVY DEFEATS – BY 10 WICKETS
(WITH OVER 100 RUNS SCORED IN THE 4th INNINGS)

4th Innings

228:0 wkt   Yorkshire (358 and 321) lost to Somerset (452 and 228:0)
           at Taunton, 2011

148:0 wkt   Yorkshire (83 and 216) lost to Lancashire (154 and 148:0)
           at Manchester, 1875.

119:0 wkt   Yorkshire (92 and 109) lost to Nottinghamshire (86 and 119:0 wkt)
           at Leeds, 1989.

108:0 wkt   Yorkshire (236 and 107) lost to Hampshire (236 and 108:0 wkt)
           at Southampton, 2008

100:0 wkt   Yorkshire (95 and 91) lost to Gloucestershire (88 and 100:0)
           at Bristol, 1956.

NARROW VICTORIES – BY 1 WICKET

Yorkshire (70 and 91:9) beat Cambridgeshire (86 and 74) at Wisbech, 1867.
Yorkshire (91 and 145:9) beat MCC (73 and 161) at Lord's, 1870.
Yorkshire (265 and 154:9) beat Derbyshire (234 and 184) at Derby, 1897.
Yorkshire (177 and 197:9) beat MCC (188 and 185) at Lord's, 1899.
Yorkshire (391 and 241:9) beat Somerset (349 and 281) at Taunton, 1901.
Yorkshire (239 and 168:9) beat MCC (179 and 226) at Scarborough, 1935.
Yorkshire (152 and 90:9) beat Worcestershire (119 and 121) at Leeds, 1946.
Yorkshire (229 and 175:9) beat Glamorgan (194 and 207) at Bradford, 1960.
Yorkshire (265.9 dec and 191:9) beat Worcestershire (227 and 227) at Worcester, 1961.
Yorkshire (329:6 dec and 167:9) beat Essex (339.9 dec and 154) at Scarborough, 1979.
Yorkshire (Innings forfeited and 251:9) beat Sussex (195 and 55.1 dec) at Leeds, 1986.
Yorkshire (314 and 150:9) beat Essex (200 and 261) at Scarborough, 1998.

NARROW VICTORIES – BY 5 RUNS OR LESS

By 1 run   Yorkshire (228 and 214) beat Middlesex (206 and 235) at Bradford, 1976.
By 1 run   Yorkshire (383 and inns forfeited) beat Loughborough UCCE (93: 3 dec.
           and 289) at Leeds, 2007.
By 2 runs   Yorkshire (108 and 122) beat Nottinghamshire (56 and 172)
           at Nottingham, 1870.
By 2 runs   Yorkshire (304:9 dec and 135) beat Middlesex (225:2 dec and 212)
           at Leeds, 1985.
By 3 runs   Yorkshire (446:9 dec and 172:4 dec) beat Essex (300:3 dec and 315)
           at Colchester, 1991.
By 5 runs   Yorkshire (271 and 147:6 dec) beat Surrey (198 and 215) at Sheffield, 1950.
By 5 runs   Yorkshire (151 and 176) beat Hampshire (165 and 157) at Bradford, 1962.
By 5 runs   Yorkshire (376:4 and 106) beat Middlesex (325:8 and 152) at Lord's, 1975.
By 5 runs   Yorkshire (323:5 dec and inns forfeited) beat Somerset (inns forfeited
           and 318) at Taunton, 1986.

NARROW DEFEATS – BY 1 WICKET

Yorkshire (224 and 210) lost to Australian Imperial Forces XI (265 and 170:9)
           at Leeds, 1919.
Yorkshire (101 and 159) lost to Warwickshire (45 and 216:9) at Scarborough, 1934.
Yorkshire (239 and 184:9 dec.) lost to Warwickshire (125 and 302:9)
           at Birmingham, 1983.
Yorkshire (289 and 153) lost to Surrey (250:2 dec and 193:9) at Guildford, 1991.
Yorkshire (341 and Inns forfeited) lost to Surrey (39:1 dec and 306:9) at Bradford, 1992.

NARROW DEFEATS – BY 5 RUNS OR LESS

By 1 run	Yorkshire (135 and 297) lost to Essex (139 and 294) at Huddersfield, 1897.
By 1 run	Yorkshire (159 and 232) lost to Gloucestershire (164 and 228) at Bristol, 1906.
By 1 run	Yorkshire (126 and 137) lost to Worcestershire (101 and 163) at Worcester, 1968.
By 1 run	Yorkshire (366 and 217) lost to Surrey (409 and 175) at The Oval, 1995.
By 2 runs	Yorkshire (172 and 107) lost to Gloucestershire (157 and 124) at Sheffield, 1913.
By 2 runs	Yorkshire (179:9 dec and 144) lost to MCC (109 and 216) at Lord's, 1957.
By 3 runs	Yorkshire (126 and 181) lost to Sussex (182 and 128) at Sheffield, 1883.
By 3 runs	Yorkshire (160 and 71) lost to Lancashire (81 and 153) at Huddersfield, 1889.
By 3 runs	Yorkshire (134 and 158) lost to Nottinghamshire (200 and 95) at Leeds, 1923.
By 4 runs	Yorkshire (169 and 193) lost to Middlesex (105 and 261) at Bradford, 1920.
By 5 runs	Yorkshire (58 and 51) lost to Lancashire (64 and 50) at Manchester, 1893.
By 5 runs	Yorkshire (119 and 115) lost to Warwickshire (167 and 72) at Bradford, 1969.

HIGH FOURTH INNINGS SCORES – 300 AND OVER

By Yorkshire

To Win:	406:4	beat Leicestershire by 6 wkts at Leicester, 2005
	402:6	beat Gloucestershire by 4 wkts at Bristol, 2012
	400:4	beat Leicestershire by 6 wkts at Scarborough, 2005
	339:6	beat Durham by 4 wkts at Chester-le-Street, 2013
	331:8	beat Middlesex by 2 wkts at Lord's, 1910.
	327:6	beat Nottinghamshire by 4 wkts at Nottingham, 1990.*
	323:5	beat Nottinghamshire by 5 wkts at Nottingham, 1977.
	318:3	beat Glamorgan by 7 wkts at Middlesbrough, 1976.
	316:8	beat Gloucestershire by 2 wkts at Scarborough, 2012
	309:7	beat Somerset by 3 wkts at Taunton, 1984.
	308:8	beat Nottinghamshire by 2 wkts at Worksop, 1982.
	305:5	beat Hampshire by 5 wkts at West End, Southampton, 2015
	305:3	beat Lancashire by 7 wkts at Manchester, 1994.
	304:4	beat Derbyshire by 6 wkts at Chesterfield, 1959.
	300:4	beat Derbyshire by 6 wkts at Chesterfield, 1981.
	300:6	beat Derbyshire by 4 wkts at Scarborough, 1990.*
To Draw:	341:8	(set 358) drew with Derbyshire at Derby, 2004.
	333:7	(set 369) drew with Essex at Chelmsford, 2010
	316:6	(set 326) drew with Oxford University at Oxford, 1948.
	312:6	(set 344) drew with Sussex at Scarborough 2011
	316:7	(set 320) drew with Somerset at Scarborough, 1990.
	300:5	(set 392) drew with Kent at Canterbury, 2010
To Lose:	433	(set 500) lost to Warwickshire by 66 runs at Birmingham, 2006
	380	(set 406) lost to MCC. by 25 runs at Lord's, 1937.
	343	(set 490) lost to Durham by 146 runs at Leeds 2011
	324	(set 485) lost to Northamptonshire by 160 runs at Luton, 1994.
	322	(set 344) lost to Middlesex by 21 runs at Lord's, 1996.
	309	(set 400) lost to Middlesex by 90 runs at Lord's 1878.

*Consecutive matches

By Opponents:

To Win:	479:6	Somerset won by 4 wkts at Taunton, 2009
	472:3	Middlesex won by 7 wkts at Lord's, 2014
	404:5	Hampshire won by 5 wkts at Leeds, 2006
	392:4	Gloucestershire won by 6 wkts at Bristol, 1948.
	364:4	Somerset won by 6 wkts at Taunton, 2009
	354:5	Nottinghamshire won by 5 wkts at Scarborough, 1990.
	337:4	Worcestershire won by 6 wkts at Kidderminster, 2007.
	334:6	Glamorgan won by 4 wkts at Harrogate, 1955.
	329:5	Worcestershire won by 5 wkts at Worcester, 1979.
	306:9	Surrey won by 1 wkt at Bradford, 1992.
	305:7	Lancashire won by 3 wkts at Manchester, 1980.
	302:9	Warwickshire won by 1 wkt at Birmingham, 1983

HIGH FOURTH INNINGS SCORES – 300 AND OVER *(Continued)*

By Opponents:

To Draw:	366:8	(set 443) Hampshire drew at Southampton, 2007.
	334:7	(set 339) MCC. drew at Scarborough, 1911.
	322:9	(set 334) Middlesex drew at Leeds, 1988.
	317:6	(set 355) Nottinghamshire drew at Nottingham, 1910.
	300:9	(set 314) Northamptonshire drew at Northampton, 1990.
To Lose:	370	(set 539) Leicestershire lost by 168 runs at Leicester, 2001.
	319	(set 364) Gloucestershire lost by 44 runs at Leeds, 1987.
	318	(set 324) Somerset lost by 5 runs at Taunton, 1986.
	315	(set 319) Essex lost by 3 runs at Colchester, 1991.
	314	(set 334) Lancashire lost by 19 runs at Manchester, 1993.
	310	(set 417) Warwickshire lost by 106 runs at Scarborough, 1939.
	306	(set 413) Kent lost by 106 runs at Leeds, 1952.
	300	(set 330) Middlesex lost by 29 runs at Sheffield, 1930.

TIE MATCHES

Yorkshire (351:4 dec and 113) tied with Leicestershire (328 and 136) at Huddersfield, 1954.
Yorkshire (106:9 dec and 207) tied with Middlesex (102 and 211) at Bradford, 1973.

HIGHEST SCORES BY AND AGAINST YORKSHIRE

Yorkshire versus: —

	By Yorkshire:	**Against Yorkshire:**
Derbyshire:		
In Yorkshire:	677:7 dec at Leeds 2013	491 at Bradford, 1949
Away:	662 at Chesterfield, 1898	523 at Derby, 2005
Durham:		
In Yorkshire:	677:7 dec. at Leeds, 2006	573 at Scarborough, 2013
Away	589-8 dec at Chester-le-Street, 2014	507:8 dec at Chester-le-Street, 2016
Essex:		
In Yorkshire:	516 at Scarborough, 2010	622:8 dec. at Leeds, 2005
Away:	555:1 dec. at Leyton, 1932	521 at Leyton, 1905
Glamorgan:		
In Yorkshire:	580:9 dec at Scarborough, 2001	498 at Leeds, 1999
Away:	536:8 dec. at Cardiff, 1996	482:7 dec. at Cardiff, 1996
Gloucestershire:		
In Yorkshire:	504:7 dec. at Bradford, 1905	411 at Leeds, 1992
Away:	494 at Bristol, 1897	574 at Cheltenham, 1990
Hampshire:		
In Yorkshire:	593:9 dec. at Leeds 2016	498:6 dec at Scarborough, 2010
Away	585:3 dec at Portsmouth 1920	599:3 at Southampton, 2011
Kent:		
In Yorkshire	550:9 at Scarborough, 1995	537:9 dec at Leeds, 2012
Away:	559 at Canterbury, 1887	580: 9 dec. at Maidstone, 1998
Lancashire:		
In Yorkshire:	590 at Bradford, 1887	517 at Leeds, 2007.
Away	616:6 dec at Manchester, 2014	537 at Manchester, 2005
Leicestershire:		
In Yorkshire	562 { at Scarborough, 1901 / at Dewsbury, 1903	681:7 dec. at Bradford, 1996
Away:	660 at Leicester, 1896	425 at Leicester, 1906

HIGHEST SCORES BY AND AGAINST YORKSHIRE *(Continued)*

Yorkshire versus: —

	By Yorkshire:	**Against Yorkshire:**

Middlesex:
| In Yorkshire: | 575:7 dec. at Bradford, 1899 | 527 at Huddersfield, 1887 |
| Away | 538:6 dec at Lord's, 1925 | 573:8 dec at Lord's, 2015 |

Northamptonshire:
| In Yorkshire: | 673:8 dec. at Leeds, 2003 | 517:7 dec. at Scarborough, 1999 |
| Away | 546:3 dec at Northampton, 2014 | 531:4 dec at Northampton, 1996 |

Nottinghamshire:
| In Yorkshire: | 572:8 dec at Scarborough, 2013 | 545:7 dec at Leeds, 2010 |
| Away | 534:9 dec at Nottingham, 2011 | 490 at Nottingham, 1897 |

Somerset:
| In Yorkshire: | 525:4 dec. at Leeds, 1953 | 630 at Leeds, 1901 |
| Away: | 589:5 dec at Bath, 2001 | 592 at Taunton, 1892 |

Surrey:
| In Yorkshire: | 582:7 dec. at Sheffield, 1935 | 510 at Leeds, 2002 |
| Away: | 704 at The Oval, 1899 | 634:5 dec at The Oval, 2013 |

Sussex:
| In Yorkshire: | 681:5 dec. at Sheffield, 1897 | 566 at Sheffield, 1937 |
| Away: | 522:7 dec. at Hastings, 1911 | 597:8 dec. at Hove, 2007 |

Warwickshire:
In Yorkshire	561:7 dec at Scarborough 2007	482 at Leeds, 2011
Away:	887 at Birmingham, 1896	601:9 dec. at Birmingham, 2002
	(Highest score by a First-Class county)	

Worcestershire:
| In Yorkshire: | 600: 4 dec. at Scarborough, 1995 | 453:5 dec. at Scarborough, 1995 |
| Away: | 560:6 dec. at Worcester, 1928 | 456:8 at Worcester, 1904 |

Australians:
| In Yorkshire: | 377 at Sheffield, 1953 | 470 at Bradford, 1893 |

Indians:
| In Yorkshire: | 385 at Hull, 1911 | 490:5 dec. at Sheffield, 1946 |

New Zealanders:
| In Yorkshire: | 419 at Bradford, 1965 | 370:7 dec. at Bradford, 1949 |

Pakistanis:
| In Yorkshire: | 433:9 dec. at Sheffield, 1954 | 356 at Sheffield, 1954 |

South Africans:
| In Yorkshire: | 579 at Sheffield, 1951 | 454:8 dec at Sheffield, 1951 |

Sri Lankans:
| In Yorkshire: | 314:8 dec. at Leeds, 1991 | 422:8 dec. at Leeds, 1991 |

West Indians:
| In Yorkshire: | 312:5 dec. at Scarborough, 1973 | 426 at Scarborough, 1995 |

Zimbabweans:
| In Yorkshire: | 298:9 dec at Leeds, 1990 | 235 at Leeds, 2000 |

Cambridge University:
| In Yorkshire: | 359 at Scarborough, 1967 | 366 at Leeds, 1998 |
| Away: | 540 at Cambridge, 1938 | 425:7 at Cambridge, 1929 |

Durham MCCU:
| Away: | 355 at Durham, 2011 | 287 at Durham, 2011 |

Leeds/Bradford MCCU:
| In Yorkshire | 454 at Leeds, 2014 | 211 at Leeds, 2012 |

Loughborough MCCU:
| In Yorkshire: | 383:6 dec at Leeds, 2007 | 289 at Leeds, 2007 |

Yorkshire versus: —

MCC:	**By Yorkshire:**	**Against Yorkshire:**
In Yorkshire:	557:8 dec. at Scarborough, 1933	478:8 at Scarborough, 1904
Away:	528:8 dec. at Lord's, 1919	488 at Lord's, 1919
Oxford University:		
In Yorkshire:	173 at Harrogate, 1972	190:6 dec at Harrogate, 1972
Away:	468:6 dec. at Oxford, 1978	422:9 dec. at Oxford, 1953

LOWEST SCORES BY AND AGAINST YORKSHIRE

Yorkshire versus:

Derbyshire:	**By Yorkshire:**	**Against Yorkshire:**
In Yorkshire:	50 at Sheffield, 1894	20 at Sheffield, 1939
Away:	44 at Chesterfield, 1948	26 at Derby, 1880
Durham:		
In Yorkshire:	93 at Leeds, 2003	125 at Harrogate, 1995
Away:	108 at Durham, 1992	74 at Chester-le-Street, 1998
Essex:		
In Yorkshire:	31 at Huddersfield, 1935	52 at Harrogate, 1900
Away:	98 at Leyton, 1905	30 at Leyton, 1901
Glamorgan:		
In Yorkshire:	83 at Sheffield, 1946	52 at Hull, 1926
Away:	92 at Swansea, 1956	48 at Cardiff, 1924
Gloucestershire:		
In Yorkshire:	61 at Leeds, 1894	36 at Sheffield, 1903
Away:	35 at Bristol, 1959	42 at Gloucester, 1924

Hampshire:

	By Yorkshire:	Against Yorkshire:
In Yorkshire:	23 at Middlesbrough, 1965	36 at Leeds, 1904
	Away:	96 at Bournemouth, 1971 36 at
	Southampton, 1898	

Kent:

	By Yorkshire:	Against Yorkshire:
In Yorkshire:	30 at Sheffield, 1865	39 { at Sheffield, 1882 { at Sheffield, 1936
Away:	62 at Maidstone, 1889	63 at Canterbury, 1901

Lancashire:		
In Yorkshire:	33 at Leeds, 1924	30 at Holbeck, 1868
Away:	51 { at Manchester, 1888 { at Manchester, 1893	39 at Manchester, 1874
Leicestershire:	By Yorkshire:	Against Yorkshire:
In Yorkshire:	93 at Leeds, 1935	34 at Leeds, 1906
Away:	47 at Leicester, 1911	57 at Leicester, 1898
Middlesex:		
In Yorkshire:	45 at Leeds, 1898	45 at Huddersfield, 1879
Away:	43 at Lord's, 1888	49 at Lord's in 1890
Northamptonshire:		
In Yorkshire:	85 at Sheffield, 1919	51 at Bradford, 1920
Away	64 at Northampton, 1959	15 at Northampton, 1908 (and 27 in first innings)
Nottinghamshire:		
In Yorkshire:	32 at Sheffield, 1876	24 at Sheffield, 1888
Away:	43 at Nottingham, 1869	13 at Nottingham, 1901 (second smallest total by a First-Class county)

Yorkshire versus:

Somerset:	**By Yorkshire:**	**Against Yorkshire:**
In Yorkshire:	73 at Leeds, 1895	43 at Bradford, 1930
Away:	83 at Wells, 1949	35 at Bath, 1898

Surrey:

In Yorkshire:	54 at Sheffield, 1873	31 at Holbeck, 1883
Away:	26 at The Oval, 1909	44 at The Oval, 1935

Sussex:

In Yorkshire:	61 at Dewsbury, 1891	20 at Hull, 1922
Away:	42 at Hove, 1922	24 at Hove, 1878

Warwickshire:

In Yorkshire:	49 at Huddersfield, 1951	35 at Sheffield, 1979
Away:	54 at Birmingham, 1964	35 at Birmingham, 1963

Worcestershire:

In Yorkshire:	62 at Bradford, 1907	24 at Huddersfield, 1903
Away:	72 at Worcester, 1977	65 at Worcester, 1925

Australians:

In Yorkshire:	48 at Leeds, 1893	23 at Leeds, 1902

Indians:

In Yorkshire:	146 at Bradford, 1959	66 at Harrogate, 1932

New Zealanders:

In Yorkshire:	189 at Harrogate, 1931	134 at Bradford, 1965

Pakistanis:

In Yorkshire:	137 at Bradford, 1962	150 at Leeds, 1967

South Africans:

In Yorkshire:	113 at Bradford, 1907	76 at Bradford, 1951

Sri Lankans:

In Yorkshire:	Have not been dismissed. Lowest is 184:1 dec at Leeds, 1991	287:5 dec at Leeds, 1988

West Indians:

In Yorkshire:	50 at Harrogate, 1906	58 at Leeds, 1928

Zimbabweans:

In Yorkshire:	124 at Leeds, 2000	68 at Leeds, 2000

Cambridge University:

In Yorkshire:	110 at Sheffield, 1903	39 at Sheffield, 1903
Away:	51 at Cambridge, 1906	30 at Cambridge, 1928

Durham MCCU:

Away:	355 at Durham, 2011	196 at Durham, 2011

Leeds/Bradford MCCU:

In Yorkshire:	135 at Leeds, 2012	118 at Leeds, 2013

Loughborough MCCU:

In Yorkshire:	348:5 dec at Leeds, 2010	289 at Leeds, 2007

MCC:

In Yorkshire:	46 { at Scarborough, 1876 at Scarborough, 1877	31 at Scarborough, 1877
Away:	44 at Lord's, 1880	27 at Lord's, 1902

Oxford University:

In Yorkshire:	Have not been dismissed. Lowest is 115:8 at Harrogate, 1972	133 at Harrogate, 1972
Away:	141 at Oxford, 1949	46 at Oxford, 1956

INDIVIDUAL INNINGS OF 150 AND OVER

A complete list of all First-class Centuries up to and including 2007 is to be found in the 2008 edition

J M BAIRSTOW (7)

205	v. Nottinghamshire	Nottingham	2011
182	v. Leicestershire	Scarborough	2012
186	v. Derbyshire	Leeds	2013
161*	v. Sussex	Arundel	2014
219*	v. Durham	Chester-le-Street	2015
246	v. Hampshire	Leeds	2016
198	v. Surrey	Leeds	2016

G S BALLANCE (2)

174	v. Northamptonshire	Leeds	2014
165	v. Sussex	Hove	2015

W BARBER (7)

162	v. Middlesex	Sheffield	1932
168	v. MCC	Lord's	1934
248	v. Kent	Leeds	1934
191	v. Sussex	Leeds	1935
255	v. Surrey	Sheffield	1935
158	v. Kent	Sheffield	1936
157	v. Surrey	Sheffield	1938

M G BEVAN (2)

153*	v. Surrey	The Oval	1995
160*	v. Surrey	Middlesbrough	1996

H D BIRD (1)

181*	v. Glamorgan	Bradford	1959

R J BLAKEY (3)

204*	v. Gloucestershire	Leeds	1987
196	v. Oxford University	Oxford	1991
223*	v. Northamptonshire	Leeds	2003

G BLEWETT (1)

190	v. Northamptonshire	Scarborough	1999

M W BOOTH (1)

210	v. Worcestershire	Worcester	1911

G BOYCOTT (32)

165*	v. Leicestershire	Scarborough	1963
151	v. Middlesex	Leeds	1964
151*	v. Leicestershire	Leicester	1964
177	v. Gloucestershire	Bristol	1964
164	v. Sussex	Hove	1966
220*	v. Northamptonshire	Sheffield	1967
180*	v. Warwickshire	Middlesbrough	1968
260*	v. Essex	Colchester (Garrison Ground)	1970
169	v. Nottinghamshire	Leeds	1971
233	v. Essex	Colchester (Garrison Ground)	1971
182*	v. Middlesex	Lord's	1971
169	v. Lancashire	Sheffield	1971
151	v. Leicestershire	Bradford	1971
204*	v. Leicestershire	Leicester	1972

INDIVIDUAL INNINGS OF 150 AND OVER *(Continued)*

G BOYCOTT (Continued)

152*	v. Worcestershire	Worcester	1975
175*	v. Middlesex	Scarborough	1975
201*	v. Middlesex	Lord's	1975
161*	v. Gloucestershire	Leeds	1976
207*	v. Cambridge University	Cambridge	1976
156*	v. Glamorgan	Middlesbrough	1976
154	v Nottinghamshire	Nottingham	1977
151*	v Derbyshire	Leeds	1979
167	v Derbyshire	Chesterfield	1979
175*	v Nottinghamshire	Worksop	1979
154*	v Derbyshire	Scarborough	1980
159	v Worcestershire	Sheffield (Abbeydale Park)	1982
152*	v Warwickshire	Leeds	1982
214*	v Nottinghamshire	Worksop	1983
163	v Nottinghamshire	Bradford	1983
169*	v Derbyshire	Chesterfield	1983
153*	v Derbyshire	Harrogate	1984
184	v Worcestershire	Worcester	1985

T T BRESNAN (1)

169*	v. Durham	Chester-le-Street	2015

G L BROPHY (1)

177*	v Worcestershire	Worcester	2011

J T BROWN (8)

168*	v Sussex	Huddersfield	1895
203	v Middlesex	Lord's	1896
311	v Sussex	Sheffield	1897
300	v Derbyshire	Chesterfield	1898
150	v Sussex	Hove	1898
168	v Cambridge University	Cambridge	1899
167	v Australians	Bradford	1899
192	v Derbyshire	Derby	1899

D BYAS (5)

153	v Nottinghamshire	Worksop	1991
156	v Essex	Chelmsford	1993
181	v Cambridge University	Cambridge	1995
193	v Lancashire	Leeds	1995
213	v Worcestershire	Scarborough	1995

D B CLOSE (5)

164	v Combined Services	Harrogate	1954
154	v Nottinghamshire	Nottingham	1959
198	v Surrey	The Oval	1960
184	v Nottinghamshire	Scarborough	1960
161	v Northamptonshire	Northampton	1963

D DENTON (11)

153*	v Australians	Bradford	1905
165	v Hampshire	Bournemouth	1905
172	v Gloucestershire	Bradford	1905
184	v Nottinghamshire	Nottingham	1909
182	v Derbyshire	Chesterfield	1910

D DENTON *(Continued)*

200*	v Warwickshire	Birmingham	1912
182	v Gloucestershire	Bristol	1912
221	v Kent	Tunbridge Wells	1912
191	v Hampshire	Southampton	1912
168*	v Hampshire	Southampton	1914
209*	v Worcestershire	Worcester	1920

A W GALE *(4)*

150	v. Surrey	The Oval	2008
151*	v. Nottinghamshire	Nottingham	2010
272	v. Nottinghamshire	Scarborough	2013
164	v. Worcestershire	Scarborough	2015

P A GIBB *(1)*

157*	v. Nottinghamshire	Sheffield	1935

S HAIGH *(1)*

159	v. Nottinghamshire	Sheffield	1901

L HALL *(1)*

160	v. Lancashire	Bradford	1887

J H HAMPSHIRE *(5)*

150	v. Leicestershire	Bradford	1964
183*	v. Sussex	Hove	1971
157*	v. Nottinghamshire	Worksop	1974
158	v. Gloucestershire	Harrogate	1974
155*	v. Gloucestershire	Leeds	1976

I J HARVEY *(1)*

209*	v. Somerset	Leeds	2005

LORD HAWKE *(1)*

166	v. Warwickshire	Birmingham	1896

G H HIRST *(15)*

186	v. Surrey	The Oval	1899
155	v. Nottinghamshire	Scarborough	1900
214	v. Worcestershire	Worcester	1901
153	v. Leicestershire	Dewsbury	1903
153	v. Oxford University	Oxford	1904
152	v. Hampshire	Portsmouth	1904
157	v. Kent	Tunbridge Wells	1904
341	v. Leicestershire	Leicester (Aylestone Road)	1905
232*	v. Surrey	The Oval	1905
169	v. Oxford University	Oxford	1906
158	v. Cambridge University	Cambridge	1910
156	v. Lancashire	Manchester	1911
218	v. Sussex	Hastings	1911
166*	v. Sussex	Hastings	1913
180*	v. MCC	Lord's	1919

P HOLMES *(16)*

302*	v. Hampshire	Portsmouth	1920
150	v. Derbyshire	Chesterfield	1921
277*	v. Northamptonshire	Harrogate	1921
209	v. Warwickshire	Birmingham	1922

INDIVIDUAL INNINGS OF 150 AND OVER (Continued)

P HOLMES (Continued)

220*	v. Warwickshire	Huddersfield	1922
199	v. Somerset	Hull	1923
315*	v. Middlesex	Lord's	1925
194	v. Leicestershire	Hull	1925
159	v. Hampshire	Southampton	1925
180	v. Gloucestershire	Gloucester	1927
175*	v. New Zealanders	Bradford	1927
179*	v. Middlesex	Leeds	1928
275	v. Warwickshire	Bradford	1928
285	v. Nottinghamshire	Nottingham	1929
250	v. Warwickshire	Birmingham	1931
224*	v. Essex	Leyton	1932

L HUTTON (31)

196	v. Worcestershire	Worcester	1934
163	v. Surrey	Leeds	1936
161	v. MCC	Lord's	1937
271*	v. Derbyshire	Sheffield	1937
153	v. Leicestershire	Hull	1937
180	v. Cambridge University	Cambridge	1938
158	v. Warwickshire	Birmingham	1939
280*	v. Hampshire	Sheffield	1939
151	v. Surrey	Leeds	1939
177	v. Sussex	Scarborough	1939
183*	v. Indians	Bradford	1946
171*	v. Northamptonshire	Hull	1946
197	v. Glamorgan	Swansea	1947
197	v. Essex	Southend-on-Sea	1947
270*	v. Hampshire	Bournemouth	1947
176*	v. Sussex	Sheffield	1948
155	v. Sussex	Hove	1948
167	v. New Zealanders	Bradford	1949
201	v. Lancashire	Manchester	1949
165	v. Sussex	Hove	1949
269*	v. Northamptonshire	Wellingborough	1949
156	v. Essex	Colchester (Castle Park)	1950
153	v. Nottinghamshire	Nottingham	1950
156	v. South Africans	Sheffield	1951
151	v. Surrey	The Oval	1951
194*	v. Nottinghamshire	Nottingham	1951
152	v. Lancashire	Leeds	1952
189	v. Kent	Leeds	1952
178	v. Somerset	Leeds	1953
163	v. Combined Services	Harrogate	1954
194	v. Nottinghamshire	Nottingham	1955

R A HUTTON (1)

189	v. Pakistanis	Bradford	1971

R ILLINGWORTH (2)

150	v. Essex	Colchester (Castle Park)	1959
162	v. Indians	Sheffield	1959

Hon F S JACKSON (3)

160	v. Gloucestershire	Sheffield	1898
155	v. Middlesex	Bradford	1899
158	v. Surrey	Bradford	1904

TOP NOTCH: Alex Lees enjoyed his most successful Championship season in 2016, when he was Yorkshire's leading run-scorer in the competition with 1,165 runs including three centuries and seven half-centuries. His nearest rival was his opening partner, Adam Lyth, who made 1,133 runs with four centuries and three half-centuries. It was the second time Alex had topped the 1,000 mark — he also did it in 2014 when he rapped out 1,018 runs.

RED SAILS IN THE SUNSET: The breathtaking view over Headingly as England meet Pakistan on September 1 for the Fourth Royal London One-Day International, which England won by four wickets. Five of the England team were Yorkshire players.

CLUB FIELDER OF THE YEAR: Adam Lyth puts everything into this dive in Yorkshire's Royal London One-Day Cup Semi-Final against Surrey at Headingley. Adam held 25 catches in Yorkshire's County Championship games, three more in the Royal London Cup, and he was easily top with 10 in *T20* matches.

MOMENTOUS BOOST: Women's cricket took a giant step forward with the launch of Yorkshire Diamonds to play in the KIA Super League hosted by Yorkshire County Cricket Club. Back Row, left to right: Clare Taylor, mentor; Anna Nicholls, Hollie Armitage, Katie Thompson and Jenny Owst, physiotherapist. Middle Row: Tom Geeson-Brown, strength-and-conditioning coach; Laura Spragg, Steph Butler, Katie Levick, Teresa Graves, Alice Davidson-Richards, Danielle Hazell and Ruan Louw, assistant coach. Front Row: Alex Blackwell, Katherine Brunt, Jane Hildreth, manager; Lauren Winfield, captain; Richard Pyrah, head coach; Beth Mooney and Jenny Gunn.

IN DEFEAT DEFIANCE: Katie Levick hits out against Loughborough Lightning before she is stumped by Amy Jones. Diamonds lost by 43 runs.

YORKSHIRE ACADEMY SILVER HAT-TRICK

LEAGUE CUP THREE IN A ROW: Yorkshire Academy had to be content with third place in the ECB Yorkshire Premier League North in 2016, but they were still League Cup winners for the third successive year. Back row, left to right: Ian Dews, Academy Director; Sarah Smith, scorer; Mosun Hussain, Jack Shutt, Eddie Barnes, Matthew Fisher, James Logan, Jonathan Read and Richard Damms, Academy Coach. Front row: Matthew Waite, Harry Brook, Jordan Thompson, captain, Yaasar Imtiaz, Ben Ainsley and Blaine Clancy, Strength and Conditioning Coach. *(Photo: Richard Damms)*

TOP GUN: Seam bowler Jared Warner, whose 9-19 for Yorkshire Academy against Castleford at Weetwood was the best performance of 2016 in the ECB Yorkshire League North. Jared, who is yet to make his first-team debut, has impressed with the Second Eleven as well as England Under-19s, with whom he toured Australia in April 2015, playing in the drawn four-day Test at Perth. He has since toured Sri Lanka with the Under-19s, and was in their World Cup squad in Bangladesh in early 2016.

PLAQUE HONOUR: A service commemorating the life of Sir Leonard Hutton, who was born at Fulneck on June 23, 1916, and learned his cricket at nearby Pudsey St Lawrence CC, was held at Fulneck Moravian Church on Sunday, October 30.

The address was given by the Right Reverend Richard Frith, Bishop of Hereford and a former Bishop of Hull.

Many then moved on to Pudsey St Lawrence, where a Leeds Civic Trust plaque was unveiled by Sir Leonard's sons, John, left opposite, and Richard in memory of their father and the great Herbert Sutcliffe, who played for St Lawrence's Second Eleven as a 13-year-old before moving to Pudsey Britannia.

(Yorkshire Post pictures by James Hardisty)

CHAMPIONSHIP GOLD: Yorkshire Cricket Foundation Archives Committee last year acquired a gold cigarette case presented by the Club to captain Frank Greenwood to commemorate his side winning the 1931 County Championship. Archives chairman David Allan, left, is seen receiving the case in the Yorkshire Cricket Museum at Headingley from its previous owner, David Copland, of Reeth, North Yorkshire.

CENTENARY WALK: Founder manager of Yorkshire Cricket School Ralph Middlebrook, extreme left, welcomes archivists to Pudsey Congs Cricket Ground to begin a Pudsey and Fulneck walk to commemorate the 100th anniversary of the death of Yorkshire and England all-rounder Major Booth on the first day of the Battle of the Somme on July 1, 1916, and the centenary of the birth of Sir Leonard Hutton nine days earlier.

BESIDE THE SEASIDE: Although the Championship programme is reduced from 16 matches to 14 this season, Yorkshire will continue to play two of their home games at Scarborough's North Marine Road. A poll showed that 84 per cent of members and stakeholders were supportive of two Championship games remaining at the venue, and Yorkshire Chief Executive Mark Arthur said: "Scarborough is the jewel in the crown of Championship cricket in this country, let alone Yorkshire." And where else could you watch such closely fought contests as this?

CLUBS RISE FROM THE DEPTHS

NOT SUCH A PRETTY PICTURE: Bolton Percy club secretary Bill Preacher, canoes at the ready, surveys the devastation left by the floods of Christmas 2015. BELOW: The llamas statue at Saltaire resembles mythical images of the Loch Ness monster coming up for air. Thanks to central emergency funding and the Herculean labours of club stalwarts both grounds were returned to green and pleasant lands.

INDIVIDUAL INNINGS OF 150 AND OVER *(Continued)*

P A JAQUES (7)

243	v. Hampshire	Southampton (Rose Bowl)	2004
173	v. Glamorgan	Leeds	2004
176	v. Northamptonshire	Leeds	2005
219	v. Derbyshire	Leeds	2005
172	v. Durham	Scarborough	2005
160	v. Gloucestershire	Bristol	2012
152	v. Durham	Scarborough	2013

R KILNER (5)

169	v. Gloucestershire	Bristol	1914
206*	v. Derbyshire	Sheffield	1920
166	v. Northamptonshire	Northampton	1921
150	v. Northamptonshire	Harrogate	1921
150	v. Middlesex	Lord's	1926

F LEE (1)

165	v. Lancashire	Bradford	1887

A Z LEES (1)

275*	v. Derbyshire	Chesterfield	2013

D S LEHMANN (13)

177	v. Somerset	Taunton	1997
163*	v. Leicestershire	Leicester	1997
182	v. Hampshire	Portsmouth	1997
200	v. Worcestershire	Worcester	1998
187*	v. Somerset	Bath	2001
252	v. Lancashire	Leeds	2001
193	v. Leicestershire	Leicester	2001
216	v. Sussex	Arundel	2002
187	v. Lancashire	Leeds	2002
150	v. Warwickshire	Birmingham	2006
193	v. Kent	Canterbury	2006
172	v. Kent	Leeds	2006
339	v. Durham	Leeds	2006

E I LESTER (5)

186	v. Warwickshire	Scarborough	1949
178	v. Nottinghamshire	Nottingham	1952
157	v. Cambridge University	Hull	1953
150	v. Oxford University	Oxford	1954
163	v. Essex	Romford	1954

M LEYLAND (17)

191	v. Glamorgan	Swansea	1926
204*	v. Middlesex	Sheffield	1927
247	v. Worcestershire	Worcester	1928
189*	v. Glamorgan	Huddersfield	1928
211*	v. Lancashire	Leeds	1930
172	v. Middlesex	Sheffield	1930
186	v. Derbyshire	Leeds	1930
189	v. Middlesex	Sheffield	1932
153	v. Leicestershire	Leicester (Aylestone Road)	1932
166	v. Leicestershire	Bradford	1932
153*	v. Hampshire	Bournemouth	1932
192	v. Northamptonshire	Leeds	1933
210*	v. Kent	Dover	1933

INDIVIDUAL INNINGS OF 150 AND OVER *(Continued)*

M LEYLAND *(Continued)*

263	v. Essex	Hull	1936
163*	v. Surrey	Leeds	1936
167	v. Worcestershire	Stourbridge	1937
180*	v. Middlesex	Lord's	1939

E LOCKWOOD *(1)*

208	v. Kent	Gravesend	1883

J D LOVE *(4)*

163	v. Nottinghamshire	Bradford	1976
170*	v. Worcestershire	Worcester	1979
161	v. Warwickshire	Birmingham	1981
154	v. Lancashire	Manchester	1981

F A LOWSON *(10)*

155	v. Kent	Maidstone	1951
155	v. Worcestershire	Bradford	1952
166	v. Scotland	Glasgow	1953
259*	v. Worcestershire	Worcester	1953
165	v. Sussex	Hove	1954
164	v. Essex	Scarborough	1954
150*	v. Kent	Dover	1954
183*	v. Oxford University	Oxford	1956
154	v. Somerset	Taunton	1956
154	v. Cambridge University	Cambridge	1957

R G LUMB *(2)*

159	v. Somerset	Harrogate	1979
165*	v. Gloucestershire	Bradford	1984

A LYTH *(4)*

248 *	v. Leicestershire	Leicester	2012
230	v. Northamptonshire	Northampton	2014
251	v. Lancashire	Manchester	2014
202	v. Surrey	The Oval	2016

A McGRATH *(7)*

165	v. Lancashire	Leeds	2002
174	v. Derbyshire	Derby	2004
165*	v. Leicestershire	Leicester	2005
173*	v. Worcestershire	Leeds	2005
158	v. Derbyshire	Derby	2005
188*	v. Warwickshire	Birmingham	2007
211	v. Warwickshire	Birmingham	2009

D R MARTYN *(1)*

238	v. Gloucestershire	Leeds	2003

A A METCALFE *(7)*

151	v. Northamptonshire	Luton	1986
151	v. Lancashire	Manchester	1986
152	v. MCC	Scarborough	1987
216*	v. Middlesex	Leeds	1988
162	v. Gloucestershire	Cheltenham	1990
150*	v. Derbyshire	Scarborough	1990
194*	v. Nottinghamshire	Nottingham	1990

INDIVIDUAL INNINGS OF 150 AND OVER *(Continued)*

A MITCHELL (7)

189	v. Northamptonshire	Northampton	1926
176	v. Nottinghamshire	Bradford	1930
177*	v. Gloucestershire	Bradford	1932
150*	v. Worcestershire	Worcester	1933
158	v. MCC	Scarborough	1933
152	v. Hampshire	Bradford	1934
181	v. Surrey	Bradford	1934

F MITCHELL (2)

194	v. Leicestershire	Leicester	1899
162*	v. Warwickshire	Birmingham	1901

M D MOXON (14)

153	v. Lancashire	Leeds	1983
153	v. Somerset	Leeds	1985
168	v. Worcestershire	Worcester	1985
191	v. Northamptonshire	Scarborough	1989
162*	v. Surrey	The Oval	1989
218*	v. Sussex	Eastbourne	1990
200	v. Essex	Colchester (Castle Park)	1991
183	v. Gloucestershire	Cheltenham	1992
171*	v. Kent	Leeds	1993
161*	v. Lancashire	Manchester	1994
274*	v. Worcestershire	Worcester	1994
203*	v. Kent	Leeds	1995
213	v. Glamorgan	Cardiff (Sophia Gardens)	1996
155	v. Pakistan 'A'	Leeds	1997

E OLDROYD (5)

151*	v. Glamorgan	Cardiff	1922
194	v. Worcestershire	Worcester	1923
162*	v. Glamorgan	Swansea	1928
168	v. Glamorgan	Hull	1929
164*	v. Somerset	Bath	1930

D E V PADGETT (1)

161*	v. Oxford University	Oxford	1959

R PEEL (2)

158	v. Middlesex	Lord's	1889
210*	v. Warwickshire	Birmingham	1896

A U RASHID (3)

157*	v. Lancashire	Leeds	2009
180	v. Somerset	Leeds	2013
159*	v. Lancashire	Manchester	2014

W RHODES (8)

196	v. Worcestershire	Worcester	1904
201	v. Somerset	Taunton	1905
199	v. Sussex	Hove	1909
176	v. Nottinghamshire	Harrogate	1912
152	v. Leicestershire	Leicester (Aylestone Road)	1913
167*	v. Nottinghamshire	Leeds	1920
267*	v. Leicestershire	Leeds	1921
157	v. Derbyshire	Leeds	1925

INDIVIDUAL INNINGS OF 150 AND OVER *(Continued)*

P E ROBINSON (2)

150*	v. Derbyshire	Scarborough	1990
189	v. Lancashire	Scarborough	1991

J E ROOT (5)

160	v. Sussex	Scarborough	2011
222 *	v. Hampshire	Southampton (West End)	2012
182	v. Durham	Chester-le-Street	2013
236	v. Derbyshire	Leeds	2013
	2013 innings consecutive		
213	v.Surrey	Leeds	2016

J W ROTHERY (1)

161	v. Kent	Dover	1908

J A RUDOLPH (5)

220	v. Warwickshire	Scarborough	2007
155	v. Somerset	Taunton	2008
198	v. Worcestershire	Leeds	2009
191	v. Somerset	Taunton	2009
228*	v. Durham	Leeds	2010

H RUDSTON (1)

164	v. Leicestershire	Leicester (Aylestone Rd)	1904

J J SAYERS (3)

187	v. Kent	Tunbridge Wells	2007
173	v. Warwickshire	Birmingham	2009
152	v. Somerset	Taunton	2009

A B SELLERS (1)

204	v. Cambridge University	Cambridge	1936

K SHARP (2)

173	v. Derbyshire	Chesterfield	1984
181	v. Gloucestershire	Harrogate	1986

P J SHARPE (4)

203*	v. Cambridge University	Cambridge	1960
152	v. Kent	Sheffield	1960
197	v. Pakistanis	Leeds	1967
172*	v. Glamorgan	Swansea	1971

G A SMITHSON (1)

169	v. Leicestershire	Leicester	1947

W B STOTT (2)

181	v. Essex	Sheffield	1957
186	v. Warwickshire	Birmingham	1960

H SUTCLIFFE (39)

174	v. Kent	Dover	1919
232	v. Surrey	The Oval	1922
213	v. Somerset	Dewsbury	1924
160	v. Sussex	Sheffield	1924
255*	v. Essex	Southend-on-Sea	1924
235	v. Middlesex	Leeds	1925
206	v. Warwickshire	Dewsbury	1925
171	v. MCC	Scarborough	1925

H SUTCLIFFE *(Continued)*

200	v. Leicestershire	Leicester (Aylestone Road)	1926
176	v. Surrey	Leeds	1927
169	v. Nottinghamshire	Bradford	1927
228	v. Sussex	Eastbourne	1928
150	v. Northamptonshire	Northampton	1929
150*	v. Essex	Dewsbury	1930
173	v. Sussex	Hove	1930
173*	v. Cambridge University	Cambridge	1931
230	v. Kent	Folkestone	1931
183	v. Somerset	Dewsbury	1931
195	v. Lancashire	Sheffield	1931
187	v. Leicestershire	Leicester (Aylestone Road)	1931
153*	v. Warwickshire	Hull	1932
313	v. Essex	Leyton	1932
270	v. Sussex	Leeds	1932
182	v. Derbyshire	Leeds	1932
194	v. Essex	Scarborough	1932
205	v. Warwickshire	Birmingham	1933
177	v. Middlesex	Bradford	1933
174	v. Leicestershire	Leicester (Aylestone Road)	1933
152	v. Cambridge University	Cambridge	1934
166	v. Essex	Hull	1934
203	v. Surrey	The Oval	1934
187*	v. Worcestershire	Bradford	1934
200*	v. Worcestershire	Sheffield	1935
212	v. Leicestershire	Leicester (Aylestone Road)	1935
202	v. Middlesex	Scarborough	1936
189	v. Leicestershire	Hull	1937
165	v. Lancashire	Manchester	1939
234*	v. Leicestershire	Hull	1939
175	v. Middlesex	Lord's	1939

W H H SUTCLIFFE (3)

171*	v. Worcestershire	Worcester	1952
181	v. Kent	Canterbury	1952
161*	v. Glamorgan	Harrogate	1955

K TAYLOR (8)

168*	v. Nottinghamshire	Nottingham	1956
159	v. Leicestershire	Sheffield	1961
203*	v. Warwickshire	Birmingham	1961
178*	v. Oxford University	Oxford	1962
163	v. Nottinghamshire	Leeds	1962
153	v. Lancashire	Manchester	1964
160	v. Australians	Sheffield	1964
162	v. Worcestershire	Kidderminster	1967

T L TAYLOR (1)

156	v. Hampshire	Harrogate	1901

J TUNNICLIFFE (2)

243	v. Derbyshire	Chesterfield	1898
158	v. Worcestershire	Worcester	1900

G ULYETT (1)

199*	v. Derbyshire	Sheffield	1887

M P VAUGHAN (7)

183	v. Glamorgan	Cardiff (Sophia Gardens)	1996
183	v. Northamptonshire	Northampton	1996
161	v. Essex	Ilford	1997
177	v. Durham	Chester-le-Street	1998
151	v. Essex	Chelmsford	1999
153	v. Kent	Scarborough	1999
155*	v. Derbyshire	Leeds	2000

E WAINWRIGHT (3)

171	v. Middlesex	Lord's	1897
153	v. Leicestershire	Leicester	1899
228	v. Surrey	The Oval	1899

W WATSON (7)

153*	v. Surrey	The Oval	1947
172	v. Derbyshire	Scarborough	1948
162*	v. Somerset	Leeds	1953
163	v. Sussex	Sheffield	1955
174	v. Lancashire	Sheffield	1955
214*	v. Worcestershire	Worcester	1955
162	v. Northamptonshire	Harrogate	1957

C WHITE (6)

181	v. Lancashire	Leeds	1996
172*	v. Worcestershire	Leeds	1997
186	v. Lancashire	Manchester	2001
183	v. Glamorgan	Scarborough	2001
161	v. Leicestershire	Scarborough	2002
173*	v. Derbyshire	Derby	2003

K S WILLIAMSON (1)

189	v. Sussex	Scarborough	2014

B B WILSON (2)

150	v. Warwickshire	Birmingham	1912
208	v. Sussex	Bradford	1914

J V WILSON (7)

157*	v. Sussex	Leeds	1949
157	v. Essex	Sheffield	1950
166*	v. Sussex	Hull	1951
223*	v. Scotland	Scarborough	1951
154	v. Oxford University	Oxford	1952
230	v. Derbyshire	Sheffield	1952
165	v. Oxford University	Oxford	1956

M J WOOD (5)

200*	v. Warwickshire	Leeds	1998
157	v. Northamptonshire	Leeds	2003
207	v. Somerset	Taunton	2003
155	v. Hampshire	Scarborough	2003
202*	v. Bangladesh 'A'	Leeds	2005

N W D YARDLEY (2)

177	v. Derbyshire	Scarborough	1947
183*	v. Hampshire	Leeds	1951

YOUNUS KHAN (2)

202*	v. Hampshire	Southampton (Rose Bowl)	2007
217*	v. Kent	Scarborough	2007

CENTURIES BY CURRENT PLAYERS

A complete list of all First-class Centuries up to and including 2007 is to be found in the 2008 edition

AZEEM RAFIQ (1)

100	v. Worcestershire	Worcester	2009

J M BAIRSTOW (15)

205	v. Nottinghamshire	Nottingham	2011
136	v. Somerset	Taunton	2011
182	v. Leicestershire	Scarborough	2012
118	v. Leicestershire	Leicester	2012
107	v. Kent	Leeds	2012
186	v. Derbyshire	Leeds	2013
123	v. Leeds/Bradford	Leeds	2014
161*	v. Sussex	Arundel	2014
102	v. Hampshire	Leeds	2015
125*	v. Middlesex	Leeds	2015
219*	v. Durham	Chester-le-Street **	2015
108	v. Warwickshire	Birmingham **	2015

(** consecutive innings)

139	v. Worcestershire	Scarborough	2015
246	v. Hampshire	Leeds	2016
198	v. Surrey	Leeds	2016

G S BALLANCE (15)

111	v. Warwickshire	Birmingham	2011
121*	v. Gloucestershire	Bristol	2012
112	v. Leeds/Bradford MCCU	Leeds	2013
107	v. Somerset	Leeds	2013
141	v. Nottinghamshire	Scarborough	2013
112	v. Warwickshire	Leeds	2013
148	v. Surrey 1st inns	The Oval **	2013
108*	v. Surrey 2nd inns	The Oval **	2013
101	v. Leeds/Bradford MCCU	Leeds **	2014

(** consecutive innings)

174	v. Northamptonshire	Leeds	2014
130	v. Middlesex	Lord's	2014
165	v. Sussex	Hove	2015
105	v. MCC	Abu Dhabi	2016
132	v. Middlesex	Scarborough	2016
101*	v. Nottinghamshire	Scarborough	2016

T T BRESNAN (5)

116	v. Surrey	The Oval	2007
101*	v. Warwickshire	Scarborough	2007
100*	v. Somerset	Taunton	2015
169*	v. Durham	Chester-le-Street	2015
142*	v. Middlesex	Lord's	2016

J A LEANING (3)

116	v. Nottinghamshire	Nottingham	2015
123	v. Somerset	Taunton	2015
110	v. Nottinghamshire	Leeds	2015

A Z LEES (9)

121	v. Leeds/Bradford MCCU	Leeds	2013
100	v. Middlesex	Lord's	2013
275*	v. Derbyshire	Chesterfield	2013
138	v. Northamptonshire	Northampton	2014

CENTURIES BY CURRENT PLAYERS (Continued)

A Z LEES (Continued)

108	v. Durham	Leeds	2014
100	v. Nottinghamshire	Nottingham	2015
107	v. Nottinghamshire	Nottingham	2016
114*	v. Lancashire	Manchester	2016
132	v. Durham	Leeds	2016

J S LEHMANN (1)

116	v. Somerset	Leeds	2016

A LYTH (19)

132	v. Nottinghamshire	Nottingham	2008
142	v. Somerset	Taunton	2010
133	v. Hampshire	Southampton	2010
100	v. Lancashire	Manchester	2010
248*	v. Leicestershire	Leicester	2012
111	v. Leeds/Bradford	Leeds	2013
105	v. Somerset	Taunton	2013
130	v. Leeds/Bradford MCCU	Leeds	2014
104	v. Durham	Chester-le-Street	2014
230	v. Northamptonshire	Northampton	2014
143	v. Durham	Leeds	2014
117	v. Middlesex	Scarborough	2014
251	v. Lancashire	Manchester	2014
122	v. Nottinghamshire	Nottingham	2014
113	v. MCC	Abu Dhabi	2015
111	v. Hampshire	Leeds	2016
106	v. Somerset	Taunton	2016
202	v. Surrey	The Oval	2016
114*	v. Durham	Leeds	2016

L E PLUNKETT (1)

126	v. Hampshire	Leeds	2016

A U RASHID (10)

108	v. Worcestershire	Kidderminster	2007
111	v. Sussex	Hove	2008
117*	v. Hampshire	Basingstoke	2009
157*	v. Lancashire	Leeds	2009
180	v. Somerset	Leeds	2013
110*	v. Warwickshire	Birmingham	2013
103	v. Somerset	Taunton	2013
	(2013 consecutive innings)		
108	v. Somerset	Taunton	2014
159*	v. Lancashire	Manchester	2014
127	v. Durham	Scarborough	2015

J E ROOT (6)

160	v. Sussex	Scarborough	2011
222 *	v. Hampshire	Southampton (West End)	2012
125	v. Northamptonshire	Leeds	2012
182	v. Durham	Chester-le-Street	2013
236	v. Derbyshire	Leeds	2013
213	v. Surrey	Leeds	2016

K S WILLIAMSON (1)

189	v. Sussex	Scarborough	2014

CENTURIES

(Including highest score)

112	H Sutcliffe	313	v Essex	at Leyton	1932
103	G Boycott	260*	v Essex	at Colchester (Garrison Gd)	1970
85	L Hutton	280*	v Hampshire	at Sheffield	1939
62	M Leyland	263	v Essex	at Hull	1936
61	D Denton	221	v Kent	at Tunbridge Wells	1912
60	P Holmes	315*	v Middlesex	at Lord's	1925
56	G H Hirst	341	v Leicestershire	at Leicester (Aylestone Rd)	1905
46	W Rhodes	267*	v Leicestershire	at Leeds	1921
41	M D Moxon	274*	v Worcestershire	at Worcester	1994
39	A Mitchell	189	v Northamptonshire	at Northampton	1926
37	E Oldroyd	194	v Worcestershire	at Worcester	1923
34	J H Hampshire	183*	v Sussex	at Hove	1971
34	A McGrath	211	v Warwickshire	at Birmingham	2009
33	D B Close	198	v Surrey	at The Oval	1960
30	F A Lowson	259*	v Worcestershire	at Worcester	1953
29	D E V Padgett	161*	v Oxford University	at Oxford	1959
29	J V Wilson	230	v Derbyshire	at Sheffield	1952
28	D Byas	213	v Worcestershire	at Scarborough	1995
27	W Barber	255	v Surrey	at Sheffield	1935
26	D S Lehmann	339	v Durham	at Leeds	2006
26	W Watson	214*	v Worcestershire	at Worcester	1955
25	A A Metcalfe	216*	v Middlesex	at Leeds	1988
24	E I Lester	186	v Warwickshire	at Scarborough	1949
23	J T Brown	311	v Sussex	at Sheffield	1897
23	P J Sharpe	203*	v Cambridge University	at Cambridge	1960
22	R G Lumb	165*	v Gloucestershire	at Bradford	1984
22	J Tunnicliffe	243	v Derbyshire	at Chesterfield	1898
21	Hon F S Jackson	160	v Gloucestershire	at Sheffield	1898
20	M P Vaughan	183	v Glamorgan	at Cardiff (Sophia Gardens)	1996
and		183	v. Northamptonshire	at Northampton	1996
19	A W Gale	272	v. Nottinghamshire	at Scarborough	2013
19	A Lyth	251	v. Lancashire	at Manchester	2014
19	C White	186	v. Lancashire	at Manchester	2001
and		183	v Northamptonshire	at Northampton	1996
19	A W Gale	272	v. Nottinghamshire	at Scarborough	2013
19	C White	186	v Lancashire	at Manchester	2001
18	J A Rudolph	228*	v Durham	at Leeds	2010
18	E Wainwright	228	v Surrey	at The Oval	1899
17	W B Stott	186	v Warwickshire	at Birmingham	1960
17	N W D Yardley	183*	v Hampshire	at Leeds	1951
16	K Taylor	203*	v. Warwickshire	at Birmingham	1961
16	M J Wood	207	v. Somerset	at Taunton	2003
15	J M Bairstow	246	v. Hampshire	at Leeds	2016
15	G S Ballance	174	v. Northamptonshire	at Leeds	2014
15	R Kilner	206*	v. Derbyshire	at Sheffield	1920
15	G Ulyett	199*	v. Derbyshire	at Sheffield	1887
15	B B Wilson	208	v. Sussex	at Bradford	1914
14	R Illingworth	162	v. Indians	at Sheffield	1959
13	J D Love	170*	v. Worcestershire	at Worcester	1979
12	R J Blakey	223*	v. Northamptonshire	at Leeds	2003
12	H Halliday	144	v. Derbyshire	at Chesterfield	1950
11	P A Jaques	243	v. Hampshire	at Southampton (Rose Bowl)	2004
11	K Sharp	181	v. Gloucestershire	at Harrogate	1986
10	C W J Athey	134	v. Derbyshire	at Derby	1982
10	Lord Hawke	166	v. Warwickshire	at Birmingham	1896
10	F Mitchell	194	v. Leicestershire	at Leicester	1899
10	A U Rashid	180	v. Somerset	at Leeds	2013

9	D L Bairstow	145	v. Middlesex	at Scarborough	1980
9	M G Bevan	160*	v. Surrey	at Middlesbrough	1996
9	L Hall	160	v. Lancashire	at Bradford	1887
9	A Z Lees	275*	v. Derbyshire	at Chesterfield	2013
9	J J Sayers	187	v. Kent	at Tunbridge Wells	2007
8	W Bates	136	v. Sussex	at Hove	1886
8	M J Lumb	144	v. Middlesex	at Southgate	2006
8	T L Taylor	156	v. Hampshire	at Harrogate	1901
7	J B Bolus	146*	v. Hampshire	at Portsmouth	1960
7	E Robinson	135*	v. Leicestershire	at Leicester (Aylestone Rd)	1921
7	P E Robinson	189	v. Lancashire	at Scarborough	1991
6	E Lockwood	208	v. Kent	at Gravesend	1883
6	R Peel	210*	v. Warwickshire	at Birmingham	1896
6	J E Root	236	v. Derbyshire	at Leeds	2013
6	W H H Sutcliffe	181	v. Kent	at Canterbury	1952
5	T T Bresnan	169*	v. Durham	at Chester-le-Street	2015
5	C M Old	116	v. Indians	at Bradford	1974
4	I Grimshaw	129*	v. Cambridge University	at Sheffield	1885
4	S Haigh	159	v. Nottinghamshire	at Sheffield	1901
4	S N Hartley	114	v. Gloucestershire	at Bradford	1982
4	R A Hutton	189	v. Pakistanis	at Bradford	1971
4	A B Sellers	204	v. Cambridge University	at Cambridge	1936
3	G L Brophy	177*	v. Worcestershire	at Worcester	2011
3	P Carrick	131*	v. Northamptonshire	at Northampton	1980
3	A J Dalton	128	v. Middlesex	at Leeds	1972
3	A Drake	147*	v. Derbyshire	at Chesterfield	1911
3	J A Leaning	123	v. Somerset	at Taunton	2015
3	F Lee	165	v. Lancashire	at Bradford	1887
3	G G Macaulay	125*	v. Nottinghamshire	at Nottingham	1921
3	R Moorhouse	113	v. Somerset	at Taunton	1896
3	R M Pyrah	134*	v. Loughborough MCCU	at Leeds	2010
3	J W Rothery	161	v. Kent	at Dover	1908
3	J Rowbotham	113	v. Surrey	at The Oval	1873
3	T F Smailes	117	v. Glamorgan	at Cardiff	1938
3	Younus Khan	217*	v. Kent	at Scarborough	2007
2	M W Booth	210	v. Worcestershire	at Worcester	1911
2	D C F Burton	142*	v. Hampshire	at Dewsbury	1919
2	K R Davidson	128	v. Kent	at Maidstone	1934
2	P A Gibb	157*	v. Nottinghamshire	at Sheffield	1935
2	P J Hartley	127*	v. Lancashire	at Manchester	1988
2	I J Harvey	209*	v. Somerset	at Leeds	2005
2	C Johnson	107	v. Somerset	at Sheffield	1973
2	S A Kellett	125*	v. Derbyshire	at Chesterfield	1991
2	N Kilner	112	v. Leicestershire	at Leeds	1921
2	B Parker	138*	v. Oxford University	at Oxford	1997
2	A Sellers	105	v. Middlesex	at Lord's	1893
2	E Smith (Morley)	129	v. Hampshire	at Bradford	1899
2	G A Smithson	169	v. Leicestershire	at Leicester	1947
2	G B Stevenson	115*	v. Warwickshire	at Birmingham	1982
2	F S Trueman	104	v. Northamptonshire	at Northampton	1963
2	C Turner	130	v. Somerset	at Sheffield	1936
2	D J Wainwright	104*	v. Sussex	at Hove	2008
2	T A Wardall	106	v. Gloucestershire	at Gloucester (Spa Ground)	1892
1	Azeem Rafiq	100	v. Worcestershire	at Worcester	2009
1	A T Barber	100	v. England XI	at Sheffield	1929
1	H D Bird	181*	v. Glamorgan	at Bradford	1959

1	T J D Birtles	104	v. Lancashire	at Sheffield	1914
1	G S Blewett	190	v. Northamptonshire	at Scarborough	1999
1	M T G Elliott	127	v, Warwickshire	at Birmingham	2002
1	T Emmett	104	v. Gloucestershire	at Clifton	1873
1	G M Fellows	109	v. Lancashire	at Manchester	2002
1	A J Finch	110	v. Warwickshire	at Birmingham	2014
1	J N Gillespie	123*	v. Surrey	at The Oval	2007
1	D Gough	121	v. Warwickshire	at Leeds	1996
1	A K D Gray	104	v. Somerset	at Taunton	2003
1	A P Grayson	100	v. Worcestershire	at Worcester	1994
1	F E Greenwood	104*	v. Glamorgan	at Hull	1929
1	G M Hamilton	125	v. Hampshire	at Leeds	2000
1	W E Harbord	109	v. Oxford University	at Oxford	1930
1	R Iddison	112	v. Cambridgeshire	at Hunslet	1869
1	W G Keighley	110	v. Surrey	at Leeds	1951
1	R A Kettleborough	108	v. Essex	at Leeds	1996
1	B Leadbeater	140*	v. Hampshire	at Portsmouth	1976
1	J S Lehmann	116	v. Somerset	at Leeds	2016
1	D R Martyn	238	v. Gloucestershire	at Leeds	2003
1	G J Maxwell	140	v. Durham	at Scarborough	2015
1	J T Newstead	100*	v. Nottinghamshire	at Nottingham	1908
1	L E Plunkett	126	v. Hampshire	at Leeds	2016
1	C A Pujara	133*	v. Hampshire	at Leeds	2015
1	R B Richardson	112	v. Warwickshire	at Birmingham	1993
1	H Rudston	164	v. Leicestershire	at Leicester (Aylestone Rd)	1904
1	A Sidebottom	124	v. Glamorgan	at Cardiff (Sophia Gardens)	1977
1	I G Swallow	114	v. MCC	at Scarborough	1987
1	S R Tendulkar	100	v. Durham	at Durham	1992
1	J Thewlis	108	v. Surrey	at The Oval	1868
1	C T Tyson	100*	v. Hampshire	at Southampton	1921
1	H Verity	101	v. Jamaica	at Kingston (Sabina Park)	1935/36
1	A Waddington	114	v. Worcestershire	at Leeds	1927
1	W A I Washington	100*	v. Surrey	at Leeds	1902
1	H Wilkinson	113	v. MCC	at Scarborough	1904
1	W H Wilkinson	103	v. Sussex	at Sheffield	1909
1	K S Williamson	189	v. Sussex	at Scarborough	2014
1	E R Wilson	104*	v. Essex	at Bradford	1913
1	A Wood	123*	v. Worcestershire	at Sheffield	1935
1	J D Woodford	101	v. Warwickshire	at Middlesbrough	1971

FOR YORKSHIRE				AGAINST YORKSHIRE		
Total	In Yorkshire	Away		Total	In Yorkshire	Away
110	65	45	**Derbyshire**	57	27	30
32	16	16	**Durham**	24	13	11
75	34	41	**Essex**	46	21	25
68	38	30	**Glamorgan**	23	13	10
87	41	46	**Gloucestershire**	53	27	26
94	41	53	**Hampshire**	59	27	32
81	37	44	**Kent**	60	29	31
112	56	56	**Lancashire**	115	58	57
97	52	45	**Leicestershire**	46	23	23
97	49	48	**Middlesex**	91	38	53
81	35	46	**Northamptonshire**	53	25	28
127	60	67	**Nottinghamshire**	84	33	51
102	50	52	**Somerset**	59	21	38
117	50	67	**Surrey**	108	39	69
90	42	48	**Sussex**	77	33	44
105	36	69	**Warwickshire**	74	28	46
74	32	42	**Worcestershire**	42	15	27
1	1	0	**Cambridgeshire**	0	0	0
1550	**735**	**815**	**Totals**	**1071**	**470**	**601**
9	9	0	**Australians**	16	16	0
9	9	0	**Indians**	7	7	0
8	8	0	**New Zealanders**	3	3	0
5	5	0	**Pakistanis**	1	1	0
9	9	0	**South Africans**	7	7	0
5	5	0	**Sri Lankans**	1	1	0
5	5	0	**West Indians**	6	6	0
1	1	0	**Zimbabweans**	0	0	0
3	3	0	**Bangladesh 'A'**	1	1	0
0	0	0	**India 'A'**	1	1	0
1	1	0	**Pakistan 'A'**	1	1	0
45	1	44	**Cambridge University**	20	2	18
2	2	0	**Combined Services**	0	0	0
1	0	1	**Durham MCCU**	1	0	1
4	3	1	**England XI's**	3	2	1
0	0	0	**International XI**	1	1	0
1	0	1	**Ireland**	0	0	0
3	0	3	**Jamaica**	3	0	3
6	6	0	**Leeds/Bradford MCCU**	0	0	0
1	0	1	**Liverpool & District**	0	0	0
2	2	0	**Loughborough MCCU**	1	1	0
1	0	1	**Mashonaland**	0	0	0
2	0	2	**Matabeleland**	1	0	1
54	38	16	**MCC**	52	34	18
39	0	39	**Oxford University**	11	0	11
6	0	6	**Rest of England**	15	0	15
9	5	4	**Scotland**	1	0	1
3	3	0	**C I Thornton's XI**	4	4	0
0	0	0	**Western Province**	1	0	1
1	1	0	**I Zingari**	1	1	0
235	**116**	**119**	**Totals**	**161**	**91**	**70**
1785	**851**	**934**	**Grand Totals**	**1232**	**561**	**671**

FOUR CENTURIES IN ONE INNINGS

		F S Jackson	117
		E Wainwright	126
1896	v. Warwickshire	Lord Hawke	166
	at Birmingham	R Peel	*210

(First instance in First-Class cricket)

THREE CENTURIES IN ONE INNINGS

1884	v. Cambridge University	L Hall	116
	at Cambridge	W Bates	133
		I Grimshaw	115
1887	v. Kent	G Ulyett	124
	at Canterbury	L Hall	110
		F Lee	119
1897	v. Sussex	J T Brown	311
	at Sheffield	J Tunnicliffe	147
		E Wainwright	*104
1899	v. Middlesex	F S Jackson	155
	at Bradford	D Denton	113
		F Mitchell	121
1904	v. Surrey	D Denton	105
	at The Oval	G H Hirst	104
		J Tunnicliffe	*139
1919	v. Gloucestershire	H Sutcliffe	118
	at Leeds	D Denton	122
		R Kilner	*115
1925	v. Glamorgan	P Holmes	130
	at Huddersfield	H Sutcliffe	121
		E Robinson	*108
1928	v. Middlesex	P Holmes	105
	at Lord's	E Oldroyd	108
		A Mitchell	105
1928	v. Essex	H Sutcliffe	129
	at Leyton	P Holmes	136
		M Leyland	*133
1929	v. Glamorgan	E Oldroyd	168
	at Hull	W Barber	114
		F E Greenwood	*104
1933	v. MCC	H Sutcliffe	107
	at Scarborough	A Mitchell	158
		M Leyland	133
1936	v. Surrey	H Sutcliffe	129
	at Leeds	L Hutton	163
		M Leyland	*163
1937	v. Leicestershire	H Sutcliffe	189
	at Hull	L Hutton	153
		M Leyland	*118
1947	v. Leicestershire	L Hutton	137
	at Leicester	N W D Yardley	100
		G.A Smithson	169
1971	v. Oxford University	J H Hampshire	*116
	at Oxford	R A Hutton	101
		A J Dalton	111
1975	v. Gloucestershire	G Boycott	141
	at Bristol	R G Lumb	101
		J H Hampshire	*106

269

THREE CENTURIES IN ONE INNINGS *(Continued)*

		M D Moxon	.130
1995	v. Cambridge University	D Byas	.181
	at Cambridge	M G Bevan	*113
		M J Wood	.102
2001	v. Leicestershire	M J Lumb	.122
	at Leeds	D S Lehmann	.104
		C White	.183
2001	v. Glamorgan	M J Wood	.124
	at Scarborough	D Byas	.104
		J A Rudolph	.122
2007	v. Surrey	T T Bresnan	.116
	at The Oval	J N Gillespie	*123
		A Lyth	.130
2014	v. Leeds/Bradford MCCU	G S Ballance	.101
	at Leeds	J M Bairstow	.123
		A Lyth	.111
2016	v. Hampshire	J M Bairstow	.246
	at Leeds	L E Plunkett	.126

CENTURY IN EACH INNINGS

D Denton	107 and 109*	v. Nottinghamshire at Nottingham, 1906
G H Hirst	111 and 117*	v. Somerset at Bath, 1906
D Denton	133 and 121	v. MCC at Scarborough, 1908
W Rhodes	128 and 115	v. MCC at Scarborough, 1911
P Holmes	126 and 111*	v. Lancashire at Manchester, 1920
H Sutcliffe	107 and 109*	v. MCC at Scarborough, 1926
H Sutcliffe	111 and 100*	v. Nottinghamshire at Nottingham, 1928
E I Lester	126 and 142	v. Northamptonshire at Northampton, 1947
L Hutton	197 and 104	v. Essex at Southend, 1947
E I Lester	125* and 132	v. Lancashire at Manchester, 1948
L Hutton	165 and 100	v. Sussex at Hove, 1949
L Hutton	103 and 137	v. MCC at Scarborough, 1952
G Boycott	103 and 105	v. Nottinghamshire at Sheffield, 1966
G Boycott	163 and 141*	v. Nottinghamshire at Bradford, 1983
M D Moxon	123 and 112*	v. Indians at Scarborough, 1986
A A Metcalfe	194* and 107	v. Nottinghamshire at Nottingham, 1990
M P Vaughan	100 and 151	v. Essex at Chelmsford, 1999
Younus Khan	106 and 202*	v. Hampshire at Southampton, 2007
G S Ballance	148 and 108*	v. Surrey at The Oval, 2013

HIGHEST INDIVIDUAL SCORES
FOR AND AGAINST YORKSHIRE

Highest For Yorkshire:
341 G H Hirst v. Leicestershire at Leicester, 1905

Highest Against Yorkshire:
318* W G Grace for Gloucestershire at Cheltenham, 1876

Yorkshire versus:

Derbyshire	*For Yorkshire:*	300 — J T Brown at Chesterfield, 1898
	Against:	270* — C F Hughes at Leeds, 2013
Most Centuries	*For Yorkshire:*	G Boycott 9
	Against:	K J Barnett and W Storer 4 each
Durham	*For Yorkshire:*	339 — D S Lehmann at Leeds, 2006
	Against:	221* — K K Jennings at Chester-le-Street, 2016
Most Centuries	*For Yorkshire:*	A McGrath 5
	Against:	M J Di Venuto 4

Yorkshire versus

Essex	*For Yorkshire:*	313 — H Sutcliffe at Leyton, 1932
	Against:	219* — D J Insole at Colchester, 1949
Most Centuries	*For Yorkshire:*	H Sutcliffe 9
	Against:	F L Fane, K W R Fletcher, G A Gooch and D J Insole 3 each
Glamorgan	*For Yorkshire:*	213 — M D Moxon at Cardiff, 1996
	Against:	202* — H Morris at Cardiff, 1996
Most Centuries	*For Yorkshire:*	G Boycott, P Holmes and H Sutcliffe 5 each
	Against:	H Morris 5
Gloucestershire	*For Yorkshire:*	238 — D R Martyn at Leeds, 2003
	Against:	318* — W G Grace at Cheltenham, 1876
Most Centuries	*For Yorkshire:*	G Boycott 6
	Against:	W G Grace 9
Hampshire	*For Yorkshire:*	302* — P Holmes at Portsmouth, 1920
	Against:	300* — M A Carberry at Southampton, 2011
Most Centuries	*For Yorkshire:*	H Sutcliffe 6
	Against:	C P Mead 10
Kent	*For Yorkshire:*	248 — W Barber at Leeds, 1934.
	Against:	207 — D P Fulton at Maidstone, 1998
Most Centuries	*For Yorkshire:*	A McGrath 6
	Against:	F E Woolley 5
Lancashire	*For Yorkshire:*	252 — D S Lehmann at Leeds, 2001
	Against:	225 — G D Lloyd at Leeds, 1997 (Non-Championship)
		206 — S G Law at Leeds, 2007
Most Centuries	*For Yorkshire:*	G Boycott and H Sutcliffe 9 each
	Against:	M A Atherton and C H Lloyd 6 each.
Leicestershire	*For Yorkshire:*	341 — G H Hirst at Leicester, 1905
	Against:	218 — J J Whitaker at Bradford, 1996
Most Centuries	*For Yorkshire:*	H Sutcliffe 10
	Against:	J J Whitaker and C J B Wood 5 each
Middlesex	*For Yorkshire:*	315* — P Holmes at Lord's, 1925
	Against:	243* — A J Webbe at Huddersfield, 1887
Most Centuries	*For Yorkshire:*	P Holmes and H Sutcliffe 7 each
	Against:	M W Gatting 8
Northamptonshire	*For Yorkshire:*	277* — P Holmes at Harrogate, 1921
	Against:	235 — A J Lamb at Leeds, 1990
Most Centuries	*For Yorkshire:*	H Sutcliffe 5
	Against:	W Larkins 5
Nottinghamshire	*For Yorkshire:*	285 — P Holmes at Nottingham, 1929
	Against:	251* — D J Hussey at Leeds, 2010
Most Centuries	*For Yorkshire:*	G Boycott 15
	Against:	R T Robinson 6
Somerset	*For Yorkshire:*	213 — H Sutcliffe at Dewsbury, 1924
	Against:	297 — M J Wood at Taunton, 2005
Most Centuries	*For Yorkshire:*	G Boycott 6
	Against:	L C H Palairet, IVA. Richards, M E Trescothick 5 each
Surrey	*For Yorkshire:*	255 — W Barber at Sheffield, 1935
	Against:	273 — T W Hayward at The Oval, 1899
Most Centuries	*For Yorkshire:*	H Sutcliffe 9
	Against:	J B Hobbs 8

Yorkshire versus

Sussex	*For Yorkshire:*	311 — J T Brown at Sheffield, 1897
	Against:	274* — M W Goodwin at Hove, 2011
Most Centuries	*For Yorkshire:*	L Hutton 8
	Against:	C B Fry 7
Warwickshire	*For Yorkshire:*	275 — P Holmes at Bradford, 1928
	Against:	225 — D P Ostler at Birmingham, 2002
Most Centuries	*For Yorkshire:*	G Boycott and H Sutcliffe 8 each
	Against:	D L Amiss, H E Dollery, R B Khanhai and W G Quaife 4 each.
Worcestershire	*For Yorkshire:*	274* — M D Moxon at Worcester, 1994
	Against:	259 — D Kenyon at Kidderminster, 1956
Most Centuries	*For Yorkshire:*	M Leyland 6
	Against:	D Kenyon and G M Turner 5 each
Australians	*For Yorkshire:*	167 — J T Brown at Bradford, 1899
	Against:	193* — B C Booth at Bradford, 1964
Most Centuries	*For Yorkshire:*	G Boycott and D Denton 2 each
	Against:	N C O'Neill 2
Indians	*For Yorkshire:*	183* — L Hutton at Bradford, 1946
	Against:	244* — V S Hazare at Sheffield, 1946
Most Centuries	*For Yorkshire:*	M D Moxon 2
	Against:	V S Hazare, V Mankad, P R Umrigar D K Gaekwad, G A Parkar and R Lamba 1 each
New Zealanders	*For Yorkshire:*	175 — P Holmes at Bradford, 1927
	Against:	126 — W M Wallace at Bradford, 1949
Most Centuries	*For Yorkshire:*	L Hutton and D B Close 2 each
	Against:	H G Vivian, W M Wallace and J G Wright 1 each
Pakistanis	*For Yorkshire:*	197 — P J Sharpe at Leeds, 1967
	Against:	139 — A H Kardar at Sheffield, 1954
Most Centuries	*For Yorkshire:*	P J Sharpe 2
	Against:	A H Kardar 1
South Africans	*For Yorkshire:*	156 — L Hutton at Sheffield, 1951
	Against:	168 — I J Seidle at Sheffield, 1929
Most Centuries	*For Yorkshire:*	L Hutton 2
	Against:	H B Cameron, J D Lindsay, B Mitchell, D P B Morkel, I J Seidle, L J Tancred, C B van Ryneveld 1 each
Sri Lankans	*For Yorkshire:*	132 — M D Moxon at Leeds, 1988
	Against:	112 — S A R Silva at Leeds, 1988
Most Centuries	*For Yorkshire:*	K Sharp 2
	Against:	S A R Silva 1
West Indians	*For Yorkshire:*	112* — D Denton at Harrogate, 1906
	Against:	164 — S F A Bacchus at Leeds, 1980
Most Centuries	*For Yorkshire:*	M G Bevan, D Denton, L Hutton, R G Lumb and A A Metcalfe 1 each
	Against:	S F A Bacchus, C O Browne, S Chanderpaul P A Goodman, C L Hooper and G St A Sobers 1 each

HIGHEST INDIVIDUAL SCORES FOR AND AGAINST
YORKSHIRE *(continued)*

Yorkshire versus

Zimbabweans | *For Yorkshire:* | 113 — M D Moxon at Leeds, 1990
| | *Against:* | 89 — G J Whittall at Leeds, 2000
Most Centuries | *For Yorkshire:* | M D Moxon 1
| | *Against:* | None

Cambridge University | *For Yorkshire:* | 207* — G Boycott at Cambridge, 1976
| | *Against:* | 171* — G L Jessop at Cambridge, 1899
| | | 171 — P B H May at Cambridge, 1952
Most Centuries | *For Yorkshire:* | H Sutcliffe 4
| | *Against:* | G M Kemp 2

Durham MCCU | *For Yorkshire:* | 139 — J J Sayers at Durham, 2011
| | *Against:* | 127 — T Westley at Durham, 2011
Most Centuries | *For Yorkshire:* | J J Sayers 1
| | *Against:* | T Westley 1

Leeds Bradford MCCU | *For Yorkshire:* | 130 — A Lyth at Leeds, 2014
| | *Against:* | 69 — A MacQueen at Leeds, 2012
Most Centuries | *For Yorkshire:* | J M Bairstow and A Lyth, 2 each

Loughborough MCCU | *For Yorkshire:* | 134* — R M Pyrah at Leeds, 2010
| | *Against:* | 107 — C P Murtagh at Leeds, 2007
Most Centuries | *For Yorkshire:* | R M Pyrah 2
| | *Against:* | C P Murtagh 1

MCC | *For Yorkshire:* | 180* — G H Hirst at Lord's, 1919
| | *Against:* | 214 — E H Hendren at Lord's, 1919
Most Centuries | *For Yorkshire:* | L Hutton 8
| | *Against:* | R E S Wyatt 5

Oxford University | *For Yorkshire:* | 196 — R J Blakey at Oxford, 1991
| | *Against:* | 201 — J E Raphael at Oxford, 1904
Most Centuries | *For Yorkshire:* | M Leyland 4
| | *Against:* | A A Baig and Nawab of Pataudi (Jun.) 2 each

J B Hobbs scored 11 centuries against Yorkshire – the highest by any individual (8 for Surrey and 3 for the Rest of England).

Three players have scored 10 centuries against Yorkshire – W G Grace (9 for Gloucestershire and 1 for MCC). E H Hendren (6 for Middlesex, 3 for MCC and 1 for the Rest of England) and C P Mead (all 10 for Hampshire).

CARRYING BAT THROUGH A COMPLETED INNINGS

Batsman	Score	Total	Against	Season
G R Atkinson	30*	73	Nottinghamshire at Bradford	1865
L Hall	31*	94	Sussex at Hove	1878
L Hall	124*	331	Sussex at Hove	1883
L Hall	128*	285	Sussex at Huddersfield	1884
L Hall	32*	81	Kent at Sheffield	1885
L Hall	79*	285	Surrey at Sheffield	1885
L Hall	37*	96	Derbyshire at Derby	1885
L Hall	50*	173	Sussex at Huddersfield	1886
L Hall	74*	172	Kent at Canterbury	1886
G Ulyett	199*	399	Derbyshire at Sheffield	1887
L Hall	119*	334	Gloucestershire at Dewsbury	1887
L Hall	82*	218	Sussex at Hove	1887
L Hall	34*	104	Surrey at The Oval	1888
L Hall	129*	461	Gloucestershire at Clifton	1888
L Hall	85*	259	Middlesex at Lord's	1889
L Hall	41*	106	Nottinghamshire at Sheffield	1891
W Rhodes	98*	184	MCC at Lord's	1903
W Rhodes	85*	152	Essex at Leyton	1910
P Holmes	145*	270	Northamptonshire at Northampton	1920
H Sutcliffe	125*	307	Essex at Southend	1920
P Holmes	175*	377	New Zealanders at Bradford	1927
P Holmes	110*	219	Northamptonshire at Bradford	1929
H Sutcliffe	104*	170	Hampshire at Leeds	1932
H Sutcliffe	114*	202	Rest of England at The Oval	1933
H Sutcliffe	187*	401	Worcestershire at Bradford	1934
H Sutcliffe	135*	262	Glamorgan at Neath	1935
H Sutcliffe	125*	322	Oxford University at Oxford	1939
L Hutton	99*	200	Leicestershire at Sheffield	1948
L Hutton	78*	153	Worcestershire at Sheffield	1949
F A Lowson	76*	218	MCC at Lord's	1951
W B Stott	144*	262	Worcestershire at Worcester	1959
D E V Padgett	115*	230	Gloucestershire at Bristol	1962
G Boycott	114*	297	Leicestershire at Sheffield	1968
G Boycott	53*	119	Warwickshire at Bradford	1969
G Boycott	182*	320	Middlesex at Lord's	1971
G Boycott	138*	232	Warwickshire at Birmingham	1971
G Boycott	175*	360	Nottinghamshire at Worksop	1979
G Boycott	112*	233	Derbyshire at Sheffield	1983
G Boycott	55*	183	Warwickshire at Leeds	1984
G Boycott	55*	131	Surrey at Sheffield	1985
M J Wood	60*	160	Somerset at Scarborough	2004
J J Sayers	122*	326	Middlesex at Scarborough	2006
J J Sayers	149*	414	Durham at Leeds	2007
A Lyth	248*	486	Leicestershire at Leicester	2012

44 instances, of which L Hall (14 times), G Boycott (8) and H Sutcliffe (6) account for 28 between them.

The highest percentage of an innings total is 61.17 by H. Sutcliffe (104* v. Hampshire at Leeds in 1932) but P Holmes was absent ill, so only nine wickets fell.

Other contributions exceeding 55% are:

59.48%	G Boycott	(138* v. Warwickshire at Birmingham, 1971)
56.87%	G Boycott	(182* v. Middlesex at Lord's, 1971)
56.43%	H Sutcliffe	(114* v. Rest of England at The Oval, 1933)
55.92%	W Rhodes	(85* v. Essex at Leyton, 1910)

2,000 RUNS IN A SEASON

Batsman	Season	M	I	NO	Runs	HS	Avge	100s
G H Hirst	1904	32	44	3	2257	157	55.04	8
D Denton	1905	33	52	2	2258	172	45.16	8
G H Hirst	1906	32	53	6	2164	169	46.04	6
D Denton	1911	32	55	4	2161	137*	42.37	6
D Denton	1912	36	51	4	2088	221	44.23	6
P Holmes	1920	30	45	6	2144	302*	54.97	7
P Holmes	1925	35	49	9	2351	315*	58.77	6
H Sutcliffe	1925	34	48	8	2236	235	55.90	7
H Sutcliffe	1928	27	35	5	2418	228	80.60	11
P Holmes	1928	31	40	4	2093	275	58.13	6
H Sutcliffe	1931	28	33	8	2351	230	94.04	9
H Sutcliffe	1932	29	41	5	2883	313	80.08	12
M Leyland	1933	31	44	4	2196	210*	54.90	7
A Mitchell	1933	34	49	10	2100	158	53.84	6
H Sutcliffe	1935	32	47	3	2183	212	49.61	8
L Hutton	1937	28	45	6	2448	271*	62.76	8
H Sutcliffe	1937	32	52	5	2054	189	43.70	4
L Hutton	1939	29	44	5	2316	280*	59.38	10
L Hutton	1947	19	31	2	2068	270*	71.31	10
L Hutton	1949	26	44	6	2640	269*	69.47	9
F A Lowson	1950	31	54	5	2067	141*	42.18	5
D E V Padgett	1959	35	60	8	2158	161*	41.50	4
W B Stott	1959	32	56	2	2034	144*	37.66	3
P J Sharpe	1962	36	62	8	2201	138	40.75	7
G Boycott	1971	18	25	4	2221	233	105.76	11
A A Metcalfe	1990	23	44	4	2047	194*	51.17	6

1,000 RUNS IN A SEASON

Batsman	Runs scored	Runs scored	Runs scored
C W J Athey	(2) 1113 in 1980	1339 in 1982	—
D L Bairstow	(3) 1083 in 1981	1102 in 1983	1163 in 1985
J M Bairstow	(2) 1015 in 2011	1108 in 2015	—
G S Ballance	(1) 1363 in 2013	—	—
W Barber	(8) 1000 in 1932	1595 in 1933	1930 in 1934
	1958 in 1935	1466 in 1937	1455 in 1938
	1501 in 1939	1170 in 1946	—
M G Bevan	(2) 1598 in 1995	1225 in 1996	—
R J Blakey	(5) 1361 in 1987	1159 in 1989	1065 in 1992
	1236 in 1994	1041 in 2002	—
J B Bolus	(2) 1245 in 1960	1970 in 1961	—
M W Booth	(2) 1189 in 1911	1076 in 1913	—
G Boycott	(19) 1628 in 1963	1639 in 1964	1215 in 1965
	1388 in 1966	1530 in 1967	1004 in 1968
	1558 in 1970	2221 in 1971	1156 in 1972
	1478 in 1974	1915 in 1975	1288 in 1976
	1259 in 1977	1074 in 1978	1160 in 1979
	1913 in 1982	1941 in 1983	1567 in 1984
	1657 in 1985	—	—
J T Brown	(9) 1196 in 1894	1260 in 1895	1755 in 1896
	1634 in 1897	1641 in 1898	1375 in 1899
	1181 in 1900	1627 in 1901	1291 in 1903
D Byas	(5) 1557 in 1991	1073 in 1993	1297 in 1994
	1913 in 1995	1319 in 1997	—

Batsman		Runs scored	Runs scored	Runs scored
D B Close	(13)	1192 in 1952	1287 in 1954	1131 in 1955
		1315 in 1957	1335 in 1958	1740 in 1959
		1699 in 1960	1821 in 1961	1438 in 1962
		1145 in 1963	1281 in 1964	1127 in 1965
		1259 in 1966	—	—
K R Davidson	(1)	1241 in 1934	—	—
D Denton	(20)	1028 in 1896	1357 in 1897	1595 in 1899
		1378 in 1900	1400 in 1901	1191 in 1902
		1562 in 1903	1919 in 1904	2258 in 1905
		1905 in 1906	1128 in 1907	1852 in 1908
		1765 in 1909	1106 in 1910	2161 in 1911
		2088 in 1912	1364 in 1913	1799 in 1914
		1213 in 1919	1324 in 1920	—
A Drake	(2)	1487 in 1911	1029 in 1913	—
A W Gale	(2)	1076 in 2013	1045 in 2015	—
A P Grayson	(1)	1046 in 1994	—	—
S Haigh	(1)	1031 in 1904	—	—
L Hall	(1)	1120 in 1887	—	—
H Halliday	(4)	1357 in 1948	1484 in 1950	1351 in 1952
		1461 in 1953	—	—
J H Hampshire	(12)	1236 in 1963	1280 in 1964	1424 in 1965
		1105 in 1966	1244 in 1967	1133 in 1968
		1079 in 1970	1259 in 1971	1124 in 1975
		1303 in 1976	1596 in 1978	1425 in 1981
Lord Hawke	(1)	1005 in 1895	—	—
G H Hirst	(19)	1110 in 1896	1248 in 1897	1546 in 1899
		1752 in 1900	1669 in 1901	1113 in 1902
		1535 in 1903	2257 in 1904	1972 in 1905
		2164 in 1906	1167 in 1907	1513 in 1908
		1151 in 1909	1679 in 1910	1639 in 1911
		1119 in 1912	1431 in 1913	1655 in 1914
		1312 in 1919	—	—
P Holmes	(14)	1876 in 1919	2144 in 1920	1458 in 1921
		1614 in 1922	1884 in 1923	1610 in 1924
		2351 in 1925	1792 in 1926	1774 in 1927
		2093 in 1928	1724 in 1929	1957 in 1930
		1431 in 1931	1191 in 1932	—
L Hutton	(12)	1282 in 1936	2448 in 1937	1171 in 1938
		2316 in 1939	1322 in 1946	2068 in 1947
		1792 in 1948	2640 in 1949	1581 in 1950
		1554 in 1951	1956 in 1952	1532 in 1953
R Illingworth	(5)	1193 in 1957	1490 in 1959	1029 in 1961
		1610 in 1962	1301 in 1964	—
F S Jackson	(4)	1211 in 1896	1300 in 1897	1442 in 1898
		1468 in 1899	—	—
P A Jaques	(2)	1118 in 2004	1359 in 2005	—
S A Kellett	(2)	1266 in 1991	1326 in 1992	—
R Kilner	(10)	1586 in 1913	1329 in 1914	1135 in 1919
		1240 in 1920	1137 in 1921	1132 in 1922
		1265 in 1923	1002 in 1925	1021 in 1926
		1004 in 1927	—	—
A Z Lees	(2)	1018 in 2014	1285 in 2016	—
D S Lehmann	(5)	1575 in 1997	1477 in 2000	1416 in 2001
		1136 in 2002	1706 in 2006	—

1,000 RUNS IN A SEASON *(Continued)*

Batsman		Runs scored	Runs scored	Runs scored
E I Lester	(6)	1256 in 1948	1774 in 1949	1015 in 1950
		1786 in 1952	1380 in 1953	1330 in 1954
M Leyland	(17)	1088 in 1923	1203 in 1924	1560 in 1925
		1561 in 1926	1478 in 1927	1554 in 1928
		1407 in 1929	1814 in 1930	1127 in 1931
		1821 in 1932	2196 in 1933	1228 in 1934
		1366 in 1935	1621 in 1936	1120 in 1937
		1640 in 1938	1238 in 1939	—
J D Love	(2)	1161 in 1981	1020 in 1983	
F A Lowson	(8)	1678 in 1949	2067 in 1950	1607 in 1951
		1562 in 1952	1586 in 1953	1719 in 1954
		1082 in 1955	1428 in 1956	
M J Lumb	(1)	1038 in 2003	—	—
R G Lumb	(5)	1002 in 1973	1437 in 1975	1070 in 1978
		1465 in 1979	1223 in 1980	
A Lyth	(3)	1509 in 2010	1619 in 2014	1153 in 2016
A McGrath	(3)	1425 in 2005	1293 in 2006	1219 in 2010
A A Metcalfe	(6)	1674 in 1986	1162 in 1987	1320 in 1988
		1230 in 1989	2047 in 1990	1210 in 1991
A Mitchell	(10)	1320 in 1928	1633 in 1930	1351 in 1932
		2100 in 1933	1854 in 1934	1530 in 1935
		1095 in 1936	1602 in 1937	1305 in 1938
		1219 in 1939	—	—
F Mitchell	(2)	1678 in 1899	1801 in 1901	—
R Moorhouse	(1)	1096 in 1895	—	—
M D Moxon	(11)	1016 in 1984	1256 in 1985	1298 in 1987
		1430 in 1988	1156 in 1989	1621 in 1990
		1669 in 1991	1314 in 1992	1251 in 1993
		1458 in 1994	1145 in 1995	
E Oldroyd	(10)	1473 in 1921	1690 in 1922	1349 in 1923
		1607 in 1924	1262 in 1925	1197 in 1926
		1390 in 1927	1304 in 1928	1474 in 1929
		1285 in 1930		
D E V Padgett	(12)	1046 in 1956	2158 in 1959	1574 in 1960
		1856 in 1961	1750 in 1962	1380 in 1964
		1220 in 1965	1194 in 1966	1284 in 1967
		1163 in 1968	1078 in 1969	1042 in 1970
R Peel	(1)	1193 in 1896	—	—
W Rhodes	(17)	1251 in 1904	1353 in 1905	1618 in 1906
		1574 in 1908	1663 in 1909	1355 in 1910
		1961 in 1911	1030 in 1912	1805 in 1913
		1325 in 1914	1138 in 1919	1329 in 1921
		1368 in 1922	1168 in 1923	1030 in 1924
		1256 in 1925	1071 in 1926	—
E Robinson	(2)	1104 in 1921	1097 in 1929	—
P E Robinson	(3)	1173 in 1988	1402 in 1990	1293 in 1991
J A Rudolph	(4)	1078 in 2007	1292 in 2008	1366 in 2009
		1375 in 2010	—	—
J J Sayers	(1)	1150 in 2009	—	—
A B Sellers	(1)	1109 in 1938	—	—
K Sharp	(1)	1445 in 1984	—	—

1,000 RUNS IN A SEASON (Continued)

Batsman		Runs scored	Runs scored	Runs scored
P J Sharpe	(10)	1039 in 1960	1240 in 1961	2201 in 1962
		1273 in 1964	1091 in 1965	1352 in 1967
		1256 in 1968	1012 in 1969	1149 in 1970
		1320 in 1973		
W B Stott	(5)	1362 in 1957	1036 in 1958	2034 in 1959
		1790 in 1960	1409 in 1961	—
H Sutcliffe	(21)	†1839 in 1919	1393 in 1920	1235 in 1921
		1909 in 1922	1773 in 1923	1720 in 1924
		2236 in 1925	1672 in 1926	1814 in 1927
		2418 in 1928	1485 in 1929	1636 in 1930
		2351 in 1931	2883 in 1932	1986 in 1933
		1511 in 1934	2183 in 1935	1295 in 1936
		2054 in 1937	1660 in 1938	1416 in 1939

† First season in First-Class cricket – The record for a debut season.

Batsman		Runs scored	Runs scored	Runs scored
W H H Sutcliffe	(1)	1193 in 1955	—	—
K Taylor	(6)	1306 in 1959	1107 in 1960	1494 in 1961
		1372 in 1962	1149 in 1964	1044 in 1966
T L Taylor	(2)	1236 in 1901	1373 in 1902	—
S R Tendulkar	(1)	1070 in 1992	—	—
J Tunnicliffe	(12)	1333 in 1895	1368 in 1896	1208 in 1897
		1713 in 1898	1434 in 1899	1496 in 1900
		1295 in 1901	1274 in 1902	1650 in 1904
		1096 in 1905	1232 in 1906	1195 in 1907
C Turner	(1)	1153 in 1934	—	—
G Ulyett	(4)	1083 in 1878	1158 in 1882	1024 in 1885
		1285 in 1887	—	—
M P Vaughan	(4)	1066 in 1994	1235 in 1995	1161 in 1996
		1161 in 1998	—	—
E Wainwright	(3)	1492 in 1897	1479 in 1899	1044 in 1901
W A I Washington	(1)	1022 in 1902	—	—
W Watson	(8)	1331 in 1947	1352 in 1948	1586 in 1952
		1350 in 1953	1347 in 1954	1564 in 1955
		1378 in 1956	1455 in 1957	—
W H Wilkinson	(1)	1282 in 1908	—	—
B B Wilson	(5)	1054 in 1909	1455 in 1911	1453 in 1912
		1533 in 1913	1632 in 1914	—
J V Wilson	(12)	1460 in 1949	1548 in 1950	1985 in 1951
		1349 in 1952	1531 in 1953	1713 in 1954
		1799 in 1955	1602 in 1956	1287 in 1957
		1064 in 1960	1018 in 1961	1226 in 1962
A Wood	(1)	1237 in 1935	—	—
M J Wood	(4)	1080 in 1998	1060 in 2001	1432 in 2003
		1005 in 2005		
N W D Yardley	(4)	1028 in 1939	1299 in 1947	1413 in 1949
		1031 in 1950	—	—

BATSMEN WHO HAVE SCORED OVER 10,000 RUNS

Player	M	I	NO	Runs	HS	Av'ge	100s
H Sutcliffe	602	864	96	38558	313	50.20	112
D Denton	676	1058	61	33282	221	33.38	61
G Boycott	414	674	111	32570	260*	57.85	103
G H Hirst	717	1050	128	32024	341	34.73	56
W Rhodes	883	1195	162	31075	267*	30.08	46
P Holmes	485	699	74	26220	315*	41.95	60
M Leyland	548	720	82	26180	263	41.03	62
L Hutton	341	527	62	24807	280*	53.34	85
D B Close	536	811	102	22650	198	31.94	33
J H Hampshire	456	724	89	21979	183*	34.61	34
J V Wilson	477	724	75	20548	230	31.66	29
D E V Padgett	487	774	63	20306	161*	28.55	29
J Tunnicliffe	472	768	57	19435	243	27.33	22
M D Moxon	277	476	42	18973	274*	43.71	41
A Mitchell	401	550	69	18189	189	37.81	39
P J Sharpe	411	666	71	17685	203*	29.72	23
E Oldroyd	383	509	58	15891	194	35.23	37
J T Brown	345	567	41	15694	311	29.83	23
W Barber	354	495	48	15315	255	34.26	27
R Illingworth	496	668	131	14986	162	27.90	14
D Byas	268	449	42	14398	213	35.37	28
G Ulyett	355	618	31	14157	199*	24.11	15
R J Blakey	339	541	84	14150	223*	30.96	12
A McGrath	242	405	29	14091	211	37.47	34
W Watson	283	430	65	13953	214*	38.22	26
F A Lowson	252	404	31	13897	259*	37.25	30
Lord Hawke	510	739	91	13133	166	20.26	10
R Kilner	365	478	46	13018	206*	30.13	15
D L Bairstow	429	601	113	12985	145	26.60	9
K Taylor	303	505	35	12864	203*	27.37	16
N W D Yardley	302	420	56	11632	183*	31.95	17
R G Lumb	239	395	30	11525	165*	31.57	22
E Wainwright	352	545	30	11092	228	21.53	18
S Haigh	513	687	110	10993	159	19.05	4
E I Lester	228	339	27	10616	186	34.02	24
A A Metcalfe	184	317	19	10465	216*	35.11	25
C White	221	350	45	10376	186	34.01	19
Hon F S Jackson	207	328	22	10371	160	33.89	21
J D Love	247	388	58	10263	170*	31.10	13

PLAYERS WHO HAVE SCORED CENTURIES
FOR AND AGAINST YORKSHIRE

Player		For	Venue	Season
C W J Athey (5)	114*	Gloucestershire	Bradford	1984
(10 for Yorkshire)	101	Gloucestershire	Gloucester	1985
	101*	Gloucestershire	Leeds	1987
	112	Sussex	Scarborough	1993
	100	Sussex	Eastbourne	1996
M G Bevan (1)	142	Leicestershire	Leicester	2002
(9 for Yorkshire)				
J B Bolus (2)	114	Nottinghamshire	Bradford	1963
(7 for Yorkshire)	138	Derbyshire	Sheffield	1973
D B Close (1)	102	Somerset	Taunton	1971
(33 for Yorkshire)				
M T G Elliott (1)	125	Glamorgan	Leeds	2004
(1 for Yorkshire)				
P A Gibb (1)	107	Essex	Brentwood	1951
(2 for Yorkshire)				
P A Jaques (1)	222	Northamptonshire	Northampton	2003
(7 for Yorkshire)				
N Kilner (2)	119	Warwickshire	Hull	1932
(2 for Yorkshire)	197	Warwickshire	Birmingham	1933
M J Lumb (1)	135	Nottinghamshire	Scarborough	2013
(8 for Yorkshire)				
P J Sharpe (1)	126	Derbyshire	Chesterfield	1976
(23 for Yorkshire)				

RECORD PARTNERSHIPS FOR YORKSHIRE

1st wkt	555	P Holmes (224*)	and H Sutcliffe (313)	v. Essex at Leyton	1932
2nd wkt	346	W Barber (162)	and M Leyland (189)	v. Middlesex at Sheffield	1932
3rd wkt	346	J J Sayers (173)	and A McGrath (211)	v. Warwickshire at Birmingham	2009
4th wkt	358	D S Lehmann (339)	and M J Lumb (98)	v. Durham at Leeds	2006
5th wkt	340	E Wainwright (228)	and G H Hirst (186)	v. Surrey at The Oval	1899
6th wkt	276	M Leyland (191)	and E Robinson (124*)	v. Glamorgan at Swansea	1926
7th wkt	366*	J M Bairstow (219*)	and T T Bresnan (169*)	v. Durham at Chester-le-Street	2015
8th wkt	292	R Peel (210*)	and Lord Hawke (166)	v. Warwickshire at Birmingham	1896
9th wkt	246	T T Bresnan (116)	and J N Gillespie (123*)	v. Surrey at The Oval	2007
10th wkt	149	G Boycott (79)	and G B Stevenson (115*)	v. Warwickshire at Birmingham	1982

RECORD PARTNERSHIPS AGAINST YORKSHIRE

1st wkt	372	R R Montgomerie (127)	and M B Loye (205)	for Northamptonshire	at Northampton	1996
2nd wkt	417	K J Barnett (210*)	and TA Tweats (189)	for Derbyshire	at Derby	1997
3rd wkt	523	M A Carberry (300*)	and N D McKenzie (237)	for Hampshire	at Southampton	2011
4th wkt	447	R Abel (193)	and T Hayward (273)	for Surrey at The Oval		1899
5th wkt	261	W G Grace (318*)	and W O Moberley (103)	for Gloucestershire	at Cheltenham	1876
6th wkt	294	D R Jardine (157)	and P G H Fender (177)	for Surrey at Bradford		1928
7th wkt	315	D M Benkenstein (151)	and O D Gibson (155)	for Durham at Leeds		2006
8th wkt	178	A P Wells (253*)	and B T P Donelan (59)	for Sussex	at Middlesbrough	1991
9th wkt	233	I J L Trott (161*)	and J S Patel (120)	for Warwickshire	at Birmingham	2009
10th wkt	132	A Hill (172*)	and M Jean-Jacques (73)	for Derbyshire	at Sheffield	1986

CENTURY PARTNERSHIPS FOR THE FIRST WICKET IN BOTH INNINGS

128	108	G Ulyett (82 and 91)	and L Hall (87 and 37)	v. Sussex at Hove	1885
		(First instance in First-Class cricket)			
138	147*	J T Brown (203 and 81*)	and J Tunnicliffe (62 and 63*)	v. Middlesex at Lord's	1896
		(Second instance in First-Class cricket)			
105	265*	P Holmes (51 and 127*)	and H Sutcliffe (71 and 131*)	v. Surrey at The Oval	1926
184	210*	P Holmes (83 and 101*)	and H Sutcliffe (111 and 100*)	v. Nottinghamshire at Nottingham	1928
110	117	L Hutton (95 and 86)	and W Watson (34 and 57)	v. Lancashire at Manchester	1947
122	230	W B Stott (50 and 114)	and K Taylor (79 and 140)	v. Nottinghamshire at Nottingham	1957
136	138	J B Bolus (108 and 71)	and K Taylor (89 and 75)	v. Cambridge University at Cambridge	1962
105	105	G Boycott (38 and 64)	and K Taylor (85 and 49)	v. Leicestershire at Leicester	1963
116	112*	K Taylor (45 and 68)	and J H Hampshire (68 and 67*)	v. Oxford University at Oxford	1964
104	104	G Boycott (117 and 49*)	and R G Lumb (47 and 57)	v. Sussex at Leeds	1974
134	185*	M D Moxon (57 and 89*)	and A A Metcalfe (216* and 78*)	v. Middlesex at Leeds	1988
118	129*	G S Ballance (72 and 73*)	and J J Sayers (139 and 53*)	v. Durham MCCU at Durham	2011

CENTURY PARTNERSHIPS FOR THE FIRST WICKET IN BOTH INNINGS BUT WITH CHANGE OF PARTNER

109		W H H Sutcliffe (82) and F A Lowson (46)
	143	W H H Sutcliffe (88) and W Watson (52) v. Canadians at Scarborough, 1954
109		G Boycott (70) and R G Lumb (44)
	135	G Boycott (74) and JH Hampshire (58) v. Northamptonshire at Bradford, 1977

CENTURY PARTNERSHIPS

FIRST WICKET (Qualification 200 runs)

555	P Holmes (224*) and H Sutcliffe (313) v. Essex at Leyton, 1932	
554	J T Brown (300) and J Tunnicliffe (243) v. Derbyshire at Chesterfield, 1898	
378	J T Brown (311) and J Tunnicliffe (147) v. Sussex at Sheffield, 1897	
375	A Lyth (230) and (A Z Lees (138) v. Northamptonshire at Northampton, 2014	
362	M D Moxon (213) and M P Vaughan (183) v. Glamorgan at Cardiff, 1996	
351	G Boycott (184) and M D Moxon (168) v. Worcestershire at Worcester, 1985	
347	P Holmes (302*) and H Sutcliffe (131) v. Hampshire at Portsmouth, 1920	
323	P Holmes (125) and H Sutcliffe (195) v. Lancashire at Sheffield, 1931	
315	H Sutcliffe (189) and L Hutton (153) v. Leicestershire at Hull, 1937	
315	H Sutcliffe (116) and L Hutton (280*) v. Hampshire at Sheffield, 1939	
309	P Holmes (250) and H Sutcliffe (129) v. Warwickshire at Birmingham, 1931	
309	C White (186) and M J Wood (115) v. Lancashire at Manchester, 2001	
290	P Holmes (179*) and H Sutcliffe (104) v. Middlesex at Leeds, 1928	
288	G Boycott (130*) and H Sutcliffe (159) v. Somerset at Harrogate, 1979	
286	L Hutton (156) and F A Lowson (115) v. South Africans at Sheffield, 1951	
282	M D Moxon (147) and A A Metcalfe (151) v. Lancashire at Manchester, 1986	
281*	W B Stott (138*) and K Taylor (130*) v. Sussex at Hove, 1960	
279	P Holmes (133) and H Sutcliffe (145) v. Northamptonshire at Northampton, 1919	
274	P.Holmes (199) and H Sutcliffe (139) v. Somerset at Hull, 1923	
274	P Holmes (180) and H Sutcliffe (134) v. Gloucestershire at Gloucester, 1927	
272	P Holmes (194) and H Sutcliffe (129) v. Leicestershire at Hull, 1925	
272	M J Wood (202*) and J J Sayers (115) v. Bangladesh 'A' at Leeds, 2005	
270	A Lyth (143) and A Z Lees (108) v. Durham at Leeds, 2014	
268	P Holmes (136) and H Sutcliffe (129) v. Essex at Leyton, 1928	
267	W Barber (248) and L Hutton (70) v. Kent at Leeds, 1934	
265*	P Holmes (127*) and H Sutcliffe (131*) v. Surrey at The Oval, 1926	
264	G Boycott (161*) and R G Lumb (132) v. Gloucestershire at Leeds, 1976	
253	P Holmes (123) and H Sutcliffe (132) v. Lancashire at Sheffield, 1919	
248	G Boycott (163) and A A Metcalfe (122) v. Nottinghamshire at Bradford, 1983	
245	L Hutton (152) and F A Lowson (120) v. Lancashire at Leeds, 1952	
244	J A Rudolph (149) and J J Sayers (86) v. Nottinghamshire at Nottingham, 2009	
241	P Holmes (142) and H Sutcliffe (123*) v. Surrey at The Oval, 1929	
240	G Boycott (233) and P J Sharpe (92) v. Essex at Colchester, 1971	
238*	P Holmes (126*) and H Sutcliffe (105*) v. Cambridge University at Cambridge, 1923	
236	G Boycott (131) and K Taylor (153) v. Lancashire at Manchester, 1964	
235	P Holmes (130) and H Sutcliffe (132*) v. Glamorgan at Sheffield, 1930	
233	G Boycott (141*) and R G Lumb (90) v. Cambridge University at Cambridge, 1973	
233	H Halliday (116) and W Watson (108) v. Northamptonshire at Northampton, 1948	
231	M P Vaughan (151) and D Byas (90) v. Essex at Chelmsford, 1999	
230	H Sutcliffe (129) and L Hutton (163) v. Surrey at Leeds, 1936	
230	W B Stott (114) and K Taylor (140*) v. Nottinghamshire at Nottingham, 1957	
228	H Halliday (90) and J V Wilson (223*) v. Scotland at Scarborough, 1951	
228	G Boycott (141) and R G Lumb (101) v. Gloucestershire at Bristol, 1975	
227	P Holmes (110) and H Sutcliffe (119) v. Leicestershire at Leicester, 1928	
225	R G Lumb (101) and C W J Athey (125*) v. Gloucestershire at Sheffield, 1980	
224	C W J Athey (114) and J D Love (104) v. Warwickshire at Birmingham, 1980	
222	W B Stott (141) and K Taylor (90) v. Sussex at Bradford, 1958	
221	P Holmes (130) and H Sutcliffe (121) v. Glamorgan at Huddersfield, 1925	
221	M D Moxon (141) and A A Metcalfe (73) v. Surrey at The Oval, 1992	
221	A Lyth (111) and A Z Lees (121) v. Leeds/Bradford MCCU at Leeds, 2013	
219	P Holmes (102) and A Mitchell (130*) v. Somerset at Bradford, 1930	
218	M Leyland (110) and H Sutcliffe (235) v. Middlesex at Leeds, 1925	
218	R G Lumb (145) and M D Moxon (111) v. Derbyshire at Sheffield, 1981	
210*	P Holmes (101*) and H Sutcliffe (100*) v. Nottinghamshire at Nottingham, 1928	
210	G Boycott (128) and P J Sharpe (197) v. Pakistanis at Leeds, 1967	
209	F A Lowson (115) and D E V Padgett (107) v. Scotland at Hull, 1956	

282

CENTURY PARTNERSHIPS *(Continued)*

208	A Mitchell (85) and E Oldroyd (111) v. Cambridge University at Cambridge, 1929
207	A Mitchell (90) and W Barber (107) v. Middlesex at Lord's, 1935
206	G Boycott (118) and R G Lumb (87) v. Glamorgan at Sheffield, 1978
204	M D Moxon (66) and A A Metcalfe (162) v. Gloucestershire at Cheltenham, 1990
203	L Hutton (119) and F A Lowson (83) v. Somerset at Huddersfield, 1952
203	M D Moxon (117) and S A Kellett (87) v. Somerset at Middlesbrough, 1992
203	M D Moxon (134) and M P Vaughan (106) v. Matebeleland at Bulawayo, 1996
200*	P Holmes (107*) and H Sutcliffe (80*) v. Oxford University at Oxford, 1930

Note: P Holmes and H Sutcliffe shared 69 century opening partnerships for Yorkshire; G Boycott and R G Lumb 29; L Hutton and F A Lowson 22; M D Moxon and A A Metcalfe 21; J T Brown and J Tunnicliffe 19; H Sutcliffe and L Hutton 15, and L Hall and G Ulyett 12.

SECOND WICKET (Qualification 200 runs)

346	W Barber (162) and M Leyland (189) v. Middlesex at Sheffield, 1932
343	F A Lowson (183*) and J V Wilson (165) v. Oxford University at Oxford, 1956
333	P Holmes (209) and E Oldroyd (138*) v. Warwickshire at Birmingham, 1922
314	H Sutcliffe (255*) and E Oldroyd (138) v. Essex at Southend-on-Sea, 1924
311	A Z Lees (275*) and P A Jaques (139) v. Derbyshire at Chesterfield, 2013
305	J W.Rothery (134) and D Denton (182) v. Derbyshire at Chesterfield, 1910
302	W Watson (172) and J V Wilson (140) v. Derbyshire at Scarborough, 1948
301	P J Sharpe (172*) and D E V Padgett (133) v. Glamorgan at Swansea, 1971
288	H Sutcliffe (165) and A Mitchell (136) v. Lancashire at Manchester, 1939
280	L Hall (160) and F Lee (165) v. Lancashire at Bradford, 1887
266*	K Taylor (178*) and D E V Padgett (107*) v. Oxford University at Oxford, 1962
264	P A Jaques (152) and K S Williamson (97) v. Durham at Scarborough, 2013
261*	L Hutton (146*) and J V Wilson (110*) v. Scotland at Hull, 1949
260	R G Lumb (144) and K Sharp (132) v. Glamorgan at Cardiff, 1984
258	H Sutcliffe (230) and E Oldroyd (93) v. Kent at Folkestone, 1931
253	B B Wilson (150) and D Denton (200*) v. Warwickshire at Birmingham, 1912
248	H Sutcliffe (200) and M. Leyland (116) v. Leicestershire at Leicester, 1926
244	P. Holmes (138) and E Oldroyd (151*) v. Glamorgan at Cardiff, 1922
243	G Boycott (141) and J D Love (163) v. Nottinghamshire at Bradford, 1976
243	C White (183) and M J Wood (124) v. Glamorgan at Scarborough, 2001
237	H Sutcliffe (118) and D Denton (122) v. Gloucestershire at Leeds, 1919
237	M D Moxon (132) and K Sharp (128) v. Sri Lankans at Leeds, 1988
236	F A Lowson (112) and J V Wilson (157) v. Essex at Leeds, 1950
235	M D Moxon (130) and D Byas (181) v. Cambridge University at Cambridge, 1995
230	L Hutton (180) and A Mitchell (100) v. Cambridge University at Cambridge, 1938
230	M P Vaughan (109) and B Parker (138*) v. Oxford University at Oxford, 1997.
227	M J Wood (102) and M J Lumb (122) v. Leicestershire at Leeds, 2001
225	H Sutcliffe (138) and E Oldroyd (97) v. Derbyshire at Dewsbury, 1928
223	M D Moxon (153) and R J Blakey (90) v. Somerset at Leeds, 1985
222	H Sutcliffe (174) and D Denton (114) v. Kent at Dover, 1919
219	F S Jackson (155) and D Denton (113) v. Middlesex at Bradford, 1899
217	R G Lumb (107) and J D Love (107) v. Oxford University at Oxford, 1978
216	M P Vaughan (105) and D Byas (102) v. Somerset at Bradford, 1994
215	A W Gale (136) and A McGrath (99) v. Lancashire at Manchester, 2008
211	J A Rudolph (141) and A McGrath (80) v. Nottinghamshire at Leeds, 2010
207	P A Jaques (115) and A McGrath (93) v. Essex at Chelmsford, 2004
206	J Tunnicliffe (102) and F S Jackson (134*) v. Lancashire at Sheffield, 1898
206	H Sutcliffe (187) and M Leyland (90) v. Leicestershire at Leicester, 1931
205	H Sutcliffe (174) and A Mitchell (95) v. Leicestershire at Leicester, 1933
205	G Boycott (148) and P J Sharpe (108) v. Kent at Sheffield, 1970
203	A T Barber (100) and E Oldroyd (143) v. An England XI at Sheffield, 1929
203	J J Sayers (187) and A McGrath (100) v. Kent at Tunbridge Wells, 2007
202*	W Rhodes (115*) and G H Hirst (117*) v. Somerset at Bath, 1906
202	G Boycott (113) and C W J Athey (114) v. Northamptonshire at Northampton, 1978

CENTURY PARTNERSHIPS *(Continued)*

THIRD WICKET (Qualification 200 runs)

346	J J Sayers (173) and A McGrath (211) v. Warwickshire at Birmingham, 2009
323*	H Sutcliffe (147*) and M Leyland (189*) v. Glamorgan at Huddersfield, 1928
317	A McGrath (165) and D S Lehmann (187) v. Lancashire at Leeds, 2002
310	A McGrath (134) and P A Jaques (219) v. Derbyshire at Leeds, 2005
301	H Sutcliffe (175) and M Leyland (180*) v. Middlesex at Lord's, 1939
293*	A A Metcalfe (150*) and P E Robinson (117) v. Derbyshire at Scarborough, 1990
269	D Byas (101) and R J Blakey (196) v. Oxford University at Oxford, 1991
258*	J T Brown (134*) and F Mitchell (116*) v. Warwickshire at Bradford, 1901
252	D E V Padgett (139*) and D B Close (154) v. Nottinghamshire at Nottingham, 1959
249	D E V Padgett (95) and D B Close (184) v. Nottinghamshire at Scarborough, 1960
248	C Johnson (102) and J H Hampshire (155*) v. Gloucestershire at Leeds, 1976
247	P Holmes (175*) and M Leyland (118) v. New Zealanders at Bradford, 1927
244	D E V Padgett (161*) and D B Close (144) v. Oxford University at Oxford, 1959
240	L Hutton (151) and M Leyland (95) v. Surrey at Leeds, 1939
237	J A Rudolph (198) and A McGrath (120) v. Worcestershire at Leeds, 2009
236	H Sutcliffe (107) and R Kilner (137) v. Nottinghamshire at Nottingham, 1920
236	M J Wood (94) and D S Lehmann (200) v. Worcestershire at Worcester, 1998
234*	D Byas (126*) and A McGrath (105*) v. Oxford University at Oxford, 1997.
233	L Hutton (101) and M Leyland (167) v. Worcestershire at Stourbridge, 1937
230	D Byas (103) and M J Wood (103) v. Derbyshire at Leeds, 1998
229	L Hall (86) and R Peel (158) v. Middlesex at Lord's, 1889
228	A Mitchell (142) and M Leyland (133) v. Worcestershire at Sheffield, 1933
228	W Barber (141) and M Leyland (114) v. Surrey at The Oval, 1939
228	J V Wilson (132*) and D E V Padgett (115) v. Warwickshire at Birmingham, 1955
226	D E V Padgett (117) and D B Close (198) v. Surrey at The Oval, 1960
224	J V Wilson (110) and D B Close (114) v. Cambridge University at Cambridge, 1955
224	G Boycott (140*) and K Sharp (121) v. Gloucestershire at Cheltenham, 1983
221	A Mitchell (138) and M Leyland (134) v. Nottinghamshire at Bradford, 1933
219	L Hall (116) and W Bates (133) v. Cambridge University at Cambridge, 1884
218	J A Rudolph (127) and A W Gale (121) v. Lancashire at Manchester, 2009
217	A McGrath (144) and J A Rudolph (129) v. Kent at Canterbury, 2008
216	R G Lumb (118) and J H Hampshire (127) v. Surrey at The Oval, 1975
215	A Mitchell (73) and M Leyland (139) v. Surrey at Bradford, 1928
213	E Oldroyd (168) and W Barber (114) v. Glamorgan at Hull, 1929
208	J V Wilson (157*) and E I Lester (112) v. Sussex at Leeds, 1949
206	A McGrath (105) and J A Rudolph (228*) v Durham at Leeds, 2010
205*	E Oldroyd (122*) and M Leyland (100*) v. Hampshire at Harrogate, 1924
205	F S Jackson (124) and D Denton (112) v. Somerset at Taunton, 1897
205	D E V Padgett (83) and D B Close (128) v. Somerset at Bath, 1959
204	M P Vaughan (113) and A McGrath (70) v. Essex at Scarborough, 2001
203	D Denton (132) and J Tunnicliffe (102) v. Warwickshire at Birmingham, 1905
203	A A Metcalfe (216*) and P E Robinson (88) v. Middlesex at Leeds, 1988
201	J Tunnicliffe (101) and T L Taylor (147) v. Surrey at The Oval, 1900
201	H Sutcliffe (87) and W Barber (130) v. Leicestershire at Leicester, 1938
200	M D Moxon (274*) and A P Grayson (100) v. Worcestershire at Worcester, 1994

FOURTH WICKET (Qualification 175 runs)

372	J E Root (213) and J M Bairstow (198) v. Surrey at Leeds, 2016
358	D S Lehmann (339) and M J Lumb (98) v. Durham at Leeds, 2006
330	M J Wood (116) and D R Martyn (238) v. Gloucestershire at Leeds, 2003
312	D Denton (168*) and G H Hirst (146) v. Hampshire at Southampton, 1914
299	P Holmes (277*) and R Kilner (150) v. Northamptonshire at Harrogate, 1921
272	D Byas (138) and A McGrath (137) v. Hampshire at Harrogate, 1996
271	B B Wilson (208) and W Rhodes (113) v. Sussex at Bradford, 1914
259	A Drake (115) and G H Hirst (218) v. Sussex at Hastings, 1911
258	J Tunnicliffe (128) and G H Hirst (152) v. Hampshire at Portsmouth, 1904
258	P E Robinson (147) and D Byas (117) v. Kent at Scarborough, 1989

255 A W Gale (148) and J A Leaning (110) v. Nottinghamshire at Leeds, 2015
254 A W Gale (164) and J M Bairstow (139) v. Worcestershire at Scarborough, 2015
249 W B Stott (143) and G Boycott (145) v. Lancashire at Sheffield, 1963
247* R G Lumb (165*) and S N Hartley (104*) v. Gloucestershire at Bradford, 1984
247 M Leyland (263) and L Hutton (83) v. Essex at Hull, 1936
238 D S Lehmann (216) and M J Lumb (92) v. Sussex at Arundel, 2002
233 D Byas (120) and P E Robinson (189) v. Lancashire at Scarborough, 1991
231 J E Root (236) and J M Bairstow (186) v. Derbyshire at Leeds, 2013
226 W H Wilkinson (89) and G H Hirst (140) v. Northamptonshire at Hull, 1909
225 C H Grimshaw (85) and G H Hirst (169) v. Oxford University at Oxford, 1906
212 B B Wilson (108) and G H Hirst (166*) v. Sussex at Hastings, 1913
212 G Boycott (260*) and J H Hampshire (80) v. Essex at Colchester, 1970
211 J V Wilson (120) and W Watson (108) v. Derbyshire at Harrogate, 1951
210* A Mitchell (150*) and M Leyland (117*) v. Worcestershire at Worcester, 1933
210 E I. Lester (178) and W Watson (97) v. Nottinghamshire at Nottingham, 1952
207 D Byas (213) and C White (107*) v. Worcestershire at Scarborough, 1995
206 J A Rudolph (121) and A W Gale (150) v. Surrey at The Oval, 2008
205* J H Hampshire (151*) and P J Sharpe (79*) v. Leicestershire at Leicester, 1964
205 E Oldroyd (121) and R Kilner (117) v. Worcestershire at Dudley, 1922
205 W Watson (162*) and E I Lester (98) v. Somerset at Leeds, 1953
205 A Lyth (111) and J M Bairstow (246) v. Hampshire at Leeds 2016
204 A W Gale (148) and G S Ballance (90) v. Surrey at Leeds, 2013
201* J H Hampshire (105*) and D B Close (101*) v. Surrey at Bradford, 1965
203 P A Jaques (160) and G S Ballance (121*) v. Gloucestershire at Bristol, 2012
201 W H H Sutcliffe (181) and L Hutton (120) v. Kent at Canterbury, 1952
200 J V Wilson (92) and W Watson (122) v. Somerset at Taunton, 1950
198 A A Metcalfe (138) and D Byas (95) v. Warwickshire at Leeds, 1989
198 A W Gale (124) and J M Bairstow (95) v. Durham at Chester-le-Street, 2014
197 N W D Yardley (177) and A Coxon (58) v. Derbyshire at Scarborough, 1947
197 A Lyth (248*) and J M Bairstow (118) v. Leicestershire at Leicester, 2012
196 M D Moxon (130) and D L Bairstow (104) v. Derbyshire at Harrogate, 1987
193 A Drake (85) and G H Hirst (156) v. Lancashire at Manchester, 1911
192 J V Wilson (132) and W Watson (105) v. Essex at Bradford, 1955
191 M Leyland (114) and C Turner (94) v. Essex at Ilford, 1938
190 A W Gale (125) and J A Leaning (76) v. Hampshire at West End, Southampton, 2015
188 H Myers (60) and G H Hirst (158) v. Cambridge University at Cambridge, 1910
187 E Oldroyd (168) and F E Greenwood (104*) v. Glamorgan at Hull, 1929
187 K Taylor (203*) and W B Stott (57) v. Warwickshire at Birmingham, 1961
186 D S Lehmann (193) and D Byas (100) v. Leicestershire at Leicester, 2001
184 J H Hampshire (96) and R Illingworth (100*) v. Leicestershire at Sheffield, 1968
182* E I Lester (101*) and W Watson (103*) v. Nottinghamshire at Bradford, 1952
180* G Boycott (207*) and B Leadbeater (50*) v. Cambridge University
                                                at Cambridge, 1976
180 J Tunnicliffe (139*) and G H Hirst (108) v. Surrey at The Oval, 1904
179 J H Hampshire (179) and S N Hartley (63) v. Surrey at Harrogate, 1981
179 M D Moxon (171*) and R J Blakey (71) v. Kent at Leeds, 1993
178 E I Lester (186) and J V Wilson (71) v. Warwickshiire at Scarborough, 1949
177 J D Love (105*) and J H Hampshire (89) v. Lancashire at Manchester, 1980
175 L Hutton (177) and W Barber (84) v. Sussex at Scarborough, 1939
175 A McGrath (188*) and J A Rudolph (82) v. Warwickshire at Birmingham, 2007

FIFTH WICKET (Qualification 150 runs)

340 E Wainwright (228) and G H Hirst (186) v. Surrey at The Oval, 1899
329 F Mitchell (194) and E Wainwright (153) v. Leicestershire at Leicester, 1899
297 A W Gale (272) and G S Ballance (141) v. Nottinghamshire at Scarborough, 2013
276 W Rhodes (104*) and R Kilner (166) v. Northamptonshire at Northampton, 1921
273 L Hutton (270*) and N W D Yardley (136) v. Hampshire at Bournemouth, 1947
245* H Sutcliffe (107*) and W Barber (128*) v. Northamptonshire at Northampton, 1939

CENTURY PARTNERSHIPS *(Continued)*

229	D S Lehmann (193) and C White (79) v. Kent at Canterbury, 2006	
217	D B Close (140*) and R Illingworth (107) v. Warwickshire at Sheffield, 1962	
207	G S Ballance (107) and A U Rashid (180) v. Somerset at Leeds, 2013	
198	E Wainwright (145) and R Peel (111) v. Sussex at Bradford, 1896	
198	W Barber (168) and K R Davidson (101*) v. MCC at Lord's, 1934	
196*	R Kilner (115*) and G H Hirst (82*) v. Gloucestershire at Leeds, 1919	
195	M J Lumb (93) and C White (173*) v. Derbyshire at Derby, 2003	
194*	Younus Khan (202*) and G L Brophy (100*) v. Hampshire at Southampton, 2007	
193	A Mitchell (189) and W Rhodes (88) v. Northamptonshire at Northampton, 1926	
193	J D Love (106) and S N Hartley (108) v. Oxford University at Oxford, 1985	
192	C W J Athey (114*) and J D Love (123) v. Surrey at The Oval, 1982	
191*	L Hutton (271*) and C Turner (81*) v. Derbyshire at Sheffield, 1937	
191	M G Bevan (105) and A A Metcalfe (100) v. West Indians at Scarborough, 1995	
190*	R J Blakey (204*) and J D Love (79*) v. Gloucestershire at Leeds, 1987	
189	J E Root (160) and G S Ballance (87) v. Sussex at Scarborough 2011	
188	D E V Padgett (146) and J V Wilson (72) v. Sussex at Middlesbrough, 1960	
187	J V Wilson (230) and H Halliday (74) v. Derbyshire at Sheffield, 1952	
185	G Boycott (104*) and K Sharp (99) v. Kent at Tunbridge Wells, 1984	
182	E Lockwood (208) and E Lumb (40) v. Kent at Gravesend, 1882	
182	B B Wilson (109) and W Rhodes (111) v. Sussex at Hove, 1910	
182	D B Close (164) and J V Wilson (55) v. Combined Services at Harrogate, 1954	
182	A W Gale (126*) and J A Leaning (76) v. Middlesex at Scarborough, 2014	
181	A A Metcalfe (149) and J D Love (88) v. Glamorgan at Leeds, 1986	
177	Hon F S Jackson (87) and G H Hirst (232*) v. Surrey at The Oval, 1905	
176	L Hutton (176*) and A Coxon (72) v. Sussex at Sheffield, 1948	
175	A Drake (108) and R Kilner (77) v. Cambridge University at Cambridge, 1913	
173	H Sutcliffe (206) and R Kilner (124) v. Warwickshire at Dewsbury, 1925	
170	W Rhodes (157) and R Kilner (87) v. Derbyshire at Leeds, 1925	
170	J V Wilson (130*) and N W D Yardley (67) v. Lancashire at Manchester, 1954	
169	W Watson (147) and A B Sellers (92) v. Worcestershire at Worcester, 1947	
168	A T Barber (63) and A Mitchell (122*) v. Worcestershire at Worcester, 1929	
167	J M Bairstow (136) and G S Ballance (61) v. Somerset at Taunton 2011	
165	E Oldroyd (143) and W Rhodes (110) v. Glamorgan at Leeds, 1922	
165	K Sharp (100*) and P Carrick (73) v. Middlesex at Lord's, 1980	
164	A A Metcalfe (151) and D L Bairstow (88) v. Northamptonshire at Luton, 1986	
159*	J D Love (170*) and D L Bairstow (52*) v. Worcestershire at Worcester, 1979	
159	D B Close (128) and R Illingworth (74) v. Lancashire at Sheffield, 1959	
159	J H Hampshire (183*) and C Johnson (53) v. Sussex at Hove, 1971	
158*	G Boycott (153*) and P E Robinson (74*) v. Derbyshire at Harrogate, 1984	
157	T L Taylor (135*) and G H Hirst (72) v. An England XI at Hastings, 1901	
157	G H Hirst (142) and F Smith (51) v. Somerset at Bradford, 1903	
157	W Barber (87) and N W D Yardley (101) v. Surrey at The Oval, 1937	
156	A McGrath (158) and I J Harvey (103) v. Derbyshire at Derby, 2005	
155	J M Bairstow (102) and J A Leaning (82) v. Hampshire at Leeds, 2015	
153	S N Hartley (87) and M D Moxon (112*) v. Indians at Scarborough, 1986	
152	J H Hampshire (83) and S N Hartley (106) v. Nottinghamshire at Nottingham, 1981	
151*	G H Hirst (102*) and R Kilner (50*) v. Kent at Bradford, 1913	
151	G H Hirst (120) and F Smith (55) v. Kent at Leeds, 1903	
151	W Rhodes (57) and R Kilner (90) v. Nottinghamshire at Nottingham, 1925	

SIXTH WICKET (Qualification 150 runs)

296	A Lyth (251) and A U Rashid (159*) v. Lancashire at Manchester, 2014	
276	M Leyland (191) and E Robinson (124*) v. Glamorgan at Swansea, 1926	
252	C White (181) and R J Blakey (109*) v. Lancashire at Leeds, 1996	
248	G J Maxwell (140) and A U Rashid (127) v. Durham at Scarborough, 2015	
233	M W Booth (210) and G H Hirst (100) v. Worcestershire at Worcester, 1911	
229	W Rhodes (267*) and N Kilner (112) v. Leicestershire at Leeds, 1921	

225	E Wainwright (91) and Lord Hawke (127) v. Hampshire at Southampton, 1899
217*	H Sutcliffe (200*) and A Wood (123*) v. Worcestershire at Sheffield, 1935
214	W Watson (214*) and N W D Yardley (76) v. Worcestershire at Worcester, 1955
205	G H Hirst (125) and S Haigh (159) v. Nottinghamshire at Sheffield, 1901
200	D Denton (127) and G H Hirst (134) v. Essex at Bradford, 1902
198	M Leyland (247) and W Rhodes (100*) v. Worcestershire at Worcester, 1928
190	W Rhodes (126) and M Leyland (79) v. Middlesex at Bradford, 1923
190	J A Rudolph (122) and A U Rashid (86) v. Surrey at The Oval, 2007
188	W Watson (174) and R Illingworth (53) v. Lancashire at Sheffield, 1955
188	M P Vaughan (161) and R J Blakey (92) v. Essex at Ilford, 1997.
188	G S Ballance (111) and A U Rashid (82) v. Warwickshire at Birmingham 2011
184	R Kilner (104) and M W Booth (79) v. Leicestershire at Leeds, 1913
183	G H Hirst (131) and E Smith (129) v. Hampshire at Bradford, 1899
183	W Watson (139*) and R Illingworth (78) v. Somerset at Harrogate, 1956
178*	D Denton (108*) and G H Hirst (112*) v. Lancashire at Manchester, 1902
178*	N W D Yardley (100*) and R Illingworth (71*) v. Gloucestershire at Bristol, 1955
178	E Robinson (100) and D C F Burton (83) v. Derbyshire at Hull, 1921
178	H Sutcliffe (135) and P A Gibb (157*) v. Nottinghamshire at Sheffield, 1935
175	G M Fellows (88) and R J Blakey (103) v. Warwickshire at Birmingham, 2002
174	D S Lehmann (136) and G M Hamilton (73) v. Kent at Maidstone, 1998
172	A J Dalton (119*) and D L Bairstow (62) v. Worcestershire at Dudley, 1971
170*	A U Rashid 103*) and A J Hodd (68*) v. Somerset at Taunton, 2013
170	A W Gale (101) and T T Bresnan (97) v. Worcestershire at Worcester, 2009
169	W Barber (124) and H Verity (78*) v. Warwickshire at Birmingham, 1933
169	R Illingworth (162) and J Birkenshaw (37) v. Indians at Sheffield, 1959
166	E Wainwright (116) and E Smith (61) v. Kent at Catford, 1900
166	D B Close (161) and F S Trueman (104) v. Northamptonshire at Northampton, 1963
162*	G Boycott (220*) and J G Binks (70*) v. Northamptonshire at Sheffield, 1967
161*	D L Bairstow (100*) and P Carrick (59*) v. Middlesex at Leeds, 1983
159	D S Lehmann (187*) and R J Blakey (78*) v. Somerset at Bath, 2001
159	J M Bairstow (182) and A McGrath (90) v. Leicestershire at Scarborough, 2012
156	W Rhodes (82*) and E Robinson (94) v. Derbyshire at Chesterfield, 1919
154	C Turner (84) and A Wood (79) v. Glamorgan at Swansea, 1936
153*	J A Rudolph (92*) and A U Rashid (73*) v. Worcestershire at Kidderminster, 2007
153	J A Rudolph (69*) and J M Bairstow (81) v. Warwickshire at Birmingham, 2010
151	D Denton (91) and W Rhodes (76) v. Middlesex at Bradford, 1904
151	G Boycott (152*) and P Carrick (75) v. Warwickshire at Leeds, 1982
150	G Ulyett (199*) and J M Preston (93) v. Derbyshire at Sheffield, 1887

SEVENTH WICKET (Qualification 125 runs)

366*	J M Bairstow (219*) and T T Bresnan (169*) v. Durham at Chester-le-Street, 2015
254	W Rhodes (135) and D C F Burton (142*) v. Hampshire at Dewsbury, 1919
247	P Holmes (285) and W Rhodes (79) v. Nottinghamshire at Nottingham, 1929
227	J M Bairstow (246) and L E Plunkett (126) v. Hampshire at Leeds, 2016
215	E Robinson (135*) and D C F Burton (110) v. Leicestershire at Leicester, 1921
197	G S Ballance (165*) and T T Bresnan (78) v. Sussex at Hove, 2015
185	E Wainwright (100) and G H Hirst (134) v. Gloucestershire at Bristol, 1897
183	G H Hirst (341) and H Myers (57) v. Leicestershire at Leicester, 1905
183	J A Rudolph (220) and T T Bresnan (101*) v. Warwickshire at Scarborough, 2007
180	C Turner (130) and A Wood (67) v. Somerset at Sheffield, 1936
170	G S Blewett (190) and G M Hamilton (84*) v. Northamptonshire at Scarborough, 1999
168	G L Brophy (99) and A U Rashid (157*) v. Lancashire at Leeds, 2009
166	R Peel (55) and I Grimshaw (122*) v. Derbyshire at Holbeck, 1886
162	E Wainwright (109) and S Haigh (73) v. Somerset at Taunton, 1900
162	R J Blakey (90) and R K J Dawson (87) v. Kent at Canterbury, 2002
162	A W Gale (149) and G L Brophy (97) v. Warwickshire at Scarborough, 2006
161	R G Lumb (118) and C M Old (89) v. Worcestershire at Bradford, 1980

160	J Tunnicliffe (158) and D Hunter (58*) v. Worcestershire at Worcester, 1900
157*	F A Lowson (259*) and R Booth (53*) v. Worcestershire at Worcester, 1953
157	K S Wiiliamson (189) and T T Bresnan (61) v. Sussex at Scarborough, 2014
155	D Byas (122*) and P Carrick (61) v. Leicestershire at Leicester.1991.
154*	G H Hirst (76*) and J T Newstead (100*) v. Nottinghamshire at Nottingham, 1908
148	J Rowbotham (113) and J Thewlis (50) v. Surrey at The Oval, 1873
147	E Wainwright (78) and G Ulyett (73) v. Somerset at Taunton, 1893
147	M P Vaughan (153) and R J Harden (64) v. Kent at Scarborough, 1999
143	C White (135*) and A K D Gray (60) v. Durham at Chester-le-Street, 2003
141	G H Hirst (108*) and S Haigh (48) v. Worcestershire at Worcester, 1905
141	J H Hampshire (149*) and J G Binks (72) v. MCC at Scarborough, 1965
140	E Wainwright (117) and S Haigh (54) v. CI Thornton's XI at Scarborough, 1900
140	D Byas (67) and P J Hartley (75) v. Derbyshire at Chesterfield, 1990
138	D Denton (78) and G H Hirst (103*) v. Sussex at Leeds, 1905
136	GH Hirst (93) and S Haigh (108*) v. Warwickshire at Birmingham, 1904
136	E Robinson (77*) and A Wood (65) v. Glamorgan at Scarborough, 1931
133*	W Rhodes (267*) and M Leyland (52*) v. Leicestershire at Leeds, 1921
133*	E I Lester (86*) and A B Sellers (73*) v. Northamptonshire at Northampton, 1948
133	D Byas (100) and P W Jarvis (80) v. Northamptonshire at Scarborough, 1992
132	W Rhodes (196) and S Haigh (59*) v. Worcestershire at Worcester, 1904
132	A J Hodd (96*) and Azeem Rafiq (74) v. Nottinghamshire at Scarborough, 2016
131*	D L Bairstow (79*) and A Sidebottom (52*) v. Oxford University at Oxford, 1981
130	P J Sharpe (64) and J V Wilson (134) v. Warwickshire at Birmingham, 1962
128	W Barber (66) and T F Smailes (86) v. Cambridge University at Cambridge, 1938
128	D B Close (88*) and A Coxon (59) v. Essex at Leeds, 1949
126	E Wainwright (171) and R Peel (46) v. Middlesex at Lord's, 1897
126	W Rhodes (91) and G G Macaulay (63) v. Hampshire at Hull, 1925
126	J C Balderstone (58) and J G Binks (95) v. Middlesex at Lord's, 1964
126	J M Bairstow (70) and A U Rashid (59) v. Kent at Canterbury, 2010
125	A B Sellers (109) and T F Smailes (65) v. Kent at Bradford, 1937

EIGHTH WICKET (Qualification 125 runs)

292	R Peel (210*) and Lord Hawke (166) v. Warwickshire at Birmingham, 1896
238	I J Harvey (209*) and T T Bresnan (74) v. Somerset at Leeds, 2005
192*	W Rhodes (108*) and G G Macaulay (101*) v. Essex at Harrogate, 1922
192	A U Rashid (117*) and A Shahzad (78) v. Hampshire at Basingstoke, 2009
180	W Barber (191) and T F Smailes (89) v. Sussex at Leeds, 1935
165	S Haigh (62) and Lord Hawke (126) v. Surrey at The Oval, 1902
163	G G Macaulay (67) and A Waddington (114) v. Worcestershire at Leeds, 1927
159	E Smith (95) and W Rhodes (105) v. MCC at Scarborough, 1901
157	A Shahzad (88) and D J Wainwright (85*) v. Sussex at Hove, 2009
156	G S Ballance (112) and R J Sidebottom (40) v. Leeds/Bradford MCCU at Leeds, 2013
152	W Rhodes (98) and J W Rothery (79) v. Hampshire at Portsmouth, 1904
151	W Rhodes (201) and Lord Hawke (51) v. Somerset at Taunton, 1905
151	R J Blakey (80*) and P J Hartley (89) v. Sussex at Eastbourne, 1996
149	G L Brophy (177*) and R J Sidebottom (61) v. Worcestershire at Worcester 2011
147	J P G Chadwick (59) and F S Trueman (101) v. Middlesex at Scarborough, 1965
146	S Haigh (159) and Lord Hawke (89) v. Nottinghamshire at Sheffield, 1901
144	G L Brophy (85) and D J Wainwright (102*) v. Warwickshire at Scarborough, 2009
138	E Wainwright (100) and Lord Hawke (81) v. Kent at Tonbridge, 1899
137	E Wainwright (171) and Lord Hawke (75) v. Middlesex at Lord's, 1897
135	P W Jarvis (55) and P J Hartley (69) v. Nottinghamshire at Scarborough, 1992
133	R Illingworth (61) and F S Trueman (74) v. Leicestershire at Leicester, 1955
132	G H Hirst (103) and E Smith (59) v. Middlesex at Sheffield, 1904
132	W Watson (119) and J H Wardle (65) v. Leicestershire at Leicester, 1949
131	P E Robinson (85) and P Carrick (64) v. Surrey at Harrogate, 1990
130	E Smith (98) and Lord Hawke (54) v. Lancashire at Leeds, 1904
128	H Verity (96*) and T F Smailes (77) v. Indians at Bradford, 1936
128	D L Bairstow (145) and G B Stevenson (11) v. Middlesex at Scarborough, 1980

CENTURY PARTNERSHIPS *(Continued)*

127	E Robinson (70*) and A Wood (62) v. Middlesex at Leeds, 1928
126	R Peel (74) and E Peate (61) v. Gloucestershire at Bradford, 1883
126	M W Booth (56) and E R Wilson (104*) v. Essex at Bradford, 1913
126	J D Middlebrook (84) and C E W Silverwood (70) v. Essex at Chelmsford, 2001
126	M J Lumb (115*) and D Gough (72) v. Hampshire at Southampton, 2003

NINTH WICKET (Qualification 100 runs)

246	T T Bresnan (116) and J N Gillespie (123*) v. Surrey at The Oval, 2007
192	G H Hirst (130*) and S Haigh (85) v. Surrey at Bradford, 1898
179	R A Hutton (189) and G A Cope (30*) v. Pakistanis at Bradford, 1971
176*	R Moorhouse (59*) and G H Hirst (115*) v. Gloucestershire at Bristol, 1894
173	S Haigh (85) and W Rhodes (92*) v. Sussex at Hove, 1902
162	H Verity (89) and T F Smailes (80) v. Somerset at Bath, 1936
162	W Rhodes (94*) and S Haigh (84) v. Lancashire at Manchester, 1904
161	E Smith (116*) and W Rhodes (79) v. Sussex at Sheffield, 1900
154	R M Pyrah (117) and R J Sidebottom (52) v.Lancashire at Leeds 2011
151	J M Bairstow (205) and R J Sidebottom (45*) v. Nottinghamshire at Nottingham 2011
150	Azeem Rafiq (100) and M J Hoggard (56*) v. Worcestershire at Worcester, 2009
149*	R J Blakey (63*) and A K D Gray (74*) v. Leicestershire at Scarborough, 2002
149	G H Hirst (232*) and D Hunter (40) v. Surrey at The Oval, 1905
146	G H Hirst (214) and W Rhodes (53) v. Worcestershire at Worcester, 1901
144	T T Bresnan (91) and J N Gillespie (44) v. Hampshire at Leeds, 2006
140	A U Rashid (111) and D J Wainwright (104) v. Sussex at Hove, 2008
136	R Peel (210*) and G H Hirst (85) v. Warwickshire at Birmingham, 1896
125*	L Hutton (269*) and A Coxon (65*) v. Northamptonshire at Wellingborough, 1949
124	P J Hartley (87*) and P W Jarvis (43) v. Essex at Chelmsford, 1986
122	G H Hirst (138) and W Rhodes (38) v. Nottinghamshire at Nottingham, 1899
119	A B Sellers (80*) and E P Robinson (66) v. Warwickshire at Birmingham, 1938
118	S Haigh (96) and W Rhodes (44) v. Somerset at Leeds, 1901
114	E Oldroyd (194) and A Dolphin (47) v. Worcestershire at Worcester, 1923
114	N Kilner (102*) and G G Macaulay (60) v. Gloucestershire at Bristol, 1923
113	G G Macaulay (125*) and A Waddington (44) v. Nottinghamshire at Nottingham, 1921
113	A Wood (69) and H.Verity (45*) v. MCC at Lord's, 1938
112	G H Hirst (78) and Lord Hawke (61*) v. Essex at Leyton, 1907
109	Lees Whitehead (60) and W Rhodes (81*) v. Sussex at Harrogate, 1899
108	A McGrath (133*) and C E W Silverwood (80) v. Durham at Chester-le-Street, 2005
106	L E Plunkett (86) and S A Patterson (43) v. Warwickshire at Leeds, 2014
105	J V Wilson (134) and A G Nicholson (20*) v. Nottinghamshire at Leeds, 1962
105	C M Old (100*) and H P Cooper (30) v. Lancashire at Manchester, 1978
105	C White (74*) and J D Batty (50) v. Gloucestershire at Sheffield, 1993
104	L Hall (129*) and R Moorhouse (86) v. Gloucestershire at Clifton, 1888
100	G Pollitt (51) and Lees Whitehead (54) v. Hampshire at Bradford, 1899

TENTH WICKET (Qualification 100 runs)

149	G Boycott (79) and G B Stevenson (115*) v. Warwickshire at Birmingham, 1982
148	Lord Hawke (107*) and D Hunter (47) v. Kent at Sheffield, 1898
144	A Sidebottom (124) and A L Robinson (30*) v. Glamorgan at Cardiff, 1977
121	J T Brown (141) and D Hunter (25*) v. Liverpool & District at Liverpool, 1894
118	Lord Hawke (110*) and D Hunter (41) v. Kent at Leeds, 1896
113	P J Hartley (88*) and R D Stemp (22) v. Middlesex at Lord's, 1996
110	C E W. Silverwood (45*) and R D Stemp (65) v. Durham at Chester-le-Street, 1996
109	A Shahzad (70) and R J Sidebottom (28*) v. Worcestershire at Scarborough, 2011
108	Lord Hawke (79) and Lees Whitehead (45*) v. Lancashire at Manchester, 1903
108	G Boycott (129) and M K Bore (37*) v. Nottinghamshire at Bradford, 1973
106	A B Sellers (79) and D V Brennan (30) v. Worcestershire at Worcester, 1948
103	A Dolphin (62*) and E Smith (49) v. Essex at Leyton, 1919
102	D Denton (77*) and D Hunter (45) v. Cambridge University at Cambridge, 1895

FIFTEEN WICKETS OR MORE IN A MATCH

A complete list of 12, 13 and 14 wickets in a match up to and including 2007 is to be found in the 2008 edition

W E BOWES (1)

16 for 35 (8 for 18 and 8 for 17) v. Northamptonshire at Kettering, 1935

A DRAKE (1)

15 for 51 (5 for 16 and 10 for 35) v. Somerset at Weston-super-Mare, 1914

T EMMETT (1)

16 for 38 (7 for 15 and 9 for 23) v. Cambridgeshire at Hunslet, 1869

G H HIRST (1)

15 for 63 (8 for 25 and 7 for 38) v. Leicestershire at Hull, 1907

R ILLINGWORTH (1)

15 for 123 (8 for 70 and 7 for 53) v. Glamorgan at Swansea, 1960

R PEEL (1)

15 for 50 (9 for 22 and 6 for 28) v. Somerset at Leeds, 1895

W RHODES (1)

15 for 56 (9 for 28 and 6 for 28) v. Essex at Leyton, 1899

H VERITY (4)

17 for 91 (8 for 47 and 9 for 44) v. Essex at Leyton, 1933
15 for 129 (8 for 56 and 7 for 73) v. Oxford University at Oxford, 1936
15 for 38 (6 for 26 and 9 for 12) v. Kent at Sheffield, 1936
15 for 100 (6 for 52 and 9 for 48) v. Essex at Westcliffe-on-Sea, 1936

J H WARDLE (1)

16 for 112 (9 for 48 and 7 for 64) v. Sussex at Hull, 1954

TEN WICKETS IN A MATCH
(including best analysis)

61	W Rhodes	15 for	56	v Essex	at Leyton	1899
48	H Verity	17 for	91	v Essex	at Leyton	1933
40	G H Hirst	15 for	63	v Leicestershire	at Hull	1907
31	G G Macaulay	14 for	92	v Gloucestershire	at Bristol	1926
28	S Haigh	14 for	43	v Hampshire	at Southampton	1898
27	R Peel	14 for	33	v Nottinghamshire	at Sheffield	1888
25	W E Bowes	16 for	35	v Northamptonshire	at Kettering	1935
25	J H Wardle	16 for	112	v Sussex	at Hull	1954
22	E Peate	14 for	77	v Surrey	at Huddersfield	1881
20	F S Trueman	14 for	123	v Surrey	at The Oval	1960
19	T Emmett	16 for	38	v Cambridgeshire	at Hunslet	1869
17	R Appleyard	12 for	43	v Essex	at Bradford	1951
15	E Wainwright	14 for	77	v Essex	at Bradford	1896
11	R Illingworth	15 for	123	v Glamorgan	at Swansea	1960
10	A Waddington	13 for	48	v Northamptonshire	at Northampton	1920
9	M W Booth	14 for	160	v Essex	at Leyton	1914
9	R Kilner	12 for	55	v Sussex	at Hove	1924
8	W Bates	11 for	47	v Nottinghamshire	at Nottingham	1881
8	G Freeman	13 for	60	v Surrey	at Sheffield	1869
7	E P Robinson	13 for	115	v Lancashire	at Leeds	1939
7	D Wilson	13 for	52	v Warwickshire	at Middlesbrough	1967

6 G A Cope	12 for 116	v Glamorgan	at Cardiff (Sophia Gardens)	1968
6 A Hill	12 for 59	v Surrey	at The Oval	1871
6 T F Smailes	14 for 58	v Derbyshire	at Sheffield	1939
5 P Carrick	12 for 89	v Derbyshire	at Sheffield (Abbeydale Pk)	1983
5 J M Preston	13 for 63	v MCC	at Scarborough	1888
5 E Robinson	12 for 95	v Northamptonshire	at Huddersfield	1927
4 J T Newstead	11 for 72	v Worcestershire	at Bradford	1907
3 T W Foster	11 for 93	v Liverpool & District	at Liverpool	1894
3 G P Harrison	11 for 76	v Kent	at Dewsbury	1883
3 F S Jackson	12 for 80	v Hampshire	at Southampton	1897
3 P W Jarvis	11 for 92	v Middlesex	at Lord's	1986
3 S P Kirby	13 for 154	v Somerset	at Taunton	2003
3 A G Nicholson	12 for 73	v Glamorgan	at Leeds	1964
3 R K Platt	10 for 87	v Surrey	at The Oval	1959
3 A Sidebottom	11 for 64	v Kent	at Sheffield (Abbeydale Pk)	1980
3 R J Sidebottom	11 for 43	v Kent	at Leeds	2000
3 G Ulyett	12 for 102	v Lancashire	at Huddersfield	1889
2 T Armitage	13 for 46	v Surrey	at Sheffield	1876
2 R Aspinall	14 for 65	v Northamptonshire	at Northampton	1947
2 J T Brown (Darfield)	12 for 109	v Gloucestershire	at Huddersfield	1899
2 R O Clayton	12 for 104	v Lancashire	at Manchester	1877
2 D B Close	11 for 116	v Kent	at Gillingham	1965
2 M J Cowan	12 for 87	v Warwickshire	at Birmingham	1960
2 A Coxon	10 for 57	v Derbyshire	at Chesterfield	1949
2 D Gough	10 for 80	v Lancashire	at Leeds	1995
2 G M Hamilton	11 for 72	v Surrey	at Leeds	1998
2 P J Hartley	11 for 68	v Derbyshire	at Chesterfield	1995
2 R A Hutton	11 for 62	v Lancashire	at Manchester	1971
2 E Leadbeater	11 for 162	v Nottinghamshire	at Nottingham	1950
2 M A Robinson	12 for 124	v Northamptonshire	at Harrogate	1993
2 M Ryan	10 for 77	v Leicestershire	at Bradford	1962
2 E Smith (Morley)	10 for 97	v MCC	at Scarborough	1893
2 G B Stevenson	11 for 74	v Nottinghamshire	at Nottingham	1980
2 S Wade	11 for 56	v Gloucestershire	at Cheltenham	1886
2 E R Wilson	11 for 109	v Sussex	at Hove	1921
1 A B Bainbridge	12 for 111	v Essex	at Harrogate	1961
1 J Birkenshaw	11 for 134	v Middlesex	at Leeds	1960
1 A Booth	10 for 91	v Indians	at Bradford	1946
1 H P Cooper	11 for 96	v Northamptonshire	at Northampton	1976
1 A Drake	15 for 51	v Somerset	at Weston-Super-Mare	1914
1 L Greenwood	11 for 71	v Surrey	at The Oval	1867
1 P M Hutchison	11 for 102	v Pakistan 'A'	at Leeds	1997
1 L Hutton	10 for 101	v Leicestershire	at Leicester (Aylestone Rd)	1937
1 R Iddison	10 for 68	v Surrey	at Sheffield	1864
1 M Leyland	10 for 94	v Leicestershire	at Leicester (Aylestone Rd)	1933
1 J D Middlebrook	10 for 170	v Hampshire	at Southampton	2000
1 F W Milligan	12 for 110	v Sussex	at Sheffield	1897
1 H Myers	12 for 192	v Gloucestershire	at Dewsbury	1904
1 C M Old	11 for 46	v Gloucestershire	at Middlesbrough	1969
1 D Pickles	12 for 133	v Somerset	at Taunton	1957
1 A U Rashid	11 for 114	v Worcestershire	at Worcester	2011
1 W Ringrose	11 for 135	v Australians	at Bradford	1905
1 C E W Silverwood	12 for 148	v Kent	at Leeds	1997
1 W Slinn	12 for 53	v Nottinghamshire	at Nottingham	1864
1 J Waring	10 for 63	v Lancashire	at Leeds	1966
1 F Wilkinson	10 for 129	v Hampshire	at Bournemouth	1938
1 A C Williams	10 for 66	v Hampshire	at Dewsbury	1919

TEN WICKETS IN AN INNINGS

Bowler				Year
A Drake	10 for 35	v.	Somerset at Weston-super-Mare	1914
H Verity	10 for 36	v.	Warwickshire at Leeds	1931
*H Verity	10 for 10	v.	Nottinghamshire at Leeds	1932
T F Smailes	10 for 47	v.	Derbyshire at Sheffield	1939

*Includes the hat trick.

EIGHT WICKETS OR MORE IN AN INNINGS

(Ten wickets in an innings also listed above)

A complete list of seven wickets in an innings up to and including 2007 is to be found in the 2008 edition

R APPLEYARD (1)

8 for 76 v. MCC at Scarborough, 1951

R ASPINALL (1)

8 for 42 v. Northamptonshire at Northampton, 1947

W BATES (2)

8 for 45 v. Lancashire at Huddersfield, 1878
8 for 21 v. Surrey at The Oval, 1879

M W BOOTH (4)

8 for 52 v. Leicestershire at Sheffield, 1912
8 for 47 v. Middlesex at Leeds, 1912
8 for 86 v. Middlesex at Sheffield, 1913
8 for 64 v. Essex at Leyton, 1914

W E BOWES (9)

8 for 77 v. Leicestershire at Dewsbury, 1929
8 for 69 v. Middlesex at Bradford, 1930
9 for 121 v. Essex at Scarborough, 1932
8 for 62 v. Sussex at Hove, 1932
8 for 69 v. Gloucestershire at Gloucester, 1933
8 for 40 v.Worcestershire at Sheffield, 1935
8 for 18 v. Northamptonshire at Kettering, 1935
8 for 17 v. Northamptonshire at Kettering, 1935
8 for 56 v. Leicestershire at Scarborough, 1936

J T BROWN (Darfield) (1)

8 for 40 v. Gloucestershire at Huddersfield, 1899

P CARRICK (2)

8 for 33 v. Cambridge University at Cambridge, 1973
8 for 72 v. Derbyshire at Scarborough, 1975

R O CLAYTON (1)

8 for 66 v. Lancashire at Manchester, 1877

D B CLOSE (2)

8 for 41 v. Kent at Leeds, 1959
8 for 43 v. Essex at Leeds, 1960

H P COOPER (1)

8 for 62 v. Glamorgan at Cardiff, 1975

G A COPE (1)

8 for 73 v. Gloucestershire at Bristol, 1975

M J COWAN (1)

9 for 43 v. Warwickshire at Birmingham, 1960

A COXON (1)

8 for 31 v. Worcestershire at Leeds, 1946

A DRAKE (2)

8 for 59 v. Gloucestershire at Sheffield, 1913
10 for 35 v. Somerset at Weston-super-Mare, 1914

T EMMETT (8)

9 for 34 v. Nottinghamshire at Dewsbury, 1868
9 for 23 v. Cambridgeshire at Hunslet, 1869
8 for 31 v. Nottinghamshire at Sheffield, 1871
8 for 46 v. Gloucestershire at Clifton, 1877
8 for 16 v. MCC at Scarborough, 1877
8 for 22 v. Surrey at The Oval, 1881
8 for 52 v. MCC at Scarborough, 1882
8 for 32 v. Sussex at Huddersfield, 1884

S D FLETCHER (1)

8 for 58 v. Essex at Sheffield, 1988

T W FOSTER (1)

9 for 59 v. MCC at Lord's, 1894

G FREEMAN (2)

8 for 11 v. Lancashire at Holbeck, 1868
8 for 29 v. Surrey at Sheffield, 1869

L GREENWOOD (1)

8 for 35 v. Cambridgeshire at Dewsbury, 1867

S HAIGH (5)

8 for 78 v. Australians at Bradford, 1896
8 for 35 v. Hampshire at Harrogate, 1896
8 for 21 v. Hampshire at Southampton, 1898
8 for 33 v. Warwickshire at Scarborough, 1899
9 for 25 v. Gloucestershire at Leeds, 1912

P J HARTLEY (2)

8 for 111 v. Sussex at Hove, 1992
9 for 41 v. Derbyshire at Chesterfield, 1995

G H HIRST (8)

8 for 59 v. Warwickshire at Birmingham, 1896
8 for 48 v. Australians at Bradford, 1899
8 for 25 v. Leicestershire at Hull, 1907
9 for 45 v. Middlesex at Sheffield, 1907
9 for 23 v. Lancashire at Leeds, 1910
8 for 80 v. Somerset at Sheffield, 1910
9 for 41 v. Worcestershire at Worcester, 1911
9 for 69 v. MCC at Lord's, 1912

EIGHT WICKETS OR MORE IN AN INNINGS *(Continued)*

R ILLINGWORTH (5)

8 for 69 v. Surrey at The Oval, 1954
9 for 42 v. Worcestershire at Worcester, 1957
8 for 70 v. Glamorgan at Swansea, 1960
8 for 50 v. Lancashire at Manchester, 1961
8 for 20 v. Worcestershire at Leeds, 1965

R KILNER (2)

8 for 26 v. Glamorgan at Cardiff, 1923
8 for 40 v. Middlesex at Bradford, 1926

S P KIRBY (1)

8 for 80 v. Somerset at Taunton, 2003

E LEADBEATER (1)

8 for 83 v. Worcestershire at Worcester, 1950

M LEYLAND (1)

8 for 63 v. Hampshire at Huddersfield, 1938

G G MACAULAY (3)

8 for 43 v. Gloucestershire at Bristol, 1926
8 for 37 v. Derbyshire at Hull, 1927
8 for 21 v. Indians at Harrogate, 1932

H MYERS (1)

8 for 81 v. Gloucestershire at Dewsbury, 1904

A G NICHOLSON (2)

9 for 62 v. Sussex at Eastbourne, 1967
8 for 22 v. Kent at Canterbury, 1968

E PEATE (6)

8 for 24 v. Lancashire at Manchester, 1880
8 for 30 v. Surrey at Huddersfield, 1881
8 for 69 v. Sussex at Hove, 1881
8 for 32 v. Middlesex at Sheffield, 1882
8 for 5 v. Surrey at Holbeck, 1883
8 for 63 v. Kent at Gravesend, 1884

R PEEL (6)

8 for 12 v. Nottinghamshire at Sheffield, 1888
8 for 60 v. Surrey at Sheffield, 1890
8 for 54 v. Cambridge University at Cambridge, 1893
9 for 22 v. Somerset at Leeds, 1895
8 for 27 v. South of England XI at Scarborough, 1896
8 for 53 v. Kent at Halifax, 1897

J M PRESTON (2)

8 for 27 v. Sussex at Hove, 1888
9 for 28 v. MCC at Scarborough, 1888

EIGHT WICKETS OR MORE IN AN INNINGS *(Continued)*

W RHODES (18)

9 for 28 v. Essex at Leyton, 1899
8 for 38 v. Nottinghamshire at Nottingham, 1899
8 for 68 v. Cambridge University at Cambridge, 1900
8 for 43 v. Lancashire at Bradford, 1900
8 for 23 v. Hampshire at Hull, 1900
8 for 72 v. Gloucestershire at Bradford, 1900
8 for 28 v. Essex at Harrogate, 1900
8 for 53 v. Middlesex at Lord's, 1901
8 for 55 v. Kent at Canterbury, 1901
8 for 26 v. Kent at Catford, 1902
8 for 87 v. Worcestershire at Worcester, 1903
8 for 61 v. Lancashire at Bradford, 1903
8 for 90 v. Warwickshire at Birmingham, 1905
8 for 92 v. Northamptonshire at Northampton, 1911
8 for 44 v. Warwickshire at Bradford, 1919
8 for 39 v. Sussex at Leeds, 1920
8 for 48 v. Somerset at Huddersfield, 1926
9 for 39 v. Essex at Leyton, 1929

W RINGROSE (1)

9 for 76 v. Australians at Bradford, 1905

E ROBINSON (3)

9 for 36 v. Lancashire at Bradford, 1920
8 for 32 v. Northamptonshire at Huddersfield, 1927
8 for 13 v. Cambridge University at Cambridge, 1928

E P ROBINSON (2)

8 for 35 v. Lancashire at Leeds, 1939
8 for 76 v. Surrey at The Oval, 1946

M A ROBINSON (1)

9 for 37 v. Northamptonshire at Harrogate, 1993

A SIDEBOTTOM (1)

8 for 72 v. Leicestershire at Middlesbrough, 1986

T F SMAILES (2)

8 for 68 v. Glamorgan at Hull, 1938
10 for 47 v. Derbyshire at Sheffield, 1939

G B STEVENSON (2)

8 for 65 v. Lancashire at Leeds, 1978
8 for 57 v. Northamptonshire at Leeds, 1980

F S TRUEMAN (8)

8 for 70 v. Minor Counties at Lord's, 1949
8 for 68 v. Nottinghamshire at Sheffield, 1951
8 for 53 v. Nottinghamshire at Nottingham, 1951
8 for 28 v. Kent at Dover, 1954
8 for 84 v. Nottinghamshire at Worksop, 1962
8 for 45 v. Gloucestershire at Bradford, 1963
8 for 36 v. Sussex at Hove, 1965
8 for 37 v. Essex at Bradford, 1966

EIGHT WICKETS OR MORE IN AN INNINGS *(Continued)*

H VERITY (20)

9 for 60 v. Glamorgan at Swansea, 1930
10 for 36 v. Warwickshire at Leeds, 1931
8 for 33 v. Glamorgan at Swansea, 1931
8 for 107 v. Lancashire at Bradford, 1932
8 for 39 v. Northamptonshire at Northampton, 1932
10 for 10 v. Nottinghamshire at Leeds, 1932
8 for 47 v. Essex at Leyton, 1933
9 for 44 v. Essex at Leyton, 1933
9 for 59 v. Kent at Dover, 1933
8 for 28 v. Leicestershire at Leeds, 1935
8 for 56 v. Oxford University at Oxford, 1936
8 for 40 v. Worcestershire at Stourbridge, 1936
9 for 12 v. Kent at Sheffield, 1936
9 for 48 v. Essex at Westcliff-on-Sea, 1936
8 for 42 v. Nottinghamshire at Bradford, 1936
9 for 43 v. Warwickshire at Leeds, 1937
8 for 80 v. Sussex at Eastbourne, 1937
8 for 43 v. Middlesex at The Oval, 1937
9 for 62 v. MCC at Lord's, 1939
8 for 38 v. Leicestershire at Hull, 1939

A WADDINGTON (3)

8 for 34 v. Northamptonshire at Leeds, 1922
8 for 39 v. Kent at Leeds, 1922
8 for 35 v. Hampshire at Bradford, 1922

E WAINWRIGHT (3)

8 for 49 v. Middlesex at Sheffield, 1891
9 for 66 v. Middlesex at Sheffield, 1894
8 for 34 v. Essex at Bradford, 1896

J H WARDLE (4)

8 for 87 v. Derbyshire at Chesterfield, 1948
8 for 26 v. Middlesex at Lord's, 1950
9 for 48 v. Sussex at Hull, 1954
9 for 25 v. Lancashire at Manchester, 1954

C WHITE (1)

8 for 55 v. Gloucestershire at Gloucester, 1998

A C WILLIAMS (1)

9 for 29 v. Hampshire at Dewsbury, 1919

R WOOD (1)

8 for 45 v. Scotland at Glasgow, 1952

SIX WICKETS IN AN INNINGS AT LESS THAN FOUR RUNS EACH

A complete list of 5 wickets at less than 4 runs each up to and including 2007 is to be found in the 2008 edition

R APPLEYARD (2)

6 for 17 v. Essex at Bradford, 1951
6 for 12 v. Hampshire at Bournemouth, 1954

T ARMITAGE (1)

6 for 20 v. Surrey at Sheffield, 1876

R ASPINALL (1)

6 for 23 v. Northamptonshire at Northampton, 1947

W BATES (5)

6 for 11 v. Middlesex at Huddersfield, 1879
6 for 22 v. Kent at Bradford, 1881
6 for 17 v. Nottinghamshire at Nottingham, 1881
6 for 12 v. Kent at Sheffield, 1882
6 for 19 v. Lancashire at Dewsbury, 1886

A BOOTH (1)

6 for 21 v. Warwickshire at Birmingham, 1946

W E BOWES (4)

6 for 17 v. Middlesex at Lord's, 1934
6 for 16 v. Lancashire at Bradford, 1935
6 for 20 v. Gloucestershire at Sheffield, 1936
6 for 23 v. Warwickshire at Birmingham, 1947

J T BROWN (Darfield) (1)

6 for 19 v. Worcestershire at Worcester, 1899

R.O CLAYTON (1)

6 for 20 v. Nottinghamshire at Sheffield, 1876

A COXON (1)

6 for 17 v. Surrey at Sheffield, 1948

T EMMETT (6)

6 for 7 v. Surrey at Sheffield, 1867
6 for 13 v. Lancashire at Holbeck, 1868
6 for 21 v. Middlesex at Scarborough, 1874
6 for 12 v. Derbyshire at Sheffield, 1878
6 for 19 v. Derbyshire at Bradford, 1881
6 for 22 v. Australians at Bradford, 1882

H FISHER (1)

6 for 11 v. Leicestershire at Bradford, 1932

SIX WICKETS IN AN INNINGS AT LESS THAN FOUR RUNS EACH *(Continued)*

S HAIGH (10)

6 for 18 v. Derbyshire at Bradford, 1897
6 for 22 v. Hampshire at Southampton, 1898
6 for 21 v. Surrey at The Oval, 1900
6 for 23 v. Cambridge University at Cambridge, 1902
6 for 19 v. Somerset at Sheffield, 1902
6 for 22 v. Cambridge University at Sheffield, 1903
6 for 21 v. Hampshire at Leeds, 1904
6 for 21 v. Nottinghamshire at Sheffield, 1905
6 for 13 v. Surrey at Leeds, 1908
6 for 14 v. Australians at Bradford, 1912

A HILL (2)

6 for 9 v. United South of England XI at Bradford, 1874
6 for 18 v. MCC at Lord's, 1881

G H HIRST (7)

6 for 23 v. MCC at Lord's, 1893
6 for 20 v. Lancashire at Bradford, 1906
6 for 12 v. Northamptonshire at Northampton, 1908
6 for 7 v. Northamptonshire at Northampton, 1908
6 for 23 v. Surrey at Leeds, 1908
6 for 23 v. Lancashire at Manchester, 1909
6 for 20 v. Surrey at Sheffield, 1909

R ILLINGWORTH (2)

6 for 15 v. Scotland at Hull, 1956
6 for 13 v. Leicestershire at Leicester, 1963

F S JACKSON (1)

6 for 19 v. Hampshire at Southampton, 1897

R KILNER (5)

6 for 22 v. Essex at Harrogate, 1922
6 for 13 v. Hampshire at Bournemouth, 1922
6 for 14 v. Middlesex at Bradford, 1923
6 for 22 v. Surrey at Sheffield, 1923
6 for 15 v. Hampshire at Portsmouth, 1924

G G MACAULAY (10)

6 for 10 v. Warwickshire at Birmingham, 1921
6 for 3 v. Derbyshire at Hull, 1921
6 for 8 v. Northamptonshire at Northampton, 1922
6 for 12 v. Glamorgan at Cardiff, 1922
6 for 18 v. Northamptonshire at Bradford, 1923
6 for 19 v. Northamptonshire at Northampton, 1925
6 for 22 v. Leicestershire at Leeds, 1926
6 for 11 v. Leicestershire at Hull, 1930
6 for 22 v. Leicestershire at Bradford, 1933
6 for 22 v. Middlesex at Leeds, 1934

SIX WICKETS IN AN INNINGS AT LESS THAN FOUR
RUNS EACH *(Continued)*

E PEATE (5)

6 for 14 v. Middlesex at Huddersfield, 1879
6 for 12 v. Derbyshire at Derby, 1882
6 for 13 v. Gloucestershire at Moreton-in-Marsh, 1884
6 for 16 v. Sussex at Huddersfield, 1886
6 for 16 v. Cambridge University at Sheffield, 1886

R PEEL (4)

6 for 21 v. Nottinghamshire at Sheffield, 1888
6 for 19 v. Australians at Huddersfield, 1888
6 for 22 v. Gloucestershire at Bristol, 1891
6 for 19 v. Leicestershire at Scarborough, 1896

A C RHODES (1)

6 for 19 v. Cambridge University at Cambridge, 1932

W RHODES (12)

6 for 21 v. Somerset at Bath, 1898
6 for 16 v. Gloucestershire at Bristol, 1899
6 for 4 v. Nottinghamshire at Nottingham, 1901
6 for 15 v. MCC at Lord's, 1902
6 for 16 v. Cambridge University at Cambridge, 1905
6 for 9 v. Essex at Huddersfield, 1905
6 for 22 v. Derbyshire at Glossop, 1907
6 for 17 v. Leicestershire at Leicester, 1908
6 for 13 v. Sussex at Hove, 1922
6 for 23 v. Nottinghamshire at Leeds, 1923
6 for 22 v. Cambridge University at Cambridge, 1924
6 for 20 v. Gloucestershire at Dewsbury, 1927

W RINGROSE (1)

6 for 20 v. Leicestershire at Dewsbury, 1903

R J SIDEBOTTOM (1)

6 for 16 v. Kent at Leeds, 2000

W SLINN (1)

6 for 19 v. Nottinghamshire at Nottingham, 1864

G B STEVENSON(1)

6 for 14 v. Warwickshire at Sheffield, 1979

F S TRUEMAN (4)

6 for 23 v. Oxford University at Oxford, 1955
6 for 23 v. Oxford University at Oxford, 1958
6 for 18 v. Warwickshire at Birmingham, 1963
6 for 20 v. Leicestershire at Sheffield, 1968

H VERITY (5)

6 for 11 v. Surrey at Bradford, 1931
6 for 21 v. Glamorgan at Swansea, 1931
6 for 12 v. Derbyshire at Hull, 1933
6 for 10 v. Essex at Ilford, 1937
6 for 22 v. Hampshire at Bournemouth, 1939

SIX WICKETS IN AN INNINGS AT LESS THAN FOUR
RUNS EACH *(Continued)*

A WADDINGTON (2)

6 for 21 v. Northamptonshire at Harrogate, 1921
6 for 21 v. Northamptonshire at Northampton, 1923

S WADE (1)

6 for 18 v. Gloucestershire at Dewsbury, 1887

E WAINWRIGHT (4)

6 for 16 v. Sussex at Leeds, 1893
6 for 23 v. Sussex at Hove, 1893
6 for 18 v. Sussex at Dewsbury, 1894
6 for 22 v. MCC at Scarborough, 1894

J H WARDLE (8)

6 for 17 v. Sussex at Sheffield, 1948
6 for 10 v. Scotland at Edinburgh, 1950
6 for 12 v. Gloucestershire at Hull, 1950
6 for 20 v. Kent at Scarborough, 1950
6 for 23 v. Somerset at Sheffield, 1951
6 for 21 v. Glamorgan at Leeds, 1951
6 for 18 v. Gloucestershire at Bristol, 1951
6 for 6 v. Gloucestershire at Bristol, 1955

D WILSON (3)

6 for 22 v. Sussex at Bradford, 1963
6 for 15 v. Gloucestershire at Middlesbrough, 1966
6 for 22 v. Middlesex at Sheffield, 1966

FOUR WICKETS IN FOUR BALLS

A Drake v. Derbyshire at Chesterfield, 1914

FOUR WICKETS IN FIVE BALLS

F S Jackson v. Australians at Leeds, 1902
A Waddington v. Northamptonshire at Northampton, 1920
G G Macaulay v. Lancashire at Manchester, 1933
P J Hartley v. Derbyshire at Chesterfield, 1995
D Gough v. Kent at Leeds, 1995
J D Middlebrook v. Hampshire at Southampton, 2000

BEST BOWLING ANALYSES IN A MATCH
FOR AND AGAINST YORKSHIRE

Best For Yorkshire:
17 for 91 (8 for 47 and 9 for 44) H Verity v Essex at Leyton, 1933

Against Yorkshire:
17 for 91 (9 for 62 and 8 for 29) H Dean for Lancashire at Liverpool, 1913
(non-championship)

County Championship
16 for 114 (8 for 48 and 8 for 66) G Burton for Middlesex at Sheffield, 1888

Yorkshire versus:

Derbyshire	*For Yorkshire:*	14 for 58 (4 for 11 and 10 for 47) T F Smailes at Sheffield, 1939
	Against:	13 for 65 (7 for 33 and 6 for 32) W Mycroft at Sheffield, 1879
Most 10 wickets in a match	*For Yorkshire:*	P Carrick and E Peate 4 each
	Against:	W Mycroft 3
Durham	*For Yorkshire:*	10 for 101 (6 for 57 and 4 for 44) M A Robinson at Durham, 1992
	Against:	10 for 144 (7 for 81 and 3 for 63) O D Gibson at Chester-le-Street, 2007
Most 10 wickets in a match	*For Yorkshire:*	M A Robinson 1
	Against:	G R Breese and O D Gibson 1 each
Essex	*For Yorkshire:*	17 for 91 (8 for 47 and 9 for 44) H Verity at Leyton, 1933
	Against:	14 for 127 (7 for 37 and 7 for 90) W Mead at Leyton, 1899
Most 10 wickets in a match	*For Yorkshire:*	W Rhodes 7
	Against:	J K Lever, W Mead 2 each
Glamorgan	*For Yorkshire:*	15 for 123 (8 for 70 and 7 for 53) R Illingworth at Swansea. 1960
	Against:	12 for 76 (7 for 30 and 5 for 46) D J Shepherd at Cardiff, 1957
Most 10 wickets in a match	*For Yorkshire:*	H Verity 5
	Against:	D J Shepherd, J S Pressdee 1 each
Gloucestershire	*For Yorkshire:*	14 for 64 (7 for 58 and 7 for 6) R Illingworth at Harrogate, 1967
	Against:	15 for 79 (8 for 33 and 7 for 46) W G Grace at Sheffield, 1872
Most 10 wickets in a match	*For Yorkshire:*	W Rhodes 8
	Against:	E G Dennett 5
Hampshire	*For Yorkshire:*	14 for 43 (8 for 21 and 6 for 22) S Haigh at Southampton, 1898
	Against:	12 for 145 (7 for 78 and 5 for 67) D Shackleton at Bradford, 1962
Most 10 wickets in a match	*For Yorkshire:*	W Rhodes, E Robinson, H Verity 3 each
	Against:	A S Kennedy 3

301

Yorkshire versus

Kent	*For Yorkshire:*	15 for 38 (6 for 26 and 9 for 12)
		H Verity at Sheffield, 1936
	Against:	13 for 48 (5 for 13 and 8 for 35)
		A Hearne at Sheffield, 1885
Most 10 wickets	*For Yorkshire:*	E Peate and J H Wardle 4 each
in a match	*Against:*	C Blythe 6
Lancashire	*For Yorkshire:*	14 for 80 (6 for 56 and 8 for 24)
		E Peate at Manchester, 1880
	Against:	17 for 91 (9 for 62 and 8 for 29)
		H Dean at Liverpool, 1913 (non-championship)
		14 for 90 (6 for 47 and 8 for 43)
		R Tattersall at Leeds, 1956 (championship)
Most 10 wickets	*For Yorkshire:*	T Emmett 5
in a match	*Against:*	J Briggs 8
Leicestershire	*For Yorkshire:*	15 for 63 (8 for 25 and 7 for 38)
		G H Hirst at Hull, 1907
	Against:	12 for 139 (8 for 85 and 4 for 54)
		A D Pougher at Leicester, 1895
Most 10 wickets	*For Yorkshire:*	G H Hirst 5
in a match	*Against:*	A D Pougher 2
Middlesex	*For Yorkshire:*	13 for 94 (6 for 61 and 7 for 33)
		S Haigh at Leeds, 1900
	Against:	16 for 114 (8 for 48 and 8 for 66)
		G Burton at Sheffield, 1888
Most 10 wickets	*For Yorkshire:*	W Rhodes 5
in a match	*Against:*	J T Hearne 7
Northamptonshire	*For Yorkshire:*	16 for 35 (8 for 18 and 8 for 17)
		W E Bowes at Kettering, 1935
	Against:	15 for 31 (7 for 22 and 8 for 9)
		G E Tribe at Northampton, 1958
Most 10 wickets	*For Yorkshire:*	W E Bowes, G G Macaulay, H Verity,
in a match		A Waddington 3 each
	Against:	G E Tribe 3
Nottinghamshire	*For Yorkshire:*	14 for 33 (8 for 12 and 6 for 21)
		R Peel at Sheffield, 1888
	Against:	14 for 94 (8 for 38 and 6 for 56)
		F Morley at Nottingham, 1878
Most 10 wickets	*For Yorkshire:*	G H Hirst 5
in a match	*Against:*	F Morley, J C Shaw 4 each
Somerset	*For Yorkshire:*	15 for 50 (9 for 22 and 6 for 28)
		R Peel at Leeds, 1895
	Against:	15 for 71 (6 for 30 and 9 for 41)
		L C Braund at Sheffield, 1902
Most 10 wickets	*For Yorkshire:*	G H Hirst 7
in a match	*Against:*	L C Braund 3

Yorkshire versus

Surrey	*For Yorkshire:*	14 for 77 (6 for 47 and 8 for 30)
		E Peate at Huddersfield, 1881
	Against:	15 for 154 (7 for 55 and 8 for 99)
		T Richardson at Leeds, 1897
Most 10 wickets	*For Yorkshire:*	W Rhodes 7
in a match	*Against:*	G A Lohmann, T Richardson 6 each
Sussex	*For Yorkshire:*	16 for 112 (9 for 48 and 7 for 64)
		J H Wardle at Hull, 1954
	Against:	12 for 110 (6 for 71 and 6 for 39)
		G R Cox at Sheffield, 1907
Most 10 wickets	*For Yorkshire:*	R Peel, E Wainwright 3 each
in a match	*Against:*	Twelve players 1 each
Warwickshire	*For Yorkshire:*	14 for 92 (9 for 43 and 5 for 49)
		H Verity at Leeds, 1937
	Against:	12 for 55 (5 for 21 and 7 for 34)
		T W Cartwright at Bradford, 1969
Most 10 wickets	*For Yorkshire:*	S Haigh 4
in a match	*Against:*	E F Field 4
Worcestershire	*For Yorkshire:*	14 for 211 (8 for 87 and 6 for 124)
		W Rhodes at Worcester, 1903
	Against:	13 for 76 (4 for 38 and 9 for 38)
		J A Cuffe at Bradford, 1907
Most 10 wickets	*For Yorkshire:*	S Haigh, G G Macaulay 4 each
in a match	*Against:*	N Gifford 2
Australians	*For Yorkshire:*	13 for 149 (8 for 48 and 5 for 101)
		G H Hirst at Bradford, 1899
	Against:	13 for 170 (6 for 91 and 7 for 79)
		J M Gregory at Sheffield, 1919
Most 10 wickets	*For Yorkshire:*	S Haigh 2
in a match	*Against:*	C V Grimmett, F R Spofforth, C T B Turner, H Trumble 2 each

BEST BOWLING ANALYSES IN AN INNINGS
FOR AND AGAINST YORKSHIRE

Best For Yorkshire:
10 for 10 H Verity v Nottinghamshire at Leeds, 1932

Against Yorkshire:
10 for 37 C V Grimmett for Australians at Sheffield, 1930
(non-championship)

County Championship
10 for 51 H Howell for Warwickshire at Birmingham, 1923

Yorkshire versus:

Derbyshire	*For Yorkshire:*	10 for 47	T F Smailes at Sheffield, 1939
	Against:	9 for 27	J J Hulme at Sheffield, 1894
Most 5 wickets	*For Yorkshire:*	S Haigh, E Peat, W Rhodes 11 each	
in an innings	*Against:*	W Mycroft 10	

BEST BOWLING ANALYSES IN AN INNINGS
FOR AND AGAINST YORKSHIRE *(continued)*

Yorkshire versus

Durham
For Yorkshire: 6 for 37   R D Stemp at Durham, 1994
6 for 37   J N Gillespie at Chester-le-Street, 2006
Against: 7 for 58   J Wood at Leeds, 1999
Most 5 wickets in an innings
For Yorkshire: D Gough and M J Hoggard 2 each
Against: G R Breese, S J E Brown, S J Harmison and G Onions 2 each

Essex
For Yorkshire: 9 for 28   W Rhodes at Leyton, 1899
Against: 8 for 44   F G Bull at Bradford, 1896
Most 5 wickets in an innings
For Yorkshire: W Rhodes 18
Against: W Mead 14

Glamorgan
For Yorkshire: 9 for 60   H Verity at Swansea, 1930
Against: 9 for 43   J S Pressdee at Swansea, 1965
Most 5 wickets in an innings
For Yorkshire: H Verity 12
Against: D J Shepherd 6

Gloucestershire
For Yorkshire: 9 for 25   S Haigh at Leeds, 1912
Against: 9 for 36   C W L Parker at Bristol, 1922
Most 5 wickets in an innings
For Yorkshire: W Rhodes 22
Against: T W J Goddard 17

Hampshire
For Yorkshire: 9 for 29   A C Williams at Dewsbury, 1919
Against: 8 for 49   O W Herman at Bournemouth, 1930
Most 5 wickets in an innings
For Yorkshire: G H Hirst 10
Against: A S Kennedy 10

Kent
For Yorkshire: 9 for 12   H Verity at Sheffield, 1936
Against: 8 for 35   A Hearne at Sheffield, 1885
Most 5 wickets in an innings
For Yorkshire: W Rhodes 12
Against: A P Freeman 14

Lancashire
For Yorkshire: 9 for 23   G H Hirst at Leeds, 1910
Against: 9 for 41   A Mold at Huddersfield, 1890
Most 5 wickets in an innings
For Yorkshire: T Emmett 16
Against: J Briggs 19

Leicestershire
For Yorkshire: 8 for 25   G H Hirst at Hull, 1907
Against: 9 for 63   C T Spencer at Huddersfield, 1954
Most 5 wickets in an innings
For Yorkshire: G H Hirst 15
Against: H A Smith 7

Middlesex
For Yorkshire: 9 for 45   G H Hirst at Sheffield 1907
Against: 9 for 57   F A Tarrant at Leeds, 1906
Most 5 wickets in an innings
For Yorkshire: W Rhodes 18
Against: J T Hearne 21

Northamptonshire
For Yorkshire: 9 for 37   M A Robinson at Harrogate, 1993
Against: 9 for 30   A E Thomas at Bradford, 1920
Most 5 wickets in an innings
For Yorkshire: G G Macaulay 14
Against: G E Tribe, W Wells 7 each

Nottinghamshire
For Yorkshire: 10 for 10   H Verity at Leeds, 1932
Against: 8 for 32   J C Shaw at Nottingham, 1865
Most 5 wickets in an innings
For Yorkshire: W Rhodes 17
Against: F Morley 17

Yorkshire versus

Somerset	*For Yorkshire:*	10 for 35	A Drake at Weston-super-Mare, 1914
	Against:	9 for 41	L C Braund at Sheffield, 1902
Most 5 wickets	*For Yorkshire:*	G H Hirst 16	
in an innings	*Against:*	E J Tyler 8	
Surrey	*For Yorkshire:*	8 for 5	E Peate at Holbeck, 1883
	Against:	9 for 47	T Richardson at Sheffield, 1893
Most 5 wickets	*For Yorkshire:*	W Rhodes 17	
in an innings	*Against:*	W Southerton 19	
Sussex	*For Yorkshire:*	9 for 48	J H Wardle at Hull, 1954
	Against:	9 for 34	James Langridge at Sheffield, 1934
Most 5 wickets	*For Yorkshire:*	W Rhodes 14	
in an innings	*Against:*	G R Cox, J A Snow 6 each	
Warwickshire	*For Yorkshire:*	10 for 36	H Verity at Leeds, 1930
	Against:	10 for 51	H Howell at Birmingham, 1923
Most 5 wickets	*For Yorkshire:*	W Rhodes 18	
in an innings	*Against:*	E F Field, W E Hollies 7 each	
Worcestershire	*For Yorkshire:*	9 for 41	G H Hirst at Worcester, 1911
	Against:	9 for 38	J A Cuffe at Bradford, 1907
Most 5 wickets	*For Yorkshire:*	S Haigh, W Rhodes 11 each	
in an innings	*Against:*	R T D Perks 7	
Australians	*For Yorkshire:*	9 for 76	W Ringrose at Bradford, 1905
	Against:	10 for 37	C V Grimmett at Sheffield, 1930
Most 5 wickets	*For Yorkshire:*	R Peel 7	
in an innings	*Against:*	F R Spofforth 7	

HAT-TRICKS

G Freeman v. Lancashire at Holbeck, 1868
G Freeman v. Middlesex at Sheffield, 1868
A Hill v. United South of England XI at Bradford, 1874
A Hill v. Surrey at The Oval, 1880
E Peate v. Kent at Sheffield, 1882
G Ulyett v. Lancashire at Sheffield, 1883
E Peate v. Gloucestershire at Moreton-in-Marsh, 1884
W Fletcher v. MCC at Lord's, 1892
E Wainwright v. Sussex at Dewsbury, 1894
G H Hirst v. Leicestershire at Leicester, 1895
J T Brown v. Derbyshire at Derby, 1896
R Peel v. Kent at Halifax, 1897
S Haigh v. Derbyshire at Bradford, 1897
W Rhodes v. Kent at Canterbury, 1901
S Haigh v. Somerset at Sheffield, 1902
H A Sedgwick v. Worcestershire at Hull, 1906
G Deyes v. Gentlemen of Ireland at Bray, 1907
G H Hirst v. Leicestershire at Hull, 1907
J T Newstead v. Worcestershire at Bradford, 1907
S Haigh v. Lancashire at Manchester, 1909
M W Booth v. Worcestershire at Bradford, 1911
A Drake v. Essex at Huddersfield, 1912

HAT-TRICKS *(Continued)*

M W Booth v. Essex at Leyton, 1912
A Drake v. Derbyshire at Chesterfield, 1914 (4 in 4)
W Rhodes v. Derbyshire at Derby, 1920
A Waddington v. Northamptonshire at Northampton, 1920 (4 in 5)
G G Macaulay v. Warwickshire at Birmingham, 1923
E Robinson v. Sussex at Hull, 1928
G G Macaulay v. Leicestershire at Hull, 1930
E Robinson v. Kent at Gravesend, 1930
H Verity v. Nottinghamshire at Leeds, 1932
H Fisher v. Somerset at Sheffield, 1932 (all lbw)
G G Macaulay v. Glamorgan at Cardiff, 1933
G G Macaulay v. Lancashire at Manchester, 1933 (4 in 5)
M.Leyland v. Surrey at Sheffield, 1935
E Robinson v. Kent at Leeds, 1939
A Coxon v. Worcestershire at Leeds, 1946
F S Trueman v. Nottinghamshire at Nottingham, 1951
F S Trueman v. Nottinghamshire at Scarborough, 1955
R Appleyard v. Gloucestershire at Sheffield, 1956
F S.Trueman v. MCC at Lord's, 1958
D Wilson v. Nottinghamshire at Middlesbrough, 1959
F S Trueman v. Nottinghamshire at Bradford, 1963
D Wilson v. Nottinghamshire at Worksop, 1966
D Wilson v. Kent at Harrogate, 1966
G A Cope v. Essex at Colchester, 1970
A L Robinson v. Nottinghamshire at Worksop, 1974
P W Jarvis v. Derbyshire at Chesterfield, 1985
P J Hartley v. Derbyshire at Chesterfield, 1995 (4 in 5)
D Gough v. Kent at Leeds, 1995 (4 in 5)
C White v. Gloucestershire at Gloucester, 1998
M J Hoggard v. Sussex at Hove, 2009

52 Hat-Tricks: G G Macaulay and F S Trueman took four each, S Haigh and D Wilson three each. There have been seven hat-tricks versus Kent and Nottinghamshire, and six versus Derbyshire.

200 WICKETS IN A SEASON

Bowler	Season	Overs	Maidens	Runs	Wickets	Average
W Rhodes	1900	1366.4	411	3054	240	12.72
W Rhodes	1901	1455.3	474	3497	233	15.00
G H Hirst	1906	1111.1	262	3089	201	15.36
G G Macaulay	1925	1241.2	291	2986	200	14.93
R Appleyard†	1951	1323.2	394	2829	200	14.14

† First full season in First-Class cricket.

100 WICKETS IN A SEASON

Bowler		Wickets taken	Wickets taken	Wickets taken
R Appleyard	(3)	200 in 1951	141 in 1954	110 in 1956
A Booth	(1)	111 in 1946	—	—
M W Booth	(3)	104 in 1912	167 in 1913	155 in 1914
W E Bowes	(8)	117 in 1931	168 in 1932	130 in 1933
		109 in 1934	154 in 1935	113 in 1936
		106 in 1938	107 in 1939	—

Bowler		Wickets taken	Wickets taken	Wickets taken
D B Close	(2)	105 in 1949	114 in 1952	—
A Coxon	(2)	101 in 1949	129 in 1950	—
A Drake	(2)	115 in 1913	158 in 1914	—
T Emmett	(1)	112 in 1886	—	—
S Haigh	(10)	100 in 1898	160 in 1900	154 in 1902
		102 in 1903	118 in 1904	118 in 1905
		161 in 1906	120 in 1909	100 in 1911
		125 in 1912		
G H Hirst	(12)	150 in 1895	171 in 1901	121 in 1903
		114 in 1904	100 in 1905	201 in 1906
		169 in 1907	164 in 1908	138 in 1910
		130 in 1911	113 in 1912	100 in 1913
R Illingworth	(5)	103 in 1956	120 in 1961	116 in 1962
		122 in 1964	105 in 1968	
R Kilner	(4)	107 in 1922	143 in 1923	134 in 1924
		123 in 1925		
G G Macaulay	(10)	101 in 1921	130 in 1922	163 in 1923
		184 in 1924	200 in 1925	133 in 1926
		130 in 1927	117 in 1928	102 in 1929
		141 in 1933		
J T Newstead	(1)	131 in 1908	—	—
A G Nicholson	(2)	113 in 1966	101 in 1967	—
E Peate	(3)	131 in 1880	133 in 1881	165 in 1882
R Peel	(6)	118 in 1888	132 in 1890	106 in 1892
		134 in 1894	155 in 1895	108 in 1896
W Rhodes	(22)	141 in 1898	153 in 1899	240 in 1900
		233 in 1901	174 in 1902	169 in 1903
		118 in 1904	158 in 1905	113 in 1906
		164 in 1907	100 in 1908	115 in 1909
		105 in 1911	117 in 1914	155 in 1919
		156 in 1920	128 in 1921	100 in 1922
		127 in 1923	102 in 1926	111 in 1928
		100 in 1929		
E Robinson	(1)	111 in 1928	—	—
E P Robinson	(4)	104 in 1938	120 in 1939	149 in 1946
		108 in 1947	—	—
T F Smailes	(4)	105 in 1934	125 in 1936	120 in 1937
		104 in 1938	—	—
F S Trueman	(8)	129 in 1954	140 in 1955	104 in 1959
		150 in 1960	124 in 1961	122 in 1962
		121 in 1965	107 in 1966	—
H Verity	(9)	169 in 1931	146 in 1932	168 in 1933
		100 in 1934	199 in 1935	185 in 1936
		185 in 1937	137 in 1938	189 in 1939
A Waddington	(5)	100 in 1919	140 in 1920	105 in 1921
		132 in 1922	105 in 1925	—
E Wainwright	(3)	114 in 1893	157 in 1894	102 in 1896
J H Wardle	(10)	148 in 1948	100 in 1949	172 in 1950
		122 in 1951	169 in 1952	126 in 1953
		122 in 1954	159 in 1955	146 in 1956
		106 in 1957	—	—
D Wilson	(3)	100 in 1966	107 in 1968	101 in 1969

BOWLERS WHO HAVE TAKEN OVER 500 WICKETS

Player	M	Runs	Wkts	Av'ge	Best
W Rhodes	883	57634	3598	16.01	9 for 28
G H Hirst	717	44716	2481	18.02	9 for 23
S Haigh	513	29289	1876	15.61	9 for 25
G G Macaulay	445	30554	1774	17.22	8 for 21
F S Trueman	459	29890	1745	17.12	8 for 28
H Verity	278	21353	1558	13.70	10 for 10
J H Wardle	330	27917	1539	18.13	9 for 25
R Illingworth	496	26806	1431	18.73	9 for 42
W E Bowes	301	21227	1351	15.71	9 for 121
R Peel	318	20638	1311	15.74	9 for 22
T Emmett	299	15465	1216	12.71	9 for 23
D Wilson	392	22626	1104	20.49	7 for 19
P Carrick	425	30530	1018	29.99	8 for 33
E Wainwright	352	17744	998	17.77	9 for 66
D B Close	536	23489	967	24.29	8 for 41
Emmott Robinson	413	19645	893	21.99	9 for 36
A G Nicholson	.282	17296	876	19.74	9 for 62
R Kilner	365	14855	857	17.33	8 for 26
A Waddington	255	16203	835	19.40	8 for 34
T F Smailes	262	16593	802	20.68	10 for 47
E Peate	154	9986	794	12.57	8 for 5
Ellis P Robinson	208	15141	735	20.60	8 for 35
C M Old	222	13409	647	20.72	7 for 20
R Appleyard	133	9903	642	15.42	8 for 76
W Bates	202	10692	637	16.78	8 for 21
G A Cope	230	15627	630	24.80	8 for 73
P J Hartley	195	17438	579	30.11	9 for 41
A Sidebottom	216	13852	558	24.82	8 for 72
M W Booth	144	11017	557	19.17	8 for 47
A Hill	140	7002	542	12.91	7 for 14
Hon F S Jackson	207	9690	506	19.15	7 for 42

BOWLERS UNCHANGED IN A MATCH
(IN WHICH THE OPPONENTS WERE DISMISSED TWICE)

**There have been 31 instances. The first and most recent are listed below.
A complete list is to be found in the 2008 edition.**

First: L Greenwood (11 for 71) and G Freeman (8 for 73) v. Surrey
at The Oval, 1867
Yorkshire won by an innings and 111 runs

Most Recent: E Robinson (8 for 65) and G G Macaulay (12 for 50) v. Worcestershire
at Leeds, 1927
Yorkshire won by an innings and 106 runs

FIELDERS (IN MATCHES FOR YORKSHIRE)

MOST CATCHES IN AN INNINGS

6	E P Robinson	v. Leicestershire	at Bradford, 1938
5	J Tunnicliffe	v. Leicestershire	at Leeds, 1897
5	J Tunnicliffe	v. Leicestershire	at Leicester, 1900
5	J Tunnicliffe	v. Leicestershire	at Scarborough, 1901
5	A B Sellers	v. Essex	at Leyton, 1933
5	D Wilson	v. Surrey	at The Oval, 1969
5	R G Lumb	v. Gloucestershire	at Middlesbrough, 1972

MOST CATCHES IN A MATCH

7	J Tunnicliffe	v. Leicestershire	at Leeds, 1897
7	J Tunnicliffe	v. Leicestershire	at Leicester, 1900
7	A B Sellers	v Essex	at Leyton, 1933
7	E P Robinson	v. Leicestershire	at Bradford, 1938
7	A Lyth	v. Middlesex	at Scarborough, 2014

MOST CATCHES IN A SEASON

70	J Tunnicliffe	in 1901
70	P J Sharpe	in 1962
61	J Tunnicliffe	in 1895
60	J Tunnicliffe	in 1904
59	J Tunnicliffe	in 1896
57	J V Wilson	in 1955
54	J V Wilson	in 1961
53	J V Wilson	in 1957
51	J V Wilson	in 1951

MOST CATCHES IN A CAREER

665	J Tunnicliffe	(1.40 per match)
586	W Rhodes	(0.66 per match)
564	D B Close	(1.05 per match)
525	P J Sharpe	(1.27 per match)
520	J V Wilson	(1.09 per match)
518	G H Hirst	(0.72 per match)

WICKET-KEEPERS IN MATCHES FOR YORKSHIRE

MOST DISMISSALS IN AN INNINGS

7	(7ct)	D L Bairstow	v. Derbyshire	at Scarborough	1982
6	(6ct)	J Hunter	v. Gloucestershire	at Gloucester	1887
6	(5ct,1st)	D Hunter	v. Surrey	at Sheffield	1891
6	(6ct)	D Hunter	v. Middlesex	at Leeds	1909
6	(2ct,4st)	W R Allen	v. Sussex	at Hove	1921
6	(5ct,1st)	J G Binks	v. Lancashire	at Leeds	1962
6	(6ct)	D L Bairstow	v. Lancashire	at Manchester	1971
6	(6ct)	D L Bairstow	v. Warwickshire	at Bradford	1978
6	(5ct,1st)	D L Bairstow	v. Lancashire	at Leeds	1980
6	(6ct)	D L Bairstow	v. Derbyshire	at Chesterfield	1984
6	(6ct)	R J Blakey	v. Sussex	at Eastbourne	1990
6	(5ct,1st)	R J Blakey	v. Gloucestershire	at Cheltenham	1992
6	(5ct,1st)	R J Blakey	v. Glamorgan	at Cardiff	1994
6	(6ct)	R J Blakey	v. Glamorgan	at Leeds	2003
6	(6ct)	G L Brophy	v. Durham	at Chester-le-Street	2009
6	(6ct)	J M Bairstow	v. Middlesex	at Leeds	2013
6	(6ct)	J M Bairstow	v. Sussex	at Arundel	2014

MOST DISMISSALS IN A MATCH

11	(11ct)	D L Bairstow	v. Derbyshire	at Scarborough	1982
		(Equalled World Record)			
9	(9ct)	J.Hunter	v. Gloucestershire	at Gloucester	1887
9	(8ct,1st)	A Dolphin	v. Derbyshire	at Bradford	1919
9	(9ct)	D L Bairstow	v. Lancashire	at Manchester	1971
9	(9ct)	R J Blakey	v. Sussex	at Eastbourne	1990
8	(2ct,6st)	G Pinder	v. Lancashire	at Sheffield	1872
8	(2ct,6st)	D Hunter	v. Surrey	at Bradford	1898
8	(7ct,1st)	A Bairstow	v. Cambridge University	at Cambridge	1899
8	(8ct)	A Wood	v. Northamptonshire	at Huddersfield	1932
8	(8ct)	D L Bairstow	v. Lancashire	at Leeds	1978
8	(7ct,1st)	D L Bairstow	v. Derbyshire	at Chesterfield	1984
8	(6ct,2st)	D L Bairstow	v. Derbyshire	at Chesterfield	1985
8	(8ct)	R J Blakey	v. Hampshire	at Southampton	1989
8	(8ct)	R J Blakey	v. Northamptonshire	at Harrogate	1993
8	(8ct)	A J Hodd	v. Glamorgan	at Leeds	2012
8	(8ct)	J M Bairstow	v. Middlesex	at Leed	2013

MOST DISMISSALS IN A SEASON   MOST DISMISSALS IN A CAREER

107	(96ct,11st)	J G Binks, 1960		1186	(863ct,323st)	D Hunter (2.29 per match)
94	(81ct,13st)	JG Binks, 1961		1044	(872ct,172st)	J G Binks (2.12 per match)
89	(75ct,14st)	A Wood, 1934		1038	(907ct,131st)	D L Bairstow (2.41 per match)
88	(80ct,8st)	J G Binks, 1963		855	(612ct,243st)	A Wood (2.09 per match)
86	(70ct,16st)	J G Binks, 1962		829	(569ct,260st)	A Dolphin (1.94 per match)
82	(52ct,30st)	A Dolphin, 1919		824	(768ct, 56st)	R J Blakey (2.43 per match)
80	(57ct,23st)	A. Wood, 1935				

YORKSHIRE PLAYERS WHO HAVE
COMPLETED THE "DOUBLE"

(all First-Class matches)

Player	Year	Runs	Average	Wickets	Average
M W Booth (1)	1913	1,228	27.28	181	18.46
D B Close (2)	†1949	1,098	27.45	113	27.87
	1952	1,192	33.11	114	24.08
A Drake (1)	1913	1,056	23.46	116	16.93
S Haigh (1)	1904	1,055	26.37	121	19.85
G H Hirst (14)	1896	1,122	28.20	104	21.64
	1897	1,535	35.69	101	23.22
	1901	1,950	42.39	183	16.38
	1903	1,844	47.28	128	14.94
	1904	2,501	54.36	132	21.09
	1905	2,266	53.95	110	19.94
	††1906	2,385	45.86	208	16.50
	1907	1,344	28.38	188	15.20
	1908	1,598	38.97	114	14.05
	1909	1,256	27.30	115	20.05
	1910	1,840	32.85	164	14.79
	1911	1,789	33.12	137	20.40
	1912	1,133	25.75	118	17.37
	1913	1,540	35.81	101	20.13
R Illingworth (6)	1957	1,213	28.20	106	18.40
	1959	1,726	46.64	110	21.46
	1960	1,006	25.79	109	17.55
	1961	1,153	24.53	128	17.90
	1962	1,612	34.29	117	19.45
	1964	1,301	37.17	122	17.45
F S Jackson (1)	1898	1,566	41.21	104	15.67
R Kilner (4)	1922	1,198	27.22	122	14.73
	1923	1,404	32.24	158	12.91
	1925	1,068	30.51	131	17.92
	1926	1,187	37.09	107	22.52
R Peel (1)	1896	1,206	30.15	128	17.50
W Rhodes (16)	1903	1,137	27.07	193	14.57
	1904	1,537	35.74	131	21.59
	1905	1,581	35.93	182	16.95
	1906	1,721	29.16	128	23.57
	1907	1,055	22.93	177	15.57
	1908	1,673	31.56	115	16.13
	1909	2,094	40.26	141	15.89
	1911	2,261	38.32	117	24.07
	1914	1,377	29.29	118	18.27
	1919	1,237	34.36	164	14.42
	1920	1,123	28.07	161	13.18
	1921	1,474	39.83	141	13.27
	1922	1,511	39.76	119	12.19
	1923	1,321	33.02	134	11.54
	1924	1,126	26.18	109	14.46
	1926	1,132	34.30	115	14.86
T F Smailes (1)	1938	1,002	25.05	113	20.84
E Wainwright (1)	1897	1,612	35.82	101	23.06

† First season in First-Class cricket.

†† The only instance in First-Class cricket of 2,000 runs and 200 wickets in a season.

H Sutcliffe (194) and M Leyland (45) hit 102 off six consecutive overs for Yorkshire v. Essex at Scarborough in 1932.

From 1898 to 1930 inclusive, Wilfred Rhodes took no less than 4,187 wickets, and scored 39,969 runs in First-Class cricket at home and abroad, a remarkable record. He also took 100 wickets and scored 1,000 in a season 16 times, and G H Hirst 14 times.

Of players with a qualification of not less than 50 wickets, Wilfred Rhodes was first in bowling in First-Class cricket in 1900, 1901, 1919, 1920, 1922, 1923 and 1926; Schofield Haigh in 1902, 1905, 1908 and 1909; Mr E R Wilson in 1921; G G Macaulay in 1924; H Verity in 1930, 1933, 1935, 1937 and 1939; W E Bowes in 1938; A Booth in 1946; R Appleyard in 1951 and 1955, and F S Trueman in 1952 and 1963.

The highest aggregate of runs made in one season in First-Class cricket by a Yorkshire player is 3,429 by L Hutton in 1949. This total has been exceeded three times, viz: D C S Compton 3,816 and W J Edrich 3,539 in 1947, and 3,518 by T Hayward in 1906. H Sutcliffe scored 3,336 in 1932.

Three players have taken all 10 Yorkshire wickets in an innings. G Wootton, playing for All England XI at Sheffield in 1865, took all 10 wickets for 54 runs. H Howell performed the feat for Warwickshire at Edgbaston in 1923 at a cost of 51 runs; and C V Grimmett, Australia, took all 10 wickets for 37 runs at Sheffield in 1930.

The match against Sussex at Dewsbury on June 7th and 8th, 1894, was brought to a summary conclusion by a remarkable bowling performance on the part of Edward Wainwright. In the second innings of Sussex, he took the last five wickets in seven balls, including the "hat trick". In the whole match he obtained 13 wickets for only 38 runs.

M D Moxon has the unique distinction of scoring a century in each of his first two First-Class matches in Yorkshire — 116 (2nd inns.) v. Essex at Leeds and 111 (1st inns.) v. Derbyshire at Sheffield, June 1981).

In the Yorkshire v. Norfolk match — played on the Hyde Park Ground, Sheffield, on July 14th to 18th, 1834 — 851 runs were scored in the four innings, of which no fewer than 128 were extras: 75 byes and 53 wides. At that time wides were not run out, so that every wide included in the above total represents a wide actually bowled. This particular achievement has never been surpassed in the annals of county cricket.

L Hutton reached his 1,000 runs in First-Class cricket in 1949 as early as June 9th.

W Barber reached his 1,000 runs in 1934 on June 13th. P Holmes reached his 1,000 in 1925 on June 16th, as also did H Sutcliffe in 1932. J T Brown reached his 1,000 in 1899 on June 22nd. In 1905, D Denton reached his 1,000 runs on June 26th; and in 1906 G H Hirst gained the same total on June 27th.

In 1912, D Denton scored over 1,000 runs during July, while M Leyland and H Sutcliffe both scored over 1,000 runs in August 1932.

L Hutton scored over 1,000 in June and over 1,000 runs in August 1949.

H Verity took his 100th wicket in First-Class cricket as early as June 19th in 1936 and on June 27th in 1935. In 1900, W Rhodes obtained his 100th wicket on June 21st, and again on the same date in 1901, while G H Hirst obtained his 100th wicket on June 28th, 1906.

In 1930, Yorkshiremen (H Sutcliffe and H Verity) occupied the first places by English players in the batting and the bowling averages of First-Class cricket, which is a record without precedent. H Sutcliffe was also first in the batting averages in 1931 and 1932.

G Boycott was the first player to have achieved an average of over 100 in each of two English seasons. In 1971, he scored 2,503 runs for an average of 100.12, and in 1979 he scored 1,538 runs for an average of 102.53.

FIRST-CLASS MATCHES BEGUN AND FINISHED IN ONE DAY

Yorkshire v. Somerset, at Huddersfield, July 9th, 1894.

Yorkshire v. Hampshire, at Southampton, May 27th, 1898

Yorkshire v. Worcestershire, at Bradford, May 7th, 1900

For England

YORKSHIRE TEST CRICKETERS 1877–2016 (Correct to December 21, 2016)

Player	M.	I	NO	Runs	HS.	Av'ge	100s	50s	Balls	R	W	Av'ge	Best	5wI	10wM	c/st
APPLEYARD, R ...1954-56	9	9	6	51	19*	17.00	—	—	1,596	554	31	17.87	5-51	1	—	4
ARMITAGE, T ...1877	2	3	0	33	21	11.00	—	—	12	15	0	—	—	—	—	0
ATHEY, C W J ...1980-88	23	41	1	919	123	22.97	—	4	—	—	—	—	—	—	—	13
BAIRSTOW, D L ...1979-81	4	7	1	125	59	20.83	—	1	—	—	—	—	—	—	—	12/1
BAIRSTOW, J M .2012-16/17	38	65	6	2,435	167*	41.27	3	14	12	5	0	—	—	—	—	93/5
BALLANCE, G S 2013/14-16/17	21	38	2	1,413	156	39.25	4	7	—	—	—	—	—	—	—	20
BARBER, W ...1935	2	4	0	83	44	20.75	—	—	12	5	0	0.00	1-0	—	—	1
BATES, W ...1881-87	15	26	2	656	64	27.33	—	5	2,364	821	50	16.42	7-28	4	1	9
BINKS, J G ...1964	2	4	0	91	55	22.75	—	1	—	—	—	—	—	—	—	8/0
BLAKEY, R J ...1993	2	4	0	7	6	1.75	—	—	—	—	—	—	—	—	—	2/0
BOOTH, M W ...1913-14	2	2	0	46	32	23.00	—	—	312	130	7	18.57	4-49	—	—	0
BOWES, W E ...1932-46	15	11	5	28	10*	4.66	—	—	3,655	1,519	68	22.33	6-33	6	—	2
†BOYCOTT, G ...1964-82	108	193	23	8,114	246*	47.72	22	42	944	382	7	54.57	3-47	—	—	33
BRENNAN, D V ...1951	2	2	0	16	16	8.00	—	—	—	—	—	—	—	—	—	0/1
BRESNAN, T T ...2009-13/14	23	26	4	575	91	26.13	—	3	4,674	2,357	72	32.73	5-48	1	—	8
BROWN, J T ...1894-99	8	16	3	470	140	36.15	1	—	35	22	0	—	—	—	—	7
†CLOSE, D B ...1949-76	22	37	2	887	70	25.34	—	4	1,212	532	18	29.55	4-35	—	—	24
COPE, G A ...1977-78	3	2	2	40	22	13.33	—	—	864	277	8	34.62	3-102	—	—	1
COXON, A ...1948	1	2	0	19	19	9.50	—	—	378	172	3	57.33	2-90	—	—	0
DAWSON, R K J ...2002-03	7	13	3	114	19*	11.40	—	—	1,116	677	11	61.54	4-134	—	—	3
DENTON, D ...1905-10	11	22	1	424	104	20.19	—	1	—	—	—	—	—	—	—	8
DOLPHIN, A ...1921	1	2	0	1	1	0.50	—	—	—	—	—	—	—	—	—	1/0
EMMETT, T ...1877-82	7	13	1	160	48	13.33	—	—	728	284	9	31.55	7-68	1	—	9
GIBB, P A ...1938-46	8	13	0	581	120	44.69	2	3	—	—	—	—	—	—	—	3/1
GOUGH, D ...1994-2003	58	86	18	855	65	12.57	—	2	11,821	6,503	229	28.39	6-42	9	—	13

For England

YORKSHIRE TEST CRICKETERS 1877-2016 (Continued)

Player	M.	I	NO	Runs	HS.	Av'ge.	100s	50s	Balls	R	W	Av'ge	Best	5wI	10wM	c/st
GREENWOOD, A 1877	2	4	0	77	49	19.25	—	—								2
HAIGH, S 1899-1912	11	18	3	113	25	7.53	—	—	1,294	622	24	25.91	6-11	1	—	8
HAMILTON, G.M. 1999	1	2	0	0	0	0.00	—	—	90	63	0	—	—	—	—	0
HAMPSHIRE, J H ...1969-75	8	16	1	403	107	26.86	1	2								9
†HAWKE, LORD ...1896-99	5	8	1	55	30	7.85	—	—								3
HILL, A 1877	2	4	2	101	49	50.50	—	—	340	130	7	18.57	4-27	—	—	1
HIRST, G H 1897-1909	24	38	3	790	85	22.57	—	5	3,967	1,770	59	30.00	5-48	3	—	18
HOGGARD, M J ..2000-2008	67	92	27	473	38	7.27	—	—	13,909	7,564	248	30.50	7-61	7	1	24
HOLMES, P 1921-32	7	14	1	357	88	27.46	—	4								3
HUNTER, J 1884-85	5	7	2	93	39*	18.60	—	—								8/3
†HUTTON, L 1937-55	79	138	15	6,971	364	56.67	19	33	260	232	3	77.33	1-2	—	—	57
HUTTON, R A 1971	5	8	2	219	81	36.50	—	2	738	257	9	28.55	3-72	—	—	9
†ILLINGWORTH, R .1958-73	61	90	11	1,836	113	23.24	2	5	11,934	3,807	122	31.20	6-29	3	—	45
†JACKSON, Hon F S1893-1905	20	33	4	1,415	144*	48.79	5	6	1,587	799	24	33.29	5-52	1	—	10
JARVIS, P W 1988-93	9	15	2	132	29*	10.15	—	—	1,912	965	21	45.95	4-107	—	—	2
KILNER, R 1924-26	9	8	1	233	74	33.28	—	2	2,368	734	24	30.58	4-51	—	—	6
LEADBEATER, E ...1951-52	2	2	0	40	38	20.00	—	—	289	218	2	109.00	1-38	—	—	3
LEYLAND, M 1928-38	41	65	5	2,764	187	46.06	9	10	1,103	585	6	97.50	3-91	—	—	13
LOWSON, F A 1951-55	7	13	0	245	68	18.84	—	2								5
LYTH A 2015	7	13	0	265	107	20.38	1	—	6	0	0	—	—	—	—	8
McGRATH, A 2003	4	5	0	201	81	40.20	—	2	102	56	4	14.00	3-16	—	—	3
MACAULAY, G G ...1923-33	8	10	4	112	76	18.66	—	1	1,701	662	24	27.58	5-64	1	—	5
MILLIGAN, F W 1899	2	4	0	58	38	14.50	—	—	45	29	0	—	—	—	—	1
MITCHELL, A 1933-36	6	10	0	298	72	29.80	—	2	6	4	0	—	—	—	—	9
*MITCHELL, F 1899	2	4	0	88	41	22.00	—	—								2

YORKSHIRE TEST CRICKETERS 1877-2016 (Continued)

For England

Player	M.	I	NO	Runs	HS.	Av'ge.	100s	50s	Balls	R	W	Av'ge	Best	5wI	10wM	c/st
MOXON, M D 1986-89	10	17	1	455	99	28.43	—	3	48	30	0	—	—	—	—	10
OLD, C M 1972-81	46	66	9	845	65	14.82	—	2	8,858	4,020	143	28.11	7-50	4	—	22
PADGETT, D E V 1960	2	4	0	51	31	12.75	—	—	12	8	0	—	—	—	—	0
PEATE, E 1881-86	9	14	8	70	13	11.66	—	—	2,096	682	31	22.00	6-85	2	—	2
PEEL, R 1884-96	20	33	4	427	83	14.72	—	3	5,216	1,715	101	16.98	7-31	5	1	17
PLUNKETT, L E .2005/6-2014	13	20	5	238	55*	15.86	—	1	2,659	1,536	41	37.46	5-64	1	—	3
RASHID, A U .2015/16-16/17	10	18	2	295	61	18.43	—	2	2,544	1,626	38	42.78	5-64	1	—	3
RHODES, W 1899-1930	58	98	21	2,325	179	30.19	2	11	8,231	3,425	127	26.96	8-68	6	1	60
ROOT, J E 2012-16/17	53	98	11	4,594	254	52.80	11	27	1,427	721	15	48.06	2- 9	—	—	65
SHARPE, P J 1963-69	12	21	4	786	111	46.23	1	4	—	—	—	—	—	—	—	17
SHAHZAD, A 2010	1	1	0	5	5	5.00	—	—	102	63	4	15.75	3-45	—	—	2
SIDEBOTTOM, A 1985	1	1	0	2	2	2.00	—	—	112	65	1	65.00	1-65	—	—	1
SIDEBOTTOM, R J .2001-10	22	31	11	313	31	15.65	—	—	4,812	2,231	79	28.24	7-47	5	—	5
SILVERWOOD, C E W1997-2003	6	7	3	29	10	7.25	—	—	828	444	11	40.36	5-91	1	—	2
SMAILES, T F 1946	1	1	0	25	25	25.00	—	—	120	62	3	20.66	3-44	—	—	0
SMITHSON, G A 1948	2	3	0	70	35	23.33	—	—	—	—	—	—	—	—	—	0
†STANYFORTH, R T 1927-28	4	6	1	13	6*	2.60	—	—	—	—	—	—	—	—	—	7/2
STEVENSON, G B .1980-81	2	3	1	28	27*	28.00	—	—	312	183	5	36.60	3-111	—	—	0
SUTCLIFFE, H 1924-35	54	84	9	4,555	194	60.73	16	23	—	—	—	—	—	—	—	23
TAYLOR, K 1959-64	3	5	0	57	24	11.40	—	—	12	6	0	—	—	—	—	1
TRUEMAN, F S ..1952-65	67	85	14	981	39*	13.81	—	—	15,178	6,625	307	21.57	8-31	17	3	64
ULYETT, G 1877-90	25	39	0	949	149	24.33	1	7	2,627	1,020	50	20.40	7-36	1	—	19
†VAUGHAN M P .1999-2008	82	147	9	5,719	197	41.44	18	18	978	561	6	93.50	2-71	—	—	44
VERITY, H 1931-39	40	44	12	669	66*	20.90	—	3	11,173	3,510	144	24.37	8-43	5	2	30
WADDINGTON, A ..1920-21	2	4	0	16	7	4.00	—	—	276	119	1	119.00	1-35	—	—	1
WAINWRIGHT, E ..1893-98	5	9	0	132	49	14.66	—	—	127	73	0	—	—	—	—	2

For England

Player	M.	I	NO	Runs	HS.	Av'ge	100s	50s	Balls	R	W	Av'ge	Best	5wI	10wM	c/st
WARDLE, J H 1948-57	28	41	8	653	66	19.78	—	2	6,597	2,080	102	20.39	7-36	5	1	12
WATSON, W 1951-59	23	37	3	879	116	25.85	2	3	—	—	—	—	—	—	—	8
WHITE, C 1994-2002	30	50	7	1,052	121	24.46	1	5	3,959	2,220	59	37.62	5-32	3	—	14
WILSON, C E M 1899	2	4	1	42	18	14.00	—	—	—	—	—	—	—	—	—	0
WILSON, D 1964-71	6	7	1	75	42	12.50	—	—	1,472	466	11	42.36	2-17	—	—	1
WILSON, E R 1921	1	1	0	10	5	5.00	—	—	123	36	3	12.00	2-28	—	—	0
WOOD, A 1938-39	4	5	1	80	53	20.00	—	1	—	—	—	—	—	—	—	10/1
†YARDLEY, N W D ...1938-50	20	34	2	812	99	25.37	—	4	1,662	707	21	33.66	3-67	—	—	14

†Captained England
*Also represented and captained South Africa

For South Africa

Player	M.	I	NO	Runs	HS.	Av'ge	100s	50s	Balls	R	W	Av'ge	Best	5wI	10wM	c/st
†MITCHELL, F 1912	3	6	0	28	12	4.66	—	—	—	—	—	—	—	—	—	0

†Captained South Africa

Overseas Players

(Qualification: 20 first-class matches for Yorkshire)

For Australia

Player	M.	I	NO	Runs	HS.	Av'ge	100s	50s	Balls	R	W	Av'ge	Best	5wI	10wM	c/st
BEVAN, M G 1994-98	18	30	3	785	91	29.07	—	6	1,285	703	29	24.24	6-82	1	1	8
GILLESPIE, J N ...1996-2006	71	93	28	1,218	201*	18.73	1	2	14,234	6,770	259	26.13	7-37	8	—	27
JAQUES, P A 2005-2008	11	19	0	902	150	47.47	3	6	—	—	—	—	—	—	—	7
LEHMANN, D S ...1999-2004	27	42	2	1,798	177	44.95	5	10	974	412	15	27.46	3-42	—	—	11

For South Africa

Player	M.	I	NO	Runs	HS.	Av'ge	100s	50s	Balls	R	W	Av'ge	Best	5wI	10wM	c/st
RUDOLPH, J A ...2003-12/13	48	83	9	2,622	222*	35.43	6	11	664	432	4	108.00	1-1	—	—	29

For West Indies

Player	M.	I	NO	Runs	HS.	Av'ge	100s	50s	Balls	R	W	Av'ge	Best	5wI	10wM	c/st
RICHARDSON, R B 1983-84/95	86	146	12	5,949	194	44.39	16	27	66	18	0	—	—	—	—	90

CENTURIES FOR ENGLAND

C W J ATHEY (1)

123 v Pakistan at Lord's, 1987

J M BAIRSTOW (3)

150* v. South Africa at Cape Town 2016
140 v. Sri Lanka at Leeds 2016
167* v. Sri Lanka at Lord's 2016

G S BALLANCE (4)

104* v. Sri Lanka at Lord's, 2014 110 v. India at Lord's, 2014
256 v. India at Southampton, 2014 122 v. West Indies at North Sound, 2015

G BOYCOTT (22)

113 v. Australia at The Oval, 1964 112 v West Indies at Port-of-Spain, 1974
117 v. South Africa at Port Elizabeth, 1965 107 v. Australia at Nottingham, 1977
246* v. India at Leeds, 1967 191 v. Australia at Leeds, 1977
116 v. West Indies at Georgetown, 1968 100* v. Pakistan at Hyderabad, 1978
128 v. West Indies at Manchester, 1969 131 v. New Zealand at Nottingham, 1978
106 v. West Indies at Lord's, 1969 155 v. India at Birmingham, 1979
142* v. Australia at Sydney, 1971 125 v. India at The Oval, 1979
119* v. Australia at Adelaide, 1971 128* v. Australia at Lord's, 1980
121* v. Pakistan at Lord's, 1971 104* v. West Indies at St John's, 1981
112 v. Pakistan at Leeds, 1971 137 v. Australia at The Oval, 1981
115 v. New Zealand at Leeds, 1973 105 v. India at Delhi, 1981

J T BROWN (1)

140 v. Australia at Melbourne, 1895

D DENTON (1)

104 v. South Africa at Old Wanderers, Johannesburg, 1910

P A GIBB (2)

106 v. South Africa at Old Wanderers, Johannesburg, 1938
120 v. South Africa at Kingsmead, Durban, 1939

J H HAMPSHIRE (1)

107 v. West Indies at Lord's, 1969

L HUTTON (19)

100 v. New Zealand at Manchester, 1937 206 v. New Zealand at The Oval, 1949
100 v. Australia at Nottingham, 1938 202* v. West Indies at The Oval, 1950
364 v. Australia at The Oval, 1938 156* v. Australia at Adelaide, 1951
196 v. West Indies at Lord's, 1939 100 v. South Africa at Leeds, 1951
165* v. West Indies at The Oval, 1939 150 v. India at Lord's, 1952
122* v. Australia at Sydney, 1947 104 v. India at Manchester, 1952
100 v. South Africa at Leeds, 1947 145 v. Australia at Lord's, 1953
158 v. South Africa at Ellis Park, J'b'rg, 1948 169 v. West Indies at Georgetown, 1954
123 v. South Africa at Ellis Park, J'b'rg, 1949 205 v. West Indies at Kingston, 1954
101 v. New Zealand at Leeds, 1949

R ILLINGWORTH (2)

113 v. West Indies at Lord's, 1969
107 v. India at Manchester, 1971

Hon. F S JACKSON (5)

103 v. Australia at The Oval, 1893 144* v. Australia at Leeds, 1905
118 v. Australia at The Oval, 1899 113 v. Australia at Manchester, 1905
128 v. Australia at Manchester, 1902

CENTURIES FOR ENGLAND

M LEYLAND (9)

137 v. Australia at Melbourne, 1929
102 v. South Africa at Lord's, 1929
109 v. Australia at Lord's, 1934
153 v. Australia at Manchester, 1934
110 v. Australia at The Oval, 1934

161 v. South Africa at The Oval, 1935
126 v. Australia at Woolloongabba, Brisbane, 1936
111* v. Australia at Melbourne, 1937
187 v. Australia at The Oval, 1938

A LYTH (1)

107 v. New Zealand at Leeds 2015

W RHODES (2)

179 v. Australia at Melbourne, 1912
152 v. South Africa at Old Wanderers, Johannesburg, 1913

J E ROOT (11)

104 v. New Zealand at Leeds, 2013
200* v. Sri Lanka at Lord's, 2014
149* v. India at The Oval, 2014
134 v. Australia at Cardiff 2015
110 v. South Africa at Johannesburg, 2016
124 v. India at Rajkot, 2016

180 v. Australia at Lord's, 2013
154* v. India at Nottingham, 2014
182* v. West Indies at St George's, 2015
130 v. Australia at Nottingham, 2015
254 v. Pakistan at Manchester, 2016

P J SHARPE (1)

111 v. New Zealand at Nottingham, 1969

H SUTCLIFFE (16)

122 v. South Africa at Lord's, 1924
115 v. Australia at Sydney, 1924
176 v. Australia at Melbourne, 1925 (1st Inns)
127 v. Australia at Melbourne, 1925 (2nd Inns)
143 v. Australia at Melbourne, 1925
161 v. Australia at The Oval, 1926
102 v. South Africa at Old Wanderers, Jbg.1927
135 v. Australia at Melbourne, 1929

114 v. South Africa at Birmingham, 1929
100 v. South Africa at Lord's, 1929
104 v. South Africa at The Oval, 1929 (1st inns)
109* v. South Africa at The Oval, 1929 (2nd inns)
161 v. Australia at The Oval, 1930
117 v. New Zealand at The Oval, 1931
109* v. New Zealand at Manchester, 1931
194 v. Australia at Sydney, 1932

G ULYETT (1)

149 v. Australia at Melbourne, 1882

M P VAUGHAN (18)

120 v. Pakistan at Manchester, 2001
115 v. Sri Lanka at Lord's, 2002
100 v. India at Lord's, 2002
197 v. India at Nottingham, 2002
195 v. India at The Oval, 2002
177 v. Australia at Adelaide, 2002
145 v. Australia at Melbourne, 2002
183 v. Australia at Sydney, 2003
156 v. South Africa at Birmingham, 2003

105 v. Sri Lanka at Kandy, 2003
140 v. West Indies at Antigua, 2004
103 v. West Indies at Lord's (1st inns) 2004
101* v. West Indies at Lord's (2nd inns) 2004
120 v. Bangladesh at Lord's, 2005
166 v. Australia at Manchester,2005
103 v. West Indies at Leeds, 2007
124 v. India at Nottingham, 2007
106 v. New Zealand at Lord's, 2008

W WATSON (2)

109 v. Australia at Lord's, 1953

116 v. West Indies at Kingston, 1954

CENTURIES FOR ENGLAND *(Continued)*

C WHITE (1)

121 v. India at Ahmedabad, 2001

Summary of the Centuries

versus	Total	In England	Away
Australia	43	24	19
Bangladesh	1	1	0
India	17	14	3
New Zealand	11	11	0
Pakistan	6	5	1
South Africa	20	10	10
Sri Lanka	6	5	1
West Indies	19	10	9
Totals	123	80	43

For Australia

J N GILLESPIE (1)

201* v. Bangladesh at Chittagong, 2006

P A JAQUES (3)

100	v. Sri Lanka at Brisbane, 2007	108 v. West Indies at Bridgetown, 2008
150	v. Sri Lanka at Hobart, 2007	

D S LEHMANN (5)

160	v. West Indies at Port of Spain, 2003	129 v. Sri Lanka at Galle, 2004
110	v. Bangladesh at Darwin, 2003	153 v. Sri Lanka at Columbo, 2004
177	v. Bangladesh at Cairns, 2003	

10 WICKETS IN A MATCH FOR ENGLAND

W BATES (1)
14 for 102 (7 for 28 and 7 for 74) v. Australia at Melbourne, 1882

M J HOGGARD (1)
12 for 205 (5 for 144 and 7 for 61) v. South Africa at Johannesburg, 2005

R PEEL (1)
11 for 68 (7 for 31 and 4 for 37) v. Australia at Manchester, 1888

Note: The scorebook for the Australia v. England Test match at Sydney in February 1888
shows that the final wicket to fall was taken by W Attewell, and not by Peel
Peel therefore took 9, and not 10 wickets, in the match
His career totals have been amended to take account of this alteration

W RHODES (1)
15 for 124 (7 for 56 and 8 for 68) v. Australia at Melbourne, 1904

R J SIDEBOTTOM (1)
10 for 139 (4 for 90 and 6 for 49) v. New Zealand at Hamilton, 2008

F S TRUEMAN (3)
11 for 88 (5 for 58 and 6 for 30) v. Australia at Leeds, 1961
11 for 152 (6 for 100 and 5 for 52) v. West Indies at Lord's, 1963*
12 for 119 (5 for 75 and 7 for 44) v. West Indies at Birmingham, 1963*
consecutive Tests

H VERITY (2)
11 for 153 (7 for 49 and 4 for 104) v. India at Chepauk, Madras, 1934
15 for 104 (7 for 61 and 8 for 43) v. Australia at Lord's, 1934

J H WARDLE (1)
12 for 89 (5 for 53 and 7 for 36) v. South Africa at Cape Town, 1957

Summary of Ten Wickets in a Match

versus	Total	In England	Away
Australia	5	3	2
India	1	—	1
New Zealand	1	—	1
Pakistan	—	—	—
South Africa	2	—	2
Sri Lanka	—	—	—
West Indies	2	2	—
Totals	11	5	6

For Australia

M G BEVAN (1)
10 for 113 (4 for 31 and 6 for 82) v. West Indies at Adelaide, 1997

5 WICKETS IN AN INNINGS FOR ENGLAND

R APPLEYARD (1)
5 for 51 v. Pakistan at Nottingham, 1954

W BATES (4)
7 for 28 v. Australia at Melbourne, 1882   5 for 31 v. Australia at Adelaide, 1884
7 for 74 v. Australia at Melbourne, 1882   5 for 24 v. Australia at Sydney, 1885

5 WICKETS IN AN INNINGS FOR ENGLAND *(Continued)*

W E BOWES (6)

6-34	v. New Zealand	at Auckland	1933	5-100	v. South Africa	at Manchester	1935
6-142	v. Australia	at Leeds	1934*	5-49	v. Australia	at The Oval	1938
5-55	v. Australia	at The Oval	1934*	6-33	v. West Indies	at Manchester	1939

consecutive Test matches

T T BRESNAN (1)

5-48 v. India   at Nottingham 2011

T EMMETT (1)

7-68 v. Australia   at Melbourne 1879

D GOUGH (9)

6-49	v. Australia	at Sydney	1995	5-70	v. South Africa	at Johannesburg	1999
5-40	v.New Zealand	at Wellington	1997	5-109	v. West Indies	at Birmingham	2000
5-149	v. Australia	at Leeds	1997	5-61	v. Pakistan	at Lord's	2001
6-42	v.South Africa	at Leeds	1998	5-103	v. Australia	at Leeds	2001
5-96	v. Australia	at Melbourne	1998				

S HAIGH (1)

6-11 v. South Africa at Cape Town 1909

G H HIRST (3)

5-77	v. Australia	at The Oval	1902	5-58	v. Australia	at Birmingham	1909
5-48	v. Australia	at Melbourne	1904				

M J HOGGARD (7)

7-63	v. New Zealand	at Christchurch	2002	5-73	v. Bangladesh	at Chester-le-Street	
5-92	v. Sri Lanka	at Birmingham	2002				2005
5-144	v. South Africa	at Johannesburg	2005*	6-57	v. India	at Nagpur	2006
7-61	v. South Africa	at Johannesburg	2005*	7-109	v. Australia	at Adelaide	2006

Consecutive Test innings

R ILLINGWORTH (3)

6-29	v. India	at Lord's	1967	5-70	v. India	at The Oval	1971
6-87	v. Australia	at Leeds	1968				

Hon F S JACKSON (1)

5-52 v. Australia   at Nottingham 1905

G G MACAULAY (1)

5-64 v. South Africa at Cape Town 1923

C M OLD (4)

5-113	v. New Zealand	at Lord's	1973	6-54	v. New Zealand	at Wellington	1978
5-21	v. India	at Lord's	1974	7-50	v. Pakistan	at Birmingham	1978

E PEATE (2)

5-43   v. Australia   at Sydney 1882   6-85 v. Australia   at Lord's   1884

R PEEL (5)

5-51	v. Australia	at Adelaide	1884	6-67	v. Australia	at Sydney	1894
5-18	v. Australia	at Sydney	1888	6-23	v. Australia	at The Oval	1896
7-31	v. Australia	at Manchester	1888				

L E PLUNKETT (1)

5-64 v. Sri Lanka   at Leeds   2014

A U RASHID (1)

5-64 v. Pakistan   at Abu Dhabi   2015

W RHODES (6)

7-17	v. Australia	at Birmingham	1902		7-56	v. Australia	at Melbourne	1904*
5-63	v. Australia	at Sheffield	1902		8-68	v. Australia	at Melbourne	1904*
5-94	v. Australia	at Sydney	1903*		5-83	v. Australia	at Manchester	1909

*consecutive Test innings

C E W SILVERWOOD (1)

5-91   v. South Africa   at Cape Town   2000

R J SIDEBOTTOM (5)

5-88	v. West Indies	at Chester-le-Street			5-105	v. New Zealand	at Wellington	2008
			2007		7-47	v. New Zealand	at Napier	2008
6-49	v. New Zealand	at Hamilton	2008		6-47	v. New Zealand	at Nottingham	2008

F S TRUEMAN (17)

8-31	v. India	at Manchester	1952		6-31	v. Pakistan	at Lord's	1962
5-48	v. India	at The Oval	1952		5-62	v. Australia	at Melbourne	1963
5-90	v. Australia	at Lord's	1956		7-75	v. New Zealand	at Christchurch	1963
5-63	v. West Indies	at Nottingham	1957		6-100	v. West Indies	at Lord's	1963*
5-31	v. New Zealand	at Birmingham	1958		5-52	v. West Indies	at Lord's	1963*
5-35	v. West Indies	at Port-of-Spain	1960		5-75	v. West Indies	at Birmingham	1963*
5-27	v. South Africa	at Nottingham	1960		7-44	v. West Indies	at Birmingham	1963*
5-58	v. Australia	at Leeds	1961*		5-48	v. Australia	at Lord's	1964
6-30	v. Australia	at Leeds	1961*					

G ULYETT (1)

7-36   v. Australia   at Lord's   1884

H VERITY (5)

5-33	v. Australia	at Sydney	1933		8-43	v. Australia	at Lord's	1934*
7-49	v. India	at Chepauk, Madras	1934		5-70	v. South Africa	at Cape Town	1939
7-61	v. Australia	at Lord's	1934*					

J H WARDLE (5)

7-56	v. Pakistan	at The Oval	1954		7-36	v. South Africa	at Cape Town	1957*
5-79	v. Australia	at Sydney	1955		5-61	v. South Africa	at Kingsmead Durban	1957*
5-53	v. South Africa	at Cape Town	1957*					

C WHITE (3)

5-57	v. West Indies	at Leeds	2000		5-32	v. West Indies	at The Oval	2000
		5-127	v. Australia	at Perth	2002			

*consecutive Test innings

Summary of Five Wickets in an Innings

versus	Total	In England	Away
Australia	42	22	20
Bangladesh	1	1	0
India	8	6	2
New Zealand	11	3	8
Pakistan	6	5	1
South Africa	13	3	10
Sri Lanka	2	2	0
West Indies	11	10	1
Totals	94	52	42

5 WICKETS IN AN INNINGS

M G BEVAN (1)

6-82	v. West Indies	at Adelaide	1997

J N GILLESPIE (8)

5-54	v. South Africa	at Port Elizabeth	1997
7-37	v. England	at Leeds	1997
5-88	v. England	at Perth	1998
5-89	v. West Indies	at Adelaide	2000
6-40	v. West Indies	at Melbourne	2000
5-53	v. England	at Lord's	2001
5-39	v. West Indies	at Georgetown	2003
5-56	v. India	at Nagpur	2004

HAT-TRICKS

W Bates	v. Australia	at Melbourne	1882
D Gough	v. Australia	at Sydney	1998
M J Hoggard	v. West Indies	at Bridgetown	2004
R J Sidebottom	v. New Zealand	at Hamilton	2008

FOUR WICKETS IN FIVE BALLS

C M Old	v. Pakistan	at Birmingham	1978

THREE WICKETS IN FOUR BALLS

R Appleyard	v. New Zealand	at Auckland	1955
D Gough	v. Pakistan	at Lord's	2001

YORKSHIRE PLAYERS WHO PLAYED ALL THEIR TEST CRICKET AFTER LEAVING YORKSHIRE

For England

Player	M.	I	NO	Runs	HS.	Av'ge	100s	50s	Balls	R	W	Av'ge	Best	5wI	10wM	c/st
BALDERSTONE, J C ...1976	2	4	0	39	35	9.75	—	—	96	80	1	80.00	1:80	—	—	1
BATTY, G J ...2003/4-16/17	9	12	2	149	38	14.90	—	1	1,714	914	15	60.93	3-55	—	—	3
BIRKENSHAW, J ...1973-74	5	7	0	148	64	21.14	—	—	1,017	469	13	36.07	5:57	1	—	3
BOLUS, J B ...1963-64	7	12	0	496	88	41.33	—	4	18	16	0	—	—	—	—	2
†PARKIN, C H ...1920-24	10	16	3	160	36	12.30	—	—	2,095	1,128	32	35.25	5:38	2	—	3
RHODES, S J ...1994-95	11	17	5	294	65*	24.50	—	1	—	—	—	—	—	—	—	46/3
†SUGG, F H ...1888	2	2	0	55	31	27.50	—	—	—	—	—	—	—	—	—	0
WARD, A ...1893-95	7	13	0	487	117	37.46	1	3	—	—	—	—	—	—	—	1
WOOD, B ...1972-78	12	21	0	454	90	21.61	—	2	98	50	0	—	—	—	—	6

For South Africa

Player	M.	I	NO	Runs	HS.	Av'ge	100s	50s	Balls	R	W	Av'ge	Best	5wI	10wM	c/st
THORNTON, P G ...1902	1	1	1	1	1*	—	—	—	24	20	1	20.00	1:20	—	—	1

†Born outside Yorkshire

324

CENTURIES
FOR ENGLAND

A WARD (1)
117 v. Australia at Sydney, 1894

5 WICKETS IN AN INNINGS
FOR ENGLAND

J BIRKENSHAW (1)
5 : 57 v. Pakistan at Karachi, 1973

C H PARKIN (2)
5 : 60 v. Australia at Adelaide, 1921
5 : 38 v. Australia at Manchester, 1921

YORKSHIRE'S TEST CRICKET RECORDS

R APPLEYARD

Auckland 1954-55: took 3 wickets in 4 balls as New Zealand were dismissed for the lowest total in Test history (26).

C W J ATHEY

Perth 1986-87: shared an opening stand of 223 with B C Broad – England's highest for any wicket at the WACA Ground.

J M BAIRSTOW

Cape Town, January 2016: scored his maiden Test Century (150*). His sixth- wicket partnership of 399 with B A Stokes (258) was the highest in Test cricket and the highest First Class partnership for any wicket at Newlands. There was only one higher partnership for England. This was 411 by P B H May and M C Cowdrey for the fourth wicket against the West Indies at Birmingham in 1957.

Chittagong, October 2016: scored 52 in the first innings, which passed his 1,000 Test runs in a calendar year. He became only the third Yorkshire player to do this after M P Vaughan with 1,481 in 2002 and J E Root 1,385 in 2015. He was only the second Test wicket-keeper to pass this mark. His first scoring shot in the second inning broke a 16-year record set by Zimbabwe's A Flower (1,045 in 2000) to give him the highest total of runs scored in a calendar year by a Test wicket-keeper. His final tally for 2016 was 1,470.

Mohali, November 2016: his third catch of India's first innings (U T Yadav) was his 68th dismissal of the year to pass the previous best in a calendar year (67) by I A Healy (Australia) in 1991 and M V Boucher (South Africa) in 1998. Bairstow's final tally for the calendar year was 70 (66 caught and 4 stumped).

W BATES

Melbourne 1882-83 (Second Test): achieved the first hat-trick for England when he dismissed P S McDonnell, G Giffen and G J Bonnor in Australia's first innings. Later in the match, he became the first player to score a fifty (55) and take 10 or more wickets (14 for 102) in the same Test.

W E BOWES

Melbourne 1932-33: enjoyed the unique satisfaction of bowling D G Bradman first ball in a Test match (his first ball to him in Test cricket).

G BOYCOTT

Leeds 1967: scored 246 not out off 555 balls in 573 minutes to establish the record England score against India. His first 100 took 341 minutes (316 balls) and he was excluded from the next Test as a disciplinary measure; shared in hundred partnerships for three successive wickets.

Adelaide 1970-71: with J H Edrich, became the third opening pair to share hundred partnerships in both innings of a Test against Australia.

Port-of-Spain 1973-74: first to score 99 and a hundred in the same Test.

Nottingham 1977: with A P E Knott, equalled England v. Australia sixth-wicket partnership record of 215 – the only England v. Australia stand to be equalled or broken since 1938. Batted on each day of the five-day Test (second after M L Jaisimha to achieve this feat).

Leeds 1977: first to score his 100th First Class hundred in a Test; became the fourth England player to be on the field for an entire Test.

YORKSHIRE'S TEST CRICKET RECORDS *(Continued)*

G BOYCOTT *(Continued)*

Perth: 1978-79: eighth to score 2,000 runs for England against Australia.

Birmingham 1979: emulated K F Barrington by scoring hundreds on each of England's six current home grounds.

Perth: 1979-80: fourth to carry his bat through a completed England innings (third v. Australia) and the first to do so without scoring 100; first to score 99 not out in a Test.

Lord's 1981: 100th Test for England – second after M C Cowdrey (1968).

The Oval, 1981: second after Hon F S Jackson to score five hundreds v. Australia in England.

Gained three Test records from M C Cowdrey: exceeded England aggregate of 7,624 runs in 11 fewer Tests (Manchester 1981); 61st fifty – world record (The Oval 1981); 189th innings – world record (Bangalore 1981-82).

Delhi, 4.23p.m. on 23 December 1981: passed G St.A Sobers's world Test record of 8,032 runs, having played 30 more innings and batted over 451 hours (cf. 15 complete five-day Tests); his 22nd hundred equalled the England record.

J T BROWN

Melbourne 1894-95: his 28-minute fifty remains the fastest in Test cricket, and his 95-minute hundred was a record until 1897-98; his third-wicket stand of 210 with A Ward set a Test record for any wicket.

D B CLOSE

Manchester 1949: at 18 years 149 days he became – and remains – the youngest to represent England.

Melbourne 1950-51: became the youngest (19 years 301 days) to represent England against Australia.

T EMMETT

Melbourne 1878-79: first England bowler to take seven wickets in a Test innings.

P A GIBB

Johannesburg 1938-39: enjoyed a record England debut, scoring 93 and 106 as well as sharing second-wicket stands of 184 and 168 with E Paynter.

Durban 1938-39: shared record England v. South Africa second-wicket stand of 280 with W J Edrich, his 120 in 451 minutes including only two boundaries.

D GOUGH

Sydney 1998-99: achieved the 23rd hat-trick in Test cricket (ninth for England and first for England v. Australia since 1899).

Lord's 2001: took 3 wickets in 4 balls v. Pakistan.

S HAIGH

Cape Town 1898-99: bowled unchanged through the second innings with A E Trott, taking 6 for 11 as South Africa were dismissed for 35 in the space of 114 balls.

J H HAMPSHIRE

Lord's 1969: became the first England player to score 100 at Lord's on his debut in Tests.

A HILL

Melbourne 1876-77: took the first wicket to fall in Test cricket when he bowled N Thompson, and held the first catch when he dismissed T P Horan.

YORKSHIRE'S TEST CRICKET RECORDS *(Continued)*

G H HIRST

The Oval: 1902: helped to score the last 15 runs in a match-winning tenth-wicket partnership with W Rhodes.

Birmingham 1909: shared all 20 Australian wickets with fellow left-arm spinner C Blythe (11 for 102).

M J HOGGARD

Bridgetown 2004: became the third Yorkshire player to take a hat-trick in Test cricket (see W Bates and D Gough). It was the 10th hat-trick for England and the third for England versus West Indies.

L HUTTON

Nottingham 1938: scored 100 in his first Test against Australia.

The Oval 1938: his score (364) and batting time (13 hours 17 minutes – the longest innings in English First-Class cricket) remain England records, and were world Test records until 1958. It remains the highest Test score at The Oval. His stand of 382 with M Leyland is the England second-wicket record in all Tests and the highest for any wicket against Australia. He also shared a record England v. Australia sixth-wicket stand of 216 with J Hardstaff Jr. – the first instance of a batsman sharing in two stands of 200 in the same Test innings. 770 runs were scored during his innings (Test record) which was England's 100th century against Australia, and contained 35 fours. England's total of 903 for 7 declared remains the Ashes Test record.

Lord's 1939: added 248 for the fourth wicket with D C S Compton in 140 minutes.

The Oval 1939: shared (then) world-record third-wicket stand of 264 with W R Hammond, which remains the record for England v. West Indies. Hutton's last eight Tests had brought him 1,109 runs.

The Oval 1948: last out in the first innings, he was on the field for all but the final 57 minutes of the match.

Johannesburg 1948-49: shared (then) world-record first-wicket stand of 359 in 310 minutes with C Washbrook on the opening day of Test cricket at Ellis Park; it remains England's highest opening stand in all Tests.

The Oval 1950: scored England's first 200 in a home Test v. West Indies, and remains alone in carrying his bat for England against them; his 202 not out (in 470 minutes) is the highest score by an England batsman achieving this feat.

Adelaide 1950-51: only England batsman to carry his bat throughout a complete Test innings twice, and second after R Abel (1891-92) to do so for any country against Australia.

Manchester 1951: scored 98 not out, just failing to become the first to score his 100th First Class hundred in a Test match.

The Oval 1951: became the only batsman to be out 'obstructing the field' in Test cricket.

1952: first professional to be appointed captain of England in the 20th Century.

The Oval 1953: first captain to win a rubber after losing the toss in all five Tests.

Kingston 1953-54: scored the first 200 by an England captain in a Test overseas.

R ILLINGWORTH

Manchester 1971: shared record England v. India eighth-wicket stand of 168 with P Lever.

YORKSHIRE'S TEST CRICKET RECORDS *(Continued)*

Hon. F S JACKSON

The Oval 1893: his 100 took 135 minutes, and was the first in a Test in England to be completed with a hit over the boundary (then worth only four runs).

The Oval 1899: his stand of 185 with T W Hayward was then England's highest for any wicket in England, and the record opening partnership by either side in England v. Australia Tests.

Nottingham 1905: dismissed M A Noble, C Hill and J Darling in one over (W01W0W).

Leeds 1905: batted 268 minutes for 144 not out – the first hundred in a Headingley Test.

Manchester 1905: first to score five Test hundreds in England.

The Oval 1905: first captain to win every toss in a five-match rubber.

M LEYLAND

Melbourne 1928-29: scored 137 in his first innings against Australia.

1934: first to score three hundreds in a rubber against Australia in England.

Brisbane 1936-37: scored England's only 100 at 'The Gabba' before 1974-75.

The Oval 1938: contributed 187 in 381 minutes to the record Test total of 903 for 7 declared, sharing in England's highest stand against Australia (all wickets) and record second-wicket stand in all Tests: 382 with L Hutton. First to score hundreds in his first and last innings against Australia.

G G MACAULAY

Cape Town 1922-23: fourth bowler (third for England) to take a wicket (G A L Hearne) with his first ball in Test cricket. Made the winning hit in the fourth of only six Tests to be decided by a one-wicket margin.

Leeds 1926: shared a match-saving ninth-wicket stand of 108 with G Geary.

C M OLD

Birmingham 1978: took 4 wickets in 5 balls in his 19th over (0WW no-ball WW1) to emulate the feat of M J C Allom.

R PEEL

Took his 50th wicket in his ninth Test and his 100th in his 20th Test – all against Australia.

Kingston 1929-30: ended the world's longest Test career (30 years 315 days) as the oldest Test cricketer (52 years 165 days).

W RHODES

Birmingham 1902: his first-innings analysis of 7 for 17 remains the record for all Tests at Edgbaston.

The Oval 1902: helped to score the last 15 runs in a match-winning tenth-wicket partnership with G H Hirst.

Sydney 1903-04: shared record England v. Australia tenth-wicket stand of 130 in 66 minutes with R E Foster.

Melbourne 1903-04: first to take 15 wickets in England v. Australia Tests; his match analysis of 15 for 124 remains the record for all Tests at Melbourne.

Melbourne 1911-12: shared record England v. Australia first-wicket stand of 323 in 268 minutes with J B Hobbs.

YORKSHIRE'S TEST CRICKET RECORDS (Continued)

W RHODES (Continued)

Johannesburg 1913-14: took his 100th wicket and completed the first 'double' for England (in 44 matches).

Sydney 1920-21: first to score 2,000 runs and take 100 wickets in Test cricket.

Adelaide 1920-21: third bowler to take 100 wickets against Australia.

The Oval 1926: set (then) record of 109 wickets against Australia.

J E ROOT

Chittagong, October 2016: his score (40) in England's first innings took him passed 1,000 runs in a calendar year. He also did this in 2015 (1,385) and became the first Yorkshire player to do this twice. His final tally (1,477) in 2016 left him four short of M P Vaughan's total in 2002

Visakhapatnam, November 2016: Played his 50th Test match, which was also his 100th first-class match

H SUTCLIFFE

Birmingham 1924: shared the first of 15 three-figure partnerships with J B Hobbs at the first attempt.

Lord's 1924: shared stand of 268 with J B Hobbs, which remains the first-wicket record for all Lord's Tests, and was then the England v. South Africa record.

Sydney 1924-25: his first opening stands against Australia with J B Hobbs realised 157 and 110.

Melbourne 1924-25 (Second Test): with J B Hobbs achieved the first instance of a batting partnership enduring throughout a full day's Test match play; they remain the only England pair to achieve this feat, and their stand of 283 in 289 minutes remains the longest for the first wicket in this series. Became the first to score 100 in each innings of a Test against Australia, and the first Englishman to score three successive hundreds in Test cricket.

Melbourne 1924-25 (Fourth Test): first to score four hundreds in one rubber of Test matches; it was his third 100 in successive Test innings at Melbourne. Completed 1,000 runs in fewest Test innings (12) – since equalled.

Sydney 1924-25: his aggregate of 734 runs was the record for any rubber until 1928-29.

The Oval 1926: shared first-wicket stand of 172 with J B Hobbs on a rain-affected pitch.

The Oval 1929: first to score hundreds in each innings of a Test twice; only England batsman to score four hundreds in a rubber twice.

Sydney 1932-33: his highest England innings of 194 overtook J B Hobbs's world record of 15 Test hundreds.

F S TRUEMAN

Leeds 1952: reduced India to 0 for 4 in their second innings by taking 3 wickets in 8 balls on his debut.

Manchester 1952: achieved record England v. India innings analysis of 8 for 31.

The Oval 1952: set England v. India series record with 29 wickets.

Leeds 1961: took 5 for 0 with 24 off-cutters at a reduced pace v. Australia.

Lord's 1962: shared record England v. Pakistan ninth-wicket stand of 76 with T W Graveney.

Christchurch 1962-63: passed J B Statham's world Test record of 242 wickets; his analysis of 7-75 remains the record for Lancaster Park Tests and for England in New Zealand.

YORKSHIRE'S TEST CRICKET RECORDS *(Continued)*

F S TRUEMAN *(Continued)*

Birmingham 1963: returned record match analysis (12-119) against West Indies in England and for any Birmingham Test, ending with a 6-4 spell from 24 balls.

The Oval 1963: set England v. West Indies series record with 34 wickets.

The Oval 1964: first to take 300 wickets in Tests.

G ULYETT

Sydney 1881-82: with R G Barlow shared the first century opening partnership in Test cricket (122).

Melbourne 1881-82: his 149 was the first Test hundred for England in Australia, and the highest score for England on the first day of a Test in Australia until 1965-66.

M P VAUGHAN

Scored 1481 runs in 2002 – more than any other England player in a calendar year, surpassing the 1379 scored by D L Amiss in 1979. It was the fourth highest in a calendar year.

Scored 633 runs in the 2002-3 series versus Australia – surpassed for England in a five Test series versus Australia only by W R Hammond, who scored 905 runs in 1928-29, H Sutcliffe (734 in 1924-25), J B Hobbs (662 in 1911-12) and G Boycott (657 in 1970-71), when he played in five of the six Tests.

Scored six Test Match centuries in 2002 to equal the record set for England by D C S Compton in 1947.

Lord's 2004: scored a century in each innings (103 and 101*) versus West Indies and so became the third player (after G A Headley and G A Gooch) to score a century in each innings of a Test match at Lord's.

Lord's 2005: only the second player (J B Hobbs is the other) to have scored centuries in three consecutive Test match innings at Lord's. Scored the 100th century for England by a Yorkshire player.

H VERITY

Lord's 1934: took 14 for 80 on the third day (six of them in the final hour) to secure England's first win against Australia at Lord's since 1896. It remains the most wickets to fall to one bowler in a day of Test cricket in England. His match analysis of 15 for 104 was then the England v. Australia record, and has been surpassed only by J C Laker.

W WATSON

Lord's 1953: scored 109 in 346 minutes in his first Test against Australia.

N W D YARDLEY

Melbourne 1946-47: dismissed D G Bradman for the third consecutive innings without assistance from the field. Became the first to score a fifty in each innings for England and take five wickets in the same match.

Nottingham 1947: shared record England v. South Africa fifth-wicket stand of 237 with D C S Compton.

* * *

Facts adapted by Bill Frindall from his *England Test Cricketers – The Complete Record from 1877* (Collins Willow, 1989). With later additions.

YORKSHIRE'S TEST CRICKET RECORDS *(Continued)*

M P VAUGHAN

Scored 1481 runs in 2002 – more than any other England player in a calendar year, surpassing the 1379 scored by D L Amiss in 1979. It was the fourth highest in a calendar year.

Scored 633 runs in the 2002-3 series versus Australia – surpassed for England in a five Test series versus Australia only by W R Hammond, who scored 905 runs in 1928-29, H Sutcliffe (734 in 1924-25), J B Hobbs (662 in 1911-12) and G Boycott (657 in 1970-71), when he played in five of the six Tests.

Scored six Test Match centuries in 2002 to equal the record set for England by D C S Compton in 1947.

Lord's 2004: scored a century in each innings (103 and 101*) versus West Indies and so became the third player (after G A Headley and G A Gooch) to score a century in each innings of a Test match at Lord's.

Lord's 2005: only the second player (J B Hobbs is the other) to have scored centuries in three consecutive Test match innings at Lord's. Scored the 100th century for England by a Yorkshire player.

H VERITY

Lord's 1934: took 14 for 80 on the third day (six of them in the final hour) to secure England's first win against Australia at Lord's since 1896. It remains the most wickets to fall to one bowler in a day of Test cricket in England. His match analysis of 15 for 104 was then the England v. Australia record, and has been surpassed only by J C Laker.

W WATSON

Lord's 1953: scored 109 in 346 minutes in his first Test against Australia.

N W D YARDLEY

Melbourne 1946-47: dismissed D G Bradman for the third consecutive innings without assistance from the field. Became the first to score a fifty in each innings for England and take five wickets in the same match.

Nottingham 1947: shared record England v. South Africa fifth-wicket stand of 237 with D C S Compton.

* * *

Facts adapted by Bill Frindall from his *England Test Cricketers – The Complete Record from 1877* (Collins Willow, 1989). With later additions.

TEST MATCHES AT HEADINGLEY, LEEDS 1899-2016

1899 **Australia 172** (J Worrall 76) and **224** (H Trumble 56, J T Hearne hat-trick). **England 220** (A F A Lilley 55, H Trumble 5 for 60) and **19 for 0 wkt.**
Match drawn Toss: Australia

1905 **England 301** (Hon F S Jackson 144*) and **295 for 5 wkts dec** (J T Tyldesley 100, T W Hayward 60, W W. Armstrong 5 for 122). **Australia 195** (W W Armstrong 66, A R Warren 5 for 57) and **224 for 7 wkts** (M A Noble 62).
Match drawn Toss: England

1907 **England 76** (G A Faulkner 6 for 17) and **162** (C B Fry 54). **South Africa 110** (C Blythe 8 for 59) and **75** (C Blythe 7 for 40).
England won by 53 runs Toss: England

1909 **Australia 188** and **207** (S F Barnes 6 for 63). **England 182** (J Sharp 61, J T Tyldesley 55, C G Macartney 7 for 58) and **87** (A Cotter 5 for 38).
Australia won by 126 runs Toss: Australia

1912 **England 242** (F E Woolley 57) and **238** (R H Spooner 82, J B Hobbs 55). **South Africa 147** (S F Barnes 6 for 52) and **159.**
England won by 174 runs Toss: England

1921 **Australia 407** (C G Macartney 115, W W Armstrong 77, C E Pellew 52, J M Taylor 50) and **273 for 7 wkts dec** (T J E Andrew 92). **England 259** (J W H T Douglas 75, Hon L H Tennyson 63, G Brown 57) and **202.**
Australia won by 219 runs Toss: Australia

1924 **England 396** (E H Hendren 132, H Sutcliffe 83) and **60 for 1 wkt. South Africa 132** (H W Taylor 59*, M W Tate 6 for 42) and **323** (H W Taylor 56, R H Catterall 56).
England won by 9 wickets Toss: England

1926 **Australia 494** (C G Macartney 151, W M Woodfull 141, A J Richardson 100). **England 294** (G G Macaulay 76, C V Grimmett 5 for 88) and **254 for 3 wkts** (H Sutcliffe 94, J B Hobbs 88).
Match drawn Toss: England

1929 **South Africa 236** (R H Catterall 74, C L Vincent 60, A P Freeman 7 for 115) and **275** (H G Owen-Smith 129). **England 328** (F E Woolley 83, W R Hammond 65, N A Quinn 6 for 92) and **186 for 5 wkts** (F E Woolley 95*).
England won by 5 wickets Toss: South Africa

1930 **Australia 566** (D G Bradman 334, A F Kippax 77, W M Woodfull 50, M W Tate 5 for 124). **England 391** (W R Hammond 113, C V Grimmett 5 for 135) and **95 for 3 wkts.**
Match drawn Toss: Australia

1934 **England 200** and **229 for 6 wkts. Australia 584** (D G Bradman 304, W H Ponsford 181, W E Bowes 6 for 142).
Match drawn Toss: England

1935 **England 216** (W R Hammond 63, A Mitchell 58) and **294 for 7 wkts dec** (W R Hammond 87*, A Mitchell 72, D Smith 57). **South Africa 171** (E A B Rowan 62) and **194 for 5 wkts** (B Mitchell 58).
Match drawn Toss: England

1938 **England 223** (W R Hammond 76, W J O'Reilly 5 for 66) and **123** (W J O'Reilly 5 for 56). **Australia 242** (D G Bradman 103, B A Barnett 57) and **107 for 5 wkts.**
Australia won by 5 wickets Toss: England

1947 **South Africa 175** (B Mitchell 53, A Nourse 51) and **184** (A D Nourse 57). **England 317 for 7 wkts dec** (L Hutton 100, C Washbrook 75) and **47 for 0 wkt.**
England won by 10 wickets Toss: South Africa

1948 **England 496** (C Washbrook 143, W .J Edrich 111, L Hutton 81, A V Bedser 79) and **365 for 8 wkts dec** (D C S. Compton 66, C Washbrook 65, L Hutton 57, W J Edrich 54). **Australia 458** (R N Harvey 112, S J E Loxton 93, R R Lindwall 77, K R Miller 58) and **404 for 3 wkts** (A R Morris 182, D G Bradman 173*).
Australia won by 7 wickets Toss: England

1949 **England 372** (D C S Compton 114, L Hutton 101, T B Burtt 5 for 97, J Cowie 5 for 127) and **267 for 4 wkts dec** (C Washbrook 103*, W J Edrich 70). **New Zealand 341** (F B Smith 96, M P Donnelly 64, T E Bailey 6 for 118) and **195 for 2 wkts** (B Sutcliffe 82, F Smith 54*).
Match drawn   Toss: England

1951 **South Africa 538** (E A B Rowan 236, P N F Mansell 90, C B. van Ryneveld 83, R A McLean 67) and **87 for 0 wkt** (E A B Rowan 60*). **England 505** (P B H May 138, L Hutton 100, T E Bailey 95, F A Lowson 58, A M B Rowan 5 for 174).
Match drawn   Toss: South Africa

1952 **India 293** (V L Manjrekar 133, V S Hazare 89) and 165 (D G Phadkar 64, V S Hazare 56). **England 334** (T W Graveney 71, T G Evans 66, Ghulam Ahmed 5 for 100) and **128 for 3 wkts** (R T Simpson 51).
England won by 7 wickets   Toss: India

1953 **England 167** (T W Graveney 55, R R Lindwall 5 for 54) and **275** (W J Edrich 64, D C S Compton 61). **Australia 266** (R N Harvey 71, G B Hole 53, A V Bedser 6 for 95) and **147 for 4 wkts.**
Match drawn   Toss: Australia

1955 **South Africa 171** and **500** (D J McGlew 133, W R Endean 116*, T L Goddard 74, H J Keith 73). **England 191** (D C S Compton 61) and **256** (P B H May 97, T L Goddard 5 for 69, H J Tayfield 5 for 94).
South Africa won by 224 runs   Toss: South Africa

1956 **England 325** (P B H May 101, C Washbrook 98). **Australia 143** (J C Laker 5 for 58) and **140** (R N Harvey 69, J C Laker 6 for 55).
England won by an innings and 42 runs   Toss: England

1957 **West Indies 142** (P J Loader 6 for 36, including hat-trick) and **132**. **England 279** (P B H May 69, M C Cowdrey 68, Rev D S Sheppard 68, F M M Worrell 7 for 70).
England won by an innings and 5 runs   Toss: West Indies

1958 **New Zealand 67** (J C Laker 5 for 17) and **129** (G A R Lock 7 for 51). **England 267 for 2 wkts dec** (P B H May 113*, C A Milton 104*).
England won by an innings and 71 runs   Toss: New Zealand

1959 **India 161** and **149**. **England 483 for 8 wkts dec** (M C Cowdrey 160, K F Barrington 80, W G A Parkhouse 78, G Pullar 75).
England won by an innings and 173 runs   Toss: India

1961 **Australia 237** (R N Harvey 73, C C McDonald 54, F S Trueman 5 for 58) and **120** (R N Harvey 53, F S Trueman 6 for 30); **England 299** (M C Cowdrey 93, G Pullar 53, A K Davidson 5 for 63) and **62 for 2 wkts.**
England won by 8 wickets   Toss: Australia

1962 **England 428** (P H Parfitt 119, M J Stewart 86, D A Allen 62, Munir Malik 5 for 128). **Pakistan 131** (Alimuddin 50) and **180** (Alimuddin 60, Saeed Ahmed 54).
England won by an innings and 117 runs   Toss: Pakistan

1963 **West Indies 397** (G St A Sobers 102, R B Kanhai 92, J S Solomon 62) and **229** (B F Butcher 78, G St.A Sobers 52). **England 174** (G A R Lock 53, C C Griffith 6 for 36) and **231** (J M Parks 57, D B Close 56).
West Indies won by 221 runs   Toss: West Indies

1964 **England 268** (J M Parks 68, E R Dexter 66, N J N Hawke 5 for 75) and 229 (K F Barrington 85). **Australia 389** (P J P Burge 160, W M Lawry 78) and **111 for 3 wkts** (I R Redpath 58*).
Australia won by 7 wickets   Toss: England

1965 **England 546 for 4 wkts dec** (J H Edrich 310*, K F Barrington 163). **New Zealand 193** (J R Reid 54) and **166** (V Pollard 53, F J Titmus 5 for 19).
England won by an innings and 187 runs   Toss: England

1966 **West Indies 500 for 9 wkts dec** (G St A Sobers 174, S M Nurse 137). **England 240** (B L D'Oliveira 88, G St A Sobers 5 for 41) and **205** (R W Barber 55, L R Gibbs 6 for 39).
West Indies won by an innings and 55 runs   Toss: West Indies

333

1967 **England 550 for 4 wkts dec** (G Boycott 246*, B L D'Oliveira 109, K F Barrington 93, T W Graveney 59) and **126 for 4 wkts. India 164** (Nawab of Pataudi jnr 64) and **510** (Nawab of Pataudi jnr 148, A L Wadekar 91, F M Engineer 87, Hanumant Singh 73). **England won by 6 wickets** Toss: England

1968 **Australia 315** (I R Redpath 92, I M Chappell 65) and **312** (I M Chappell 81, K D Walters 56, R Illingworth 6 for 87). **England 302** (R M Prideaux 64, J H Edrich 62, A N Connolly 5 for 72) and **230 for 4 wkts** (J H Edrich 65). **Match drawn** Toss: Australia

1969 **England 223** (J H Edrich 79) and **240** (G.St A Sobers 5 for 42). **West Indies 161** and **272** (B F Butcher 91, G S Camacho 71). **England won by 30 runs** Toss: England

1971 **England 316** (G Boycott 112, B L D'Oliveira 74) and **264** (B L D'Oliveira 72, D L Amiss 56) **Pakistan 350** (Zaheer Abbas 72, Wasim Bari 63, Mushtaq Mohammad 57) and **205** (Sadiq Mohammad 91). **England won by 25 runs** Toss: England

1972 **Australia 146** (K R Stackpole 52) and **136** (D L Underwood 6 for 45). **England 263** (R Illingworth 57, A A Mallett 5 for 114) and **21 for 1 wkt.** **England won by 9 wickets** Toss: Australia

1973 **New Zealand 276** (M G Burgess 87, V Pollard 62) and **142** (G M Turner 81, G G Arnold 5 for 27). **England 419** (G Boycott 115, K W R Fletcher 81, R Illingworth 65, RO Collinge 5 for 74). **England won by an innings and 1 run** Toss: New Zealand

1974 **Pakistan 285** (Majid Khan 75, Safraz Nawaz 53) and **179. England 183** and **238 for 6 wkts** (J H Edrich 70, K W R Fletcher 67*). **Match drawn** Toss: Pakistan

1975 **England 288** (D S Steele 73, J H Edrich 62, A W Greig 51, G J Gilmour 6 for 85) and **291** (D S Steele 92). **Australia 135** (P H Edmonds 5 for 28) and **220 for 3 wkts** (R B McCosker 95*, I M Chappell 62). **Match drawn** Toss: England

1976 **West Indies 450** (C G Greenidge 115, R C Fredericks 109, I V A Richards 66, L G Rowe 50) and **196** (C L King 58, R G D Willis 5 for 42). **England 387** (A W Greig 116, A P E Knott 116) and **204** (A W Greig 76*). **West Indies won by 55 runs** Toss: West Indies

1977 **England 436** (G Boycott 191, A P E Knott 57). **Australia 103** (I T Botham 5 for 21) and **248** (R W Marsh 63). **England won by an innings and 85 runs** Toss: England

1978 **Pakistan 201** (Sadiq Mohammad 97). **England 119 for 7 wkts** (Safraz Nawaz 5 for 39). **Match drawn** Toss: Pakistan

1979 **England 270** (I T Botham 137). **India 223 for 6 wkts** (S M Gavaskar 78, D B Vengsarkar 65*). **Match drawn** Toss: England

1980 **England 143 and 227 for 6 wkts dec** (G A Gooch 55). **West Indies 245.** **Match drawn** Toss: West Indies

1981 **Australia 401 for 9 wkts dec** (J Dyson 102, K J Hughes 89, G N Yallop 58, I T Botham 6 for 95) and **111** (R G D Willis 8 for 43). **England 174** (I T Botham 50) and **356** (I T Botham 149*, G R Dilley 56, T M Alderman 6 for 135). **England won by 18 runs** Toss: Australia

1982 **Pakistan 275** (Imran Khan 67*, Mudassar Nazar 65, Javed Miandad 54) and **199** (Javed Miandad 52, I T Botham 5 for 74). **England 256** (D I Gower 74, I T Botham 57, Imran Khan 5 for 49) and **219 for 7 wkts** (G Fowler 86). **England won by 3 wickets** Toss: Pakistan

1983 **England 225** (C J Tavaré 69, A J Lamb 58, B L Cairns 7 for 74) and **252** (D I Gower 112*, E J Chatfield 5 for 95). **New Zealand 377** (J G Wright 93, B A Edgar 84, R J Hadlee 75) and **103 for 5 wkts** (R G D Willis 5 for 35). **New Zealand won by 5 wickets** Toss: New Zealand

334

1984 **England 270** (A J Lamb 100) and **159** (G Fowler 50, M D Marshall 7 for 53). **West Indies 302** (H A Gomes 104*, M A Holding 59, P J W Allott 6 for 61) and **131 for 2 wkts.**
West Indies won by 8 wickets   Toss: England

1985 **Australia 331** (A M J Hilditch 119) and **324** (W B Phillips 91, A M J Hilditch 80, K C Wessels 64, J E Emburey 5 for 82). **England 533** (R T Robinson 175, I T Botham 60, P R Downton 54, M W Gatting 53) and **123 for 5 wkts.**
England won by 5 wickets   Toss: Australia

1986 **India 272** (D B Vengsarkar 61) and **237** (D B Vengsarkar 102*). **England 102** (R M H Binny 5 for 40) and **128.**
India won by 279 runs   Toss: India

1987 **England 136** (D J Capel 53) and **199** (D I Gower 55, Imran Khan 7 for 40). **Pakistan 353** (Salim Malik 99, Ijaz Ahmed 50, N A Foster 8 for 107).
Pakistan won by an innings and 18 runs   Toss: England

1988 **England 201** (A J Lamb 64*) and **138** (G A Gooch 50). **West Indies 275** (R A Harper 56, D L Haynes 54, D R Pringle 5 for 95) and **67 for 0 wkt.**
West Indies won by 10 wickets   Toss: West Indies

1989 **Australia 601 for 7 wkts dec** (S R Waugh 177*, M A Taylor 136, D M Jones 79, M G Hughes 71, A R Border 66) and **230 for 3 wkts dec** (M A Taylor 60, A R Border 60*). **England 430** (A J Lamb 125, K J Barnett 80, R A Smith 66, T M Alderman 5 for 107) and **191.** (G A Gooch 68, T M Alderman 5 for 44).
Australia won by 210 runs   Toss: England

1991 **England 198** (R A Smith 54) and **252** (G A Gooch 154*, C E L Ambrose 6 for 52). **West Indies 173** (I V A Richards 73) and **162** (R B Richardson 68).
England won by 115 runs   Toss: West Indies

1992 **Pakistan 197** (Salim Malik 82*) and **221** (Salim Malik 84*, Ramiz Raja 63, N A Mallinder 5 for 50). **England 320** (G A Gooch 135, M A Atherton 76, Waqar Younis 5 for 117) and **99 for 4 wkts.**
England won by 6 wickets   Toss: Pakistan

1993 **Australia 653 for 4 wkts dec** (A R Border 200*, S R Waugh 157*, D C Boon 107, M J Slater 67, M E Waugh 52). **England 200** (G A Gooch 59, M A Atherton 55, P R Reiffel 5 for 65) and **305** (A J Stewart 78, M A Atherton 63).
Australia won by an innings and 148 runs   Toss: Australia

1994 **England 477 for 9 wkts dec** (M A Atherton 99, A J Stewart 89, G P Thorpe 72, S J Rhodes 65*) and **267 for 5 wkts dec** (G A Hick 110, G P Thorpe 73). **South Africa 447** (P N Kirsten 104, B M McMillan 78, C R Matthews 62*) and **116 for 3 wkts** (G Kirsten 65).
Match drawn   Toss: England

1995 **England 199** (M A Atherton 81, I R Bishop 5 for 32) and **208** (G P Thorpe 61). **West Indies 282** (S L Campbell 69, J C Adams 58, B C Lara 53) and **129 for 1 wkt** (C L Hooper 73*).
West Indies won by 9 wickets   Toss: West Indies

1996 **Pakistan 448** (Ijaz Ahmed 141, Mohin Khan 105, Salim Malik 55, Asif Mujtaba 51, D G Cork 5 for 113) and **242 for 7 wkts dec** (Inzamam-ul-Haq 65, Ijaz Ahmed sen 52) **England 501** (A J Stewart 170, N V Knight 113, J P Crawley 53).
Match drawn   Toss: England

1997 **England 172** (J N. Gillespie 7 for 37) and **268** (N Hussain 105, J P Crawley 72, P R Reiffel 5 for 49). **Australia 501 for 9 wkts dec** (M T G Elliott 199, R T Ponting 127, P R Reiffel 54*, D Gough 5 for 149).
Australia won by an innings and 61 runs   Toss: Australia

1998 **England 230** (M A Butcher 116) and **240** (N Hussain 94, S M Pollock 5 for 53, A A Donald 5 for 71). **South Africa 252** (W J. Cronje 57, A R C Fraser 5 for 42) and **195** (J N Rhodes 85, B M McMillan 54, D Gough 6 for 42).
England won by 23 runs   Toss: England

2000 **West Indies 172** (R R Sarwan 59*, C White 5 for 57) and **61** (A R Caddick 5 for 14). **England 272** (M P Vaughan 76, G A Hick 59).
England won by an innings and 39 runs   Toss: West Indies

2001 **Australia 447** (R T Ponting 144, D R Martyn 118, M E Waugh 72, D Gough 5 for 103) and **176 for 4 wkts dec** (R T Ponting 72). **England 309** (A J Stewart 76*, G D McGrath 7 for 76) and **315 for 4 wkts** (M A Butcher 173*, N Hussain 55).
England won by 6 wickets   Toss: Australia

2002 **India 628 for 8 wkts dec** (S R Tendulkar 193, R S Dravid 148, S C Ganguly 128, S B Bangar 68). **England 273** (A J Stewart 78*, M P Vaughan 61) and **309** (N Hussain 110.)
India won by an innings and 46 runs   Toss: India

2003 **South Africa 342** (G Kirsten 130, M Zondeki 59, J A Rudolph 55) and **365** (A J Hall 99*, G Kirsten 60). **England 307** (M A Butcher 77, M E Trescothick 55, A Flintoff 55) and **209** (M A Butcher 61, A Flintoff 50, J H Kallis 6 for 54.)
South Africa won by 191 runs   Toss: South Africa

2004 **New Zealand 409** (S P Fleming 97, M H W Papps 86, B B McCullum 54) and **161.** **England 526** (M E Trescothick 132, G O Jones 100, A Flintoff 94, A J Strauss 62) and **45 for 1 wkt**
England won by 9 wickets   Toss: England

2006 **England 515** (K P Pietersen 135, I R Bell 119, Umar Gul 5 for 123) and **345** (A J Strauss 116, M E Trescothick 58, C M W Reid 55). **Pakistan 538** (Mohammad Yousuf 192, Younis Khan 173) and **155**.
England won by 167 runs   Toss: England

2007 **England 570 for 7 wkts dec** (K P Pietersen 226, M P Vaughan 103, M J Prior 75). **West Indies 146** and **141** (D J Bravo 52).
England won by an innings and 283 runs   Toss: England

2008 **England 203** and **327** (S C J Broad 67*, A N Cook 60). **South Africa 522** (A B de Villiers 174, A G Prince 149) and **9 for 0 wkt**.
South Africa won by 10 wickets   Toss: South Africa

2009 **England 102** (P M Siddle 5 for 21) and **263** (G P Swann 62, S C J Broad 61, M G Johnson 5 for 69). **Australia 445** (M J North 110, M J Clarke 93, R T Ponting 78, S R Watson 51, S C J Broad 6 for 91).
Australia won by an innings and 80 runs   Toss: England

2010 **Australia 88** and **349** (R T Ponting 66, M J Clarke 77, S P D Smith 77). **Pakistan 258** (S R Watson 6-33) and **180-7** (Imran Farhat 67, Azhar Ali 51).
Pakistan won by 3 wickets   Toss: Australia
(This was a Home Test Match for Pakistan)

2012 **South Africa 419** (A N Petersen 182, G C Smith 52) and **258-9 dec** (J A Rudolph 69, GC Smith 52, S C J Broad 5-69). **England 425** (K P Pietersen 149, M J Prior 68) and **130-4.**
Match drawn   Toss: England

2013 **England 354** (J E Root 104, J M Bairstow 64, T A Boult 5-57) and **287-5 dec** (A N Cook 130, I J L Trott 76). **New Zealand 174** and **220** (L R P L Taylor 70, G P Swann 6-90)
England won by 247 runs   Toss: England

2014 **Sri Lanka 257** (K C Sangakkara 79, L E Plunkett 5-64) and **457** (K C Sangakkara 55, DPMD Jayawardene 79, A D Mathews 160). **England 365** (S D Robson 127, G S Ballance 74, I R Bell 64) and **249** (M M Ali 108*, K T G D Prasad 5-50)
Sri Lanka won by 100 runs   Toss: England

2015 **New Zealand 350** (T W M Latham 84, L Ronchi 88, S C J Broad 5-109) and **454-8 dec** (M J Guptill 70, B B McCullum 55, B J Watling 120, M D Craig 58*). **England 350** (A Lyth 107, A N Cook 75) and **255** (A N Cook 56, J C Buttler 73)
New Zealand won by 199 runs   Toss: England

2016 **England 298** (A D Hales 86, J M Bairstow 140). **Sri Lanka 91** (J M Anderson 5-16) and **119** (B K G Mendis 53, J N Anderson 5-29)
England won by an innings and 88 runs   Toss: Sri Lanka

336

SUMMARY OF RESULTS

ENGLAND	First played	Last played	Played	Won	Lost	Drawn
v. Australia	1899	2009	24	7	9	8
v. India	1952	2002	6	3	2	1
v. New Zealand	1949	2015	8	5	2	1
v. Pakistan	1962	2006	9	5	1	3
v. South Africa	1907	2012	13	6	3	4
v. Sri Lanka	2014	2016	2	1	1	0
v. West Indies	1957	2007	12	5	6	1
Totals	1899	2016	74	32	24	18

SIX HIGHEST AGGREGATES

Runs	Wkts	
1723	31	in 1948 (England 496 and 365 for 8 wkts dec; Australia 458 and 404 for 3 wkts)
1553	40	in 2006 (England 515 and 345; Pakistan 538 and 155)
1452	30	in 1989 (Australia 601 for 7 wkts dec and 230 for 3 wkts dec; England 430 and 191)
1409	40	in 2015 (New Zealand 350 and 454 for 8 wkts dec; England 350 and 255)
1350	28	in 1967 (England 550 for 4 wkts dec and 126 for 4 wkts; India 164 and 510)
1311	35	in 1985 (Australia 331 and 324; England 533 and 123 for 5 wkts)

Note: The highest aggregate prior to the Second World War

1141	37	in 1921 (Australia 407 and 272 for 7 wkts dec; England 259 and 202)

SIX LOWEST AGGREGATES

Runs	Wkts	
423	40	in 1907 (England 76 and 162; South Africa 110 and 75)
463	22	in 1958 (New Zealand 67 and 129; England 267 for 2 wkts)
505	30	in 2000 (West Indies 172 and 61; England 272)
508	30	in 2016 (England 298; Sri Lanka 91 and 119)
553	30	in 1957 (West Indies 142 and 132; England 279)
566	31	in 1972 (Australia 146 and 136; England 263 and 21 for 1 wkt)

SIX HIGHEST TOTALS

653 for 4 wkts dec	Australia v. England, 1993
608 for 8 wkts dec	India v. England, 2002
601 for 7 wkts dec	Australia v. England, 1989
584	Australia v. England, 1934
570 for 7 wkts dec	England v. West Indies, 2007
566	Australia v. England, 1930

SIX LOWEST TOTALS

61	West Indies v. England, 2000
67	New Zealand v. England, 1958
75	South Africa v. England, 1907
76	England v. South Africa, 1907
87	England v Australia, 1909
88	Australia v. Pakistan, 2010

SIX HIGHEST INDIVIDUAL SCORES
For England

310*	J H Edrich versus New Zealand, 1965
246*	G Boycott versus India, 1967
226	K P Pietersen versusWest Indies, 2007
191	G Boycott versus Australia, 1977
175	R T Robinson versus Australia, 1985
173*	M A Butcher versus Australia, 2001

SIX HIGHEST INDIVIDUAL SCORES *(Continued)*

For Australia		For Pakistan	
334	D G Bradman, 1930	192	Mohammad Yousuf, 2006
304	D G Bradman, 1934	173	Younis Khan, 2006
200*	A R Border, 1993	141	Ijaz Ahmed, 1996
199	M T G Elliott, 1997	105	Moin Khan, 1996
182	A R Morris, 1948	99	Salim Malik, 1987
181	W H Ponsford, 1934	97	Sadiq Mohammad, 1978

For India		For South Africa	
193	S R Tendulkar, 2002	236	E A B Rowan, 1951
148	Nawab of Pataudi jnr, 1967	182	A N Petersen, 2012
148	R S Dravid, 2002	174	A B de Villiers, 2008
133	V L Manjrekar, 1952	149	A G Prince, 2008
128	S C Ganguly, 2002	133	D J McGlew, 1955
102*	D B Vengsarkar, 1986	130	G Kirsten, 2003

For New Zealand		For Sri Lanka	
120	B J Watling , 2015	160*	A D Mathews, 2014
97	S P Fleming, 2004	79	K C Sangakkara, 2014
96	F B Smith, 1949	55	K C Sangakkara, 2014
93	J G Wright, 1983	53*	B K G Mendis, 2016
88	L Ronchi, 2015	48	H M R K B Herath, 2014
87	M G Burgess, 1973	45	L D Chandimal, 2014
		45	F D M Karunaratne, 2014

For West Indies	
174	G St.A Sobers, 1966
137	S M Nurse, 1966
115	C G. Greenidge, 1976
109	R C Fredericks, 1976
104*	H A Gomes, 1984
102	G St A Sobers, 1963

HUNDRED BEFORE LUNCH

First day

112*	C G Macartney for Australia, 1926
105*	D G Bradman for Australia, 1930

Third day

102	(from 27* to 129) H G Owen-Smith for South Africa, 1929

CARRYING BAT THROUGH A COMPLETED INNINGS

154* out of 252 G A Gooch, England v. West Indies, 1991

MOST CENTURIES IN AN INNINGS

3	1926	C G Macartney (151), W M Woodfull (141) and A J Richardson for Australia
3	1993	A R Border (200*), S R Waugh (157*) and D C Boon (107) for Australia
3	2002	S R Tendulkar (193), R S Dravid (148) and S C Ganguly (128) for India

MOST CENTURIES IN A MATCH

5	1948	C Washbrook (143) and W J Edrich (111) for England; R N Harvey (112), A R Morris (182) and D G Bradman (173*) for Australia
5	2006	K P Pietersen (135), I R Bell (119) and A J Strauss (116) for England: Younis Khan (173) and Mohammad Yousuf (192) for Pakistan
4	1976	C G Greenidge (115) and R C Fredericks (109) for West Indies; A W Greig (116) and A P E Knott (116) for England
4	1996	Ijaz Ahmed (141) and Moin Khan (105) for Pakistan; A J Stewart (170) and N V Knight (113) for England
4	2002	S R Tendulkar (193), R S Dravid (148) and S C Ganguly (128) for India; N Hussain (110) for England

CENTURY PARTNERSHIPS

For England
(six highest)
For the 1st wicket

177	A Lyth (107) and A N Cook (75) v. New Zealand, 2015
168	L Hutton (81) and C Washbrook (143) v. Australia, 1948 (1st inns)
168	G A Gooch (135) and M A Atherton (76) v. Pakistan, 1992
158	M E Trescothick (58) and A J Strauss (116) v. Pakistan, 2006
156	J B Hobbs (88) and H Sutcliffe (94) v. Australia, 1926
153	M E Trescothick (132) and A J Strauss (62) v. New Zealand, 2004

For all other wickets

369	(2nd wkt) J H Edrich (310*) and K F Barrington (163) v. New Zealand, 1965
252	(4th wkt) G Boycott (246*) and B L D'Oliveira (109) v. India, 1967
194*	(3rd wkt) C A Milton (104*) and P B H May (113*) v. New Zealand, 1958
193	(4th wkt) M C Cowdrey (160) and K F Barrington (80) v. India, 1959
187	(4th wkt) P B H May (101) and C Washbrook (98) v. Australia, 1956
181	(3rd wkt) M A Butcher (173*) and N Hussain (55) v. Australia, 2001

For Australia
(six highest)
For the 1st wkt – none

For all other wickets

388	(4th wkt) W H Ponsford (181) and D G Bradman (304), 1934
332*	(5th wkt) A R Border (200*) and S R Waugh (157*), 1993
301	(2nd wkt) A R Morris (182) and D G Bradman (173*), 2002
268	(5th wkt) M T G Elliott (199) and R T Ponting (127), 1997
235	(2nd wkt) W M Woodfull (141) and C G Macartney (151), 1926
229	(3rd wkt) D G Bradman (334) and A F Kippax (77), 1930

For other countries in total

India

249	(4th wkt) S R Tendulkar (193) and S C Ganguly (128), 2002
222	(4th wkt) V S Hazare (89) and V L Manjrekar (133), 1952
170	(2nd wkt) S B Bangar (68) and R S Dravid (148), 2002
168	(2nd wkt) F M Engineer (87) and A L Wadekar (91), 1967
150	(3rd wkt) R S Dravid (148) and S R Tendulkar (193), 2002
134	(5th wkt) Hanumant Singh (73) and Nawab of Pataudi jnr (148), 1967
105	(6th wkt) V S Hazare (56) and D G Phadkar (64), 1952

New Zealand

169	(2nd wkt) M H W Papps (86) and S P Fleming (97), 2004
121	(5th wkt) B B McCullum (55) and B J Watling (120), 2015
120	(5th wkt) M P Donnelly (64) and F B Smith (96), 1949
120	(6th wkt) T W M Latham (84) and L Ronchi (88), 2015
116	(2nd wkt) J G Wright (93) and M D Crowe (37), 1983
112	(1st wkt) B Sutcliffe (82) and V J Scott (43), 1949
106	(5th wkt) M G Burgess (87) and V Pollard (62), 1973

Pakistan

363	(3rd wkt) Younis Khan (173) and Mohammad Yousuf (192), 2006
130	(4th wkt) Ijaz Ahmed (141) and Salim Malik (55), 1996
129	(3rd wkt) Zaheer Abbas (72) and Mushtaq Mohammed (57), 1971
112	(7th wkt) Asif Mujtaba (51) and Moin Khan (105), 1996
110	(2nd wkt) Imran Farhat (67) and Azhar Ali (51), 2010 v. Australia
100	(3rd wkt) Mudassar Nazar (65) and Javed Miandad (54), 1982
100	(4th wkt) Majid Khan (75) and Zaheer Abbas (48), 1974

CENTURY PARTNERSHIPS *(Continued)*

South Africa

212	(5th wkt)	A G Prince (149)	and A B de Villiers (174)	2008
198	(2nd wkt)	E A B Rowan (236)	and C B van Ryneveld (83)	1951
176	(1st wkt)	D J McGlew (133)	and T L Goddard (74)	1955
150	(8th wkt)	G Kirsten (130)	and M Zondeki (59)	2003
120	(1st wkt)	A N Petersen (182)	and G C Smith (52)	2012
120	(1st wkt)	J A Rudolph (69)	and G C Smith (52)	2012
117	(6th wkt)	J N Rhodes (85)	and B M McMillan (54)	1998
115	(7th wkt)	P N Kirsten (104)	and B M McMillan (78)	1994
108	(5th wkt)	E A B Rowan (236)	and R A McLean (67)	1951
103	(10th wkt)	H G Owen-Smith (129)	and A J Bell (26*)	1929

Sri Lanka

149	(8th wkt)	A D Mathews (160)	and H M R K B Herath (48)	2014

West Indies

265	(5th wkt)	S M Nurse (137)	and G St A Sobers (174)	1966
192	(1st wkt)	R C Fredericks (109)	and C G Greenidge (115)	1976
118*	(2nd wkt)	C L Hooper (73*)	and B C Lara (48*)	1995
143	(4th wkt)	R B Kanhai (92)	and G St A Sobers (102)	1963
108	(3rd wkt)	G S Camacho (71)	and B F Butcher (91)	1969
106	(1st wkt)	C G Greenidge (49)	and D L Haynes (43)	1984

6 BEST INNINGS ANALYSES

For England

8-43	R G D Willis	v. Australia	1981
8-59	C Blythe	v. South Africa	1907 (1st inns)
8-107	N A Foster	v. Pakistan	1987
7-40	C Blythe	v. South Africa,	1907 (2nd inns)
7-51	G A R Lock	v. New Zealand	1958
7-115	A P Freeman	v. South Africa	1929

For Australia

7-37	J N Gilliespie	1997	
7-58	C G Macartney	1909	
7-76	G D McGrath	2001	
6-33	S R Watson	2010	v. Pakistan
6-85	G J Gilmour	1975	
6-135	T M Alderman	1981	

5 WICKETS IN AN INNINGS

For India (2)

5-40	R M H Binny	1986
5-100	Ghulam Ahmed	1952

For New Zealand (6)

7-74	B L Cairns	1983
5-57	T A Boult	2013
5-74	R O Collinge	1973
5-95	E J Chatfield	1983
5-97	T B Burtt	1949
5-127	J Cowie	1949

For Pakistan (6)

7-40	Imran Khan	1987
5-39	Sarfraz Nawaz	1978
5-49	Imran Khan	1982
5-117	Waqar Younis	1992
5-123	Umar Gul	2006
5-128	Munir Malik	1962

For South Africa (8)

6-17	G A Faulkner	1907
6-92	N A Quinn	1929
6-54	J H Kallis	2003
5-53	S M Pollock	1998
5-69	T L Goddard	1955
5-71	A A Donald	1998
5-94	H J Tayfield	1955
5-174	A M B Rowan	1951

For Sri Lanka

5-50	K T G D Prasad	2014

For West Indies (8)

7-53	M D Marshall	1984
7-70	F M Worrell	1957
6-36	C C Griffith	1963
6-39	L R Gibbs	1996
6-52	C E L Ambrose	1991
5-32	I R Bishop	1995
5-41	G.St.A Sobers	1966
5-42	G.St A Sobers	1969

10 WICKETS IN A MATCH

For England (8)

15-99	(8-59 and 7-40)	C Blythe	v. South Africa	1907
11-65	(4-14 and 7-51)	G A R Lock	v. New Zeland	1958
11-88	(5-58 and 6-30)	F S Trueman	v. Australia	1961
11-113	(5-58 and 6-55)	J C Laker	v. Australia	1956
10-45	(5-16 and 5-29)	J M Anderson	v. Sri Lanka	2016
10-82	(4-37 and 6-45)	D L Underwood	v. Australia	1972
10-115	(6-52 and 4-63)	S F Barnes	v. South Africa	1912
10-132	(4-42 and 6-90)	G P Swann	v. New Zealand	2013
10-207	(7-115 and 3-92)	A P Freeman	v. South Africa	1929

For Australia (3)

11-85	(7-58 and 4-27)	C G Macartney	1909
10-122	(5-66 and 5-56)	W J O'Reilly	1938
10-151	(5-107 and 5-44)	T M Alderman	1989

For New Zealand (1)

10-144	(7-74 and 3-70)	B L Cairns	1983

For Pakistan (1)

10-77	(3-37 and 7-40)	Imran Khan	1987

Note: Best bowling in a match for:

India	7-58	(5-40 and 2-18)	R M H Binny	1986
Sri Lanka	6-125	(1-75 and 5-50)	K T G D Prasad	2014
South Africa	9-75	(6-17 and 3-58)	G A Faulkner	1907
West Indies	9-81	(6 -36 and 3-45)	C C Griffith	1963

HAT-TRICKS

J T Hearne	v. Australia	1899
P J Loader	v. West Indies	1957

TEST MATCH AT BRAMALL LANE, SHEFFIELD 1902

1902 **Australia 194** (S F Barnes 6 for 49) and **289** (C Hill 119, V T Trumper 62, W Rhodes 5 for 63) **England 145** (J V Saunders 5 for 50, M A Noble 5 for 51) and **195** (A C MacLaren 63, G L Jessop 55, M A Noble 6 for 52).
Australia won by 143 runs   Toss: Australia

For England

YORKSHIRE ONE-DAY INTERNATIONAL CRICKETERS 1971-2016/17 (Correct to October 27, 2016)

Player	M	I	NO	Runs	HS	Av'ge	100s	50s	Balls	Runs	W	Av'ge	Best	4wI	Ct/St
ATHEY, C W J 1980-88	31	30	3	848	142*	31.40	2	4	—	—	—	—	—	0	16
BAIRSTOW, D L ...1979-84	21	20	6	206	23*	14.71	0	0	—	—	—	—	—	0	17/4
BAIRSTOW, J M .2011-16/17	22	18	3	458	83*	30.53	0	2	—	—	—	—	—	0	15/2
BALLANCE, G S .2013-14/15	16	15	1	297	79	21.21	0	2	—	—	—	—	—	0	8
BLAKEY, R J ...1992-93	3	2	0	25	25	12.50	0	0	—	—	—	—	—	0	2/1
BOYCOTT, G ...1971-81	36	34	4	1,082	105	36.06	1	9	168	105	5	21.00	2-14	0	5
BRESNAN, T T ...2006-15	85	64	20	871	80	19.79	0	1	4,221	3,813	109	34.98	5-48	4	20
COPE, G A ...1977-78	2	1	1	1	1*	—	0	0	112	35	2	17.50	1-16	0	0
GOUGH, D ...1994-2006	158	87	38	609	46*	12.42	0	0	8,422	6,154	234	26.29	5-44	10	24
HAMPSHIRE, J H ...1971-72	3	3	1	48	25*	24.00	0	0	—	—	—	—	—	0	0
HOGGARD, M J ...2001-06	26	6	2	17	7	4.25	0	0	1,306	1,152	32	36.00	5-49	1	5
JARVIS, P W ...1988-93	16	8	2	31	16*	5.16	0	0	879	672	24	28.00	5-35	2	1
LOVE, J D 1981	3	3	0	61	43	20.33	0	0	—	—	—	—	—	0	1
McGRATH, A ...2003-04	14	12	2	166	52	16.60	0	1	228	175	4	43.75	1-13	0	4
MOXON, M D ...1985-88	8	8	0	174	70	21.75	0	1	—	—	—	—	—	0	5
OLD, C M ...1973-81	32	25	7	338	51*	18.77	0	1	1,755	999	45	22.20	4- 8	2	8
PLUNKETT, L E 2005/6-16/17	44	32	12	445	56	22.25	0	1	2,143	2,093	60	34.88	3-24	0	15
RASHID, A U ...2009-16/17	37	18	6	327	69	27.25	0	1	1,922	1,794	51	35.17	4-43	4	10
ROOT, J E ...2012/13-16	78	73	7	3,017	125	45.71	8	17	888	855	13	65.76	2-15	0	35
SHAHZAD, A ...2010-11	11	8	2	39	9	6.50	0	0	588	490	17	28.82	3-41	0	4
SIDEBOTTOM, R J .2001-10	25	18	8	133	24	13.30	0	0	1,277	1,039	29	35.82	3-19	0	6
SILVERWOOD, C E W 1996-2001	7	4	4	17	12	4.25	0	0	306	244	6	40.66	3-43	0	0
STEVENSON, G B ..1980-81	4	3	0	43	28*	43.00	0	0	192	125	7	17.85	4-33	1	2
VAUGHAN, M P ...2001-07	86	83	10	1,982	90*	27.15	0	16	796	649	16	40.56	4-22	1	25
WHITE, C ...1994-2003	51	41	5	568	57*	15.77	0	0	2,364	1,726	65	26.55	5-21	2	12
WILLEY, D J ..2015-2016/17	22	12	5	84	13*	12.00	0	0	1,042	961	29	33.13	4-34	1	11
For Scotland															
BLAIN, J A R ...1999-2009	33	25	6	284	41	14.94	0	0	1,329	1,173	41	28.60	5-22	4	8
HAMILTON, G M .1999-2010	38	38	3	1,231	119	35.17	2	7	220	160	3	53.33	2-36	0	6/1
WARDLAW, I ..2012/14/15	22	14	8	21	7*	3.50	0	0	1,108	1,036	36	28.77	4-22	2	1

YORKSHIRE PLAYERS WHO PLAYED ALL THEIR ONE-DAY INTERNATIONAL CRICKET AFTER LEAVING YORKSHIRE

For England

Player	M	I	NO	Runs	HS	Av'ge	100s	50s	Balls	Runs	W	Av'ge	Best	4wI	Ct/St
BATTY, G J 2002-09	10	8	2	30	17	5.00	0	0	440	366	5	73.20	2-40	—	4
CLOSE, D B 1972	3	3	0	49	43	16.33	0	0	18	21	0	—	—	—	1
GRAYSON, A P ...2000-01	2	2	0	6	6	3.00	0	0	90	60	3	20.00	3-40	—	1
ILLINGWORTH, R .1971-72	3	2	0	5	4	2.50	0	0	130	84	4	21.00	3-50	—	1
LUMB, M J 2013/14	3	3	0	165	106	55.00	1	0	—	—	—	—	—	—	—
RHODES, S J 1989-95	9	8	2	107	56	17.83	0	1	—	—	—	—	—	—	9/2
WHARF, A G 2004-05	13	5	3	19	9	9.50	0	0	584	428	18	23.77	4-24	1	1
WOOD, B 1972-82	13	12	2	314	78*	31.40	0	2	420	224	9	24.88	2-14	—	6

Overseas Players

(Qualification: 24 List A matches for Yorkshire)

For Australia

BEVAN, M G ...1994-2004	232	196	67	6,912	108*	53.58	6	46	1,966	1,655	36	45.97	3-36	—	128
HARVEY, I J .1997/98-2004	73	51	11	715	48*	17.87	0	0	3,279	2,577	85	30.31	4-16	4	17
JAQUES, P A 2006-2007	6	6	0	125	94	20.83	0	1	—	—	—	—	—	—	3
LEHMANN, D S .1996-2005	117	101	22	3,078	119	38.96	4	17	1,793	1,445	52	27.78	4-7	1	26

For South Africa

RUDOLPH, J A 2003-06	43	37	6	1,157	81	37.32	0	7	24	26	0	—	—	—	11

For West Indies

RICHARDSON, R B 1983-96	224	217	30	6,248	122	33.41	5	44	58	46	1	46.00	1-4	—	75

343

LIMITED-OVERS INTERNATIONAL MATCHES
AT HEADINGLEY, LEEDS 1973-2016

1973 **West Indies 181** (54 overs) (R B Kanhai 55). **England 182 for 9 wkts** (54.3 overs) (M H Denness 66).
England won by 1 wicket Award: M H Denness

1974 **India 265** (53.5 overs) (B P Patel 82, A L Wadekar 67). **England 266 for 6 wkts** (51.1 overs) (J H Edrich 90).
England won by 4 wickets Award: J H Edrich

1975 **Australia 278 for 7 wkts** (60 overs) (R Edwards 80*). **Pakistan 205** (53 overs) (Majid Khan 65, Asif Iqbal 53, D K Lillee 5 for 34).
Australia won by 73 runs Award: D K Lillee

1975 **East Africa 120** (55.3 overs). **India 123 for 0 wkt** (29.5 overs) (S M Gavaskar 65* F M Engineer 54*).
India won by 10 wickets Award: F M Engineer

1975 **England 93** (36.2 overs) (G J Gilmour 6 for 14). **Australia 94 for 6 wkts** (28.4 overs).
Australia won by 4 wickets Award: G J Gilmour

1979 **Canada 139 for 9 wkts** (60 overs). **Pakistan 140 for 2 wkts** (40.1 overs) (Sadiq Mohammed 57*).
Pakistan won by 8 wickets Award: Sadiq Mohammed

1979 **India 182** (55.5 overs) (S M Gavaskar 55). **New Zealand 183 for 2 wkts** (57 overs) (B A Edgar 84*).
New Zealand won by 8 wickets Award: B A Edgar

1979 **England 165 for 9 wkts** (60 overs). **Pakistan 151** (56 overs) (Asif Iqbal 51, M Hendrick 4 for 15)
England won by 14 runs Award: M Hendrick

1980 **West Indies 198** (55 overs) (C G Greenidge 78). **England 174** (51.2 overs) (C J Tavaré 82*).
West Indies won by 24 runs Award: C J Tavaré

1981 **Australia 236 for 8 wkts** (55 overs) (G M Wood 108). **England 165** (46.5 overs) (R M Hogg 4 for 29).
Australia won by 71 runs Award: G M Wood

1982 **India 193** (55 overs) (Kapil Dev 60, I T Botham 4 for 56). **England 194 for 1 wkt** (50.1 overs) (B Wood 78*, C J Tavaré 66).
England won by 9 wickets Award: B Wood

1983 **West Indies 252 for 9 wkts** (60 overs) (H A Gomes 78). **Australia 151** (30.3 overs) (W W Davis 7 for 51).
West Indies won by 101 runs Award: W W Davis

1983 **Pakistan 235 for 7 wkts** (60 overs) (Imran Khan 102*, Shahid Mahboob 77, A L F de Mel 5 for 39). **Sri Lanka 224** (58.3 overs) (S Wettimuny 50, Abdul Qadir 5 for 44).
Pakistan won by 11 runs Award: Abdul Qadir

1983 **Sri Lanka 136** (50.4 overs). **England 137 for 1 wkt** (24.1 overs) (G Fowler 81*).
England won by 9 wickets Award: R G D Willis

1986 **New Zealand 217 for 8 wkts** (55 overs) (J J Crowe 66). **England 170** (48.2 overs).
New Zealand won by 47 runs Award: J J Crowe

1988 **England 186 for 8 wkts** (55 overs). **West Indies 139** (46.3 overs).
England won by 47 runs Award: D R Pringle

1990 **England 295 for 6 wkts** (55 overs) (R A Smith 128, G A Gooch 55). **New Zealand 298 for 6 wkts** (54.5 overs) (M J Greatbatch 102*, J G Wright 52, A H Jones 51).
New Zealand won by 4 wickets Award: M J Greatbatch

1990 **England 229** (54.3 overs) (A J Lamb 56, D I Gower 50). **India 233 for 4 wkts** (53 overs) (S V Manjrekar 82, M Azharuddin 55*)
India won by 6 wickets Award: A Kumble

1996 **India 158** (40.2 overs). **England 162 for 4 wkts** (39.3 overs) (G P Thorpe 79*).
England won by 6 wickets **Award: G P Thorpe**

1997 **Australia 170 for 8 wkts** (50 overs).**England 175 for 4 wkts** (40.1 overs) (G P Thorpe 75*, A J Hollioake 66*).
England won by 6 wickets **Award: G P Thorpe**

1998 **South Africa 205 for 8 wkts** (50 overs) (S M Pollock 56). **England 206 for 3 wkts** (35 overs) (A D Brown 59, N V Knight 51).
England won by 7 wickets **Award: A D Brown**

1999 **Pakistan 275 for 8 wkts** (50 overs) (Inzamam-ul-Haq 81, Abdur Razzaq 60). **Australia 265** (49.5 overs) (M G Bevan 61, Wasim Akram 4-40).
Pakistan won by 10 runs **Award: Inazmam-ul-Haq**

1999 **Zimbabwe 175** (49.3 overs) (M A Goodwin 57). **New Zealand 70 for 3 wkts** (15 overs).
No result **No Award**

1999 **South Africa 271 for 7 wkts** (50 overs) (H H Gibbs 101, D J Cullinan 50). **Australia 275 for 5 wkts** (49.4 overs) (S R. Waugh 120*, R T Ponting 69).
Australia won by 5 wickets **Award: S R Waugh**

2001 **England 156 (45.2 overs)** (B C Hollioake 53, Waqar Younis 7 for 36). **Pakistan 153 for 4 wkts** (39.5 overs) (Abdur Razzaq 75).
Pakistan won — England conceding the match following a pitch invasion.
Award: Waqar Younis

2002 **Sri Lanka 240 for 7 wkts** (32 overs) (S T Jayasuriya 112). **England 241 for 7 wkts** (31.2 overs) (M E Trescothick 82).
England won by 3 wkts **Award: S T Jayasuriya**

2003 **England 81 for 4 wkts. Zimbabwe** did not bat.
No result **No Award**

2004 **West Indies 159** (40.1 overs). **England 160 for 3 wkts** (22 overs) (M E Trescothick 55).
England won by 7 wickets **Award: S J Harmison**

2005 **Bangladesh 208 for 7 wkts** (50 overs) (Belim 81, A Flintoff 4-29). **England 209 for 5 wkts** (38.5 overs) (A J Strauss 98).
England won by 5 wickets **Award: A J Strauss**

Australia 219 for 7 wkts (50 overs) (P D Collingwood 4-34). **England 221 for 1 wkt** (46 overs) (M E Trescothick 104*, M P Vaughan 59*).
England won by 9 wickets **Award: M E Trescothick**

2006 **England 321 for 7 wkts** (50 overs) (M E Trescothick 121, S L Malinga 4-44). **Sri Lanka 324 for 2 wkts** (37.3 overs) (S T Jayasuriya 152, W U Tharanga 109).
Sri Lanka won by 8 wickets **Award: S T Jayasuriya**

2007 **India 324 for 6 wkts** (50 overs) (Yuvraj Singh 72, S R Tendulkar 71, S C Ganguly 59, G Gambhir 51). **England 242 for 8 wkts** (39 overs) (P D Collingwood 91*)
India won by 38 runs *(D/L Method)* **Award: S C Ganguly**

2008 **England 275 for 4 wkts** (50 overs) (K P Pietersen 90*, A Flintoff 78). **South Africa 255** (J H Kallis 52).
England won by 20 runs **Award: K P Pietersen**

2009 **England v. West Indies** **Match abandoned without a ball bowled**

2010 **Pakistan 294 for 8 wkts** (50 overs) (Kamran Akmal 74, Asad Shafiq 50, S C J Broad 4-81). **England 295 for 6 wkts** (A J Strauss 126, I J L Trott 53)
England won by 4 wickets **Award: A J Strauss**

2011 **Sri Lanka 309 for 5 wkts** (50 overs) (D P M D Jayawardene 144, K C Sangakkara 69) **England 240 all out** (E J A Morgan 52)
Sri Lanka won by 69 runs **Award: D P M D Jayawardene**

2012 **England v. West Indies** **Match abandoned without a ball bowled**

2013 **England v. Australia** **Match abandoned without a ball bowled**

2014 **England 294 for 7 wkts** (50 overs) (J E Root 113). **India** 253 all out (48.4 overs) (R A Jadeja 87)
England won by 41 runs   **Award: J E Root**

2015 **Australia 299 for 7 wkts** (50 overs) (G J Bailey 75, G J Maxwell 85, M S Wade 50*). **England 304 for 7 wkts** (48.2 overs) (E J G Morgan 92, P J Cummins 4-49)
England won by 7 wickets   **Award: E J G Morgan**

2016 **Pakistan 247 for 8 wkts** (50 overs) (Azhar Ali 80, Imad Wasim 57*); **England 252 for 6 wkts** (48 overs) (B A Stokes 69, J M Bairstow 61)
England won by 6 wickets   **Award: J M Bairstow**

SUMMARY OF RESULTS

ENGLAND	Played	Won	Lost
v. Australia	5	3	2
v. Bangladesh	1	1	0
v. India	6	4	2
v. New Zealand	2	0	2
v. Pakistan	4	3	1
v. South Africa	2	2	0
v. Sri Lanka	4	2	2
v. West Indies	4	3	1
v. Zimbabwe	1*	0	0
Totals	29	18	10

*No result. In addition to two matches v. West Indies abandoned and one match v. Australia abandoned

AUSTRALIA	Played	Won	Lost
v. England	5	2	3
v. Pakistan	2	1	1
v. South Africa	1	1	0
v. West Indies	1	0	1
Totals	9	4	5

In addition to one match abandoned

BANGLADESH	Played	Won	Lost
v. England	1	0	1

INDIA	Played	Won	Lost
v. England	6	2	4
v. East Africa	1	1	0
v. New Zealand	1	0	1
Totals	8	3	5

NEW ZEALAND	Played	Won	Lost
v. England	2	2	0
v. India	1	1	0
v. Zimbabwe	1*	0	0
Totals	4	3	0

*No result

PAKISTAN	Played	Won	Lost
v. Australia	2	1	1
v. Canada	1	1	0
v. England	4	1	3
v. Sri Lanka	1	1	0
Totals	8	4	4

SOUTH AFRICA	Played	Won	Lost
v. Australia	1	0	1
v. England	2	0	2
Totals	3	0	3

SRI LANKA	Played	Won	Lost
v. England	4	2	2
v. Pakistan	1	0	1
Totals	5	2	3

WEST INDIES	Played	Won	Lost
v. Australia	1	1	0
v. England	4	1	3
Totals	5	2	3

In addition to two matches abandoned

ZIMBABWE	Played	Won	Lost
v. England	1*	0	0
v. New Zealand	1*	0	0
Totals	2*	0	0

*No result

CANADA	Played	Won	Lost
v. Pakistan	1	0	1

EAST AFRICA	Played	Won	Lost
v. India	1	0	1

CENTURIES

152	S J Jayasuriya	for Sri Lanka	v. England	2006
144	D P M D Jayawardene	for Sri Lanka	v. England	2011
128	R A Smith	for England	v. New Zealand	1990
126	A J Strauss	for England	v. Pakistan	2010
121	M E Trescothick	for England	v. Sri Lanka	2006
120*	S R Waugh	for Australia	v. South Africa	1999
113	J E Root	for England	v. India	2014
112	S J Jayasuriya	for Sri Lanka	v. England	2002
109	W U Tharanga	for Sri Lanka	v. England	2006
108	G M Wood	for Australia	v. England	1981
104*	M E Trescothick	for England	v. Australia	2005
102*	Imran Khan	for Pakistan	v. Sri Lanka	1983
102*	M J Greatbatch	for New Zealand	v. England	1990
101	H H Gibbs	for South Africa	v. Australia	1999

4 WICKETS IN AN INNINGS

7-36	Waqar Younis	for Pakistan	v. England	2001
7-51	W W Davis	for West Indies	v. Australia	1983
6-14	G J Gilmour	for Australia	v. England	1975
5-34	D K Lillee	for Australia	v. Pakistan	1975
5-39	A L F de Mel	for Sri Lanka	v. Pakistan	1983
5-44	Abdul Qadir	for Pakistan	v. Sri Lanka	1983
4-15	M Hendrick	for England	v. Pakistan	1979
4-29	R M Hogg	for Australia	v England	1981
4-29	A Flintoff	for England	v. Bangladesh	2005
4-34	P D Collingwood	for England	v. Australia	2005
4-40	Wasim Akram	for Pakistan	v. Australia	1999
4-44	S L Malinga	for Sri Lanka	v. England	2006
4-49	P J Cummins	Australia	v. England	2015
4-56	I T Botham	for England	v. India	1982
4-81	S J C Broad	for England	v. Pakistan	2010

LIMITED-OVERS INTERNATIONAL MATCHES
AT NORTH MARINE ROAD, SCARBOROUGH 1976-1978

1976 **England 202 for 8 wkts** (55 overs) (G D Barlow 80*, A M E Roberts 4 for 32).
West Indies 207 for 4 wkts (41 overs) (I V A Richards 119*).
West Indies won by 6 wickets   **Award: I V A Richards**

1978 **England 206 for 8 wkts** (55 overs) (G A Gooch 94, B L Cairns 5 for 28).
New Zealand 187 for 8 wkts (55 overs) (B E Congdon 52*).
England won by 19 runs   **Award: G A Gooch**

LIST OF PLAYERS AND CAREER AVERAGES IN ALL FIRST-CLASS MATCHES FOR YORKSHIRE 1863-2016

Based on research by John T Potter, Roy D Wilkinson and the late Anthony Woodhouse

The Editor and Statistics Editor welcome any information which will help in keeping this list up to date. The present compilers do not believe that we should alter the status of matches from that determined at the time they were played. Therefore, these averages include the match versus Gentlemen of Scotland in 1878, and exclude the matches versus Liverpool and District played in 1889, 1891, 1892 and 1893 in line with what appear to be the decisions of the Club at the time.

* Played as an amateur   © Awarded County Cap   § Born outside Yorkshire

Player	Date of Birth	Date of Death (if known)	First Played	Last Played	M	Inns	NO	Runs	HS	Av'ge	100s	Runs	Wkts	Av'ge	Ct/St
Ackroyd, A *	Aug. 29, 1858	Oct. 3, 1927	1879	1879	1	1	1	2	2*	—	0	7	0	—	0
Allen, S *	Dec 20, 1893	Oct 9, 1978	1924	1924	1	2	0	8	6	4.00	0	116	2	58.00	0
Allen, W R	Apr4, 1893	Oct 14, 1950	1921	1925	30	32	10	475	95*	21.59	0	—	—	—	45/21
Ambler, J	Feb 12, 1860		1886	1886	4	7	0	68	25	9.71	0	22	0	—	2
Anderson, G	Jan 20, 1826	Nov 27, 1902	1851	1869	19	31	6	520	99*	20.80	0	—	—	—	19
Anderson, P N	Apr. 28, 1966		1988	1988	1			0	0	0.00	0	47	1	47.00	0
Anson, C E *	Oct 14, 1889		1924	1924	1	2	0	27	14	13.50	0	—	—	—	1
Appleton, C *	May15, 1844	Feb 26, 1925	1865	1865	3	6	1	56	18	11.20	0	—	—	—	1
Appleyard, R	© June 27, 1924	Mar 17, 2015	1950	1958	133	122	43	679	63	8.59	0	9,903	642	15.42	70
Armitage, C1 *	Apr 24, 1849	Apr 24, 1917	1872	1878	3	5	0	26	12	5.20	0	29	0	—	2
Armitage, T	Apr 25, 1848	Sept 21, 1922	1873	1878	52	85	8	1,053	95	13.67	0	1,614	107	15.08	20
Ash, D L	Feb 18, 1944		1965	1965	3	3	0	22	12	7.33	0	22	0	—	0
Ashman, J R	May 20, 1926		1951	1951	1	1	0	0	0*	0.00	0	116	4	29.00	0
Ashraf, Moin A	Jan 5, 1992		2010	2013	21	19	5	56	10	4.00	0	1,268	43	29.48	2
Aspinall, R	© Oct 26, 1918	Aug 16, 1999	1946	1950	36	48	8	763	75*	19.07	0	2,670	131	20.38	18
Aspinall, W	Mar 24, 1858	Jan 27, 1910	1880	1880	2	3	0	16	14	5.33	0	—	—	—	—
Asquith, F T	Sept 5, 1870	Jan 11, 1916	1903	1903	1	1	0	0	0	0.00	0	—	—	—	2
Athey, C W J	© Sept 27, 1957		1976	1983	151	246	21	6,320	134	28.08	10	1,003	21	47.76	144/2
Atkinson, G R	Sept 21, 1830	May 3, 1906	1861	1870	27	38	8	399	44	13.30	0	1,146	54	21.22	14
Atkinson, H T	Feb 1, 1881	Dec 23, 1959	1907	1907	1	2	0	0	0	0.00	0	17	0	0.00	0
Azeem Rafiq	**© Feb 27, 1991**		**2009**	**2016**	**29**	**34**	**4**	**760**	**100**	**25.33**	**1**	**2,052**	**53**	**38.71**	**14**
Backhouse, E N	May 13, 1901	Nov 1, 1936	1931	1931	1	1	0	2	2	2.00	0	4	0	—	0
Badger, H D *	Mar7, 1900	Aug 10, 1975	1921	1922	2	4	2	6	6*	3.00	0	145	6	24.16	0
Bainbridge, A B	Oct 15, 1932		1961	1963	5	10	0	93	24	9.30	0	358	20	17.90	3

Player	Date of Birth	Date of Death (if known)	First Played	Last Played	M	Inns	NO	Runs	HS	Av'ge	100s	Runs	Wkts	Av'ge	Ct/St
Baines, F E *	June 18, 1864	Nov 17, 1948	1888	1888	1	1	0	0	0	0.00	0	—	—	—	0
Bairstow, A	Aug 14, 1868	Dec 7, 1945	1896	1900	24	24	10	69	12	4.92	0	—	—	—	41/18
Bairstow, D L	©Sept 1, 1951	Jan 5, 1998	1970	1990	429	601	113	12,985	145	26.60	9	192	6	32.00	907/131
Bairstow, J M	**©Sept 26, 1989**		2009	2016	87	138	22	6,072	246	52.34	15	1	0	—	219/10
Baker, G R	Apr 18, 1862	Feb 6, 1938	1884	1884	7	11	1	42	13	4.20	0	43	0	—	5
Baker, R *	July 13, 1849	June 21, 1896	1874	1875	3	5	1	45	22	11.25	0	—	—	—	3
Balderstone, J C	Nov 16, 1940	Mar 6, 2000	1961	1969	68	81	6	1,332	82	17.76	0	790	37	21.35	24
§ Ballance, G S	**©Nov 22, 1989**		2008	2016	77	122	14	4,970	174	46.01	15	143	0	—	56
Barber, A T *	©June 17, 1905	Mar 10, 1985	1929	1930	42	54	3	1,050	100	20.58	1	0	0	—	40
Barber, W	©Apr 18, 1901	Sept 10, 1968	1926	1947	354	495	48	15,315	255	34.26	27	404	14	28.85	169
Barraclough, E S	Mar 30, 1923	May 21, 1999	1949	1950	2	4	2	43	24*	21.50	0	136	4	34.00	1
Bates, W	©Nov 19, 1855	Jan 8, 1900	1877	1887	202	331	12	6,499	136	20.37	8	10,692	637	16.78	163
Bates, W E	Mar 5, 1884	Jan 17, 1957	1907	1913	113	167	15	2,634	81	17.32	0	57	2	28.50	64
Batty, G J	Oct 13, 1977		1997	1997	1	2	0	18	18	9.00	0	70	2	35.00	0
Batty, J D	May 15, 1971		1989	1994	64	67	20	703	51	14.95	0	5,286	140	37.75	25
Bayes, G W	Feb 27, 1884	Dec 6, 1960	1910	1921	28	24	11	165	36	12.69	0	1,534	48	31.95	7
Beaumont, J	Oct 14, 1916	Nov 15, 2003	1946	1947	28	46	6	716	60	17.90	0	236	9	26.22	11
Beaumont, J	Sept 16, 1855	May 1, 1920	1877	1878	5	9	3	60	24	10.00	0	50	2	25.00	1
Bedford, H	July 1, 1907	July 5, 1968	1928	1928	5	5	1	57	24	14.25	0	179	8	22.37	1
Bedford, W	Feb 24, 1879	July 28, 1939	1903	1903	2	2	1	38	30*	38.00	0	117	2	58.50	—
Bell, J T	June 14, 1895	Aug 8, 1974	1921	1923	7	7	0	125	54	17.85	0	—	—	—	12
Berry, John	Jan 10, 1823	Feb 26, 1895	1849	1867	18	32	2	492	78	16.40	0	149	8	18.62	—
Berry, Joseph	Nov 29, 1829	Apr 20, 1894	1861	1874	3	4	0	68	30	17.00	0	—	—	—	1
Berry, P J	Dec 28, 1966		1986	1990	7	4	3	76	31*	76.00	0	401	7	57.28	6
§ Best, T L	Aug 26, 1981		2010	2010	7	9	0	86	44*	9.55	0	793	18	44.05	—
Betts, G	Sept 19, 1843	Sept 26, 1902	1873	1874	9	3	0	56	40	18.66	0	—	—	—	—
§ Bevan, M G	©May 8, 1970		1995	1996	32	56	8	2,823	160*	58.81	9	720	10	72.00	24
Binks, J G	©Oct 5, 1935		1955	1969	491	587	128	6,745	95	14.69	0	66	0	—	872/172
Binns, J	Mar 31, 1870	Dec 8, 1934	1898	1898	2	4	3	4	4	4.00	0	—	—	—	0/3
Bird, H D	Apr 19, 1933		1956	1959	14	25	2	613	181*	26.65	1	—	—	—	3
Birkenshaw, J	Nov 13, 1940		1958	1960	30	42	7	588	42	16.80	0	1,819	69	26.36	21

LIST OF PLAYERS AND CAREER AVERAGES IN ALL FIRST-CLASS MATCHES FOR YORKSHIRE (Continued)

Player	Date of Birth	Date of Death (if known)	First Played	Last Played	M	Inns	NO	Runs	HS	Av'ge	100s	Runs	Wkts	Av'ge	Ct/St
Birtles, T J D	Oct 26, 1886	Jan 13, 1971	1913	1924	37	57	11	876	104	19.04	1	20	0	—	19
Blackburn, J D H *	Oct 27, 1924	Feb 19, 1987	1956	1956	2	2	1	18	15	9.00	0				0
Blackburn, J S	Sept 24, 1852	July 8, 1922	1877	1877	6	11	1	102	28	10.20	0	173	7	24.71	4
§ Blackburn, W E *	Nov 24, 1888	June 3, 1941	1919	1920	10	13	6	26	6*	3.71	0	1,113	45	24.73	9
§ Blain J A R	Jan 4, 1979		2004	2010	15	17	7	137	28*	13.70	0	1,312	38	34.52	4
Blake, W	Nov 29, 1854*	Nov 28, 1931	1880	1880	2	3	0	44	21	14.66	0	17	1	17.00	4
© Blakey, R J	Jan 15, 1967		1985	2003	339	541	84	14,150	223*	30.96	12	68	1	68.00	768/56
Blamires, E	July 31, 1850	Mar 22, 1886	1877	1877	1	2	0	23	17	11.50	0	82	5	16.40	0
§ Blewett, G S	Oct 28, 1971		1999	1999	12	23	1	655	190	31.19	1	212	5	42.40	5
Bloom, G R	Sept 13, 1941		1964	1964	1	2	0	14	11	7.00	0			—	2
Bocking, H	Dec 10, 1835	Feb 22, 1907	1865	1865	1	2	0	6	6	6.00	0			—	2
Boden, J G *	Dec 27, 1848	Jan 3, 1928	1878	1878	1	1	0	2	2	2.00	0			—	1
§ Bolton, B C *	Sept 23, 1862	Nov 18, 1910	1890	1891	4	6	0	25	11	4.16	0	252	13	19.38	2
© Bolus, J B	Jan 31, 1934		1956	1962	107	179	18	4,712	146*	29.26	7	407	13	31.30	45
Booth, A	Nov 3, 1902	Aug 17, 1974	1931	1947	36	36	18	114	29	5.70	0	1,684	122	13.80	10
© Booth, M W	Dec 10, 1886	July 1, 1916	1908	1914	144	218	31	4,244	210	22.69	2	11,017	557	19.17	114
Booth, P A	Sept 5, 1965		1982	1989	23	29	9	193	33*	9.65	0	1,517	35	43.34	7
Booth, R	Oct 1, 1926		1951	1955	65	76	28	730	53*	15.20	0			—	79/29
Bore, M K	June 2, 1947		1969	1977	74	78	21	481	37*	8.43	0	4,866	162	30.03	27
Borrill, P D	July 4, 1951		1971	1971	2							61	5	12.20	0
Bosomworth W E	Mar 8, 1847	June 7, 1891	1872	1880	4	7	1	20	7	3.33	0	140	9	15.55	2
Bottomley, I H *	Apr 9, 1855	Apr 23, 1922	1878	1880	9	12	0	166	32	13.83	0	75	1	75.00	0
Bottomley, T	Dec 26, 1910	Feb 19, 1977	1934	1935	6	7	0	142	51	20.28	0	188	1	188.00	5
Bower, W H	Oct 17, 1857	Jan 31, 1943	1883	1883	1	2	0	10	5	5.00	0			—	0
© Bowes, W E	July 25, 1908	Sept 4, 1987	1929	1947	301	257	117	1,251	43*	8.93	0	21,227	1,351	15.71	118
© Boycott, G	Oct 21, 1940		1962	1986	414	674	111	32,570	260*	57.85	103	665	28	23.75	200
Brackin, T	Jan 5, 1859	Oct 7, 1924	1882	1882	3	3	0	12	9	2.00	0			—	0
Brayshay, P B *	Oct 14, 1916	July 6, 2004	1952	1952	2	3	0	20	13	6.66	0	104	3	34.66	0
Brearley, H *	June 26, 1913	Aug 14, 2007	1937	1937	1	2	0	17	9	8.50	0			—	0
© Brennan, D V *	Feb 10, 1920	Jan 9, 1985	1947	1953	204	221	66	1,653	47	10.66	0			—	280/100

LIST OF PLAYERS AND CAREER AVERAGES IN ALL FIRST-CLASS MATCHES FOR YORKSHIRE (Continued)

Player	Date of Birth	Date of Death (if known)	First Played	Last Played	M	Inns	NO	Runs	HS	Av'ge	100s	Runs	Wks	Av'ge	Ct/St
Bresnan, T T ....©	Feb 28, 1985		2003	2016	135	186	32	4,736	169*	30.75	5	11,498	374	30.74	70
Britton, G	Feb 7, 1843	Jan 3, 1910	1867	1867	1	1	0	3	3	1.50	0	—	—	—	0
Broadbent, A	June 7, 1879	July 19, 1958	1909	1910	3	5	0	66	29	13.20	0	252	5	50.40	1
Broadhead, W B	May 31, 1903	Apr 2, 1986	1929	1929	2	2	0	5	5	2.50	0	—	—	—	1
Broadhurst, M	June 20, 1974		1991	1994	5	3	0	7	6	2.33	0	231	7	33.00	0
Brook, H C	Feb 22, 1999		2016	2016	1	1	0	0	0	0.00	0	—	—	—	0
Brook, J W	Feb 1, 1897		1923	1923	1	2	0	0	0	0.00	0	—	—	—	0
Brooke, B	Mar 3, 1930	Mar.3 1989	1950	1950	2	4	0	16	14	4.00	0	191	2	95.50	0
§ Brooks J A ....©	June 4, 1984		2013	2016	60	69	27	748	50*	17.80	0	6,046	242	24.98	18
§ Brophy, G L ....©	Nov 26, 1975		2006	2012	73	112	12	3,012	177*	30.12	3	6	0	—	176/15
Broughton, P N	Oct 22, 1935		1956	1956	6	5	2	19	12	6.33	0	—	—	—	1
Brown, A	June 10, 1854	Nov 2, 1900	1872	1872	2	2	0	9	5	3.00	0	47	3	15.66	4
Brown, J T (Driffield) ©	Aug 20, 1869	Nov 4, 1904	1889	1904	345	567	41	15,694	311	29.83	23	5,183	177	29.28	188
Brown, J T (Darfield) ©	Nov 24, 1874	Apr 12, 1950	1897	1903	30	32	3	333	37*	11.48	0	2,071	97	21.35	18
Brown, W	Nov 19, 1876	July 27, 1945	1902	1908	2	2	0	2	2	2.00	0	84	4	21.00	0
Brownhill, T	Oct 10, 1838	Jan 6, 1915	1861	1871	14	20	3	185	25	10.88	0	—	—	—	7
Brumfitt, J *	Feb. 18, 1917	Mar 16, 1987	1938	1938	1	1	0	9	9	9.00	0	—	—	—	0
Buller, J S	Aug 23, 1909	Aug 7, 1970	1930	1930	1	2	0	5	3	2.50	0	—	—	—	2
Bulmer, J R L	Dec 28, 1867	Jan 20, 1917	1891	1891	1	2	1	0	0*	0.00	0	—	—	—	2
Burgess, T	Feb 15, 1859	Jan 20, 1922	1895	1895	1	2	0	0	0*	0.00	0	79	1	79.00	0
Burgin, E	Jan 4, 1924	Nov 11, 2012	1952	1953	12	10	3	92	32	13.14	0	795	31	25.64	2
Burman, C	Oct 5, 1838	May 14, 1900	1867	1867	1	2	1	1	1*	1.00	0	—	—	—	0
Burnet, J R * ....©	Oct 11, 1918	Mar 6, 1999	1958	1959	54	75	6	889	54	12.88	0	26	1	26.00	7
§ Burrows, M	Aug 18, 1855	May 29, 1893	1880	1880	6	10	0	82	23	8.20	0	—	—	—	2
Burton, D C F * ....©	Sept 13, 1887	Sept 24, 1971	1907	1921	104	130	15	2,273	142*	19.76	2	—	—	—	44
Burton, R C *	Apr 11, 1891	Apr 30, 1971	1914	1914	2	2	0	47	47	23.50	0	73	6	12.16	2
Butterfield, E B *	Oct 22, 1848	May 6, 1899	1870	1870	1	2	0	18	10	9.00	0	—	—	—	0
Byas, D ....©	Aug 26, 1963		1986	2001	268	449	42	14,398	213	35.37	28	727	12	60.58	351
Byrom, J L *	July, 20, 1851	Aug 24, 1931	1874	1874	2	4	0	19	11	4.75	0	—	—	—	1
Callis, E	Nov 8, 1994		2016	2016	1	2	1	114	84	114.00	0	—	—	—	1

LIST OF PLAYERS AND CAREER AVERAGES IN ALL FIRST-CLASS MATCHES FOR YORKSHIRE (Continued)

Player	Date of Birth	Date of Death (if known)	First Played	Last Played	M	Inns	NO	Runs	HS	Av'ge	100s	Runs	Wkts	Av'ge	Ct/St
Cammish, J W	May 21, 1921	July 16, 1974	1954	1954	2	2	0	0	0	0.00	0	155	3	51.66	0
Carrick, P	© July, 16 1952		1970	1993	425	543	102	9,994	131*	22.66	3	30,530	1,018	29.99	183
Carter, Rev E S *	Feb 3, 1845	May 23, 1923	1876	1881	14	21	2	210	39*	11.05	0	104	8	13.00	4
Carter, W H	June 20, 1861	Jan 16, 1935	1891	1891	3	6	0	57	49	9.50	0	—	—	—	0
Carver, K	**Mar 26, 1996**		**2014**	**2016**	**5**	**7**	**4**	**59**	**16**	**19.66**	**0**	**425**	**14**	**30.35**	**2**
Cawthray, G	Sept 28, 1913	Jan 5, 2001	1939	1952	4	6	0	114	30	19.00	0	304	4	76.00	1
Chadwick, J P G	Nov 8, 1934		1960	1965	6	9	3	106	59	17.66	0	67	2	33.50	7
Champion, A	Dec 27, 1851	June 26, 1909	1876	1879	14	23	4	148	29	7.78	0	17	1	17.00	7
Chapman, C A	June 8, 1971		1990	1998	8	13	2	238	80	21.63	0	—	—	—	13/3
Charlesworth, A P	Feb 19, 1865	May 11, 1926	1894	1895	7	12	1	241	63	21.90	0	—	—	—	2
§ Chichester															
Constable, R C J *	Dec 21, 1890	May 26, 1963	1919	1919	1	1	0	0	0	0.00	0	6	0	—	0
Clarkson, A	Sept 5, 1939		1963	1963	6	8	1	80	30	11.42	0	92	5	18.40	5
§ Claughton, H M	Dec 24, 1891	Oct 17, 1980	1914	1919	4	6	0	39	15	6.50	0	176	3	58.66	1
§ Clayton, R O	Nov 25, 1982	Nov 26, 1901	1870	1879	3	2	0	38	38	19.00	0	263	3	87.66	0
§ Cleary, M F	July 19, 1980		2005	2005	70	115	23	992	62	10.78	0	2,478	153	16.19	26
Clegg, H	Dec 8, 1850	Dec 30, 1920	1881	1881	2	2	0	23	12	11.50	0	250	8	31.25	0
Clifford, C C	July 5, 1942		1972	1972	6	8	1	63	25*	9.00	0	666	26	25.61	2
Close, D B	© Feb 24, 1931	Sept 14, 2015	1949	1970	536	811	102	22,650	198	31.94	33	23,489	967	24.29	564
Clough, G D	May 23, 1978		1998	1998	2	2	0	34	33	17.00	0	11	—	—	0
Coad, B O	**Jan 10, 1994**		**2016**	**2016**	**2**	**3**	**1**	**18**	**17***	**18.00**	**0**	**108**	**1**	**108.00**	**0**
Collinson, R W *	Nov 6, 1875	Dec 26, 1963	1897	1897	2	3	0	58	34	19.33	0	—	—	—	0
Cooper, H P	Apr 17, 1949		1971	1980	98	107	29	1,159	56	14.85	0	6,327	227	27.87	60
Cooper, P E *	Feb 1885	May 21, 1950	1910	1910	1	1	0	0	0	0.00	0	—	—	—	0
Cope, G A	© Feb 23, 1947		1966	1980	230	249	89	2,241	78	14.00	0	15,627	630	24.80	64
Corbett, A M	Nov 25, 1855	Oct 7, 1934	1881	1881	1	2	0	0	0	0.00	0	—	—	—	0
Coverdale, S P	Nov 25, 1954		1973	1980	6	4	0	31	18	7.75	0	—	—	—	11/4
Coverdale, W *	July 8, 1862	Sept 23, 1934	1888	1888	2	2	0	2	1	1.00	0	—	—	—	2
Cowan, M J	© June 10, 1933		1953	1962	91	84	48	170	19*	4.72	0	6,389	266	24.01	37

LIST OF PLAYERS AND CAREER AVERAGES IN ALL FIRST-CLASS MATCHES FOR YORKSHIRE (Continued)

Player	Date of Birth	Date of Death (if known)	First Played	Last Played	M	Inns	NO	Runs	HS	Av'ge	100s	Runs	Wkts	Av'ge	Ct/St
Cownley, J M	Feb 24, 1929	Nov 7, 1998	1952	1952	2	2	—	19	19	19.00	0	119	1	119.00	0
Coxon, A ......©	Jan 18, 1916	Jan 22, 2006	1945	1950	142	182	33	2,747	83	18.43	0	9,528	464	20.53	124
Craven, V J	July 31, 1980		2000	2004	33	55	6	1,206	81*	24.61	0	584	15	38.93	18
Crawford, G H	Dec 15, 1890	June 28, 1975	1914	1926	9	8	2	46	21	5.75	0	541	21	25.76	3
Crawford, M G *	July 30, 1920	Dec 2, 2012	1951	1951	1	1	0	22	13	11.00	0	—	—	—	1
Creighton, E	July 9, 1859	Feb 17, 1931	1888	1888	4	8	2	33	10	5.50	0	—	—	—	—
Crick, H	Jan 29, 1910	Feb 10, 1960	1937	1947	8	10	0	88	20	8.80	0	181	10	18.10	18/4
Crookes, R	Oct 9, 1846	Feb 15, 1897	1879	1879	1	2	1	2	2*	2.00	0	—	0	—	—
Crossland, S M	Aug 16, 1851	April 11, 1906	1883	1886	4	6	2	32	20	8.00	0	14	0	—	3/5
Crowther, A	Aug 1, 1878		1905	1905	1	2	0	0	0	0.00	0	—	—	—	0
Cuttell, W	Jan 28, 1835	June 10, 1896	1862	1871	15	27	6	271	56	12.90	0	596	36	16.55	4
Dalton, A J	Mar 14, 1947		1969	1972	21	31	1	710	128	24.48	3	—	—	—	6
§ Darnton, T	Feb 12, 1836	Oct 18, 1874	1864	1868	13	22	1	314	81*	14.95	0	349	12	29.08	3
Davidson, K R	Dec 24, 1905	Dec 25, 1954	1933	1935	30	46	5	1,331	128	32.46	2	—	—	—	18
Dawes, J	Feb 14, 1836	Not known	1865	1865	5	9	3	93	28*	13.28	0	196	5	39.20	3
Dawood, I	July 23, 1976		2004	2005	20	31	7	636	75	26.50	0	—	—	—	46/3
Dawson, E	May 1, 1835	Dec 1, 1888	1863	1874	16	25	2	224	20	9.33	0	—	—	—	5
Dawson, R K J ......©	Aug 4, 1980		2001	2006	72	106	9	2,179	87	22.46	0	6,444	157	41.04	39
Dawson, W A *	Dec 3, 1850	Mar 6, 1916	1870	1870	1	2	0	2	2*	0.00	0	—	—	—	1
Day, A G *	Sept 20, 1865	Oct 16, 1908	1885	1888	6	10	0	78	25	7.80	0	—	0	—	3
Dennis, F ......©	June 11, 1907	Nov 21, 2000	1928	1933	89	100	28	1,332	67	18.50	0	4,517	156	28.95	58
Dennis, S J ......©	Oct 18, 1960		1980	1988	67	62	24	338	53*	8.89	0	5,548	173	32.06	19
Denton, D ......©	July 4, 1874	June 16, 1950	1894	1920	676	1,058	61	33,282	221	33.38	61	957	34	28.14	360/1
Denton, J	Feb 3, 1865	July 19, 1946	1887	1888	15	24	1	222	59	9.65	0	—	—	—	6
Dewse, H	Feb 23, 1836	July 8, 1910	1873	1873	1	2	0	14	12	7.00	0	15	0	—	1
Deyes, G	Feb 11, 1879	Jan 11, 1963	1905	1907	17	24	4	44	12	2.20	0	944	41	23.02	6
Dick, R D *	Apr 16, 1889	Dec 14, 1983	1911	1911	1	1	0	2	2	2.00	0	37	2	18.50	1
Dobson, M J	Feb 22, 1854	Sept 17, 1932	1879	1879	2	3	0	1	1	0.33	0	—	—	—	—
Doidge, M J	July 2, 1970		1990	1990	1	—	—	—	—	—	0	106	0	—	0
Dolphin, A ......©	Dec 24, 1885	Oct 23, 1942	1905	1927	427	446	157	3,325	66	11.50	0	28	1	28.00	569/260

LIST OF PLAYERS AND CAREER AVERAGES IN ALL FIRST-CLASS MATCHES FOR YORKSHIRE (Continued)

Player	Date of Birth	Date of Death (if known)	First Played	Last Played	M	Inns	NO	Runs	HS	Av'ge	100s	Runs	Wkts	Av'ge	Ct/St
Douglas, J S	Apr 4, 1903	Dec 27, 1971	1925	1934	23	26	8	125	19	6.94	0	1,310	49	26.73	14
Drake, A ©	Apr 16, 1884	Feb 14, 1919	1909	1914	156	244	24	4,789	147*	21.76	3	8,623	479	18.00	93
Drake, J	Sept 1, 1893	May 22, 1967	1923	1924	3	4	1	21	10	7.00	0	117	1	117.00	2
Driver, J	May 16, 1861	Dec 10, 1946	1889	1889	2	4	1	24	8	8.00	0	—	—	—	2
Dury, T S *	June 12, 1854	May 1, 1881	1878	1881	13	24	1	329	46	14.30	0	21	0	—	3
Dyson, W L	Dec 11, 1857	May 1, 1936	1887	1887	2	4	0	8	6	2.00	0	—	—	—	2
Earnshaw, D	Sept 20, 1867	Nov 24, 1941	1893	1896	6	7	3	44	23	11.00	0	349	11	31.72	6/2
Eastwood, D	Mar 30, 1848	May 17, 1903	1870	1877	29	51	2	591	68	12.06	0	62	0	—	16
Eckersley, R	Sept 4, 1925	May 30, 2009	1945	1945	1	1	1	9	9*	—	0	—	—	—	0
Elam, F W *	Sept 13, 1871	Mar 19, 1943	1900	1902	9	3	1	48	28	24.00	0	77	1	77.00	7
§ Elliott, M T G	Sept 28, 1971		2002	2002	5	10	1	487	127	54.11	1	—	—	—	—
Ellis, J E	Nov 10, 1864	Dec 1, 1927	1888	1892	11	15	6	14	4*	1.55	0	28	1	28.00	11/10
Ellis, S *	Nov 23, 1851	Oct 28, 1930	1880	1880	2	2	2	12	9*	—	0	—	—	—	—
Elms, J E	Dec 24, 1874	Nov 1, 1951	1905	1905	1	2	0	20	20	10.00	0	—	—	—	1
Elstub, C J	Feb 3, 1981		2000	2002	6	7	6	28	18*	28.00	0	356	9	39.55	2
Emmett, T ©	Sept 3, 1841	June 29, 1904	1866	1888	299	484	65	6,315	104	15.07	1	15,465	1,216	12.71	179
Farrar, A	Apr 29, 1884	Dec 25, 1954	1906	1906	1	1	0	2	2	2.00	0	133	6	22.16	1
Fearnley, M C	Aug 21, 1936	July 7, 1979	1962	1964	3	4	2	19	11*	9.50	0	12	0	—	0
Featherby, W D	Aug 18, 1888	Nov 20, 1958	1920	1920	2	—	—	—	—	—	—	—	—	—	—
Fellows, G M	July 30, 1978		1998	2003	46	71	6	1,526	109	23.47	1	1,202	32	37.56	23
Fiddling, K	Oct 13, 1917	June 19, 1992	1938	1946	18	24	6	182	25	10.11	0	—	—	—	24/13
§ Finch, A J ©	Nov 27, 1986		2014	2015	8	10	1	415	110	46.11	1	40	1	40.00	11
Firth, A *	Sept 3, 1847	Jan 16, 1927	1869	1869	1	1	0	4	4	4.00	0	—	—	—	0
Firth, Rev E B *	Apr 11, 1863	July 25, 1905	1894	1894	1	1	0	1	1	1.00	0	—	—	—	0
Firth, J	June 27, 1918	Sept 7, 1981	1949	1950	8	4	1	134	67*	44.66	0	—	—	—	14/2
Fisher, H ©	Aug 3, 1903	Apr 16, 1974	1928	1936	52	58	14	681	76*	15.47	0	2,621	93	28.18	22
Fisher, I D	Mar 31, 1976		1996	2001	24	32	9	545	68*	23.69	0	1,382	43	32.13	1
Fisher, M D	**Nov 9, 1997**		**2015**	**2015**	**3**	**3**	**2**	**0**	**0***	**0.00**	**0**	**243**	**5**	**48.60**	**1**
Flaxington, S	Oct 14, 1860	Mar 10, 1895	1882	1882	4	8	0	121	57	15.12	0	—	—	—	—
§ Fleming, S P ©	Apr 1, 1973		2003	2003	7	14	2	469	98	39.08	0	—	—	—	13

LIST OF PLAYERS AND CAREER AVERAGES IN ALL FIRST-CLASS MATCHES FOR YORKSHIRE (Continued)

Player	Date of Birth	Date of Death (if known)	First Played	Last Played	M	Inns	NO	Runs	HS	Av'ge	100s	Runs	Wkts	Av'ge	Ct/St
Fletcher, S D	© June 8, 1964		1983	1991	107	91	31	410	28*	6.90	0	7,966	234	34.04	25
Fletcher, W	Feb 16, 1866	June 1, 1935	1892	1892	5	8	1	31*	31*	11.42	0	157	7	22.42	4
Foord, C W	June 11, 1924	July 8, 2015	1947	1953	51	34	16	114	35	6.33	0	3,412	126	27.07	19
Foster, I	Nov 23, 1873	April 16, 1956	1901	1901	1	1	0	2	2	2.00	0	27	—	—	0
Foster, M J	Sept 17, 1972		1993	1994	5	7	1	165	63*	27.50	0	156	6	25.00	6
§ Foster, T W	Nov 12, 1871	Jan 31, 1947	1894	1895	14	20	5	138	25	9.20	0	952	58	16.41	6
Frank, J *	Dec 17, 1857	Oct 22, 1940	1881	1881	1	2	0	10	7	5.00	0	17	1	17.00	3
Frank, R W *	© May 29, 1864	Sept 9, 1950	1889	1903	18	28	4	298	58	12.41	0	9	—	—	8
Freeman, G	July 27, 1843	Nov 18, 1895	1865	1880	32	54	2	752	53	14.46	0	2,079	209	9.94	16
Gale, A W	© Nov 28, 1983		2004	2016	149	235	17	7,726	272	35.44	19	238	1	238.00	46
Geldart, C J	Dec 17, 1991		2010	2011	2	2	0	51	34	25.50	0	—	—	—	1
Gibb, P A *	July 11, 1913	Dec 7, 1977	1935	1946	36	54	1	1,545	157*	32.87	2	82	3	27.33	25/8
Gibson, B P **	Mar 31, 1996		2011	2011	1	1	0	1	1*	1.00	0	—	—	—	6/0
Gibson, R	**Jan 22, 1996**		**2016**	**2016**	**1**	**1**	**0**	**0**	**0**	**0.00**	**0**	**42**	**1**	**42.00**	**0**
§ Gifkins, C J *	Feb 19, 1856	Jan 31, 1897	1880	1880	2	3	0	30	23	10.00	0	—	—	—	1
Gilbert, C R	Apr 16, 1984		2007	2007	1	2	0	64	64	64.00	0	11	0	—	1
Gill, F	Sept 3, 1883	Nov 1, 1917	1906	1906	2	4	0	18	11	4.50	0	—	—	—	1
§ Gillespie, J N	© April 19, 1975		2006	2007	26	34	11	640	123*	27.82	1	2,013	59	34.11	4
Gillhouley, K	Aug 8, 1934		1961	1961	24	31	7	323	56*	13.45	0	1,702	77	22.10	16
Gough, D	© Sept 18, 1970		1989	2008	146	188	29	2,922	121	18.37	1	12,487	453	27.56	30
Goulder, A	Aug 16, 1907	June 11, 1986	1929	1929	2	1	0	3	3	3.00	0	—	—	—	0
§ Gray, A K D	May 19, 1974		2001	2004	18	26	3	649	104	28.21	0	1,357	30	45.23	16
Grayson, A P	Mar 31, 1971		1990	1995	52	80	10	1,958	100	27.97	1	846	13	65.07	36
Greenwood, A	Aug 20, 1847	Feb 12, 1889	1869	1880	95	166	12	2,762	91	17.93	0	9	0	—	33
Greenwood, F E *	© Sept 28, 1905	July 30, 1963	1929	1932	57	66	8	1,458	104*	25.13	1	36	2	18.00	37
Greenwood, I	July 13, 1834	Nov 1, 1909	1861	1874	50	84	12	885	83	12.29	0	1,615	85	19.00	24
Grimshaw, C H	May 12, 1880	Sept 25, 1947	1904	1908	54	75	14	1,219	85	17.92	0	221	7	31.57	42
Grimshaw, I	May 4, 1857	Jan 18, 1911	1880	1887	125	194	14	3,354	129*	18.63	4				76/3

356

** At 15 years and 27 days on April 27, 2011, First Day of Yorkshire's match v. Durham MCCU, he became the youngest ever English First Class cricketer.

LIST OF PLAYERS AND CAREER AVERAGES IN ALL FIRST-CLASS MATCHES FOR YORKSHIRE (Continued)

Player	Date of Birth	Date of Death (if known)	First Played	Last Played	M	Inns	NO	Runs	HS	Av'ge	100s	Runs	Wkts	Av'ge	Ct/St
Guy S M	Nov 17, 1978		2000	2011	37	52	6	742	52*	16.13	0	8	0	—	98/12
Haggas, S	Apr 18, 1856	Mar 14, 1926	1878	1882	31	47	3	478	43	10.86	0	—	—	—	10
◎ Haigh, S	Mar 19, 1871	Feb 27, 1921	1895	1913	513	687	110	10,993	159	19.05	4	29,289	1,876	15.61	276
Hall, B	Sept 16, 1929	Feb 27, 1989	1952	1952	2	2	0	14	10	7.00	0	55	1	55.00	1
Hall, C H	Apr 5, 1906	Dec 11, 1976	1928	1934	23	22	9	67	15*	5.15	0	1,226	45	27.24	11
§ Hall, J	Nov 11, 1815	Apr 17, 1888	1844	1863	1	2	0	4	3	2.00	0	—	—	—	2
Hall, L	Nov 1, 1852	Nov 19, 1915	1873	1894	275	477	58	9,757	160	23.28	9	781	15	52.06	173
◎ Halliday, H	Feb 9, 1920	Aug 27, 1967	1938	1953	182	279	18	8,361	144	32.03	12	3,119	101	30.88	140
Halliday, C	Dec 5, 1852	Mar 23, 1929	1872	1872	3	5	0	27	17	5.40	0	—	—	—	2
Hamer, A	Dec 8, 1916	Nov 3, 1993	1938	1938	2	2	0	3	3	1.50	0	64	1	64.00	2
§ Hamilton, G M	Sept 16, 1974		1994	2003	73	108	18	2,228	125	24.75	1	5,479	222	24.68	25
Hampshire, A W	Oct 18, 1950		1975	1975	1	2	0	18	17	9.00	0	—	—	—	1
Hampshire, J	Oct 5, 1913	May 23, 1997	1937	1937	3	2	0	5	5	2.50	0	109	5	21.80	1
◎ Hampshire, J H	Feb 10, 1941		1961	1981	456	724	89	21,979	183*	34.61	34	1,108	24	46.16	368
Hannon-Dalby, O J	Jun 20, 1989		2008	2012	24	25	10	45	11*	3.00	0	1,938	43	45.06	7
§ Harbord, W E *	Dec 15, 1908	July 28, 1992	1929	1935	16	21	1	411	69	20.55	0	—	—	—	7
Harden, R J	Aug 16, 1965		1999	2000	12	22	3	439	84	23.10	0	—	—	—	2
◎ Hardisty, C H	Dec 10, 1885	Mar 2, 1968	1906	1909	38	55	5	991	84	19.82	0	51	1	—	18
Hargreaves, H S	Mar 22, 1913	Sept 29, 1990	1934	1938	18	20	6	51	9	3.64	0	1,145	55	20.81	3
§ Harmison, S J	Oct 23, 1978		2012	2012	3	3	0	25	23	8.33	0	195	8	24.37	1
Harris, W	Nov 21, 1861	May 23, 1923	1884	1887	4	8	2	45	25	7.50	0	18	0	—	1
◎ Harrison, G P	Feb 11, 1862	Sept 14, 1940	1883	1892	59	87	26	407	28	6.67	0	3,276	226	14.49	36
Harrison, H	Jan 26, 1885	Feb 11, 1962	1907	1907	2	1	1	4	4*	—	0	39	2	19.50	1
Harrison, W H	May 27, 1863	July 15, 1939	1888	1888	3	6	1	12	7	2.40	0	—	—	—	0
Hart, H W *	Sept 21, 1859	Nov 2, 1895	1888	1888	1	2	0	6	6	3.00	0	32	2	16.00	0
Hart, P R	Jan 12, 1947		1981	1981	3	5	0	23	11	4.60	0	140	2	70.00	1
Hartington, H E	Sept 18, 1881	Feb 16, 1950	1910	1911	10	10	4	51	16	8.50	0	764	23	33.21	2
◎ Hartley, P J	Apr 18, 1960		1985	1997	195	237	51	3,844	127*	20.66	2	17,438	579	30.11	60
◎ Hartley, S N	Mar 18, 1956		1978	1988	133	199	27	4,193	114	24.37	2	2,052	42	48.85	47
§ Harvey, I J	Apr 10, 1972		2004	2005	20	31	2	1,045	209*	36.03	2	831	37	22.45	12

LIST OF PLAYERS AND CAREER AVERAGES IN ALL FIRST-CLASS MATCHES FOR YORKSHIRE (Continued)

Player	Date of Birth	Date of Death (if known)	First Played	Last Played	M	Inns	NO	Runs	HS	Av'ge	100s	Runs	Wkts	Av'ge	Ct/St
Hatton, A G	Mar 25, 1937		1960	1961	1	1	—	4	4*	—	0	202	6	33.66	—
§ Hawke, Lord *	© Aug 16, 1860	Oct 10, 1938	1881	1911	510	739	91	13,133	166	20.26	10	16	0	—	159
Hayley, H	Feb 22, 1860	June 3, 1922	1884	1898	7	12	1	122	24	11.09	0	48	0	—	3
Haywood, W J	Feb 25, 1841	Jan 7, 1912	1878	1878	1	2	0	7	7	3.50	0	14	1	14.00	—
§ Head, T M	**Dec 29, 1993**		**2016**	**2016**	**1**	**2**	**0**	**56**	**54**	**28.00**	**0**	**16**	**0**	**—**	**0**
Hicks, J	Dec 10, 1850	June 10, 1912	1872	1876	15	25	3	313	66	14.22	0	17	0	—	12
Higgins, J	Mar 13, 1877	July 19, 1954	1901	1905	9	14	5	93	28*	10.33	0	—	—	—	10/3
Hill, A	Nov 14, 1843	Aug 29, 1910	1871	1882	140	223	25	1,705	49	8.61	0	7,002	542	12.91	91
Hill, H *	Nov 29, 1858	Aug 14, 1935	1888	1891	14	27	2	337	34	13.48	0	—	—	—	10
Hill, L G *	Nov 2, 1860	Aug 27, 1940	1882	1882	1	2	0	13	8	6.50	0	—	—	—	1
Hirst, E T *	May 6, 1857	Oct 26, 1914	1877	1888	21	33	2	328	87*	10.58	0	—	—	—	7
Hirst, E W *	Feb 27, 1855	Oct 24, 1933	1881	1881	2	3	0	33	28	11.00	0	3	0	—	0
Hirst, G H	© Sept 7, 1871	May 10, 1954	1891	1921*	717	1,050	128	32,024	341	34.73	56	44,716	2,481	18.02	518
Hirst, T H	May 21, 1865	Apr 3, 1927	1899	1899	1	1	0	5	5*	—	0	27	0	—	0
§ Hodd A J	**© Jan 12, 1984**		**2012**	**2016**	**41**	**53**	**8**	**1,192**	**96***	**26.48**	**0**	**14**	**0**	**—**	**114/10**
Hodgson, D M	Feb 26, 1990		2014	2015	2	3	0	72	35	24.00	0	—	—	—	2
Hodgson, G	July 24, 1938		1964	1964	1	1	0	4	4	4.00	0	—	—	—	0/2
Hodgson, I	Nov 15, 1828	Nov 24, 1867	1855	1866	21	35	14	164	21*	7.80	0	1,537	88	17.46	11
Hodgson, L J	Jun 29, 1986		2009	2010	3	2	2	99	34	33.00	0	158	2	79.00	1
Hodgson, P	Sept 21, 1935	Mar 30, 2015	1954	1956	13	6	2	33	8*	8.25	0	648	22	29.45	6
Hoggard, M J	© Dec 31, 1976		1996	2009	102	120	34	956	89*	11.11	0	8,956	331	27.05	23
Holdsworth, W E N	Sept 17, 1928		1952	1953	27	26	12	111	22*	7.92	0	1,598	53	30.15	7
Holgate, G	June 23, 1839	July 11, 1895	1865	1867	12	19	0	174	38	9.15	0	—	—	—	17/1
Holmes, P	Nov 25, 1886	Sept 3, 1971	1913	1933	485	699	74	26,220	315*	41.95	60	124	1	124.00	319
Horner, N F	May 10, 1926	Dec 24, 2003	1950	1950	2	4	1	114	43	28.50	0	—	—	—	2
Houseman I J	Oct 12, 1969		1989	1991	5	2	2	18	18	18.00	0	311	3	103.66	2
Hoyle, T H	Mar 19, 1884	June 2, 1953	1919	1919	1	2	0	7	5	3.50	0	—	—	—	0/1
Hudson, B	June 29, 1852	Nov 11, 1901	1880	1880	3	4	0	13	5	3.25	0	—	—	—	0
Hunter, D	© Feb 23, 1860	Jan 11, 1927	1888	1909	517	681	323	4,177	58*	11.66	0	43	0	—	863/323
Hunter, J	Aug 3, 1855	Jan 4, 1891	1878	1888	143	213	61	1,183	60*	7.78	0	—	—	—	207/102

LIST OF PLAYERS AND CAREER AVERAGES IN ALL FIRST-CLASS MATCHES FOR YORKSHIRE (Continued)

Player	Date of Birth	Date of Death (if known)	First Played	Last Played	M	Inns	NO	Runs	HS	Av'ge	100s	Runs	Wkts	Av'ge	Ct/St
Hutchison, P M ...... ©	June 9, 1977		1996	2001	39	39	23	187	30	11.68	0	3,244	143	22.68	8
Hutton, L ...... ©	June 23, 1916	Sept, 6, 1990	1934	1955	341	527	62	24,807	280*	53.34	85	4,221	154	27.40	278
Hutton, R A ...... ©	Sept 6, 1942		1962	1974	208	292	45	4,986	189	20.18	4	10,254	468	21.91	160
Iddison, R	Sept 15, 1834	Mar 19, 1890	1855	1876	72	108	15	1,916	112	20.60	0	1,540	102	15.09	70
Illingworth, R ...... ©	June 8, 1932		1951	1983	496	668	131	14,986	162	27.90	14	26,806	1,431	18.73	286
§ Imran Tahir	Mar 27, 1979		2007	2007	1	2	0	5	5	2.50	0	141	0	—	0
Ingham, P G	Sept 28, 1956		1979	1981	8	14	0	290	64	20.71	0	—	—	—	0
Inglis, J W	Oct 19, 1979		2000	2000	1	2	0	4	2	2.00	0	—	—	—	0
§ Inzamam-ul-Haq	Mar 3, 1970		2007	2007	3	4	0	89	51	22.25	0	—	—	—	5
Jackson, Hon F S * ...... ©	Nov 21, 1870	Mar 9, 1947	1890	1907	207	328	22	10,371	160	33.89	21	9,690	506	19.15	129
Jackson, S R *	Jan 15, 1859	July 19, 1941	1891	1891	1	2	0	9	9	4.50	0	—	—	—	0
Jacques, T A	Feb 19, 1905	Feb 23, 1995	1927	1936	28	20	7	162	35*	12.46	0	1,786	57	31.33	12
Jakeman, F	Jan 10, 1920	May 18, 1986	1946	1947	10	16	2	262	51	18.71	0	—	—	—	3
James, B	Apr 23, 1934	May 1999	1954	1954	4	5	3	22	11*	11.00	0	228	8	28.50	0
§ Jaques, P A ...... ©	May 3, 1979		2004	2013	53	82	3	4,039	243	51.12	11	112	1	112.00	46
Jarvis, P W	June 29, 1965		1981	1993	138	160	46	1,898	80	16.64	0	11,990	449	26.70	36
Johnson, C	Sept 5, 1947		1969	1979	100	152	14	2,960	107	21.44	2	265	4	66.25	50
Johnson, J	May 16, 1916	Jan 16, 2011	1936	1939	3	3	1	5	4*	5.00	0	27	5	5.40	1
Johnson, M	Apr 23, 1958		1981	1981	4	4	2	2	2	1.00	0	301	7	43.00	1
Joy, J	Sept 29, 1826	Sept 27, 1889	1849	1867	3	5	0	107	74	21.40	0	5	0	—	3
Judson, A	July 10, 1885	Apr 8, 1975	1920	1920	1	—	—	—	—	—	—	5	0	—	0
§ Katich, S M	Aug 21, 1975		2002	2002	1	2	0	37	21	18.50	0	25	0	—	1
Kaye, Harold S *	May 9, 1882	Nov 6, 1953	1907	1908	18	25	1	243	37	10.12	0	—	—	—	9
Kaye, Haven	June 11, 1846	Jan 24, 1892	1872	1873	8	14	0	117	33	8.35	0	—	—	—	3
Keedy, G ...... ©	Nov 27, 1974		1994	1994	1	1	1	1	1*	1.00	0	—	—	—	0
§ Keighley, W G *	Jan 10, 1925	June 14, 2005	1947	1951	35	51	5	1,227	110	26.67	1	18	0	—	12
Kellett, S A	Oct 16, 1967		1989	1995	86	147	10	4,204	125*	30.68	7	7	0	—	74
Kennie, C	May 17, 1904		1927	1927	1	2	0	6	6	3.00	0	—	—	—	1
Ketleborough, R A	Mar 15, 1973	Apr 11, 1994	1994	1997	13	19	2	446	108	26.23	1	153	3	51.00	9

Player	Date of Birth	Date of Death (if known)	First Played	Last Played	M	Inns	NO	Runs	HS	Av'ge	100s	Runs	Wkts	Av'ge	Ct/St
Kilburn, S	Oct 16, 1868	Sept 25, 1940	1896	1896	1	1	0	8	8	8.00	0	—	—	—	0
Kilner, N	July 21, 1895	Apr 28, 1979	1919	1923	69	73	7	1,253	112	18.98	2	—	—	—	34
Kilner, R	Oct 17, 1890	Apr 5, 1928	1911	1927	365	478	46	13,018	206*	30.13	15	14,855	857	17.33	231
King, A M	Oct 8, 1932		1955	1955	1	1	0	12	12	12.00	0	—	—	—	0
Kippax, P J	Oct 15, 1940		1961	1962	4	7	2	37	9	7.40	0	279	8	34.87	0
§ Kirby, S P	Oct 4, 1977	⊙	2001	2004	47	61	14	342	57	7.27	0	5,143	182	28.25	11
§ Kruis, G J	May 9, 1974	⊙	2005	2009	54	64	31	617	50*	18.69	0	5,431	154	35.26	11
§ Lambert, G A	Jan 4, 1980		2000	2000	2	3	2	6	3*	6.00	0	133	4	33.25	1
Lancaster, W W	Feb 4, 1873	Dec 30, 1938	1895	1895	2	3	0	163	51	16.30	0	29	0	—	1
§ Landon, C W *	May 30, 1850	Mar 5, 1903	1878	1882	7	13	0	51	18	3.92	0	74	0	—	7
§ Law, W *	Apr 9, 1851	Dec 20, 1892	1871	1873	4	7	0	51	22	7.28	0	—	—	—	3
Lawson, M A K	Oct 24, 1985	⊙	2004	2007	15	21	5	197	44	12.31	0	1,699	42	40.45	7
Leadbeater, B	Aug 14, 1943	⊙	1966	1979	81	236	27	5,247	140*	25.10	1	5	—	5.00	80
Leadbeater, E	Aug 15, 1927	Apr 17, 2011	1949	1956	81	94	29	898	91	13.81	0	5,657	201	28.14	49
Leadbeater, H *	Dec 31, 1863	Oct 9, 1928	1884	1890	6	10	2	141	65	17.62	0	11	0	—	4
§ Leaning, J A	Oct 18, 1993	⊙	2013	2016	40	63	7	1,751	123	31.26	3	244	3	81.33	33
Leatham, G A B *	Apr 30, 1851	June 19, 1932	1874	1886	12	18	5	61	14	4.69	0	—	—	—	21/7
Leather, R S *	Aug 17, 1880	Jan 3, 1913	1906	1906	1	2	0	19	14	9.50	0	—	—	—	0
Lee, C	Mar 17, 1924	Sept 4, 1999	1952	1952	2	4	0	98	74	24.50	0	—	—	—	2
Lee, F	Nov 18, 1856	Sept 13, 1896	1882	1890	105	182	10	3,622	165	21.05	3	—	—	—	53/1
Lee, G H	Aug 24, 1854	Oct 4, 1919	1879	1879	1	2	0	13	9	6.50	0	—	—	—	0
Lee, Herbert	July 2, 1856	Feb 4, 1908	1885	1885	2	3	0	20	12	3.33	0	—	—	—	2
Lee, J E *	Mar 23, 1838	Apr 2, 1880	1867	1867	2	3	0	9	6	3.00	0	—	—	—	0
Lee, J E	Dec 23, 1988		2006	2009	2	3	1	24	21*	12.00	0	149	2	74.50	1
§ Leeds, A Z	Apr 14, 1993		2010	2016	63	106	8	3,847	275*	39.25	9	77	2	38.50	47
Legard, A D *	June 19, 1878	Aug 15, 1939	1910	1910	4	5	0	50	15	10.00	0	26	0	—	1
§ Lehmann, D S	Feb 5, 1970	⊙	1997	2006	88	137	8	8,871	339	68.76	26	1,952	61	32.00	35
§ Lehmann, J S	Jul 8, 1992	⊙	2016	2016	5	8	1	384	116	54.85	1	—	—	—	2
§ Lester, E I	Feb 18, 1923	Mar 23, 2015	1945	1956	228	339	12	10,616	186	34.02	24	160	3	53.33	106
§ Leyland, M	July 20, 1900	Jan 1, 1967	1920	1946	548	720	82	26,180	263	41.03	62	11,079	409	27.08	204

LIST OF PLAYERS AND CAREER AVERAGES IN ALL FIRST-CLASS MATCHES FOR YORKSHIRE (Continued)

Player	Date of Birth	Date of Death (if known)	First Played	Last Played	M	Inns	NO	Runs	HS	Av'ge	100s	Runs	Wks	Av'ge	Ct/St
Lilley, A E	Apr 17, 1992		2011	2011	1	1	0	0	0	0.00	0	34	0	—	0
Linaker, L	Apr 8, 1885	Nov 17, 1961	1909	1909	1	1	0	0	0	0.00	0	28	1	28.00	0
Lister, B	Dec 9, 1850	Dec 3, 1919	1874	1878	7	11	1	36	10	3.60	0	—	—	—	2
§ Lister-Kaye, K A *	Mar 27, 1892	Feb 28, 1955	1928	1928	2	2	1	13	7*	13.00	0	64	1	64.00	2
Lister, J *	May 14, 1930	Jan 28, 1991	1954	1954	2	4	0	35	16	8.75	0	—	—	—	2
Lockwood, E	Apr 4, 1845	Dec 19, 1921	1868	1884	214	364	29	7,789	208	23.25	6	2,265	141	16.06	164/2
Lockwood, H	Oct 20, 1855	Feb 18, 1930	1877	1882	16	27	2	408	90	16.32	0	37	0	—	8
Lodge, J T	Apr 16, 1921	July 9, 2002	1948	1948	2	3	0	48	30	16.00	0	17	0	—	0
Love, J D	Apr 22, 1955		1975	1989	247	388	58	10,263	170*	31.10	13	835	12	69.58	123
Lowe, G E	Jan 12, 1878	Aug 15, 1932	1902	1902	1	1	0	5	5*	5.00	0	—	—	—	1
Lowe J R	Oct 19, 1991		2010	2010											0
Lowson, F A	© July 1, 1925	Sept 8, 1984	1949	1958	252	404	31	13,897	259*	37.25	30	15	0	—	180
§ Loxley-Firth, E *	Mar 7, 1886	Jan 8, 1949	1912	1912	2	4	0	43	37	10.75	0	—	—	—	1
§ Lucas, D S	Aug 19, 1978		2005	2005	2							84	8	10.50	5
Lumb, E *	© Sept 12, 1852	Apr 5, 1891	1872	1886	14	23	4	311	70*	16.36	0	199	5	39.80	43
§ Lumb, M J	© Feb 12, 1980		2000	2006	78	135	12	4,194	144	34.09	8	5	0	—	25
Lumb, R G	© Feb 27, 1950		1970	1984	239	395	30	11,525	165*	31.57	22	88	0	—	129
Lupton, A W *	Feb 23, 1879	Apr 14, 1944	1908	1927	104	79	15	668	43*	10.43	0	—	—	—	25
Lynas, G G	© Sept 7, 1832	Dec 8, 1896	1867	1867	2	3	1	4	4*	2.00	0	—	—	—	2
Lyth, A	**© Sept 25, 1987**		**2007**	**2016**	**119**	**196**	**10**	**7,825**	**251**	**42.06**	**19**	**1,088**	**25**	**43.52**	**154**
Macaulay, G G	Dec 7, 1897	Dec 13, 1940	1920	1935	445	430	112	5,717	125*	17.97	3	30,554	1,774	17.22	361
McGrath, A	© Oct 6, 1975		1995	2012	242	405	29	14,091	211	37.47	34	4,652	128	36.34	168
McHugh, F P	Nov 15, 1925		1949	1949	3	3	0	0	0	0.00	0	147	4	36.75	1
Marshall, A	July 10, 1849	Aug 3, 1891	1874	1874	3	2	0	2	2	1.00	0	11	0	—	0
§ Martyn, D R	Oct 21, 1971		2003	2003	2	3	1	342	238	171.00	2	—	—	—	6
Mason, A	May 2, 1921	Mar, 2006.	1947	1950	18	19	3	105	22	6.56	0	1,473	51	28.88	2
Maude, E *	Dec 31, 1839	July 2, 1876	1866	1866	2	2	0	17	16	8.50	0	—	—	—	6
§ Maxwell, G J	© Oct 14, 1988		2015	2015	2	7	1	244	140	40.66	1	144	4	36.00	3
Metcalfe, A A *	© May 25, 1963		1983	1995	184	317	19	10,465	216*	35.11	25	344	3	114.66	72
Micklethwait, W H *	Dec 13, 1885	Oct 7, 1947	1911	1911	1	1	0	44	44	44.00	0	—	—	—	0

LIST OF PLAYERS AND CAREER AVERAGES IN ALL FIRST-CLASS MATCHES FOR YORKSHIRE (Continued)

Player	Date of Birth	Date of Death (if known)	First Played	Last Played	M	Inns	NO	Runs	HS	Av'ge	100s	Runs	Wkts	Av'ge	Ct/St
Middlebrook, J D	May 13, 1977		1998	2015	29	38	3	534	84	15.25	0	1,899	66	28.77	1
Middlebrook, W	May 23, 1858	Apr 26, 1919	1888	1889	37	27	7	88	19*	4.40	0	895	50	17.90	17
Midgley, C A *	Nov 11, 1877	June 24, 1942	1906	1906	4	6	2	115	59*	28.75	0	149	8	18.62	3
Milburn, S M	Sept 29, 1972		1992	1995	6	8	2	22	7	3.66	0	431	14	30.78	0
§ Milligan, F W *	© Mar 19, 1870	Mar 31, 1900	1894	1898	81	113	10	1,879	74	18.24	0	2,736	112	24.42	40
Mitchell, A	© Sept 13, 1902	Dec 25, 1976	1922	1945	401	550	69	18,189	189	37.81	39	291	5	58.20	406
Mitchell, F *	© Aug 13, 1872	Oct 11, 1935	1894	1904	83	125	5	4,104	194	34.20	10	16	1	16.00	52
Monks, G D	Sept 3, 1929		1952	1952	1	1	0	3	3	3.00	0	—	—	—	1
Moorhouse, R	© Sept 7, 1866	Jan 7, 1921	1888	1899	206	315	45	5,217	113	19.32	3	1,232	43	28.65	92
§ Morkel, M	Oct 6, 1984		2008	2008	1	2	0	8	8	4.00	0	33	1	33.00	0
Morris, A C	Oct 4, 1976		1995	1997	16	23	2	362	60	17.23	0	508	9	56.44	12
Mosley, H	Mar 8, 1852	Nov 29, 1933	1881	1881	2	4	0	1	1	0.25	0	34	3	11.33	1
Mosley, A *	Feb 5, 1858	Sept 28, 1897	1879	1879	2	2	1	10	8*	10.00	0	135	7	19.28	1
Mounsey, J T	© Aug 30, 1871	Apr 6, 1949	1891	1897	92	145	21	1,939	64	15.63	0	444	10	44.40	45
Moxon, M D	© May 4, 1960		1981	1997	277	476	42	18,973	274*	43.71	41	1,213	22	55.13	190
Myers, H	Jan 2, 1875	June 12, 1944	1901	1910	201	289	46	4,450	91	18.31	0	7,095	282	25.15	106
Myers, M	Apr 12, 1847	Dec 8, 1919	1876	1878	22	40	4	537	49	14.91	0	20	—	—	11
§ Naved-ul-Hasan, Rana	Feb 28, 1978		2008	2009	11	16	3	207	32	15.92	0	1,018	26	39.15	3
Naylor, J E	Dec 11, 1930	June 26, 1996	1953	1953	1	—	—	—	—	—	—	88	2	44.00	1
§ Newstead, J T	© Sept 8, 1877	Mar 25, 1952	1903	1913	96	128	17	1,791	100*	16.13	0	5,555	297	18.70	75
Nicholson, A G	© June 25, 1938	Nov 3, 1985	1962	1975	282	267	125	1,667	50	11.73	0	17,296	876	19.74	85
Nicholson, N G	Oct 17, 1963		1988	1989	5	8	3	134	56*	26.80	0	25	—	—	5
Oates, William	Jan 11, 1852	Dec 9, 1940	1874	1875	7	7	1	34	14*	5.66	0	—	—	—	5
Oates, W F	June 11, 1929	May 15, 2001	1956	1956	3	3	0	20	9	6.66	0	—	—	—	5/1
Old, C M	© Dec 22, 1948		1966	1982	222	262	56	4,785	116	23.22	5	13,409	647	20.72	131
Oldham, S	© July 26, 1948		1974	1985	59	39	18	212	50	10.09	0	3,849	130	29.60	18
Oldroyd, E	© Oct 1, 1888	Dec 29, 1964	1910	1931	383	509	58	15,891	194	35.23	37	1,658	42	39.47	203
Oyston, C	© May 12, 1869	July 15, 1942	1900	1909	15	21	8	96	22	7.38	0	872	31	28.12	3
Padgett, D E V	© July 20, 1934		1951	1971	487	774	63	20,306	161*	28.55	29	208	6	34.66	250

LIST OF PLAYERS AND CAREER AVERAGES IN ALL FIRST-CLASS MATCHES FOR YORKSHIRE (Continued)

Player	Date of Birth	Date of Death (if known)	First Played	Last Played	M	Inns	NO	Runs	HS	Av'ge	100s	Runs	Wkts	Av'ge	Ct/St
Padgett, G H	Oct 9, 1931		1952	1952	6	7	4	56	32*	18.66	0	336	4	84.00	5
Padgett, J	Nov 21, 1860		1882	1889	6	9	0	92	22	10.22	0				2
Parker, B	June 23, 1970		1992	1998	44	71	10	1,839	138*	30.14	2	3	0	—	19
§ Parkin, C H	Feb 18, 1886	June 15, 1943	1906	1906	1	1	0	0	0	0.00	0	25	2	12.50	0
Parratt, J	Mar 24, 1859	May 6, 1905	1888	1890	2	2	0	11	11	5.50	0	75	1	75.00	4
§ Parton, J W	Jan 31, 1863	Jan. 30, 1906	1889	1889	2	2	0	16	14	8.00	0	4	1	4.00	0
Patterson, S A ......©	Oct 3, 1983		2005	2016	122	139	35	1,674	63	16.09	0	8,957	321	27.90	17
Pearson, H E	Aug 7, 1851	July 8, 1903	1878	1880	4	7	5	31	10*	15.50	0	90	5	18.00	1
Pearson, J H	May 14, 1915	May 13, 2007	1934	1936	3	3	0	54	44	18.00	0				1
Peate, E ......©	Mar 2, 1855	Mar 11, 1900	1879	1887	154	226	61	1,793	95	10.86	0	9,986	794	12.57	97
Peel, R ......©	Feb 12, 1857	Aug 12, 1941	1882	1897	318	510	42	9,322	210*	19.91	0	20,638	1,311	15.74	141
Penny, J H	Sept 29, 1856	July 29, 1902	1891	1891	1	1	0	8	8*		0	31	2	15.50	1
Pickles, C S	Jan 30, 1966		1985	1992	58	76	21	1,336	66	24.29	0	3,638	83	43.83	24
Pickles D	Nov 16, 1935		1957	1960	41	40	20	74	12	3.70	0	2,062	96	21.47	5
Pinder, G	July 15, 1841	Jan 15, 1903	1867	1880	125	199	44	1,639	57	10.57	0	325	19	17.10	145/102
Platt, R K ......©	Dec 26, 1932		1955	1963	96	103	47	405	57*	7.23	0	6,389	282	22.65	35
Plunkett, L E ......©	Apr 6, 1985		2013	2016	34	48	7	1,149	126	28.02	1	2,789	92	30.31	20
Pollard, D	Aug 7, 1835	Mar 26, 1909	1865	1865	1	2	0	3	3	1.50	0	19	—		1
Pollitt, G	June 3, 1874	May 19, 1942	1899	1899	1	2	0	51	51	51.00	0				—
Prest, C H *	Dec 9, 1841	Mar 4, 1875	1864	1864	1	2	0	57	31	14.25	0				3
Preston, D ......©	Nov 26, 1890	Feb 16, 1919	1885	1889	79	134	11	1,935	93	15.73	0	3,232	178	18.15	36
Pride, T	July 23, 1864		1887	1887	1	2	1	1	1	1.00	0				4/3
Priestley, J M	Sept 25, 1967		1989	1989	1	2	0	25	23	12.50	0	119	4	29.75	—
Pullan, P	Mar 29, 1857	Mar 3, 1901	1884	1884	1	2	0	14	14	14.00	0	5	0	—	1
§ Pujara, C A ......©	Jan 25, 1988		2015	2015	4	6	1	264	133*	52.80	1	5	0	—	2
Pyrah, R M	Nov 1, 1982		2004	2015	51	61	8	1,621	134*	30.58	3	2527	55	45.94	22
§ Radcliffe, E J R H * ......©	Jan 27, 1884	Nov 23, 1969	1909	1911	64	89	13	826	54	10.86	0	134	2	67.00	21
Ramage, A	Nov 29, 1957		1979	1983	23	22	9	219	52	16.84	0	1,649	44	37.47	8
Ramsden, G	Mar 2, 1983		2000	2000	1	1	0	0	0*		0	68	1	68.00	—
Randhawa, G S	Jan 25, 1992		2011	2011	1	1	0	5	5	5.00	0	62	2	31.00	—

Player	Date of Birth	Date of Death (if known)	First Played	Last Played	M	Inns	NO	Runs	HS	Av'ge	100s	Runs	Wkts	Av'ge	Ct/St
Raper, J R S *	Aug 9, 1909	Mar 9, 1997	1936	1947	3	4	0	24	15	6.00	0	—	—	—	0
Rashid, A U	**Feb 17, 1988** ©		2006	2016	133	186	32	5,409	180	35.12	10	13,636	410	33.25	70
Rawlin, E R	Oct 4, 1897	Jan 11, 1943	1927	1936	8	10	1	72	35	8.00	0	498	21	23.71	2
Rawlin, J T	Nov 10, 1856	Jan 19, 1924	1880	1885	27	36	2	274	31	8.05	0	258	11	23.45	13
Rawlinson, E B	Apr 10, 1837	Feb 17, 1892	1867	1875	37	68	5	991	55	15.73	0	62	5	12.40	16
Read, J	**Feb 2, 1998** ©		2016	2016	1	1	0	14	14	14.00	0	—	—	—	4
Redfearn, J	May 13, 1862	Jan 14, 1931	1890	1890	1	1	0	5	5	5.00	0	—	—	—	0
Render, G W A	Jan 5, 1887	Sept 17, 1922	1919	1919	1	1	0	5	5	5.00	0	—	—	—	0
Rhodes, A C	Oct 14, 1906	May 21, 1957	1932	1934	61	70	19	917	64*	17.98	0	3,026	107	28.28	45
§ Rhodes, H E *	Jan 11, 1852	Sept 10, 1889	1878	1883	10	16	1	269	64	17.93	0	—	—	—	1
Rhodes, S J	June 17, 1964		1981	1984	3	2	1	41	35	41.00	0	—	—	—	3
Rhodes, Wilfred	Oct 29, 1877 ©	July 8, 1973	1898	1930	883	1,195	162	31,075	267*	30.08	46	57,634	3,598	16.01	586
Rhodes, William	Mar 4, 1841	Aug 5, 1941	1911	1911	1	1	1	—	1*	—	0	40	—	—	0
§ Rhodes, W M H	**Mar 2, 1995** ©		2015	2016	15	25	2	689	95	29.95	0	551	16	34.43	8
Richardson, J A *	Aug 4, 1908	Apr 2, 1985	1936	1947	7	12	2	308	61	30.80	0	90	2	45.00	3
§ Richardson, R B	Jan 12, 1962		1993	1994	23	39	1	1,310	112	34.47	1	23	1	23.00	18
§ Richardson, S A	Sept 5, 1977		2000	2003	13	23	3	377	69	17.95	0	—	—	—	11
Riley, H	Aug 17, 1875	Nov 6, 1922	1895	1900	4	5	1	36	25*	9.00	0	54	1	54.00	1
Riley, M *	Apr 5, 1851	June 1, 1899	1878	1882	17	28	9	361	92	13.37	0	10	0	—	3
Ringrose, W	Sept 2, 1871 ©	Sept 14, 1943	1901	1906	57	66	9	353	23	6.19	0	3,224	155	20.80	25
Robinson, A L	Aug 17, 1946 ©		1971	1977	84	69	31	365	30*	9.60	0	4,927	196	25.13	48
Robinson, Edward *	Dec 27, 1862	Sept 3, 1942	1887	1887	1	2	1	23	22*	23.00	0	—	—	—	0
Robinson, Emmott	Nov 16, 1883	Nov 17, 1969	1919	1931	413	455	77	9,651	135*	25.53	7	19,645	893	21.99	318
Robinson, E P	Aug 10, 1911 ©	Nov 10, 1998	1934	1949	208	253	46	2,596	75*	12.54	0	15,141	735	20.60	189
Robinson, H	May 12, 1858	Dec 14, 1909	1879	1879	1	2	0	5	4	2.50	0	20	1	20.00	0
§ Robinson, M A	Nov 23, 1966		1991	1995	90	93	36	240	23	4.21	0	6,866	218	31.49	17
Robinson, P E	Aug 3, 1963 ©		1984	1991	132	217	31	6,668	189	35.84	7	238	1	238.00	96
Robinson, W	Nov 29, 1851	Aug 14, 1919	1876	1877	1	1	0	23	23	23.00	0	—	—	—	3
Roebuck C G	Aug 14, 1991		2010	2010	1	1	—	—	—	—	0	—	—	—	0
Root, J E	**Dec 30, 1990** ©		2010	2016	40	66	7	2,703	236	45.81	6	579	11	52.63	24

Player	Date of Birth	Date of Death (if known)	First Played	Last Played	M	Inns	NO	Runs	HS	Av'ge	100s	Runs	Wkts	Av'ge	Ct/St
Roper, E *	Apr 8, 1851	Apr 27, 1921	1878	1880	5	7	1	85	68	14.16	0	44	2	22.00	2
Rothery, J W ...©	Sept 5, 1877	June 2, 1919	1903	1910	150	236	18	4,614	161	21.16	3	—	—	—	45
Rowbotham, J	July 8, 1831	Dec 22, 1899	1861	1876	94	162	9	2,624	113	17.15	3	37	1	311.00	52
§ Rudolph, J A ...©	May 4, 1981		2007	2011	68	112	8	5,429	228*	52.20	18	311	1	311.00	79
Rudston, H	Nov 22, 1879	Apr 14, 1962	1902	1907	21	30	0	609	164	20.30	1	—	—	—	3
Ryan, M ...©	June 23, 1933	Nov 16, 2015	1954	1965	150	149	58	682	26*	7.49	0	9,466	413	22.92	59
Ryder, L	Aug 28, 1899	Jan 24, 1955	1924	1924	2	2	1	1	1	1.00	0	151	4	37.75	2
Sanderson B W	Jan 3, 1989		2008	2010	3	2	1	6	6	6.00	0	190	6	31.66	0
Savile, G *	Apr 26, 1847	Sept 4, 1904	1867	1874	3	3	0	140	65	20.00	0	—	—	—	2
Sayers, J J ...©	Nov 5, 1983		2004	2113	97	161	13	4,855	187	32.80	9	166	6	27.66	60
Schofield, C J	Mar 21, 1976		1996	1996	1	1	0	25	25	25.00	0	—	—	—	0
Schofield, D	Oct 9, 1947		1970	1974	3	4	4	13	6*	—	0	112	5	22.40	0
Scott, E	July 6, 1834	Dec 3, 1898	1864	1864	1	1	0	8	8	8.00	0	27	2	13.50	1
Sedgwick, H A	Apr 8, 1883	Dec 28, 1957	1906	1906	2	2	0	53	34	17.66	0	327	16	20.43	2
Sellers, Arthur * ...©	May 31, 1870	Sept 25, 1941	1890	1899	49	88	1	1,643	105	18.88	2	84	2	42.00	40
Sellers, A B * ...©	Mar 5, 1907	Feb 20, 1981	1932	1948	334	437	51	8,949	204	23.18	4	653	8	81.62	264
Shackleton, W A	Mar 9, 1908	Nov 16, 1971	1928	1934	5	6	0	49	25	8.16	0	130	6	21.66	3
Shahzad, Ajmal ...©	July 27, 1985		2006	2012	45	58	14	1,145	88	26.02	0	4,196	125	33.56	5
Sharp, K	Apr 6, 1959		1976	1990	195	320	35	8,426	181	29.56	11	836	12	69.66	95
§ Sharpe, C M *	Sept 6, 1851	June 25, 1935	1875	1875	1	2	1	15	15	15.00	0	17	0	—	0
Sharpe, P J ...©	Dec 27, 1936	May 19, 2014	1958	1974	411	666	71	17,685	203*	29.72	23	140	2	70.00	526
Shaw C	Feb 17, 1964		1984	1988	61	58	27	340	31	10.96	0	4,101	123	33.34	9
Shaw, J (Linthwaite)	Mar 12, 1865	Jan 22, 1921	1896	1897	3	3	0	3	3	2.66	0	181	7	25.85	2
Shaw, J (Wakefield)	**Jan 3, 1996**		**2016**	**2016**	**2**	**2**	**1**	**31**	**24**	**31.00**	**0**	**177**	**5**	**35.40**	**1**
Sheepshanks, E R *	Mar 22, 1910	Dec 31, 1937	1929	1929	1	1	0	26	26	26.00	0	—	—	—	0
Shepherd, D A *	Mar 10, 1916	May 29, 1998	1938	1938	1	0	0	0	0	—	0	—	—	—	0
Shotton, W	Dec 1, 1840	May 26, 1909	1865	1874	2	4	0	13	7	3.25	0	—	—	—	1
Sidebottom, A ...©	Apr 1, 1954		1973	1991	216	249	50	4,243	124	22.33	1	13,852	558	24.82	60
Sidebottom, R J ...©	**Jan 15, 1978**		**1997**	**2016**	**129**	**161**	**47**	**1,617**	**61**	**14.18**	**0**	**9,610**	**425**	**22.61**	**35**
Sidgwick, R *	Aug 7, 1851	Oct 23, 1933	1882	1882	9	13	0	64	17	4.92	0	—	—	—	7

LIST OF PLAYERS AND CAREER AVERAGES IN ALL FIRST-CLASS MATCHES FOR YORKSHIRE (Continued)

Player	Date of Birth	Date of Death (if known)	First Played	Last Played	M	Inns	NO	Runs	HS	Av'ge	100s	Runs	Wkts	Av'ge	Ct/St
Silverwood, C E W ..©	Mar 5, 1975		1993	2005	131	179	33	2,369	80	16.22	0	11,413	427	27.62	30
Silvester, S	Mar 12, 1951		1976	1977	6	7	2	30	14	10.00	0	313	12	26.08	2
Simpson, E T B *	Mar 5, 1867		1889	1889	1	2	0	1	1	0.50	0	—	—	—	0
§ Sims, Rev H M *	Mar 15, 1853	Oct 5, 1885	1875	1877	5	10	1	109	35*	12.11	0	—	—	—	2
Slinn, W	Dec 13, 1826	June 19, 1888	1861	1864	9	14	3	22	11	2.00	0	742	48	15.45	5
Smailes, T F ...©	Mar 27, 1910	Dec 1, 1970	1932	1948	262	339	42	5,686	117	19.14	3	16,593	802	20.68	153
Smales, K F	Sept 15, 1927	Mar 10, 2015	1948	1950	13	19	3	165	45	10.31	0	766	22	34.81	4
Smith, A F	Mar 7, 1847	Jan 6, 1915	1868	1874	28	49	4	692	89	15.37	0	1,090	46	23.69	11
Smith, E (Barnsley)	July 11, 1888	Jan 2, 1972	1914	1926	16	21	5	169	49	10.56	0	—	—	—	5
Smith, Ernest (Morley)*©	Oct 19, 1869	Feb 9, 1945	1888	1907	154	234	18	4,453	129	20.61	2	6,278	248	25.31	112
Smith, Fred (Idle)	Dec 26, 1885	Not known	1911	1911	1	1	0	11	11	11.00	0	—	—	—	0
Smith, Fred (Yeadon)	Dec 18, 1879	Oct 20, 1905	1903	1903	13	19	1	292	55	16.22	0	45	2	22.50	3
Smith, G	Jan 16, 1876	Jan 16, 1929	1901	1906	2	3	1	1	1	0.50	0	62	0	—	0
Smith, J	Mar 23, 1833	Feb 12, 1909	1865	1865	2	3	0	28	16	9.33	0	72	6	12.00	3
Smith, N	Apr 1, 1949	Mar 4, 2003	1970	1971	8	11	5	82	20	13.66	0	—	—	—	3
Smith, R	Apr 6, 1944		1969	1970	5	9	4	99	37*	19.80	0	—	—	—	14/3
Smith, Walker	Aug 14, 1847	July 7, 1900	1874	1874	5	9	0	152	59	16.88	0	—	—	—	0
§ Smith, William	Nov 1, 1839	Apr 19, 1897	1865	1874	11	19	3	260	90	16.25	0	—	—	—	3
Smithson, G A ...©	Nov 1, 1926	Sept 6, 1970	1946	1950	39	60	5	1,449	169	26.34	2	84	1	84.00	8
Smurthwaite, J	Oct 17, 1916	Oct 20, 1989	1938	1939	7	9	5	29	20*	7.25	0	237	12	19.75	21
Sowden, A	Dec 1, 1853	July 5, 1921	1878	1887	8	13	2	137	37	12.45	0	22	0	—	4
Squire, D	Dec 31, 1864	Apr 28, 1922	1893	1893	1	2	0	1	1	0.00	0	25	0	—	1
Squires, P J	Aug 4, 1951		1972	1976	49	84	8	1,271	70	16.72	0	32	0	—	0
Stanley, H C *	Feb 16, 1888	May 18, 1934	1911	1913	8	13	0	155	42	11.92	0	—	—	—	14
§ Stanyforth, R T *	May 30, 1892	Feb 20, 1964	1928	1928	3	3	0	26	11	8.66	0	—	—	—	6
§ Starc, M A	Jan 13, 1990		2012	2012	2	3	1	28	28*	—	0	153	7	21.85	2
Stead, B	June 21, 1939	Apr 15, 1980	1959	1959	2	3	0	8	8	2.66	0	115	7	16.42	0
§ Stemp, R D ...©	Dec 11, 1967		1993	1998	104	135	36	1,267	65	12.79	0	8,557	241	35.50	49
Stephenson, E	June 5, 1832	July 5, 1898	1861	1873	36	61	5	803	67	14.33	0	65	0	—	30/27
Stephenson, J S *	Nov 10, 1903	Oct 7, 1975	1923	1926	16	19	2	182	60	10.70	0	—	—	—	6

LIST OF PLAYERS AND CAREER AVERAGES IN ALL FIRST-CLASS MATCHES FOR YORKSHIRE (Continued)

Player	Date of Birth	Date of Death (if known)	First Played	Last Played	M	Inns	NO	Runs	HS	Av'ge	100s	Runs	Wkts	Av'ge	Ct/St
Stevenson, G B	◎ Dec 16, 1955	Jan 21, 2014	1973	1986	177	217	32	3,856	115*	20.84	2	13,254	464	28.56	73
Stott, W B	◎ July 18, 1934		1952	1963	187	309	19	9,168	186	31.61	17	112	7	16.00	91
Stringer, P M	Feb 23, 1943		1967	1969	19	17	8	101	15*	11.22	0	696	32	21.75	17
Stuchbury, S	June 22, 1954		1978	1981	3	3	2	7	4*	7.00	0	236	8	29.50	0
§ Sugg, F H	Jan 11, 1862	May 29, 1933	1883	1883	8	12	4	80	13*	10.00	0	—	—	—	4/1
§ Sugg, W	May 21, 1860	May 21, 1933	1881	1881	1	1	0	9	9	9.00	0	—	—	—	0
Sullivan, J H B *	Sept 21, 1890	Feb 8, 1932	1912	1912	1	2	0	41	26	20.50	0	43	0	—	0
Sutcliffe, H	◎ Nov 24, 1894	Jan 22, 1978	1919	1945	602	864	96	38,558	313	50.20	112	381	8	47.62	402
Sutcliffe, W H H *	Oct 10, 1926	Sept 16, 1998	1948	1957	177	273	34	6,247	181	26.13	6	152	6	25.33	80
Swallow, I G	Dec 18, 1962		1983	1989	61	82	18	1,296	114	20.25	1	3,270	64	51.09	28
§ Swanepoel, P J	Mar 30, 1977		2003	2003	2	3	0	20	17	6.66	0	129	3	43.00	1
§ Tait, T	Oct 7, 1872	Sept 6, 1954	1898	1899	2	3	1	7	3	3.50	0	—	—	—	1
Tasker, J *	Feb 4, 1887	Aug 24, 1975	1912	1913	31	43	4	586	67	15.02	0	—	—	—	14
Tattersall, G *	Apr 21, 1882	June 29, 1972	1905	1905	1	2	0	26	26	13.00	0	—	—	—	0
Taylor, C R	Feb 21, 1981		2001	2005	16	27	3	416	52*	17.33	0	—	—	—	8
Taylor, H	Dec 18, 1900	Oct 28, 1988	1924	1925	9	13	0	153	36	11.76	0	—	—	—	1
Taylor, H S	Dec 11, 1856	Nov 16, 1896	1879	1879	3	5	0	36	22	7.20	0	—	—	—	0
Taylor, J	Apr 2, 1850	May 27, 1924	1880	1881	9	13	1	107	44	8.91	0	—	—	—	4
Taylor, K	◎ Aug 21, 1935		1953	1968	303	505	35	12,864	203*	27.37	16	3,680	129	28.52	146
Taylor, N S	June 2, 1963		1982	1983	8	6	1	10	4	2.00	0	720	22	32.72	22
Taylor, T L *	May 25, 1878	Mar. 16, 1960	1899	1906	82	122	2	3,933	156	35.11	8	—	—	—	47/2
§ Tendulkar, S R	◎ Apr 24, 1973		1992	1992	16	25	2	1,070	100	46.52	1	195	4	48.75	4
§ Thewlis, H	Aug 31, 1865	Nov 30, 1920	1888	1888	2	4	1	4	2*	1.33	0	—	—	—	2
Thewlis, John Jun.	Sept 21, 1850	Aug 9, 1901	1879	1879	3	4	0	21	10	5.25	0	—	—	—	0
Thewlis, John Sen.	Mar 11, 1828	Dec 29, 1899	1861	1875	44	80	3	1,280	108	16.62	1	—	—	—	21/1
Thornicroft, N D	Jan 23, 1985		2002	2007	7	10	4	50	30	8.33	0	545	16	34.06	2
Thornton, A	July 20, 1854	Apr 18, 1915	1881	1881	2	4	0	21	21	5.25	0	—	—	—	2
Thornton, G *	Dec 24, 1867	Jan 31, 1939	1891	1891	3	4	0	21	16	5.25	0	74	2	37.00	0
Thorpe, G	Feb 20, 1834	Mar 2, 1899	1864	1864	1	2	1	14	9*	14.00	0	—	—	—	2

LIST OF PLAYERS AND CAREER AVERAGES IN ALL FIRST-CLASS MATCHES FOR YORKSHIRE (Continued)

Player	Date of Birth	Date of Death (if known)	First Played	Last Played	M	Inns	NO	Runs	HS	Av'ge	100s	Runs	Wkts	Av'ge	Ct/St
Threapleton, J W	July 20, 1857	July 30, 1918	1881	1881	1	1	0	8	8*	8.00	0	57	4	14.25	2/1
Tinsley, H J	Feb 20, 1865	Dec 10, 1938	1890	1891	9	13	0	56	15	4.30	0	0	—	—	1
Townsley, R A J	June 24, 1952	—	1974	1975	1	4	0	22	12	5.50	0	—	—	—	—
Towse, A D	Apr 22, 1968	—	1988	1988	1	1	0	1	1	1.00	0	50	3	16.66	—
Trueman, F S ©	Feb 6, 1931	July 1, 2006	1949	1968	459	533	81	6,852	104	15.15	2	29,890	1,745	17.12	325
Tunnicliffe, J ©	Aug 26, 1866	July 11, 1948	1891	1907	472	768	57	19,435	243	27.33	22	388	7	55.42	665
Turner, A	Sept 2, 1885	Aug 29, 1951	1910	1911	11	16	1	163	37	10.86	0	—	—	—	7
Turner, B	July 25, 1938	Dec 27, 2015	1960	1961	2	4	2	7	3*	3.50	0	47	4	11.75	2
Turner, C ©	Jan 11, 1902	Nov 19, 1968	1925	1946	200	266	32	6,132	130	26.20	2	5,320	173	30.75	181
Turner, F I	Sept 3, 1894	Oct 18, 1954	1924	1924	5	7	0	33	12	4.71	0	—	—	—	2
Tyson, C T	Jan 24, 1889	Apr 3, 1940	1921	1921	3	5	2	232	100*	77.33	1	—	—	—	1
Ullathorne, C E ©	Apr 11, 1845	May 2, 1904	1868	1875	27	46	8	283	28	7.44	0	—	—	—	19
Ulyett, G ©	Oct 21, 1851	June 18, 1898	1873	1893	355	618	31	14,157	199*	24.11	15	8,181	457	17.90	235
§ Usher, J	Feb 26, 1859	Aug 9, 1905	1888	1888	1	2	0	7	5	3.50	0	31	2	15.50	1
van Geloven, J	Jan 4, 1934	Aug 21, 2003	1955	1955	3	2	1	17	16	17.00	0	224	6	37.33	2
§ Vaughan, M P ©	Oct 29, 1974	—	1993	2009	151	267	14	9,160	183	36.20	20	4,268	92	46.39	55
§ Verelst, H W *	July 2, 1846	Apr 5, 1918	1868	1869	3	4	1	66	33*	22.00	0	—	—	—	—
Verity, H ©	May 18, 1905	July 31, 1943	1930	1939	278	294	77	3,898	101	17.96	1	21,353	1,558	13.70	191
Waddington, A ©	Feb 4, 1893	Oct 28, 1959	1919	1927	255	250	65	2,396	114	12.95	1	16,203	835	19.40	222
Wade, S ©	Feb 8, 1858	Nov 5, 1931	1886	1890	65	111	20	1,438	74*	15.80	0	2,498	133	18.78	31
Wainwright, D J ©	Mar 21, 1985	—	2004	2011	29	36	11	914	104*	36.56	2	2,480	69	35.94	6
Wainwright, E ©	Apr 8, 1865	Oct 28, 1919	1888	1902	352	545	30	11,092	228	21.53	18	17,744	998	17.77	327
Wainwright, W	Jan 21, 1882	Oct 28, 1961	1903	1905	24	36	3	648	62	19.63	1	582	19	30.63	21
Wake, W R *	May 21, 1852	Mar 14, 1896	1881	1881	3	3	0	13	11	4.33	0	—	—	—	2
Walker, A *	June 22, 1844	May 26, 1927	1863	1870	11	16	1	138	26	9.20	0	74	1	74.00	1
Walker, C	June 26, 1919	Dec 3, 1992	1947	1948	9	9	2	268	91	38.28	1	71	2	35.50	—
Walker, T	Apr 3, 1854	Aug 28, 1925	1879	1880	14	22	2	179	30	8.95	0	7	0	—	3
Waller, G	Dec 3, 1864	Dec 11, 1937	1893	1894	3	4	0	17	13	4.25	0	70	4	17.50	1

LIST OF PLAYERS AND CAREER AVERAGES IN ALL FIRST-CLASS MATCHES FOR YORKSHIRE (Continued)

Player	Date of Birth	Date of Death (if known)	First Played	Last Played	M	Inns	NO	Runs	HS	Av'ge	100s	Runs	Wkts	Av'ge	Ct/St
Wallgate, L *	Nov 12, 1849	May 5, 1887	1875	1878	3	3	0	9	6	3.00	0	17	1	17.00	3
Ward, A	Nov 21, 1865	Jan 6, 1939	1886	1886	4	7	1	41	22	6.83	0	1	0	—	1
Ward, F	Aug 31, 1881	Feb 28, 1948	1903	1903	1	1	1	0	0	0.00	0	16	0	—	0
Ward, H P *	Jan 20, 1899	Dec 16, 1946	1920	1920	1	1	0	10	10*	—	0	—	—	—	1
Wardall, T A ©	Apr 19, 1862	Dec 20, 1932	1884	1894	43	73	2	1,003	106	14.12	2	489	23	21.26	25
Wardlaw, I	Jun 29, 1985		2011	2012	4	3	2	31	17*	31.00	0	368	4	92.00	2
Wardle, J H ©	Jan 8, 1923	July 23, 1985	1946	1958	330	418	57	5,765	79	15.96	0	27,917	1,539	18.13	210
Waring, J S ©	Oct 1, 1942		1963	1966	28	27	15	137	26	11.41	0	1,122	53	21.16	17
Waring, S	Nov 4, 1838	Apr 17, 1919	1870	1870	1	1	0	9	9	9.00	0	—	—	—	0
Washington, W A I ©	Dec 11, 1879	Oct 20, 1927	1900	1902	44	62	6	1,290	100*	23.03	1	—	—	—	18
Watson, H	Sept 26, 1880	Apr 24, 1951	1908	1914	29	35	11	141	41	5.87	0	—	—	—	46/10
Watson, W ©	Mar 7, 1920	Apr 24, 2004	1939	1957	283	430	65	13,953	214*	38.22	26	75	0	—	170
Waud, B W *	June 4, 1837	May 31, 1889	1862	1864	6	10	1	165	42	18.33	0	2	—	—	2
Webster, C	June 9, 1838	Jan 6, 1881	1861	1868	3	5	1	30	10	7.50	0	1	—	—	1
Webster, H H	May 8, 1844	Mar 5, 1915	1868	1868	2	3	0	10	10	3.33	0	—	—	—	0
§ Weekes, L C	July 19, 1971		1994	2000	2	2	0	20	10	10.00	0	191	10	19.10	2
West, J	Oct 16, 1844	Jan 27, 1890	1868	1876	38	64	13	461	41	9.03	0	853	53	16.09	14
Wharf, A G	June 4, 1975		1994	1997	7	9	1	186	62	23.25	0	454	11	41.27	2
Whatmough, F J	Dec 4, 1856	June 3, 1904	1878	1882	7	11	1	51	20	5.10	0	111	5	22.20	4
Wheater, C H *	Mar 4, 1860	May 11, 1885	1880	1880	2	4	1	45	27	15.00	0	—	—	—	3
White, Sir A W * ©	Oct 14, 1877	Dec 16, 1945	1908	1920	97	128	28	1,457	55	14.57	0	7	0	—	50
White, C ©	Dec 16, 1969		1990	2007	221	350	45	10,376	186	34.01	19	7,649	276	27.71	140
Whitehead, J P	Sept 3, 1925	Aug 15, 2000	1946	1951	37	38	17	387	58*	18.42	0	2,610	96	27.47	11
Whitehead, Lees ©	Mar 14, 1864	Nov 22, 1913	1889	1904	119	172	38	2,073	67*	15.47	0	2,408	99	24.32	68
Whitehead, Luther	June 25, 1869	Jan 16, 1931	1893	1893	2	4	0	21	13	5.25	0	—	—	—	0
Whiteley, J P	June 28, 1955		1978	1982	45	38	17	231	20	11.00	0	2,410	70	34.42	21
Whiting, C P	Apr 18, 1888	Jan 14, 1959	1914	1920	6	10	2	92	26	11.50	0	416	15	27.73	2
Whitwell, J F *	Feb 22, 1869	Nov 6, 1932	1890	1890	1	2	0	8	4	4.00	0	11	1	11.00	0

LIST OF PLAYERS AND CAREER AVERAGES IN ALL FIRST-CLASS MATCHES FOR YORKSHIRE (Continued)

Player	Date of Birth	Date of Death (if known)	First Played	Last Played	M	Inns	NO	Runs	HS	Av'ge	100s	Runs	Wkts	Av'ge	Ct/St
§ Whitwell, W F *	Dec 12, 1867	Apr 12, 1942	1890	1890	10	14	2	67	26	5.58	0	518	25	20.72	2
Widdup, S	Nov 10, 1977		2000	2001	11	18	1	245	44	14.41	0	22	1	22.00	5
Wigley, D H	Oct 26, 1981		2002	2002	1	2	1	19	15	19.00	0	116	1	116.00	0
§ Wilkinson, A J A *	May 28, 1835	Dec 11, 1905	1865	1868	5	6	0	57	53	21.50	0	57	0	—	1
Wilkinson, F	May 23, 1914	Mar 26, 1984	1937	1939	14	14	1	73	18*	5.61	0	590	26	22.69	12
Wilkinson, H *	Dec 11, 1877	Apr 15, 1967	1903	1905	48	75	3	1,382	113	19.19	1	121	3	40.33	19
Wilkinson, R	Nov 11, 1977		1998	1998	1	1	0	9	9	9.00	0	35	1	35.00	0
© Wilkinson, W H	Mar 12, 1881	June 4, 1961	1903	1910	126	192	14	3,812	103	21.41	0	971	31	31.32	93
§ Willey D J ©	Feb 28, 1990		2016	2016	4	5	0	58	22	11.60	0	334	9	37.11	2
Williams, A C	Mar 1, 1887	June 1, 1966	1911	1919	12	14	10	95	48*	23.75	0	678	30	22.60	6
§ Williamson, K S ©	Sept 8, 1990		2013	2016	16	26	3	1,074	189	46.49	0	466	11	42.64	17
Wilson, B B	Dec 11, 1879	Sept 14, 1957	1906	1914	185	308	13	8,053	208	27.50	15	278	2	139.00	53
Wilson, C E M *	May 15, 1875	Feb 8, 1944	1896	1899	8	13	3	256	91*	25.60	0	257	12	21.41	3
© Wilson, D	Aug 7, 1937	July 21, 2012	1957	1974	392	502	85	5,788	83	13.88	0	22,626	1,104	20.49	235
© Wilson, E R *	Mar 25, 1879	July 21, 1957	1899	1923	66	72	18	902	104*	16.70	0	3,106	197	15.76	30
© Wilson, Geoffrey *	Aug 21, 1895	Nov 29, 1960	1919	1924	92	94	14	983	70	12.28	0	11	0	—	33
Wilson, G A *	Feb 2, 1916	Sept 24, 2002	1936	1939	15	25	5	352	55*	17.60	0	138	1	138.00	7
Wilson, John *	June 30, 1857	Oct 3, 1959	1887	1888	4	5	1	17	13*	4.25	0	165	12	13.75	3
© Wilson, J P *	Apr 3, 1889		1911	1912	9	14	1	81	36	6.23	0	24	1	24.00	2
© Wilson, J V	Jan 17, 1921	June 5, 2008	1946	1962	477	724	75	20,548	230	31.66	29	313	3	104.33	520
© Wood, A	Aug 25, 1898	Apr 1, 1973	1927	1946	408	481	80	8,579	123*	21.39	0	33	1	33.00	612/243
Wood, B	Dec 26, 1942		1964	1964	5	7	1	63	35	12.60	0				4
Wood, C H	July 26, 1934	June 28, 2006	1959	1959	4	4	1	22	10	7.33	0	319	11	29.00	1
Wood, G W	Nov 18, 1862	Dec 4, 1948	1895	1895	2	4	2	2	2	1.00	0			—	0/1
Wood, H *	Mar 22, 1855	July 31, 1941	1879	1880	10	16	1	156	36	10.40	0	212	10	21.20	8
Wood, J H *			1881	1881	2	1	0	14	14	14.00	0				0
© Wood, M J	Apr 6, 1977		1997	2007	128	222	20	6,742	207	33.37	16	27	2	13.50	113
Wood, R	June 3, 1929	May 22, 1990	1952	1956	22	18	4	60	17	4.28	0	1,346	51	26.39	5

LIST OF PLAYERS AND CAREER AVERAGES IN ALL FIRST-CLASS MATCHES FOR YORKSHIRE (Continued)

Player	Date of Birth	Date of Death (if known)	First Played	Last Played	M	Inns	NO	Runs	HS	Av'ge	100s	Runs	Wkts	Av'ge	Ct/St
Woodford, J D	Sept 9, 1943		1968	1972	38	61	2	1,204	101	20.40	1	185	4	46.25	12
Woodhead, F E *	May 29, 1868	Aug 25, 1943	1893	1894	4	8	0	57	18	7.12	0	—	—	—	3
Woodhouse, W H *	Apr 16, 1856	Mar 4, 1938	1884	1885	9	13	0	218	63	16.76	0	—	—	—	6
Wormald, A	May 10, 1855	Feb 6, 1940	1885	1891	7	11	3	161	80	20.12	0	—	—	—	10/2
Worsley, W A * ....©	Apr 5, 1890	Dec 4, 1973	1928	1929	60	50	4	722	60	15.69	0	—	—	—	32
Wrathmell, L F	Jan 22, 1855	Sept 16, 1928	1886	1886	1	2	0	18	17	9.00	0	—	—	—	0
Wright, R	July 19, 1852	May 25, 1891	1877	1877	2	4	1	28	22	9.33	0	—	—	—	0
Wright, T J *	Mar 5, 1900	Nov 7, 1962	1919	1919	1	1	0	12	12	12.00	0	—	—	—	0
Yardley, N W D * ...©	Mar 19, 1915		1936	1955	302	420	56	11,632	183*	31.95	17	5,818	195	29.83	220
Yeadon, J §	Dec 10, 1861	May 30, 1914	1888	1888	3	6	2	41	22	10.25	0	—	—	—	5/3
§ Younus Khan .....©	Nov 29, 1977		2007	2007	13	19	2	824	217*	48.47	3	342	8	42.75	11
§ Yuvraj Singh	Dec 12, 1981		2003	2003	7	12	2	145	56	14.50	0	130	3	43.33	4

In the career averages it should be noted that the bowling analysis for the second Cambridgeshire innings at Ashton-under-Lyne in 1865 has not been found. G R Atkinson took 3 wickets, W Cuttell 2, G Freeman 4 and R Iddison 1. The respective bowling averages have been calculated excluding these wickets.

MOST FIRST-CLASS APPEARANCES FOR YORKSHIRE

Matches	Player	Matches	Player	Matches	Player
883	W Rhodes (1898-1930)	496	R Illingworth (1951-1983)	429	D L Bairstow (1970-1990)
717	G H Hirst (1891-1929)	491	† J G Binks (1955-1969)	427	A Dolphin (1905-1927)
676	D Denton (1894-1920)	487	D E V Padgett (1951-1971)	425	P Carrick (1970-1993)
602	H Sutcliffe (1919-1945)	485	P Holmes (1913-1933)	414	G Boycott (1962-1986)
548	M Leyland (1920-1947)	477	J V Wilson (1946-1962)	413	E Robinson (1919-1931)
536	D B Close (1949-1970)	472	J Tunnicliffe (1891-1907)	411	P J Sharpe (1958-1974)
517	D Hunter (1888-1909)	459	F S Trueman (1949-1968)	408	A Wood (1927-1946)
513	S Haigh (1895-1913)	456	J H Hampshire (1961-1981)	401	A Mitchell (1922-1945)
510	Lord Hawke (1881-1911)	445	G G Macaulay (1920-1935)		

† Kept wicket in 412 consecutive Championship matches 1955-1969

MOST TOTAL APPEARANCES FOR YORKSHIRE
(First-Class, Domestic List A and t20)

Matches	Player	Matches	Player
883	W Rhodes (1898-1930)	513	S Haigh (1895-1913)
832	D L Bairstow (1970-1990)	510	Lord Hawke (1881-1911)
729	P Carrick (1970-1993)	502	P J Sharpe (1958-1974)
719	R J Blakey (1985-2004)	485	P Holmes (1913-1933)
717	G H Hirst (1891-1929)	477	J V Wilson (1946-1962)
690	J H Hampshire (1961-1981)	472	J Tunnicliffe (1891-1907)
678	G Boycott (1962-1986)	470	F S Trueman (1949-1968)
676	D Denton (1894-1920)	467	J D Love (1975-1989)
602	H Sutcliffe (1919-1945)	453	D Wilson (1957-1974)
583	A McGrath (1995-2012)	452	A Sidebottom (1973-1991)
581	D Byas (1986-2001)	445	G G Macaulay(1920-1935)
568	D B Close (1949-1970)	443	C M Old (1966-1982)
548	M Leyland (1920-1947)	427	A Dolphin (1905-1927)
546	C White (1990-2007)	414	P J Hartley (1985-1997)
544	D E V Padgett (1951-1971)	413	E Robinson (1919-1931)
537	R Illingworth (1951-1983)	408	A Wood (1927-1946)
521	J G Binks (1955-1969)	402	A G Nicholson (1962-1975)
517	D Hunter (1888-1909)	401	A Mitchell (1922-1945)
514	M D Moxon (1980-1997)		

ONE DAY RECORDS SECTION

Yorkshire County Cricket Club thanks Statistician JOHN T. POTTER, who in 2014 has revamped and streamlined Yorkshire's One-Day Records Section. John's symbols in the pages that follow are:

$ = Sunday and National Leagues, Pro 40, Clydesdale Bank 40 and Yorkshire Bank 40

= Benson & Hedges Cup

+ = Gillette Cup, NatWest Trophy, Cheltenham & Gloucester Trophy, Friends Provident Trophy and Royal London Cup

LIST A
WINNERS OF THE GILLETTE CUP, NATWEST TROPHY, CHELTENHAM & GLOUCESTER TROPHY FRIENDS PROVIDENT TROPHY AND ROYAL LONDON ONE-DAY CUP

		Yorkshire's Position
GILLETTE CUP		
1963	Sussex	Quarter-Final
1964	Sussex	Round 2
1965	**Yorkshire**	**Winner**
1966	Warwickshire	Round 2
1967	Kent	Quarter-Final
1968	Warwickshire	Round 2
1969	**Yorkshire**	**Winner**
1970	Lancashire	Round 1
1971	Lancashire	Round 2
1972	Lancashire	Round 1
1973	Gloucestershire	Round 1
1974	Kent	Quarter-Final
1975	Lancashire	Round 2
1976	Northamptonshire	Round 1
1977	Middlesex	Round 2
1978	Sussex	Quarter-Final
1979	Somerset	Quarter-Final
1980	Middlesex	Semi-Final
NATWEST TROPHY		
1981	Derbyshire	Round 1
1982	Surrey	Semi-Final
1983	Somerset	Round 2
1984	Middlesex	Round 1
1985	Essex	Round 2
1986	Sussex	Quarter-Final
1987	Nottinghamshire	Quarter-Final

		Yorkshire's Position
1988	Middlesex	Round 2
1989	Warwickshire	Round 2
1990	Lancashire	Quarter-Final
1991	Hampshire	Round 1
1992	Northamptonshire	Round 2
1993	Warwickshire	Quarter-Final
1994	Worcestershire	Round 2
1995	Warwickshire	Semi-Final
1996	Lancashire	Semi-Final
1997	Essex	Quarter-Final
1998	Lancashire	Round 2
1999	Gloucestershire	Semi-Final
2000	Gloucestershire	Round 4
CHELTENHAM & GLOUCESTER TROPHY		
2001	Somerset	Quarter-Final
2002	**Yorkshire**	**Winner**
2003	Gloucestershire	Round 4
2004	Gloucestershire	Semi-Final
2005	Hampshire	Semi-Final
2006	Sussex	North 7 (10)
FRIENDS PROVIDENT TROPHY		
2007	Durham	North 5 (10)
2008	Essex	Semi-Final
2009	Hampshire	Group C 3 (5)
ROYAL LONDON ONE-DAY CUP		
2014	Durham	Quarter-Final

WINNERS OF THE NATIONAL AND SUNDAY LEAGUES, PRO 40, CLYDESDALE BANK 40 AND YORKSHIRE BANK 40 1969-2014

		Yorkshire's Position				Yorkshire's Position
SUNDAY LEAGUE				1993	Glamorgan	9th
1969	Lancashire	8th		1994	Warwickshire	5th
1970	Lancashire	14th		1995	Kent	12th
1971	Worcestershire	15th		1996	Surrey	3rd
1972	Kent	4th		1997	Warwickshire	10th
1973	Kent	2nd		1998	Lancashire	9th
1974	Leicestershire	=6th		**NATIONAL LEAGUE**		
1975	Hampshire	=5th				
1976	Kent	15th		1999	Lancashire	5th Div 1
1977	Leicestershire	=13th		2000	Gloucestershire	2nd Div 1
1978	Hampshire	7th		2001	Kent	6th Div 1
1979	Somerset	=4th		2002	Glamorgan	4th Div 1
1980	Warwickshire	=14th		2003	Surrey	8th Div 1
1981	Essex	=7th		2004	Glamorgan	4th Div 2
1982	Sussex	16th		2005	Essex	8th Div 2
1983	**Yorkshire**	**1st**		2006	Essex	9th Div 2
1984	Essex	=14th		2007	Worcestershire	6th Div 2
1985	Essex	6th		2008	Sussex	2nd Div 2
1986	Hampshire	8th		2009	Sussex	7th Div 1
1987	Worcestershire	=13th		**CLYDESDALE BANK 40**		
1988	Worcestershire	8th				
1989	Lancashire	11th		2010	Warwickshire	Group B 1 (7) (Semi-Final)
1990	Derbyshire	6th				
1991	Nottinghamshire	7th		2011	Surrey	Group A 6 (7)
1992	Middlesex	15th		2012	Hampshire	Group C 5 (7)
				2013	Nottinghamshire	Group C 6 (7)

BENSON & HEDGES WINNERS 1972-2002

		Yorkshire's Position				Yorkshire's Position
1972	Leicestershire	Final		1988	Hampshire	Group B 4 (5)
1973	Kent	Group N 3 (5)		1989	Nottinghamshire	Group C 3 (5)
1974	Surrey	Quarter-Final		1990	Lancashire	Group C 3 (5)
1975	Leicestershire	Quarter-Final		1991	Worcestershire	Semi-Final
1976	Kent	Group D 3 (5)		1992	Hampshire	Group C 5 (5)
1977	Gloucestershire	Group D 3 (5)		1993	Derbyshire	Round One
1978	Kent	Group D 4 (5)		1994	Warwickshire	Round One
1979	Essex	Semi-Final		1995	Lancashire	Quarter-Final
1980	Northamptonshire	Group B 4 (5)		1996	Lancashire	Semi-Final
1981	Somerset	Quarter-Final		1997	Surrey	Quarter-Final
1982	Somerset	Group A 5 (5)		1998	Essex	Semi-Final
1983	Middlesex	Group B 5 (5)		1999	Gloucestershire	Final
1984	Lancashire	Semi-Final		2000	Gloucestershire	Quarter-Final
1985	Leicestershire	Group B 3 (5)		2001	Surrey	Semi-Final
1986	Middlesex	Group B 3 (5)		2002	Warwickshire	Quarter-Final
1987	**Yorkshire**	**Winner**				

SEASON-BY-SEASON RECORD OF ALL LIST A
MATCHES PLAYED BY YORKSHIRE 1963-2016

Season	Played	Won	Lost	Tie	N R	Abd	Season	Played	Won	Lost	Tie	N R	Abd
1963	2	1	1	0	0	0	1991	24	13	10	0	1	0
1964	1	0	1	0	0	0	1992	21	8	13	0	0	2
1965	4	4	0	0	0	1	1993	21	10	10	0	1	0
1966	1	0	1	0	0	0	1994	19	11	8	0	0	1
1967	2	1	1	0	0	0	1995	27	15	11	0	1	1
1968	1	0	1	0	0	0	1996	27	18	9	0	0	0
1969	19	12	7	0	0	2	1997	25	14	10	1	0	1
1970	17	5	10	0	2	0	1998	25	14	10	0	1	0
1971	15	5	10	0	0	2	1999	23	13	10	0	0	0
1972	25	15	8	0	2	1	2000	24	13	10	0	1	0
1973	21	14	7	0	0	0	2001	26	13	13	0	0	0
1974	22	12	9	0	1	1	2002	27	16	10	0	0	1
1975	22	12	10	0	0	0	2003	18	6	12	0	0	0
1976	22	9	13	0	0	0	2004	23	13	8	0	2	0
1977	19	5	10	0	4	2	2005	22	8	14	0	0	0
1978	22	10	11	0	1	2	2006	15	4	10	0	1	2
1979	21	12	6	0	3	3	2007	17	8	7	0	2	1
1980	23	9	14	0	0	0	2008	18	10	4	1	3	0
1981	19	9	8	0	2	3	2009	16	6	9	0	1	0
1982	23	7	14	1	1	1	2010	13	10	3	0	0	0
1983	19	11	7	0	1	3	2011	12	5	7	0	0	0
1984	23	10	13	0	0	0	2012	11	4	7	0	0	1
1985	19	9	9	0	1	3	2013	13	4	9	0	0	0
1986	22	11	9	1	1	1	2014	10	6	4	0	0	0
1987	24	14	9	0	1	2	2015	10	5	3	0	2	0
1988	21	9	9	0	3	1	2016	10	5	4	0	1	0
1989	23	10	13	0	0	0							
1990	22	13	9	0	0	1		971	481	446	4	40	39

Abandoned matches are not included in the list of matches played.

ABANDONED LIST A MATCHES (39)

1965	v. South Africa at Bradford
1969 (2)	v. Warwickshire at Harrogate $
	v. Lancashire at Manchester $
1971 (2)	v. Gloucestershire at Sheffield $
	v. Somerset at Weston-Super-Mare $
1972	v. Sussex at Leeds $
1974	v. Warwickshire at Leeds $
1977 (2)	v. Warwickshire at Birmingham $
	v. Surrey at Leeds $
1978 (2)	v. Essex at Bradford $
	v. Gloucestershire at Hull $
1979 (3)	v. Leicestershire at Middlesbrough $
	v. Kent at Huddersfield $
	v. Worcestershire at Worcester $
1981 (3)	v. Warwickshire at Birmingham $
	v. Lancashire at Leeds #
	v. Sussex at Hove $
1982	v. Glamorgan at Bradford $
1983 (3)	v. Derbyshire at Chesterfield #
	v. Surrey at Leeds $
	v. Essex at Chelmsford $

1985 (3)	v. Derbyshire at Scarborough $
	v. Warwickshire at Birmingham $
	v. Lancashire at Leeds $
1986	v. Kent at Canterbury $
1987 (2)	v. Sussex at Hull $
	v. Hampshire at Leeds $
1988	v. Northamptonshire
	at Northampton $
1990	v. Glamorgan at Newport $
1992 (2)	v. Sussex at Hove $
	v. Durham at Darlington $
1994	v. Essex at Leeds $
1995	v. Derbyshire at Chesterfield #
1997	v. Sussex at Scarborough $
2002	v. Nottinghamshire at Nottingham $
2006 (2)	v. Nottinghamshire at Leeds +
	v. Derbyshire at Derby $
2007	v. Warwickshire at Birmingham +
2012	v. Northamptonshire at Leeds $

ANALYSIS OF LIST A RESULTS V. ALL TEAMS 1963-2016
DOMESTIC MATCHES

		HOME				AWAY				
Opponents	*Played*	*Won*	*Lost*	*Tied*	*N. R*	*Won*	*Lost*	*Tied*	*N. R*	*Abd*
Derbyshire	62	19	9	0	1	19	9	1	4	4
Durham	28	9	5	0	0	6	7	0	1	1
Essex	46	12	12	0	0	9	12	0	0	3
Glamorgan	39	9	8	0	0	9	13	0	0	2
Gloucestershire	55	12	12	0	2	8	19	0	2	2
Hampshire	44	11	9	0	1	9	14	0	0	1
Kent	55	13	11	0	1	10	20	0	0	2
Lancashire	61	9	16	0	2	14	18	0	2	3
Leicestershire	65	18	16	0	0	12	16	1	2	1
Middlesex	48	14	4	0	3	9	16	0	2	0
Northamptonshire	57	17	11	0	3	18	7	0	1	2
Nottinghamshire	58	19	8	1	2	9	16	0	3	2
Somerset	54	13	14	0	1	11	15	0	0	1
Surrey	55	12	14	0	0	11	18	0	0	2
Sussex	46	11	11	0	1	11	12	0	0	5
Warwickshire	60	11	17	1	2	13	16	0	0	6
Worcestershire	62	13	19	0	2	17	11	0	0	1
Bedfordshire	1	0	0	0	0	1	0	0	0	0
Berkshire	2	0	0	0	0	2	0	0	0	0
Cambridgeshire	3	2	0	0	0	1	0	0	0	0
Cheshire	1	0	0	0	0	1	0	0	0	0
Combined Universities	3	0	2	0	0	1	0	0	0	0
Devon	4	0	0	0	0	4	0	0	0	0
Dorset	1	0	0	0	0	1	0	0	0	0
Durham (M C)	3	1	1	0	0	1	0	0	0	0
Herefordshire	1	0	0	0	0	1	0	0	0	0
Ireland	4	3	0	0	0	1	0	0	0	0
Minor Counties	11	6	0	0	0	5	0	0	0	0
Netherlands	4	1	1	0	0	1	1	0	0	0
Norfolk	2	1	0	0	0	1	0	0	0	0
Northumberland	1	1	0	0	0	0	0	0	0	0
Scotland	16	8	0	0	0	8	0	0	0	0
Shropshire	2	0	0	0	0	1	1	0	0	0
Unicorns	4	2	0	0	0	2	0	0	0	0
Wiltshire	1	0	0	0	0	1	0	0	0	0
Yorkshire Cricket Board	1	0	0	0	0	1	0	0	0	0
Total	**960**	**247**	**200**	**2**	**21**	**230**	**241**	**2**	**17**	**38**

OTHER MATCHES

Australia	3	0	1	0	2	0	0	0	0	0
Bangladesh A	1	1	0	0	0	0	0	0	0	0
South Africa	0	0	0	0	0	0	0	0	0	1
Sri Lanka A	3	0	3	0	0	0	0	0	0	0
West Indies	1	1	0	0	0	0	0	0	0	0
West Indies A	1	0	1	0	0	0	0	0	0	0
Young Australia	1	1	0	0	0	0	0	0	9	0
Zimbabwe	1	1	0	0	0	0	0	0	0	0
Total	**11**	**4**	**5**	**0**	**2**	**0**	**0**	**0**	**0**	**1**
Grand Total	**971**	**251**	**205**	**2**	**23**	**230**	**241**	**2**	**17**	**39**

Abandoned matches are not included in the list of matches played.

LIST A HIGHEST AND LOWEST SCORES BY AND AGAINST YORKSHIRE
PLUS INDIVIDUAL BEST BATTING AND BOWLING

The lowest score is the lowest all-out total or the lowest score at completion of the allotted overs, 10-over matches not included

Yorkshire versus:

Derbyshire

		By Yorkshire		Against Yorkshire	
Highest Score:	In Yorkshire	241:4	at Leeds 2006 +	251:6	at Leeds 2010 $
	Away	288:6	at Derby 2002 #	268:8	at Derby 2002 #
Lowest Score:	In Yorkshire	117	at Huddersfield 1978 $	87	at Huddersfield 1978 $
	Away	132	at Chesterfield 1986 $	127	at Chesterfield 1986 $
Best Batting:	In Yorkshire	S A Kellett 118*	at Leeds 1992 $	K J Barnett 101	at Leeds 1989 #
	Away	M J Wood 115*	at Derby 2002 #	C J Adams 109*	at Derby 1997 $
Best Bowling:	In Yorkshire	S A Patterson 6-32	at Leeds 2010 $	F E Rumsey 4-20	at Bradford 1973 #
	Away	C W J Athey 5-35	at Chesterfield 1981 $	C J Tunnicliffe 5-24	at Derby 1981 #

Durham

		By Yorkshire		Against Yorkshire	
Highest Score:	In Yorkshire	269:5	at Leeds 1998 $	266:8	at Leeds 1998 $
	Away	271:7	at Chester-le-Street 2002 #	281:7	at Chester-le-Street 2002 #
Lowest Score:	In Yorkshire	133	at Leeds 1995 $	121	at Leeds 1995 $
	Away	122	at Chester-le-Street 2007 $	136	at Chester-le-Street 1996 $
Best Batting:	In Yorkshire	D S Lehmann 119	at Leeds 1998 #	W Larkins 114	at Leeds 1993 $
	Away	C White 101*	at Chester-le-Street 2006 +	J P Maher 124*	at Chester-le-Street 2006 +
Best Bowling:	In Yorkshire	C White 4-18	at Scarborough 1997 $	S J E Brown 4-20	at Leeds 1995 $
	Away	C E W Silverwood 4-26	at Chester-le-Street 1996 $	P D Collingwood 4-31	at Chester-le-Street 2000 #

Essex

		By Yorkshire		Against Yorkshire	
Highest Score:	In Yorkshire	290:6	at Scarborough 2014 +	291:5	at Scarborough 2014 +
	Away	307:3	at Chelmsford 1995 +	285:8	at Chelmsford 2008 +
Lowest Score:	In Yorkshire	54	at Leeds 2003 $	108	at Leeds 1996 $
	Away	119:8	at Colchester 1987 $	123	at Colchester 1974 $
Best Batting:	In Yorkshire	J A Leaning 111*	at Scarborough 2014 +	R N ten Doeschate 119*	at Scarborough 2014 +
	Away	A W Gale 125*	at Chelmsford 2002 #	N Hussain 136*	at Chelmsford 2002 #
Best Bowling:	In Yorkshire	G B Stevenson 4-20	at Barnsley 1977 #	R E East 6-18	at Hull 1969 $
	Away	A L Robinson 4-31	at Leyton 1976 $	R E East 5-20	at Colchester 1979 $

Yorkshire versus:

Glamorgan

	By Yorkshire			Against Yorkshire		
Highest Score:	253:4		at Leeds 1991 $	216:6		at Leeds 2013 $
Lowest Score:	257		In Yorkshire	285:7		at Colwyn Bay 2013 $
	139		at Colwyn Bay 2013 $	83		at Leeds 1987 +
	93-8		at Hull 1981 $	90		at Neath 1969 $
Best Batting:	96	A A Metcalfe	at Swansea 1985 $	97*	G P Ellis	at Leeds 1976 $
	141*	M D Moxon	at Cardiff 1991 #	127	A R Butcher	at Cardiff 1991 #
Best Bowling:	5-22	P Carrick	at Leeds 1991 $	5-26	D S Harrison	at Leeds 2002 $
	6-40	R J Sidebottom	at Cardiff 1998 $	5-16	G C Holmes	at Swansea 1985 $

Gloucestershire

	By Yorkshire			Against Yorkshire		
Highest Score:	263:9		In Yorkshire	269		at Leeds 2009 +
Lowest Score:	262:7		at Bristol 1996 $	294:6		at Cheltenham 2010 $
	115		at Leeds 1973 $	91		at Scarborough 2001 $
	133		at Cheltenham 1999 $	90		at Tewkesbury 1972 $
Best Batting:	118	J A Rudolph	at Leeds 2009 +	146*	S Young	at Leeds 1997 $
	100*	J D Love	at Gloucester in 1985 $	143*	C M Spearman	at Bristol 2004 $
	100*	R J Blakey	at Cheltenham 1990 $			
Best Bowling:	5-42	N D Thornicroft	at Leeds 2003 $	5-33	M C J Ball	at Leeds 2003 $
	4-25	R D Stemp	at Bristol 1996 $	5-42	M C J Ball	at Cheltenham 1999 $

Hampshire

	By Yorkshire			Against Yorkshire		
Highest Score:	259:4		In Yorkshire	257:6		at Middlesbrough 1985 $
Lowest Score:	264:2		at Southampton 1995 $	261		at Bournemouth 1977 +
	74:9		In Yorkshire	50		at Leeds 1991 $
	118		at Southampton 1990 +	133		at Bournemouth 1976 $
Best Batting:	104*	D Byas	at Leeds 1999 #	155*	B A Richards	at Hull 1970 $
	97*	M G Bevan	at Southampton 1995 $	125*	C G Greenidge	at Bournemouth 1986 $
Best Bowling:	5-16	G M Hamilton	at Leeds 1998 $	5-33	A J Murtagh	at Huddersfield 1977 $
	5-33	A U Rashid	at Southampton 2014 +	5-31	D W White	at Southampton 1969 $

LIST A HIGHEST AND LOWEST SCORES BY AND AGAINST YORKSHIRE PLUS INDIVIDUAL BEST BATTING AND BOWLING (Continued)

Yorkshire versus:

Kent

		By Yorkshire		Against Yorkshire	
Highest Score:	In Yorkshire	299:3	at Leeds 2002 $	232:8	at Leeds 2011 $
	Away	263:3	at Maidstone 1998 $	266:5	at Maidstone 1998 $
Lowest Score:	In Yorkshire	75	at Leeds 1995 $	133	at Leeds 1974 $
				133	at Leeds 1979 #
	Away			105	at Canterbury 1969 $
Best Batting:	Away	114	at Canterbury 1978 #		
	In Yorkshire	130* R J Blakey	at Scarborough 1991 $	118* M H Denness	at Scarborough 1976 $
	Away	102 A McGrath	at Canterbury 2001 $	118* C J Tavare	at Canterbury 1981 +
Best Bowling:	In Yorkshire	4-15 A G Nicholson	at Leeds 1974 $	6-32 M T Coles	at Canterbury 2012 $
	Away	6-18 D Wilson	at Canterbury 1969 $	5-25 B D Julien	at Canterbury 1971 +

Lancashire

		By Yorkshire		Against Yorkshire	
Highest Score:	In Yorkshire	292:4	at Leeds 2006 +	287:9	at Leeds 2006 +
	Away	325:7	at Manchester 2016 +	293:9	at Manchester 1996 +
Lowest Score:	In Yorkshire	81	at Leeds 1998 $	68	at Leeds 2000 $
		81	at Leeds 2002 #		
	Away	125	at Manchester 1973 #	84	at Manchester 2016 +
Best Batting:	In Yorkshire	111* D Byas	at Leeds 1996 $	102* N J Speak	at Leeds 1992 $
	Away	136 A Lyth	at Manchester 2016 +	141* B J Hodge	at Manchester 2007 +
Best Bowling:	In Yorkshire	5-25 C White	at Leeds 2000 #	6-25 G Chapple	at Leeds 1998 $
	Away	4-18 G S Blewett	at Manchester 1999 +	5-49 M Watkinson	at Manchester 1991 #

Leicestershire

		By Yorkshire		Against Yorkshire	
Highest Score:	In Yorkshire	303:4	at Leeds 2008 $	302:7	at Leeds 2008 $
	Away	376:3	at Leicester 2016 +	298:9	at Leicester 1997 $
Lowest Score:	In Yorkshire	93	at Leeds 1998 $	141	at Hull 1975 $
	Away	89:9	at Leicester 1989 $	53	at Leicester 2000 $
Best Batting:	In Yorkshire	120 J A Rudolph	at Leeds 2008 $	108 N E Briers	at Bradford 1984 $
	Away	176 T M Head	at Leicester 2016 +	108 E J H Eckersley	at Leicester 2013 $
Best Bowling:	In Yorkshire	4-18 H P Cooper	at Leeds 1975 +	5-24 C W Henderson	at Leeds 2004 $
	Away	5-16 S Stuchbury	at Leicester 1982 $	4-25 J Ormond	at Leicester 2001 #

LIST A HIGHEST AND LOWEST SCORES BY AND AGAINST YORKSHIRE PLUS INDIVIDUAL BEST BATTING AND BOWLING (Continued)

Yorkshire versus:

Middlesex

	By Yorkshire		Against Yorkshire	
Highest Score: In Yorkshire	271:7	at Scarborough 1990 $	245:8	at Scarborough 2010 $
Away	275:4	at Lord's 2011 $	273:6	at Southgate 2004 $
Lowest Score: In Yorkshire	148	at Leeds 1974 $	23	at Leeds 1974 $
Away	90	at Lord's 1964 +	107	at Lord's 1979 #
Best Batting: In Yorkshire	124* J A Rudolph	at Lord's 1991	104 P N Weekes	at Leeds 1996 +
Away	116 A A Metcalfe	at Hull 1983 $	125* O A Shah	at Southgate 2004 $
Best Bowling: In Yorkshire	4-6 R Illingworth	at Lord's 1979 #	4-24 N G Cowans	at Leeds 1986 +
Away	4-28 H P Cooper		5-44 T M Lamb	at Lord's 1975 #

Northamptonshire

	By Yorkshire		Against Yorkshire	
Highest Score: In Yorkshire	314:8	at Scarborough 2016 +	314:4	at Leeds 2007 +
Away	341:3	at Northampton 2006 +	339:7	at Northampton 2006 +
Lowest Score: In Yorkshire	129	at Leeds 2000 $	127	at Huddersfield 1974 $
Away	112	at Northampton 1975 $	109	at Northampton 2000 $
Best Batting: In Yorkshire	125 A Lyth	at Scarborough 2016 +	132 U Afzaal	at Leeds 2007 +
Away	118* D S Lehmann	at Northampton 2006 +	161 D J G Sales	at Northampton 2006 +
Best Bowling: In Yorkshire	5-38 C M Old	at Sheffield 1972 $	5-16 B S Crump	at Bradford 1969 $
Away	5-29 P W Jarvis	at Northampton 1992 $	5-15 Sarfraz Nawaz	at Northampton 1975 $

Nottinghamshire

	By Yorkshire		Against Yorkshire	
Highest Score: In Yorkshire	352:6	at Scarborough 2001 $	251:5	at Scarborough 1996 $
Away	280:4	at Nottingham 2007 +	251:9	at Scarborough 2016 +
Lowest Score: In Yorkshire	120:9	at Scarborough 1998 $	291:6	at Nottingham 2004 $
Away	147	at Nottingham 1975 $	66	at Bradford 1969 $
Best Batting: In Yorkshire	191 D S Lehmann	at Scarborough 2001 $	101 M J Harris	at Hull 1973 +
Away	103 R B Richardson	at Nottingham 1993 $	123 D W Randall	at Nottingham 1987 $
Best Bowling: In Yorkshire	5-17 A G Nicholson	at Hull 1972 $	5-41 C L Cairns	at Scarborough 1996 $
Away	4-12 C M Old	at Nottingham 1977 $	5-30 F D Stephenson	at Nottingham 1991 #

LIST A HIGHEST AND LOWEST SCORES BY AND AGAINST YORKSHIRE PLUS INDIVIDUAL BEST BATTING AND BOWLING (Continued)

Yorkshire versus:

Somerset

		By Yorkshire	Against Yorkshire
Highest Score:	In Yorkshire	283:9 at Scarborough 2002 $	338:5 at Leeds 2013 $
	Away	343:9 at Taunton 2005 $	345:4 at Taunton 2005 $
Lowest Score:	In Yorkshire	110 at Scarborough 1977 $	103 at Sheffield 1972 $
	Away	120 at Taunton 1992 #	63 at Taunton 1965 #
Best Batting:	In Yorkshire	127 J A Rudolph at Scarborough 2007 $	113 R T Ponting at Scarborough 2004 $
	Away	148 A McGrath at Taunton 2006 $	140* P D Trego at Taunton 2013 $
Best Bowling:	In Yorkshire	6-36 A G Nicholson at Sheffield 1972 $	4-10 I T Botham at Scarborough 1979 $
	Away	6-15 F S Trueman at Taunton 1965 +	5-27 J Garner at Bath 1985 $

Surrey

		By Yorkshire	Against Yorkshire
Highest Score:	In Yorkshire	263:8 at Bradford 1985 $	375:4 at Scarborough 1994 $
	Away	334:5 at The Oval 2005 $	329:8 at The Oval 2009 +
Lowest Score:	In Yorkshire	76 at Harrogate 1970 +	90 at Leeds 1996 $
	Away	128:8 at The Oval 1971 $	134 at The Oval 1969 +
Best Batting:	In Yorkshire	118* J D Love at Leeds 1987 $	136 M A Lynch at Bradford 1985 $
	Away	146 G Boycott at Lord's 1965 +	177 S A Newman at The Oval 2009 +
Best Bowling:	In Yorkshire	5-25 D Gough at Leeds 1998 $	7-33 R D Jackman at Harrogate 1970 +
	Away	5-29 R Illingworth at Lord's 1965 +	5-22 R D Jackman at The Oval 1978 $

Sussex

		By Yorkshire	Against Yorkshire
Highest Score:	In Yorkshire	302:4 at Scarborough 2011 $	267 at Scarborough 2011 $
	Away	270 at Hove 1963 +	292 at Hove 1963 +
Lowest Score:	In Yorkshire	89:7 at Huddersfield 1969 $	85 at Bradford 1972 #
	Away	89 at Hove 1998 $	108 at Hove 1971 $
Best Batting:	In Yorkshire	132* J A Rudolph at Scarborough 2011 $	129 A W Greig at Scarborough 1976 $
	Away	111* J H Hampshire at Hastings 1973 $	103 L J Wright at Hove 2012 $
Best Bowling:	In Yorkshire	5-34 G M Hamilton at Scarborough 2000 $	4-15 Imran Khan at Sheffield 1985 $
	Away	5-13 D Gough at Hove 1994 $	4-10 M H Yardy at Hove 2011 $

LIST A HIGHEST AND LOWEST SCORES BY AND AGAINST YORKSHIRE PLUS INDIVIDUAL BEST BATTING AND BOWLING (*Continued*)

Yorkshire versus:

Warwickshire

		By Yorkshire			Against Yorkshire		
Highest Score:	In Yorkshire	274:3		at Leeds 2003 $	283:6		at Leeds 2016 +
	Away	247:8		at Birmingham 1984 #	309-3		at Birmingham 2005 $
Lowest Score:	In Yorkshire	158		at Scarborough 2012 $	59		at Leeds 2001 $
	Away	56		at Birmingham 1995 $	158:9		at Birmingham 2003 $
Best Batting:	In Yorkshire	139*	S P Fleming	at Leeds 2003 $	118	I J L Trott	at Leeds 2016 +
	Away	100*	J H Hampshire	at Birmingham 1975 $	137	I R Bell	at Birmingham 2005 $
Best Bowling:	In Yorkshire	5-31	M D Moxon	at Leeds 1991 #	4-16	N M Carter	at Scarborough 2012 $
	Away	4-27	H P Cooper	at Birmingham 1973 $	7-32	R G D Willis	at Birmingham 1981 #

Worcestershire

		By Yorkshire			Against Yorkshire		
Highest Score:	In Yorkshire	290:7		at Leeds 1982 +	286:5		at Leeds 1982 +
	Away	346:6		at Worcester 2015 +	289:3		at Worcester 1996 #
Lowest Score:	In Yorkshire	88		at Leeds 1995 #	86		at Leeds 1969 $
	Away	90		at Worcester 1987 $	122		at Worcester 1975 $
Best Batting:	In Yorkshire	101	M G Bevan	at Leeds 1982 +	113*	G A Hick	at Scarborough 1995 $
	Away	142	G Boycott	at Worcester 1980 #	115	Younis Ahmed	at Worcester 1980 #
Best Bowling:	In Yorkshire	7-15	R A Hutton	at Leeds 1969 $	5-36	Kabir Ali	at Leeds 2002 $
	Away	6-14	H P Cooper	at Worcester 1975 $	5-30	R J Chapman	at Worcester 1998 $

Bedfordshire +

		By Yorkshire			Against Yorkshire		
Highest Score:	Away	212:6		at Luton 2001	211:9		at Luton 2001
Best Batting:	Away	88	D S Lehmann	at Luton 2001	34	O J Clayton	at Luton 2001
Best Bowling:	Away	4-39	R J Sidebottom	at Luton 2001	4-54	S R Rashid	at Luton 2001

Berkshire +

		By Yorkshire			Against Yorkshire		
Highest Score:	Away	131:3		at Reading 1983	128:9		at Reading 1983
Lowest Score:	Away				105		at Finchampstead 1988
Best Batting:	Away	74*	A A Metcalfe	at Finchampstead 1988	29	G R J Roope	at Reading 1983
Best Bowling:	Away	5-27	G B Stevenson	at Reading 1983	1-15	M Lickley	at Reading 1983

LIST A HIGHEST AND LOWEST SCORES BY AND AGAINST YORKSHIRE PLUS INDIVIDUAL BEST BATTING AND BOWLING (Continued)

Yorkshire versus:

Cambridgeshire +

		By Yorkshire			Against Yorkshire		
Highest Score:	In Yorkshire	177:1		at Leeds 1986	176: 8		at Leeds 1986
	Away	299:5		at March 2003	214:8		at March 2003
Lowest Score:	In Yorkshire				176:8		at Leeds 1986
	Away	299:5		at March 2003	214:8		at March 2003
Best Batting:	In Yorkshire	75	M D Moxon	at Leeds 1986	85	J D R Benson	at Leeds 1986
	Away	118*	M J Wood	at March 2003	53	N T Gadsby	at March 2003
Best Bowling:	In Yorkshire	3-11	A G Nicholson	at Castleford 1967	2-8	D H Fairey	at Castleford 1967
	Away	3-37	A K D Gray	at March 2003	3-53	Ajaz Akhtar	at March 2003

Cheshire +

		By Yorkshire			Against Yorkshire		
Highest Score:	Away	160:0		at Oxton 1985	159:7		at Oxton 1985
Best Batting:	Away	82*	M D Moxon	at Oxton 1985	46	K Teasdale	at Oxton 1985
Best Bowling:	Away	2-17	G B Stevenson	at Oxton 1985			

Combined Universities

		By Yorkshire			Against Yorkshire		
Highest Score:	In Yorkshire	197:8		at Leeds 1990	200:8		at Leeds 1990
	Away	151:1		at Oxford 1980	150:7		at Oxford 1980
Lowest Score:	In Yorkshire	197:8		at Leeds 1990	200:8		at Leeds 1990
	Away	151:1		at Oxford 1980	150:7		at Oxford 1980
Best Batting:	In Yorkshire				63	S P James	at Leeds 1990
	Away	74*	C W J Athey	at Oxford 1980	63	J O D Orders	at Oxford 1980
Best Bowling:	In Yorkshire	3-34	P J Hartley	at Leeds 1990	3-44	M E W Brooker	at Barnsley 1976
	Away	2-43	H P Cooper	at Oxford 1980	1-16	C J Ross	at Oxford 1980

Devon +

		By Yorkshire			Against Yorkshire		
Highest Score:	Away	411:6		at Exmouth 2004	279-8		at Exmouth 2004
Lowest Score:	Away	259:5		at Exmouth 2002	80		at Exmouth 1998
Best Batting:	Away	160	M J Wood	at Exmouth 2004	83	P M Roebuck	at Exmouth 1994
Best Bowling:	Away	4-26	D S Lehmann	at Exmouth 2002	2-42	A O F Le Fleming	at Exmouth 1994

383

LIST A HIGHEST AND LOWEST SCORES BY AND AGAINST YORKSHIRE
PLUS INDIVIDUAL BEST BATTING AND BOWLING (Continued)

Yorkshire versus:

		By Yorkshire		Against Yorkshire	
Dorset +					
Highest Score:	Away	101:2	at Bournemouth 2004	97	at Bournemouth 2004
Best Batting:	Away	71* M J Wood	at Bournemouth 2004	23 C L Park	at Bournemouth 2004
Best Bowling:	Away	4-18 C E W Silverwood	at Bournemouth 2004	2-31 D J Worrad	at Bournemouth 2004
Durham M C +					
Highest Score:	In Yorkshire	249:6	at Middlesbrough 1978	138:5	at Middlesbrough 1978
	Away	214:6	at Chester-le-Street 1979	213:9	at Chester-le-Street 1979
Lowest Score:	In Yorkshire	135	at Harrogate 1973	136:7	at Harrogate 1973
	Away			213:9	at Chester-le-Street 1979
Best Batting:	In Yorkshire	110 J H Hampshire	at Middlesbrough 1978	52 N A Riddell	at Middlesbrough 1978
	Away	92 G Boycott	at Chester-le-Street 1979	52 Wasim Raja	at Chester-le-Street 1979
Best Bowling:	In Yorkshire	4-9 C M Old	at Middlesbrough 1978	5-15 B R Lander	at Middlesbrough 1978
	Away	3-39 H P Cooper	at Chester-le-Street 1979	2-35 B L Cairns	at Chester-le-Street 1979
Herefordshire +					
Highest Score:	Away	275:8	at Kington 1999	124:5	at Kington 1999
Best Batting:	Away	77 G S Blewett	at Kington 1999	39 R D Hughes	at Kington 1999
Best Bowling:	Away	2-22 G M Hamilton	at Kington 1999	2-41 C W Boroughs	at Kington 1999
Ireland +					
Highest Score:	In Yorkshire	299:6	at Leeds 1995	228:7	at Leeds 1995
	Away	202:4	at Belfast 2005	201:7	at Belfast 2005
Lowest Score:	In Yorkshire	249	at Leeds 1997	53	at Leeds 1997
	Away			201:7	at Belfast 2005
Best Batting:	In Yorkshire	113 C White	at Leeds 1995	82 S J S Warke	at Leeds 1995
	Away	58 M P Vaughan	at Belfast 2005	59 E J G Morgan	at Belfast 2005
Best Bowling:	In Yorkshire	7-27 D Gough	at Leeds 1997	3-26 P McCrum	at Leeds 1997
	Away	4-43 C White	at Belfast 2005	1-29 W K McCallan	at Belfast 2005

LIST A HIGHEST AND LOWEST SCORES BY AND AGAINST YORKSHIRE
PLUS INDIVIDUAL BEST BATTING AND BOWLING (Continued)

Yorkshire versus:

		By Yorkshire		Against Yorkshire	
Minor Counties #					
Highest Score:	In Yorkshire	309:5	at Leeds 1997	206:6	at Leeds 1988
	Away	218:3	at Scunthorpe 1975	182	at Scunthorpe 1975
		218:9	at Jesmond 1979		
Lowest Score:	In Yorkshire	309:5	at Leeds 1997	109	at Leeds 1974
	Away	218:3	at Scunthorpe 1975	85	at Jesmond 1979
		218:9	at Jesmond 1979		
Best Batting:	In Yorkshire	109* A McGrath	at Leeds 1997	80* J D Love	at Leeds 1991
	Away	83* G Boycott	at Chester-le-Street 1973	61 N A Folland	at Jesmond 1989
Best Bowling:	In Yorkshire	6-27 A G Nicholson	at Middlesbrough 1972	3-37 S Oakes	at Leeds 1997
	Away	5-32 S Oldham	at Scunthorpe 1975	3-27 I E Conn	at Jesmond 1989
Netherlands $					
Highest Score:	In Yorkshire	204:6	at Leeds 2010	200:8	at Leeds 2010
	Away	158:5	at Rotterdam 2010	154:9	at Rotterdam 2010
Lowest Score:	In Yorkshire	188:9	at Leeds 2011	190:8	at Leeds 2011
	Away	123	at Amsterdam 2011	154:9	at Rotterdam 2010
Best Batting:	In Yorkshire	83* J A Rudolph	at Leeds 2010	62 M G Dighton	at Leeds 2010
	Away	46* J M Bairstow	at Rotterdam 2010	34 P W Borren	at Rotterdam 2010
Best Bowling:	In Yorkshire	3-34 S A Patterson	at Leeds 2010	3-26 Mudassar Bukhari	at Leeds 2011
	Away	4-24 R M Pyrah	at Rotterdam 2010	3-28 Mudassar Bukhari	at Amsterdam 2011
Norfolk +					
Highest Score:	In Yorkshire	106:0	at Leeds 1990	104	at Leeds 1990
	Away	167	at Lakenham 1969	78	at Lakenham 1969
Lowest Score:	In Yorkshire	167	at Leeds 1990	104	at Leeds 1990
	Away			78	at Lakenham 1969
Best Batting:	In Yorkshire	56* M D Moxon	at Leeds 1990	25 R J Finney	at Leeds 1990
	Away	55 J H Hampshire	at Lakenham 1969	21 G J Donaldson	at Lakenham 1969
Best Bowling:	In Yorkshire	3-8 P Carrick	at Leeds 1990		
	Away	3-14 C M Old	at Lakenham 1969	6-48 T I Moore	at Lakenham 1969

LIST A HIGHEST AND LOWEST SCORES BY AND AGAINST YORKSHIRE PLUS INDIVIDUAL BEST BATTING AND BOWLING (Continued)

Yorkshire versus:

		By Yorkshire			Against Yorkshire		
Northumberland +							
Highest Score:	In Yorkshire	138: 2		at Leeds 1992	137		at Leeds 1992
Best Batting:	In Yorkshire	38	S A Kellett	at Leeds 1992	47	G R Morris	at Leeds 1992
Best Bowling:	In Yorkshire	3-18	M A Robinson	at Leeds 1992	2-22	S Greensword	at Leeds 1992
Scotland							
Highest Score:	In Yorkshire	317:5		at Leeds 1986 #	244		at Leeds 2008 +
	Away	259:8		at Edinburgh 2007 +	217		at Edinburgh 2007 +
Lowest Score:	In Yorkshire	228:6		at Bradford 1981 #	142		at Leeds 1996 #
	Away	199:8		at Edinburgh 2004 $	129		at Glasgow 1995 #
Best Batting:	In Yorkshire	118*	J D Love	at Bradford 1981 #	73	I L Philip	at Leeds 1989 +
	Away	91	A A Metcalfe	at Glasgow 1987 #	78	J A Beukes	at Edinburgh 2005 $
Best Bowling:	In Yorkshire	5-28	C E W Silverwood	at Leeds 1996 #	2-22	P J C Hoffman	at Edinburgh 2006 +
	Away	4-20	R K J Dawson	at Edinburgh 2004 $	3-42	Asim Butt	at Linlithgow 1998 #
Shropshire +							
Highest Score:	Away	192		at Telford 1984	229.5		at Telford 1984
Lowest Score:	Away	192		at Telford 1984	185		at Wellington 1976
Best Batting:	Away	59	J H Hampshire	at Wellington 1976	80	Mushtaq Mohammad	at Telford 1984
Best Bowling:	Away	3-17	A L Robinson	at Wellington 1976	3-26	Mushtaq Mohammad	at Telford 1984
Unicorns $							
Highest Score:	In Yorkshire	266:6		at Leeds 2013	234		at Leeds 2013
	Away	191:5		at Chesterfield 2013	189:9		at Chesterfield 2013
Lowest Score:	In Yorkshire				150:6		at Leeds 2012
	Away				184		at Scarborough 2012
Best Batting:	In Yorkshire	139	G S Ballance	at Leeds 2013	107	M S Lineker	at Leeds 2013
	Away	103*	G S Ballance	at Scarborough 2012	83*	T J New	at Scarborough 2012
Best Bowling:	In Yorkshire	5-22	J A Leaning	at Leeds 2013	2-25	R J Woolley	at Leeds 2012
	Away	3-34	R M Pyrah	at Chesterfield 2013	2-31	W W Lee	at Chesterfield 2013

LIST A HIGHEST AND LOWEST SCORES BY AND AGAINST YORKSHIRE PLUS INDIVIDUAL BEST BATTING AND BOWLING (Continued)

Yorkshire versus:

Wiltshire +

	By Yorkshire				Against Yorkshire		
Highest Score:	Away	304:7		at Trowbridge 1987	175	J J Newman	at Trowbridge 1987
Best Batting:	Away	85	A A Metcalfe	at Trowbridge 1987	62	J J Newman	at Trowbridge 1987
Best Bowling:	Away	4-40	K Sharp	at Trowbridge 1987	2-38	R C Cooper	at Trowbridge 1987

Yorkshire Cricket Board +

	By Yorkshire				Against Yorkshire		
Highest Score:	Away	240:5		at Harrogate 2000	110		at Harrogate 2000
Best Batting:	Away	70	M P Vaughan	at Harrogate 2000	31	R A Kettleborough	at Harrogate 2000
Best Bowling:	Away	5-30	D Gough	at Harrogate 2000	1-25	A E McKenna	at Harrogate 2000

Australians

	By Yorkshire				Against Yorkshire		
Highest Score:	In Yorkshire	188		at Leeds 1989	297:3		at Leeds 1989
Lowest Score:	In Yorkshire	140		at Bradford 1972	297:3		at Leeds 1989
Best Batting:	In Yorkshire	105	G Boycott	at Bradford 1972	172	D C Boon	at Bradford 1972
Best Bowling:	In Yorkshire	2-23	D Wilson	at Bradford 1972	3-30	D J Colley	at Bradford 1972

Bangladesh A

	By Yorkshire				Against Yorkshire		
Highest Score:	In Yorkshire	198		at Leeds 2013	191		at Leeds 2013
Best Batting:	In Yorkshire	47*	L E Plunkett	at Leeds 2013	69	Anamul Haque	at Leeds 2013
Best Bowling:	In Yorkshire	5-30	Azeem Rafiq	at Leeds 2013	3-25	Elias Sunny	at Leeds 2013

Sri Lanka A

	By Yorkshire				Against Yorkshire		
Highest Score:	In Yorkshire	249		at Leeds 2014	275:9		at Leeds 2014
Lowest Score:	In Yorkshire	179:7		at Leeds 2004			
Best Batting:	In Yorkshire	81	A W Gale	at Leeds 2007	100	L D Chandimal	at Leeds 2007
Best Bowling:	In Yorkshire	5-51	A Shahzad	at Leeds 2007	4-42	S Prasanna	at Leeds 2007

West Indians

	By Yorkshire				Against Yorkshire		
Highest Score:	In Yorkshire	253:4		at Scarborough 1995	242		at Scarborough 1995
Best Batting:	In Yorkshire	106	A McGrath	at Scarborough 1995	54	R B Richardson	at Scarborough 1995
Best Bowling:	In Yorkshire	3-42	G M Hamilton	at Scarborough 1995	3-48	R Dhanraj	at Scarborough 1995

LIST A HIGHEST AND LOWEST SCORES BY AND AGAINST YORKSHIRE PLUS INDIVIDUAL BEST BATTING AND BOWLING (*Continued*)

Yorkshire versus:

	West Indians A		By Yorkshire		Against Yorkshire		
Highest Score:	In Yorkshire	139		at Leeds 2002	140:2		at Leeds 2002
Best Batting:	In Yorkshire	48	M J Wood	at Leeds 2002	57	D Ganga	at Leeds 2002
Best Bowling:	In Yorkshire	1-31	C J Elstub	at Leeds 2002	4-24	J J C Lawson	at Leeds 2002
	Young Australians						
Highest Score:	In Yorkshire	224:6		at Leeds 1995	156		at Leeds 1995
Best Batting:	In Yorkshire	76	M P Vaughan	at Leeds 1995	51	A C Gilchrist	at Leeds 1995
Best Bowling:	In Yorkshire	5-32	A C Morris	at Leeds 1995	2-21	S Young	at Leeds 1995
	Zimbabwe						
Highest Score:	In Yorkshire	203:7		at Sheffield 1982	202		at Sheffield 1982
Best Batting:	In Yorkshire	98*	G Boycott	at Sheffield 1982	53	D A G Fletcher	at Sheffield 1982
Best Bowling:	In Yorkshire	3-47	P W Jarvis	at Sheffield 1982	3-30	D A G Fletcher	at Sheffield 1982

388

LIST A HIGHEST TEAM TOTALS

BY YORKSHIRE

411:6	v.	Devon at Exmouth	2004 +
376:3	v.	Leicestershire at Leicester	2016 +
352:6	v.	Nottinghamshire at Scarborough	2001 $
345:5	v.	Nottinghamshire at Leeds	1996 +
345:6	v.	Worcestershire at Worcester	2015 +
343:9	v.	Somerset at Taunton	2005 $
341:3	v.	Northamptonshire at Northampton	2006 +
334:5	v.	Surrey at The Oval	2005 $
330:6	v	Surrey at The Oval	2009 +
325:7	v.	Lancashire at Manchester	2016 +
324:7	v.	Lancashire at Manchester	2014 +
318:7	v.	Leicestershire at Leicester	1993 $
317:4	v.	Surrey at Lord's	1965 +
317:5	v.	Scotland at Leeds	1986 #
314:8	v.	Northamptonshire at Scarboough	2016 +
310:5	v.	Leicestershire at Leicester	1997 +
309:5	v.	Minor Counties at Leeds	1997 #
307:3	v.	Essex at Chelmsford	1995 +
307:4	v.	Somerset at Taunton	2002 $
304:7	v.	Wiltshire at Trowbridge	1986 +
303:3	v.	Northamptonshire at Northampton	2002 +
303:4	v.	Leicestershire at Leeds	2008 $
302:4	v.	Sussex at Scarborough	2011 $

AGAINST YORKSHIRE

375:4	for Surrey at Scarborough	1994 $
345:4	for Somerset at Taunton	2005 $
339:7	fo r Northamptonshire at Northampton	2006 +
338:5	for Somerset at Leeds	2013 $
329:8	for Surrey at The Oval	2009 +
325:7	for Northamptonshire at Northampton	1992 $
314:4	for Northamptonshire at Leeds	2007 +
310:7	for Northamptonshire at Sacrborough	2016 +
309:3	for Warwickshire at Birmingham	2005
308:6	for Surrey at The Oval	1995 $
306:8	for Somerset at Taunton	2002 $
302:7	for Leicestershire at Leicester	2008 $
298:9	for Leicestershire at Leicester	1997 $
297:3	for Australians at Leeds	1989
294:6	for Gloucestershire at Cheltenham	2010 $
293:9	for Lancashire at Manchester	1996 +
292	for Sussex at Hove	1963 +
291:5	for Essex at Scarborough	2014 +
291:6	for Nottinghamshire at Nottingham	2004 $
291:9	for Gloucestershire at Lord's	1999 #
291	for Surrey at The Oval	2005 $
289:3	for Worcestershire at Worcester	1996 #
287:9	for Lancashire at Leeds	2006 $

LIST A HIGHEST INDIVIDUAL SCORES

BY YORKSHIRE

191	D S Lehmann	v.	Nottinghamshire at Scarborough	2001 $
175	T M Head	v.	Leicestershire at Leicester	2016 +
160	M J Wood	v.	Devon at Exmouth	2004 +
148	C White	v.	Leicestershire at Leicester	1997 $
148	A McGrath	v.	Somerset at Taunton	2006 $
146	G Boycott	v.	Surrey at Lord's	1965 +
142	G Boycott	v.	Worcestershire at Worcester	1980 #
141*	M D Moxon	v	Glamorgan at Cardiff	1991 #
139*	S P Fleming	v.	Warwickshire at Leeds	2003 $
139	G S Ballance	v.	Unicorns at Leeds	2013 $
137	M D Moxon	v.	Nottinghamshire at Leeds	1996 +
136	A Lyth	v.	Lancashire at Manchester	2016 +
135*	A McGrath	v.	Lancashire at Manchester	2007 +
132*	J A Rudolph	v.	Sussex at Scarborough	2011 $
131*	J A Leaning	v.	Leicestershire at Leicester	2016 +

AGAINST YORKSHIRE

177	S A Newman for	Surrey at The Oval	2009 +
172	D C Boon for	Australia at Leeds	1989
161	D J G Sales for	Northamptonshire at Northampton	2006 +
155*	B A Richards for	Hampshire at Hull	1970 $
146*	S Young for	Gloucestershire at Leeds	1997 $
143*	C M Spearman for	Gloucestershire at Bristol	2004 $
141*	B J Hodge for	Lancashire at Manchester	2007 +
140*	P D Trego for	Somerset at Taunton	2013 $
137*	M Klinger for	Gloucestershire at Leeds	2015 +
137	I R Bell for	Warwickshire at Birmingham	2005 $
136*	N Hussain for	Essex at Chelmsford	2002 #
136	M A Lynch for	Surrey at Bradford	1985 $
135*	D J Bicknell for	Surrey at The Oval	1989 +
133	A D Brown for	Surrey at Scarborough	1994 $
132	U Afzaal for	Northamptonshire at Leeds	2007 +

MOST RUNS IN LIST A MATCHES

690	v.	Devon at Exmouth	2004 +	Y 411:6	D 279:8
688	v.	Somerset at Taunton	2005 $	S 345:4	Y 343:9
680	v.	Northamptonshire at Northampton	2006 +	Y 342:3	N 339:7
659	v.	Surrey at The Oval	2009 +	S 329:8	Y 330:6
625	v.	Surrey at The Oval	2005 $	Y 334:5	S 291
624	v.	Northamptonshire at Scarborough	2016 +	N 310:7	Y 314:8
613	v.	Somerset at Taunton	2002 $	Y 307:4	S 306:8
605	v.	Leicestershire at Leeds	2008 $	Y 303:4	L 302:7
604	v.	Surrey at The Oval	1995 $	S 308:6	Y 296:6
601	v.	Lancashire at Manchester	2014 +	Y 324:7	L 277
596	v.	Leicestershire at Leicester	1997 $	L 298:9	Y 298:9
581	v.	Worcestershire at Worcester	1996 #	W 289:3	Y 292:3
581	v.	Essex at Scarborough	2014 +	Y 290:6	E 291:5

LIST A BEST BOWLING

BY YORKSHIRE

7-15	R A Hutton	v.	Worcestershire at Leeds	1969 $
7-27	D Gough	v.	Ireland at Leeds	1997 +
6-14	H P Cooper	v.	Worcestershire at Worcester	1975 $
6-15	F S Trueman	v.	Somerset at Taunton	1965 +
6-18	D Wilson	v.	Kent at Canterbury	1969 $
6-27	A G Nicholson	v.	Minor Counties at Middlesbrough	1972 #
6-27	P W Jarvis	v.	Somerset at Taunton	1989 $
6-32	S A Patterson	v.	Derbyshire at Leeds	2010 $
6-36	A G Nicholson	v	Somerset At Sheffield	1972 $
6-40	R J Sidebottom	v.	Glamorgan at Cardiff	1998 $
5-13	D Gough	v.	Sussex at Hove	1994 $
5-16	S Stuchbury	v.	Leicestershire at Leicester	1982 $
5-16	G M Hamilton	v.	Hampshire at Leeds	1998 $
5-17	A G Nicholson	v.	Nottinghamshire at Hull	1972 $
5-18	P W Jarvis	v.	Derbyshire at Leeds	1990 $

AGAINST YORKSHIRE

7-32	R G D Willis	for	Warwickshire at Birmingham	1981 #
7-33	R D Jackman	for	Surrey at Harrogate	1970 +
6-15	A A Donald	for	Warwickshire at Birmingham	1995 $
6-18	R E East	for	Essex at Hull	1969 $
6-25	G Chapple	for	Lancashire at Leeds	1998 $
6-32	M T Coles	for	Kent at Leeds	2012 $
6-48	T I Moore	for	Norfolk at Lakenham	1969 +
5-15	B R Lander	for	Durham M C at Harrogate	1973 +
5-15	Sarfraz Nawaz	for	Northamptonshire at Northampton	1975 $
5-16	B S Crump	for	Northamptonshire at Bradford	1969 $
5-16	G C Holmes	for	Glamorgan at Swansea	1985 $
5-20	R E East	for	Essex at Colchester	1979 $
5-22	R D Jackman	for	Surrey at The Oval	1978 $
5-24	C J Tunnicliffe	for	Derbyshire at Derby	1981 #
5-24	C W Henderson	for	Leicestershire at Leeds	2004 $

LIST A ECONOMICAL BOWLING

BY YORKSHIRE

11-9-3-1	C M Old	v.	Middlesex at Lord's	1979 #
8-5-3-3	A L Robinson	v.	Derbyshire at Scarborough	1973 $

AGAINST YORKSHIRE

8-4-6-2	P J Sainsbury	for	Hampshire at Hull	1970 $
8-5-6-3	M J Procter	for	Gloucestershire at Cheltenham	1979 $

LIST A MOST EXPENSIVE BOWLING

BY YORKSHIRE

9-0-87-1	T T Bresnan	v.	Somerset at Taunton	2005 $

AGAINST YORKSHIRE

12-1-96-0	M E Waugh	for	Essex at Chelmsford	1995 +

LIST A HAT-TRICKS FOR YORKSHIRE (4)

P W Jarvis v. Derbyshire at Derby 1982 $ D Gough v. Ireland at Leeds 1997 +
D Gough   v. Lancashire at Leeds 1998 $ C White v. Kent at Leeds 2000 $

LIST A MAN-OF-THE-MATCH AWARDS (136)

M D Moxon	12	M P Vaughan	5	M J Wood	3
G Boycott	11	A Sidebottom	4	R J Blakey	2
D L Bairstow	8	C E W Silverwood	4	G L Brophy	2
C White	8	D Byas	3	P Carrick	2
A A Metcalfe	7	D Gough	3	R A Hutton	2
J H Hampshire	6	P J Hartley	3	L E Plunkett	2
D S Lehmann	6	J D Love	3	P J Sharpe	2
C W J Athey	5	A McGrath	3	G B Stevenson	2
M G Bevan	5	C M Old	3		

One each: T T Bresnan, D B Close, M T G Elliott, G M Fellows, S D Fletcher, G M Hamilton, S N Hartley, P M Hutchinson, R Illingworth, C Johnson, S A Kellett, B Leadbeater, M J Lumb, A G Nicholson, S Oldham, R M Pyrah, P E Robinson, R D Stemp, F S Trueman and D Wilson.

ALL LIST A CENTURIES 1963-2016 (107)

C W J ATHEY (2)

118	v.	Leicestershire	at Leicester	1978 $
115	v.	Kent	at Leeds	1980 +

D L BAIRSTOW (1)

103 *	v	Derbyshire	at Derby	1981 #

J M BAIRSTOW (1)

114	v	Middlesex	at Lord's	2011 $

G S BALLANCE (2)

139	v	Unicorns	at Leeds	2013 $
103 *	v	Unicorns	at Scarborough	2012 $

M G BEVAN (2)

103 *	v	Gloucestershire	at Middlesbrough	1995 $
101	v	Worcestershire	at Scarborough	1995 $

G BOYCOTT (7)

146	v	Surrey	at Lord's	1965 +
142	v	Worcestershire	at Worcester	1980 #
108 *	v	Northamptonshire	at Huddersfield	1974 $
106	v	Northamptonshire	at Bradford	1984 #
105	v	Australians	at Bradford	1972
104 *	v	Glamorgan	at Colwyn Bay	1973 $
102	v	Northamptonshire	at Middlesbrough	1977 #

R J BLAKEY (3)

130	v	Kent	at Scarborough	1991 $
105 *	v	Warwickshire	at Scarborough	1992 $
100 *	v	Gloucestershire	at Cheltenham	1990 $

D BYAS (5)

116 *	v	Surrey	at The Oval	1996 #
111 *	v	Lancashire	at Leeds	1996 $
106 *	v	Derbyshire	at Chesterfield	1993 $
104 *	v	Hampshire	at Leeds	1999 #
101 *	v	Nottinghamshire	at Leeds	1994 $

M T G ELLIOTT (3)

128 *	v	Somerset	at Lord's	2002 +
115 *	v	Kent	at Leeds	2002 $
109	v	Leicestershire	at Leicester	2002 $

S P FLEMING (1)

139 *	v	Warwickshire	at Leeds	2003 $

M J FOSTER (1)

118	v	Leicestershire	at Leicester	1993 $

A W GALE (2)

125 *	v	Essex	at Chelmsford	2010 $
112	v	Kent	at Canterbury	2011 $

J H HAMPSHIRE (7)

119	v	Leicestershire	at Hull	1971 $
114 *	v	Northamptonshire	at Scarborough	1978 $
111 *	v	Sussex	at Hastings	1973 $
110	v	Durham M C	at Middlesbrough	1978 +
108	v	Nottinghamshire	at Sheffield	1970 $
106 *	v	Lancashire	at Manchester	1972 $
100 *	v	Warwickshire	at Birmingham	1975 $

T M HEAD (1))

175	v.	Leicestershire	at Leicester	2016 +

P A JAQUES (1)

105	v.	Sussex	at Leeds	2004 $

S A KELLETT (2)

118 *	v	Derbyshire	at Leeds	1992 $
107	v	Ireland	at Leeds	1995 +

J A LEANING (2)

131 *	v.	Leicestershire	at Leicester	2016 +
111 *	v.	Essex	at Scarborough	2014 +

A Z LEES (1)

102	v	Northamptonshire	at Northampton	2014 +

D S LEHMANN (8)

191	v	Nottinghamshire	at Scarborough	2001 $
119	v	Durham	at Leeds	1998 #
118 *	v	Northamptonshire	at Northampton	2006 +
105	v	Glamorgan	at Cardiff	1995 +
104	v	Somerset	at Taunton	2002 $
103	v	Derbyshire	at Leeds	2001 #
103	v	Leicestershire	at Scarborough	2001 $
102 *	v	Derbyshire	ar Derby	1998 #

J D LOVE (4)

118 *	v	Scotland	at Bradford	1981 #
118 *	v	Surrey	at Leeds	1987 $
104 *	v	Nottinghamshire	at Hull	1986 $
100 *	v	Gloucestershire	at Gloucester	1985 $

R G LUMB (1)

101	v	Nottinghamshire	at Scarborough	1976 $

A LYTH (3)

136 $	v. Lancashire	at Manchester	2016 +
125 $	v. Northamptonshire	at Scarborough	2016 +
109 *	v. Sussex	at Scarborough	2009 $

($ consecutive days)

A McGRATH (7)

148	v	Somerset	at Taunton	2006 $
135 *	v	Lancashire	at Manchester	2007 +
109 *	v	Minor Counties	at Leeds	1997 #
106	v	West Indies	at Scarborough	1995
105 *	v	Scotland	at Leeds	2008 +
102	v	Kent	at Canterbury	2001 $
100	v	Durham	at Leeds	2007 +

G J MAXWELL (1)

111	v	Worcestershire	at Worcester	2015 +

A A METCALFE (4)

127 *	v	Warwickshire	at Leeds	1990 +
116	v	Middlesex	at Lord's	1991 $
115 *	v	Gloucestershire	at Scarborough	1984 $
114	v	Lancashire	at Manchester	1991 #

M D MOXON (7)

141 *	v	Glamorgan	at Cardiff	1991 #
137	v	Nottinghamshire	at Leeds	1996+
129 *	v	Surrey	at The Oval	1991 $
112	v	Sussex	at Middlesbrough	1991 $
107 *	v	Warwickshire	at Leeds	1990 +
106 *	v	Lancashire	at Manchester	1986 #
105	v	Somerset	at Scarborough	1990 $

R B RICHARDSON (1)

103	v	Nottinghamshire	at Nottingham	1993 $

J A RUDOLPH (9)

132 *	v	Sussex	at Scarborough	2011 $
127	v	Somerset	at Scarborough	2007 $
124 *	v	Middlesex	at Scarborough	2010 $
120	v	Leicestershire	at Leeds	2008 $
118	v	Gloucestershire	at Leeds	2009 +
106	v	Warwickshire	at Scarborough	2010 $
105	v	Derbyshire	at Chesterfield	2010 $
101 *	v	Essex	at Chelmsford	2010 $
100	v	Leicestershire	at Leeds	2007 +

ALL LIST A CENTURIES 1963-2016 *(Continued)*

K SHARP (3)

114		v	Essex	at Chelmsford	1985 $
112	*	v	Worcestershire	at Worcester	1985 $
105	*	v	Scotland	at Leeds	1984 #

S R TENDULKAR (1)

107		v	Lancashire	at Leeds	1992 $

M P VAUGHAN (3)

125	*	v	Somerset	at Taunton	2001 #
116	*	v	Lancashire	at Manchester	2004 +
116	*	v	Kent	at Leeds	2005 $

C WHITE (5)

148		v	Leicestershire	at Leicester	1997 $
113		v	Ireland	at Leeds	1995 +
112		v	Northamptonshire	at Northampton	2006 +
101	*	v	Durham	at Chester-le-Street	2006 +
100	*	v	Surrey	at Leeds	2002 +

M J WOOD (5)

160		v	Devon	at Exmouth	2004 +
118	*	v	Cambridgeshire	at March	2003 +
115	*	v	Derbyshire	at Derby	2002 #
111		v	Surrey	at The Oval	2005 $
105	*	v	Somerset	at Taunton	2002$

YOUNUS KHAN (1)

100		v	Nottinghamshire	at Nottingham	2007 +

LIST A PARTNERSHIPS OF 150 AND OVER 1963-2016 (44)

274 3rd wkt T M Head (175)   and J A Leaning (131*)   v. Leicestershire at Leicester 2016+
242* 1st wkt M D Moxon (107*)   and A A Metcalfe (127*) v. Warwickshire at Leeds   1990 +
233* 1st wkt A W Gale (125*)   and J A Rudolph (101*)   v. Essex at Chelmsford   2010 $
213 1st wkt M D Moxon (141*)   and A A Metcalfe (84)   v. Glamorgan at Cardiff   1991 #
211* 1st wkt M D Moxon (93*)   and A A Metcalfe (94*)   v. Warwickshire at Birmingham
                                                                                        1987 $
207 4th wkt S A Kellett (107)   and C White (113)   v. Ireland at Leeds   1995 +
202 2nd wkt G Boycott (87)   and C W J Athey (115)   v. Kent at Leeds   1980 +
201 1st wkt J H Hampshire (86)   and C W J Athey (118)   v. Leicestershire at Leicester
                                                                                        1978 $
198* 4th wkt M T G Elliott (115*) and A McGrath (85*)   v. Kent at Leeds   2002 $
195 1st wkt A Lyth (84)   and A Z Lees (102)   v. Northamptonshire
                                                               at Northampton 2014 +
192 2nd wkt G Boycott (146)   and D B Close (79)   v. Surrey at Lord's   1965 +
190 1st wkt G Boycott (89*)   and R G Lumb (101)   v. Nottinghamshire
                                                               at Scarborough 1976 $
190 5th wkt R J Blakey (96)   and M J Foster (118)   v. Leicestershire at Leicester
                                                                                        1993 $
186 1st wkt G Boycott (99)   and J H Hampshire (92*) v. Gloucestershire
                                                               at Scarborough 1975 $
186 1st wkt G S Blewett (71)   and D Byas (104*)   v. Hampshire at Leeds   1999 #
184 3rd wkt M P Vaughan (70)   and D S Lehmann (119)   v. Durham at Leeds   1998 #
181 5th wkt M T G Elliott (109)   and A McGrath (78)   v. Leicestershire at Leicester
                                                                                        2002 $
176 3rd wkt R J Blakey (86)   and S R Tendulkar (107) v. Lancashire at Leeds   1992 $
172 2nd wkt D Byas (86)   and D S Lehmann (99)   v. Kent at Maidstone   1998 $
172 3rd wkt A McGrath (38)   and D S Lehmann (191)   v. Nottinghamshire
                                                               at Scarborough 2001 $
171 1st wkt M D Moxon (112)   and A A Metcalfe (68)   v. Sussex at Middlesbrough 1991 $
170 4th wkt M J Wood (105*)   and D S Lehmann (104)   v. Somerset at Taunton   2002 $
170 1st wkt A W Gale (89)   and J A Rudolph (120)   v. Leicestershire at Leeds 2008 $
167* 6th wkt M G Bevan (95*)   and R J Blakey ((80*)   v. Lancashire at Manchester
                                                                                        1996 #
167* 1st wkt C White (100*)   and M J Wood (57*)   v. Surrey at Leeds   2002 +
167 1st wkt M D Moxon(64)   and A A Metcalfe (116)   v. Middlesex at Lord's   1991 $
167 1st wkt M J Wood (65)   and S P Fleming (139*)   v. Warwickshire at Leeds   2003 $
166 1st wkt M D Moxon (82*)   and A A Metcalfe (70)   v. Northamptonshire at Leeds
                                                                                        1988 #
165 1st wkt M D Moxon (80)   and D Byas (106*)   v. Derbyshire at Chesterfield
                                                                                        1993 $
165 1st wkt M D Moxon (70)   and D Byas (88*)   v. Northamptonshire at Leeds
                                                                                        1993 $
164* 2nd wkt G Boycott (91*)   and C W J Athey (79*)   v. Worcestershire at Worcester
                                                                                        1981 $
164 3rd wkt A McGrath (105*)   and J A Rudolph (82)   v. Scotland at Leeds   2008 +
164 3rd wkt J A Rudolph (84)   and A McGrath (73)   v. Glamorgan at Scarborough
                                                                                        2008 $
161 1st wkt M D Moxon (74)   and A A Metcalfe (85)   v. Wiltshire at Trowbridge 1987 +
160* 1st wkt G Boycott (70*)   and M D Moxon (82*)   v. Cheshire at Oxton   1985 +
160* 5th wkt G M Fellows (80*)   and C White (73*)   v. Surrey at Leeds   2001 +
160* 3rd wkt A Lyth (60*)   and G S Ballance (103*) v. Unicorns at Scarborough
                                                                                        2012 $
160 1st wkt G Boycott (67)   and J H Hampshire (84)   v. Warwickshire at Birmingham
                                                                                        1973 $

396

LIST A PARTNERSHIPS OF 150 AND OVER *(Continued)*

159	2nd wkt	G Boycott (92)	and D B Close (96)	v. Surrey at The Oval	1969 +
157	2nd wkt	K Sharp (71)	and R J Blakey (79)	v. Worcestershire at Worcester	
					1990 $
155	*1st wkt	A Lyth (67*)	and A Z Lees (69*)	v. Derbyshire at Scarborough	
					2014 +
154*	2nd wkt	J H Hampshire (111*)			
			and B Leadbeater (57*)	v. Sussex at Hove	1973 $
153	4th wkt	Younus Khan (100)	and A W Gale ((69*)	v. Nottinghamshire	
				at Nottingham 2007 +	
150*	5th wkt	S N Hartley (67*)	and J D Love (82*)	v. Hampshire at Middlesbrough	
					1983 $

LIST A HIGHEST PARTNERSHIPS FOR EACH WICKET

1st wkt	242*	M D Moxon (107*)	and A A Metcalfe (127*)	v Warwickshire at Leeds 1990 +	
2nd wkt	202	G Boycott (87)	and C W J Athey (115)	v. Kent at Leeds	1980 +
3rd wkt	274	T M Head (175)	and J A Leaning (131*)	v.Leicestershire at Leiceater	
					2016+
4th wkt	207	S A Kellett (107)	and C White (113)	v. Ireland at Leeds	1995 +
5th wkt	190	R J Blakey (96)	and M J Foster (118)	v. Leicestershire at Leicester	
					1993 $
6th wkt	167*	M G Bevan (95*)	and R J Blakey ((80*)	v. Lancashire at Manchester	
					1996 #
7th wkt	149 *	J D Love (118*)	and C M Old (78*)	v. Scotland at Bradford	1981 #
8th wkt	89	R J Blakey (60)	and R K J Dawson (41)	v. Leicestershire at Scarborough	
					2002 $
9th wkt	88	S N Hartley (67)	and A Ramage (32*)	v. Middlesex at Lord's	1982 $
10th wkt	80*	D L Bairstow (103*)			
			and M Johnson (4*)	v. Derbyshire at Derby	1981 #

ALL LIST A 5 WICKETS IN AN INNINGS 1963-2016 (56)

C W J ATHEY (1)

5-35	v	Derbyshire	at Chesterfield	1981 $

AZEEM RAFIQ (1)

5-30	v	Bangladesh A	at Leeds	2013

M G BEVAN (1)

5-29	v	Sussex	at Eastbourne	1996 $

P CARRICK (2)

5-22	v	Glamorgan	at Leeds	1991 $
5-40	v	Sussex	at Middlesbrough	1991 $

H P COOPER (2)

6-14	v	Worcestershire	at Worcester	1975 $
5-30	v	Worcestershire	at Middlesbrough	1978 $

D GOUGH (4)

5-13	v	Sussex	at Hove	1994 $
7-27	v	Ireland	at Leeds	1997 +
5-25	v	Surrey	at Leeds	1998 $
5-30	v	Yorkshire C B	at Harrogate	2000 +

G M HAMILTON (2)

5-16	v	Hampshire	at Leeds	1998 $
5-34	v	Sussex	at Scarborough	2000 $

P J HARTLEY (4)

5-36	v	Sussex	at Scarborough	1993 $
5-38	v	Worcestershire	at Worcester	1990 $
5-43	v	Scotland	at Leeds	1986 #
5-46	v	Hampshire	at Southampton	1990 +

M J HOGGARD (3)

5-28	v	Leicestershire	at Leicester	2000 $
5-30	v	Northamptonshire	at Northampton	2000 $
5-65	v	Somerset	at Lord's	2002 +

R A HUTTON (1)

7-15	v	Worcestershire	at Leeds	1969 $

R ILLINGWORTH (1)

5-29	v	Surrey	at Lord's	1965 +

P W JARVIS (3)

6-27	v	Somerset	at Taunton	1989 $
5-18	v	Derbyshire	at Leeds	1990 $
5-29	v	Northamptonshire	at Northampton	1992 $

J A LEANING (1)

5-22	v	Unicorns	at Leeds	2013 $

A C MORRIS (1)

5-32	v	Young Australia	at Leeds	1995

M D MOXON (1)

5-31	v	Warwickshire	at Leeds	1991 #

A G NICHOLSON (4)

6-27	v	Minor Counties	at Middlesbrough	1972 #
6-36	v	Somerset	at Sheffield	1972 $
5-17	v	Nottinghamshire	at Hull	1972 $
5-24	v	Derbyshire	at Bradford	1975 #

C M OLD (2)

5-33	v	Sussex	at Hove	1971 $
5-38	v	Northamptonshire	at Sheffield	1972 $

S OLDHAM (1)

5-32	v	Minor Counties	at Scunthorpe	1975 #

S A PATTERSON (2)

6-32	v	Derbyshire	at Leeds	2010 $
5-24	v	Worcestershire	at Worcester	2015 +

A U RASHID (1)

5-33	v	Hampshire	at Southampton	2014 +

A SHAHZAD (1)

5-51	v	Sri Lanka A	at Leeds	2007

C SHAW (1)

5-41	v	Hampshire	at Bournemouth	1984 $

A SIDEBOTTOM (2)

5-27	v	Worcestershire	at Bradford	1985 #
5-27	v	Glamorgan	at Leeds	1987 +

R J SIDEBOTTOM (2)

6-40	v	Glamorgan	at Cardiff	2003 $
5-42	v	Leicestershire	at Leicester	2003 $

C E W SILVERWOOD (1)

5-28	v	Scotland	at Leeds	1996 #

G B STEVENSON (4)

5-27	v	Berkshire	at Reading	1983 +
5-28	v	Kent	at Canterbury	1978 #
5-41	v	Leicestershire	at Leicester	1976 $
5-50	v	Worcestershire	at Leeds	1982 #

S STUCHBURY (1)

5-16	v	Leicestershire	at Leicester	1982 $

N D THORNICROFT (1)

5-42	v	Gloucestershire	at Leeds	2003 $

F S TRUEMAN (1)

6-15	v	Somerset	at Taunton	1965 +

C WHITE (2)

5-19	v	Somerset	at Scarborough	2002 $
5-25	v	Lancashire	at Leeds	2000 #

D WILSON (2)

6-18	v	Kent	at Canterbury	1969 $
5-25	v	Lancashire	at Bradford	1972 #

ALL LIST A PLAYERS WHO HAVE TAKEN 4 WICKETS IN AN INNINGS 1963-2016 (159) AND BEST FIGURES

11	C M Old	4-9	v	Durham M C	at Middlesbrough	1978 +
10	C White	4-14	v	Lancashire	at Leeds	2000 $
		4-14	v	Surrey	at The Oval	2005 $
9	A Sidebottom	4-15	v	Worcestershire	at Leeds	1987 #
8	P W Jarvis	4-13	v	Worcestershire	at Leeds	1986 $
8	D Gough	4-17	v	Nottinghamshire	at Nottingham	2000 #
8	G B Stevenson	4-20	v	Essex	at Barnsley	1977 #
7	S D Fletcher	4-11	v	Kent	at Canterbury	1988 $
6	C E W Silverwood	4-11	v	Leicestershire	at Leicester	2000 $
6	H P Cooper	4-18	v	Leicestershire	at Leeds	1975 +
5	S Oldham	4-13	v	Nottinghamshire	at Nottingham	1989 $
5	R M Pyrah	4-24	v	Netherlands	at Rotterdam	2010 $
4	P Carrick	4-13	v	Derbyshire	at Bradford	1983 $
4	R K J Dawson	4-13	v	Derbyshire	at Derby	2002 #
4	T T Bresnan	4-25	v	Somerset	at Leeds	2005 $
4	G M Hamilton	4-27	v	Warwickshire	at Birmingham	1995 $
3	R A Hutton	4-18	v	Surrey	at The Oval	1972 $
3	A G Nicholson	4-15	v	Kent	at Leeds	1974 $
3	P J Hartley	4-21	v	Scotland	at Glasgow	1995 #
3	A L Robinson	4-25	v	Surrey	at The Oval	1974 $
3	R D Stemp	4-25	v	Gloucestershire	at Bristol	1996 $
3	M P Vaughan	4-27	v	Gloucestershire	at Bristol	2000 $
2	M K Bore	4-21	v	Sussex	at Middlesbrough	1970 $
		4-21	v	Worcestershire	at Worcester	1970 $
2	J D Woodford	4-23	v	Northamptonshire	at Northampton	1970 $
		4-23	v	Warwickshire	at Middlesbrough	1971 $
2	G J Kruis	4-17	v	Derbyshire	at Leeds	2007 $
2	D Wilson	4-22	v	Nottinghamshire	at Bradford	1969 $
2	V J Craven	4-22	v	Kent	at Scarborough	2003 $
2	M A Robinson	4-23	v	Northamptonshire	at Leeds	1993 $
2	S N Hartley	4-32	v	Derbyshire	at Leeds	1989 #
2	A U Rashid	4-38	v	Northamptonshire	at Northampton	2012 $
2	A McGrath	4-41	v	Surrey	at Leeds	2003 $
1	R Illingworth	4-6	v	Middlesex	at Hull	1983 $
1	M Johnson	4-18	v	Scotland	at Bradford	1981 $
1	G S Blewett	4-18	v	Lancashire	at Manchester	1999 +
1	G M Fellows	4-19	v	Durham	at Leeds	2002 $
1	A P Grayson	4-25	v	Glamorgan	at Cardiff	1994 $
1	C J Elstub	4-25	v	Surrey	at Leeds	2001 $
1	D S Lehmann	4-26	v	Devon	at Exmouth	2002 +
1	S A Patterson	4-28	v	Worcestershire	at Worcester	2011 $
1	C Shaw	4-29	v	Middlesex	at Leeds	1988 +
1	A G Wharf	4-29	v	Nottinghamshire	at Leeds	1996 #
1	F S Trueman	4-30	v	Nottinghamshire	at Middlesbrough	1963 +
1	J D Batty	4-33	v	Kent	at Scarborough	1991 $
1	P M Hutchinson	4-34	v	Gloucestershire	at Gloucester	1998 $
1	A K D Gray	4-34	v	Kent	at Leeds	2002 $
1	A Shahzad	4-34	v	Middlesex	at Lord's	2010 $
1	P M Stringer	4-35	v	Derbyshire	at Sheffield	1969 $
1	C S Pickles	4-36	v	Somerset	at Scarborough	1990 $
1	M J Hoggard	4-39	v	Surrey	at Leeds	2000 #
1	R J Sidebottom	4-39	v	Bedfordshire	at Luton	2001 +
1	K Sharp	4-40	v	Wiltshire	at Trowbridge	1987 +
1	T L Best	4-46	v	Essex	at Chelmsford	2010 $
1	A C Morris	4-49	v	Leicestershire	at Leicester	1997 $
1	L E Plunkett	4-52	v	Kent	Canterbury	2016 +
1	D B Close	4-60	v	Sussex	at Hove	1963 +

CAREER AVERAGES FOR YORKSHIRE

ALL LIST A MATCHES OF 40 TO 65 OVERS 1963-2016

Player	M	Inns	NO	Runs	HS	Av'ge	100s	50s	Runs	Wkts	Av'ge	Ct/St
Ashraf, M A ...	22	6	4	3	3*	1.50	0	0	895	23	38.91	4
Athey, C W J ...	140	129	14	3662	118	31.84	2	25	431	19	22.68	46
Azeem Rafiq ..	**21**	**16**	**6**	**144**	**34***	**14.40**	**0**	**0**	**752**	**23**	**32.69**	**7**
Bairstow, D L ..	403	317	71	5180	103*	21.05	1	19	17	0	—	390/31
Bairstow, J M .	**38**	**34**	**4**	**783**	**114**	**26.10**	**1**	**3**	**0**	**0**	**—**	**28/2**
Baker, T M	4	1	0	3	3	3.00	0	0	89	4	22.25	3
Balderstone, J C	13	11	2	173	46	19.22	0	0	38	2	19.00	3
Ballance, G S ..	**45**	**42**	**7**	**1829**	**139**	**52.25**	**2**	**12**	**0**	**0**	**—**	**19**
Batty, J D	38	16	7	50	13*	5.55	0	0	1297	42	30.88	18
Berry, P J	1	0	0	0	—	—	0	0	28	0	—	0
Best, T L	5	1	1	8	8*	—	0	0	166	10	16.60	1
Bevan, M G	48	45	12	2110	103*	63.93	2	19	540	28	19.28	11
Binks, J G	30	21	3	247	34	13.72	0	0	0	0	—	26/8
Blain, J A R ...	15	8	3	34	11*	6.80	0	0	462	14	33.00	3
Blakey, R J ...	373	319	84	7361	130*	31.32	3	35	0	0	—	369/59
Blewett, G S ...	17	17	0	345	77	20.29	0	2	196	11	17.81	7
Booth, P A	5	2	1	7	6*	7.00	0	0	147	3	49.00	1
Bore, M K	55	24	10	90	15	6.42	0	0	1600	50	32.00	15
Boycott, G ...	264	255	38	8699	146	40.08	7	63	1095	25	43.80	92
Bresnan, T T .	**160**	**112**	**28**	**1729**	**95**	**20.58**	**0**	**6**	**5583**	**174**	**32.08**	**45**
Brooks, J A ..	**12**	**4**	**1**	**7**	**6**	**2.33**	**0**	**0**	**461**	**15**	**30.73**	**3**
Brophy, G L ...	68	57	12	1240	93*	27.55	0	9	0	0	—	67/14
Byas, D	313	301	35	7782	116*	29.25	5	44	659	25	26.36	128
Callis, E	**1**	**1**	**0**	**0**	**0**	**0.00**	**0**	**0**	**0**	**0**	**—**	**0**
Carrick, P	304	206	53	2159	54	14.11	0	2	7408	236	31.38	70
Carver, K	**9**	**2**	**2**	**47**	**35***	**—**	**0**	**0**	**163**	**7**	**23.28**	**1**
Chapman, C A..	10	7	4	94	36*	31.33	0	0	0	0	—	7
Claydon, M E ..	7	2	0	15	9	7.50	0	0	293	8	36.62	0
Cleary, M F ...	4	3	1	50	23*	25.00	0	0	159	2	79.50	0
Close, D B	32	31	2	631	96	21.75	0	3	475	23	20.65	14
Coad, B O	**7**	**3**	**3**	**2**	**2***	**—**	**0**	**0**	**282**	**3**	**94.00**	**3**
Cooper, H P ...	142	74	34	483	29*	12.07	0	0	4184	177	23.63	26
Cope, G A	37	20	13	96	18*	13.71	0	0	1020	24	42.50	9
Coverdale, S P .	3	3	2	18	17*	18.00	0	0	0	0	—	3
Craven, V J ...	42	39	5	580	59	17.05	0	2	353	21	16.80	14
Dalton, A J ...	17	16	1	280	55	18.66	0	1	0	0	—	7
Dawood, I	25	20	4	260	57	16.25	0	1	0	0	—	18/8
Dawson, R K J .	92	58	12	431	41	9.36	0	0	2784	91	30.59	31
Dennis, S J ...	56	24	11	114	16*	8.76	0	0	1736	42	41.33	7
Elliott, M T G ..	6	6	3	394	128*	131.33	3	0	0	0	—	0
Elstub, C J	10	4	4	6	4*	—	0	0	290	12	24.16	0
Fellows, G M ..	95	79	15	1342	80*	20.96	0	4	836	22	38.00	27
Fisher, I D	28	12	3	68	20	7.55	0	0	708	29	24.41	6
Fisher, M D ..	**13**	**5**	**3**	**62**	**34**	**31.00**	**0**	**0**	**431**	**11**	**39.18**	**2**
Fleming, S P ...	7	7	1	285	139*	47.50	1	1	0	0	—	3
Fletcher, S D ...	129	32	18	109	16*	7.78	0	0	4686	164	28.57	34
Foster, M J	20	14	1	199	118	15.30	1	0	370	6	61.66	6
Gale, A W	125	116	11	3256	125*	31.00	2	17	0	0	—	24
Gibson, R	**5**	**4**	**1**	**19**	**9**	**6.33**	**0**	**0**	**158**	**5**	**31.60**	**1**
Gilbert, C R ...	5	4	0	55	37	13.75	0	0	199	8	24.87	2
Gillespie, J N ...	18	4	1	29	15*	9.66	0	0	601	18	33.38	6
Gough, D	214	120	33	1280	72*	14.71	0	1	6798	291	23.36	43
Gray, A K D ...	31	19	7	130	30*	10.83	0	0	843	25	33.72	8
Grayson, A P ...	66	49	8	587	55	14.31	0	1	1441	39	36.94	19
Guy, S M	32	23	4	282	40	14.84	0	0	0	0	—	35/11
Hamilton, G M .	101	70	18	1059	57*	20.36	0	2	2803	121	23.16	15
Hampshire, A W	4	3	0	3	3	1.00	0	0	0	0	—	1

Player	M	Inns	NO	Runs	HS	Av'ge	100s	50s	Runs	Wkts	Av'ge	Ct/St
Hampshire, J H .	234	223	24	6296	119	31.63	7	36	26	1	26.00	69
Hannon-Dalby, O J	5	1	1	21	21*	—	0	0	202	5	40.40	3
Harden, R J	19	16	2	230	42	16.42	0	0	0	0	—	1
Hartley, P J	219	145	49	1609	83	16.76	0	4	7476	283	26.41	40
Hartley, S N	171	154	31	2815	83*	22.88	0	13	2153	67	32.13	52
Harvey, I J	28	27	2	637	74	25.48	0	3	950	30	31.66	8
Head, T M	**4**	**4**	**0**	**277**	**175**	**69.25**	**1**	**1**	**0**	**0**	**—**	**1**
Hodd, A J	**29**	**21**	**4**	**350**	**69***	**20.58**	**0**	**1**	**0**	**0**	**—**	**35/8**
Hodgson, D M .	12	10	1	272	90	30.22	0	3	0	0	—	10/2
Hodgson, L J ..	6	2	0	9	9	4.50	0	0	161	4	40.25	1
Hoggard, M J ..	83	28	19	41	7*	4.55	0	0	2682	118	22.72	4
Hutchinson, P M .	32	11	8	18	4*	6.00	0	0	844	43	19.62	3
Hutton, R A ...	107	80	25	1075	65	19.54	0	4	3000	128	23.43	27
Illingworth, R ..	41	15	11	171	45	42.75	0	0	793	40	19.82	14
Ingham, P G	12	10	4	312	87*	52.00	0	2	0	0	—	2
Inzamam ul Haq	3	3	0	69	53	23.00	0	1	0	0	—	0
Jaques, P A	43	42	2	1588	105	39.70	1	13	0	0	—	16
Jarvis, P W	144	74	28	529	42	11.50	0	0	4684	213	21.99	33
Johnson, C	129	102	22	1615	73*	20.18	0	4	28	2	14.00	33
Johnson, M	14	6	3	34	15*	11.33	0	0	455	12	37.91	2
Katich, S M ...	3	3	2	79	40*	79.00	0	0	0	0	—	0
Kellett, S A	56	51	3	1207	118*	25.14	2	4	16	0	—	13
Kettleborough, R A	10	6	3	71	28	23.66	0	0	72	3	24.00	4
Kirby, S P	29	12	3	38	15	4.22	0	0	1061	24	44.20	6
Kruis, G J	55	22	11	138	31*	12.54	0	0	1793	62	28.91	9
Lawson, M A K .	4	4	0	30	20	7.50	0	0	141	3	47.00	1
Leadbeater, B ..	105	100	19	2245	90	27.71	0	11	95	5	19.00	26
Leaning, J A ...	**32**	**28**	**6**	**786**	**131***	**35.72**	**2**	**4**	**141**	**7**	**20.14**	**13**
Lee, J E	4	0	0	0	0	—	0	0	116	7	16.57	0
Lees, A Z	**37**	**35**	**2**	**1032**	**102**	**31.27**	**1**	**8**	**0**	**0**	**—**	**14**
Lehmann, D S ..	130	126	20	5229	191	49.33	8	38	1990	79	25.18	41
Lester, E I	1	1	0	0	0	0.00	0	0	0	0	—	0
Love, J D	220	203	33	4298	118*	25.28	4	18	129	5	25.80	44
Lucas, D S	5	2	0	40	32	20.00	0	0	187	3	62.33	1
Lumb, M J	104	98	8	2606	92	28.95	0	18	28	0	—	31
Lumb, R G	137	123	13	2784	101	25.30	1	16	0	0	—	21
Lyth, A	**96**	**89**	**7**	**2816**	**136**	**34.34**	**3**	**13**	**217**	**3**	**72.33**	**39**
McGrath, A	275	253	39	7220	148	33.73	7	44	2514	79	31.82	91
Maxwell, G J ...	8	7	1	312	111	52.00	1	2	144	3	48.00	4
Metcalfe, A A ..	194	189	15	5584	127*	32.09	4	36	44	2	22.00	44
Middlebrook, J D	18	11	3	61	15*	7.62	0	0	530	13	40.76	5
Milburn, S M ..	4	2	1	14	13*	14.00	0	0	118	2	59.00	1
Miller, D A	3	3	0	45	44	15.00	0	0	0	0	—	0
Morris, A C	27	17	5	212	48*	17.66	0	0	464	21	22.09	5
Moxon, M D ...	237	229	21	7380	141*	35.48	7	49	1202	34	35.35	77
Nicholson, A G .	120	46	22	155	15*	6.45	0	0	2951	173	17.05	16
Nicholson, N G .	2	2	1	1	1*	1.00	0	0	0	0	—	2
Old, C M	221	169	38	2572	82*	19.63	0	10	5841	308	18.96	56
Oldham, S	106	40	21	192	38*	10.10	0	0	3136	142	22.08	17
Padgett, D E V .	57	54	3	1069	68	20.96	0	2	25	1	25.00	13
Parker, B	73	61	9	965	69	18.20	0	1	18	0	—	12
Patterson, S A .	**76**	**32**	**19**	**201**	**25***	**15.46**	**0**	**0**	**2648**	**92**	**28.78**	**12**
Pickles, C S ...	71	48	20	375	37*	13.39	0	0	2403	63	38.14	23
Plunkett, L E ..	**21**	**17**	**7**	**309**	**53**	**30.90**	**0**	**1**	**743**	**29**	**25.62**	**13**
Pyrah, R M ...	114	75	20	978	69	17.78	0	2	3572	133	26.85	35
Ramage, A	34	17	8	134	32*	14.88	0	0	1178	30	39.26	3
Ramsden, J	1	0	0	0	—	—	0	0	26	2	13.00	0
Rana Naved -ul-Hasan ..	17	16	1	375	74	25.00	0	3	681	26	26.19	5
Rashid, A U ...	**92**	**65**	**19**	**948**	**71**	**20.60**	**0**	**1**	**3244**	**115**	**28.20**	**26**
Rhodes, S J	2	1	0	6	6	6.00	0	0	0	0	—	3

ALL LIST A MATCHES OF 40 TO 65 OVERS 1963-2016 *(Continued)*

Player	M	Inns	NO	Runs	HS	Av'ge	100s	50s	Runs	Wkts	Av'ge	Ct/St
Rhodes W M H	19	16	2	242	46	17.28	0	0	344	10	34.40	6
Richardson. R B	28	28	6	993	103	45.13	1	8	0	0	—	5
Richardson, S A	1	1	0	7	7	7.00	0	0	0	0	—	0
Robinson, A L ..	92	36	19	127	18*	7.47	0	0	2588	105	24.64	14
Robinson, M A ..	89	30	16	41	7	2.92	0	0	2795	91	30.71	7
Robinson, O E ..	3	2	2	16	12*	—	0	0	66	0	—	4
Robinson, P E ..	135	123	15	2738	78*	25.35	0	14	0	0	—	47
Root, J E	17	16	2	488	63	34.85	0	2	222	7	31.71	9
Rudolph, J A ...	65	62	10	3090	132*	59.42	9	19	37	0	—	32
Ryan, M	3	2	1	7	6*	7.00	0	0	149	5	29.80	3
Sadler, J L	1	1	0	19	19	19.00	0	0	0	0	—	0
Sanderson, B W	10	2	1	14	12*	14.00	0	0	247	8	30.87	5
Sayers, J J	31	30	2	594	62	21.21	0	5	79	1	79.00	2
Scofield, D	3	1	0	0	0	0.00	0	0	111	2	55.50	1
Shahzad. A	30	22	7	243	59*	16.20	0	1	1182	34	34.76	7
Sharp, K	206	191	18	4776	114	27.60	3	28	48	4	12.00	68
Sharpe, P J	91	86	4	1515	89*	18.47	0	8	11	0	—	53
Shaw, C	48	20	10	127	26	12.70	0	0	1396	58	24.06	8
Sidebottom, A ..	236	131	47	1279	52*	15.22	0	1	6918	260	26.60	51
Sidebottom, R J	51	22	22	303	30*	10.44	0	0	3631	124	29.28	24
Silverwood, C E W												
	166	94	33	892	61	14.62	0	4	5212	224	23.26	25
Smith, N	7	2	1	5	5	5.00	0	0	0	0	—	2
Smith, R	3	2	0	17	17	8.50	0	0	0	0	—	1
Squires, P J ...	56	48	5	708	79*	16.46	0	3	4	0	—	10
Starc, M A	4	2	2	5	4*	—	0	0	181	8	22.62	1
Stemp, R D	88	28	10	118	23*	6.55	0	0	2996	100	29.96	14
Stevenson, G B .	217	158	23	1710	81*	12.66	0	2	6820	290	23.51	38
Stott, W B	2	2	0	30	30	15.00	0	0	0	0	—	0
Stringer, P M ...	11	8	6	29	13*	14.50	0	0	256	15	17.06	0
Stuchbury, S ...	22	8	4	21	9*	5.25	0	0	677	29	23.34	2
Swallow, I G ...	8	5	3	37	17*	18.50	0	0	198	2	99.00	5
Swanepoel, P J .	3	2	2	9	8*	—	0	0	100	3	33.33	0
Tattersall, J A ..	1	1	0	0	0	0.00	0	0	0	0	—	0
Taylor, C R	6	5	0	102	28	20.40	0	0	0	0	—	0
Taylor, K	10	10	0	135	30	13.50	0	0	168	11	15.27	3
Taylor, N S	1	0	0	0	0	—	0	0	45	1	45.00	1
Tendulkar, S R .	17	17	2	540	107	36.00	1	1	167	6	27.83	3
Thornicroft, N D	14	7	4	52	20	17.33	0	0	591	17	34.76	3
Townsley, R A J	5	4	1	81	34	27.00	0	0	62	0	—	1
Trueman, F S ..	11	9	1	127	28	15.87	0	0	348	21	16.57	5
Vaughan, M P ..	183	178	13	4966	125*	30.09	3	29	1860	60	31.00	56
Wainman, J C .	1	1	0	33	33	33.00	0	0	51	3	17.00	1
Wainwright, D J	48	21	13	150	26	18.75	0	0	1427	38	37.55	16
Waite, M E	3	3	1	61	38	30.50	0	0	117	3	39.00	0
Wardlaw, I	17	10	4	56	18	9.33	0	0	686	24	28.58	3
Waring, J	1	1	1	1	1*	—	0	0	11	0	—	0
Warren, A C ...	1	1	0	3	3	3.00	0	0	35	1	35.00	0
Wharf, A G	6	1	1	2	2*	—	0	0	176	8	22.00	1
White, C	292	266	39	6384	148	28.12	5	28	6120	248	24.67	84
Whiteley, J P ...	6	4	0	19	14	4.75	0	0	195	2	97.50	1
Widdup, S	4	4	0	49	38	12.25	0	0	0	0	—	2
Wigley, D H ...	1	1	0	0	0	0.00	0	0	38	0	—	0
Willey, D J	9	7	1	123	26*	20.50	0	0	361	11	32.81	2
Williamson, K A	13	11	0	279	70	25.36	0	1	42	1	42.00	6
Wilson, D	61	47	8	430	46	11.02	0	0	1527	76	20.09	22
Wood, G L	1	1	0	26	26	26.00	0	0	0	0	—	0
Wood, M J	145	134	14	3270	160	27.25	5	14	76	3	25.33	57
Woodford, J D..	72	57	14	890	69*	20.69	0	2	1627	77	21.12	25
Younus Khan ...	11	8	0	248	100	31.00	1	0	144	2	72.00	5
Yuvraj Singh ...	9	9	0	196	50	21.77	0	1	197	3	65.66	0

YORKSHIRE T20i CRICKETERS 2003-2016 (Correct to October 27, 2016)

For England

Player	M	I	NO	Runs	HS	Av'ge	100s	50s	Balls	Runs	W	Av'ge	Best	4wI	Ct/St
BAIRSTOW, J M ...2011-16	20	15	4	195	60*	17.72	0	1	—	—	—	—	—	0	23
BRESNAN, T T ..2006-13/14	34	22	9	216	47*	16.61	0	0	663	887	24	36.95	3-10	0	10
PLUNKETT, L E ..2006-16	9	3	1	5	4	2.50	0	0	203	244	11	22.18	3-21	0	2
RASHID, A U ...2009-16	20	8	5	28	9*	9.33	0	0	384	500	15	33.33	2-18	0	5
ROOT, J E ...2012-16	21	19	3	600	90*	37.50	0	2	72	128	6	21.33	2-9	0	12
SHAHZAD, A ...2010-11	3	1	1	0	0*	—	0	0	66	97	3	32.33	2-38	0	1
VAUGHAN, M P* ..2005-7	2	2	0	27	27	13.50	0	0	—	—	—	—	—	—	0
WILLEY, D J ...2015-16	12	8	3	73	21	14.60	0	0	236	325	18	18.05	3-20	0	6

For Scotland

Player	M	I	NO	Runs	HS	Av'ge	100s	50s	Balls	Runs	W	Av'ge	Best	4wI	Ct/St
BLAIN, J A R ...2007-8	6	3	1	4	3*	2.00	0	0	120	108	6	18.00	2-23	0	1
HAMILTON, G M ..2007-10	12	8	0	90	32	11.25	0	0	—	—	—	—	—	0	3
WARDLAW, I 2012/13-13/14	4	1	0	1	1	1.00	0	0	96	145	9	16.11	4-40	0	0

YORKSHIRE PLAYERS WHO PLAYED ALL THEIR T20i CRICKET AFTER LEAVING YORKSHIRE

For England

Player	M	I	NO	Runs	HS	Av'ge	100s	50s	Balls	Runs	W	Av'ge	Best	4wI	Ct/St
BATTY, G J ...2009	1	1	0	4	4	4.00	0	0	18	17	0	—	—	0	0
GOUGH, D ...2005-06	2	0	0	0	—	—	0	—	41	49	3	16.33	3-16	0	0
LUMB, M J ...2010-13/14	27	27	1	552	63	21.23	0	3	—	—	—	—	—	—	8
SIDEBOTTOM, R J .2007-10	18	1	1	5	5*	—	0	0	367	437	23	19.00	3-16	0	5

Overseas Players

(Qualification: 20 t20 matches for Yorkshire)

For South Africa

Player	M	I	NO	Runs	HS	Av'ge	100s	50s	Balls	Runs	W	Av'ge	Best	4wI	Ct/St
RUDOLPH, J A ...2006	1	1	1	6	6*	—	0	0	—	—	—	—	—	—	0

TROPHY WINNERS 2003-2016

		Yorkshire's Position			*Yorkshire's Position*
2003	Surrey	Group N 2 (6)	2010	Hampshire	Group N 6 (9)
2004	Leicestershire	Group N 5 (6)	2011	Leicestershire	Group N 6 (9)
2005	Somerset	Group N 4 (6)	2012	Hampshire	Final
2006	Leicestershire	Quarter-Final	2013	Northamptonshire	Group N 6 (6)
2007	Kent	Quarter-Final	2014	Warwickshire	Group N 5 (9)
2008	Middlesex	Group N 3 (6)	2015	Lancashire	Group N 8 (9)
2009	Sussex	Group N 5 (6)	2016	Northamptonshire	Semi-Final

SEASON-BY-SEASON RECORD OF ALL T20 MATCHES PLAYED BY YORKSHIRE 2003-2016

Season	Played	Won	Lost	Tie	N R	Abd	Season	Played	Won	Lost	Tie	N R	Abd
2003	5	3	2	0	0	0	2012	12	9	2	0	1	1
2004	5	2	3	0	0	0	2012/13	6	2	3	0	1	0
2005	8	3	5	0	0	0	2013	10	2	7	1	0	0
2006	9	4	4	0	1	0	2014	11	6	5	0	0	3
2007	8	4	4	0	0	1	2015	14	5	8	1	0	0
2008	9	5	3	1	0	1	2016	15	8	6	0	1	1
2009	10	4	6	0	0	0							
2010	16	6	9	1	0	0		153	69	74	4	6	8
2011	15	6	7	0	2	1							

Abandoned matches are not included in the list of matches played.

ANALYSIS OF T20 RESULTS V. ALL TEAMS 2003-2016
DOMESTIC MATCHES

		HOME				AWAY				
Opponents	Played	Won	Lost	Tied	N. R	Won	Lost	Tied	N. R	Abd
Derbyshire	23	8	5	0	0	8	1	0	1	0
Durham	27	8	4	1	0	5	8	0	1	0
Essex	1	0	0	0	0	0	1	0	0	0
Glamorgan	1	0	0	0	0	1	0	0	0	0
Hampshire	1	0	0	0	0	0	1	0	0	0
Lancashire	23	7	3	1	0	4	8	0	0	3
Leicestershire	19	4	5	0	0	3	6	1	0	1
Northamptonshire	9	1	3	0	0	3	1	1	0	1
Nottinghamshire	25	5	6	0	1	4	9	0	0	1
Sussex	2	0	0	0	0	1	1	0	0	0
Warwickshire	9	2	3	0	0	0	2	0	2	1
Worcestershire	7	3	1	0	0	0	3	0	0	1
Total	**147**	**38**	**30**	**2**	**1**	**29**	**41**	**2**	**4**	**8**

OTHER MATCHES

Uva	1	0	0	0	0	1	0	0	0	0
Trinidad and Tobago	1	0	0	0	0	1	0	0	0	0
Sydney Sixers	1	0	0	0	0	0	1	0	0	0
Mumbai	1	0	0	0	0	0	0	0	1	0
Highveld	1	0	0	0	0	0	1	0	0	0
Chennai	1	0	0	0	0	0	1	0	0	0
Total	**6**	**0**	**0**	**0**	**0**	**2**	**3**	**0**	**1**	**0**
Grand Total	**153**	**38**	**30**	**2**	**1**	**31**	**44**	**2**	**5**	**8**

ABANDONED T20 MATCHES (7)

2007	v. Lancashire at Leeds	2014	v. Warwickshire at Birmingham
2008	v. Leicestershire at Leeds		v. Lancashire at Leeds
2011	v. Northamptonshire at Leeds		v. Worcestershire at Worcester
2012	v. Lancashire at Manchester	2016	v. Nottinghamshire at Leeds

T20 HIGHEST TEAM TOTALS

BY YORKSHIRE

213:7	v.	Worcestershire at Leeds	2010
212:5	v.	Worcestershire at Leeds	2012
211:6	v.	Leicestershire at Leeds	2004
210:3	v.	Derbyshire at Derby	2006
209:4	v.	Nottinghamshire at Leeds	2015
207:7	v.	Nottinghamshire at Nottingham	2004
202:8	v.	Lancashire at Manchester	2015
200:5	v.	Nottinghamshire at Leeds	2014
198:4	v.	Durham at Leeds	2003
198:4	v.	Derbyshire at Leeds	2005
196:5	v.	Nottinghamshire at Leeds	2003
194:5	v.	Durham at Leeds	2015
187:7	v.	Worcestershire at Worcester	2010
186:5	v.	Derbyshire at Leeds	2003
186:8	v.	Durham at Chester-le-Street	2014

AGAINST YORKSHIRE

231:6	for Lancashire at Manchester	2015
222:6	for Derbyshire at Leeds	2010
221:3	for Leicestershire at Leeds	2004
215:6	for Nottinghamshire at Nottingham	2011
215:6	for Durham at Chester-le-Street	2013
210:7	for Nottinghamshire at Nottingham	2004
208:7	for Worcestershire at Worcester	2010
207:6	for Lancashire at Manchester	2005
201:5	for Nottinghamshire at Leeds	2014
195:4	for Nottinghamshire at Nottingham	2006
195:8	for Derbyshire at Leeds	2005
193:5	for Sussex at Hove	2007
191:4	for Leicestershire at Leeds	2011
191:6	for Durham at Leeds	2015
191:6	for Worcestershire at Leeds	2015

T20 HIGHEST INDIVIDUAL SCORES

BY YORKSHIRE

109	I J Harvey	v.	Derbyshire at Leeds	2005
108*	I J Harvey	v.	Lancashire at Leeds	2004
102*	J M Bairstow	v.	Durham at Chester-le-Street	2014
101*	H H Gibbs	v	Northamptonshire at Northampton	2010
96*	M J Wood	v.	Nottinghamshire at Nottingham	2004
92*	G J Maxwell	v.	Nottinghamshire at Leeds	2015
92	P A Jaques	v.	Leicestershire at Leeds	2004
92	J M Bairstow	v.	Durham at Leeds	2015
91	A W Gale	v.	Nottinghamshire at Leeds	2009
89	A J Finch	v.	Nottinghamshire at Leeds	2014
88	A J Finch	v.	Lancashire at Manchester	2014
84*	M J Lumb	v.	Lancashire at Leeds	2006
79*	A W Gale	v.	Derbyshire at Chesterfield	2009

AGAINST YORKSHIRE

111	D L Maddy	for	Leicestershire at Leeds	2004
101	S G Law	for	Lancashire at Manchester	2005
100*	G M Smith	for	Derbyshire at Leeds	2008
97	B J Hodge	for	Leicestershire at Leicester	2003
96*	A M McDonald	for	Leicestershire at Leeds	2011
94	L E Bosman	for	Derbyshire at Leeds	2010
91*	G Clark	for	Durham at Leeds	2015
91*	R A Whiteley	for	Worcestershire at Leeds	2015
91	M A Ealham	for	Nottinghamshire at Nottingham	2004
91	P Mustard	for	Durham at Chester-le-Street	2013
90*	S R Patel	for	Nottinghamshire at Leeds	2015
85	A Flintoff	for	Lancashire at Leeds	2004
83	J Moss	for	Derbyshire at Leeds	2005
82*	A C Voges	for	Nottinghamshire at Leeds	2009

T20 BEST BOWLING

BY YORKSHIRE

5-16	R M Pyrah	v.	Durham at Scarborough	2011
5-21	J A Brooks	v.	Leicestershire at Leeds	2013
5-22	M D Fisher	v.	Derbyshire at Leeds	2015
4-18	M A Ashraf	v.	Derbyshire at Derby	2012
4-20	R M Pyrah	v.	Durham at Leeds	2008
4-20	A U Rashid	v.	Leicestershire at Leeds	2010
4-21	R M Pyrah	v.	Worcestershire at Leeds	2011
4-21	B W Sanderson	v.	Derbyshire at Derby	2011
4-21	J A Brooks	v.	Derbyshire at Leeds	2013
4-23	Rana Naved	v.	Nottinghamshire at Leeds	2009
4-24	A U Rashid	v.	Nottinghamshire at Nottingham	2008
4-25	R J Sidebottom	v.	Durham at Chester-le-Street	2012
4-26	A U Rashid	v.	Lancashire at Leeds	2011
4-30	S A Patterson	v.	Lancashire at Leeds	2010
4-33	C J McKay	v.	Derbyshire at Leeds	2010

AGAINST YORKSHIRE

4-9	C K Langeveldt	for	Derbyshire at Leeds	2008
4-19	K H D Barker	for	Warwickshire at Birmingham	2010
4-19	J S Patel	for	Warwickshire at Leeds	2014
4-21	J Needham	for	Derbyshire at Leeds	2009
4-23	A J Hall	for	Northamptonshire at Northampton	2011
4-25	J A Morkel	for	Derbyshire at Chesterfield	2013
4-25	I G Butler	for	Northamptonshire at Leeds	2014
4-31	Shakib al Hasan	for	Worcestershire at Worcester	2011
4-37	K K Jennings	for	Durham at Chester-le-Street	2015
4-38	S J Harmison	for	Durham at Leeds	2008
3-3	J K H Naik	for	Leicestershire at Leeds	2011
3-6	B J Hodge	for	Leicestershire at Leicester	2003
3-6	J N Snape	for	Leicestershire at Leicester	2007
3-9	J J Cobb	for	Leicestershire at Leicester	2013
3-10	D M Benkenstein	for	Durham at Leeds	2005
3-10	D G Cork	for	Lancashire at Manchester	2005
3-10	D L Maddy	for	Warwickshire at Leeds	2011

T20 ECONOMICAL BOWLING

BY YORKSHIRE

4-0-12-2	T T Bresnan	v.	Lancashire at Manchester	2008

AGAINST YORKSHIRE

4-0-9-4	C K Langeveldt	for	Derbyshire at Leeds	2008

T20 MOST EXPENSIVE BOWLING

BY YORKSHIRE

4-0-65-2	M J Hoggard	v.	Lancashire at Leeds	2005

AGAINST YORKSHIRE

4-0-58-0	G Welsh	for	Derbyshire at Leeds	2003

T20 HIGHEST AND LOWEST SCORES BY AND AGAINST YORKSHIRE PLUS INDIVIDUAL BEST BATTING AND BOWLING

The lowest score is the lowest all-out score or the lowest score at completion of the allotted overs, five-over matches not included.

Yorkshire versus:

		By Yorkshire		Against Yorkshire	
Derbyshire					
Highest Score:	In Yorkshire	198:4	at Leeds 2005	222:5	at Leeds 2010
	Away	210:3	at Derby 2006	158:6	at Chesterfield 2008
Lowest Score:	In Yorkshire	119:8	at Leeds 2013	124	at Chesterfield 2014
	Away	109	at Derby 2012	119:7	at Leeds 2007
Best Batting:	In Yorkshire	109	I J Harvey at Leeds 2005	100*	G M Smith at Leeds 2008
	Away	79*	A W Gale at Chesterfield 2009	68	G M Smith at Chesterfield 2008
Best Bowling:	In Yorkshire	5-22	M D Fisher at Leeds 2015	4-9	C K Langeveldt at Leeds 2008
	Away	4-18	M A Ashraf at Derby 2012	4-25	J A Morkel at Chesterfield 2013
Durham					
Highest Score:	In Yorkshire	223:6	at Leeds 2016	191:6	at Leeds 2015
	Away	186:8	at Chester-le-Street 2014	215:6	at Chester-le-Street 2013
Lowest Score:	In Yorkshire	95	at Leeds 2014	116:8	at Leeds 2009
	Away	90:9	at Chester-le-Street 2009	98	at Chester-le-Street 2006
Best Batting:	In Yorkshire	92	J M Bairstow at Leeds 2015	91*	G Clark at Leeds 2015
	Away	102*	J M Bairstow at Chester-le-Street 2014	91	P Mustard at Chester-le-Street 2013
Best Bowling:	In Yorkshire	5-16	R M Pyrah at Scarborough 2011	4-38	S J Harmison at Leeds 2008
	Away	4-25	R J Sidebottom at Chester-le-Street 2012	4-25	M A Wood at Birmingham 2016
Essex					
Highest Score:	Away	143:7	at Chelmsford 2006	149:5	at Chelmsford 2006
Best Batting:	Away	43	G L Brophy at Chelmsford 2006	48*	J S Foster at Chelmsford 2006
Best Bowling:	Away	2-22	A Shahzad at Chelmsford 2006	2-11	T J Phillips at Chelmsford 2006
Glamorgan					
Highest Score:	Away	180:8	at Cardiff 2016	90	at Cardiff 2016
Best Batting:	Away	79	D J Willey at Cardiff 2016	26	J A Rudolph at Cardiff 2016
Best Bowling:	Away	4-26	A U Rashid at Cardiff 2016	4-32	C A Ingram at Cardiff 2016
Hampshire					
Highest Score:	Away	140:6	at Cardiff 2012	150:6	at Cardiff 2012
Best Batting:	Away	72*	D A Miller at Cardiff 2012	43	J H K Adams at Cardiff 2012
Best Bowling:	Away	2-20	R J Sidebottom at Cardiff 2012	3-26	C P Wood at Cardiff 2012

T20 HIGHEST AND LOWEST SCORES BY AND AGAINST YORKSHIRE PLUS INDIVIDUAL BEST BATTING AND BOWLING (Continued)

The lowest score is the lowest all-out score or the lowest score at completion of the allotted overs, five-over matches not included.

Yorkshire versus:

Lancashire

		By Yorkshire	Against Yorkshire
Highest Score:	In Yorkshire	185:8 at Leeds 2015	186:6 at Leeds 2015
	Away	202:8 at Manchester 2015	231:4 at Manchester 2015
Lowest Score:	In Yorkshire	111:8 at Leeds 2009	131:9 at Leeds 2004
	Away	97 at Manchester 2005	104:3 at Manchester 2003
Best Batting:	In Yorkshire	108* I J Harvey at Leeds 2004	85 A Flintoff at Leeds 2004
	Away	92* J E Root at Manchester 2016	101 S G Law at Manchester 2005
Best Bowling:	In Yorkshire	4-26 A U Rashid at Leeds 2011	3-25 N L Buck at Leeds 2016
	Away	3-15 Azeem Rafiq at Manchester 2011	3-10 D G Cork at Manchester 2005

Leicestershire

		By Yorkshire	Against Yorkshire
Highest Score:	In Yorkshire	211:6 at Leeds 2004	221:3 at Leeds 2004
	Away	177:5 at Leicester 2005	175:4 at Leicester 2010
Lowest Score:	In Yorkshire	134 at Leeds 2006	113:9 at Leeds 2013
	Away	105 at Leicester 2013	147:9 at Leicester 2012
Best Batting:	In Yorkshire	92 P A Jaques at Leeds 2004	111 D L Maddy at Leeds 2004
	Away	77 I J Harvey at Leicester 2005	97 B J Hodge at Leicester 2003
Best Bowling:	In Yorkshire	5-21 J A Brooks at Leeds 2013	3-3 J K H Naik at Leeds 2011
	Away	2-19 R M Pyrah at Leicester 2010	3-6 B J Hodge at Leicester 2003
	Away	2-19 M A Starc at Leicester 2012	

Northamptonshire

		By Yorkshire	Against Yorkshire
Highest Score:	In Yorkshire	215:8 at Leeds 2016	165:7 at Leeds 2014
	Away	181:3 at Northampton 2014	180:5 at Northampton 2010
Lowest Score:	In Yorkshire	144 at Leeds 2016	140 at Leeds 2016
	Away	74 at Northampton 2011	132:7 at Northampton 2011
Best Batting:	In Yorkshire	101* D J Willey at Leeds 2016	76 B M Duckett at Leeds 2016
	Away	74 H H Gibbs at Northampton 2010	51 R E Levi at Northampton 2014
Best Bowling:	In Yorkshire	3-23 A U Rashid at Leeds 2010	4-25 I G Butler at Leeds
	Away	3-15 T T Bresnan at Northampton 2016	4-23 A J Hall at Northampton 2011

T20 HIGHEST AND LOWEST SCORES BY AND AGAINST YORKSHIRE PLUS INDIVIDUAL BEST BATTING AND BOWLING (*Continued*)

The lowest score is the lowest all-out score or the lowest score at completion of the allotted overs, five-over matches not included.

Yorkshire versus:

		By Yorkshire		Against Yorkshire	
Nottinghamshire					
Highest Score:	In Yorkshire	209:4	at Leeds 2015	201:4	at Leeds 2014
	Away	207:7	at Nottingham 2004	215:6	at Nottingham 2011
Lowest Score:	In Yorkshire	141:8	at Leeds 2008	155:6	at Leeds 2009
	Away	112:7	at Nottingham 2010	136:6	at Nottingham 2008
Best Batting:	In Yorkshire	92* G J Maxwell	at Leeds 2015	90* S R Patel	at Leeds 2015
	Away	96* M J Wood	at Nottingham 2004	91 M A Ealham	at Nottingham 2004
Best Bowling:	In Yorkshire	4-23 Rana Naved-ul-Hasan	at Leeds 2009	3-38 J T Ball	at Leeds 2014
	Away	4-24 A U Rashid	at Nottingham 2008	3-16 H F Gurney	at Nottingham 2016
Sussex					
Highest Score:	Away	172:6	at Cardiff 2012	193:5	at Hove 2007
Lowest Score:	Away	155	at Hove 2007	136:8	at Cardiff 2012
Best Batting:	Away	68* J M Bairstow	at Cardiff 2012	80* C D Nash	at Cardiff 2012
Best Bowling:	Away	2-22 T T Bresnan	at Cardiff 2012	3-22 S B Styris	at Cardiff 2012
Warwickshire					
Highest Score:	In Yorkshire	161:8	at Leeds 2011	164:5	at Leeds 2011
	Away	132:7	at Birmingham 2015	145:8	at Birmingham 2010
Lowest Score:	In Yorkshire	121:9	at Leeds 2010	145	at Leeds 2015
	Away	131	at Birmingham 2010		
Best Batting:	In Yorkshire	63 A Z Lees	at Leeds 2015	69* L J Evans	at Leeds 2014
	Away	45 J A Leaning	at Birmingham 2015	49* J O Troughton	at Birmingham 2011
Best Bowling:	In Yorkshire	3-22 R M Pyrah	at Leeds 2010	4-19 J S Patel	at Leeds 2014
	Away	3-25 S A Patterson	at Birmingham 2010	4-19 K H D Barker	at Birmingham 2010

411

T20 HIGHEST AND LOWEST SCORES BY AND AGAINST YORKSHIRE PLUS INDIVIDUAL BEST BATTING AND BOWLING (Continued)

Yorkshire versus:

		By Yorkshire	Against Yorkshire
Worcestershire			
Highest Score:	In Yorkshire	213:7 at Leeds 2010	191:6 at Leeds 2015
	Away	187:7 at Worcester 2010	208:7 at Worcester 2010
Lowest Score:	In Yorkshire	117 at Leeds 2015	109 at Leeds 2010
	Away	142 at Worcester 2011	183:7 at Worcester 2011
Best Batting:	In Yorkshire	65 J E Root at Leeds 2012	91* R A Whiteley at Leeds 2015
	Away	39 A McGrath at Worcester 2010	56 A N Kervezee at Worcester 2011
Best Bowling:	In Yorkshire	4-21 R M Pyrah at Leeds 2011	3-29 B L d'Oliveira at Leeds 2015
	Away	3-30 A Shahzad at Worcester 2011	4-31 Shakib al Hasan at Worcester 2011
Chennai			
Highest Score:	Away	140:6 at Durban 2012	141:6 at Durban 2012
Best Batting:	Away	58 G S Ballance at Durban 2012	47 S Badrinath at Durban 2012
Best Bowling:	Away	3-23 I Wardlaw at Durban 2012	2-12 J A Morkel at Durban 2012
Highveld			
Highest Score:	Away	131:7 at Johannesburg 2012	134:5 at Johannesburg 2012
Best Batting:	Away	31 P A Jaques at Johannesburg 2012	32 Q de Kock at Johannesburg 2012
Best Bowling:	Away	2-21 S A Patterson at Johannesburg 2012	2-23 A M Phangiso at Johannesburg 2012
Mumbai			
Highest Score:	Away		156:6 at Cape Town 2012
Best Batting:	Away		37 D R Smith at Cape Town 2012
Best Bowling:	Away	2-36 Azeem Rafiq at Cape Town 2012	
Sydney Sixers			
Highest Score:	Away	96:9 at Cape Town 2012	98:2 at Cape Town 2012
Best Batting:	Away	25 J E Root at Cape Town 2012	43* M J Lumb at Cape Town 2012
Best Bowling:	Away	1-21 Azeem Rafiq at Cape Town 2012	3-22 M A Starc at Cape Town 2012
Trinidad and Tobago			
Highest Score:	Away	154:4 at Centurion 2012	148:9 at Centurion 2012
Best Batting:	Away	64* G S Ballance at Centurion 2012	59 D Ramdin at Centurion 2012
Best Bowling:	Away	3-13 R J Sidebottom at Centurion 2012	1-16 K Y G Ottley at Centurion 2012
Uva			
Highest Score:	Away	151:5 at Johannesburg 2012	150:7 at Johannesburg 2012
Best Batting:	Away	39* D A Miller at Johannesburg 2012	29 S H T Kandamby at Johannesburg 2012
Best Bowling:	Away	2-29 M A Ashraf at Johannesburg 2012	3-32 E M D Y Munaweera at Johannesburg 2012

T20 MAN OF THE MATCH AWARDS (70)

A W Gale	8	D A Miller	3	P A Jaques	2
A McGrath	6	J M Bairstow	3	A Z Lees	2
R M Pyrah	5	J A Leaning	3	M J Lumb	2
A Lyth	4	T T Bresnan	3	A U Rashid	2
Azeem Rafiq	4	A J Finch	2	D J Willey	2
I J Harvey	3	H H Gibbs	2		

One each: G S Ballance, J A Brooks, M E Claydon, M D Fisher, S P Fleming, D S Lehmann,
G J Maxwell, J E Root, J A Rudolph, B W Sanderson, J J Sayers, A Shahzad,
D J Wainwright, C White and K S Williamson

T20 PARTNERSHIPS OF 100 AND OVER 2003-2016 (16)

137*	2nd wkt	A W Gale	(60*)	and H H Gibbs	(76*)	v. Durham at Leeds	2010
131	1st wkt	A Lyth	(78)	and P A Jaques	(64)	v. Derbyshire at Leeds	2012
129	2nd wkt	A W Gale	(91)	and M P Vaughan	(41*)	v. Nottinghamshire at Leeds	2009
124	2nd wkt	I J Harvey	(109)	and P A Jaques	(37)	v. Derbyshire at Leeds	2005
121	3rd wkt	J A Rudolph	(56)	and A McGrath	(59)	v. Leicestershire at Leicester	2008
116	1st wkt	A W Gale	(70)	and A U Rashid	(48)	v. Leicestershire at Leeds	2012
108	2nd wkt	I J Harvey	(108*)	and P A Jaques	(39)	v. Lancashire at Leeds	2004
108	2nd wkt	A Lyth	(59)	and H H Gibbs	(40)	v. Worcestershire at Leeds	2010
106	2nd wkt	D J Willey	(74)	and A Z Lees	(35)	v. Northamptonshire at Leeds	2016
104	1st wkt	A W Gale	(43)	and J A Rudolph	(61)	v. Leicestershire at Leicester	2009
104	2nd wkt	A Z Lees	(63)	and J A Leaning	(60*)	v. Warwickshire at Leeds	2015
103*	5th wkt	G S Ballance	(64*)	and A U Rashid	(33*)	v. Trinidad & Tobago at Centurion	2012/13
103	1st wkt	A W Gale	(65*)	and J A Rudolp	(53)	v. Leicestershire at Leicester	2010
101	2nd wkt	M J Wood	(57)	and M J Lumb	(55)	v. Nottinghamshire at Leeds	2003
101	3rd wkt	A J Hodd	(70)	and G J Maxwell	(92*)	v. Nottinghamshire at Leeds	2015
100	4th wkt	A Z Lees	(59)	and J A Leaning	(64)	v. Northamptonshire at Northampton	2016

T20 HIGHEST PARTNERSHIPS FOR EACH WICKET

1st wkt	131	A Lyth	(78)	and P A Jaques	(64)	v. Derbyshire at Leeds	2012
2nd wkt	137*	A W Gale	(60*)	and H H Gibbs	(76*)	v. Durham at Leeds	2010
3rd wkt	121	J A Rudolph	(56)	and A McGrath	(59)	v. Leicestershire at Leicester	2008
4th wkt	100	A Z Lees	(59)	and J A Leaning	(64)	v. Northamptonshire at Northampton	2016
5th wkt	103*	G S Ballance	(64*)	and A U Rashid	(33*)	v. Trinidad & Tobago at Centurion	2012/13
6th wkt	76	J E Root	(92*)	and L E Plunkett	(22)	v. Lancashire at Manchester	2016
7th wkt	68*	T T Bresnan	(45*)	and A U Rashid	(29*)	v. Warwickshire at Leeds	2014
8th wkt	54	T T Bresnan	(51)	and J D Middlebrook	(29*)	v. Lancashire at Manchester	2015
9th wkt	33*	A U Rashid	(5*)	and D Gough	(20*)	v. Lancashire at Leeds	2008
10th wkt	28*	A U Rashid	(28*)	and G J Kruis	(12*)	v. Durham at Chester-le-Street	2009

ALL WHO HAVE TAKEN 4 WICKETS IN AN INNINGS (16)

A U RASHID (4)

4-20	v. Leicestershire	at Leeds	2011
4-24	v. Nottingham	at Nottingham	2008
4-26	v. Lancashire	at Leeds	2011
4-26	v. Glamorgan	at Cardiff	2016

R M PYRAH (3)

5-16	v. Durham	at Scarborough	2011
4-20	v. Durham	at Leeds	2006
4-21	v. Worcestershire	at Leeds	2011

J A BROOKS (2)

5-21	v. Leicestershire	at Leeds	2013
4-21	v. Derbyshire	at Leeds	2013

M D FISHER (1)

5-22	v. Derbyshire	at Leeds	2015

M A ASHRAF (1)

4-18	v. Derbyshire	at Derby	2012

B W SANDERSON (1)

4-21	v. Derbyshire	at Derby	2011

RANA NAVED-UL-HASAN (1)

4-23	v. Nottinghamshire	at Leeds	2009

R J SIDEBOTTOM (1)

4-25	v. Durham	at Chester-le-Street	2012

S A PATTERSON (1)

4-30	v. Lancashire	at Leeds	2010

C J MCKAY (1)

4-33	v. Derbyshire	at Leeds	2010

CAREER AVERAGES FOR YORKSHIRE

ALL t20 MATCHES 2003-2016

Player	M	Inns	NO	Runs	HS	Av'ge	100s	50s	Runs	Wkts	Av'ge	Ct/St
Ashraf, M A ...	17	1	0	4	4	4.00	0	0	462	17	27.17	1
Azeem Rafiq ..	71	30	19	144	21*	13.09	0	0	1,787	77	23.20	31
Bairstow, J M .	63	58	11	1,231	102*	26.19	1	4	0	0	—	27/8
Ballance, G S ..	57	50	7	1,064	68	24.74	0	3	0	0	—	36
Best, T L	8	3	2	10	10*	10.00	0	0	243	7	34.71	4
Blakey, R J	7	5	1	119	32	29.75	0	0	0	0	—	5/1
Bresnan, T T ..	86	65	24	922	51	22.48	0	1	2,106	86	24.48	33
Brooks, J A	13	0	0	—		—	0	0	314	13	24.15	4
Brophy, G L ...	54	46	9	717	57*	19.37	0	2	0	0	—	25/7
Carver, K	8	2	1	2	2	2.00	0	0	132	6	22.00	3
Claydon, M E ..	7	2	2	14	12*	—	0	0	188	5	37.60	2
Coad, B O	5	2	1	3	2*	—	0	0	154	6	25.66	3
Craven, V J	6	6	4	76	44*	38.00	0	0	67	0	—	1
Dawood, I	11	8	3	44	15	8.80	0	0	0	0	—	5/2
Dawson, R K J .	22	8	3	71	22	14.20	0	0	558	24	23.25	7
Finch, A J	16	16	0	332	89	20.75	0	2	24	1	24.00	16
Fisher, M D ...	13	1	1	0	0*	—	0	0	362	16	22.62	5
Fleming, S P ...	4	4	0	62	58	15.50	0	1	0	0	—	1
Gale, A W ...	104	97	8	2,260	91	25.39	0	16	0	0	—	30
Gibbs, H H	15	15	3	443	101*	36.91	1	2	0	0	—	8
Gibson, R	3	2	0	32	18	16.00	0	0	30	0	—	1
Gilbert, C R ...	13	9	2	107	38*	15.28	0	0	0	0	—	7
Gillespie, J N ..	17	4	2	14	8*	7.00	0	0	422	17	24.82	5
Gough, D	17	7	3	42	20*	10.50	0	0	416	16	26.00	2
Gray, A K D ...	8	3	0	17	13	5.66	0	0	211	9	23.44	4
Guy, S M	10	6	1	44	13	8.80	0	0	0	0	—	2
Hamilton, G M .	3	3	1	41	41*	20.50	0	0	0	0	—	1
Hannon-Dalby, O J	2	0	0	0	—		0	0-	58	3	19.33	
Harvey, I J	10	10	1	438	109	48.66	2	2	258	10	25.80	4
Head, T M	4	4	0	113	40	28.25	0	0	4	0	—	
Hodd, A J	26	17	4	147	70	11.30	0	1	0	0	—	9/6
Hodgson, D M ..	16	14	2	213	52*	17.75	0	1	0	0	—	9/1
Hodgson, L J ...	2	1	1	39	39*	—	0	0	59	2	29.50	1
Hoggard, M J ..	15	2	1	19	18	19.00	0	0	472	13	36.30	4
Jaques, P A	34	32	3	907	92	31.27	0	6	15	0	—	5
Kirby, S P	3	0	0	0	—		0	0	119	4	29.75	1
Kruis, G J	20	5	3	41	22	20.50	0	0	486	19	25.57	6
Lawson, M A K .	2	1	1	4	4*	—	0	0	87	3	29.00	1
Leaning, J A ...	30	28	7	624	64	29.71	0	2	30	0	—	10
Lees, A Z	35	34	2	817	67*	25.53	0	4	0	0	—	12
Lehmann, D S ..	9	9	3	252	48	42.00	0	0	180	8	22.50	4
Lumb, M J	26	26	3	442	84*	19.21	0	4	65	3	21.66	8
Lyth, A	73	64	2	1,251	87	20.17	0	4	88	4	22.00	35
McGrath, A	66	61	12	1,403	73*	28.63	0	8	698	23	30.34	26
McKay, C J	8	6	3	54	21*	18.00	0	0	258	10	25.80	1
Maxwell, G J ...	12	12	1	229	92*	20.81	0	1	264	12	22.00	6
Middlebrook, J D	4	2	2	33	29*	—	0	0	101	4	25.25	1
Miller, D A	14	13	4	457	74*	50.77	0	4	0	0	—	7
Patterson S A ..	38	7	4	9	3*	3.00	0	0	1,062	35	30.34	4
Plunkett, L E ..	33	26	7	306	36	16.10	0	0	894	36	24.83	10

Player	M	Inns	NO	Runs	HS	Av'ge	100s	50s	Runs	Wkts	Av'ge	Ct/St
Pyrah, R M	105	71	21	593	42	11.86	0	0	2,315	108	21.43	40
Naved-ul-Hasan Rana	8	8	2	63	20*	10.50	0	0	159	11	14.45	2
Rashid, A U ...	**88**	**56**	**15**	**532**	**36***	**12.97**	**0**	**0**	**2,245**	**92**	**24.40**	**28**
Rhodes, W M H	**18**	**16**	**3**	**128**	**45**	**9.84**	**0**	**0**	**283**	**13**	**21.76**	**2**
Robinson, O E ..	7	3	0	5	3	1.66	0	0	162	6	27.00	3
Root, J E	**32**	**28**	**6**	**582**	**92***	**26.45**	**0**	**3**	**269**	**4**	**67.25**	**10**
Rudolph, J A ...	39	35	5	710	61	23.66	0	3	145	6	24.16	7
Sanderson, B W	4	0	0	0	0	—	0	0	74	6	12.33	0
Sayers, J J	17	14	0	253	44	18.07	0	0	0	0	—	5
Shahzad, A	22	16	4	129	20	10.75	0	0	576	17	33.88	5
Shaw, J	**3**	**2**	**1**	**1**	**1**	**1.00**	**0**	**0**	**71**	**0**	**—**	**1**
Sidebottom, R J	40	16	10	87	16*	14.50	0	0	1,069	42	25.45	9
Silverwood, C E W	9	5	2	32	13*	10.66	0	0	264	7	37.71	4
Starc, M A	10	2	1	0	0*	0.00	0	0	218	21	10.38	1
Swanepoel, P J .	2	1	1	2	2*	—	0	0	60	3	20.00	1
Taylor, C R	2	2	1	10	10*	10.00	0	0	0	0	—	0
Vaughan, M P ..	16	16	1	292	41*	19.46	0	0	81	1	81.00	2
Wainman, J C .	**2**	**1**	**1**	**12**	**12***	**—**	**0**	**0**	**49**	**1**	**49.00**	**0**
Wainwright, D J	26	9	6	23	6*	7.66	0	0	551	21	26.23	9
Waite, M J	**3**	**2**	**2**	**33**	**19***	**—**	**0**	**0**	**51**	**1**	**51.00**	**2**
Wardlaw, I	10	1	1	1	1	—	0	0	179	5	35.80	0
Warren, A C ...	2	0	0	0	—	—	0	0	70	4	17.50	0
White, C	33	31	0	570	55	18.38	0	2	132	2	66.00	8
Willey, D J	**11**	**10**	**0**	**272**	**79**	**27.20**	**0**	**2**	**214**	**9**	**23.77**	**5**
Williamson, K S	**12**	**11**	**0**	**302**	**65**	**27.45**	**0**	**1**	**37**	**3**	**12.33**	**3**
Wood, M J	15	15	3	328	96*	27.33	0	2	32	2	16.00	11
Younus Khan ...	2	2	0	55	40	27.50	0	0	32	2	16.00	0
Yuvraj Singh ...	5	5	0	154	71	30.80	0	1	51	5	10.20	0

SECOND ELEVEN RECORDS
in the
SECOND ELEVEN CHAMPIONSHIP 1959-1961 AND 1975-2016

SUMMARY OF RESULTS BY SEASON

Season	Played	Won	Lost	Drawn	Tied	Abandoned	Position in Championship
1959	10	4	1	5	0	0	7
1960	10	1	3	6	0	0	14
1961	9	2	2	5	0	1	11
1975	14	4	0	10	0	0	4
1976	14	5	5	4	0	0	5
1977	**16**	**9**	**0**	**7**	**0**	**1**	**1**
1978	15	5	2	8	0	1	4
1979	16	5	0	11	0	0	3
1980	14	5	2	7	0	1	5
1981	16	2	3	11	0	0	11
1982	16	2	3	11	0	0	14 =
1983	11	5	1	5	0	3	2
1984	**15**	**9**	**3**	**3**	**0**	**0**	**1**
1985	14	3	3	8	0	1	12
1986	16	5	1	10	0	0	5
1987	**15**	**5**	**2**	**8**	**0**	**1**	**1 =**
1988	16	4	1	11	0	0	9
1989	17	2	3	12	0	0	9 =
1990	16	1	6	9	0	0	17
1991	**16**	**8**	**1**	**7**	**0**	**0**	**1**
1992	17	5	2	10	0	0	5
1993	17	6	1	10	0	0	3
1994	17	6	2	9	0	0	2
1995	17	7	1	9	0	0	5
1996	17	6	3	8	0	0	4
1997	16	8	5	3	0	1	2
1998	15	4	2	9	0	0	9
1999	16	3	8	5	0	1	14
2000	14	5	2	7	0	1	5
2001	12	8	2	2	0	1	2
2002	12	5	1	6	0	0	3
2003	**10**	**7**	**1**	**2**	**0**	**0**	**1**
2004	7	2	0	5	0	1	8
2005	12	2	4	6	0	0	10
2006	14	6	4	4	0	0	3
2007	12	4	5	3	0	0	10
2008	12	4	4	4	0	2	5
2009	9	5	0	4	0	0	(Group A) 2
2010	9	2	4	3	0	0	(Group A) 8
2011	9	0	4	4	1	0	(Group A) 10
2012	7	1	2	4	0	2	(North) 9
2013	9	3	4	2	0	0	(North) 4
2014	9	2	1	6	0	0	(North) 4
2015	9	2	4	3	0	0	(North) 7
2016	9	2	3	4	0	0	(North) 5
Totals	593	191	111	290	1	18	

Matches abandoned without a ball being bowled are not counted as a match played.
The Championship was divided into two groups from 2009, each team playng each other
once. The two group winners play for the Championship

ANALYSIS OF RESULTS AGAINST EACH OPPONENT

County	Played	Won	Lost	Drawn	Tied	Abandoned	First Played
Derbyshire	56	13	8	35	0	3	1959
Durham	31	11	6	14	0	2	1992
Essex	13	9	2	2	0	0	1990
Glamorgan	40	11	3	26	0	2	1975
Gloucestershire	10	3	3	4	0	0	1990
Hampshire	12	4	1	7	0	0	1990
Kent	26	5	4	17	0	1	1981
Lancashire	68	14	19	35	0	3	1959
Leicestershire	30	12	7	10	1	1	1975
MCC Young Cricketers	5	3	1	1	0	0	2005
MCC Universities	4	1	1	2	0	0	2011
Middlesex	18	7	2	9	0	0	1977
Northamptonshire	48	15	6	27	0	2	1959
Nottinghamshire	59	17	12	30	0	2	1959
Scotland	2	1	0	1	0	0	2007
Somerset	18	9	3	6	0	0	1988
Surrey	36	9	9	18	0	2	1976
Sussex	16	6	5	5	0	0	1990
Warwickshire	61	21	13	27	0	0	1959
Worcestershire	40	20	6	14	0	0	1961
Totals	593	191	111	290	1	18	

Note: Matches abandoned are not included in the total played.

Highest Total

By Yorkshire: 538 for 9 wkts dec v. Worcestershire at Stamford Bridge, 2007
Against Yorkshire: 567 for 7 wkts dec by Middlesex at RAF Vine Lane, Uxbridge, 2000

Lowest Total

By Yorkshire: 66 v Nottinghamshire at Trent College, 2016
Against Yorkshire: 36 by Lancashire at Elland, 1979

Highest Individual Score

For Yorkshire: 273* by R J Blakey v. Northamptonshire at Northampton, 1986
Against Yorkshire: 235 by O A Shah for Middlesex at Leeds, 1999

Century in Each Innings

For Yorkshire:	C White	209* and 115*	v. Worcestershire at Worcester, 1990
	K Sharp	150* and 127	v. Essex at Elland, 1991
	A A Metcalfe	109 and 136*	v. Somerset at North Perrott, 1994
	R A Kettleborough	123 and 192*	v. Nottinghamshire at Todmorden, 1996
	C R Taylor	201* and 129	v. Sussex at Hove, 2005
	A W Gale	131 and 123	v. Somerset at Taunton, 2006
	J J Sayers	157 and 105	v. Lancashire at Leeds, 2007
Against Yorkshire:	N Nannan	100 and 102*	for Nottinghamshire at Harrogate, 1979
	G D Lloyd	134 and 103	for Lancashire at Scarborough, 1989
	A J Swann	131 and 100	for Northamptonshire at York, 1998
	G J Kennis	114 and 114	for Somerset at Taunton, 1999

Best Bowling in an Innings

For Yorkshire: 9 for 27 by G A Cope v. Northamptonshire at Northampton, 1979
Against Yorkshire: 8 for 15 by I Folley for Lancashire at Heywood, 1983

Best Bowling in a Match

For Yorkshire: 13 for 92 (6 for 48 and 7 for 44) by M K Bore v. Lancashire at Harrogate, 1976
Against Yorkshire: 13 for 100 (7 for 45 and 6 for 55) by N J Perry for Glamorgan at Cardiff, 1978

Totals of 450 and over

By Yorkshire (27)

Score	Versus	Ground	Season
538 for 9 wkts dec	Worcestershire	Stamford Bridge	2007
534 for 5 wkts dec	Lancashire	Stamford Bridge	2003
530 for 8 wkts dec	Nottinghamshire	Middlesbrough	2000
514 for 3 wkts dec	Somerset	Taunton	1988
509 for 4 wkts dec	Northamptonshire	Northampton	1986
502	Derbyshire	Chesterfield	2003
501 for 5 wkts dec	MCC Young Cricketers	Stamford Bridge	2009
497	Derbyshire	Chesterfield	2005
495 for 5 wkts dec	Somerset	Taunton	2006
488 for 8 wkts dec	Warwickshire	Harrogate	1984
486 for 6 wkts dec	Glamorgan	Leeds	1986
480	Leicestershire	Market Harborough	2013
476 for 3 wkts dec	Glamorgan	Gorseinon	1984
475 for 9 wkts dec	Nottinghamshire	Nottingham	1995
474 for 3 wkts dec	Glamorgan	Todmorden	2003
474	Durham	Stamford Bridge	2003
470	Lancashire	Leeds	2006
469	Warwickshire	Castleford	1999
462	Scotland	Stamford Bridge	2007
461 for 8 wkts dec	Essex	Stamford Bridge	2006
459 for 3 wkts dec	Leicestershire	Oakham	1997
459 for 6 wkts dec	Glamorgan	Bradford	1992
457 for 9 wkts dec	Kent	Canterbury	1983
456 for 5 wkts dec	Gloucestershire	Todmorden	1990
456 for 6 wkts dec	Nottinghamshire	York	1986
454 for 9 wkts dec	Derbyshire	Chesterfield	1959
452 for 9 wkts dec	Glamorgan	Cardiff	2005

Against Yorkshire (14)

Score	For	Ground	Season
567 for 7 wkts dec	Middlesex	RAF Vine Lane, Uxbridge	2000
555 for 7 wkts dec	Derbyshire	Stamford Bridge	2002
530 for 9 wkts dec	Leicestershire	Hinckley	2015
525 for 7 wkts dec	Sussex	Hove	2005
502 for 4 wkts dec	Warwickshire	Edgbaston Community Foundation Sports Ground	2016
493 for 8 wkts dec	Nottinghamshire	Lady Bay, Nottingham	2002
488 for 8 wkts dec	Warwickshire	Castleford	1999
486	Essex	Chelmsford	2000
485	Gloucestershire	North Park, Cheltenham	2001
477	Lancashire	Headingley	2006
471	Warwickshire	Clifton Park, York	2010
458	Lancashire	Bradford	1997
454 for 7 wkts dec	Lancashire	Todmorden	1993
450 for 7 wkts (inns closed)	Derbyshire	Bradford	1980

Completed Innings under 75

By Yorkshire (6)

Score	Versus	Ground	Season
66	Nottinghamshire	Trent College	2016
67	Worcestershire	Barnt Green (1st inns)	2013
68	Worcestershire	Barnt Green (2nd inns)	2013
69	Lancashire	Heywood	1983
74	Derbyshire	Chesterfield	1960
74	Nottinghamshire	Bradford	1998

Against Yorkshire (10)

Score	By	Ground	Season
36	Lancashire	Elland	1979
49	Leicestershire	Leicester	2008
50	Lancashire	Liverpool	1984
60	Derbyshire	Bradford	1977
60	Surrey	Sunbury-on-Thames	1977
62	MCC YC	High Wycombe	2005
64	Nottinghamshire	Brodsworth	1959
66	Leicestershire	Lutterworth	1977
72	Sussex	Horsham	2003
74	Worcestershire	Barnsley	1978

Individual Scores of 150 and over (64)

Score	Player	Versus	Ground	Season
273*	R J Blakey	Northamptonshire	Northampton	1986
238*	K Sharp	Somerset	Taunton	1988
233	P E Robinson	Kent	Canterbury	1983
221*	K Sharp	Gloucestershire	Todmorden	1990
219	G M Hamilton	Derbyshire	Chesterfield	2003
218*	A McGrath	Surrey	Elland	1994
212	G S Ballance	MCC Young Cricketers	Stamford Bridge	2009
209*	C White	Worcestershire	Worcester	1990
205	C R Taylor	Glamorgan	Todmorden	2003
204	B Parker	Gloucestershire	Bristol	1993
203	A McGrath	Durham	Headingley	2005
202*	J M Bairstow	Leicestershire	Oakham	2009
202	M J Wood	Essex	Stamford Bridge	2006
201*	C R Taylor	Sussex	Hove	2005
200*	D Byas	Worcestershire	Worcester	1992
200*	A McGrath	Northamptonshire	Northampton	2012
192*	R A Kettleborough	Nottinghamshire	Todmorden	1996
191	P E Robinson	Warwickshire	Harrogate	1984
191	M J Wood	Derbyshire	Rotherham	2000
191	M J Lumb	Nottinghamshire	Middlesbrough	2000
189*	C S Pickles	Gloucestershire	Bristol	1991
186	A McGrath	MCC Universities	York	2011
184	J D Love	Worcestershire	Headingley	1976
183	A W Gale	Durham	Stamford Bridge	2006
174	G L Brophy	Worcestershire	Stamford Bridge	2007
173	S N Hartley	Warwickshire	Edgbaston	1980
173	A A Metcalfe	Glamorgan	Gorseinon	1984
173	B Parker	Sussex	Hove	1996
173	R A Kettleborough	Leicestershire	Oakham School	1997

Individual Scores of 150 and over *(Continued)*

Score	Player	Versus	Ground	Season
172	A C Morris	Lancashire	York	1995
170*	R A J Townsley	Glamorgan	Harrogate	1975
169	J E Root	Warwickshire	York	2010
168	M J Wood	Leicestershire	Oakham School	1997
166	A A Metcalfe	Lancashire	York	1984
166	C A Chapman	Northamptonshire	York	1998
165*	A Lyth	Durham	Stamford Bridge	2006
165	J J Sayers	Sussex	Hove	2006
164*	A W Gale	Leicestershire	Harrogate	2002
164	J C Balderstone	Nottinghamshire	Harrogate	1960
163*	J E Root	Leicestershire	Oakham	2009
163	A A Metcalfe	Derbyshire	Chesterfield	1992
162*	D Byas	Surrey	Scarborough	1987
162*	R Gibson	Leicestershire	York	2016
160	A A Metcalfe	Somerset	Bradford	1993
157	J J Sayers	Lancashire	Headingley	2007
155	S M Guy	Derbyshire	Chesterfield	2005
154*	C R Taylor	Surrey	Whitgift School	2005
153*	A A Metcalfe	Warwickshire	Bingley	1995
153	C White	Worcestershire	Marske-by-the-Sea	1991
153	R A Stead	Surrey	Todmorden	2002
152	A A Metcalfe	Gloucestershire	Bristol	1993
151*	P E Robinson	Nottinghamshire	York	1986
151*	S J Foster	Kent	Elland	1992
151*	J J Sayers	Durham	Stamford Bridge	2004
151	P J Hartley	Somerset	Clevedon	1989
151	A McGrath	Somerset	Elland	1995
151	V J Craven	Glamorgan	Todmorden	2003
150*	K Sharp	Essex	Elland	1991
150*	G M Fellows	Hampshire	Todmorden	1998
150*	S M Guy	Nottinghamshire	Headingley	2005
150*	J A Leaning	Worcestershire	Worcester	2011
150	K Sharp	Glamorgan	Ebbw Vale	1983
150	S N Hartley	Nottinghamshire	Worksop	1988
150	C R Taylor	Derbyshire	Chesterfield	2003

7 Wickets in an Innings (30)

Analysis	Player	Versus	Ground	Season
9 for 27	G A Cope	Northamptonshire	Northampton	1977
9 for 62	M K Bore	Warwicshire	Scarborough	1976
8 for 53	S J Dennis	Nottinghamshire	Nottingham	1983
8 for 57	M K Bore	Lancashire	Manchester	1977
8 for 79	P J Berry	Derbyshire	Harrogate	1991
7 for 13	P Carrick	Northamptonshire	Marske-by-the-Sea	1977
7 for 21	S Silvester	Surrey	Sunbury-on-Thames	1977
7 for 22	J A R Blain	Surrey	Purley	2004
7 for 32	P W Jarvis	Surrey	The Oval	1984
7 for 34	P Carrick	Glamorgan	Leeds	1986
7 for 37	P M Hutchison	Warwickshire	Coventry	2001

7 Wickets in an Innings *(Continued)*

Analysis	Player	Versus	Ground	Season
7 for 39	G M Hamilton	Sussex	Leeds	1995
7 for 40	M K Bore	Worcestershire	Old Hill	1976
7 for 44	M K Bore	Lancashire	Harrogate	1976
7 for 44	J P Whiteley	Worcestershire	Leeds	1979
7 for 51	J D Middlebrook	Derbyshire	Rotherham	2000
7 for 53	J P Whiteley	Warwickshire	Birmingham	1980
7 for 55	C White	Leicestershire	Bradford	1990
7 for 58	K Gillhouley	Derbyshire	Chesterfield	1960
7 for 58	P J Hartley	Lancashire	Leeds	1985
7 for 63	M J Hoggard	Worcestershire	Harrogate	1998
7 for 65	M K Bore	Nottinghamshire	Steetley	1976
7 for 70	J D Batty	Leicestershire	Bradford	1992
7 for 71	J D Batty	Hampshire	Harrogate	1994
7 for 81	K Gillhouley	Lancashire	Scarborough	1960
7 for 84	I J Houseman	Kent	Canterbury	1989
7 for 88	I G Swallow	Nottinghamshire	Nottingham	1983
7 for 90	A P Grayson	Kent	Folkestone	1991
7 for 93	D Pickles	Nottinghamshire	Nottingham	1960
7 for 94	K Gillhouley	Northamptonshire	Redcar	1960

12 Wickets in a Match (6)

Analysis		Player	Versus	Ground	Season
13 for 92	(6-48 and 7-44)	M K Bore	Lancashire	Harrogate	1976
13 for 110	(7-70 and 6-40)	J D Batty	Leicestershire	Bradford	1992
13 for 111	(4-49 and 9-62)	M K Bore	Warwickshire	Scarborough	1976
12 for 69	(5-32 and 7-37)	P M Hutchison	Warwickshire	Coventry	2001
12 for 120	(5-39 and 7-81)	K Gillhouley	Lancashire	Scarborough	1960
12 for 162	(5-78 and 7-84)	I J Houseman	Kent	Canterbury	1989

Hat-tricks (4)

Player	Versus	Ground	Season
I G Swallow	Warwickshire	Harrogate	1984
S D Fletcher	Nottinghamshire	Marske-by-the-Sea	1987
I G Swallow	Derbyshire	Chesterfield	1988
M Broadhurst	Essex	Southend-on-Sea	1992

Second Eleven Performance Of The Year Award

The Trophy was instituted in 2013 to reward a Second Eleven performance with either bat or ball that stood out from the ordinary and turned the course of the game.

2013	M D Fisher	6-25	v. Leicestershire (One-Day Trophy)	
				Grace Road, Leicester
2014	J A Leaning	102	v. Nottinghamshire (T20)	Trent College, Nottingham
2015	M J Waite	143	v. Lancashire (Friendly)	Scarborough
2016	W M H Rhodes	137		
		and 114*	v Lancashire (Friendly)	Liverpool

ANNUAL REPORT
and
Statement of Account
for the year ended
December 31, 2016

CHAIRMAN'S STATEMENT

So close!

It was an unbelievably exciting but ultimately heartbreaking end to the 2016 season at Lord's, but I was incredibly proud of the team's approach to the game and their decision to go for the win.

Watching Tim Bresnan steer us to the bonus point we needed to keep our Championship hopes alive was one of the most nerve-wracking times of my life, but Middlesex were the most consistent team throughout the season and wor-

STEVE DENISON

thy winners, further developing some fine young talent of their own in the process.

Semi-Final heartache

We entered the season determined to win at least one of the white-ball competitions, and so the two semi-final defeats in 2016 were particularly disappointing. It's fair to say that we weren't helped by the constant team changes caused by international call-ups/releases — just look at the stability in Northamptonshire's *NatWest T20 Blast* winning team — and achieving greater consistency remains a priority.

International success

I was lucky enough to be at Newlands last January to see Jonny Bairstow's maiden Test century in his outstanding partnership with Ben Stokes, where they scored 399 off 346 balls, the highest sixth-wicket partnership in Test history. The rest of the 2016 international season turned out to be exceptional for both Jonny and Joe Root, who further cemented his place as one of the top three batsmen in the world. The prospect of seeing them both — together with our other England internationals — at Headingley this year is a very exciting one, and ticket

423

sales for the ODI against South Africa and the Test Match against the West Indies are going well. Please come along and support!

All change

We said farewell to Jason Gillespie at the end-of-season gala dinner. In his five years as First Eleven Coach Dizzy led Yorkshire out of the second division to consecutive County Championship titles, suffering just a handful of defeats in nearly 80 games and making a huge number of friends along the way. Dizzy will forever occupy a special place in our hearts, and we wish him, Anna and the kids health, happiness and every success in their new lives in Australia.

After a wide-ranging and rigorous search process conducted by Martyn Moxon I was personally delighted that Andrew Gale was chosen to replace Dizzy. No one embodies the values of YCCC more than Galey, and the leadership qualities he has demonstrated throughout his time as captain and the huge respect he commands throughout the dressing room mean that he is ideally placed to drive further success.

I'm equally delighted that Gary Ballance has been appointed Club Captain. His experience and tactical awareness will be invaluable, as will the contribution of Tim Bresnan as vice-captain.

The Kolpak debate

Whether you feel that Kolpak signings in county cricket are bad for the game or just the result of routine market forces, we have a clear policy of growing our own at YCCC. Our No. 1 priority is to nurture and grow cricketers of the highest quality, and to that end we invest substantially in developing our own talent. The production line of players who have emerged from our Academy, broken into the Yorkshire team and gone on to international glory is testament to that policy and the unrivalled quality of our coaching staff. Long may it continue.

Twenty 20 in 2020

Much has been written and said about the ECB's proposals for a new "city based" *T20* competition from 2020 onwards. Unfortunately, commentators have often lost sight of the twin goals of the new competition: securing the financial stability of all 18 first-class counties and driving significantly increased audiences for cricket, particularly families.

Both of these objectives are fundamental to the long-term future of YCCC, and we are supportive of the new initiative while maintaining our belief that the continued integrity and success of the County Championship remains paramount. For the avoidance of doubt we don't want any team that plays at Headingley to have Leeds in its name, even though I'm a LUFC fan! Please remain open-minded about the proposed new competition, and come along to the AGM where more details will be provided, and you can join in the debate.

Headingley Stadium

I said last year that we are determined to make Headingley one of the best sporting venues in the country, and thereby secure its future as an international cricket ground. This remains a complicated and expensive goal, but one which we and our friends at Leeds Rugby are totally committed to, despite the difficulties of planning and funding. Leeds City Council and the Leeds City Region Local Enterprise Partnership are very supportive, but we are in a crucial period if the new North-South stand is to be ready for the World Cup and Ashes Test in 2019. Further details will be provided to members at the AGM.

Thank you

Everyone involved with your Club demonstrates a passion and commitment which goes above and beyond, and none more so than John Hampshire, who is an outstanding ambassador for YCCC as our President. John was a wonderful player and umpire, and is a truly exceptional man. It was an absolute privilege and a joy to spend time with him over the year. Thanks to Mark Arthur for his day-to-day management of the Club, and also for his partnership with Andrew Watson of the Yorkshire Cricket Board in transforming the league structure across the county. We are also indebted to the Yorkshire Cricket Foundation and Yorkshire Schools Cricket Association for their tremendous work in driving participation among the younger age groups. Thanks to the rest of the board and every member of staff for their hard work and commitment. You are all amazing!

We are also indebted to our sponsors and commercial partners who have been with us every step of the way, and we're very proud to have each of them as part of the Yorkshire cricket family.

Steve Mann is stepping down after 10 years as chairman of the Members' Committee. Steve has been a passionate advocate of members' interests, and the board are extremely grateful for his terrific contribution and advice over the years.

A big thank-you to each of you as members. Your support is massively appreciated by everyone at the Club, and there has been an 11 per cent increase in membership compared to the same point last year. Please keep spreading the word about the excellent value membership offers!

I hope you have a healthy and exciting year, and I wish Andrew Gale and Gary Ballance every success in both regaining the County Championship and capturing at least one of the white-ball trophies.

STEVE DENISON
Executive Chairman
The Yorkshire
County Cricket Club

CHIEF EXECUTIVE'S REPORT

MARK ARTHUR

2016 was another year of steady progress for the Club, both on and off the field. While we came agonisingly close to winning a third consecutive County Championship, and took the season into the last hour of the last day of the last match, it was not to be. We were probably not at our best at crucial times of the season, but the experience will only drive us on in the search for another Championship in 2017. In the white-ball formats two semi-finals would suggest that we are also improving as a one-day team.

Off the field, this was our first full year of trading without either the financial support of our former Chairman or the benefit of a refinancing package. So, to record a small profit from where we were in 2013, with income increasing by £2m from that year, is testimony to the ability and hard work of everyone associated with the Club.

A three-day Test match can cause issues for a hosting ground, but our excellent advanced ticket and hospitality sales, complemented by an emphatic England win, due largely to Jonny Bairstow's magnificent 140, meant that it was another successful Headingley Test. That said, we are really looking forward to hosting a Headingley Test in the summer months in 2017, and early sales would suggest bumper crowds in August for the visit of the West Indies. The ODI between England and Pakistan was practically a perfect day from a delivery perspective. Five Yorkshire players were in the England team, and the atmosphere was special. It was a tremendous game of cricket, culminating in a home victory.

Domestic success was achieved yet again by our age-group sides. The Yorkshire Girls Under-13s won their fourth consecutive title, and the Under-17s were also crowned County Champions. Sessay CC won the National Village Cup Final at Lord's, and the Black Sheep Trophy saw York CC triumph. Our Academy won the Yorkshire League Knockout Trophy, defeating Sheriff Hutton Bridge CC in the final. The inaugural Yorkshire Premier League Final took place in Abu Dhabi, where Wakefield Thornes CC beat Pudsey St Lawrence CC. The match was streamed live back to the UK to over 12,000 on-line viewers. That wasn't at all bad for a club match on a Thursday afternoon in October!

The Kia Women's Super League was launched in 2016, and the Yorkshire Diamonds represented our county. While results were hard to come by, the crowds were excellent, and we look forward to a double-header against Lancashire at Headingley in 2017.

The Scarborough Festival seems to be becoming more and more popular, if that is possible, and a members' poll indicated that two Championship matches should be retained at Scarborough. Our thanks go to their chairman, Bill Mustoe, and his team for maintaining the first-class experience that we all enjoy so much at North Marine Road.

The end of the season saw the departure of our first-team coach, Jason Gillespie. He had five outstanding years at the Club, and immersed himself in every aspect of Yorkshire Cricket. Promotion in his first year, two County Championship titles and a second and third place is a record he can be proud of. Andrew Gale stepped down as first-team Captain and retired from first-class cricket. He has been a superb leader of a very talented group of players for the last seven years, and his record will be well documented in the history of The Yorkshire County Cricket Club. We also need to record our thanks to Bernard Knowles and Chris Hassell for their dedication to Yorkshire Schools cricket for many years.

Free Wi-Fi was installed at Headingley by InTechnology, enabling members and spectators to stay in touch with the rest of the world, while being consumed by the cricket. It has set the benchmark for such a service within British stadia. A Multi Faith Room was created just prior to the ODI, thanks to Regal Foods, and this has proved to be very popular. Changes were made to the retail and ticketing areas to improve the customer experience. At the end of the season Andy Fogarty and his groundstaff created eight new pitches on the edge of the square to enable more practice in the middle. These will be in use for 2018. This year we are replacing all the balcony seating in the Carnegie Pavilion as well as commencing improvements in the Long Room.

We have much to look forward to in 2017 and beyond. A new First Team coach in Andrew Gale and a new Captain in Gary Ballance will hopefully lead us to more success in the coming years. They have an experienced first-team squad, learning to manage with all the international call-ups, and many young emerging players eager to take their chances when they arise. Developments at Headingley, Scarborough and Bradford are all on the horizon. We aim to bring more young players through the Pathways system, administered by the YCB and Pro Coach; the community work of the YCF continues to grow throughout Yorkshire, and we remain ever grateful for the loyal support of our members, partners, stakeholders and volunteers. It's an exciting time to be involved with Yorkshire Cricket.

Enjoy the season.

MARK ARTHUR
Chief Executive
Yorkshire County Cricket Club

FINANCE DIRECTOR'S REPORT

PAUL HUDSON

Financially 2016 has continued to show a steady improvement over previous years. This has been our first complete year since the refinancing of the Club was completed in December 2015. From a financial structure point of view, we have seen the impact of the refinancing on the Club's results.

Our interest charge has been approximately £300,000 lower than it would have been without the support of our lenders, as reported on last year. In addition to this we have benefited from the absence of capital repayments on our main funding loans.

Operating the Club in this environment has meant that we have been able to focus on the running of the Club, and for the first time in several years we have avoided having to raise funds through a financing exercise. It is currently envisaged that this situation will continue during the 2017 year, subject to any funding required in respect of stadium developments during 2017.

The Club has had a financial result which continues the improving trend seen in recent years. Turnover shows a year on year increase of 5.1 per cent to £8.8m. Our income is now slightly over £2m higher than it was in 2013, with improvements in all categories of income.

EBITDA generated in the year is in excess of £1m, which together with the restructured interest charge has delivered a small surplus before taxation of £3,000. Set out on the following page is a summary of our financial performance covering the 2013 year to date.

The tax charge in the year is an accounting treatment to reflect a deferred tax charge in the accounts. This does not directly result in a tax liability that requires payment.

There remain, however, many financial sensitivities within the Club's financial results. In the light of these it remains important that finances continue to be managed in a very careful manner. We are naturally grateful for all the one-off items, including prize money, and a generous legacy we have been left. However we must remain careful not to become dependent on these items.

Our cash flow for the year is an outflow of £959,000. This includes an adverse working-capital movement of £602,000 within creditors relating to items of current-year funding from the ECB which were

Historic financial trends

	2016 £'000	2015 £'000	2014 £'000	2013 £'000
International ticket and hospitality	2,399	2,441	2,181	2,239
Domestic ticket and hospitality	1,005	836	538	442
Subscriptions	740	652	564	520
ECB	2,638	2,481	2,194	1,832
Commercial income	1,881	1,905	1,797	1,633
Other	131	50	33	108
Total income	8,794	8,365	7,307	6,774
Cost of sales	(2,109)	(1,993)	(1,746)	(1,398)
Cricket expenses	(3,055)	(3,168)	(2,765)	(2,937)
Overhead	(2,554)	(2,610)	(2,311)	(2,287)
EBITDA	1,076	594	485	152
Interest	(794)	(639)	(1,050)	(1,005)
Depreciation	(465)	(435)	(439)	(458)
Capital Grants release	186	177	178	146
Surplus / (deficit) before exceptional items	3	(302)	(826)	(1,165)
Exceptional items	0	781	500	526
Surplus / (deficit) after exceptional items, before tax	3	479	(326)	(639)

received in the 2015 financial year, together with an increase of general trade creditors at the end of 2015, which were paid in the current year.

Capital expenditure in the year was £257,000, of which the main item related to the provision of WiFi in the stadium. The Club also invested in hand dryers in the toilets, which should improve the cleanliness of the toilets and reduce our annual running costs.

The 2017 year will bring its own financial challenges, including the financing of any continued development in the stadium. At the time of writing this report there are many ongoing discussions in this area, and an up to date presentation on these plans will be provided at the AGM.

PAUL HUDSON
Director of Finance
Yorkshire County Cricket Club

DIRECTOR OF PROFESSIONAL CRICKET'S REPORT

Our main objective ahead of the 2016 season was to be competitive in all three formats. After coming third in the Specsavers County Championship and reaching two semi-finals in limited-overs cricket it's fair to say that we were. Having said that, it was obviously disappointing not to win anything.

We had another good season of Specsavers County Championship cricket, culminating in the incredible finale at Lord's. The pressure and intensity of the fixture was unbelievable. The drama of the 10th wicket partnership between Tim Bresnan and Ryan Sidebottom was some-

MARTYN MOXON

thing to behold. It was deeply disappointing to fall short on that final day, but the competitiveness and spirit of the game was a fantastic advert for county cricket. To be fair to Middlesex, I think they deserved to win the title with their performances over the course of the season.

The main area for us to address in the County Championship is the top-order batting. Over the course of the season individuals did well, but the top five rarely fired at the same time. In half of our innings we were 50 or less for three wickets, which put a big strain on our middle and lower orders. From that position it's hard to win. This has been the case for a couple of years, so we need to get back into the habit of making big totals, as we did in 2014. Then we can back our bowlers to finish the job.

Our form in the Royal London One-Day Cup was consistent once again this year. However, it was frustrating to fall short in the semi-final. Unfortunately, we didn't bat well enough on the day against Surrey, and that cost us.

It was a similar story in the NatWest T20 Blast, where we put in a dis-appointing performance in the semi-final, particularly given the person-nel at our disposal. Nevertheless, I feel we made real progress in this form of the game. I've spoken previously about our need to find a method, and despite a slow start to the competition I think we eventually found that method which served us well until Finals Day. To beat the champions both home and away showed our capabilities, and hopefully this will give us confidence going into the 2017 campaign.

There have already been several changes in staff since the end of the 2016 season. I would like to express our gratitude to Jason Gillespie for his tremendous work over the last five years. It was a huge pleasure to work with him, and I would like to wish him well for the future. Jason's departure left big shoes to fill, and after speaking to several potential candidates I decided to advertise the role.

There were a number of strong candidates. However, having given the situation a lot of thought, I approached Andrew Gale to discuss his feelings on the position. I wanted to protect the environment we have created, and in the short-term appoint someone who could manage the senior players at the Club. Andrew fits the bill perfectly; he will grow into the coaching aspect of the role. Richard Pyrah will predominantly assist Andrew at First Eleven games. The entire coaching staff will also be ensuring that both Andrew and Richard receive the support they require.

Appointing Andrew as coach obviously meant we needed a new Club captain. Both Andrew and I were in total agreement that this should be Gary Ballance. He has an excellent cricket brain, and has huge respect within the dressing room. On the occasions when he has been asked to take over the reins he has done an excellent job, and I'm sure he will develop into an outstanding captain, both on and off the field. We have appointed Tim Bresnan as vice-captain, and I feel that together Gary and Tim will provide strong leadership, and will work well together.

One thing I'll be looking for this season is for the younger players to really challenge for places in the first team. Performances in the Second Eleven really matter, and I would like to see more consistency from our next generation to ensure that we continue to be competitive, both now and in the future.

The Yorkshire Academy had another good season, winning the Yorkshire League Knockout Cup with a number of players showing real promise. The excellent work of Richard Damms as Academy Coach, with the assistance of Ian Dews and Richard Pyrah, continues to be vitally important in developing our young cricketers.

I would once again like to thank all the support staff and coaches at the Club for their continued hard work, passion and commitment in supporting and developing the players. Blaine Clancy has left us to take up a position in Hong Kong, and Ian Fisher, our Senior Strength and Conditioning Coach, is in the process of finding a replacement. I would like to thank Blaine and wish him well for the future.

We were delighted that Andy Fogarty retained his title as Groundsman of the Year. Also, John Dodds (Scarborough CC), and Richard Robinson (Weetwood) received the recognition they deserve at the First-Class Groundsmen Awards, winning the Best Outground Pitches and UCCE Groundsman of the Year awards respectively. They all work tirelessly to give us the best possible surfaces to play on, and we thank them for their continued commitment.

As you may be aware, all junior cricket is now under the Yorkshire Cricket banner. However, I would like to thank the Yorkshire Schools Cricket Association for their outstanding work over many years and, in particular, Bernard Knowles for his contribution.

As we prepare for the 2017 season the players and staff are in good spirits, and we are all looking forward to, and excited by, the challenges ahead.

I would once again like to take this opportunity to thank the Board and all of the staff at YCCC for their continued support.

The support shown by our members is nothing short of incredible, and the players and staff really do appreciate it. I think it's fair to say we have the best supporters in the country, and I hope we can continue to entertain you and bring home some silverware in 2017.

MARTYN MOXON
Director of Professional Cricket
Yorkshire County Cricket Club

MEMBERS' COMMITTEE
CHAIRMAN'S REPORT

The following served on the Members' Committee during the year.

Chairman:	**Mr S J Mann**
Elected Members:	**Mrs C Evers**
	Mr R Levin
	Mr S J Mann
	Mr E Stephens (Resigned July 2016)
Appointed Members:	**Mr G Greenfield**
	Mr A Kilburn
	Mrs K Mathew
In Attendance:	**Mr R Smith,** Board Director
	Mr M Arthur, Chief Executive
	Mr A Dawson, Commercial Director

There were seven full committee meetings during the year. Each is appropriately recorded with the detailed minutes being submitted to the main Board by inclusion in papers for the Board meeting immediately thereafter.

Two Member Forums were held in the Long Room during the season. The revised format so successfully introduced in 2015 was continued with the Chairman, Chief Executive and the Commercial Director attending to answer member questions and provide insight and background. The Director of Cricket Development and the Academy and Development Coach

STEPHEN MANN

attended the second forum, and dealt with policy issues affecting the second team, academy and player development.

While there are a number of drawbacks to using the Long Room it is clearly the appropriate focal point for this gathering. Attendances continue to grow with over 120 members present at each event.

Yet again the major topic of debate throughout the season has been the latest proposals from the ECB to change the domestic structure. One of the benefits of the forums has been that members have been able to hear the Chairman and Chief Executive outline the Club's position.

433

The Club consulted members as to whether two Championship matches should remain at Scarborough or just one game. The resounding view that there should be no reduction was responded to by the Club committing to keeping the status quo for Championship matches but to moving the limited-overs games to Headingley. A popular decision if ever there was one. It is refreshing that the Club consulted as they did, not a process that would have been followed in the not-too-distant past.

The year saw yet another splendid rate of growth in membership, growth that has been consistent over the last three years and continues in to 2017. The committee continue to seek with the management team ways to build on this growth in a bid to ensure a membership platform that is solid, sustainable and provides a substantial financial income for the Club. While a number of factors have contributed to this progress the much-improved communications from the Club and the increased openness and accessibility have been crucial.

One area that continues to disappoint is the proportion of members who attend international matches at Headingley. The Club has sought to avoid First Eleven fixtures taking place while a Test match is being staged, and while a few members have taken advantage and attended some days of a Test the numbers are still low.

It is appreciated that the opposition and scheduling have not been the most attractive, yet watching international cricket at Headingley is still the cheapest in the country. £100 for all five days of a Test is real value, and the staging of the event is excellent. Hopefully, in years ahead, more members will put at least one day of a Test in their cricket-watching diary. The larger the crowd at a Test the greater the financial return to the Club, and thus the greater security. To repeat a phrase I used in this report several years ago: "Ask not what your Club can do for you, ask what you can do for your Club."

I would like to express my sincere appreciation to all my committee colleagues for this and the previous 12 years for their support and endeavour. Without exception they are passionate about the game of cricket and specifically Yorkshire County Cricket Club. They work diligently, and give up much private time to represent the membership by working progressively with management for the benefit of all, a productive approach that all too often does not achieve the acknowledgement it should.

STEPHEN MANN,
Chairman,
Members' Committee

INDEPENDENT AUDITORS' REPORT

TO THE MEMBERS OF THE YORKSHIRE
COUNTY CRICKET CLUB

We have audited the financial statements of The Yorkshire County Cricket Club ("the Club") for the year ended December 31, 2016, set out on pages 439 to 448. The financial reporting framework that has been applied in their preparation is applicable law and UK Accounting Standards (UK Generally Accepted Accounting Practice) including FRS102 The Financial Reporting Standard applicable in the UK and Republic of Ireland.

This report is made solely to the Club's members, as a body, in accordance with Section 87 of the Co-operative and Community Benefit Societies Act 2014. Our audit work has been undertaken so that we might state to the Club's members those matters we are required to state to them in an auditor's report and for no other purpose. To the fullest extent permitted by law we do not accept or assume responsibility to anyone other than the Club and the Club's members, as a body, for our audit work, for this report, or for the opinions we have formed.

Respective responsibilities of directors and auditor

As more fully explained in the Statement of Directors' Responsibilities set out on Page 438 the Club's directors are responsible for the preparation of financial statements which give a true and fair view. Our responsibility is to audit, and express an opinion on, the financial statements in accordance with applicable law and International Standards on Auditing (UK and Ireland). Those standards require us to comply with the Auditing Practices Board's Ethical Standards for Auditors.

Scope of the audit of the financial statements

A description of the scope of an audit of financial statements is provided on the Financial Reporting Council's website at: www.frc.org.uk/ auditscopeukprivate.

Opinion on financial statements

In our opinion the financial statements:

- give a true and fair view, in accordance with UK Generally Accepted Accounting Practice, of the state of the Club's affairs as at December 31, 2016, and of its deficit for the year then ended; and
- comply with the requirements of the Co-operative and Community Benefit Societies Act 2014.

Matters on which we are required to report by exception

We have nothing to report in respect of the following.

Under the Co-operative and Community Benefit Societies Act 2014 we are required to report to you if, in our opinion:

- The Club has not kept proper books of account; or
- The Club has not maintained a satisfactory system of control over its transactions; or
- The financial statements are not in agreement with the Club's books of account; or
- We have not received all the information and explanations we need for our audit.

CHRIS BUTT for and on behalf of KPMG LLP,
Statutory Auditor
Chartered Accountants
1 Sovereign Square
Sovereign Street
Leeds LS1 4DA

FEBRUARY 6, 2017

CORPORATE GOVERNANCE

The Board is accountable to the Club's members for good corporate governance, and this statement describes how the principles of governance are applied.

THE BOARD

The Board is responsible for approving Club policy and strategy. It meets bi-monthly, or more frequently if business needs require, and has a schedule of matters specifically reserved to it for decision, including all significant commercial issues and all capital expenditure.

The Executive Management Team supply the Board with appropriate and timely information, and Board Members are free to seek any further information they consider necessary.

NOMINATIONS AND GOVERNANCE COMMITTEE

The Nominations Committee is formally constituted with written terms of reference, which are defined in the Club Rules and reviewed regularly. It consists of the President, Secretary and two other Board members, currently S Denison and R A Smith.

AUDIT COMMITTEE

The Audit Committee meets to provide oversight of the financial reporting process, the audit process, systems of internal controls and compliance with laws and regulations. It meets with the external auditors as part of this process. Members of the committee are S J Denison, S Willis and Professor P Smith.

REMUNERATION COMMITTEE

The main role and function of the Remuneration Committee is to assist the Board in developing and administering a fair remuneration policy for the Club and determining remuneration of senior employees. Members of the committee are S Willis and S J Denison.

RELATIONS WITH MEMBERS

The Club encourages effective communication with its members, and a specific Committee, as defined in the Club Rules, is appointed for that purpose.

INTERNAL CONTROL

The Board acknowledges its responsibility to maintain a sound system of internal control relating to operational, financial and compliance controls and risk management to safeguard the members' interests and the Club's assets, and will regularly review its effectiveness. Such a system, however, is designed to manage and meet the Club's particular needs and mitigate the risks to which it is exposed, rather than eliminate the risk of failure to achieve business objectives, and can provide only reasonable and not absolute assurance against material mis-statement or loss. The Club considers its key components to provide effective internal control and improve business efficiency are:

- Regular meetings with senior management to review and assess progress made against objectives and deal with any problems which arise from such reviews.
- A financial reporting system of annual budgets, periodic forecasts and detailed monthly reporting which includes cash-flow forecasts. Budgets and forecasts are reviewed and approved by the Board.
- A management and organisation structure exists with defined responsibilities and appropriate authorisation limits and short lines of communication to the Non-Executive Chairman.
- A Senior Independent Director is appointed by the Board whose role is to serve as a sounding board for the Chairman and act as an intermediary for other directors. The position is currently held by R A Smith.

DIRECTORS' RESPONSIBILITIES

The directors are responsible for preparing the Annual Report and the Club's financial statements in accordance with applicable law and regulations. Co-operative and Community Benefit Society law requires the directors to prepare financial statements for each financial year. Under that law the directors have elected to prepare the financial statements in accordance with UK Accounting Standards including FRS102 The Financial Reporting Standard applicable in the UK and Republic.

The financial statements are required by law to give a true and fair view of the state of affairs of the Club and of its income and expenditure for that period. In preparing the Club's financial statements, the directors are required to:

- select suitable accounting policies and then apply them consistently;
- make judgements and estimates that are reasonable and prudent;
- state whether applicable UK Accounting Standards have been followed, subject to any material departures disclosed and explained in the financial statements, and
- prepare the financial statements on the going-concern basis unless it is inappropriate to presume that the Club will continue in business.

The directors are responsible for keeping proper books of account that disclose with reasonable accuracy at any time the financial position of the Club and enable them to ensure that its financial statements comply with the Co-operative and Community Benefit Societies Act 2014. They have general responsibility for taking such steps as are reasonably open to them to safeguard the assets of the Club and to prevent and detect fraud and other irregularities.

The directors are responsible for the maintenance and integrity of the corporate and financial information included on the Club's website. Legislation in the UK governing the preparation and dissemination of financial statements may differ from legislation in other jurisdictions.

DISCLOSURE OF INFORMATION TO AUDITOR

The members of the Board who held office at the date of approval of the Annual Report and Accounts confirm that, so far as they are aware, there is no relevant information of which the Club's auditor is unaware; or each member has taken all the steps that he ought to have taken as a member to make himself aware of any relevant audit information or to establish that the Club's auditor is aware of that information.

INCOME AND EXPENDITURE ACCOUNT
for the year ended 31st December, 2016

	Note	2016 £	2015 £
Income			
International ticket and hospitality revenue		2,398,862	2,440,612
Domestic ticket and hospitality revenue		1,004,666	835,547
Subscriptions		739,615	652,324
England and Wales Cricket Board		2,638,190	2,480,607
Commercial income		1,881,192	1,904,940
Other income		131,103	51,683
		8,793,628	8,365,713
Cost of sales			
International match and hospitality expenditure		1,368,341	1,300,521
Domestic match and hospitality costs (home fixtures)		489,547	421,390
Retail		208,954	239,447
Catering		42,272	31,518
		(2,109,114)	(1,992,876)
Cricket expenses			
Staff remuneration and employment expenses		2,370,116	2,563,753
Match expenses (away fixtures)		234,493	238,265
Development expenses		361,504	337,108
Other cricket expenses		88,641	28,926
		(3,054,754)	(3,168,052)
Overheads			
Infrastructure and ground operations		1,006,554	943,772
Commercial		800,146	767,982
Administration		573,857	697,705
Ticket and membership office		173,039	201,015
		(2,553,596)	(2,610,474)
Earnings before interest, tax, depreciation and amortisation		1,076,164	594,311
Below the line expenditure:			
Interest		(794,360)	(638,741)
Depreciation	5	(464,659)	(434,768)
Release of Capital Grants	11	186,111	177,382
		(1,072,908)	(896,127)
Surplus/(deficit) before exceptional items and taxation		3,256	(301,816)
Exceptional items	9	—	781,106
Surplus before taxation		3,256	479,290
Taxation	4,12	(108,430)	(110,877)
(Deficit)/Surplus for the year after taxation		(105,174)	368,413

BALANCE SHEET

as at 31st December, 2016

	Note	2016 £	2016 £	2015 £	2015 £
Assets employed:					
Fixed Assets	5		29,051,688		29,259,590
Current assets:					
Stocks		129,526		112,770	
Debtors	6	1,467,398		1,482,89	
Cash at bank and in hand	7	14,382		765,142	
		1,611,306		2,360.803	
Creditors: amounts falling due within one year	7, 8	(3,534,670)		(4,153,629)	
Net current liabilities			(1,923,364)		(1,792,826)
Total assets less current liabilities			27,128,324		27,466,764
Funded by:					
Creditors: amounts falling due after more than one year	9		25,013,528		25,160,683
Deferred income — capital grants	11		5,066,175		5,152,286
			30,079,703		30,312,969
Capital and Reserves					
Called up share capital	13		210		197
Capital redemption reserve			680		693
Income and expenditure account			(2,952,269)		(2,847,095)
			(2,951,379)		(2,846,205)
			27,128,324		27,466,764

These accounts were approved by the Board on 6th February 2017

S J DENISON, Chairman

P A HUDSON, Club Secretary

440

CASH FLOW STATEMENT
for the year ended 31st December, 2016

	Note	2016 £	2015 £
Cash flows from Operating Activities			
(Deficit) / surplus for the year		(105,174)	368,413
Adjustments for:			
Depreciation of tangible assets		464,659	434,768
Loan interest payable		794,360	638,741
Capital grants released		(186,111)	(177,382)
Taxation		108,430	110,877
Exceptional item	9	—	(907,000)
Adjustment to debenture debt		—	(23,696)
Increase in trade and other debtors		(92,937)	(282,622)
Increase in stocks		(16,756)	(25,017)
(Decrease)/Increase in creditors		(601,623)	493,292
Interest paid		(794,360)	(638,741)
Net cash outflow from operating activities		(429,512)	(8,367)
Cash flows from investing activities			
Purchase of tangible fixed assets		(256,757)	(658,573)
Capital grants received		100,000	310,000
Net cash outflow from investing activities		(156,757)	(348,573)
Cash flows from financing activities			
Proceeds from new loans		5,600	13,765,400
Repayment of borrowings		(300,000)	(12,200,000)
Repayment of finance lease liabilities		(78,043)	(138,549)
Net cash outflow from financing activites		(372,443)	1,426,851
(Decrease)/Increase in cash in the period		(958,712)	1,069,911
Cash and cash equivalents at January 1		765,142	(304,769)
Cash and cash equivalents at December 31	7	(193,570)	765,142

STATEMENT OF CHANGES IN EQUITY
for the year ended December 31, 2016

	Called Up Share Capital £	Capital Redemption Reserve £	Income and Expenditure Account £	Total £
Balance at January 1, 2015	199	691	(3,215,508)	(3,214,618)
Reduction in Share Capital for retiring members	(2)	2	—	—
Surplus for the year after taxation	—	—	368,413	368,413
Balance at December 31, 2015	197	693	(2,847,095)	(2,846,205)
Balance at January 1, 2016	197	693	(2,847,095)	(2,846,205)
Additional Share Capital for new members	13	(13)		
Deficit for the year after taxation	—	—	(105,174)	(105,174)
Balance at December 31, 2016	210	680	(2,952,269)	(2,951,379)

NOTES TO THE ACCOUNTS

for the year ended 31st December, 2016

1. Accounting policies

These financial statements were prepared in accordance with Financial Reporting Standard 102 The Financial Reporting Standard applicable in the UK and Republic of Ireland (FRS 102) as issued in August 2014. The amendments to FRS 102 issued in July 2015 and effective immediately have been applied. The presentation currency of these financial statements is sterling.

(a) Income

All income is accounted for on an accruals basis except for donations, which are accounted for in the year of receipt.

Income represents amounts receivable from the Club's principal activities. Income is analysed between international ticket and hospitality revenue, domestic ticket and hospitality revenue, subscriptions, England and Wales Cricket Board, commercial and other income.

Subscriptions

Subscription income comprises amounts receivable from members in respect of the current season. Subscriptions received in respect of future seasons is treated as deferred income.

Domestic-ticket and hospitality revenue

Relate to amounts received from gate charges, ticket sales, hospitality and guarantees directly attributable to staging domestic cricket matches in Yorkshire.

International-ticket and hospitality revenue

Relate to amounts received from gate charges, ticket sales, hospitality and guarantees directly attributable to staging international cricket matches in Yorkshire.

England and Wales Cricket Board (ECB)

ECB income relates to fees receivable, including performance-related elements, in the current season distributed from central funds in accordance with the First Class Memorandum of Understanding. ECB fees received in respect of future seasons are treated as deferred income. ECB distributions receivable to fund capital projects are treated as deferred income, and are released to the Income and Expenditure Account by equal instalments over the expected useful lives of the relevant assets in accordance with accounting policy (b) Fixed assets and depreciation, as set out below.

Commercial and other income

Commercial income relates to amounts received, net of related expenditure, from ground advertising, catering guarantees, box lettings, facility hire, dinners and other events. Advertising income received in respect of future seasons is treated as deferred income.

Other income relates to amounts received, net of related expenditure, from retail, Cricket Centre bar, Taverners' Club, fundraising activities and other sundry items.

(b) Fixed assets and depreciation

All expenditure in connection with the development of Headingley Carnegie Cricket Ground and the related facilities has been capitalised. Finance costs relating to and incurred during the period of construction were also capitalised. Depreciation is only charged once a discrete phase of the development is completed. Depreciation is calculated to write down the cost of fixed assets by equal annual instalments over their expected useful lives.

The periods generally applicable are:

Headingley Carnegie Cricket Ground and Cricket Centre

Buildings	Carnegie Pavilion	125 years
	Other buildings	50 years
Fixtures		4 years
Plant & Equipment	Between 4 and 10 years	
Office equipment		
— telephone system		4 years
Computer equipment		2 years
Freehold land is not depreciated.		

All other expenditure on repairs to Headingley Carnegie Cricket Ground and other grounds is written off as and when incurred.

(c) Carnegie Pavilion

The Club's contribution towards the design and build cost of the Carnegie Pavilion is £3m, of which £1.5m is payable over 20 years under a 125-year lease agreement. The £3m, together with the associated legal, professional and capital fit-out costs of the areas within the Pavilion that the Club occupies, have been capitalised and depreciated over the 125-year lease term. The £1.5m, payable under the lease agreement has been treated as a finance lease within the financial statements with the capital element reported within Creditors (Finance leases), and the interest element charged to the Income and Expenditure Account on a straight-line basis over the 20-year term.

(d) Stocks

Stocks represent goods for resale, and are stated at the lower of cost and net realisable value.

(e) Grants

Capital grants relating to the development of Headingley Carnegie Cricket Ground (including the Yorkshire Cricket Museum) and Cricket Centre are included within the Balance Sheet as deferred income, and are released to the Income and Expenditure Account by equal instalments over the expected useful lives of the relevant assets in accordance with accounting policy (b) Fixed assets and depreciation, as set out above.

Grants of a revenue nature are credited to the Income and Expenditure Account in the same period as their related expenditure.

(f) Trade and other debtors

Trade receivables are initially recognised at fair value and subsequently measured at amortised cost, less any appropriate provision for estimated irrecoverable amounts. A provision is established for irrecoverable amounts when there is objective evidence that amounts due under the original payment terms will not be collected.

(g) Cash and cash equivalents

For the purpose of presentation in the cash-flow statement cash and cash equivalents include cash on hand, deposits with financial institutions which are subject to an insignificant risk of change in value, and bank overdrafts. Bank overdrafts are presented as current borrowings on the balance sheet.

(h) Taxation

Tax on the surplus or deficit for the year comprises current and deferred tax. Tax is recognised in the income-and-expenditure account except to the extent that it relates to items recognised directly in equity or other comprehensive income, in which case it is recognised directly in equity or other comprehensive income.

Current tax is the expected tax payable or receivable on the taxable income or deficit for the year, using tax rates enacted or substantively enacted at the balance-sheet date, and any adjustment to tax payable in respect of previous years.

Deferred tax is provided in full using the balance-sheet liability method. A deferred-tax asset is recognised where it is probable that future taxable income will be sufficient to utilise the available relief. Tax is charged or credited to the income statement except when it relates to items charged or credited directly to equity, in which case the tax is also dealt with in equity. Deferred tax liabilities and assets are not discounted.

2. Financial Position

Going concern

The Club is in a net current liability position of £1.9m (2015: £1.8m). This includes current deferred income of £2.2m (2015: £2.0m). Details of the loan and overdraft maturity analysis which impact on the financial position can be found in Note 9. The Board have prepared forecasts which show that the Club will continue to operate within its current facilities and pay creditors as they fall due for at least the next 12 months. The Board expect all current facilities to be extended under the same terms. Due to this, the Board therefore considers it appropriate to prepare the financial statements on a going-concern basis.

3. Directors' Remuneration and Staff Numbers and Costs

	2016 £	2015 £
Wages and salaries	260,125	105,975
Social security costs	29,648	11,715
Pension costs	28,752	8,498
	318,525	126,188

The Board consider the above remuneration to represent that of key management personnel. The Chairman and other non-executive directors do not receive any remuneration for their services to the Club.

Staff Numbers and Costs

The average number of persons employed by the company (including directors) during the year, analysed by category, was as follows:

	2016	2015
Players (including Academy Players)	39	37
Non Playing Full Time Staff	46	42
Seasonal and Casual Staff	16	13
	101	92

The aggregate payroll costs of these persons were as follows:

	2016 £	2015 £
Wages and salaries	3,440,127	3,403,851
Social security costs	369,884	365,369
Contribution to Pension Plans	283,332	280,160
	4,093,343	4,049,380

4. Taxation

	2016 £	2015 £
(Deficit) / surplus for the year	(105,174)	368,413
Total tax expense	108,430	110,877
Surplus excluding taxation	3,256	479,290
Tax at 20.00% (2015: 20.25%)	651	97,056
Reduction in tax rate on deferred tax balances	36,805	88,454
Expenses not deductible for taxation purposes	88,821	84,523
Non taxable income	(92,229)	(112,428)
Depreciation for the period in excess of capital allowances	—	3,518
Losses utilised	—	(72,669)
Origination of timing differences	—	66,661
Adjustments in respect of prior periods	74,382	(44,238)
Total tax expense	108,430	110,877

The tax charge for the year represents deferred tax and as such is a non-cash item, which has been fully recognised in the income and expenditure account. No charges have been recognised in other comprehensive income or directly in equity. A similar situation existed in 2015 A reduction in the UK corporation tax rate from 21% to 20% (effective from April 1, 2015) was substantively enacted on July 2, 2013. Further reductions to 19% (effective from April 1, 2017) and to 18% (effective April 1, 2020) were substantively enacted on October 26, 2015, and an additional reduction to 17% (effective April 1, 2020) was substantively enacted on September 6, 2016. This will reduce the company's future current tax charge accordingly. The deferred tax asset at December 31, 2016 has been calculated based on these rates.

5. Fixed assets (See next page)

	Cricket Centre		Headingley Carnegie Cricket Ground				
	Freehold Land and Buildings £	Plant & Equipment £	Freehold Land and Buildings £	Plant and Equipment £	Improvements to Leasehold Property £	Office Equipment £	Total £
Cost							
At January 1, 2016	608,624	780,094	26,989,729	4,954,279	4,453,421	417,113	38,203,260
Additions	—	—	92,454	139,867	—	24,436	256,757
At December 31, 2016	608,624	780,094	27,082,183	5,094,146	4,453,421	441,549	38,460,017
Depreciation							
At January 1, 2016	155,777	764,847	2,864,201	4,526,016	239,653	393,176	8,943,670
Provided in the year	17,913	2,841	269,338	116,136	42,522	15,909	464,659
At December 31, 2016	173,690	767,688	3,133,539	4,642,152	282,175	409,085	9,408,329
Net book value							
At January 1, 2016	434,934	12,406	23,948,644	451,994	4,171,246	32,464	29,051,688
At December 31, 2016	**452,847**	**15,247**	**24,125,528**	**428,263**	**4,213,768**	**23,937**	**29,259,590**

6. Debtors

	2016 £	2015 £
Trade debtors	579,241	597,608
Deferred tax asset (see Note 12)	620,999	729,429
Other debtors	267,158	155,854
	1,467,398	1,482,891

7. Cash and cash equivalents

	2016	2015
Cash at bank and in hand	14,382	765,142
Bank overdraft (secured)	(207,952)	—
	(193,570)	765,142

8. Creditors: amounts falling due within one year

Bank overdraft (secured)	207,952	—
ECB loan	100,000	700,000
Trade creditors	419,359	684,254
Finance leases	98,797	96,794
Social security and other taxes	320,927	389,662
Other creditors	82,733	113,874
Accruals	148,974	197,639
Deferred income	2,155,928	1,971,406
	3,534,670	4,153,629

9. Creditors: amounts falling due after more than one year

HSBC Bank Loan	3,069,014	3,069,014
ECB Loan	300,000	—
Pride Appeal Loans	—	5,000
CJ and J Graves Accumulation and Maintenance Trusts Loans	6,703,500	6,703,500
J Graves Accumulation and Maintenance Trusts Loans	6,703,500	6,703,500
CJ Graves 1999 Settlement Trust Loan	5,500,000	5,500,000
Debentures	370,600	365,000
Finance leases	1,597,377	1,677,424
Deferred income	769,537	1,137,245
	25,013,528	25,160,683

Loan, borrowing and overdraft maturity analysis:

In one year or less or on demand	406,749	1,006,749
In more than one year but not more than two years	3,873,312	803,096
In more than two years but not more than five years	19,345,256	22,214,270
In more than five years	1,025,423	1,006,073
	24,650,740	25,030,188

Exceptional Item

As part of the 2015 refinancing Leeds City Council demonstrated by way of reviewing the actual cost of interest that the council loan had been fully repaid and accepted £6.5m in settlement of £7.4m capital outstanding on the loan. This gave rise to exceptional income, net of costs, of £781,106.

Loan descriptions

As part of the refinancing in 2015 HSBC agreed to lower their interest rate to 2.5% and defer full capital repayment until October 1, 2018, in return for a First Legal Charge over the Cricket Centre and a Third Legal Charge over Headingley Cricket Ground in respect of the bank loan and overdrafts. HSBC Bank plc also has a fixed and floating charge over all of the

assets of the Club, subject to the Legal Charges referred to above.

C J and J Graves Accumulation and Maintenance and J Graves Accumulation and Maintenance Trusts loans stand at £6.7m each, bearing an interest rate of 4.625 per cent and with initial capital repayments to be made in 2019 (£2m each Trust) and during 2020 (£1.5m each Trust) with the balance at December 31, 2020. The two Trusts have been granted by the Club joint First Legal Charge over Headingley Cricket Ground and joint Second Legal Charge over the Cricket Centre.

A further £5.5m of debt has also been incurred from the C J Graves 1999 Settlement Trust, bearing an interest rate of 0 per cent. The Club has granted Second Legal Charge over Headingley Cricket Ground and Third Legal Charge over the Cricket Centre. An additional loan was made available by the ECB towards the cost of installing the floodlights at Headingley Cricket Ground. The total available loan is £700,000, of which all was drawn down by early in 2015. £300,000 has been repaid with further payments to be made in the coming years at a rate of £100,000 per year until the loan is repaid. The current policy of the ECB is to award a capital grant of the same value as the repayment resulting in no cash out-flow for the Club.

10. Financial instruments

	2016 £	2015 £
Assets measured at cost less impairment		
Trade Debtors	579,241	597,608
Other Debtors	70,761	59,584
Accrued Income	70,000	—
Cash	14,382	765,142
Liabilities measured at amortised cost		
Term Loans	22,376,014	22,681,014
Debentures	370,660	365,000
Finance Leases	1,696,174	1,774,218
Loan commitments measured at cost less impairment		
Bank Overdraft	207,952	—
Trade Creditors	419,359	684,254
Social security and other taxes	320,927	389,662
Other creditors	82,733	113,874
Accruals	148,974	197,639

11. Deferred income - capital grants

At January 1, 2016	5,152,286	5,019,668
Received in year	100,000	310,000
Released to Income and Expenditure Account	(186,111)	(177,382)
At December 31, 2016	5,066,175	5,152,286

12. Deferred taxation asset

At January 1, 2016	(729,429)	(840,306)
Charge to Income and Expenditure Account for the year	108,430	110,877
At December 31, 2016 (see Note 6)	(620,999)	(729,429)

The elements of recognised deferred taxation are as follows:

Difference between accumulated depreciation and capital allowances	324,182	171,755
Tax losses	(945,181)	(901,184)
At December 31, 2016 (see Note 6)	(620,999)	(729,429)

The anticipated amount of deferred tax asset to reverse in the next financial year is approximately £110,000.

| | **2016** | 2015 |
| | **£** | £ |

13. Share capital

| Allotted, called up and fully paid Ordinary shares of 5p each | **210** | 197 |

During the year there was a net increase in qualifying members of 269. The total number of qualifying members as at December 31, 2016, was 4,193 (2015: 3,924). Each member of the Club owns one Ordinary share, and the rights attached thereto are contained within the Club's rules which can be found on the Club's website, or from the Secretary on request.

14. Leasing commitments

Finance lease liabilities are payable as follows:

Minimum Lease Payment	**2016**	2015
In one year or less	**98,797**	96,794
Between two and five years	**942,554**	966,351
More than five years	**654,823**	711,073
	1,696,174	1,774,218

The Club currently has two finance leases. One is with Leeds Beckett University, relating to the Carnegie Pavilion. This lease is for 125 years, with lease payments being made for 20 years until 2030, after which a peppercorn rate is due. The second lease is with Investec in relation to the floodlights installed during 2015. This lease will be repaid in 2019, at which point ownership of the floodlights will revert to the Club.

Operating lease liabilities are payable as follows:

Minimum Lease Payment	**2016**	2015
In one year or less	**41,202**	41,704
Between two and five years	**72,650**	113,853
More than five years	**—**	—
	113,852	155,557

Operating lease payments amounting to £41,704 (2015:£41,704) were recognised as an expense in the income-and-expense account in respect of operating leases.

15. Related Party Transactions

During the year Mr M A Arthur and Mr R A Smith were Board Members of YCCC and Trustees of the Yorkshire Cricket Foundation (YCF). During 2016 the YCF awarded non-capital grants of £26,457 (2015: £11,594). YCCC made donations of £3,545 to the YCF in return for events and activities co-ordinated by the YCF.

Mr M A Arthur was also Board Member and Director of the Yorkshire Cricket Board (YCB). During 2016, invoiced sales to the YCB of £118,366 (2015: £71,715) were made in return for goods or services. All invoices have been settled in cash or form part of the trade debtors balance at the year end. The balance owed at the end of 2016 was £17,422 (2015: £17,043).

16. Pensions

The Club operates defined contribution pension schemes for the benefit of certain employees. The amounts paid during the year were £283,332 (2015: £280,160). The assets of these schemes are administered in funds independent from those of the Club.

17. Audit Fee

The Club paid its auditor £17,500 (2015: £16,750) in respect of the audit of these Financial Statements.

18. Contingent liabilities

The Club is currently involved in plans to redevelop the shared South Stand with Leeds Rugby. If the stand project were to be terminated early the Club would be required to pay its fair share of a contribution towards costs incurred to date by the other party.